VERA BRITTAIN (1893-1970) grew up in provincial comfort in the north of England. In 1914 she won an exhibition to Somerville College, Oxford, but a year later abandoned her studies to enlist as a VAD nurse. She served throughout the war, working in London, Malta and the Front in France.

At the end of the war, with all those closest to her dead, Vera Brittain returned to Oxford. There she met Winifred Holtby – author of *South Riding* – and this friendship, which was to last until Winifred Holtby's untimely death in 1935, sustained her in those difficult post-war years. In 1933 Vera Brittain published *Testament of Youth* – also published by Fontana, now a BBC Television serial. This haunting autobiography, a vivid and passionate record of the years 1900-1925, conveyed to an entire generation the essence of their common experience of war: it was a bestseller in both Britain and America. In 1957 Vera Brittain continued her story in *Testament of Experience,* which covers the years 1925-1950.

Both volumes record the life and times of a remarkable woman. A convinced pacifist, a prolific speaker, lecturer, journalist and writer, Vera Brittain devoted much of her energies to the causes of peace and feminism. She travelled widely in Europe and lectured extensively in the USA and Canada, and wrote twenty-nine books in all, novels, poetry, biography and autobiography and other non-fiction.

In 1925 Vera Brittain married the political philosopher G. E. Catlin and had two children, one of whom is Shirley Williams.

VERA BRITTAIN

TESTAMENT OF EXPERIENCE

An Autobiographical
Story of the Years
1925-1950

New Introduction by Paul Berry

FONTANA PAPERBACKS
in association with Virago

First published by Victor Gollancz Ltd 1957
First published in paperback by Virago Ltd 1979
First published in this edition by Fontana Paperbacks
in association with Virago Ltd 1980

Made and printed in Great Britain by
William Collins Sons & Co. Ltd, Glasgow

To G.
Beloved companion of these rich and
challenging years
*"Confirma hoc, Deus, quod operatus es
in nobis"*

CONTENTS

AUTHOR'S ACKNOWLEDGMENTS

MY GRATEFUL THANKS are due for permission to quote the following copyright material: to Sidgwick and Jackson Ltd. for two lines from Rupert Brooke's sonnet *"The Dead"*, taken from *The Collected Poems of Rupert Brooke*; to Mr. Gerald Bullett for his Epigram on the Abdication; to Mr. Kingsley Martin for passages from an article by him in the *New Statesman*, and to "Sagittarius" for lines from a poem published in that journal; to the Association des Amis de Romain Rolland for three paragraphs from the *Déclaration d'Indépendance de l'Esprit* by Romain Rolland; to Paul Engle for two verses from his poem *"I Leave the House"*; to Mr. Rathindranath Tagore, the Trustees of Rabindranath Tagore and Macmillan & Co. Ltd. for four lines from *"The Sunset of the Century"* and for *"Quiet Moment"*, both by Rabindranath Tagore; to Cassell & Co. Ltd. for an extract from Sir Winston Churchill's *The Second World War*, Vol. IV; to Mrs. R. W. Moore and the Oxford University Press for Dr. R. W. Moore's verses from *"Trophy for an Unknown Soldier"*; to Mr. Kenneth Boulding for a sonnet from his sequence, *"There is a Spirit"*; to my husband George Catlin, Mrs. Dorothy Elliot, Miss Phyllis Bentley and Mr. George P. Brett for extracts from their letters to me; and to Mr. Henry Villard, Mr. Leonard Woolf and Mrs. Gwen Catchpool for passages from letters sent to me by Oswald Garrison Villard, Virginia Woolf and Corder Catchpool respectively.

Finally, I owe especial gratitude to Sheila Hodges for her brilliant editorial help, and to my husband for his patient reading of the manuscript and many useful suggestions.

V. B.

INTRODUCTION

The countless readers who fell under the spell of *Testament of Youth* will rejoice at this timely reissue of Vera Brittain's second volume of autobiography. Together these two *Testaments* span the first half of the twentieth century, and provide an absorbing record of the life of one woman set against the panoramic background of one of the most tumultuous periods in our history.

As she herself admitted with characteristic honesty, Vera Brittain was a complex person, and to understand her, the two books should be read in sequence. In *Testament of Youth* she tells the story of the first half of her life, and in *Testament of Experience* we see how her heredity, the circumstances of her comfortable, middle-class upbringing, and in particular her experiences as a VAD nurse in the First World War, were to influence and guide her for the rest of her life.

Vera was born in Newcastle-under-Lyme, Staffordshire, on December 29, 1893. Although her parents cannot have been aware of the significance of their choice of names, it is singularly appropriate that "Vera" is derived from the Russian "Vjera" meaning "truth" or "faith".

Almost as soon as she could hold a pen Vera decided that she was going to be a writer, and among her manuscripts when she died were five novels written before she was eleven. She was eighteen months older than her only brother, Edward, and at night when their parents supposed them to be asleep she regaled him with the adventures of *The Five School Girls* or *The Breaking-In of Dorothy*, although Edward was more absorbed in making music on his small violin than in his sister's epics.

Her vocation as a writer was the mainstay of Vera's life, and almost all her twenty-nine books reflect her feminist and pacifist convictions. She published five novels but attached greater importance to her autobiographical books. She hoped to leave a complete record of her life but *Testament of Time* remained half written when she died.

As a child Vera was prey to a variety of irrational fears—the dark, thunderstorms, the full moon, and standing under railway arches. In spite of her calm composure in later life her apprehensions remained. She had always been insufficiently tough, she said, and had always had to fight with pain and effort for such confidence as she had acquired, which was only marginally increased by her literary successes.

She was reading a book on psychoanalysis one day and found it threw a flood of light on her emotional make-up. It revealed her, she reflected, as a potential neurotic as a result of an inherited tendency to melancholia combined with her wartime experiences; the victim of an anxiety state, subjected to a perpetual conflict between fear and courage, and between spontaneity and self-preservation. The ideal of social duty triumphed but the cost was high. The air raids on London during the Second World War, and the rebuffs and ostracism she endured for her pacifist convictions, imposed a heavy strain on her emotional resources.

Vera's feminism was stimulated by the years she spent at St Monica's School in Kingswood, Surrey, where her mother's sister was one of the two principals, and it was here that she first became aware of the suffragette struggle being waged by Emmeline Pankhurst and her supporters. At home Vera carried on a running battle with her parents to be allowed to go to university, and chafed at the claustrophobia of her middle-class existence, the pointlessness of the hunt balls, and the ineptitude of the young men looking for a wife. She remembered all her life her anger at travelling in a second-class railway carriage with her mother and Edward, whilst her father ensconced himself in a first-class compartment on the same train.

Edward attended Uppingham Public School, and during the Easter vacation of 1912 he invited his friend, Roland Leighton, to stay with him, and Roland promptly fell in love with Edward's dark-haired, serious-minded sister. Vera obtained a Somerville Exhibition, but her first year was overshadowed by the war with Germany, and her anxiety for Roland and Edward, and their two friends, Victor and Geoffrey, who had all joined the army. By 1915 an academic life had become intolerably irrelevant, and interrupting her university studies Vera enlisted as a VAD nurse.

In August 1915 Vera and Roland were unofficially engaged, but on December 22—two days before he was due home on leave—he was fatally wounded on a night reconnaissance and died, whilst Vera waited for him in a Brighton hotel. Less than eighteen months later both Victor and Geoffrey were dead, and Vera clung to the hope that Edward at least might survive the war. He had been awarded the Military Cross, and in November 1917 he was posted to the comparatively less lethal battle area in Northern Italy. The following June the Austrians launched a fierce offensive across the heights above Vicenza, and less then five months before the war ended Edward was killed 5,000 feet up amidst the dark pine forests and swirling mists on the Asiago Plateau.

"I ended the First World War with my deepest emotions paralysed if not dead," Vera wrote in a letter in 1952. "This would not have happened if I had had *one* person left. It was Edward's death rather than Roland's which turned me into an automaton . . . I could have

8

married Victor in memory of Roland, and Geoffrey in memory of Edward, but the war took even the second best. It left nothing. Only ambition held me to life."

On her return to Somerville in 1919 Vera met Winifred Holtby, and the friendship began which was to last until Winifred's death sixteen years later. Winifred was four-and-a-half years younger than Vera. She had also interrupted her university training to join the Queen Mary's Army Auxiliary Corps, and it was their shared experience of war service in France that first brought them together.

Physically and temperamentally Vera and Winifred were opposites. Vera was five-foot-three, dark-haired, with amethyst coloured eyes and finely chiselled, sensitive features; whilst Winifred was tall, fair-haired and blue-eyed, and was almost always optimistic, full of gaiety, and infinitely kind. Vera's wartime experiences had accentuated her naturally introspective nature, and often she was weighed down by anxieties both large and small, but she had also, as Winifred perceived, infinite compassion and concern for other people.

"She is a person whom life has battered," Winifred wrote, "and who has been given by circumstance and heredity such a temperament that every blow and every snub, even every casual coldness, makes a wound and scar . . but never for a moment does she give way, nor lose her sweetness, nor her tenderness for suffering, nor an imagination which is constantly trying to devise ways for protecting other people from the sorrows she has known."

When they came down from Oxford with good degrees, Vera and Winifred shared several flats, and after Vera's marriage to George Catlin in 1925 Winifred remained part of the household. They wrote articles and taught, they lectured for the League of Nations, and published their first novels.

Winifred's death in 1935, two years after the publication of *Testament of Youth*, robbed Vera of a deep, rewarding friendship, and an invaluable, stabilising presence. In *Testament of Friendship* she told the story of Winifred's brief, valiant life with the same power and poignancy that had characterised *Testament of Youth*, and writing these books she discovered had been a cathartic experience.

"After my two *Testaments*," she told a friend who had been recently bereaved, "I never thought of either the First War or of Winifred with bitterness again, or any feeling of despair. Stoicism isn't enough. One must accept what has happened as part of experience—theirs and yours. Theirs because we don't know what may lie beyond death, and anyhow death itself —as for Winifred— is for some a form of victory; yours because grief is part of the total richness of life and thus part of its pattern. Somehow the real acceptance of this conclusion brings a kind of reconciliation which is quite other than stoicism."

9

Vera joined the Peace Pledge Union early in 1937, and for the rest of her life her pacifism never faltered. Her fight for peace arose principally from the losses she suffered in the 1914–18 war, and her resolution was reinforced by her nursing experiences. "Then I went back to the Hospital," she wrote in her war diary in 1916, "back to one or two dressings that make even me almost sick—that of a man with his hand blown off and the stump untrimmed, and the other man with an arm off and great hole in his back one could get one's hand into, and other wounds on his leg and sides and head. Poor, poor souls."

She never forgot her passionate fury at the wickedness of war as she stood with her hands covered with blood after assisting at a particularly gory amputation dressing, wishing she had never been born.

In the upsurge of patriotic fervour during the Second World War she paid for her convictions with courage and dignity. She incurred the animosity of friends, and was cold-shouldered by editors and fellow writers; her letters were intercepted and read; she was the subject of a Parliamentary question; and at the Home Office listed as an embryonic "Quisling".

In 1944, almost alone, Vera protested vehemently against the obliteration bombing of German cities, which massacred half-a-million civilians with insignificant effect on either war production or morale.

In *Seed of Chaos* she reproduced reports from the neutral press of the destruction of German cities in massive "area bombing" attacks which have since been shown to have been as wasteful of British pilots and aircraft as they were cruel. Her unemotional, factual booklet of 20,000 words was published in America under the more challenging title of *Massacre by Bombing*.

"The separate campaigns carried out by Vera Brittain and George Hartman," James J. Martin, of Rampart College, Colorado, commented in a 28-page article published in 1968, "stand out as about the only humanitarian protests against an all-out war against civilians fought by armies that had lost their horror of horror, and led by politicians who had done so as well."

In England Vera's booklet provoked a few sporadic attacks, but America was preparing to drop atomic bombs on Hiroshima and Nagasaki, and it would have been intolerable had she influenced public opinion to believe that it was contrary to Christian principles to kill thousands of women and children in the pursuit of victory. The reaction to her protest was immediate and overwhelming. Attacks on her occurred from coast to coast by the hundreds in every imaginable medium of communication, and the printed condemnations alone would fill a number of volumes.

Vera had predicted that unrestricted bombing would make peace with Germany impossible for many years, and James J. Martin concluded that "the absence of a peace treaty twenty-four years after her prediction suggests some commentary on her prowess as a seer, though this situation results from complications beyond even her analysis at that time. It has been remarked that self-delusion is the cardinal English weakness, but Vera Brittain demonstrated her immunity."

Massacre by Bombing completely destroyed Vera's American popularity. With it disappeared a large and lucrative market for her books, but she had always known that in adhering to her pacifist principles she was jeopardising her reputation as a writer.

"I was never half so much interested in success as in the purposes to which I had dedicated myself," she wrote to her husband. "As soon as they and success became incompatible, success had to go. There was never any question about this . . . the sacrifice of popularity and prestige was worthwhile."

In 1945 in Berlin the Americans discovered a Gestapo "Black List" containing the names of 2,000 people whose arrest—and presumably liquidation—was to have been automatic after the German victory over Britain. Owing to the alphabetical proximity of their surnames, Vera's was included with that of Winston Churchill and others splashed on the front pages of the daily newspapers. Many prominent writers who had actively supported the war were chagrined to find themselves omitted from the Gestapo list, and Vera's inclusion is a significant indication of the influence and potential power of the dedicated pacifist.

"If there had been an invasion," she remarked to me not long after the list was published, "it looks as if it would have been quite a race between the Home Office and the Gestapo to see who could get their hands on me first!"

Work was the essential vitamin of Vera's life. She was the most conscientious person I have known and carefully regulated her time to make the most of each day. She was up by 7.30, and always endeavoured to write for at least three hours each morning. She seldom received less than twenty letters a day, and to many of these she dictated replies to her part-time secretary. To her family and close friends she wrote long, graphic letters by hand, and invariably replied by return. In the afternoon she liked to take a walk, shop, or catch up on some household chores. After her evening meal she returned to her desk again, and was often there well after midnight.

Vera enjoyed living in London, but the constant interruptions were a serious impediment to concentrated writing, and whenever possible she escaped to her cottage near Lyndhurst in Hampshire, which she had bought with royalties from *Testament of Youth*. The cottage was on the edge of the New Forest, and the long country walks she enjoyed were among her happiest memories. Her bedroom overlooked the green of the small hamlet, and in the early morning she watched the Forest ponies gathering under her window, and the foals racing round the trees.

"I love it here," she wrote to me, "because I make such rapid and uninterrupted progress. Since I came here less than three weeks ago I have written the six most difficult chapters of my book. The previous six much shorter chapters took me two months."

Some people imagined that Winifred's death and the obloquy she endured for her pacifist convictions must seriously have overshadowed Vera's later life, but this was certainly not so. She had her writing and her friends, her dedication burned as brightly as ever, and she was devoted to her husband and their two gifted and highly individual children. As a wife and mother Vera was deeply involved in the lives of her husband and children, and in almost every letter she wrote about their activities, of her hopes for them, and, occasionally, of her anxieties. John, meticulous, musical and artistic, reminded her in many ways of her brother, and she attributed his business sense to his Brittain ancestry.

For so staunch a feminist it was perhaps natural that her hopes—particularly in later life—should be centred principally upon her daughter, Shirley, whom she had named "after Charlotte Brontë's 'gallant little cavalier'."

"What a child of us both she is," Vera wrote to her husband when Shirley was twenty-one. "The careful choice of words, the love of birds and small animals, plus so many of your interests and so much of your disposition. She is a darling."

On the day of the Parliamentary election in 1964, Vera had contemplated going to Hitchin, but decided that Shirley could scarcely expect to be elected, and knew she would prefer to face defeat unencumbered by her parents. She went instead to the Reform Club, and at 12.15 am heard Richard Dimbleby announce, "Here's a Labour gain from Hitchin", as her daughter's face lit up the television screen.

Sometimes thoughtlessly, but sometimes Vera suspected with an element of malice, people asked her whether she was envious of her daughter's success. She acknowledged with complete honesty that Shirley's intellectual capacity was quite different to hers, and that although she might have acquired from her such environmental qualities as a facility for public speaking, and an aptitude for sustained and concentrated effort, she inherited from her father her exceptional qualities of political thinking and economic judgment.

Each night when Parliament was sitting Vera looked across from the balcony of her Whitehall Court flat to the bright light shining from the top of Big Ben. It typified for her Shirley's political career, and the hopes she cherished for it.

"She will go, and was intended to go, much farther than I was," she prophesied, "but how far I shall probably not survive long enough to know. I think she will be one of those who will help to achieve the heights that I believe humanity can reach if it is permitted to survive."

Vera combined her writing with a love of travel, and a considerable skill for public speaking. After the publication of *Testament of Youth* she undertook three highly successful coast-to-coast American lecture tours for the Colston Leigh Bureau, and later two more for The American Friends Service Committee. She was for many years a popular speaker on lecture platforms throughout Great Britain, and in 1960 she addressed the University of Natal Jubilee Conference in Durban.

In the autumn of 1966 Vera was hurrying along Northumberland Avenue to give a talk at St Martin-in-the-Fields when she stumbled in the dark and fell over some builders' debris. Although considerably shaken and in pain she fulfilled her engagement, and discovered only later that she had broken her left arm, and the little finger of her right hand.

Her recovery was protracted and inconclusive. Imperceptibly as the months passed, the mind that had always been so clear and resolute became clouded and uncertain, her memory faltered, and she dwelt for long periods in a silent world of her own. "I know I am on my way out," she wrote to me in a brief, scarcely legible note. "I don't much mind except for George."

As time went by her illness claimed her inexorably, and she turned increasingly for comfort and reassurance to her husband, her family, and to Charles and Amy Burnett, who had joined the household in Glebe Place early in the 1930's and who remained for almost forty years, loyal and devoted.

When I visited her one afternoon early in January 1970 it was as if the mists that enveloped her had been miraculously swept aside. "Oh, Paul, I'm so glad you've come," she greeted me as I lent over and kissed her, smiling with her eyes as she had always done. "I want you to tell me everything you're doing, and all about your plans for the future." I sat down beside her and held her hand, but almost at once the mists rolled up again and enshrouded her.

On Easter Sunday, March 29, 1970, Vera came at last to the end of her journey. The world is only as good a place as the people living in it choose to make it, and we should be grateful to Vera Brittain for her valiant fight to make it better, for her dedication to peace and the continuing liberation of women, for her passion for justice and her compassion for the oppressed, and, perhaps above all, for the shining example of her rock-like integrity.

Friendship is one of life's greatest gifts, and for almost twenty-eight years Vera had suffused my existence with constant supportive help, generosity and encouragement, and love. It was not without tears that I mourned her departure, but the memory and inspiration endure of a courageous and lovable woman.

Paul Berry, Steadham, Midhurst 1979

FOREWORD

In *Testament of Youth*, published in 1933, I attempted to interpret history in terms of personal life, and to use for this purpose the technique of presentation hitherto reserved for fiction.

The story became a memorial to the generation of young men who were swept from the threshold of life by the First World War. Mirroring universal tragedy in private sorrow, it sought to give reality to their fate.

Testament of Experience continues the history of that generation, which in the second half of its journey appears to be faced with the most momentous challenge of all time. This challenge compels it to surmount its own "impulse towards death", or vanish with all man's works in an orgy of annihilation.

The personal record which accompanies a second epoch of unparalleled achievement and abysmal disaster is a different story from that through which the reader saw the first. Here is a chronicle of marriage, with its joys and tribulations, and of family relationships exposed to the ordeal of a Second World War. The fight for literary achievement again accompanies a search for the road to a civilised society. A sudden flight to fame precedes a swift descent into humiliation; and redemption finally appears as the acceptance of experience, which makes the future still a living adventure undimmed by the shadows of the past.

In the closing chapter of *Testament of Youth*, I put into words the fear with which I faced the re-creation of hopes once thought to be gone for ever. "If life should deal me a new series of blows through G. and his children, could I survive them and go on working?"

But history tends to defy the familiar aphorism; whether national or personal, it seldom repeats itself. The apprehensions which I had expressed were to prove well-founded, as anyone who has lived through the past twenty years would expect. But the new onslaughts of fate did not arise from marriage and motherhood, though sometimes tragedy—as in the episode of the *Western Prince*—came close to repetition.

The Second War brought instead a succession of sharp anxieties, common to all who endured it, and a series of moral dilemmas, peculiar to the individuals who faced them. Problems arose in which it was all too easy to make the wrong choice, and all too difficult to accept the consequences of decisions that seemed right. For myself the calamity of 1914 innocently represented "an interruption of the most exasperating kind to my personal plans". The "interruptions" of the Second War were different. They came to involve a conscious and deliberate withdrawal from popular acclaim and material reward.

Eighteen months after the publication of *Testament of Youth*, its unexpected appeal to an international public suggested the wisdom of an early sequel. When I discussed the idea with Winifred Holtby, she asked me how I proposed to continue the story.

Looking back on the decade which had followed 1925, I said: "I want to write about the menace of a dangerous world to John and Shirley, and the attempt to achieve something useful for them and their contemporaries before it's too late. Surely such a theme matters enough to make a book?"

"I should think it does!" she replied. "It's about the only theme that matters today."

But before the sequel could be started she was dead, and to tell her story in *Testament of Friendship* became more urgent than resuming my own. And directly her story was finished the Second World War eclipsed the years which had followed the First, and in its turn was eclipsed by the events that threatened a third.

During that long interval my son and daughter grew up, constructing their own patterns of life in an age not merely of catastrophe but of wonder; a century of opportunity in the fullest and deepest sense. Watching them, I perceived that to be born into an apocalyptic era may be a cause for rejoicing rather than lamentation; the problems to be resolved demand, and create, spiritual resources which the prosperous ease of a golden age will never inspire.

Thus by 1950 I had lost the compunction aroused in 1935 by the children's existence, and the celebration that summer of our Silver Wedding reminded me that two and a half decades had passed since the year which closed the story of my youth. Three years later, and exactly twenty after the publication of the first *Testament*, I began to write its successor.

The creation of this third record has been more difficult than that of the other two. In *Testament of Friendship*, though its subject was dead, the need to consider living persons whom the story affected already compelled reservations, but *Testament of Youth* belonged to a period of life in which purposes and choices, though shadowed by grief, remained comparatively simple.

My young contemporaries and I faced the obligation of dying if death were demanded; we had not attained, as those who reach maturity attain, to the necessity of living a complicated life. Time brings new forms of responsibility and a concern for the aims and reticences of others; the private aspects of public affairs impinge upon knowledge, and compel a reserve quite different from the single-minded reverence demanded by the memory of the dead.

I have written this book with two phrases in my mind. A quarter of a century ago John Grierson invented the word "documentary", which he later defined as "the creative treatment of actuality". More recently, in his *Study of History*, Professor Arnold Toynbee wrote that "we find the novelist vying with the diarist, the biographer, and the letter-writer to determine whether 'Fiction' or 'Fact' is the more propitious medium for bringing out the poetry in the private affairs of ordinary people".

To find and convey this poetry by the "creative treatment of actuality" has been my endeavour.

I have tried to show how experience is both particular and universal, each separate strand contributing to the texture of the whole. The experience of one person, as practical record and spiritual pilgrimage, may be important in itself; its significance is doubled if the personal narrative is linked with the experience of many, and approaches the experience of all.

In this sense my story reflects an epoch in history, and an epoch in history embodies the personal discovery of a faith unattained in my youth.

PART I

"What is the price of Experience? do men buy it for a song?
Or wisdom for a dance in the street? No, it is bought with the price
Of all that a man hath."

WILLIAM BLAKE, *Vala*, or *The Four Zoas*.

CHAPTER ONE
BRITISH BRIDE

*"If I were drawing up a marriage service, I think I would make it run thus:
'We who have different interests and serve God in different ways, yet knowing
that all interests are poor and worldly compared with that human devotion
which is the means whereby we enter into eternal experience, do desire to take
each other so long as love lasts, and so long as piety to ancient loyalties and to
the sacrament of unrepeatable experience binds us together.'"*

G.C. TO V.B., 1925.

(1)

WHEN G. AND I were married on June 27th, 1925, the First
World War was seven years behind us, and only a few political
specialists dreamed of the Second.

Together we left the Catholic Church of St. James's, Spanish
Place, on a mild London afternoon of grey skies lit by fleeting
glimmers of sunshine. Our only bridesmaid, Winifred Holtby, followed us down the steps of the Church accompanied by the Earl of
Stamford, G.'s New College contemporary, who had been his
best man.

Behind these two tall figures came my pretty, young-looking
mother, whose face when she died in her late seventies was to be less
lined than mine at thirty, though she never ceased to mourn my
brother Edward, whose death in the final year of the war had made
me an only child. With her walked G.'s widowed clerical parent and
my fastidiously-dressed, semi-invalid father, every button of his pale
grey waistcoat doing its duty.

The well-to-do middle-class congregation typical of every semi-
fashionable London wedding drifted after them. It included my
numerous relatives and a bevy of highly respectable neighbours
living near my parents' flat in Kensington. They were all irre-
proachably Anglican, and I concluded that curiosity about G. had
drawn them to a "mixed marriage" in a Catholic church. Because he
had recently been appointed to a professorship at an American university they thought of him as forty-five and bearded, though he was

17

actually still in his twenties and, being tall, slim, blue-eyed and wavy-haired, resembled an undergraduate rather than a don.

Hardly a shadow of the griefs and conflicts which had dominated the past decade hung over the cosy, conventional reception. Only the lovely cadences of Gounod's *Ave Maria*, swelling to the vaulted roof of the tall church as G. and I signed the register, had symbolised those poignant memories and the self-dedication which they involved.

Foremost among our wedding guests we greeted Father Bede Jarrett, the eloquent and handsome Provincial of the Dominican Order in Britain, who knew G. and had agreed to marry us. From his words to us that day I have carried through life only one sentence —"We cannot know the love of God until we have known the love of man"—but long after his premature death I had not forgotten the beauty, like a spiritual flame, of the face which appeared ten years younger than its age as he stood before us in white and gold vestments.

After speaking with him I sought out the two guests for whom, in that amiable unthinking crowd, I felt the deepest concern. Robert and Marie Connor Leighton were the parents of Roland, to whom, but for a machine-gun bullet in wartime France, I should now be married instead of marrying G. Having achieved notoriety with a pre-war best-seller, *Convict 99*, Marie Leighton was still writing Edwardian thrillers, for the dynamic energy transmuted in Roland to brilliant classic scholarship and poetry of rare promise had proved in her to be unquenchable even by grief for his death.

In spite of her fifty or sixty summers (I never knew her exact age, nor, I think, did anyone else), she wore for our wedding a pale blue muslin dress with short puffed sleeves, and a picture hat of the same girlish material. As usual her cheeks were thickly smudged with brick-coloured rouge, which contrasted oddly with the long locks of saffron-yellow-hair hanging unevenly beneath the incredible hat.

To the church I had carried the same variety of tall pink roses, with a touch of orange in their colouring and the sweetest scent in the world, which Roland had given me one New Year's Eve a lifetime ago. I offered them to Marie Leighton before going upstairs to put on my travelling dress.

"Please take them, because of Roland," I said, and turned away abruptly, knowing that behind the screen of exquisite flowers a tear or two would make pathetic runnels down the gallant mask of ill-assorted cosmetics. Roland had been her mainspring, her reason

18

for living and working; without him only her strong animal vitality held her to life. Long afterwards I learned that she had kept the bouquet untouched for years, though the roses were brown and withered, and their leaves had crumbled to dust.

To please my relatives our wedding had been as orthodox as a "mixed marriage" allowed, but from the start of the exhausting preparations I had been conscious that the long tulle veil with its crown of orange blossom was an inappropriate symbol of unsophisticated youth. For between my schooldays and my marriage lay ten years of love and sorrow, more crowded than many a long lifetime with adventure and loss.

Then, from the blue, G. had inconveniently emerged, to remind me that the human relationships which I thought I had renounced were still there for the taking. At first I had not regarded him seriously; whoever heard of a "fan-mail" writer turning into a husband? But first his letters, and then his disturbing presence, had exercised the strange and sweet compulsion which brought me, the young war-time veteran masquerading as an ingenuous bride, incredulously to the altar.

I had taken many misgivings there, for the past, with its still unresolved memories, remained vividly alive. Apart from a few weeks together the previous summer, I knew G. chiefly through his brilliant and articulate letters, which assured me that he offered as free a marriage as any man could propose.

"I ask you to give what you want to give, no more. I hope you will never be condemned to regard marriage as in any sense an impoverishment. If it is, you should give it up."

In spite of those bravely defiant words, I realised as I removed my wedding-dress that in the near future lay another conflict as harsh as any I had faced in the past, for I knew that, even if I would, I could not lay down my work unless everything in me that mattered to both G. and myself was to die.

Work, as I had learned in the past few years of minor achievement, was reality; it was bread, while emotion was wine. Life as I had known it was short, with an issue as dark and uncertain as the close of an autumn day, and each new love that it brought me was a hostage given to death. When years faced me which seemed empty and interminable as they can seem only in our early twenties, it had been the honest, pedestrian monotony of work which brought about a return to life still rich with purpose and with hope.

Yet henceforth the difficult early period of creative writing would have to be combined not only with marriage, but with life in a small

American town, and this, at least for a time, would mean my removal from the London scene where the first modest successes had been staged. A process of adaptation lay ahead which would not be easy, and might even prove too difficult to accomplish at all.

But for the moment that new problem was postponed by a holiday called a honeymoon, on which I was so strangely to embark at the summer peak of London's working season.

(2)

After a rainy weekend in Dover we travelled to Vienna, for during the previous six months we had both saved up for a European honeymoon. G., who had just returned from America, had contributed the difference between second class and steerage, while I put aside the small sums which I was already beginning to earn by free-lance journalism.

On our wedding morning a timely cheque for £18 had reached me from Mr. Andrew Dakers, then my literary agent. The profits which I brought him were negligible, but he was the most helpful and benevolent agent that I have ever had. His cheque represented the total amount in royalties earned by my second novel, *Not Without Honour*. It seemed to me then to be quite a substantial sum.

We reached Vienna in a downpour of rain. Already the leaves in the Stadtpark were turning yellow; the first heralds of autumn had touched the beds of scarlet salvia and geranium. Tired though we were, we listened for an hour to an organ recital in the Stefanskirche, which watched over the city like a tutelary god.

After the red evening light the serene darkness of the cathedral was so soothing that for a few moments I fell asleep. I woke to hear the organist playing Schubert's *Pax Vobiscum*, and to see G.'s eyes fixed dreamily upon the lamp hanging like a firefly above the altar. And I recalled a sentence from Fitzjames Stephen which he had quoted in one of his letters: "The earnest believer falls in love with his religion as a man might fall in love with a woman, without hope, but beyond the possibility of recovery."

The previous autumn I had spent several weeks in Vienna, once the proud centre of an unwieldy empire but now the incongruously large capital of a small humiliated country in a continent torn and divided by the Peace Treaties. The brilliant city had become a head without a body, an administration with nothing to administer, and the Hapsburgs, who once ran about Europe like mercury on a glass plate accumulating territory by judicious marriages, had vanished into exile and silence. Now, in 1925, the Hofburg with its

20

dilapidated façade like the scarred face of an old warrior supplied the public with postage stamps in the courts formerly trodden by kings, and beneath its arches the red motor buses pounded heavily on their way from Stefansplatz to the Burg Ring.

Yet, for all her monuments of decayed yesterday, there was life in Vienna still. Her citizens still flocked to cafés and concerts; their amiable idleness saved them from that spiritual despair which is the only true death. As the French writer Mazade once said of Prince Metternich, Vienna belonged to the old régime *"par ses goûts, par ses mémoires, et par ses regrets."* She remained dignified in defeat, without self-pity, hatred or anger. For the aggressive politicians who had trampled her down so ruthlessly in the post-war epidemic of vengeance, she had merely a gentle, tolerant contempt.

From time to time, as we explored the Kärntnerstrasse and the gardens of Schönbrunn together, speculations assailed me concerning the personality of the young man who was now my husband. One of his college contemporaries had warned me, only half humorously, that he had always regarded G. as a natural bachelor and something of a monk.

"He has a complicated mind," wrote H., "but a very simple nature, whence it follows naturally that he is genuinely devout, though rather at a loss as to where to worship. On general grounds I should have supposed him less adapted for marriage than any other man in the world except myself."

So far there had been little time in which to examine this judgment. Though G. and I had corresponded on everything under the sun, we had only been aware of each other's existence for two years, and I wondered how far my undiluted society would satisfy him. I need not have been perturbed, for it was not to be put to the test.

As a gifted interpreter of politics, G. had written me from America that he was now concerned "with an exceedingly scientific and technical post-mortem of the political system that produced the past war." This was to be the basis of his first important book, and I soon discovered that his appetite for political knowledge was insatiable.

For him a holiday, and even a honeymoon, would be incomplete unless each week contained a number of interviews with politicians and government officials. Not for several years did he learn to appreciate the frivolities of Capri and the Riviera.

In Vienna these interviews were seldom satisfactory, for the Austrians are a sociable people which prefers art to politics. An "interview" tended to become a tea-party, complete with cream

21

cakes and tempting open sandwiches arranged in appetising patterns. When a dozen guests, invited to reinforce the morale of the person interviewed, found themselves in conjunction with such delicacies, little hope existed that we should be able to outsit the rest of the company by remaining quietly but firmly in our chairs.

Not until we reached Hungary did sensational descriptions of strife and revolution thunder over our heads, and impassioned declamation lend a histrionic flavour to political inquiry.

Our travel agency had advised us that the river journey to Budapest would be a pleasant alternative to the train, but he forgot to warn us that Sunday, when only one boat made the trip, was the worst possible day to choose.

When we reached the Praterkai where the boat started, we found it littered with children, dogs, American tin travelling-trunks, beer bottles, unwieldy wicker baskets fastened with padlocks, and bird-cages occupied by green parrots loudly squawking their surprise and indignation. The official who examined our passports described the steamer as "bumvoll."

With a series of squeaks and groans it slid ponderously into midstream, accompanied by the jubilant strains of Gounod's *Faust* from the band on the upper deck. I watched the banks of the Danube, and continued to watch them for the next two or three hours. There was, indeed, no alternative to contemplating their grey-green fringe of little feathery poplars and the oily yellowish water.

Hours passed. We slept, ate and read, and grew progressively dirtier, until the curving Slovakian meadows became black silhouettes beneath the sunset. Going into the saloon for a final cup of coffee, I found an Austrian and a Hungarian vehemently discussing the Peace Treaties. The Hungarian had wild hair and a figure as rotund as the Archepiscopal Palace of Gran, which we had just passed.

"You are American, Fräulein?" he inquired as the argument momentarily slackened from sheer exhaustion.

"No," I replied. "I am English."

"Indeed!" he ejaculated. "But it is all the same! You are one of those who sent President Wilson to Paris. It is his doing that our lands were stolen from Hungary, but the Lord God was on our side and has punished him by an early death!"

In the distance, now heavy with darkness, dull yellow lights flecked the sky like a tarnished constellation. The undulating banks had changed to sharp cliffs, which hung black and menacing above the ink-blue water. As we approached the lights, the Austrian took out his watch.

"It is ten o'clock. At midnight we shall be in Budapest. We are only four hours late," he added without irony.

At Buda G. and I scrambled on to the dimly-lit quay, where a Customs officer awaited us. He pointed to the suitcase containing my new lingerie, and plunged his grubby hands among crêpe-de-chine nightgowns and silk-embroidered slips. Suddenly, with one great heave, he turned everything over from the bottom upwards, and a pair of pink and silver garters which G. had bought for me in the Kärtnerstrasse flew into the air. The crystals on the little velvet roses winked impertinently in the flickering light of the oil-lamp.

"*Sehr schön*," I murmured, holding up one garter seductively.

The official's face suddenly crumpled into a benevolent grin.

"*Fertig!*" he announced, slamming down the lid of my suitcase, and G. and I passed unhindered through the barrier.

(3)

In the white-painted hotel with its window-boxes of red geranium, G. suggested next morning that, since interviews had piled up in Buda as remorselessly as they had evaporated in Vienna, we might well divide our energies. He would go to see Mr. Jeremiah Smith, the American Director of Financial Reconstruction in Hungary, while I endeavoured to extract from the British Minister such crumbs of information as British Ministers impart.

On my way to the Legation, I found that the routine operation of obtaining £5 in kronen from a Hungarian bank was not so simple as I had expected. A clerk promptly invited me into the manager's room, where I found no manager but observed numerous maps.

We were soon to learn that, after the Treaty of the Trianon, the map had become the alternative language of Hungary. In trains, offices, hotels and restaurants, relief maps showed that the old frontiers of Hungary were her natural geographical frontiers; military maps proved them to be her strategical frontiers; and ethnographical maps demonstrated that they were her racial frontiers.

I had examined the maps for ten minutes when the manager appeared, dark, sallow, and smiling. At eleven o'clock, I explained, I had an appointment with the British Minister, and would be grateful for £5 in Hungarian currency.

"Certainly, *gnädige Frau*," he said. "It will not take one moment."

He opened a drawer, and unfastened a roll of papers. With dismay I perceived, not kronen, but the familiar colourful charts. He pointed, his finger shaking, to red splashes outside the black lines of Hungary's existing boundary. "*Gnädige Frau!*" he exclaimed, and his voice vibrated with passion. "Take this map, I entreat you, back to London, and show the men and women of England what they have done to this poor Hungary! See the red that surrounds the black line—this line that marks the infamous boundary which has mutilated my country! *Gnädige Frau*, this red—the colour of the tears of blood which Hungary has shed since you forced her to sign your Treaty—this red represents the millions of miserable Magyars whom you have transferred, contrary to their will and against law and humanity, to the harsh intolerance of inferior civilisations!"

"But," I interrupted as he paused for breath, "you mustn't blame me for the Trianon Treaty. I didn't make it—and I wouldn't have, either."

His air of courteous patience convinced me that my protests were futile.

"Ach!" he responded sadly. "Those words are the words of all your countrymen. England did not make the Treaty, but alas! she submitted to it! England and the other Western nations bowed their proud heads and allowed themselves to be dictated to by Czechs, Serbs, and Roumanians. England and the other Western nations. . . ."

The hands of the wall clock moved steadily on past eleven as I learned of the sufferings imposed by the Treaty upon Hungary's intellectuals, and their humiliation by peoples of inferior culture because Western statesmen were ignorant of geography. Twenty minutes later a clerk appeared with a formidable sheaf of documents which he placed before me.

"Please sign here, madame."

I signed here, there, and everywhere. Ten minutes afterwards I escaped into the street with nearly two million kronen, a large map, and an even larger quantity of distressing information. Noon was past when a dilapidated droschke, frantically summoned, deposited me at the Legation in the Verböczy Utca. There, to my relief, I learned that in Hungary even British Ministers did not expect their callers to be on time.

Before we left Budapest, an introduction to a Hungarian financier brought us one evening of real relaxation. Mr. Jacobi invited us to dinner at Buda's most fashionable restaurant on the Margareten Island in the Danube, where a galaxy of summer flowers flung their

24

scent into the air; and the dancers, hypnotised by the wailing of the gipsy orchestra, glided and swayed like half-intoxicated butterflies.

We dined on crab soup, fish from Lake Balaton, roast chicken, and chocolate-iced cream cakes known to Budapest as "indiennes". Best of all was a drink which our host called "Bowl", made from champagne, fruit syrup, wild strawberries, and ice. Drugged by this ambrosial diet, we listened in a beatific dream while he conversed with gentle irony, proving himself in every sentence to be that rarest of individuals, a liberal Hungarian.

"No doubt you have been told that the bloodthirsty Béla Kun was a son of the devil. But I have seen and talked with this diabolical lackey of Russia. I found him a moderate, well-intentioned man, who wanted to build up a better university for Budapest and bring in new professors from other countries. He and his Jews were better than the Roumanians, who stole everything the Bolsheviks left."

Our friend took a long drink, and pointed to the dancers.

"See how happy they are! The English and Americans respect women, but the Hungarians enjoy them. It is the same with politics. For us they are the national game, like your baseball or your cricket. It does not require a son of the devil to make a revolution in Hungary."

He continued his amiable monologue, as absorbing to us as to him, on the anatomy of revolutions and the war-time tolerance of Hungarians towards their British prisoners, until the echo of many chimes floated along the river.

"It is midnight," he announced, picking up my coat. "But before I take you back to your hotel, I shall drive you to the heights above the city and show you Budapest in the darkness."

We walked to his car along a garden path stencilled by the vivid moon with black and white patterns, in appearance as permanent but in reality as ephemeral as the complicated designs traced by politicians upon the ancient countenance of Europe. Half-an-hour later G. and I stood hand in hand on the dark edge of the world, where a little night-wind caressed our faces with a touch as gentle as a lover's.

Between the moonlit silhouettes of hills a close-set constellation of lights twinkled from the black river and the wide-awake city, which for all its age-old animosities and its bitter new regrets had given us a week of genuine happiness. I felt grateful to contemporary civilisation for establishing its Eastern limits at Vienna; too much discipline would have spoiled Budapest, that conglomeration of dust and magnificence, fleas and palaces, courtesy and crusading fervour, where nobody seemed to stop talking and no one was ever in time.

Better, I thought, a paradox with revolutions, than an orthodoxy steeped in safety and without surprises.

(4)

On his homeward voyage in the *Aquitania*, G. had shared a cabin with three companions. One had been a musical Jugoslav, who wrote poetry, spoke seven languages, and came from Ljubljana. When G. learned that this city with the unpronounceable name lay on the main railway line between Budapest and Trieste, he persuaded me to give up my plan of visiting Innsbrück and go to Ljubljana instead.

"It'll be useful to you journalistically," he urged when I asked why. Even the discovery that this mysterious place was the capital of Slovenia, and under its former name of Laibach had been the homely location of an international Congress after the Napoleonic Wars, failed to shake his determination to explore it.

From Buda the dilatory *Schnellzug* moved slowly south-west across the Hungarian plain, its jade-brown monotony unbroken by any large town up to the Jugoslav border. As I sat in the dining-car drinking coffee, I observed these gently-sloping fields with half-conscious apprehension.

Their quiet productiveness had set me thinking about one of the many problems which we had to face. If we wanted children—as we did, though I had no illusion about the degree to which they would intensify the conflict between work and marriage—we knew that we must have them soon if we were to be young enough to enjoy their companionship when they grew up. Yet the uncertainty of the immediate future made postponement inevitable.

G. hoped by way of his American appointment to return to a British academic post, more advanced than the lectureship which he had held at Sheffield before obtaining a Cornell Fellowship to study political science. But another year in the United States lay ahead of him, and where we should go after that we did not know. A settled household and a family would have to wait; our first home would be a small top-floor apartment in a frame house on the Cornell campus.

As we crossed the great plain I wished that this postponement were unnecessary, for the patient fertility of the fields, like marriage itself, had reawakened the normal instinct for motherhood which I

26

had deliberately suppressed after Roland's death. That dear obstacle to fulfilment in writing would best be surmounted at once, while the impulse towards both forms of creation was strong. But where? When? How?

"What are you thinking about?" G. inquired, turning from his own contemplation of the olive-green marshland outside the train.

"Oh, I don't know! Marriage—children—family life in general," I answered vaguely, still feeling too shy and strange to be explicit.

"Look, here's the lake!" he announced tactfully, perceiving that I did not want to talk. "It isn't too late to see it after all."

Through the pearl-grey twilight I looked towards the water, and the aching problems vanished. Lake Balaton suddenly captured me, like a huge bird poised between earth and sky, one flamingo feather of sunset trailing across its dove-coloured breast. But even as I looked the feather disappeared, and a visible curtain of darkness un-rolled itself before the smouldering clouds. With nightfall came blinding rain, putting out the bright eyes of the lamp-lit villas perched on the rocky cliffs above us.

The lake, ferociously lashed by wind, seemed suddenly hostile to the alien railway line precariously laid along the narrow belt of land between the rocks and the water. Involuntary partisans, we were caught into a fierce battle between primeval forces and the Hungarian transport system. Ghosts walked the jet-black waves and the forlorn colourless earth, and the train, as though pursued, fled screeching along the solitary shore.

The transport system won, for at 4 a.m. it deposited us, shivering, at Ljubljana. In the small splashy station yard, a dog-cart drew up which must certainly have been used for the Laibach Congress of 1821.

"Whoever comes here, and why?" I demanded.

"Who indeed but our original selves?" G. retorted, his early morning thoughts turning to Serb-Croat relations and the pluralistic basis of the Jugoslav state.

But after interviews with a *Zupan* (governor) and an eloquent doctor from the Fortschritt Partei, and a pleasant Sunday of relaxation in which the sun shone and the bells rang and the mountain breezes blew from the Julian Alps, and the round-headed German-speaking children, born Austrian but now learning to be good little Jugoslavs, hurried newly washed and plaited to church with their stiff-collared mothers and fathers, he agreed that we had exhausted the possibilities of the place.

So we took the train to Trieste, and slept until a Jugoslav official politely shook us awake at a frontier village called Rakek-Pakek.

"It sounds like a crowd of jays having a quarrel," I commented to G. as the Customs officer endeavoured to discover how much Jugoslav currency we were taking into perfidious Italy.

"*Wie viel Geld haben Sie?*" he asked me.

"*Ich habe drei hundert Dinars, nicht mehr,*" I replied, sleepy but truthful. Inquiringly, he turned to G.

"*Ich habe kein Geld. Ich habe nur Lire,*" G. answered drowsily.

A delighted smile spread responsively over the sympathetic Jugoslav countenance.

"*Bitte!*" he protested benevolently. "*Lire sind auch Geld!*" And in that tone of contemptuous appreciation we read the whole story of Fiume and Trieste.

From the dun Istrian plateau, ruthless as Fascism itself, we travelled south through Venice to Vicenza, now the site of a unique war memorial. Thirty miles from the small town, which once spelt Italy to a few marooned divisions of British troops, rose the Asiago Plateau, and in one of its two British cemeteries was Edward's grave. Winifred Holtby and I had been there just after going down from Oxford, and now I wrote to tell her that I had returned with G., driving through ivied and fortressed Marostica up hairpin roads still more terrifying than those which she and I had ascended together from Bassano.

Only the pines, sighing their minor melodies in tune with dead music, had linked the violin-playing companion of my childhood with the Edward now tersely commemorated in black letters on a white stone. Thirty years after his death I should still miss him as though he had died yesterday.

That late July evening the sun set angrily amid flaming banks of cloud, and the Angelus sounded solemnly from a hundred little churches in the Brenta Valley far below the Monte Berico memorial. Into my mind came a familiar passage from Kingsley's *Heroes*: "Through doubt and need, danger and battle, I drive them; and some are slain in the flower of youth . . . but what will be their latter end I know not, and none save Zeus, the Father of gods and men."

In front of the burning sky the grim silhouette of the mountains, range upon range as unrelenting as my childish nightmares of eternity, grew sharper as the stars came out and a thousand lights, their humble reflections, sprang like tiny beacons from the houses in the valley. A fitful wind blew across the terrace as a giant finger slowly extinguished the incandescent glow where the day had disappeared. Suddenly it blotted out the last red memory of the sun, and the long black ridge of the Asiago Plateau vanished beneath the shrouding wings of the summer night.

Edward was gone.

(5)

We had planned to spend the second half of our honeymoon in the French Alps, reading, writing and walking as a peaceful change from continuous travel. A tedious journey took us through Turin and over the Col de Sestrières, which proved even more hair-raising than the drive to the Asiago Plateau.

In Turin the charcoal countenance of Mussolini scowled at us from every other doorpost along the principal streets. The more doorways we passed, the more beetle-browed and Napoleonic that menacing countenance appeared, until the whole city became a dizzy portrait-gallery of charcoal Mussolinis, each more ferocious than the last.

After a day's complicated travelling, we reached La Grave between the green glaciers of La Meije and the restless Romanche, tumbling in petulant cascades over its rocky bed. We had only been there two days when a letter from home announced a family tragedy. My father's eldest sister, after years of marital misery, had jumped from the top of a Welsh mountain and died without recovering consciousness. Fearing that this disaster would greatly upset my highly-strung father, we hastened home.

It was a sobering end to a honeymoon, though I did not then recognise it as a portent.

When we reached London my father received us gladly, but appeared to regard his sister's end with singular detachment. Not for the first time I reflected on the indifference of the older generation of Brittains, who met chiefly at funerals, to each other's needs and sorrows. Counting three deaths in infancy, they had been eleven all told, and though large families were then still identified with morality, they did not appear to have benefited much from their numbers.

Silently I prayed that the son and daughter for whom G. and I hoped would bring more happiness to themselves and others than my grandmother's prolific family.

(6)

In September we went to America, remorsefully leaving my parents, who had lost their only son and were now parting for nearly a year with their only daughter. It was even harder to leave Winifred, for the past five years my second self. When we sailed from

Liverpool in the White Star Dominion ship *Regina*, I felt I was relinquishing my early youth and all the beloved contemporaries whom the war had taken. The vanishing coast of Britain seemed to symbolise that gigantic tragedy of young intense living—"the past's enormous disarray".

Before me lay—what? New opportunities, or a repetition of the early frustrations? A dear companionship worthy of the past, or one which would never shine with the glory of those inspired intimacies? At least we meant it to be different, if not better; a permanent relationship which would grow in depth and significance.

"Marriage vows," G. had written me during our courtship, "are merely the expression of one's honourable intentions."

Going along the Welsh coast, where the Great Orme loomed starkly against an orange sunset, those intentions seemed to provide a basis for reassurance. Then, for four days, the small liner plunged into a full gale which quenched speculation in the terror brought back from the submarine-infested voyages of the war, when fear had been ruthlessly repressed.

Such alarms now seem ludicrous after many years of travel by sea and air, but in 1925 they left me slightly distraught when we finally landed at Montreal.

G. had chosen this route through Canada in order to show me the fire-opal evening beauty of the St. Lawrence, and the scarlet maples on the banks of the gargantuan river, with its estuary which spanned the distance from London to York. But the long circuitous journey proved to be mistaken; unlike the first breath-catching sight of the New York skyline by travellers unfamiliar with America, it did nothing to redeem my apprehensive belief that I was going to the back of beyond. This expectation was not removed by the series of short expeditions through small New York State townships which eventually deposited us in Ithaca, the home of Cornell University.

After the slow-moving, dislocated countries where we had spent our honeymoon, I was soon to find overwhelming the pace and wealth of post-war America. Shortly after we arrived, a writer in *Harper's Magazine* inquired, "Is this a Christian land?" and went on to comment regretfully: "Many of us seem almost hopelessly enamoured of a religion that is little better than a sanctified commercialism. . . . Self-interest bulks large as the fuel which makes the present economic machine go."

The Prohibition experiment, tested for five years, now seemed to be firmly established, and "speak-easies" had replaced the former licensed saloons. Calvin Coolidge had succeeded Warren Harding, and already bore the popular title of "Prosperity President". Internationally, the United States remained outside the League of Nations; internally, all progressive impulses seemed dead. But in *Current History* for September, Bruce Bliven, an editor of *The New Republic*, ventured upon a prophecy: "An active progressive movement is needed as it has never been before. . . . Such a progressive movement may not play a part in the national campaign in 1928 or 1932, but when it finally comes it will amount to something."

What it did amount to was Franklin D. Roosevelt's "New Deal" on the further side of the 1929 Wall Street slump.

The local élite who welcomed me to Ithaca, set like a northern gem in the Iroquois country of lakes and forests, represented a microcosm of wealthy America. I had left a London which took its pleasures modestly at the Wembley Exhibition; here, for days on end, lavish gifts of flowers, fruit and candies descended upon our small apartment. Invitations also poured in, and with G.—a little astonished that the acquisition of a novelist wife should create such a stir—I became the guest of honour at numerous receptions and the object of continual social calls by "Faculty wives".

For a time I enjoyed these attentions, as any young woman would. But all too soon, when they showed no sign of diminishing, I began to reflect how poor a substitute they were for the satisfying and fruitful work which had claimed me during the four years between Oxford and marriage.

At that stage of my experience I was totally unable to estimate at their true value the internationally famous scholars, such as Carl Becker, Wallace Notestein and Bradford Titchener, who made Cornell one of America's most distinguished universities. G.'s own students had previously been taught by Professor (now Sir) A. E. Zimmern.

(7)

Had it not been the site of a great University, Ithaca's remarkable scenery and dramatic position might well have made it a mountain spa. From the first it reminded me of the beautiful but reactionary Derbyshire health resort where I had spent my restricted girlhood. Owing to the long struggle to get away from it, Buxton remained in my memory as the ultimate symbol of frustration. When I perceived Ithaca's similarity, my first reaction was one of sheer dismay.

I had thought Buxton remote owing to its four hours' rail

journey from London, but Ithaca, four hundred miles from New York, made escape even more difficult. Today, thanks to air travel, Fifth Avenue can be reached in two hours from the little up-state city, but I doubt whether an assistant-professor's salary makes frequent flights any more feasible than constant overnight train trips at $25 return were feasible for ourselves in 1925. Even when G. became a full professor at thirty-one, our resources seldom permitted unnecessary expeditions.

In Ithaca, Derbyshire's pleasant rocky dales became dramatic ravines crossed by swaying suspension bridges over thundering torrents, and the tinkling streamlets of my childhood turned into boisterous cascades. Tuchannock Falls were steep and fierce; at Buttermilk Falls the water, resembling delicate lace, dripped slowly from a great height over enormous rocks. Every winter huge icicles hung from the beetling cliffs for several months of sub-zero weather, and desolate winds swept the steel-cold surface of the Finger Lakes into angry waves.

But the biggest contrast came from the colours. In Derbyshire the gentle, continuous spring had taken three months to merge into pale-hued June; Ithaca had no spring at all, but leapt from stulti-fying winter into noisy summer. After August the noise became a tumult, with vermilion maples, orange oaks and flaming banners of sumac competing in a riotous woodland carnival.

Much as I love colour, this gorgeous panoply of reds and yellows brought me no comfort; it merely reminded me that until my lengthening but mediocre record included some valuable achieve-ment, I had not earned the right to enjoy it. Like Buxton's dales and moors in the previous decade, Ithaca's beauty represented in itself, a challenge to get back to constructive work.

Although we now had legions of pleasant acquaintances, I soon realised that G. and I were likely to be intimate only with each other. Loneliness made me an assiduous letter-writer during his long hours of lectures and classes, while the inexorable passing of the futile days in our small dark apartment seemed to be empha-sised by the bells in the Library tower. Every morning and evening they played one of the tunes adopted by Cornell for its own song-book—*Old Man Noah*, *The Bells of Hell*, or *Sweet Adeline*.

"I am not homesick," I insisted when acknowledging to Winifred a copy of *The Nation* which contained one of my own articles. "I have never been that, for each type of life is so interesting. But London is London, and home is home, and you are you."

From the isolation which in spite of myself I now thought of as exile, it was reassuring to see my name printed beside the names of Professor C. K. Webster and Commander Kenworthy. This tiny piece of encouragement reinforced my determination to tackle the editors of American magazines as a substitute for the precarious foothold so recently acquired in London journalism, and I set to work on my first impressions of an unfamiliar civilisation.

In addition to these articles, I was now trying to start a new book. The inspiration had come from a conversation between G. and myself at Vicenza. He had suggested then that I should write the story of a honeymoon—a combination of comments on marriage, travel experiences, and international politics.

This project, subsequently entitled *A Honeymoon in Two Worlds*, had considerable "spice" in the writing, but its ideas on marriage —now common to most intelligent people—were then uncongenial and even shocking to conventional minds. For this reason it failed to find a publisher.

At the outset I was, as usual, full of hope, but neither optimistic energy nor the critical standards of a husband on whom I inflicted these experiments could persuade American editors to publish my articles. Back they came with devastating regularity, accompanied by complimentary letters filled with amiable excuses which conveyed the dismal certainty that residence in Ithaca meant full-stop to a writer's progress.

(8)

To give me a break from provincial isolation, G. arranged in late November a visit to New York. Such revitalising trips had to be strictly rationed, for our combined annual income was £750.

New York, I reported to Winifred, had obviously been invented by H. G. Wells in a previous existence; it was "a city like no other city, full of terrestrial monstrosities". But its real enchantment lay in the contacts at last made possible. Equipped with introductions from the British League of Nations Union, which had included me amongst its voluntary lecturers, I visited its modest American equivalent, the Non-Partisan Association, and discussed the ungrateful task of attracting individual supporters in a non-Member State. An introduction from one distant relative to another—a New York lawyer named Standish Chard—also produced encouraging results. In the delightful and stimulating company of Standish and his wife when G. had to return to Ithaca, I explored New York, visited New Jersey across the Hudson, and carried out some literary business.

Galvanised by this temporary return to my normal life, I worked hard in Ithaca on three articles which the literary agents to whom Andrew Dakers had introduced me hopefully believed that they could sell. I also agreed to give a "literary polish" to G.'s first substantial book, *The Science and Method of Politics*, and, more usefully, to type it for him. Invitations now came to talk on the League of Nations from several small groups, for the University and the local Press were as pro-Geneva as all Democratic communities. The League had become a Party issue, with the Republicans opposing whatever policy its Council initiated.

Christmas went by while, surrounded by rejected typescripts in our top-floor apartment, I looked out upon hurricane, sleet, snow, and other ruthless accompaniments of below-zero temperatures. The one enduring consolation was G. himself. He too disliked small-town life, though his strenuous university post saved him from nostalgia. As the winter deepened, he entered with increasing sympathy into my consciousness of wastefully marking time after four years of promising work.

"It is just six months since our marriage," I wrote to my mother of the personal relationship which we were creating, "and I could not wish better than that the next six months and years may be as this last. . . ."

Early in February, when the endless winter seemed to have reached its nadir, a telegram from home brought a new sorrow. It reported the sudden death, at forty-five, of my mother's younger brother, the beloved "Uncle Bill" whose gallant letters had cheered my war-time nursing in Malta. The thought of my unhappy parents attending, without my support, this second family funeral made the long separation seem harder than ever.

For myself I felt as though another little piece of my life had gone; I had seen so much of Uncle Bill during the war, and he was so closely associated with Edward. It seemed strange to me that, of all the people who had known Edward intimately, only my father and mother were left. Sometimes I had a feeling almost of shock when I reflected that I had not yet known G. for two years. The person one married—at the beginning, at any rate—belonged so much more to one's future than one's past.

My uncle, in dying from the after-effects of wartime overwork, had unconsciously given me one last compensation, for the revived memories of the war gradually converged into the idea which ultimately produced *Testament of Youth*. Indifferent, for once, to my discouraging environment, I wrote to Winifred, who was then travelling in South Africa, in a glow of excitement.

"Yesterday I had a great inspiration for what will, I think, be my next novel—partly because I can write it without having to look up anything except my own letters and diaries."

The novel, I continued, was to be called *The Incidental Adam*, and it would cover the period 1913 to 1925. It would be, I admitted, "dreadfully autobiographical", but at that time I had never thought of my stormy 'teens and 'twenties as a basis for anything but fiction. Biography, and much less autobiography, did not occur to me as lying within my slowly developing powers.

As though fate, having lighted this flame, was now ready to grant further encouragement, a sudden change in our circumstances removed us only a month later from up-state isolation and the grey depression of a persistent but never completed thaw.

In New York at this time the Social Science Research Council was preparing a national investigation into the effects of Prohibition. Its board of directors wanted a trained scholar to seek out available sources of material, and G.'s name had been mentioned because, as an Englishman, he was likely to be impartial and had, while still an undergraduate, undertaken similar work on the British Liquor Control Board under Lord d'Abernon. In late March the Research Council summoned him to New York; there he telephoned me that he had been offered the job of directing the preliminary investigation.

The University gave him leave for the remaining half-semester, and the beginning of April found us both, still incredulous of our good fortune, established in a small New York hotel opposite Columbia University on the heights above the Hudson.

(9)

At first the change seemed a foretaste of Paradise. Freed from cleaning, shopping and feminine gossip, I could spend the months before me in revising and typing G.'s book, and finishing my own. Optimistically I also believed that my chances of placing articles and giving lectures would now be limited, as in London, only by my time and energy.

Our two-room apartment was tiny, but its windows were large. Half New York seemed to spread beneath our bedroom, while from the living-room we looked over the tree-dotted expanse of 116th Street to the northward sweep of the Hudson. Every evening the Jersey shore across the river deepened to the sultry red of a desert beneath the flaming sunset.

At this period New York State led the anti-Prohibition forces, and in the city itself even the police did not pretend to keep the law. G.

took an office on the twentieth floor of the Knickerbocker Building near Times Square and engaged a Radcliffe College graduate as his executive secretary. When his work took him further afield his letters dominated my days, though the frequent visits of my cousins, the kindly Chards, redeemed them from loneliness. I was still too close to the shocks of the war to regard G.'s prolonged absences with equanimity. There was always a little undercurrent of anxiety, of dread. When he was away and I went for walks by myself in Riverside Drive or Morningside Park, I thought of him with a lighthearted, zestful tenderness—the feeling of having treasure in heaven.

Although our limited income forbade me the longer journeys, I had not always to be left behind. In May I accompanied him to an International Relations Conference thirty miles from New York, where forsythia shimmered gold like celestial rain, and pink-tinged blossom foamed over the young green fruit-trees in countless orchards. In April, too, I had been with him to Philadelphia, Washington and Boston, and at a White House reception felt the cold dry hand of Calvin Coolidge as he looked resignedly over my head at the next insignificant stranger waiting in line.

From Boston I carried the memory of sunlight on terra-cotta brick and brilliant foliage tumbling in cascades over old iron balconies. There at a dinner I met Professor Manley Hudson, later America's representative on the Permanent Court of International Justice at The Hague, and Mrs. Francis Sayre, President Wilson's daughter. I was told later that she still felt Wilson's death acutely, and thought no public career worth what it cost.

When I returned to New York, the Non-Partisan Association offered me more speaking engagements. But my real hopes centred on *A Honeymoon in Two Worlds*, of which I finished the first draft in May. The eventual failure to publish it seemed to set the final seal of futility upon our months at Ithaca, where most of it had been written.

Nevertheless, this book did not stir me to the same excitement as the one which I continued to plan as a novel. I was impatient to complete my task of revision so that I could begin *The Incidental Adam*; I ached to write, at long last, about the war—all the glory and the grieving and the sacrifice and struggle and loss. It was, I felt, a book on which one ought to spend at least two years—and I wanted to finish it before I began to have a baby.

I have often since wondered whether all authors are persuaded to continue the head-cracking and too often disappointing job of book writing by similar roseate estimates of their future time-tables. The work to which I had mentally allocated less than two years was ultimately to take four; to be actually started when the first baby was two years old, and finished when the second was nearly three.

By the end of June, when we celebrated our first wedding anniversary, most of our New York acquaintances had departed on holiday, and political and social events had ceased. In the growing midsummer heat, humid and heavy, I sat in the tiny apartment, now crammed with books and papers, doggedly typing G.'s book or my own with clammy hands and swimming head.

Realistically, if reluctantly, I had to admit the greater urgency of his need, for publication of *The Science and Method of Politics* had now been arranged on both sides of the Atlantic. When the soaring temperature reached 100°, Standish and Daisy Chard invited me to stay at their country farm in Massachusetts until G. returned from his travels. There I found respite from the extinguishing counterpane of urban heat in a long low house painted white with green shutters. It stood on the edge of refreshing woods four miles from Sunderland, a pretty New England village which incongruously took its name from the industrial town where nine years later G. was to fight his second Parliamentary election. But temporary peace did not eliminate my problems.

By now it was evident that my life with G. had raised in an acute form the much-discussed issue so tritely summarised as "marriage versus career". The word "career" is a limited expression, suggesting a neat nine-to-five job of small significance; the real clash lies between the important human relationship of marriage, and every type of fulfilment—spiritual, intellectual, social—which falls outside the range of personal intimacy.

In England I had been regarded as a promising young writer whose work dealt with subjects that mattered, but in the United States I was less than the dust. Whereas G. was now happily contributing to *The New Republic, Harper's Magazine, Current History* and several academic publications, I had failed to place one article in an American magazine. I could not even persuade some minor periodical to appoint me as its representative at the coming League of Nations Assembly.

Despondently we both recognised that America would never have any use for me as an author unless, at some distant and improbable date, I became a "lion" of some special kind. Meanwhile, since G.'s research work would end with August, the only available American future appeared to be that of a "Faculty wife", increasingly depressed, frustrated and embittered.

I did not imagine this potential fate; I had seen it come in Ithaca to the few wives who had once dreamed of contributing by creative work to the thought of their generation. Deeply though I now cared for G., the self-sufficient America of 1926, which so little understood the griefs and struggles of the Old World, deprived me of mental food as completely as any Florence Nightingále in a Victorian drawing-room lamenting her "Death from Starvation".

But that was not all. Had the problem merely been one of intellectual frustration I might have believed—though I doubt whether the experiment would have lasted long—that it was my "duty" to sacrifice to domesticity the urge to write, speak, and travel which had possessed me since childhood. But what neither conscience nor reason could accept was spiritual frustration. After seeing civilisation wrecked and the brilliant loves of my early youth destroyed, I had dedicated myself in the months following the Armistice to a future which was less a "career" than a devotional crusade.

It had begun with the realisation, in a German prison camp at Étaples, that the basic fact of men's humanity is more important than the political differences which sometimes divide them. That discovery brought me as close as I had then ever been to the psychological experience of conversion, though it was to remain incomplete for nearly twenty years.

My second phase as an Oxford student from 1919 to 1921 had been a time of conscious preparation. By suffering and experience, and later through continuous reading and thinking, I had become convinced that there were certain ideas, however difficult to realise and promote, which could save mankind from its suicidal follies. And I believed that, through experiment, patience and the integrity by which the artist transcends the cruder expedients of the propagandist, I could learn to embody those ideas in my work with sufficient conviction to make others think too. Only thus could I atone to my dead contemporaries for the cruelty of having outlived them.

Could it really be my duty, I asked myself now, to sacrifice the attempt to convey a redemptive faith—so difficult to accept and so incessantly resisted by human beings anxious only to be comfortable —to the personal needs of a husband and later a family? In spite of many misgivings reinforced by the socially conditioned conscience of my youth, I did not believe it. And though my generation of women was so ruthlessly trained in childhood to put persons before convictions that its members have never been able to pursue an impersonal ideal without remorse, I do not believe it now.

Just how I should acquire a status which would command a hearing and thus enable me to create my particular memorial to the dead, I did not yet know, though the book provisionally entitled *The Incidental Adam* seemed to point a way. But whatever I achieved would have to be done through writing and speaking, for these were my only gifts—and America did not want them.

As early as the autumn of my arrival, a letter home had recorded that "G. says he would rather I did not come out at all next year if I feel that my work demands my staying in London"—a comment indicating the dismay which inspired so drastic a suggestion at this initial stage. Now it appeared to be the only way for G. to fulfil the undertakings which had led me to accept marriage nearly a decade after the eclipse of early love by war.

Many a would-be husband has made promises to his bride which he has subsequently repudiated, but betrayal did not lie in G.'s philosophy of life. With undeceived eyes he saw me responsive to his love and happy in his society yet fundamentally unsatisfied, thwarted by lack of opportunity to use that "one talent" which, however poor it might be, was "death to hide".

After much painful deliberation, we decided to try "semi-detached marriage"—an experiment which would mean living and working apart from the coming September until the following March, he at Cornell and I in London. Our original intention of returning to England together in June had already been abandoned owing to G.'s investigation, which involved a final report in August to the Social Science Research Council. We now agreed that I should sail home in time to accompany Winifred to the League Assembly. He would follow me when his report was completed, visit his father at Oxford, and see me on my return from Geneva before going back to Ithaca alone.

To my parents, pleased at the prospect of having my society for several months but startled by our unorthodox plans into protests about "duty", I wrote firmly that we were both suspicious of the word—" 'duty' is so often the name other people give to what they want you to do because it is the conventional thing".

But my love for G., undeveloped when I married him, had flowered in a year of mutual living, and the pain of our decision spilled over in a letter to Winifred which deplored "this perpetual clash between persons and ideals, one's private life and one's public. I shall nearly break my heart over being away from him next winter,

39

and the knowledge that he will be nearly breaking his won't make it any easier. What a thing life is, to condemn one to this perpetual heartache!"

Here, crudely enough stated, was the fundamental problem of our marriage. Not for many years would it be resolved.

(11)

On an August evening the White Star docks lay dark and somnolent beneath their burden of summer heat. Towards midnight the great harbour became unusually quiet; the holiday travellers to Europe had long departed, and the *Majestic*, by which I was sailing, had many empty berths.

All day, while G. worked at the final pages of his Report, I had laboured in our sultry little apartment to reduce a year's possessions to manageable proportions. We were both tired when he and Standish Chard took me to the modest second-class cabin, shared with a stranger, which seemed too restricted for the many small packages unsuited to the hold.

The conflict of the past few weeks hung heavily on our spirits, and we welcomed the cheerful presence of Standish. I felt no compunction at quitting America, which had become the symbol of thwarted hope, and though I regretted leaving G. alone to face his portentous committee, it still appeared the most practical plan for me to precede him to England. The Social Science Research Council had summoned him to Hanover, New Hampshire, for a Conference which I was not entitled to attend, and three more solitary weeks in New York would have added pointlessly to our mounting expenses.

It seemed therefore absurd to feel so guilty and depressed when in a month's time we should meet again, but over this temporary parting hung the shadow of the longer and more dangerous separation to which we had so reluctantly agreed. Alone together in the cabin, we glumly stowed away the innumerable suitcases. In putting my typewriter under the bunks G. tore his hand on a sharp fragment of wire, and suddenly the minor mishap seemed to symbolise all our mutual wretchedness. After I had tied his handkerchief round the small wound, we clung remorsefully together in the silent intensity of bewildered affection.

When he and Standish left me, I could neither sleep nor unpack. After midnight persistent sirens annihilated the previous silence, and at five o'clock, when the ship began at last to move down the river, I climbed to the upper deck.

A dull copper-red sunrise turned gradually to daylight as I gazed at the fantastic skyline, and saw many skyscrapers still so vividly illuminated that they resembled hollow structures blazing with fire. Grey-green in the vanishing mists of dawn, the Statue of Liberty seemed a living guardian standing with upraised torch to defend the spectacular harbour.

For the first time in years the uncertain future seemed longer and more complex than the crowded past, which since my marriage had gradually receded as the New York horizon was receding now. But while we moved across the midsummer Atlantic, smooth as a stagnant pool, Winifred and my parents became newly endowed with a growing reality.

Would they, I wondered, be disappointed because G. and I had not yet begun to produce a family, though the bride of June 1925 had now been a wife for thirteen months?

CHAPTER TWO

ENGLISH MOTHER

"If we have learnt nothing else as yet, we have at least learnt how to bear disappointments without giving up. There is no lesson which more justifies our having children. If we can bring them up to fight against the human tendency to resignation (which is merely 'the line of least resistance' masquerading as a moral quality) we shall have contributed to the strength and courage of our generation."

V.B. TO G.C., 1926.

(1)

ON THE AFTERNOON of August 13th, the *Majestic* reached Southampton. A canopy of pink-tinged cloud crowned the Isle of Wight, and the sandy banks on either side of the blue-green Solent glowed vermilion in the late summer sunshine. Ten years earlier I had sailed for Malta in the doomed *Britannic* on just such a day of sun and colour and clouds.

Ten years! But for once my mother, anxiously waiting on the docks with Winifred, forgot to deplore the period in which I might have provided her with a grandchild, and still had not. For the moment she seemed more concerned by the thin face and sallow complexion which I had acquired unawares owing to continuous indoor work in humid New York.

"So lovely, so cool!" I wrote appreciatively to G. of England's gentle freshness. Already some of the minor successes implacably withheld by America had reinforced my sentimental affection for my native land. A biographical vignette of Senator Borah had been accepted by *The Outlook*, while *Time and Tide* had commissioned two articles on the League Assembly.

From New Hampshire G. shortly announced that "the nabobs" had been "well-pleased" with his 130-page Report, but its financial recommendations made his future employment by the Council unlikely. The cost of research pointed to a full-scale Government inquiry, which ultimately took shape in the Wickersham Committee of 1930.

G. concluded his diagnosis of the "noble Experiment" by sending me an anecdote which illustrated the less reputable ingenuities of the law-breakers.

"A lady imported liquor on her person through the New York Customs by feigning to be *enceinte* (which Bruce Bliven thinks immoral and so do I!)."

He arrived in England while I was still at Geneva, describing the admission to the League of Stresemann's Germany after its initial rejection by the French-dominated Member States. Of that shameful episode, which contributed to the rise of Hitlerism, Dr. Fridtjof Nansen was shortly to speak in his Rectorial Address at St. Andrews University.

"Nations have hardly begun to have real morality," he said. "The proceedings of the League of Nations Assembly last March . . . should have shocked the world much more than they did."

I returned to join G. and his father at Oxford, where we walked through Port Meadow to the Trout Inn at Godstow. The saffron glory of the snapdragons in the neat flower-garden across the water seemed to glow like a letter which G. had recently written me.

"I do think that ours has been a perfect marriage. It has been just such a marriage as I could have wished, something hardening and yet *con amore*. I wanted somebody who adventured; I wanted somebody above all who would keep me keyed up to that pitch of vivid living and working which is the keenest and divinest of all experiences in life."

Separation, it seemed, was the price we had to pay if that perfection was to endure. On a radiant September morning we travelled to Southampton without as yet foreseeing that this was the poignant prototype of other partings to come. How many departures there were to be, with one or the other standing on the dock and waving farewell, or in far-off years waiting at the airport to see the beloved take wings.

With a heart newly burdened by misgivings I watched the *Mauretania* slide down Southampton Water in drenching sunlight, and then drove to the station.

"Just as the taxi turned the corner of the docks," I wrote to G. that evening, "I caught one last sight of the *Mauretania* all lit up with sunshine, her backward-leaning red funnels between a sea and a sky as colourless as a crystal. She looked so brilliant that it seemed like a good omen. . . . You are part of me—and the most important part—in all possible ways; how much truer it is that a lovely marriage makes people one spirit than that it makes them one flesh."

In similar mood he began a letter next day on the ship:

"Such a clear impression of a little figure with a red sunshade waving a handkerchief. . . . For the last twenty-four hours I have been setting my teeth against what parts us, in a determination to get back on my own conditions. And, after all, they are your conditions, for one of them is that this strange equal comradeship on which we have embarked shall not fail. . . ."

My faith in him buoyed me up with hopeful resolution when I returned to the red-brick Maida Vale mansion flat which I was again to share with Winifred for the next six months.

(2)

The work which I had vainly sought in America immediately appeared in embarrassing profusion. After Christmas I reported triumphantly to G. that in six months not one free-lance contribution has been refused.

Of the half-dozen journals to which I now contributed, the *Manchester Guardian* remained impersonal, though for years it accepted more of my articles than any other newspaper. Through Winifred I came to know Violet Scott-James, whose "London Letter" was a regular feature of the *Yorkshire Post* for many years, and became an occasional contributor to her column.

During the nineteen-twenties and thirties, several worthy weekly reviews kept afloat with a tenacity which now seems incredible. To three of these periodicals, *The Outlook*, *Time and Tide* and *The Nation*, and to a monthly, *Foreign Affairs*, I owed much gratitude for their timely encouragement.

The editor of *The Outlook*, A. Wyatt Tilby, elderly, tall and benevolent, published several of my short pieces. On *Time and Tide* Lady

43

Rhondda, the only woman editor of a weekly review, concealed a forceful personality behind a façade of deceptive shyness. Winifred was now her youngest Director, and for the next few years, until Winifred's death, she commissioned from me articles and reviews.

Another woman editor, Mrs. H. M. Swanwick, ran *Foreign Affairs* for the Union of Democratic Control. In 1924, the first Labour Government had sent her to Geneva as a British substitute-delegate. A middle-aged woman of Scandinavian appearance with undimmed golden hair and a deep beautiful voice, she gave me biographies and current histories to criticise.

But the greatest joy of these periodicals was *The Nation*, then beginning a new phase of life under the chairmanship of J. M. Keynes. It enjoyed a reputation for intellectual brilliance similar to that of the present *New Statesman*, which five years later absorbed it.

In *The Nation* I published articles with such controversial titles as "Society and the Suicide" and "Our Malthusian Middle Classes", which almost wrote themselves. Its editor was Hubert Henderson, who died in 1952 shortly after his election as Warden of All Souls' College, Oxford. Tall, thin, amiable, and still in his early thirties, he treated his contributors with exceptional courtesy.

"London and life in general are quite desperately interesting just now," I told G. in the midst of this "come back" period. "I would that one's active life lasted for 100 years and that each day were twice as long."

Our positions were now reversed, for at Cornell G. found himself exasperated by local residents retailing gossip, publishers seeking only text-books, and students wanting only lectures which they could take down verbatim. An early letter boiled with uncharacteristic bitterness into a dissertation on some incidental effects of American democracy upon education.

"All Ithaca knows of your winter plans before I told 'em. . . . Ginn of Boston asks if I have written a text-book. Knopf [the American publisher of *The Science and Method of Politics*] tells me that if I propose a text-book he is 'already interested'. Oh, were I constructing a hell I would put the text-book writers in the bottom of it and keep them there one further year for every dollar they make. What nonsense is this we talk about creative work? All we want is something that every errand boy who has scrambled into college can understand."

His own creative and original work was now scheduled for publication in December. Already he was planning his next big book, provisionally entitled *Principles and Practice of Politics*—"the

44

constants in human political method, by which I hope *inter alia* to take the lynch-pin out of war". In spite of the text-book hunters, it was this social-scientific world which for him spelt romance.

"As romance," he wrote, "I want to keep it, and you to keep it with me—all the adventure of the discovery of a new science which can 'do work'."

How revolutionary was his thinking, which I had studied so closely in the past few months, I realised even more clearly after Winifred had gone to hear Harold J. Laski's inaugural address at the London School of Economics. A year after publishing his *Grammar of Politics*, Laski had been appointed to the School's Chair of Political Science.

He lectured, Winifred admitted, very well indeed. "But," I reported to G., "the programme he laid down was, she said, quite of the old order, and entirely different from your book."

(3)

Though we had been parted only for a few weeks, it was already clear from G.'s letters that "semi-detached marriage"—so abundantly justified from my own standpoint by the work now pouring in upon me—was not succeeding as well as I had hoped.

The American college society which G. had found so enjoyable in the two years preceding our marriage now seemed to him restricted and melancholic. For this the stimulating months in New York were at least as much responsible as my absence, but the New York life could not be brought back, while I could be if my concern were sufficiently aroused. Dispirited letters alternated with gallant attempts to abide by our mutual covenant.

"Of course I shall not drop you through," he would write with rational determination. "You must not construe my gloomy letters as an endeavour to lure you out here."

Then, a page or two later, emotion would triumph over reason.

"My light and my brightness, the world without you is just horrible. Long ages of male exploitation have made it damnably difficult to be just to women. My very love for you is a snare, for when you are absent I can think of nothing else. All my unconscious self continually conspires against my will to urge me to play on every chord of compunction in you. And yet I know it is mean to do it."

As this tormenting correspondence continued, the sense of insoluble conflict weighed me down like an Old Man of the Sea. Why, I asked myself, should a man get the best of both worlds, but a woman be compelled to choose between personal relationships and the work for which she was fitted? Was any community justified in sacrificing intelligence and creative ability solely on the ground of sex? Could such a concept as "selfishness" really apply to the endeavour to put a talent to effective use? How far was resignation to "the inevitable" a duty, and how far a spineless surrender to conventions which, when closely examined, did not appear "inevitable" at all? Was not "making the best of things" just an excuse for lack of the energy to change them? And would not each woman who consciously "gave in" make it harder for all the struggling women to come?

Round and round in my head went the intolerable questions which so many of my women contemporaries had begun to ask of a civilisation that seemed to provide no answer. Perpetually they pushed my work aside, destroying concentration on urgent articles, and sacrificing significance to a last-minute scamper to produce the required number of words.

By mid-November our correspondence was approaching a remorseful quarrel in which our whole future appeared to be at stake; the tension created by our letters was destroying the very purpose for which "semi-detachment" had been undertaken. In spite of our mutual love and need, the only solution seemed to lie in a formal separation.

After much further wrestling with myself and G., I wrote desperately to propose that we arranged one, "based not on incompatibility of temper but on incompatibility of occupation". We would not, I suggested, separate judicially, or necessarily for ever, but definitely enough to announce to our orthodox acquaintances that we had done so.

The pain arising from this proposal overflowed into a letter sent to Ithaca in mid-November.

"I don't want you to think for a moment that I love you less. In so far as I can separate my personal and physical life from what I believe to be its purpose, I love you more than my life. What is wrong is not merely marriage as such—with that alone, in cooperation as we are, we could have coped quite easily. It is your banishment to such a faraway country. . . ."

Strangely enough, this drastic proposal achieved more than pages of argument. Neither of us really wanted a complete break, for we "spoke the same language" and that is a closer bond than the same household. Once convinced that I was ready to carry out my suggestion and for the second time face the ruin of my emotional life, he responded with the imaginative generosity which I had not trusted in vain. Magnanimously he told me that I must follow the way which seemed to me right: for his part, he would doubtless work out his own salvation.

"You are I, and did I lose you, I should lose all of myself but the grey duty of working on."

To prove that he meant what he said, he put himself on a strict régime of hour-by-hour work, resolved to live only in the present, and cabled me that April would be early enough for me to rejoin him in America.

When the cable came, I tried to express in halting words the measure of my gratitude for his determination to remain with such a wife.

"Without you, I could never be quite the same person again. If I achieved anything some wraith of myself would achieve it. I think I have been in so much of a panic largely because I did promise you that, unless circumstances were unutterably difficult, I would have a baby next year. And this means that all the footholds that I am to have for the next two or three years must be made this winter. . . . I feel as if I had been saved from some tremendous catastrophe."

(4)

Christmas was welcome because it coincided with the publication of G.'s book and marked the halfway period of our separation. I kept the day by going to St. James's, Spanish Place—alone because Winifred had gone home to Yorkshire. No conceivable argument would have induced my father to go to a Catholic church on Christmas morning, and my mother felt that she ought to be with him. But perhaps, I thought, by going alone I should be nearer to G., who in Ithaca would be alone too.

In St. James's Church the lights flickered before the altar where we had stood, and cold but persistent sunlight filtered through the high windows. I tried to remember the church as it had looked at our wedding, resplendent with pink peonies and roses, and wondered whether a year or so hence there would be another life to record on time's crowded page.

To both G. and Winifred I now confessed the desire for a Christmas baby. In my mind Christmas had long been linked with death because, a decade earlier, Roland had died of wounds on December 23rd, and throughout Christmas Day I had vainly awaited his arrival on leave. By marrying G. at St. James's, I had found reconciliation with the war-time months in which I knelt beneath its lofty windows grieving for Roland. Now I desired similarly to transform the recollection of tragedy which overshadowed the Christmas period.

But in the spring of 1927, though I could write to G. with a new lifting of the heart now that the tension between us was over, the propagation of the much-desired family still seemed comfortably distant, and I plunged with zeal into the fascinating present.

For the first time I was living the life which I had most desired from my earliest youth; the life of the professional writer who undertakes other activities mainly as a source of ideas for her work.

"Never before," I wrote to G., "have I felt so alive. Idea after idea comes surging up, clamouring to be written, put down in a notebook and dealt with in due course. My marriage with you is all a part of this new life."

The Incidental Adam still possessed my thoughts, but so much reading of war-time letters would be involved that it would have to wait till America was done with. America alone might part us; nothing else could. Sometimes, I told him, its claims pressed down on me like a great potential doom.

Yet as April approached this mood changed; the United States summoned me because they held G. and our future. Just then my mother, after much perturbation, decided to give herself a break from my father and accompany me to America for the eight weeks' visit. Writing to confirm our arrival in the *Leviathan*, which had been planned to coincide with G.'s Easter recess, I sent him a letter that glowed with anticipation:

"I want to tell you before I see you how much our marriage has meant to me. It has meant more joy than anything I ever dreamed possible."

And he responded in a fashion which assured me that our autumn misunderstandings had been forgotten and would never recur.

"I throw off the discipline of this six months which has forbidden me to think of the sight of you for fear of being unable to cease to think. The whole world may be lost and if you remain to share the experience it is not lost . . . you who are music to me through the entire gamut of my experience's little universe, my love, my dancer, the red light in the wine, the gleam in the sunshine on a summer's day, the peace of an autumn evening, the stillness of the stars, the adventure and wonder of all things."

(5)

As soon as I saw G. again, I realised that the conflict between us had been little more than a figment of taut nerves sharpened by separation. His admiration for the United States had not destroyed his deep interest in British politics; a return which gave opportunity for his special work was now as much his hope as mine.

I found him, as I had expected, gaily encouraged because the American philosopher, John Dewey—"one of the Olympians themselves"—had praised *The Science and Method of Politics* in *The New Republic*. More surprising was my mother's speedy adaptation to Ithaca and the small apartment, for her travels with my father had been limited to conventional Swiss or Italian hotels. In New York she actually appeared to enjoy herself, discarding for once the peculiar moral principle which normally forbade her to appreciate a pleasant experience.

We had not been long in Ithaca when an opportunity for G. to return to England suggested itself with the deceptive brightness of a promise which proves to be only a mirage.

One warm spring day the head of G.'s department invited us to meet Professor Graham Wallas, who at sixty-seven had recently retired from the Chair of Political Science at the London School of Economics. He struck me, I recorded, as "a perfect darling—rather like a large shaggy rook".

At the end of the afternoon, Professor Wallas asked G. if he was interested in returning to England. On receiving a definite affirmative, he then suggested that G. might give a course of lectures on his next book during the coming academic year at the London School, and asked him to write to the School recording this proposal. He would then, said Professor Wallas, "put over the idea to Beveridge".

G. wrote as advised, but the reply which came was sent not by Sir William Beveridge but by Harold Laski, whose political theory differed widely from that of Graham Wallas. His answer to G.'s letter gave it a subtle twist which transformed him from an invited lecturer into a supplicant for a post. He understood, he said, that G. had raised the question of his giving lectures at the School with Professor Wallas, but it was too late to make any such arrangement as all the grants for that purpose in the coming year had already been allocated. His letter ignored the possibility of any alternative date.

Clearly Harold Laski had no intention of encouraging Graham Wallas's protégés to challenge his own interpretation of political science, then a relatively new study which had hitherto been regarded as a branch of history. Laski increasingly approached the developing science from a Marxist angle, while G., like Graham Wallas, regarded it from a humanist standpoint which owed its inspiration to Erasmus and Colet, and embodied in his work

49

many revolutionary discoveries of twentieth-century psychology.

Though Laski's subtle but determined opposition remained a permanent obstacle to G.'s chances of obtaining one of the few academic posts which England had to offer in his subject, it was to be G. who sought, almost at the end of Harold Laski's life, to bring into their relationship the mutual regard which was always latent, and might have existed permanently between them had they taught different subjects or pursued different professional ends. After Laski had lost the libel action which he brought against the Press after the 1945 General Election, G. offered, his concern reinforced by his esteem for Harold's wife Frieda, to approach American friends who might help to raise the enormous sum demanded in damages.

But in 1927 we felt baffled, bewildered, and inexplicably let down, for between G.'s letter to the London School and Laski's disconcerting reply, we had become aware that the future generation which we had set out to create was already more than a speculation. As soon as the prospect of a home in London seemed to open before us, the promise of a child had appeared to me a delight unimpaired by misgiving.

When Laski's letter destroyed our hopes, the joyful anticipation of a son or daughter developed its undercurrent of consternation. The problem which had confronted us the previous winter remained unsolved and was now intensified; motherhood would inevitably double the obstacles which had still to be overcome in the struggle to be both a wife and a writer.

Eventually, after this reverse of fortune, G. exchanged his full-time appointment for a half-time post at Cornell. This arrangement, which meant that he would be in America for every second semester —from January to June each year—at least made possible the establishment of a London household. Marriage, whether semi-detached or continuously shared, must henceforth, for the new generation's sake, be accepted without question as a permanent bond.

In June we sailed for England, and I did not see America again until 1934.

(6)

When my son was born three weeks ahead of schedule, the doctor did not arrive until the event was well over. Expecting the long-drawn-out procedure usual with first babies, the staff of the small nursing-home where I had booked a room also left me severely alone until the next moment to the last.

Owing to the boy's premature arrival he was at least a Christmas baby—a feat which I had never imagined the previous year that I could achieve with my first-born. For three days, in the bleak streets outside the home, carol-singers accompanied his struggle for survival with familiar words:

> "Nowell, Nowell! Now-ow-ell, Now-ell!
> Born is the Ki-ing of Is-is-ra-el."

Throughout that week of freezing temperatures, heavy snow-storms swept the country. In the New Year they turned to floods, and the Thames, overflowing its banks, drowned fourteen people in London basements.

Early in January we carried the fragile baby up a steep dark staircase to our new home, still shared with Winifred, on the two top floors of a south-facing house in a street off the Earl's Court Road. There, for three months, with an Irish nursemaid's semi-trained help which was the best that we could afford, I waged an unremitting battle for his life.

His sudden appearance on the shortest day of an exceptionally cold winter, and my own slow recovery, had brought me some unexpected problems. John might well have succumbed to the after-effects of his catastrophic arrival but for my providential discovery of the Chelsea Babies' Club. This Welfare Centre for Subscribers was founded that spring, with the late Dr. Harold K. Waller, a pioneer paediatrician associated for many years with the British Hospital for Mothers and Babies at Woolwich, as chief consultant in charge of its periodic clinics.

When John was only four weeks old, G. returned to Cornell for the spring semester. Since he could no longer assist in the nursery campaign, I tried in writing to gloss over the precariousness of the baby's hold on life. Not until two years afterwards did I describe how I awoke each morning in dread lest I should find that he had died in the night.

My mother's Cassandra-like letters spared G. no alarming detail, but he had been so long accustomed to discount her pessimism that for some weeks he failed to recognise the real basis for her lugubrious prophecies. Then indeed he wrote anxiously and sympathetically, requesting a series of cables.

Often during that bleak spring, when I sat in the baby's modest nursery and learned to bath him with hands that trembled lest the minute body should slip from my grasp, I thought to myself: "This is what nine-tenths of the mothers in this country go through—not once, but again and again. Even now, I don't really know what they suffer. It was just a mistake that I was given no alleviation for the pain, and could come back to a pleasant home with people to help me. But they have to be up in a few days, and do everything for the baby and everyone else, and run badly-planned cottages better suited to animals than men. And government after government inists that we can't afford a national maternity service—we who spend millions a year on armaments to destroy the bodies which are produced at such cost."

At such times I was filled with a vehement anger. I wanted to batter down the solid walls of the Ministry of Health; to take the Minister himself and give him a woman's inside, and compel him to have six babies, all without anaesthetics. Then I remembered that he, after all, could only go as fast as the public insisted. Had not the aftermath of the war taught me how slowly social sentiments changed; how gradually wisdom dawned; how small was the compassion created even in enlightened human beings by the pain of the centuries?

Sometimes I gripped the chair in impotent rage because one woman could do so little, and all women were cursed with such an infinite capacity for resigned endurance.

Throughout this period I owed a debt that still seems incalculable to Winifred's sustaining encouragement, which reinforced my own faith that my son would survive. But all too soon I lost the solace of her company, for her sister Grace, a doctor's wife, died in childbirth, and she was summoned home.

Reduced to the society of two half-trained "helps", and reluctant to upset my parents, I wrote to G. of this new desolation.

"Such a queer blank world. Snow and bitter weather are back again—and Grace Morrison-Tolmie is being buried tomorrow. Winifred writes that all the country looks so bright in the snow, and somehow strange. This reminds me of the war days, when people were killed. I don't know if you have ever noticed that when someone you know well is dead, the whole earth seems to take on a kind of garish unnatural brilliance, rather as it looks after a sleepless night. I always think that if the dead could return, they would see the world like this."

(7)

A new publication entitled *Women's Work in Modern England* had kept me contentedly occupied during the weeks before John's birth. It had grown out of a suggestion to Andrew Dakers by a small firm of publishers, which thought that a series of articles originally written for *The Outlook* on "Prospects in Women's Employment" would make a useful short book.

The reconstruction of existing material seemed better suited to a period of physical uncertainty than a larger effort, and I finally corrected the typescript in the nursing-home. But even before this book had been planned, an unexpected telephone call had come one August evening from the London office of the *Yorkshire Post*.

Calvin Coolidge, I learned, had just issued a laconic Press pronouncement: "I do not choose to run for President." The *Yorkshire Post* had sought in vain for its normal "contacts" on American affairs, and most of its leader-writers were away on holiday.

"You know the United States," said the editorial voice at the other end of the line, "and you have written us a number of acceptable articles. Do you think you could manage a 'leader' on the President's statement by midnight?"

For a second the room seemed to spin and I felt temporarily suffocated. I had then been pregnant for four months and was getting used to the experience, though like other women enduring it for the first time I found it disconcerting. But my feeling of agitation was not really due to my physical condition, but to the recognition that in its minor way the request from Fleet Street was an epoch-making event.

In 1927 young women were not asked to write top-flight editorials for Conservative newspapers on major political declarations. Women were not, in fact, usually invited to contribute at all. If I could produce a good editorial on President Coolidge, it would be more useful to the women's cause than a dozen speeches from feminist platforms. This was an occasion when one pulled one's self together and acted, cost what it might.

With a confidence which I felt sure the distinguished journalist on the telephone would think I had no right to display, I said that I had indeed just returned from America. Over there I had read many newspapers on possible Presidential policies, and could certainly produce some relevant comments on the baffling statement. Since the newspaper office had no alternative, I was told to go ahead. For nearly four hours I studied notes and Press cuttings, and eventually produced my editorial.

Just before midnight I took it to Fleet Street and, tired but triumphant, handed it in. Later I learned that the editorial staff, to their surprised relief, had found it "good" by their own standards. Returning home in a late Underground train, I realised that throughout those hours of concentrated work I had completely forgotten the physical inconveniences caused by the prospective baby. From that time onwards I recognised that for pregnancy, as for other forms of tiresome indisposition, the best antidote, as always, was work.

During that holiday season I wrote several further editorials for the *Yorkshire Post*; I should have been invited, Violet Scott-James told me, to do many more if only the editor could have forgotten that I was a woman. G., too, contributed "leaders" to the same newspaper that autumn, and for some time after returning to Ithaca sent over a regular "American Letter".

The after-effects of mismanaged childbirth proved less easy to disregard than the *malaises* of pregnancy. But disregarded they had to be, since only through journalism could I make my one-third contribution to our joint household. When I left the nursing-home a woolly fog enveloped my mind, but within a few days I was again writing for the usual journals.

My satisfaction in being able to work again was doubled by a change for the better in John. At two months old the tiny dark-eyed baby had still weighed only seven pounds, but at the end of March a prescription suggested by the Babies' Club turned him into a different child. He slept through the night and rapidly put on weight. In April I cabled G. that he had reached ten pounds.

"Now that he is well and seems happy," I wrote, "he is such an inestimable joy to me. He is more than worth the four months of misery and anxiety. Sentimental as it may sound, I now realise that no one will go on trying so persistently, or believing to long, as a mother. I never thought I could love such a young baby so much."

In May the publication of *Women's Work in Modern England* brought a request from the *Daily News* for an article on "How should a Woman's Education fit her for Life?" Other demands for kindred topics followed from different newspapers.

Within forty-eight hours the book had received nearly thirty notices, including a favourable criticism in *The Observer*. By the end of that week I had added the *Daily Chronicle* and the *Evening Standard* to the list of papers which published my work.

This little success raised my spirits to a tenth heaven after the hard months just past. Soon our combined earnings made possible many small benefits. They included a better-qualified nurse for John and, during G.'s annual return to England, a short October visit to Monte Carlo. In *les Jardins Exotiques* the brilliant rock flowers glowed like celestial jewels beneath the autumn sun. How much happier was this brief holiday than the strained novelty, amounting almost to antagonism, of a honeymoon!

November brought a peculiar police-court case, which made literary history, after Radclyffe Hall's novel, *The Well of Loneliness*, had been suppressed for impropriety.

I had reviewed this earnest and harmless story on publication, and now joined the thirty-nine/"expert" witnesses who appeared before the Bow Street magistrate, Sir Chartres Biron. They included Hugh Walpole, E. M. Forster, Sheila Kaye-Smith and Julian Huxley, but apart from Desmond MacCarthy we were never called. The following year I learned from G. that the American courts had refused to condemn the book.

On the whole I felt, summing up my impressions of the case after the second hearing, that there was a profound security in normal human relationships. And I wrote gratefully to thank G. for giving me John and the family life which had seemed, ten years earlier, to be buried with other lost hopes in a grave on the Somme.

(8)

As John passed his first birthday, I watched him grow into a self-sufficient, uncomplaining child. Across the Atlantic, in the cold early spring of 1929, went reports of the kind sent by all recent mothers to their husbands overseas.

"He is like a little dark flower." "He is lovely—a fat, curly-haired, rosy-cheeked boy." Occasionally a less typical anecdote varied these rhapsodies over a triumph wrested from such unpromising beginnings. "Yesterday he enthusiastically addressed the Melanesian monstrosity in your study as 'Daddy'!" In reply G. commented ruefully: "Poor child! One questions whether one has the right to bring so bright a creature into the world to be disillusioned."

That spring G. himself had no reason for disillusionment. Two weeks before Herbert Hoover's inauguration as the next American President, a new Everyman edition of Mary Wollstonecraft's *Vindication* and John Stuart Mill's *Subjection of Women* had been published with his sympathetic Introduction.

"You *have* struck oil in that young man!" a Somerville friend commented after reading it.

In March, too, appeared the first number of an unusual publication, *The Realist* magazine. The previous November G. had founded this periodical in conjunction with its subsequent editor, Major A. G. Church, then assistant editor of *Nature* and later M.P. for

Wandsworth. In those days of ample newsprint they had both seen the need for an intellectual monthly on similar lines to the American *Harper's Magazine*, but dedicated to "Scientific Humanism". Professor Julian Huxley, who joined *The Realist's* illustrious board, had perceived almost simultaneously that such a publication had long been required.

The twenty-three other members of the board, who regularly dined together at Kettners, included Arnold Bennett, H. G. Wells, Sir Richard Gregory, Professor J. B. S. Haldane, Herbert Read, Aldous Huxley, H. J. Laski, and Rebecca West. The former Lord Melchett put up the necessary funds, and Macmillan produced the magazine with their usual distinction. A galaxy of favourable reviews greeted its appearance, and its pale orange cover became conspicuous on bookstalls throughout the country.

Soon after G.'s departure for the spring semester, his new book, *The Principles of Politics*, dedicated to Professor Graham Wallas, appeared on both sides of the Atlantic. By that time a new opportunity for "thinking things through" had also come to me with a request from Kegan Paul for a book on the future of marriage in their *Today and Tomorrow* series. Since this, though "extravagant and fantastical", enabled me to use material patiently collected for a larger book which never took shape, I began it at once and thereby found compensation for an unexpected blow. That spring the firm which had published *Women's Work in Modern England* went bankrupt, and I learned that I should receive a mere fraction of the £50 earned by royalties.

"It was a bitter disappointment to get nothing from such a successful book," I told G. when I had recovered, but I could now report the arrival of Kegan Paul's contract for *Halcyon, or the Future of Monogamy*. This little extravaganza embodied four imaginary chapters from *A History of English Moral Institutions in the Nineteenth, Twentieth, and Twenty-first Centuries: by Minerva Huxterwin, Professor of Moral History in the University of Oxford.*

When *Halcyon* appeared just before the International Sex Reform Congress held in London that autumn, Dr. C. E. M. Joad reviewed it with approval in the *Yorkshire Post*.

"Of all the brilliant books in this series I know of few more 'squib-like'. It will do everybody good to read it, even if it should shock some."

Cyril Joad was one of the many writers on sex morals to appear at the Congress, which provided a fine display of modern contraceptives and a series of "daring" lectures by up-to-date reformers.

It typified the sex obsessions of that period, which may well seem disproportionate to a generation contemplating the threat of extinction by hydrogen bombs.

At home, over nursery tea, Winifred and I cheerfully discussed the preposterous solemnity of the moralists. Two years later, when John, twenty-one months old at the time of the Congress, suddenly observed out of the blue: "I don't like my wife—I'll send him away because I want another woman," we wondered whether he could have memorised a fragment of our conversation.

In our letters that spring G. and I discussed his education with well-justified confidence that he would now grow up to need the best we could give him, and I repeated an anecdote to which the future was to lend significance.

"Jung and Adler both agree that children with some disadvantage to fight often do better than those with none. In *Time and Tide* this week there is a story of Winston Churchill. When he was twelve, and had just gone to Harrow, he went round worrying the masters and everybody to find someone who could cure him of the impediment in his speech, 'because,' he said, 'when I am a great statesman and have to make important speeches in Parliament, it will be a great handicap to me if I have to avoid all words beginning with s.' "

(9)

Winston Churchill had been Chancellor of the Exchequer in the Baldwin Government of 1924, which now, after five years of office, sought re-election. In *The Gathering Storm*, Churchill describes this administration as "a capable sedate government". It had certainly been responsible for the Locarno Treaty and the Kellogg Pact, which had brought a measure of tranquillity to the international landscape. But other historians emphasise the depression in the export trades, the distress in the mining areas, and the unemployment figures of a million-and-a-half which had made the government unpopular. In May 1929 it was turned out, and a minority Labour administration led by Ramsay MacDonald took its place.

Moved by the misery that we saw on a post-college journey through Central Europe, Winifred and I had joined the Labour Party in 1924, while G. first voted for it in 1918 as a philosophic young rifleman outside Mons. The 1929 election campaign began during the Easter recess, and we listened to several speeches on the radio which for the first time was used for political propaganda.

Our own campaign in South Kensington—usually an uncontested

Conservative stronghold—for once provided some interest. The sitting Member, Sir William Davison, had recently been through the Divorce Court, and his return to Parliament was now challenged by a young Liberal and an Independent Conservative, Mr. Rayner Goddard, K.C. When a feminist deputation of which I was a member interviewed all three candidates, the future Lord Chief Justice rewarded us with a word of approval.

"I congratulate you," he said, "on the competence with which you have prepared your brief."

Regretting his own absence during a political crisis, G. sought information especially on two contemporary figures, Harold Laski and Sir Oswald Mosley. Endeavouring to obtain for him a series of reliable judgments, I arranged an interview with Mrs. Swanwick, who had now retired from *Foreign Affairs* but was still close to Labour's inner counsels.

"Is Laski likely to be offered anything in a Labour Government?" I asked her.

"No," she replied. "Too much tarred with the academic brush. He is also regarded as unstable, and any information he gives about the Party is likely to be unreliable."

The still greater instability of Sir Oswald Mosley was then less obvious. Even Mrs. Swanwick mentioned him as a possible Foreign Secretary, though Laski himself had warned G. that Mosley "has a way of making his henchmen syllables in his mouth". For some time G. had been associated with a London group which included the Quaker politician, Charles Roden Buxton, who knowing their common interest in political research had introduced him to Mosley, another member. From Cornell G. sent the group a series of memoranda on American reactions to British politics. What became of these memoranda we never knew.

Winifred and I spent the sunny election week in the cathedral city of St. Albans, where a woman candidate, Monica Whately, was standing against a 9,000 Conservative majority. Though her defeat was inevitable, her unremitting energy and gallant eloquence created a stimulating contest which dramatised the purpose of the long suffragist campaign.

G.'s own interest was now centred in a *New York Times* account of the issues—unemployment, disarmament, relations with America and Russia—which Ramsay MacDonald proposed to tackle. They seemed to him so urgent that he cabled offering his services to Mosley, who was now Chancellor of the Duchy of Lancaster, and returned home at the end of May.

September found us both at Geneva, where the foundation stone of the new League of Nations headquarters was laid in Ariana Park during the Tenth Assembly. An annual review optimistically reported at the end of that year: "In these ten years the League has developed from a struggling experiment born in a world exhausted and embittered by the Great War . . . into a permanent feature of the political landscape."

"Permanent" is a rash word when applied to political institutions. Ten years later the League had gone, but in September 1929 nobody dreamed of its early extinction.

The first threat to world confidence descended the following month like a thunderbolt from a cloudless sky. In September the United States had reached the peak of a stock market boom which had accelerated under President Coolidge; on October 23rd came the disaster known to history as the Wall Street crash. Speculators who had started the wave of gambling which rolled over America began suddenly to sell; panic swept the country, and millions of shares changed hands. Prices went down, and unemployment figures shot up just in time to defeat the hopes of Britain's new Labour Government; American loans to Europe ceased, and disillusionment pervaded the recently hopeful League Secretariat.

One of the minor victims of the catastrophe was the promising *Realist*, from which Lord Melchett at once withdrew his subsidy. Even today it is hardly possible to estimate the blow, in long-range terms, which the collapse of this short-lived but important periodical inflicted upon G. '

But *The Realist* did not actually cease publication until 1930; nor did the "economic blizzard", with its disastrous consequences for Central Europe, immediately make another war appear inevitable. By November, when a second American panic rivalled the first, my thoughts had moved far from New York and Geneva to provincial England and the childhood years before 1914.

As soon as John grasped life firmly and began to appreciate the companionship of other children, G. and I had planned to provide him with a successor. But Nature proved unco-operative, and by the autumn of 1929 I concluded that neglect and damage at the time of his birth had perhaps made further children improbable.

This possibility hardly perturbed me, for the large, amorphous but indestructible product which I called my "war book" had now become compelling. In November, after ten years of intermittent contemplation, I began to write it.

I had barely drafted half the first chapter when I realised that the elusive fourth member of our family would eventually appear. Theoretically, I ought to have been delighted; actually, I felt as though I had fallen downstairs. A book involving a large-scale reconstruction of the history, both national and personal, which had shaped my early life could not be tackled effectually with such a major diversion as a new baby just ahead. And, in spite of the assurances of the woman doctor who now looked after me, the shadow of the previous experience lay across the near future.

So deep was the frustration soon caused by sheer inability to get the ideas seething in my head on to paper, that in spite of myself I felt an unreasonable resentment against the coming child—against my future creator of happiness, whose gay and generous existence was to compensate in fullest measure for every moment of delay and discomfort that it cost.

(10)

In March, 1930, her prospective arrival brought me a minor but memorable adventure. Two summers earlier I had attended with Winifred the funeral of Mrs. Pankhurst, who lived just long enough to see the attainment of equal suffrage. Now we were invited to the unveiling of her statue by Mr. Baldwin in Victoria Tower Gardens beside the Houses of Parliament, and given tickets which we thought entitled us to seats in the enclosure. But when we arrived we found that we were expected to stand throughout the long ceremony, and I was reluctantly going home when Cicely Hamilton, the writer and former suffragette, beckoned me across the compound to her own reserved seat.

"Stay and sit down," she commanded, for Winifred had told her about the expected infant, and I gratefully accepted her chair.

The spring sunshine was mild and pleasant. At the edge of the large crowd which covered the lawn, another "old suffragette", Dame Ethel Smyth, stood resplendent in the red and grey robes of a Doctor of Music. Vigorously she conducted the orchestra of the Metropolitan Police, whose members had once escorted her to Holloway Gaol, in a powerful rendering of "The March of the Women" which she had composed to Cicely Hamilton's words. We were enjoying this unusual demonstration of poetic justice when we saw Sylvia Pankhurst making her way through the crowd with her son in her arms. He appeared to be about the same age as John, but was a much larger child.

When I stood up and offered Miss Pankhurst my chair she would not accept it, but a friend deposited her son on my lap and carried her off to meet some old acquaintances. The reserved seats were close to the platform where Mr. Baldwin was now about to speak, and the possibility that the baby boy, suddenly consigned to the care of a stranger, would punctuate his remarks with howls seemed far from remote.

Somebody produced an old envelope, and throughout the speech I managed to keep the adaptable child amused by drawing a series of "catties". My subsequent recollections of the eulogy pronounced by Mr. Baldwin on Mrs. Pankhurst were somewhat vague, but I felt that I had contributed my quota to the success of the ceremony.

During April, in order to accommodate our growing household, Winifred and I moved our joint possessions to a tall ugly house with an attractive view of studios in Glebe Place, Chelsea. Though G. and I lived there for seven years he never became acclimatised to its third-rate architecture, but I loved and still miss the small sunny back-garden, which proved to be an ideal place for writing.

Our new abode, I told G., was a real joy after the "unutterable Earl's Courtishness" of Earl's Court, where our windows had faced a peculiarly depressing hostel for girl clerks. At week-ends, instead of seeking variety, these young women remained in their comfortless rooms, mending stockings and washing underwear. On Sundays the results of their activities festooned their window-sills, offering dreary evidence of female underpayment to anyone with eyes to see.

Our removal was timely for other reasons; as soon as the spring brought pleasant weather, the useful Square garden where John and I had spent our afternoons was closed to outsiders. His young nurse was obliged to push him a mile to Kensington Gardens, while I took refuge in Brompton Cemetery, the only adjacent open space. One friend commented, "What an extraordinary mixture of life and death!", but as I sat in the cemetery reading review books beneath the flowering shrubs, I thought not of the dead in their grey tombs but of the imminent life.

In June Sir Oswald Mosley resigned from the Labour Government owing to a difference of opinion on unemployment policy, and thereby squandered his chances of high office. His departure shook but did not upset that unlucky administration, and it was still safely in office at the end of July when Shirley—who was to become a Labour Youth delegate at seventeen and a Socialist politician at twenty-two—appropriately arrived under its auspices on a Sunday morning.

This experience eradicated a nightmare memory, for my new doctor fulfilled all her promises. By breakfast-time the baby lay sleeping placidly in her cot, while I sat up eating a poached egg with a zest that I would never have thought possible so soon after an event which I had dreaded as one dreads a major operation.

My theoretical faith in medical women had now received practical confirmation. So had my belief that the benefits which they conferred should be available to every mother who required them.

Our two children proved to be so dissimilar in type and temperament that they might have come from families at opposite ends of the earth. When I first saw Shirley's flaxen head I thought I was still dreaming, for I had expected a physical replica of John. A medical student subsequently told me that, being dark-haired and dark-eyed, I had only a rare chance of producing a child with G.'s Anglo-Saxon colouring.

From the outset Shirley sustained the nursery adage which commends "Sunday's child", for she put on weight steadily and was the easiest of infants to rear. Her affirmative attitude to life seemed to justify the instinct which had led us to name her after Charlotte Brontë's "gallant little cavalier".

Until the newcomer could walk, John guarded her like a sentinel protecting a vulnerable treasure. As she grew out of infancy she became a dynamo of energy; she never walked when she could run, and she climbed everything. At three she climbed her father's bookcase, which stretched from floor to ceiling; at thirteen she climbed the perilous roof of an hotel in Estoril; at fifteen she climbed Helvellyn; at nineteen Cader Idris; at twenty-one Snowdon; and at twenty-two the Dolomites.

She never knew defeat until, as a Labour candidate still under twenty-three, she began a series of attempts to surmount adverse majorities in Tory constituencies.

(11)

In 1930 my dreams did not reach to the girl who would be chosen at such an early age to stand for Parliament; I was glad only that a daughter had succeeded the too precious son whose highly critical intelligence now needed the challenge of a resistant contemporary. When the monthly nurse had gone and I took charge of both babies with the August thermometer suddenly rocketing into the nineties, I wrote to Winifred in Geneva of the happiness that they brought me.

"I must admit I am really rather enjoying it. If only I could eliminate the constant wish to work, forget I had ever been ambitious and cease chasing work-periods which don't materialise, I can imagine nothing much pleasanter."

Two days before that year's Labour Party Conference, the airship R101 was wrecked near Beauvais on a trial trip to India, and forty-six of its fifty-four passengers, including the Air Minister, Lord Thomson, were burned to death. This tragedy threw a shadow over the Conference, already convulsed by a storm, originating with Mosley, over unemployment. Sir Oswald's election to the National Executive of the Party at the expense of J. H. Thomas showed the hold which his policy still exercised over Socialist imagination.

Tied by the care of Shirley, I could not accompany G. to Llandudno, or even accept speaking engagements. Sometimes I felt appalled by the load of domestic detail which two small children involved; one understands, I thought after each new avalanche of interruptions, why no woman has ever achieved the concentration demanded by the work of a Shakespeare or a Bernard Shaw.

For months now my book had been laid aside; I had not even time to seek the three-guinea articles which built up my contribution to the household finances. Then, late in the year, came a stroke of luck which seemed likely to solve my problem until Shirley was old enough to join John at the open-air nursery school in Glebe Place.

The editor of *The Nation*, Harold Wright, who had recently succeeded Hubert Henderson, decided to introduce a new feature entitled *A Woman's Notebook*. After some preliminary discussion, he offered me the job at six guineas a week. I accepted with alacrity; here was work which I could do without leaving home, and a regular salary instead of the wearisome pursuit of free-lance commissions already cut down through the slump.

So absorbed was I by this assignment and the children, that G.'s annual departure for America came as a shock. When he wrote me after his arrival that he had found the unemployed selling apples in New York, and commented: "This country has the psychological malaise of economic depression far worse than England", I replied lamenting how little time we had recently been able to spend together.

"Since last June I have not had one good conversation with you. My life has been nothing but the two children, with intervals of spasmodic effort to keep my end up in the world of journalism. Why, oh why, can't one stay the same towards people? One perfect moment on the river—shy, a little embarrassing, but so exquisite. Stay there for ever, lovely moment, with all your possibilities, so much more exciting always than achievement! No—it has gone; it will never come back."

Shortly afterwards I had an unexpected disappointment: my

Woman's Notebook came to an end. In February 1931 *The Nation*, another brilliant victim of the depression, amalgamated with the *New Statesman*, now edited by Kingsley Martin. An apologetic letter from Harold Wright brought me news of this change and its possible consequences for myself.

"I think you are doing extremely well," he wrote. "Each week seems to me an improvement on the last and I am personally very much pleased with the new feature." But it would be for the new editor, he explained, to decide which sections of *The Nation* would be carried on by the combined journal. "I need scarcely add that I did not know how short the life of the paper would be when I encouraged you to embark on this experiment."

After the first periodic luncheon over which he presided, Kingsley Martin told me that *A Woman's Notebook* would be discontinued. He disapproved on principle, he said, of anything which suggested a division in the interests of intelligent men and women. At this period the liberal intelligentsia were trying to prove that the preoccupations of the sexes ought to be identical; today they perceive, more realistically, that diverse concerns may have equal value.

When I reported Kingsley Martin's explanation to Harold Wright, he remarked dryly: "How old-fashioned! But then K.M. *is* old-fashioned; he's pure nineteenth-century."

Old-fashioned or not, he was to raise the paper's circulation during the next twenty years to levels never previously attained, but when the enlarged magazine published a long list of future contributors which included practically everybody who had written for *The Nation*, Winifred and I found ourselves omitted. We were the first victims of that "discrimination" on which, with some justice, the *New Statesman* has prided itself ever since.

(12)

After nine years of endeavour to make an income through journalism, I knew that most editors had their pet authors and their pet aversions; though I had been repudiated by one, I still hoped to win the respect of others. But the renewed chase after elusive guineas was deeply discouraging when the ground which seemed at last to be so firm under my feet had revealed itself as a treacherous quagmire, shaky and uncertain.

The accumulated physical fatigue of the past months, combined with perpetual inability to salvage time for my large book, might well have led me to abandon in despair the long struggle to become an author, had not a small "feeler" appeared from another direction.

In 1930 a group of writers had seceded from *The Saturday Review* and had started yet another weekly, *The Week-end Review*, with Gerald Barry as editor. The day before I lost my job on *The Nation*, he asked me for a signed criticism of Sylvia Pankhurst's history, *The Suffragette Movement*. I had hesitated, knowing that *The New Statesman* and *The Week-end Review* regarded each other as rivals; two days later I agreed to write the notice, and subsequently reviewed a number of well-known books which included Storm Jameson's autobiographical *No Time Like the Present*.

Eventually *The Week-end Review* faded out, while *The New Statesman* continued on its triumphant way. But the ephemeral contact helped me through a period of depression, and I felt correspondingly grateful.

Meanwhile G. in America was facing his own disappointment—the realisation that one bright hope of political co-operation would have to be abandoned. At the end of February 1931, Sir Oswald Mosley broke with Labour and formed the New Party.

"You won't, I imagine, depart from the Labour Party with Young, Strachey, Brown and Lady Cynthia?" I wrote anxiously to G. "It doesn't seem to me that in a Mosley group there would be a future for anyone but Mosley."

There was, as we now know, no future at all. In mid-March I sent another cross-Atlantic diagnosis of the New Party members.

"Most of them will probably be of the aristocratic, advanced-Tory type; progressives who don't like the proletariat. You yourself are torn as ever, I suppose, between the ideals of St. Francis and those of St. Dominic. There are no St. Francises in the Mosley Party; that at least, I think, is quite clear."

Two months later, when the New Party fought a by-election at Ashton-under-Lyne and thereby handed a safe Labour seat to the Conservatives, G. cut himself off for good from the Mosley group with which he had broken the previous Christmas.

"There are two charges of substance against the New Party", he wrote me: "(*a*) That it is Fascist-militant; (*b*) That it believes not in science but in miracles by strong men."

While G. and I shared setbacks and disillusionments, Winifred maintained the prestige of our household. Her career seemed to open like a fan; nobody could have guessed how soon it would close.

When she decided to undertake a short study of Virginia Woolf, she sought an interview with the subject of her biography. Virginia Woolf seemed doubtful whether Winifred's literary standards were equal to a book about herself, and the following conversation ensued.

V.W.: "But what do you do for your living?"
W.H.: "I write articles for popular papers, like 'The Javelin Women of London' in the *Evening Standard*."
V.W.: "What a terrible life!"
W.H.: "I don't think it's terrible. I enjoy it. I like being provocative."
V.W.: "What is 'provocative'?"
W.H.: "Oh, writing the kind of thing which makes Ethel Mannin immediately send in a reply contradicting everything you say."
V.W.: "Who is Ethel Mannin?"

In the end Winifred obtained enough information to start her biography, and a letter which reached me after *Testament of Friendship* was published showed that Virginia Woolf remembered her with respect and affection.

That spring I could at least record one iota of encouragement. During the Trinity Term the Oxford University Labour Club invited me to address them on "Marriage Past and Present" in a programme which contained, as usual, a large number of distinguished names. A beautiful red-haired girl undergraduate took charge of me beforehand; I learned that she was "Peter" Spence, who subsequently became the third wife of Bertrand Russell.

Nineteen years afterwards Shirley, who had already grown from a baby into an animated small girl, was to be the first woman president of this celebrated University Club.

(13)

Throughout 1931, the weather itself appeared to be in mourning for the state of the world. When I took a furnished cottage at Rustington in Sussex for the children's summer holiday, the rains descended and the winds blew, and I spent a dismal month of shopping, cleaning, and drying wet clothes.

A period of subnormal health had followed a minor operation on an impacted wisdom tooth, and when Winifred returned from visiting friends in France, she and G. agreed that it was about time I had a proper holiday myself. He decided to take me to St. Raphael on the Riviera while she kept an eye on the family. I acquiesced, with the mental reservation that for me a "proper" holiday was one which permitted the maximum opportunity for uninterrupted writing.

Though the countryside of Northern France drowned beneath the floods of that rain-dominated year, a day spent in Arles under blue skies appeared a promising if deceptive augury. In the clean bright town on the banks of the Rhône, with its fragments of Roman architecture cream-yellow against a rich countryside framed in distant mountains, we ate an ambrosial luncheon at a flower-decorated hotel in the central square. From relative austerity I still look back with wistful nostalgia upon the delicious *hors d'oeuvres*, cold salmon, fried chicken, cream cheese, luscious golden peaches and mellow Provençal wine which we enjoyed for a trivial sum.

But by the time we reached St. Raphael the rain had started again, and the deepening political crisis, which had made G. restless from the outset, suggested that in 1931 a proper holiday was unattainable for either of us.

Throughout that summer declining trade, rising unemployment, and threatening revolution within the British Commonwealth had made the United States, as so often, much sorrier for us than we were for ourselves. In puzzled words Raymond Gram Swing commented in *Harper's Magazine* on "the complete refusal of the British public to face the serious facts of their decline", while Harold Laski sustained this verdict by writing in *The Forum* on Britain's "prevailing temper of depression" and "widespread fatalism". The only popular member of the Labour Government was George Lansbury, who as First Commissioner of Works had set up a Lido on the Serpentine and introduced mixed bathing.

In Germany, where the now senile Hindenburg had been President since 1925, events were hastening the advent of Hitler. So far only the few foresaw Europe's descent into the still deeper shadows which lay ahead. Like other parents of young children, we continued hopefully to count on bringing them up in a world at peace. Politically conscious though we were, neither G. nor I perceived, in the visit of Chancellor Brüning to Ramsay MacDonald at Chequers, a last attempt to save German sanity.

But the coming downfall of MacDonald's Government was already manifest. A fortnight before we left for St. Raphael a Bank of England crisis had precipitated its resignation; though nominal leadership in the new National Government still belonged to MacDonald, the real power was vested in Stanley Baldwin. Early in September England went off the Gold Standard, and the Government contemplated going to the country for a "doctor's mandate".

Statesmen of all parties hastened home from their holidays. By late August the only conspicuous political figures left on the Riviera were Sir Oswald Mosley and Winston Churchill. Not being invited to join the Coalition, Churchill remained, as he himself has recorded, peacefully painting at Cannes throughout the crisis.

Having offered his services to Labour after MacDonald's defection, G. found St. Raphael vexatiously irrelevant. When Winifred forwarded an invitation to him to stand for selection as Labour candidate in the Middlesex constituency of Brentford and Chiswick, which was expecting a by-election, he telegraphed his acceptance and returned joyfully home.

The Committee selected him from among the eight nominees chosen to appear before it, and he wired me that he could not return to the South of France. Throughout the previous ten days, I had steadily written my "war book" on our bedroom balcony overlooking the grey Mediterranean. Now, left alone, I tried vainly to continue it with the uncomfortable sense that G. in England was counting on my practical co-operation.

Finally, my "proper" holiday destroyed by solitude, appalling weather, and the psychological tensions of the crisis, I packed up my book and followed him. But I should not, I knew, be able to touch it again for weeks, as the anticipated by-election had become part of a General Election, and G. was now a Parliamentary candidate.

(14)

Normally Brentford and Chiswick, divided between the Conservative dormitory-dwellers of Chiswick and the Socialist workers in Brentford factories, ranks as a "marginal" constituency which in recent years has changed hands several times. But no constituencies were "marginal" in 1931. G. fought his campaign on a constructive programme, describing the contest as that of "the People versus the Bankers and their Party", and I supported him with short speeches on international relations or the importance of social services to women while the rival factions roared in our wake.

History has since recorded how ineffectual were the arguments of the progressive parties in that period of panic. The little rump of Labour M.Ps. which crept back to the House of Commons numbered only 52, with Lloyd George's "family party" of four Independent Liberals tagging on to their tail. The top-heavy Government, backed by 554 supporters, conducted legislation in its own way during four critical years.

G.'s poll of 7,572 votes, though the best result in Middlesex for seats not previously held by Labour, seemed a poor reward for so

68

much effort. When the result was declared at Chiswick Town Hall, a thick screen of autumn fog hid the candidates on the balcony from the voters in the street. Striving to reach his supporters' ears through the damp curtain which fitly symbolised the miasma descending on their spirits, G. declared pertinaciously that Labour "had lost the trick but would win the rubber"—a happy *dénouement* not to be realised till 1945.

The fog compelled us to spend the night in the constituency. Only when I telephoned Winifred in the small hours did we realise that our local defeat was but one item in a national débâcle. She had just left Lady Rhondda with a rapturous group of champagne-drinking Conservatives at a West End celebration party, and now reported the results already announced.

"It's incredible!" she said. "Everybody seems to have gone down —Herbert Morrison, and Arthur Greenwood, and Ellen, and even Henderson himself. There's almost nobody left."

The remnant which survived included Clement Attlee and George Lansbury, returned by small majorities from safe seats in London's East End. But neither then nor later was Winifred able to repeat the speeches that she had made on Labour's behalf. Three days after the election she collapsed from the mysterious illness, ultimately diagnosed as Bright's disease, which for months puzzled doctors mistakenly pursuing their theory of a nervous breakdown.

When our doctor and I had established her in a nursing-home I met her intimidating white-haired mother, for some years a pillar of East Riding local government, at King's Cross Station. After reluctantly summoning her from Yorkshire I expected anxiety and even distress, but had not been prepared for a vehement scolding the moment that she saw me on the platform. Humiliated and bewildered, and unwilling for Winifred's sake to expostulate, I felt as baffled as a twelve-year-old hauled to the headmistress's study and berated for some unknown misdemeanour. Only gradually did I grasp the reasons for this consummate indignation of which I was the immediate target.

In Winifred's childhood the future Alderman Mrs. Holtby had been the combined dictator and Lady Bountiful of their Yorkshire village, for she came from a feudal stock whose members specialised in arranging the lives of others for their own good. "One more, and you have done," she had written to me when Shirley was born.

Now strangers, whose names she hardly knew, had assumed responsibility for the care of her precious surviving daughter, so suddenly smitten. When, on the doctor's advice, I kept Winifred's friends, both eminent and humble, away from the nursing-home, her mother attributed this prohibition not to medical instructions but to unjustified self-assertion.

Another explanation of her attitude lay in a misunderstanding of Winifred's illness which persisted for months. In spite of the doctors' reports, Alice Holtby attributed the disquieting symptoms of high blood pressure to psychological causes which Winifred could "throw off" if she "pulled herself together". In answer to my summons she referred in bitter exasperation to "this brain sickness", and, even when the doctors had belatedly discovered the origin of the trouble, continued to believe that the literary life which Winifred had carried so easily, and found so congenial, was "too much" for a country-bred young woman brought up on a farm. She blamed the neurotic and unwholesome influence of Winifred's London friends for the crippling demands which, she believed, such a mode of living had made on her daughter.

This assumption, never wholly relinquished, confronted me with some formidable difficulties when eventually I became Winifred's literary executor.

(15)

At the outset of her illness, the idea that she would soon require executors never entered my head.

"She's tired out," we all admitted. "The election was the last straw. After she's had a good rest she'll be all right . . . in a few days . . . a few weeks . . . a few months."

When the months had elapsed and she was still moving in and out of nursing-homes, we said more reluctantly: "Well, perhaps she'll never be absolutely fit again. But if she takes care of herself, she can go on indefinitely."

Only at long last, heavily and incredulously, we began to face the truth. "It kills in the end," one doctor told me. "She's only got a few years at most."

Even then we tried to persuade ourselves that her courage and vitality would defeat the doctors, though she might be the only person in the world who could do it.

After Christmas I took her to South Devon for a period which we both regarded as convalescence, and stayed with her until G.'s return to the States.

Throughout that year of continued "economic blizzard", he found America climbing slowly from her own despair and fog towards domination by the Democratic Party. This began with the election of Franklin D. Roosevelt as President in November 1932, and was destined to continue for twenty years.

Not long after G.'s departure, when I was back in London again, John came home from his nursery school with chickenpox. Struggling with influenza followed by laryngitis, I caught it from him. The severe attack and the risk of pneumonia meant a trained nurse and several days in bed.

"Your isolation at Ithaca is a gay party compared to this," I told G. For a week I felt as stiff as though I had been poured into a mould and left to set; covered with calamine lotion from head to foot, I resembled a long-buried corpse.

In order to leave the children's young nurse free to look after Shirley, we brought John, whose attack was very mild, from the nursery to my bedroom. Now four years old, he was growing up sensitive, critical, self-possessed and disconcertingly intuitive. Without disturbing me he played on the floor, pretending to be a "naughty lobster" and pulling terrible faces. His "wife", now apparently restored to favour, had taken the place of an African, "Mr. Ginns", as his invisible playmate.

"My wife's got a photograph of his mother," he announced. "I'll show it you after tea if you like."

"I should love to see it," I said. "What's your wife's mother like?"

"She's rather like you. She's quite old but very pretty." Uncertain whether his tact had been impeccable, he added hastily: "Well, not so very old, but *quite* pretty. Never mind, Mummy! When you're better, and I'm better, we'll take ourselves away."

But the period of "taking ourselves away" was still distant when my father chose this period of stress for a bout of melancholia. His prolonged ill-health, which a generous but wilful and too-seldom disciplined temperament did nothing to arrest, had been precipitated by external events.

During the First World War a business dispute had led him, at the early age of fifty, into impulsive retirement from the Staffordshire firm where he was a director. Two years later, Edward's death in action eclipsed his remaining purpose in life. Though Edward had been an absorbed musician with no serious intention of entering business, my father's hopes of a successor had been centred in this only son.

After Edward was killed he drifted forlornly from one specialist to another, with periodic expeditions to health resorts and nursing-homes. How much I wished, as I tried vainly to cheer him, that he could turn from his own troubles to those of the world, which were now alarming enough to demand concern even from the most self-absorbed invalid. Though a Disarmament Conference was sitting hopefully at Geneva, its endeavours had been undermined from the start by Japan's use of arms to steal Manchuria from China, and were soon to be doomed because the German demand for equality could not be reconciled with the French desire for security.

In March a sanitary squad arrived at 19 Glebe Place from Chelsea Town Hall. They fumigated three bedrooms and a bathroom while I washed the children's hair and gave them and myself Lysol baths. We were now free from the thraldom of infection.

At the end of the month, a gentle spring sun changed the face of the earth. The children played in their sandpit while I sat writing in the garden, "on call" but seldom called. Shirley, it seemed, had actually escaped chickenpox. She had become, I reported proudly to her father, "a lovely vital creature, health personified, with a mop of bright hair".

Winifred now decided to see a specialist recommended by her medical brother-in-law. Our doctor and I met her in the Harley Street waiting-room; as we left she entertained us with a ribald account of the consultation, though for the first time she had heard the words "renal sclerosis".

Not until I read the fictitious account of this consultation four years afterwards in *South Riding* did I realise that the diagnosis then given her amounted to a verdict of early death, which she understood and accepted.

After this, doctors and relatives abandoned the absurd theory that she was a nervous invalid needing pastoral solitude. She was given a new series of tests, of which the purpose was no longer to save her life, but to prolong it. One doctor, a German-American specialist in arterial diseases named Obermer, succeeded so brilliantly in finding drugs to alleviate her most painful symptoms that he enabled her to write *South Riding*.

Because this treatment, though too late for rescue, was at least appropriate, she seemed again to become wholly herself. At first she was fit only for quiet work at home, but she recovered sufficiently to enjoy the society of Phyllis Bentley, the young Yorkshire writer from Halifax whom she had known for some years. Phyllis's novel, *Inheritance*, had become the fiction-star of that spring. We invited her to spend a few weeks with us and follow up its astounding success.

After the austere months of anxiety and illness, it was stimulating to accompany a much-sought-after author to functions and parties. Together Phyllis and I sampled the social round of literary London;

spent a day with Cecil Roberts at his Pilgrim Cottage; and visited Rebecca West, whose husband, Henry Andrews, whom she had recently married, had been G.'s New College contemporary.

Owing to the slump, new plays were few that year, but we saw Cochran's production of *The Miracle* with Lady Diana Cooper as the Madonna, and J. B. Priestley's drama, *Dangerous Corner*, at the Lyric. Soon afterwards Phyllis introduced me to J. B. Priestley at a League of Nations Union dinner where we were all speakers.

I saw a broad, short, pale Yorkshireman with vivid blue eyes, who spoke in an accent more emphatic than Phyllis's. At dinner he sat between us, and appeared to find family topics more absorbing than the League of Nations. When I mentioned my baby daughter he acknowledged five girls of his own, and suddenly inquired: "Would you rather your daughter went off with a chimney-sweep, knowing he'd make her unhappy, or have no sex adventures at all?"

"I'd rather she went off with the chimney-sweep," I answered rashly. "If she'd had one experience she might believe life would bring her another, but if nothing happened at all she'd get a dreadful inferiority complex."

Priestley laughed. "I quite agree," he commented.

(16)

In Parliament that June Mr. Baldwin had proposed the abolition of aerial bombing, but as the year moved on towards winter the vast army of the unemployed feared idleness more than war. During October a demonstration of hunger-marchers from all over England converged upon Hyde Park, but failed to invade the House of Commons. My sympathy with them was heightened by the continued effect of the slump upon free-lance journalism.

For two years the once frequently commissioned articles which represented a substantial part of our livelihood had been difficult to obtain. Since this setback occurred when we had two children under five to support, and Winifred's illness compelled her to withdraw her financial contributions for long periods, the problem of making ends meet became a real dilemma.

Although I had been writing steadily since leaving Oxford, no book had so far made even £50; only my persistent journalism had paid. Budgeting and contriving was now a vicious circle, for any cut in our young half-trained staff meant that the extra work descended on me and deprived me of time to write.

As I travelled to occasional engagements, I had only to use my eyes in order to see how complete was the depression which undermined the work of many authors besides myself. In October, going to Waterloo Station at the time of a London County Council meeting, I observed dozens of policemen assembling outside the County Hall. At these meetings complaints were heard from local Public Assistance Committees, and the previous week a riot had broken out over the Means Test.

After a lecture at Halifax in November, I saw the tall chimneys of idle mills standing smokeless in a long valley free from industrial murk. Their incongruous cleanliness seemed to symbolise the entire paradox of the slump.

Its consequences now mingled so often with the war memories revived by my perpetual book that one autumn night I had the strangest and most coherent dream of my experience. So completely did it afterwards dominate my imagination that I erased it from my mind only by making it the theme of a short story, *Re-encounter*, which appeared in *Time and Tide* the following December.

I dreamed that I was going to meet Edward, and see him off to India on an engineering assignment. How strange it was, I thought, that such an ardent violinist should become an engineer! When I met him he looked much as I remembered him in life, yet was somehow different; he seemed more depressed, less tranquil, less vital, and inexplicably older without having changed.

"Whatever do you want to go and do engineering for?" I asked.

"Well," he said, "it's as good as anything else."

"But Edward," I expostulated, "you haven't finished your education yet. Why don't you go back to Oxford?"

"They wouldn't take me after all this time," he replied with an air of resignation.

But why shouldn't they? I thought. After all, he's only eighteen—or is it twenty-two? And then I remembered that this was 1932, and reflected perturbedly: "But, good heavens, he's in his thirties, like me!"

We hailed a taxi, and drove along a dreary suburban road which led to the station. In my dream I was aware that I had not seen him for a long interval, and I inquired anxiously: "Do you ever play the violin now, Edward?"

"No," he answered, "not now. You see," he added, referring to his war-time wound on the Somme, "my arm still hurts at times, and I can't get the finer tones."

"But you do go to concerts, don't you?"

"No," he replied. "Not at all."

"Oh, Edward!" I exclaimed, deeply disappointed. "I've been to them myself because I thought you'd be going too and enjoying them."

"In that case," he said, politely but quite without interest, "I must start going again."

We drove on, and I tried desperately to penetrate his armour of indifference.

"Do you *really* want to go to India and to do this job?" I asked. "It isn't quite in your line."

Apathetically he answered: "Oh, it's as good as anything else! Nowadays you have to take what you can get. What does it matter, anyway?"

And I thought in my dream: "Wouldn't it perhaps have been better if he'd been killed in the war, like the others?"

A sudden crash interrupted us, and I awoke to find the housemaid standing beside my bed with the early morning tea. It took me several moments to remember that Edward was not a disillusioned engineer going off to India, but a promising young musician who had been killed on the Asiago Plateau fourteen years ago.

CHAPTER THREE

PERSONAL RUBICON

"There was a need to write this book, but little assurance that it would be written."

> WINIFRED HOLTBY, 1933.
> (Dust-cover description of
> *Testament of Youth*, first edition.)

(1)

JUST BEFORE MY dream occurred, I had been revising the section of my war book which described the last farewell to Edward on Waterloo Station in January 1918. This book eventually became a minor "sensation" in two continents during 1933 and 1934.

Most "books of the season" are soon forgotten by their readers, but an author's life may be completely changed by the publication which briefly becomes a fashion. and the unexpected event fundamentally altered mine. From the outset it meant far more than the sudden beginning of long-delayed recognition.

By enabling me to set down the sorrows of the First War and thus remove their bitterness, *Testament of Youth* became the final instrument of a return to life from the abyss of emotional death. It also proved that if one believes in a purpose sufficiently and persists long enough, achievement will come. What mattered was not that, at long last, this autobiography brought "success", but that it created spiritual reassurance.

In 1922 a publishing firm had offered a prize for an autobiography or personal diary. I put together some extracts from an ingenuous journal which I had kept as a student, but the compilation did not even qualify as an "also-ran". Apart from this naïve little venture, I never thought of using the war as a theme for a book until the idea of *The Incidental Adam* came to me at Ithaca.

When John was three months old I went down to Rye for a belated recapture of physical energy, and my vague literary project suddenly became a passionate impulse. The "occasion" of this change was the gift from G. of Humbert Wolfe's latest volume of poems.

"Why," I wrote him tempestuously, "did you send *Requiem* to strengthen the revolt which has deepened in me ever since I came here? It makes me want to go right away into some quiet country place, and greatly write my novel of that great decade through which, so infinitesimally and yet so grandly, I lived. Everything here reminds me of all that I want to put in that novel—the smell of the sea, the primroses in the grass, the simple Easter morning service in the old Norman church with the flying buttresses. . . . The years slip by in a host of little achievements, and I never make any great use of the gifts with which I was endowed. I come here, and every morning I see a church clock which says to me 'Our time is a very shadow that passeth away'!

"Oh, do you understand? I *can* do great things if only I can have more time, more freedom, more peace. Please help me. I have fought hard for our son's life. Help me to find a little time in which to fight hard for achievement of another kind."

But of G.'s understanding there was really no question, as his answering letter showed. In my novel, he wrote, I must perceive "the needs of your age which your age doesn't know itself."

A year later John's survival seemed assured, and another phase of consciousness came with the publication of numerous war books by men. Early in 1929 Winifred and I saw the new war play, *Journey's End*. We expected only a *succès d'estime*, but an electric atmosphere of reminiscent emotion left us subsequently unamazed by the popular success of that famous swallow which was to make a summer.

Out came the war-books in Europe and America—*Goodbye to All*

That, Death of a Hero, All Quiet on the Western Front, A Farewell to Arms. They enthralled readers already moved by two publications of the previous year—*Undertones of War* and *Memoirs of a Fox-hunting Man.*

After reading these books, I began to ask: "Why should these young men have the war to themselves? Didn't women have their war as well? They weren't, as these men make them, only suffering wives and mothers, or callous parasites, or mercenary prostitutes. Does no one remember the women who began their war work with such high ideals, or how grimly they carried on when that flaming faith had crumbled into the grey ashes of disillusion? Who will write the epic of the women who went to the war?"

Could I, who had done nothing important yet, carry through such an undertaking? A letter sent to G. in March contained a new note of resolution.

"Everything I have wanted in life has had to be fought for every step of the way, and at first it always looked as if I should not get it. . . . Do you remember what you wrote in my *Daedalus*:

> " 'Per cruciamina leti
>   Via panditur ardua justis,
>   Et ad astra doloribus itur' ?"*

With scientific precision, I studied the memoirs of Blunden, Sassoon, and Graves. Surely, I thought, my story is as interesting as theirs? Besides, I see things other than they have seen, and some of the things they perceive I see differently.

Then, suddenly, illumination came. I too must record my memories as an autobiography; nothing else is stark enough, nothing else so direct. I'll write an autobiographical study of the years that I remember, and try to assess their significance.

The kind of memoir that could only be written by a Prime Minister or an Ambassador was ceasing, I believed, to be popular. A new type of autobiography was coming into fashion, and I might, perhaps, speed its development. I meant to make my story as truthful as history but as readable as fiction, and in it I intended to speak, not for those in high places, but for my own generation of obscure young women.

(2)

Years ago, as a sixth-form girl editing the school magazine at St. Monica's, Kingswood, I had discovered the fascination of viewing

*"Beyond the agonies of death, a stern road lies before the righteous, a way that leads through sorrow to the stars."

private events against the great panorama of history, and had dimly realised the scope offered by this treatment to creative imagination.

My project, I perceived, would be a very big book. By now my twenties, like my 'teens, were a memory, and I believed, God help me, that my youth was past, but I did not want actually to start writing until I could command the long period of uninterrupted time which I still optimistically believed to be attainable. I drafted the opening chapters, under the tentative title *Chronicle of Youth*, only when the baby planned for 1929 did not materialise.

By the time I knew that she would arrive in 1930 instead, I was too deeply committed to my book to abandon it, but the occasional moments of inspiration alternated with periods of extinguishing discouragement. In April a letter from my literary agents warned me that the boom in war books was already waning, and expressed the hope that mine was nearly finished.

Two months before the baby's arrival I was obliged to relinquish the book altogether owing to the disconcerting paralysis of my mental powers, but even this unproductive period brought another valuable idea. Looking for some old diaries in my former bedroom at my parents' flat, I re-discovered the correspondence between myself and the four boys—lover, brother, and friends—who had been killed in the war.

Just as I had kept their letters, so they had kept mine, and after their deaths this correspondence had been officially returned to the sender. For years these letters had remained undisturbed because I could bear neither to re-read nor to destroy them. When I mentioned them to my mother, she remarked casually that she had kept all my war letters to her.

If, now, I could bring myself to use these letters, my new type of autobiography would become newer still. The usual retrospective view would be combined with contemporary impressions and thus create the effect of a double dimension.

After a prolonged search through the Kensington flat before Shirley's birth, I collected all the letters and diaries at 19 Glebe Place. During her first six months, I sorted these documents into years corresponding with the twelve long chapters of the book. In January 1931, fourteen months after starting it, I rewrote the first two chapters and began the third.

I knew now that, to counter frustration, I must make no exact plans. "I can only be a pragmatist, thanking God for every uninterrupted hour," I told G. "It *is* queer living in 1914. Sometimes it seems to me enormously interesting, sometimes just nothing but trivialities."

That spring I finished the fourth chapter, and took the fifth to St. Raphael. But worse obstacles than those I had already faced lay ahead. The General Election of 1931 was over, Christmas had come and gone, and Winifred was wrestling with the first onslaught of her illness, when I took up my book once more and realised, in January 1932, that I had still written less than half.

About this time an extremely cultured young acquaintance named Roy Randall invited me to lunch. Roy, destined to die prematurely of cancer, had not much creative ability, but he wore a beard, cherished an earnest ambition to become a literary arbiter, and assiduously cultivated all the writers he could reach. During lunch he asked me the question which, at this still tentative stage, I had hoped to avoid:

"What are you writing now?"

Apologetically I replied: "It's a different book from the others. I'm trying to do a kind of autobiography."

"An *autobiography*!" he exclaimed incredulously. "But I shouldn't have thought that anything in *your* life was worth recording!"

This devastating judgment, though it shook my equilibrium, did not put me off my project. It wasn't Roy's fault that I still resembled an immature young woman to whom nothing had ever happened. In spite of my deceptive exterior I did now believe my story to be worth recording, owing to the very fact—which the cultured Roy had discounted—that it was typical of so many others.

When I related this incident at a dinner with Rebecca West and her husband, Henry seemed disposed to agree with Roy. But Rebecca, echoing my private thoughts, turned on him and said: "You mean she's not a field-marshal? But it's the psychological sort of autobiography that succeeds nowadays—not the old dull kind."

This encouragement alone sustained me during the next few months, dominated by chickenpox and anxiety for Winifred. Though one or two publishers had now "expressed interest", I had still received neither contract nor advance, and dreaded lest this vast, unremunerative expenditure of time should prove abortive. What, after all, had I achieved apart from scores of ephemeral articles? Two immature novels which had sold a few hundred copies; a travel book which no one would publish; a text-book on women's careers; and a pamphlet in the *Today and Tomorrow* Series.

Now, inspired only by blind faith and the urgent need for reconciliation with the past, I gave up hoping for any real fulfilment, and wrote on in my few spare hours only because, if I did not write, I might as well cease to live. But subconsciously I knew that this was the last great effort that I could make without recognition or reward. If I failed my light would be extinguished, and I should have no more to say.

(3)

That spring an Oxford contemporary of Winifred and myself, Edward Marjoribanks, committed suicide in the midst of a conspicuously successful career as politician, barrister, and biographer. To some natures, it appeared, success must be almost as intolerable as failure; the strain of a fortnight's influenza, mentioned by the coroner, seemed hardly enough to account for so drastic an exit.

This new perspective on success brought the realisation that what mattered about a book, however costly, was not its favourable reception by the public, but the quality and significance of the work put into it. As my *Testament* slowly acquired coherence and began to give a picture of the war in time and space, the experiences recorded seemed to be less my own than those of all my near contemporaries.

I was writing, I thought, to try to console others who like myself had known despair—about the loves they had lost, perhaps, or their work's frustration—and to prove that this universal emotion could be overcome even by individuals whose courage was as small as mine. I wanted also to show that war was not glamour or glory but abysmal grief and purposeless waste, though I acknowledged its moments of grandeur.

Finally, I wrote to commemorate the lives of four young men who because they died too soon would never make books for themselves, yet deserved as much as anyone to be long remembered. Whatever happened—whether success came and tasted bitter or sweet, or whether in material terms the result was negligible—nothing could take away the significance of that memorial and its challenge to the spiritual bankruptcy of mankind.

Occasional surges of hope now increased the temporary relief from tension which these reflections brought. In May, Phyllis Bentley's visit made my task seem easier because its anxieties could be communicated to a new and sympathetic friend. At last I finished the second third of the *Testament*, and with this section rid myself of the war and its memories.

"When I had finished it," I wrote to G., "I felt empty and curiously oppressed. For eighteen years I have thought about little else but the war and the men I lost in it; now it is all down on paper and I shall never, perhaps, write of it again. I finished with myself walking up Whitehall in the chill November gloom of the evening of Armistice Day, with the lamps newly lit after four years of darkness. It was so strange to come back and find myself sitting in the June sunshine in the garden of 19 Glebe Place; for quite five minutes I felt utterly dazed."

Before she left, Phyllis talked about my book to Victor Gollancz, its subsequent English publisher, and he, with his usual promptitude, wrote at once to ask for the first refusal.

Now that the long manuscript at last seemed likely to move from the desk where it had lain for three years, Winifred asked if she could read the nine chapters which I was now revising. Terrified even of her benevolent judgment, I allowed her to take them away.

In August she wrote me from Yorkshire with urgent reassurance:

"What can I say to make you believe in your book as I believe in it? When I read those early chapters I felt 'This is *it*. This is the thing she has been waiting to do. This is the justification of those long years of waiting.' You write with your heart and nerves and sinews. You write of what you must. You have *paid* for your material by grinding work and broken youth and sorrow. I have, now that I have read it, no fears at all. It is a book of flesh and blood and intellect. No one else can do just the same."

She added, having not yet begun *South Riding*, "I wish I could think that I could ever do so *real* a thing."

Throughout September I worked ferociously, and discovered that even by leaving the war behind I had not escaped its elastic tentacles of grief. Writing one afternoon about my visit to the Asiago Plateau in 1921, I was ashamed to find myself ignominiously weeping.

(4)

An autumn luncheon for H. G. Wells, who had known G. on the board of *The Realist*, alleviated this inexorable preoccupation with the war.

The luncheon had been arranged to discuss the new Socialist League, and Wells had said that he would like Winifred and me to be invited. My diary for October 5th, 1932, recorded the impression made upon me by the writer whose *Modern Utopia* had been a beacon light of my schooldays:

"At first when he appeared I felt subdued and overwhelmed, because as long as I can remember Wells had been one of the two or three major stars on my literary horizon, and I have always regarded him as a person with whom acquaintance was quite outside my range. After a time I began to thaw—partly perhaps the effect of some dry Moselle, but chiefly because of Wells himself for he isn't terrifying at all, but genial, forthcoming, magnetic, and what Winifred calls 'cosy'. Though very 'mellow' he doesn't somehow strike one as an elderly man; his manner is young and very vital, and his eyes vividly blue."

After this luncheon Wells arranged a further discussion at his flat in Chiltern Court. I expected to be greatly impressed by the "left-wing personalities" whom we were invited to meet, but instead was sadly disappointed.

"Never in my life," I wrote in my diary, "did I hear so much 'hot air' talked or see such an exhibition of egotism, incoherence, dogmatism and turgidity of ideas, coupled with an immovable conviction on the part of everyone who spoke that he had nothing to learn from anyone, let alone one of the others."

Wells, with his anxiety to discover forward-looking people and organise them into an "Open Conspiracy", seemed to be the only person present who had a logical plan. Obviously none of the younger men really wanted to listen to him, though I would gladly have heard him talk for hours. Perhaps the *Mind at the End of Its Tether* owed its final disillusionment to many such experiences.

Early in November, my book encountered a new and formidable setback. Through consulting the Society of Authors, I discovered that copyright in personal letters remains with the writer, and belongs, if he is dead, to his heirs or executors. This meant that many of the letters which I had been using for *Testament of Youth* were other people's property. I could not even quote my love-letters from Roland, or the poems that he had sent me, without his parents' permission.

Winifred consulted Roland's artist sister Clare, who observed pessimistically that I should never get permission to quote the letters, but might possibly be allowed to use the poems if I wrote flatteringly enough to her father and mother. Eventually I sent them a careful letter, but I did not expect a favourable answer because for some time Marie Connor Leighton had disliked my political and social opinions.

Three days later an unexpectedly cordial reply from her gave me permission to use Roland's poems. I had asked only for this, intending if the book found a publisher to tell her—as I subsequently did—that I needed a few extracts from the letters too

Later that week I obtained the required permission from two other friends, and thankfully noted that "one more of *Testament of Youth*'s innumerable fences is surmounted". But the physical after-effects of perturbation were less easily overcome, and manifested themselves in an exhausting and humiliating attack of acute gastritis, precipitated by a lecture at Halifax, which lasted most of December.

One day Winifred brought me a sympathetic comment from Rebecca West; it was a great effort, she had said, to bring up young children, and she wished that I could have a real success. I was still in the trough of physical exhaustion, and nothing seemed less likely than the happy fulfilment of Rebecca's benevolent hope. But early in 1933, when effort still seemed endless and its consequences nil, Winifred was invited to a dinner-party by a visiting editor from the Macmillan Company of New York.

(5)

Even when handicapped by serious illness Winifred still reached every goal before me, and doubtless would have continued to do so had a normal share of time been permitted her. She was asked to the Macmillan dinner because the New York company had recently accepted her novel, *Mandoa! Mandoa!*, now a British "best-seller", for publication in the United States. Phyllis Bentley, also a Macmillan author in America, had promised to take her to Claridge's and introduce her to the representative of the firm which had been so successful with *Inheritance*.

They returned very late, and Winifred, who for once had enjoyed an evening free from headache, began eagerly to discuss it. At dinner, she said, she had sat next to the Macmillan editor, Mr. Harold Latham.

"He talked a lot about the war, and how he wished America understood better what it meant to England. Vera, he ought to be told about your book."

"But it isn't finished," I protested feebly.

"Never mind. There's quite enough for a publisher to judge by, and he's only here for another week. Do let me write and tell him about it."

Phyllis agreed that this was the moment. Feeling as though a chasm had opened before me when I thought I was still on the long last lap of a protracted obstacle race, I told them to do as they thought best.

"The upshot was," I reported to G. some days later of Mr.

Latham, "he got excited at once, asked if I could bring what there was of the typescript round to his hotel next morning, and when I did so was so optimistic that I felt quite ill."

Two days after I handed in the unfinished manuscript, Mr. Latham telephoned my agents to discuss terms, and within five days my book had been accepted in the United States.

The next day I met him again at his hotel. But this visit was not the delightful occasion that my wishful dreams of acceptance had pictured, for the sudden unbelievable excitement had brought back the gastric symptoms of the previous month. Before and after my interview I was obliged to take humiliating refuge in Marshall and Snelgrove's "Rest-room", and maintained equilibrium in Mr. Latham's enthusiastic presence only by doggedly reflecting that I could never confront his magnificent American firm with dignity if I collapsed into ignominious illness before its chief editor.

I have never known a literary business representative more reassuring than this huge smiling man, whose benevolent countenance so effectually concealed the shrewd skill of his critical intelligence. He could not, however, avoid inflicting on me a new period of suspense. Would I let him know as soon as possible, he asked, the name of my English publisher, so that they could "work together"?

My agents telephoned Victor Gollancz, and hearing of Macmillan's swift acceptance, he wanted to see the material at once. But I could endure no more, promised it for Monday, and went home to bed. There I remained for several days, getting up only to attend with Winifred the Westminster Abbey Memorial Service for John Galsworthy, who had died on January 31st two months after winning the Nobel Prize.

In the Abbey we sat in the enclosure reserved for writers and politicians; opposite to us were the Prime Minister and Sir James Barrie. Listening in the half-dream of convalescence to the reading from Ecclesiasticus, I heard as though for the first time the familiar words: "And some there be, which have no memorial; who are perished as though they had never been; and are become as though they had never been born; and their children after them. But these were merciful men, whose righteousness hath not been forgotten. . . ."

And I thought: "That's what I want for *Testament of Youth*. I'll put it below my dedication 'To R.A.L. and E.H.B.'—the unfulfilled poet and the unrecognised musician who died too soon to have any memorial but this unworthy one of mine." At home I added these words to the manuscript now revised for Gollancz.

My agents assured me that I need not doubt his verdict, but the expectation of disappointment had become so ingrained that I waited to hear from him as anxiously as though Macmillan did not exist. To G. I described my final spurt to finish the book.

"There are only about 20 pages more to do, so before another week this long purgatory should be OVER. I'm thoroughly done in, though pleased and happy."

On February 16th, just before midnight, I finished the final page. After that, the period of waiting for Victor Gollancz's decision seemed almost unbearable, and my legs developed an uncomfortable habit of turning to water every time the telephone went or the door-bell rang.

Five days later the morning sun shone coldly brilliant after a dark snowy week-end, and I went down to breakfast with a breathless certainty that the expected letter would be on the table. It was; and I tore it from its envelope to see only the words: "Very proud to publish."

A few moments later I found myself on the Embankment staring at the sun mirrored in the river with the consciousness that a turning-point had come at last. Here was the Rubicon between unavailing obscurity and substantial achievement—not in terms of money or fame, but of power to wage effectively the "mental fight" for the things that mattered.

I returned home knowing that I should remember the high curve of Battersea Bridge, and the shining daggers of sunlight piercing the water, until that final hour when I remembered nothing at all.

(6)

From Yorkshire, where her father was now dying, Winifred ignored her own troubles to send me a series of extravagant prophecies.

"You will make friendships and opportunies beyond all dreams. The destiny laid upon you seems to be the destiny wished by the Spanish writer Unamuno to his friends: 'May God deny you peace and give you glory.' "

As I returned slowly from exaltation to my normal routine, the practical consequences of acceptance became evident too; a double advance on royalties immediately solved the financial problems created by the slump. This made me feel so rich that I treated myself to a "glorious orgy" at the local hairdresser's.

To G. I reported that we could now have the house's shabby

exterior painted, and, humble and grateful, recalled my overwhelming debt to him.

"I think of you, my dear love, and your sense of values, with a feeling of profound relief and trust. I do thank you for your ten years' patience with me, and the tolerance and charity you have always shown."

In March Winifred took me to lunch with Victor Gollancz, whom I then hardly knew. He enjoined the utmost speed in revision, for he was anxious to have the final typescript at the earliest possible moment.

The story, he thought, would appeal to German readers if the translation rights were sold in Germany; for the moment we both overlooked the ominous fact that on January 30th Adolf Hitler had assumed office as Chancellor. But by the time I had revised 200,000 words against the clock and brought Victor his fair copy, the burning of the Reichstag on February 27th had shaken Europe, and the German elections of March 5th had confirmed Hitler's authority.

"I hope there won't be another war before your book comes out," Victor remarked grimly as he took the manuscript.

Like him I realised the errors made by politicians since 1918, but I still had faith that an alternative to war could be found. Oh for a policy of positive magnanimity, instead of the weak provocation of neighbouring countries which seemed to be all that successive governments could achieve!

But soon even the fear of another war became less insistent than concern for Winifred owing to the persistence of family demands upon her failing strength. Nevertheless, she found time to write, at Gollancz's request, the jacket description for *Testament of Youth*. By agreement with Victor, she never put her name to this lovely piece of writing; to sign it, she thought, would be a little indecent when she was so often mentioned in the book, and few people knew that it was her work. The concluding sentences were often quoted during the next two years:

"Its protest against the conventions which cripple our lives and the blind and passionate follies which destroy them is a protest true through all time, and its lamentation shares that universal quality which makes the story of the fall of Troy still relevant to our daily lives.

"When the final verdict upon our age is passed, this testament of stricken but unbroken youth must be accepted as evidence of its temper."

I read this description at Worthing, where I had taken John and Shirley for ten days' convalescence after whooping cough. A cousin had found us a pleasant lodging in a quiet by-road, and I hoped for a period of recuperation for us all.

Sometimes their piping voices and the artless prattle of their nurse sent me on long expeditions in quest of solitude. One day, walking over the Downs beyond High Salvington, I found a wood so enchanting that I took the children there for a picnic. Primroses and anemones strewed the ground beneath the trees; the air was violet-scented, and the warm sunshine of that healing spring suggested June rather than April. Huge bumble-bees blundered half-awake among the flowers; an aeroplane zoomed through the clouds, and the larks above our heads sang with the *abandon* of small prima-donnas from Paradise.

How golden the world seemed now that *Testament of Youth* was finished and accepted! How wonderful it was to have produced such a large book and brought up John and Shirley too! So often their existence had seemed likely to postpone its completion until too late for the theme to find favour with publishers or public. And in less than a year, the suddenly altered temper of Europe was indeed to show how narrow had been the margin of time against which, half-consciously, I had struggled.

Happiness is too often an episodic emotion; the idyllic mood of High Salvington was soon to be overshadowed by a series of mundane obligations. Mainly through inexperience, I had used a large amount of copyright material in my book. The impatient publishers now urged me to obtain without delay the necessary permission for my numerous quotations. In the process I learned more about the psychology of eminent authors than I have ever discovered before or since.

Adverse reactions ran all the way from Charles Morgan, who would not allow me to quote a sensitive undergraduate poem because (mistakenly, I still think) he regarded it as "not good enough" for reproduction, to Rudyard Kipling, who replied through his agent. So onerous were the conditions imposed for the use "without charge" of eight lines from "The Dirge of Dead Sisters" that I should have dropped them altogether, had not their poignant description of endurance among nurses in the South African War carried me through some terrifying hours in military hospitals.

For fear of overlooking anything, I compiled a short list of the Kipling demands:

(1) Make due acknowledgment in a form dictated by himself.

(2) Reproduce the lines exactly as they appeared in *The Five Nations* without omitting any part of either verse.

(3) Write additional letters to his publishers in Britain, the United States, and Canada.

(4) Send him copies of both my English and American editions when the book appeared.

One short quotation thus involved five letters and two presentation copies. I felt thankful that everyone wasn't Kipling; he must, I thought, have collected a good free library over the years.

After this disconcerting experience, I appreciated gratefully the courteous and unqualified "permissions" which came from Sir Owen Seaman (ex-editor of *Punch*), Walter de la Mare (who actually apologised because the precise identification of a title cost me two letters), and Wilfred Meynell, who allowed me to quote the whole of Alice Meynell's "Renouncement".

"I am proud and happy to say Yes to any request of yours," he wrote warmly, "and particularly to this one."

Still worse than copyright problems were the agitating objections of individuals mentioned or described in my narrative. As a conscientious writer anxious to hurt no feelings in such a work, I had submitted relevant sections to be "passed" by those concerned. To my growing dismay nobody seemed willing to "pass" anything, and, while my publisher daily demanded the corrected proofs, constant requests to add, alter, or eliminate material recreated the strain which I had hoped was over.

Even G. apologetically added to my troubles by demanding numerous modifications in the last chapter, where alone he appeared. I could not repudiate his desire for anonymity, but I altered my chapter with a sad and rebellious heart. I had drawn, I believed quite vivid portraits of Edward and Roland, and even of Victor and Geoffrey; now I was compelled to make a colourless cipher of the person who had become the centre of my life.

(8)

In June the President of the Macmillan Company, George P. Brett, came to London with his wife on their way to the Continent. A few days earlier the World Economic Conference—perhaps the most futile aftermath of the slump—had been opened by the King in the all too appropriate setting of South Kensington's Geological Museum.

This time the invitations to dine at Claridge's included myself. Also in the party was Charles Morgan, now a conspicuous literary figure on both sides of the Atlantic owing to the resounding success of *The Fountain*. Sitting beside me at dinner, he inquired with mild curiosity about the work for which he had refused the use of his poem.

"Is it a novel?" he asked.

"Oh, no," I replied. "Straight autobiography."

A sceptical expression appeared on my publisher's face, and I wondered why. Eighteen months later he told me in New York that, after reading my manuscript, he had taken me for a clever if unscrupulous artist who had produced what one American critic subsequently described as "a novel masquerading as an autobiography".

By July a few advance copies had come from the printer, and I sent one to Roland's parents.

"Please forgive me," I wrote, "if you find parts of this book distressing, as I know you must. I have quite deliberately not tried to mitigate any of the tragedy and horror of the war, because I wanted to make my own generation remember, and the younger generation understand, what it meant *at the time*. . . . Whatever the result may be, the intention at least transcended the personal."

My letter also told the Leightons that I was shortly going to France, leaving the children at a nursery boarding school where they were now old enough to stay. From Hardelot I had planned to re-visit the war country, which I had recently avoided lest contemporary changes should blot out memories now fifteen years old.

"I want, if I can, to go again to Louvencourt. If there is any memory, any flower or prayer, that you would like me to leave at Roland's grave, will you tell me and I will try to do it?"

When I reached Hardelot-Plage with G. and Winifred, the small country hotel where a travel agency had sent us gave me the strange "I have been here before" feeling which is supposed to provide evidence of reincarnation. Hardelot lies some eight miles from Étaples, the scene of my war service in France, and I had passed through the village only once, during a long walk on a "day-off" with another V.A.D. nurse. Eventually I recalled that, at this glorified inn, Norah and I had unwillingly surprised an Australian officer about to enjoy a clandestine "date" with a nursing sister.

Having thus identified the hotel, I sought the Pré Catalan, an old château where the two of us, so obviously *de trop*, had eventually lunched. On its site, I discovered, stood a smart "Golfer's Hotel" in modern red-brick architecture with a terrace overlooking a lake.

But the name had survived, and now belonged to a green-shuttered restaurant half-covered with climbing nasturtiums.

Here on the hot July evenings we drank coffee in a garden so rich with brilliant flowers that it was difficult to follow the flight of the red admiral and tortoiseshell butterflies which added their beauty to the colour-carnival. Magenta-pink phlox glowed in the fading light like a deep sunset against the orange of French marigolds, and beyond the lawn a tiny stream tinkled like a child's musical-box along the edge of the pinewoods.

Across the sand-dunes drifted the pungent scent of hot pine-needles, and in the marshy meadows beyond the forest, untamed clumps of willow-herb and ragwort made a changing pattern of purple and gold. So completely did this lush country capture me that I resolved to use it as part-background for the long novel slowly shaping in my mind, and subsequently entitled *Honourable Estate*.

Two years later, when I was writing this book, I vividly recalled the sweep of pinewoods and meadows which encircled the ruined Château d'Hardelot, its crumbling portals still showing the gallant boast *Gaudeam adferro*, where my younger heroine, Ruth Alleyndene, secretly met her American lover, Eugene Meury.

Though the publication of one book is usually rendered endurable for any writer only by the contemplation of the next, the letters now coming from the first recipients of advance copies of *Testament of Youth* made concentration difficult. Amid several warmly appreciative judgments came a frank note from St. John Ervine, who wrote that my book had entirely changed his opinion of me.

There was ample room for this transformation, since his opinion of me had been very low.

(9)

For five days of that summer holiday Violet Scott-James, beautiful, sensitive and fastidious, stayed with us at the Hardelot hotel. Anne, the second of her three children, promised to be as graceful and elegant, but a good deal tougher. Just before our visit to France, Anne had caused her intellectual parents much heart-burning by her determination to exchange Somerville College, where she had obtained a Classical Scholarship and a First in "Honour Mods.", for the career of a fashion-journalist.

In this controversy G., undeluded about the merits of universities, supported Anne, whose decision, he thought, showed courage and independence. After his forcibly-expressed conviction had brought Violet and himself to the verge of a quarrel, he decided that a week in the South would provide better accommodation, warmer weather, less liability to argument, and gayer methods of spending the time.

When he departed, and Violet, who shared his dislike of the primitive hotel, had returned to her work in Fleet Street, Winifred and I spent several placid days walking together in the scented pinewoods.

On the nineteenth anniversary of August 4th, 1914, we travelled to the Somme battlefields. At Louvencourt, now a peaceful Somme village, I looked down upon the carefully tended, flower-adorned grave to which my twenty-year-old lover had been carried in the second December of the war. Amid the African marigolds on the grave a rambler was growing; I picked a spray for his mother, and laid two withered roses—pink from the Leightons' garden, red from my own—against the words "Never Goodbye" on the white stone.

"Never Goodbye." Yet though I could still weep for Edward, my childhood companion, I had now no tears to shed for Roland. As I stood beside his grave I could feel only a deep impersonal sorrow for brilliant youth thrown remorselessly away, and a profound thankfulness that he never knew—as we who were left realised already—that the sacrifice had been vain.

Gradually I understood that this disappearance of personal grief was the measure of my love for G., and of the friendship created between us by nine years of companionship and correspondence. To him, too, and not to Roland, I owed John and Shirley. This was what Rupert Brooke meant when he wrote of his dead contemporaries:

"And those who would have been
Their sons, they gave; their immortality."

Yet the previous December, after reading my first nine chapters, G. had written to me at Halifax:

"Your book, I think, is a very great, a very moving book . . . powerful, significant, important—for me it is oppressive also—to it I am an outsider, intruding, shamefaced, feeling very unworthy, painfully unworthy to the verge of tears. After all Roland is entitled to you; all that is beautiful in love is between him and you. All this I foresaw must come from the book, and I have been right—perhaps shunned it—yet am glad—for your book is death unless it leads on to that courageous determination that is life."

Because, at the time I received it, I was blind and deaf to everything but the shattering attack of gastritis which finally overcame me, I never read this beautiful letter—less coherent and precise than his normal writing—with the careful attention that it deserved. By the time I recovered my equilibrium, it had been put away with other papers and I did not re-read or reply to it.

A few weeks afterwards, in America, G. wrote me in a similar strain:

"It will not be, that which I have desired. I do not know certainly why, but it will not be. Perhaps your book explains it. Sometimes I half hope that you may find your Lewis" (a reference to the lover in *The Fountain*). "But I do not think you will, for all the secret is that you have found him and lost him, and so keep him more than any living man can be kept."

He never sent this letter, though he did not destroy it, and I saw it only long afterwards when I began to collect and file our quarter-century of correspondence. For years he went on believing that Roland's passionate young ghost stood between us when he had in fact laid it by his own loving-kindness. He had taught me that, though we cannot forget the dead, we must not remember them at the expense of the living.

Beneath the external glow of my book's overwhelming reception lay this tragic undercurrent of personal misunderstanding, unknown to me until recently save as an uneasy suspicion. He had never allowed for the degree to which the actual decanting into words of past grief for lost loves is a form of exorcism, leaving the way clear for new patterns of tenderness. *Testament of Youth*, which he looked upon as evidence that "you cannot love me", was part of the very metamorphosis which meant that I could.

(10)

Even the most self-assured of authors seldom enjoys the week which precedes the publication of a major book. But when four years have been staked on one effort without the confidence created by previous success, the period can seem as slow as a steamroller and as unnerving as the prelude to a major operation. When giant advertisements of *Testament of Youth* appeared in *The Observer* and *Sunday Times* on August 27th, the day before publication, any gratification that I might have felt was submerged by a desire to sink into the ground and remain there for the next three months.

A week later my diary summarised the first unbelievable results:

"Oh, what a head-cracking week! Reviews, reviews, reviews, and reviews again. Never did I think that the *Testament* would inspire such great praise at such length, or provoke—in small doses—so much abuse!"

In those spacious days, when criticisms could be spread over two or three columns, the owners of distinguished reputations found it worthwhile to write them. My eminent advocates that week included Compton Mackenzie, Naomi Mitchison, John Brophy, Pamela Hinkson, Storm Jameson and Cecil Roberts; soon afterwards came Henry Nevinson, Rebecca West and Eric Gillett.

I had last seen Eric at Buxton, where as boy and girl we had acted together in an amateur performance of *Raffles*. Now, when he suddenly telephoned to say that he was reviewing my book for the *London Mercury*, I learned that his thigh had been smashed at Passchendaele, where Edward and his regiment had also endured a long ordeal. Later he came to tea, and I observed that the war injury had shortened by about two inches the height of the tall young man in top hat and white spats who had walked with me in Buxton's Pavilion Gardens.

By this time my notices, though ample and prominent, had not been wholly favourable. James Agate delivered a ferocious broadside in the *Daily Express*; the *New English Weekly*, in two successive issues, launched a venomous personal attack; and the consistent *New Statesman* told its readers in an anonymous review that I possessed neither originality of thought nor distinction of style.

Now I began to perceive how deep are the humiliations which the literary profession involves even for the successful author. Only politics, as I was to learn indirectly, exceeds letters in its power to mortify and abash. Like other writers (the *Diary* of Virginia Woolf has shown that even the greatest do not escape this strange form of inferiority complex) I was far more distressed by my few adverse notices than encouraged by the dozens which praised.

Some months afterwards I met James Agate; Winifred had persuaded him to take part in a Six Point Group debate, and invited him to dine with us both beforehand at the Café Royal. She could never, she said, "retain a good hate", and if I had ever felt one, she did not intend me to retain it either.

In the taxi after dinner, the perverse little man suddenly turned to me and said: "It's very sweet of you to be so nice to me."

I had not expected him to mention his review, and, taken aback, stammered with priggish stupidity: "Oh, I don't bear you any malice."

93

"Well," he remarked promptly, "you wouldn't find *me* showing that Christ-like spirit!"

Obviously he thought me a spiritless nincompoop with no fight in her. But because this irascible egotist was in fact a great man he had the magnanimity to reverse a disparaging judgment, and later commended me for work which others attacked. When he died in 1947 I felt unexpectedly grieved, and would gladly have bought his continued existence with any number of scornful reviews.

(11)

Shortly after publication the *Sunday Chronicle* offered me a substantial sum for serial rights, and Mrs. Dawson Scott, the founder of the P.E.N., invited me to dinner.

"I am told this is the literary equivalent of receiving a knighthood," I wrote to G., who was then in Germany.

At her home I met Ernst Toller, the German refugee writer who subsequently committed suicide in New York. Grey-haired and sad, with large dark eyes, he explained that he had been in Switzerland when Hitler came to power and was warned not to return to Germany. Later his flat had been sacked by the Nazis, and his mother and sister turned into the street. He was now trying—one of the first of many—to make a living in England.

By November, though once I would never have believed it, I had ceased even to read the reviews still pouring in from obscure periodicals at home and abroad. In addition, 250 letters had now reached me; in three years they were to amount to 1300 from all parts of the world.

One of the first was from Dame Ethel Smyth, the composer, whom I had last seen at the unveiling of Mrs. Pankhurst's statue. She proved to be a delightful and pertinacious letter-writer, and like many of the others invited me to tea. I visited her house at Woking on a golden October afternoon still warm enough for conversation in the garden.

Dame Ethel was now nearly seventy-five, but she appeared no older than an energetic sixty, and her lively blue eyes seemed to snap with gaiety as she talked. After tea—which consisted of a large loaf, a slab of butter, and marmalade in a grocer's pot set without ceremony on the dining-room table—she took my arm and marched me round the Woking golf-course, which she regarded as her individual kingdom. I once heard her say on a public platform that the title she would have preferred to any other was "Ethel, Duchess of Woking".

But not many of my correspondents reached her stimulating level. Because I had written on great issues of war and peace, I was harassed by crusaders, aspirants, advice-seekers and cranks, who implored me to advertise the particular "cause"—peace, feminism, socialism, or anti-fascism—with which they were identified; or showered me with hopeful pages of immature poems and the untidy manuscripts of very long books; or sought guidance on personal problems which ranged from the choice of a career to the wisdom of marrying a deaf doctor with insanity in the family.

Worst of all were the astrologists, paranoiacs and other eccentrics who wrote, telephoned, called and battered their way to an interview through every domestic and secretarial barrier. I never decided whether to award the palm for pertinacity to the lady whose father had invented a mechanical brake—its connection with a war autobiography being obvious to herself though not to me—or to the feminine disciple of Lord Beaverbrook who urged me to sign a petition to the Foreign Secretary for the repeal of the Treaty of Locarno, though she appeared to be quite unaware of its contents.

Even more embarrassing were the demands for money which poured in from every quarter. A general impression seemed to exist that I had made vast sums from my book. Aunts wrote sourly to congratulate me on this imaginary fortune, and an old acquaintance from a wartime hospital inquired, with the habitual candour of old acquaintances, why we continued to live in such a modest house when I was now so rich.

In October 1933 came American publication and a new dilemma. The previous month *Mandoa! Mandoa!* had also appeared in New York, and our agents cabled invitations to Winifred and myself to undertake American lecture tours for the Colston Leigh Bureau. Her precarious health automatically ruled out such a project, but I felt keenly tempted. Yet how could I leave the children for three months? And dare I put the Atlantic between myself and my anxious, unhappy parents?

Cautiously I acknowledged "interest", but this was enough. Before I realised what was happening, I found myself provisionally booked for a tour the following autumn.

A more sober, but to me more moving, invitation came in November from the Oxford Women's Debating Society. I had never been *persona grata* at Somerville since a humourless Senior Common Room had banned my first novel, *The Dark Tide*, a lurid but guileless caricature of life at the Oxford women's colleges. But now the Principal invited me to spend the night at her home, and during the crowded debate, in which the novelist Marjorie Bowen also took part, I caught sight of my Classical tutor, Hilda Lockhart Lorimer, who had steered me through "Pass Mods." during the poigant summer when Roland was at the front.

She had been moved, she said afterwards, by my story, in which she appeared anonymously; "it expressed what a generation of women wanted to say." A subsequent entry in my diary revealed the cathartic mood created by that visit:

"It was a lovely day with a radiant afternoon sky, and as I watched the beginnings of the sunset I thought how queer it was that, because of *Testament of Youth*, Oxford should thus have welcomed and reinstated me, and felt strangely thrilled."

Two weeks later, another crowd surpassed the audience at Oxford's Randolph Hotel. With several other authors I had been asked to give a talk at the *Sunday Times* Book Exhibition, and as I struggled to the lecture hall through a long queue massed on the stairs, I wondered why so many people had suddenly appeared. Then I was called to the rostrum, where Norman Collins introduced me, and the queue began quickly to move. With a feeling of utter incredulity, I realised that they had been waiting for me.

How can the overwhelmed individual learn to estimate these sudden reversals of experience? Why, I asked myself on the rare occasions when I now had time to think, had all this happened? What accounted for the rich and sudden flowering of life after so long a struggle in frustrated obscurity? This dizzy hurricane of attention was something I had never bargained for, and in spite of its thrilling rewards it was difficult to accept.

The most experienced publisher finds "best-sellers" perplexing; if they were easy to explain, all publishers would be millionaires. According to Frank Swinnerton's definition, "a best-seller is a book written by a sincere author whose talent is greater than the common talent but whose tastes are similar to the popular tastes".

If my publishers' judgment was to be trusted, I had shown sufficient talent to accomplish my task. But popular tastes? I did not, except very rarely, like going to the cinema or listening to the radio. I loved entertaining or being entertained on a small scale, but large parties where sustained conversation was impossible usually bored me. My chief passion was for work, which included reading; my second for travel; my third for country walks; and my fourth for intellectual drama and "problem" plays. No; I certainly did not share the popular tastes of my generation.

More significant, perhaps, than common tastes is common experience; the experience of a generation, a class, a people, a nation. If the experiences of an epoch have been memorable and poignant, a book which records them can hardly fail to make some impression.

Battered by perpetual turmoil, I struggled to keep my head and lay hold on the humility which is most needed when acutely tested. Not I, but my generation both living and dead, was the real object of acclaim; how could I avoid the self-importance—one of the least lovable of human qualities—which I had seen overtake other authors on whom fortune had suddenly smiled?

To have leapt so many rungs of the ladder after living for years on the lowest was actually a humbling experience, and I never quite believed that it was happening to me. At least I always realised how far *Testament of Youth* had fallen short of the vision that I had tried to interpret. It was only a tinsel imitation of the glory which I had glimpsed intermittently, like the gleam of dawn sunshine seen through a veil of earthbound mist upon the summits of distant hills.

(12)

During much of this unforeseen hubbub G. was providentially out of England, fulfilling an intention which had long possessed him.

In the spring of that year he had written me from Ithaca: "If I am any judge, there is another bloody war brewing. The storm-clouds are rising again. For fifteen years I have observed that cauldron boiling. It is enough to drive a man to insanity to be off the scenes."

If only, he added, he had a little spare cash, he would study Europe's troubles on the spot instead of stagnating comfortably in America.

Now, it seemed, my book was likely for the time being to produce this extra money; it would at least enable me to carry our household. I urged him to fulfil his project, and when the academic year ended he obtained twelve months' leave from Cornell in order to investigate European revolution whenever the chance occurred.

The time was certainly appropriate. On May 10th, lorry-loads of books by men and women who loved peace and taught compassion had been publicly burned on the Opera House Square of Berlin's *Unter den Linden*, while the broadcast voice of Dr. Goebbels denounced their writers to hypnotised crowds. Other German cities—Breslau, Dresden, Frankfort, Munich and Nuremberg—followed Berlin's lead.

Henceforth Nazi literature was to be purely patriotic, and books which discussed international understanding were banned even from private libraries. G. subsequently became treasurer of an international organisation, known as the Library of the Burned Books, which planned to collect in Paris, from countries outside Germany, copies of the destroyed volumes.

Publications analysing the German revolution now succeeded novels, such as Walter Greenwood's *Love on the Dole*, which showed the effect of the slump upon obscure human lives. These two types of literature were not unconnected; in our epoch totalitarianism has invariably been the answer to misery unless some better idea has previously taken root.

In August the German Government announced that the trial of Torgler, Dimitrov, Popov and van der Lubbe—prisoners accused of "complicity" in the Reichstag fire—would be held at Leipzig in September. At Ellen Wilkinson's flat, British anti-Fascists from all parties formed a body known as the Reichstag Trial Defence and German Delegation Committee. This group arranged to "defend" the Reichstag prisoners at a "counter-process" in London and to send an international delegation to the trial itself.

The selected British delegate had been H. N. Brailsford, but at the last moment he withdrew on the ground that he was already "suspect" in Germany and might find his freedom of movement impaired. Early in September the Committee asked G. to take his place. He agreed at once to travel by air to Leipzig; here was precisely the opportunity for which leave from Cornell had been obtained.

Next morning I accompanied him to Croydon Airport, whence a Dutch line connected with a Czech service to Germany. My heart seemed to turn over as I watched his tiny plane vanish into the clouds, for the pioneer commercial airlines of that period were far from reliable. That afternoon came the hardly believable telegram announcing his arrival.

At a crowded Reichstag Trial meeting next day at the Kingsway Hall, numerous friends praised G.'s prompt decision, and after the meeting Harold Laski, who had been one of the speakers, walked with me to Holborn Tube Station.

"Doesn't Pollitt make you sick!" he remarked of the vigorous oratory to which we had just listened. This comment surprised me a little, since in his own address, which followed that of the Communist leader, he had referred to "the superb speech of Mr. Pollitt".

I learned later that G.'s air trip had been both uncomfortable and adventurous, and that the Leipzig plane had barely avoided a crash-landing. He had flown, G. reported, over Essen, where only 60,000 from a population of nearly half a million were now employed. This

98

desperate economic position, he thought, explained why Thyssen, the great industrial magnate of the Ruhr, was prepared to gamble on the success of the Third Reich.

Since material for the British Press from unorthodox sources might be confiscated in this sinister Germany, we had arranged that G. should relay his articles to me. I revised and typed them, and found homes for nearly all. After them came picture-postcards showing the face of Hitler, already *"Der Führer und Vater des Volkes"*; Hitler in uniform receiving a bunch of roses from a plump blue-eyed maiden; a ferocious Hitler with fanatical eyes and arm like an automatic weapon shooting aloft.

Other cards pictured an older civilisation: the New Rathaus at Leipzig, with red roof and green copper dome; the delicate pinnacles of the historic Rathaus at Munich; the portraits of the grave, sagacious Rothschild brothers from the house dedicated to their memory at Frankfurt-am-Main. It was a doomed Germany which G.'s pictures showed me; fourteen years later, when I made an official visit of my own, these treasures of art and architecture had disappeared beneath the satanic man-made meteorites of the Second World War.

From Leipzig G. reported a significant sidelight on Nazism. At Bach's church, the Tomaskirche, he had found a total Sunday evening congregation of eighty, but the next night 3,000 German Christians attended a meeting where Protestant pastors described Jews as "unbrotherly" and eulogised the Germans as "God's creation". Outside the Supreme Court he found little evidence that an historic trial, comparable to the trial of Dreyfus, was now in progress.

Inside, apart from the jailers, only four policemen casually kept order. A hundred journalists of different nationalities surrounded the five red-robed judges in the wooden-panelled courtroom, but the ticket-holders did not fill the public galleries. Photographers behind the judges' chairs, and the undisciplined witnesses who were permitted to harangue the Court, added to the informal procedure, which now seems an odd curtain-raiser to the greatest catastrophe so far known to history.

Only one prisoner was German—Torgler, the leading Communist Deputy in the Reichstag. Van der Lubbe, the half-blind Dutch paranoiac who boasted of his incendiarism, kept silence before a bourgeois Court while the Bulgarians, Dimitroff and Popov, stole the limelight.

"Dimitroff conducts himself as a doomed man before a court of bourgeois foes," wrote G. "He doesn't expect justice but makes propaganda."

In October, when the trial moved to Berlin, G. moved with it, and there wrote me of a significant experience at the film of Noel Coward's *Cavalcade*, then being shown in Germany.

Some parts of the picture, "with its misrepresentation of the workers and snobbery", he found "as insufferable as ever". But the historic theme rang true, and though it described a war in which Britain captured the German colonies and took the German fleet, he found its reception "unforgettable". As the film ended with its toast *"Auf Würde, Macht und Frieden"*—"To Dignity, Greatness and Peace"—the packed Berlin audience which had remained silent when Hitler appeared on the newsreel applauded again and again.

"The play was over and I went out into the brilliantly lighted night streets bright with the Nazi colours. And I realised that the intense pride I felt in the English tradition was just because it was a tradition that has been content to put above England peace and humanity, and to be judged by whether it has in fact forwarded what are in God's sight eternal values."

Another letter described a luncheon with "Putzi" Hanfstaengl, head of the Nazi Propaganda Department, who explained that "Hitler had no alternative. The parsons were in politics, but they did nothing to make a national revival. They left that to the Nazis and spent their time comfortably in their homes, producing endless children."

Herr Hanfstaengl told G. that it was he who first saw the Reichstag burning from Goering's house and telephoned Hitler; vividly he described how he had gone to bed in a perspiration and was sleeping lightly. G. believed this anecdote; the medical details, he thought, rang true.

At Munich G. heard Hitler speak and reported one of his exhortations: "This is a glorious time to live, in which men are confronted by problems. The German people must advance by devotion and sacrifice."

These words, like August Kubisec's story, *Young Hitler*, suggest that at least a century must pass—as it had to pass for an objective estimate of Napoleon—before the impartial justice of history delivers its final verdict on the Führer. But even in 1933 there could be, to a perceptive observer, no question about the historic significance of that "glorious time". Travelling north along the Rhine for a visit to Cologne, G. wrote: "Unless my judgment is at fault, we are seeing the most important days now for fifteen years."

In Frankfort he walked through the short street in the old walled town where until 1806 all Jews had to live. Near the large shabby synagogue, now chalked with swastikas by small boys, he entered the four-roomed house shown on the postcard he sent me, with a ship carved over the door.

"Here with his seven children and his little counting house behind the kitchen and bedroom lived Maier Rothschild. As the Jewish caretaker said to me: 'Once a little office and great business; now great offices and no business.'"

As he left Frankfort the passengers in the train were discussing the break-up of the Disarmament Conference, and in London a *Times* editorial reproved the Führer like an outraged schoolmaster upbraiding a recalcitrant pupil.

G. remained in Germany until the November elections produced a 92 per cent vote for the Nazi régime, and returned to Berlin on Armistice Day by the same train as Hermann Goering.

"I have just been within two yards of him," he reported. "So if the Communists blow up the train they'll get me too. Five years hence I wonder what? Mosley in England? . . . This exaltation, for a whole nation, cannot go on for ever. Goering looked pink, well and not ill-favoured."

From Berlin he sent me his verdict on that autumn in an article which concluded with a prophecy:

"Germany's case is good, but Herr Hitler must reflect that the case for the reign of law is better and the power behind it greater. If he neglects to do this, he will arouse in the Anglo-Saxon lands a movement compared with which his own National Socialism will be but a Potsdam stage play."

While other nations were still lamenting the Trojan sorrows of the First World War, Germany, failing to get any response to peaceful protests, had turned her face towards the Second. After that war I learned from an acquaintance in Hamburg that *Testament of Youth*, with other books, had been removed from her flat by the Gestapo during the winter of 1933, and publicly burned in the town.

(13)

No protagonist of peace could accept Fascist doctrines, but Berlin's reception of the *Cavalcade* film suggested that those who subscribed to them by no means represented the whole German nation. And even the Nazis' philosophy of hatred might perhaps be modified by overdue concessions to their country.

"We face a choice of evils," H. N. Brailsford had written in *The New Clarion* after the break-up of the Disarmament Conference.

"Hitler's Germany will be a peril and a curse even if we disarm it and overthrow it. It will be a danger if we allow it to re-arm. There is no tolerable course before us, because we are trying to administer Europe on the impossible basis of the Versailles Treaty which, given the present balance of power, we are impotent to revise. Until we cast off that legacy there is no course open to us that merits the name of honesty and fair dealing."

Early in 1934, an offer from America of $10,000 for the film rights of my book interrupted my preoccupation with events in Germany.

"Mr. P. of the film department seems to think me mentally defective because I don't jump at the idea of selling my soul (to say nothing of other people's) for £2,000," I wrote to G., "but just think what Hollywood might do."

Could I ask the Leightons to endure the probable sentimentalisation of their dead son, with whose writings they had been so generous? Could G., in a film, preserve the anonymity which already had virtually disappeared? What would happen if the producer wanted to introduce, as a minor character, a well-known author who had given me a bad two hours over the alteration of three sentences? Feeling that for no money on earth could I endure a new series of controversies, I hesitated and was lost. *Testament of Youth* never became a film, but the publicity in which the book had involved me showed no signs of diminishing.

When I travelled to speaking engagements people now identified me from photographs, and started conversations about my past, future, and family relationships. These encounters left a pleasant feeling that the world was full of unknown friends who thought kindly of me, but by the end of March I had experienced enough even of them. Since my book's publication I had given seventy-four addresses, and felt that I never wanted to lecture again.

When G., still intent on revolutions, decided to attend the current Sociological School in Rome, the idea of a fortnight away from it all in Italy suddenly captured my mind. He then suggested that we should meet in Florence or Milan, and go on to the coast.

As soon as this plan had been broached, obstacles appeared. My father's fast-failing health, as usual, was advanced as a reason for "staying put", and a sudden attack of influenza sent my own temperature rocketing upwards. But the warning that I could not continue much longer without a break from turmoil seemed clear. From my bed I booked rooms at the small Albergo Nazionale in Portofino, on the Ligurian coast, risked a fluctuating temperature, and went. The result was the most satisfying holiday of our experience.

(14)

The enchantment began with the journey itself.

Being barely convalescent I felt entitled at last to luxurious travel, and booked a compartment on the Rome Express to Santa Margherita, where G. had promised to meet me. By the Golden Arrow, which I had never sampled before, I reached Calais in unbelievable comfort, and found Paris white and green with chestnut blossom and the vivid foliage of young larches.

Looking that evening at the French countryside unrolling beneath a mild spring sky, I became conscious of a healing tranquillity such as I had never yet known. Before I left England the seventh edition of *Testament of Youth* had come off the press; after months of crowds and clamour, I realised the inestimable boon that solitude can be.

As the train roared south into Italy, I rose early after an uneasy night and went to the breakfast car. It was empty except for a stocky man hunched in a far corner; his appearance seemed familiar, and to my surprise I recognised J. B. Priestley. He too recognised me, and beckoned me to join him; he was up so soon, he said, because he too had slept badly. After a trip to the West Indies he was now on his way to Capri with Basil Dean to see Gracie Fields, and for two hours we discussed books, authors, politics, war and peace.

When I reached Santa Margherita G. was loyally awaiting me, and we drove together into Paradise. After a rainy night, the whole Ligurian coast broke into summer. Thankfully discarding my winter clothes I put on a bright blue cotton shirt, and went out of the small hotel with its green and orange sunblinds to look at the fishing boats drawn up on the sandy beach of the miniature harbour.

Our meals were served on an open-air terrace overlooking the narrow blue inlet; round a little piazza immediately opposite, argumentative fishermen mended their nets. Violinists, guitar-players, and an itinerant piper successively performed along the shore, and the infant population danced after them like the children who followed the Pied Piper of Hamelin. Never, G. and I agreed, had we known such a ravishing spot. Here, we learned, the author of *Elizabeth and Her German Garden* had written *The Enchanted April*.

From the village a rocky path led uphill to Portofino Vetta, five miles across the mountains. As we climbed through olive groves to pinewoods, the season changed from summer back to spring. On the lower slopes wild hyacinths and milk-blue periwinkles grew like weeds amid vetch as large as sweetpeas, and buttercups and purple borage fringed the stony track. But among the pines, where the smell of sticky resin filled the air to intoxication, we saw anemones, dog-violets, and the last late primroses. At the top we found ourselves on a peak of the Ligurian Alps, with still higher peaks stretching eastward, and the huge half-circle of the Gulf of Genoa sweeping towards the west.

Along the inlet facing our hotel, the Capo di Madonna sloped high above the harbour to a lighthouse. In a small public garden, tulips, tea-roses, stocks, wallflowers, cherry blossom and lavender growing gloriously together created a heady perfume like the scent of flowers in Eden. Each hot morning I sat with my book on a sun-saturated seat against an old wall where freesias and wistaria made a delicate backcloth of colour, and the scuttling lizards stopped to inspect me fearlessly as I read.

Here was really a holiday: here was heaven. I did not know that I was looking my last for many years on the carefree Italy which only twelve months hence would become a memory. The harsh hatreds of Fascism, to be so deeply emphasised by the Abyssinian War, had not yet penetrated to this lovely coast; even in Milan the only marchers whom G. had seen belonged to a company of Catholic Boy Scouts. Beyond the turquoise Tigullian Bay, in Rapallo harbour, lay the only visible hint of Europe's reviving militarism—the British battleship *Resolution*, with nine gunboats anchored beside her.

Refreshed and transformed, we returned home to find the children, collected by Winifred from the nursery boarding-school at Burford, already installed. They examined our coloured postcards with delight while Winifred talked uneasily of the Incitement to Disaffection Bill which had passed its Second Reading while we were abroad. This undemocratic measure sought "to make better provision for the prevention and punishment of endeavours to seduce members of His Majesty's Forces from their duty or allegiance", and made the mere possession of literature capable of "seducing" the Forces an offence.

I liked the sound of the Bill no better than she; it was another "pointer" towards the impending shadow of war and its threat to human liberty. But the idea that such legislation could affect my own future never entered my head.

Shortly after our return, the Sidney Webbs invited G. and me to spend the day with them at Passfield Corner. Forty-eight hours before this visit, Gollancz had published my small volume of verse, *Poems of the War and After*.

Although I had corresponded with Beatrice Webb I had never seen her, and I awaited this experience with trepidation. These apprehensions proved to be unnecessary, though we found her at seventy-four as uncompromising and incisive as the "Altiora Bailey" of Wells's ruthless portrait in *The New Machiavelli*.

Very tall, with the face and neck of a lean, dominating eagle, she relegated to the background of whatever stage they shared her small, bearded and highly intellectual husband, though he had been a Minister of the Crown. The previous January she had undergone an operation for the removal of a kidney, but she insisted upon taking us for a two-mile walk through the Hampshire woods while she discussed the Press comments on my book.

"In youth," she remarked, "there's nothing one longs for so much as publicity. But when it comes, there's nothing that nauseates one so quickly."

Before the Italian holiday I might have agreed, but Portofino had renewed my vitality. Although I sometimes felt tempted to exclaim, with the "Tawny Island" chapter of *Testament of Youth* which described my year of hospital service in Malta, "Give me back that enchanted obscurity!", I suspected Winifred of being more realistic than I when she observed shrewdly: "I don't believe you'd really like to go back to enchanted obscurity. For one thing, as your poem says, we do not recapture the enchantment. We only resent the obscurity."

But perhaps, I now reflected, the desire might become genuine if I lived as long as Mrs. Webb, and endured publicity for nearly forty years.

I wrote later that I had been captivated by her personality— "so downright, so witty, so easy to talk to for all her slight alarmingness". Her combination of complete intelligence and social *savoir faire* seemed so irresistible that I wondered whether I was really as good a democrat as I had supposed.

"I think she liked me," my comment continued, "and she didn't make me feel in the least provincial or 'genteel', as some of the great do. She accepts you entirely for what you are now, and what you were doesn't matter. . . . Her best *bon mot* was about X., whom she can't bear though she appreciates Y.: 'I'm prepared to tolerate polygamy in a man I like, but I don't see why I should condone polyandry in a woman I detest!' "

(16)

Early in May, I learned that Robert Leighton—of whose illness I was unaware—had died from dropsy. In that casual household no one had realised until too late that his malady could be fatal.

For medical reasons the funeral had been hastened, and I went next morning to the Leightons' villa at Bishop's Stortford. I found it much as I had last seen it in 1926, when I almost believed myself back in their overcrowded cottage at Keymer in 1916.

"Every habitation they occupy," I had written to G., "looks the same after a few weeks—a sort of squalid comfort, warm, unceremonious and dirty, with piles of books and clothes on the floors of all the rooms. The loveliest thing in the house was a neurotic but very beautiful female Alsatian."

Eight more years had put further layers of dust over the uncleared accumulation of papers and garments, and nothing suggested that, throughout this period, the windows had ever been opened. The Alsatian or her successor, handsome and excitable, was still ferociously present.

The hurried arrangements meant that no one could send flowers, apart from a bouquet which I had brought from London and a few wreaths ordered locally by Clare. Nor had time been sufficient to buy mourning, which was then still expected at burials.

Marie Leighton, whatever her actual emotions, camouflaged them by rouged cheeks and a spate of inappropriate anecdotes. Her funeral attire, as grotesque as the clothes she had worn at my wedding, consisted of an ancient black velvet jacket, a large velvet hat, and a black lace petticoat barely concealed by a short silk coat. A pair of thick winter gloves with grey fur at the wrists completed, on a sweltering day, this fantastic collection. She resembled an elderly chorus-girl who had equipped herself from the acting chest at the local Repertory.

Two ageing writers who acutely disliked each other accompanied Clare and me as we walked together behind the unseasoned coffin of bright brown wood. Their names were famous, but their frock coats and enormous top hats suggested a sudden resurrection of Victorian relics from trunks stored in attics for years. As we proceeded solemnly through the small cemetery to the Catholic graves over the hill, a passer-by would certainly have taken us for an eccentric group of pauper mourners.

106

The priest, at any rate, appeared to despise us; he intoned the burial service so fast that it was over in ten minutes, and even the committal prayers sounded commonplace. Only the splendid summer afternoon, the beauty of the flowers on the coffin and the persistent singing of innumerable birds, redeemed the ceremony from caricature. Even the grave had been roughly dug by amateurs because the sexton refused to work on a Saturday.

When the cheap coffin had been lowered into the raw earth, we were obliged to leave it without even a spadeful of dust to cover it. This unceremonious leave-taking, though I had no choice, felt like a base desertion after the benevolent acceptance of me which I had owed, years ago, to Roland's father. It seemed a shabby and pathetic end for that sensible, kindly, unappreciated man, always overshadowed by the flamboyant egotism of his dynamic wife.

What would Roland have thought of them now? I wondered. But then, if he hadn't been killed, they would probably never have become what they were—any more than my father would have become what he was if Edward had lived. Bygone battles, like old sins, cast long shadows.

I left Marie Leighton, impenetrably armoured in brassy composure, with the woman friend who lived at their cottage. In the subdued light of the memories that we shared, it was a strangely inadequate farewell. She had still seven years of life before her, but such are the chances of human existence that I never saw her again.

(17)

In June G. was able to study counter-revolution without crossing the Channel. At Olympia, the great West Kensington stadium, Sir Oswald Mosley and his Blackshirts staged a melodramatic demonstration which bore an unEnglish resemblance to the noisy caperings on the Continent.

During 1932 Mosley's New Party had become the British Union of Fascists, with its headquarters in a derelict theological college off the King's Road, Chelsea. When I went out shopping, open trucks rushed past me packed with husky young men in Blackshirt uniforms waving Union Jacks. Another large flag floated over the entrance to the Fascist offices, where unoccupied Blackshirts lounged against the walls now plastered with strident posters: "SHALL JEWS DRAG BRITAIN INTO WAR?" "FASCISM IS PRACTICAL PATRIOTISM."

In 1934 Mosley launched a new campaign supported by Lord Rothermere and the *Daily Mail*. Its highlight was this mass meeting at Olympia, which I attended with G., Storm Jameson, and several other friends. In response to a planned series of Communist interruptions, the demonstrators employed a technique of organised violence which shocked the habitual equanimity of the British public.

G. and I struggled into the one available entrance through an undisciplined crowd of several thousands seething round the Stadium; among them were men and women wearing evening dress, workers in overalls, and family parties with young children. Inside the hall, huge clusters of amplifiers hung like the trumpets of arum lilies in a green mist created by the rising fumes of tobacco. Arc-lamps threw a theatrical blue light upon the Blackshirt band massed beneath their black and yellow flag. Salmon-pink drugget, which exuberantly clashed with everything else, covered the platform floor.

Half-an-hour after the advertised opening "the Leader" appeared, preceded by a fanfare of trumpets and a Blackshirt procession. Lights flickered; the band played a German march; the beams from the arc-lamps focussed on the platform, and Sir Oswald started to speak. Immediately a chorus of interruptions burst from a gallery; Blackshirts leaped over chairs, and a noisy scrimmage began. As though awaiting a signal, Sir Oswald raised his voice.

"You can see how badly a Blackshirt Force is needed to defend free speech in Britain!"

Opposite us a man cried out: "Does Hitler stand for free speech?" A group of Blackshirts promptly knocked him down and pummelled him; the struggling human mass rolled over several rows of chairs, and the interrupter was frog-marched from the hall. Shortly afterwards I saw similar treatment suffered by a man on my right who merely shouted "No!"

After listening for two hours to a dull speech on economic conditions, punctuated by wild attacks on interrupters for which he appeared deliberately to stop, I decided that Mosley was no orator. The military-looking uniformed figure with dark hair and small black moustache appeared harshly handsome, but his expression never changed. No flickers of emotion illuminated his face as they illumine the faces of great speakers, and when we could hear his speech it sounded as though it had been memorised and often repeated. He suggested a large wooden marionette with a gramophone inside him.

A long interval of scrimmages and statistics ended in a shower of leaflets which fell on our heads. Far above us a voice shouted "Down with Mosley! Down with Fascism!", and we looked up to see a figure climbing across the iron girders of the roof. The arc-lamps, swinging round from the platform, spotlighted several Blackshirts clambering after the interrupter 150 feet overhead. Sir Oswald went on speaking monotonously, but no one listened; this free cinema-show claimed the whole audience's breathless attention.

Just as the opposing forces appeared to meet, the object of pursuit suddenly climbed the girders to a still higher ledge. Pursued and pursuers disappeared from view; almost immediately a crash of glass sounded behind us. The audience, weary of economics and violence, and now concerned for its own safety, began to filter out. In the street a fight broke out and held up the traffic.

The following day a *Times* letter of protest signed by three Conservative M.Ps. typified many others. Shortly afterwards Victor Gollancz issued a pamphlet, entitled *Fascists at Olympia*, which contained statements from eye-witnesses, victims of assault, and doctors who attended the injured. Many of these statements came from well-known men and women whose integrity as witnesses was unquestionable; they included Mr. Baldwin's Parliamentary Private Secretary, Geoffrey Lloyd, M.P.; Canon H. R. L. Sheppard; Storm Jameson; Gerald Barry; A. J. Cummings of the *News Chronicle*; and Aldous Huxley.

As we left the hall, G. had correctly summed up the repulsive entertainment: "This is the biggest bear-garden I have ever been in."

(18)

But bigger and grimmer bear-gardens awaited the peoples of Western Europe. The Olympia demonstration soon appeared as a mere curtain-raiser to "the night of the long knives" on June 30th, when, by Hitler's order, Roehm, Heines, and other S.A. leaders were arrested and shot.

This massacre, short-circuiting legal formalities, horrified the countries whose delegates had attended the twelfth International P.E.N. Congress at Edinburgh. Between the Fascist meeting in Kensington and the Nazi murders in Germany, H. G. Wells, then International President of the P.E.N., gravely addressed this gathering of writers.

"The world," he warned them, "is in a state of unexampled crisis. Wars and revolutions, violent external and internal struggles, threaten mankind almost everywhere. You do not want me to talk politics. . . . But what if Politics and Politicians and Police and Soldiers . . . lift themselves up and presume to lay hands on Literature and Science? What if they attack *books*? ... When Politics reaches us, and assaults Literature and the liberty of human thought and expression, we have to take notice of Politics."

Politics, indeed, gave us no choice. On July 25th in Vienna, Chancellor Dollfuss, who had been responsible for the February bombardment of the workers' flats which killed 1500 Austrian Socialists, was himself murdered by a Nazi conspirator, Otto Planetta. That night the sullen zoom of aeroplanes, practising "defence", echoed for hours over London; from my bed I could see the brilliant streak of a lighted bomber circling the horizon. At the end of the month Mr. Baldwin woke long enough from his chronic lethargy to announce that Britain's frontier was now the Rhine.

On holiday in Devon with the children, I tried to prepare amid these alarms for the rashly accepted American lecture tour, which now loomed so near. During our stay the author of *The Diary of a Provincial Lady*, E. M. Delafield, brought her children from Cullompton to visit mine, and described her own experiences as a lecturer in America.

"She said one can really make a lot of money by these tours," I told G., "and that one comes home with such purely commercial standards of achievement that our own somewhat sentimental and studiously non-mercenary attitude is difficult to reacquire."

Hints of that realistic outlook had already reached me from my publisher and lecture-agent, who had been deluging me for the past six months with demands for photographs, press-cuttings, and descriptions of myself from birth to maturity. But these professional problems seemed trivial compared with the personal dilemma created for me by my parents, for during our brief visit to Portofino my father had displayed suicidal tendencies, and my mother wanted me to cancel my tour. She never understood that this would now involve heavy financial compensation to my agent, and my decision to go meant ignoring her wishes.

"I shall be glad to get you safely out to sea," G. wrote affectionately. "It is one's duty, when old, to keep out of the way of one's children."

But when, the day before I left, I said goodbye to my father in his nursing home, the mingled pity and exasperation habitually inspired by my parents turned wholly to compunction. For some time he had suffered from intermittent delusions, but today he was clear-headed and had compelled himself to get up and buy me a farewell present.

First he produced a miniature diamond brooch shaped like a bee;

that, he said, was for Shirley. To me he gave a silver paper-cutter with a tiny magnifying glass in the head. On the cardboard box he had inscribed his pet-name for me in childhood: "To dear Jack. Her Father's parting gift, with all love and affection."

My mother told me afterwards that the brooch had been his first choice of a present for me; at the store his failing mind had reverted to the past, showing him a picture of the small girl to whom, as a young father, he had been so deeply devoted. He had bought the diamond bee imagining me to be still a child; only as he left the shop did he remember that his daughter was now an adult woman going on a lecture tour, for whom a paper-knife was more appropriate than a baby brooch.

As I took these gifts, my heart seemed to be torn in two. His sui- cidal experiment (was it real or staged?) had occurred when I was abroad, as though he wanted me to be at an irretrievable distance before making up his mind to leave me for good. Would he wait till I reached America to make another attempt, and could I prevent it by staying? Why was a professional job, regarded as meritorious when performed by a man, so often made by circumstances to appear selfish and callous when done by a woman?

That evening, as I fastened the brooch on my four-year-old baby's frock, I knew it would always remind me of my father's love for me when I was her age, and he a normal, handsome man affec- tionately proud of his boy and girl. And so for several years it did, until Shirley, to whom the brooch meant nothing, lost it.

At midnight, when I went upstairs for a final look at the sleeping children, she half woke up and put her arms round my neck, and my resolution to fulfil my engagements, come what might, almost broke down.

(19)

When G. and I sailed together for this first American tour, an ex- cited cavalcade saw us off at Waterloo. My mother and Winifred were there with John and Shirley; the novelist John Brophy, to whom the children were much attached, gallantly appeared; and our secretary and household helpers completed the group.

The children seemed unperturbed except when the sudden shriek of a whistle made Shirley cry. Clinging one on each side to Winifred, who was accompanying us to Southampton, they only wanted to be assured that "Auntie isn't going to America too".

All the way to the coast I thought wretchedly of their faces vanishing as the train left the platform, and of my father struggling out of the nursing-home to buy me a farewell bouquet of roses. But gradually a sense of proportion returned. After all, three months wasn't long, and with Winifred in charge I need not fear for the children. Even her own precarious health had temporarily improved.

It was on this voyage that I heard a story of the only American lecture-tour ever attempted by C. E. M. Joad, who had been persuaded to come over by my own manager, thirty-three-year-old William Colston Leigh. Shrewd as a ferret and tough as a Brooklyn boy, this human dynamo had already been "talked into riches" by a series of renowned lecturers from Eleanor Roosevelt downwards.

So far the only Englishman who had proved immune to his spellbinding was Cyril Joad. Landing a year or so earlier, he had driven in obstinate solitude from the docks to his hotel. On that short journey he decided that he couldn't endure New York another moment, and telephoned Colston Leigh that he was rejoining his ship and going straight home.

The lecture-manager announced that he would come over and see him. They dined together, and he kept Joad talking about his decision until nearly midnight. Leigh then observed quietly: "You can't board your boat now; embarkation-time closed at eleven, and there isn't another ship for five days. Don't you think you might as well give the lectures booked for you this week?"

Reluctantly Joad agreed. He found the experience more tolerable than he had expected, remained another week, and saved himself and his manager from commercial loss. But not one further moment would he stay, and he never visited the United States again.

This unfamiliar America of spectacular lecture tours, the New Deal, and nineteen million citizens dependent on the Federal Emergency Relief Administration, was to capture me with its contrasts as I had never been captured by the prosperous America of the twenties. The shared experience of economic chaos had brought the United States and Britain to a closer understanding. American home-life had become simpler, entertaining less formal; perhaps for this reason I was to learn, as I had never learned during the first two years of marriage, to accept graciously America's zestful, overwhelming hospitality.

After an appreciative glance at the familiar skyline, we landed to find this hospitality lavishly extended to ourselves and my book. Scarlet-jacketed copies filled Macmillan's bookshop window, glowing like a vivid sunrise across Fifth Avenue; even my little volume of poems, in grey linen with a shiny paper cover, had gone into a second edition.

Testament of Youth, I learned, was still selling a thousand copies a month, and had become known throughout the United States. The total sales had reached 35,000, then quite a sensational figure; *Gone with the Wind* had not yet appeared to set a million-copies standard and threaten all publishing with new forms of commercial temptation.

"It'll go on selling for at least ten years!" George Brett, my publisher, said blithely of my book. He remained a true prophet until America again went to war, and books reflecting totally different values began to seduce the reading public.

(20)

When the tour was first discussed, Mr. Brett had generously offered me hospitality. The home which he now put at our disposal proved to be informal beyond my most optimistic dreams. After an annihilating day of interviewers and photographers, G. and I were driven out of the stifling city to the Bretts' luxurious country "shack" in Fairfield, Connecticut.

Here I had been allocated a few restful days until my tour officially began with a mammoth reception to publishers, editors and journalists. And restful indeed I found them, though the rôle of guest of honour at successive luncheons, teas and dinners taxed to its limit the trait which Americans charitably describe as "British reserve". A total lack of the elaborate "sport clothes" worn at American country functions also caused me acute embarrassment.

Soon G. had to leave for Ithaca. His first letter to me contained a new story.

"I hear that Hitler consulted an astrologer about the date of his death. 'It will be a Jewish holiday.' 'Which holiday?' 'I cannot say which—but if it is not a Jewish holiday now, it will be after!' "

The following weekend Archie Macdonell, author of *England, Their England*, also visited Fairfield; Macmillan had invited him to write a companion book on America, and he was about to tour the country. Archie had survived four years in the trenches of the First World War, but was destined to die at forty-five of a heart-attack amid the air-raids of the Second. Now a muscular, red-faced giant of thirty-nine, he appeared capable of living till ninety.

Walking with him through orange and scarlet Connecticut woods, where Black Swallowtail butterflies larger than humming-birds hovered above purple clumps of wild aster, I became aware of a reminiscent feeling which puzzled me. I had never been in New England during the autumn, yet for years that sense of familiarity

113

caused the colours and contours of Connecticut in late September to outlast subsequent mental pictures harvested from successive American tours.

Only recently I discovered its origin in Longfellow's *New England Tragedies*, read and re-read during my childhood when Longfellow and Matthew Arnold were the only poets in the parental library. The play *John Endicott*, based on the Quaker persecutions of 1665, first taught me the cost of self-dedication to an impersonal ideal, and up to my schooldays I could repeat from memory the lines spoken by the young Quaker, Edith Christison, which had created for me an imagined New England not so different from the reality.

> "How beautiful are these autumnal woods!
> The wilderness doth blossom like the rose
> And change into a garden of the Lord!
> How silent everywhere! Alone and lost
> Here in the forest there comes over me
> An inward awfulness. . . .
>
>   O woods, that wear
> Your golden crown of martyrdom, blood-stained,
> From you I learn a lesson of submission,
> And am obedient even unto death
> If so God wills it. . . ."

(21)

After the woods with their seventeenth-century silence came the uproar of modern America, and the adventurous journeys which added to the strange sense of being a fictitious individual in a world totally unreal.

The longer the tour continued, the faster my own personality receded. Within a few hours I ceased to identify myself with the "little bride" who had first set foot on these New World shores, and much less with the harassed young mother pursued by sick relatives, children's diseases, budgets that never quite balanced, and household "chores" which never came to an end. I was not that person at all, but an actress paid by celebrity-conscious America to play the part of a lionised best-seller.

Testament of Youth itself shared in this metamorphosis. As the incredible genesis of lectures, cocktail parties, fan-letters, and all the colourful ballyhoo of publicity, it acquired an independent life which had nothing to do with the story of love and sorrow which I had poured out with such mingled relief and anguish. For nearly two decades it was to maintain this impersonal character; except to sign innumerable title-pages I hardly looked at it again after correcting the proofs, and never read it as an ordinary reader until I began, eighteen years afterwards, to write this successor.

Long before that first tour ended, my mind had become a confused kaleidoscope of endless clapping, cheering crowds; of lectures in halls holding audiences of two thousand; of almost non-stop receptions; of successive nights with only two or three hours of sleep; and of perpetual questions which varied from the idiotic-erotic to inquiries making heavy demands on my knowledge of international history.

There is, I suppose, no experience quite comparable to that of "being a success" in the United States. It is a very deceptive experience, for only a miracle can keep a stranger in the benignant limelight for long, and the moment, for whatever reason, the illumination fades, the adulation ceases like a hose-pipe abruptly turned off. But while it lasts it is so flattering that its object tends to forget that these dynamic enthusiasms are always transitory, and in America, perhaps, more than anywhere else.

With one State, Minnesota, I felt that I had made a permanent liaison; and so I had, but not for the reason I supposed. From New York I had written my mother that my schedule included three days in Minneapolis, "where a woman who sounds very nice has asked me to stay with her, a very friendly doctor's wife who has written me so warmly about my book that I feel as though I knew her."

Breaking my manager's rule of "hotels only" I accepted this invitation, though no premonition showed me Ruth Gage Colby as the future guardian of John and Shirley, and with them of our own domestic happiness.

The Minnesota lectures had been preceded by a period of uncomfortable travel through small townships in the Middle West. But I could now tolerate the night-journeys which had once been a major affliction, for air-cooled trains had replaced the steam-heated mobile ovens of 1925. More exhausting were the long periods without food while I spoke, answered questions, shook hands, autographed books, and went for lengthy drives with well-intentioned hostesses.

No other trial quite equalled the crescendo of correspondence which usually awaited me late at night in strange hotels after long journeys, and had to be digested before I could sleep with a mind at rest. Apart from periodic reassurance from my co-operative pub-

·lishers, the only letters I welcomed were those bringing news from home.

When my mother actually reported a brief improvement in my father's health, a heavy load seemed to roll from my back. Occasional doubts whether I should really be able to fulfil my rigorous schedule gave place to the conviction that it was better to work beyond one's strength than to be the victim of inactivity, neurosis and fear.

Before I left home I had arranged with Winifred to send me weekly cables about John and Shirley. These messages, duly forwarded by the Macmillan Company, doubtless provided some entertainment for the secretary who sent them on. One, solemnly relayed to Grand Rapids, Michigan, conveyed a touching item of domestic information.

"Cable received this morning reads quote all very well no special news John pulled out his own first tooth without any fuss unquote".

Occasional contacts with G. also brought sympathy and comfort. We spent the Thanksgiving holiday in Washington and walked up and down before the Lincoln Memorial in warm rain, oddly discussing which types of behaviour really constituted infidelity. A fortnight earlier we had met on Armistice Day in New York; my notes of the commemoration service which we attended at St. Thomas's Church in Fifth Avenue contain, in G.'s handwriting, a prayer which might appropriately be used in contemporary periods of alarm and suspicion.

"Almighty God, who has given us this good land for our heritage: We humbly beseech Thee that we may always prove ourselves a people mindful of Thy favor and glad to do Thy will. Bless our land with honorable industry, sound learning, and pure manners. Save us from violence, discord and confusion, from pride and arrogancy, and from every evil way. Defend our liberties, and fashion into one united people the multitudes brought hither out of many kindreds and tongues."

At a Sunday address to a large congregation in Buffalo just before I left America, I had again the support of G.'s presence; he had driven one hundred and fifty miles from Ithaca with a Russian colleague, Vladimir Terentieff, the son of a White Army Colonel, who had fled to America, dug graves, made matches, and was now the tennis coach at Cornell. They saw me off by train to New York, and G. sent me a farewell letter to the *Majestic*, which sailed in mid-December.

"Of course we are more attached than most married couples. We genuinely enjoy each other's company; we never quarrel; we never 'scat'. I have reached an age when what matters to me is perspective. And in that perspective you stand, after the political interests that are the only religion I have left, in the foreground. So I hope you are content with me."

Content and blessed indeed, I thought, preparing to return to family life from forty-one lectures, two broadcasts, and an incalculable quantity of flowers, flattery, invitations and applause. The flowers surrounded me now as I sat up till 3 a.m. reading letters and telegrams; then I went to bed and, in a very rough sea, slept undisturbed for forty-eight hours.

Today those weeks appear as a brilliant interlude which divided the years of literary and domestic drudgery from the period, now almost upon me, when destiny struck again.

CHAPTER FOUR

"PULVIS ET UMBRA SUMUS"

" 'Dust unto dust.'
Yet, living mind, I have remembered you
All through the chequered years.
Surviving love
Pitifully softens the stark outlines of sorrow,
And the face of hope reappears.

"Within the shadows
Strong and weak alike find the quiet of mortality,
Safe from the challenging hour.
Judge not the dead,
For in the perpetual day of God's omnipotence
Only compassion has power."

V.B., 1954.

(1)

IN AUGUST E. M. Delafield had warned me that British professional standards would seem casual after America's exacting commercialism, but this was not the form of readjustment that I found most difficult when I came home.

Both children spent Christmas in bed with mumps, while the troubles of my parents, now living in an hotel, were as usual acute.

"I seem," I told G., "to have been drowned in a warm bath of domesticity ever since I arrived home."

He was now as far from these stubborn problems as geography could take him, and had spent New Year's Day in California. The new San Francisco bridge would be opened, he wrote, in 1936. Reporting two hours' conversation with Herbert Hoover at Palo Alto, he enclosed a keepsake for me—"a carnation dipped in the Pacific".

By this time I had begun the new book which has invariably provided the best solace for domestic disturbance. Both my publishers hoped to receive this long novel by April 1936, but I made my plans to meet their wishes with the usual misgivings. These, as always, were fully justified. I had hardly become absorbed in the story when my mother asked me to help her search for a new home. In an historic square off the Kensington High Street she found a small period house with a paved garden, and a serene atmosphere quite unsuited to the tragedies for which it was to provide a background. Eventually she was bombed out of it, but now it absorbed all her time and thoughts.

In the midst of my parents' move came the news of fresh perturbations from Europe. On January 13th the Saar Valley had held its 1935 plebiscite under the League of Nations, and vociferously elected to return to Germany. Soon afterwards a new decree by Hitler had reintroduced conscription. While the British Cabinet sent protest notes to the Führer, meetings organised by the League of Nations Union sprang up throughout the country.

From Hornsea, where she was now working on *South Riding*, Winifred reported an impressive demonstration in Hull—"the place packed in every corridor with people who stood motionless through two-hour speeches, and then drafted resolutions to be sent to Simon. . . . The most living L.N.U. meeting I was ever at."

But by now the League had become an instrument of French policy; however strongly the people might favour constructive peace-making, French politicians were timid and British politicians supine. Between them they allowed the best practical instrument hitherto created for maintaining peace to become rusty and finally useless.

(2)

G. returned from the United States in February. Before the end of March he had departed to Russia in search of another revolution.

I saw him off from Liverpool Street with a sense of desolation, for I could not count on his letters reaching me from Soviet territory. I felt that he was virtually disappearing for two months, and seemed to watch him vanish into eternity.

He himself shared none of these misgivings, for he journeyed to Moscow in exhilarating society. On that day Sir John Simon and Anthony Eden left London by the same train for Berlin, whence they subsequently reported "divergencies of view" between the British and German Governments. Thence Anthony Eden went on to Moscow and a cordial welcome from Stalin.

G. accompanied this second delegation, travelling "in the utmost luxury" by the Manchurian Express. On his tour, which took him to Kiev, Kharkhov, Sevastopol, Odessa and several smaller cities, he had arranged to travel "hard". This austerity he usually maintained, though he soon discovered that Russians of comparable status went by *Wagon-lit*.

In April, when he was due to leave Moscow for Rostov, no letters from me had reached him. Just then I chanced to meet Cicely Hamilton, an intrepid European traveller, who told me that during six weeks in Russia she had received only one postcard. The rest of her correspondence filtered back to England long after her return.

On the strength of this information I wrote to the Soviet Ambassador, Mr. Ivan Maisky, whom I had met at political gatherings. G. subsequently scolded me for this drastic expedient; the Ambassador's job, he said, was to revive the Triple Entente, and not to look after the private correspondence of travellers. Mr. Maisky nevertheless replied in a courteous note, and from that moment our letters went through.

G.'s communications had begun with a picture postcard showing the red roofs and spires of the Kremlin. There he attended the full-dress reception at which Litvinoff, the Commissar for Foreign Affairs, received Eden and the British delegates. Bidding Eden farewell, Litvinoff had said: "We wish you every success. Our interests are your interests now."

Behind that scene G. had already perceived three Russias. First came the Russia of diplomacy, in which distinguished guests consumed caviar and vodka, and drank coffee from cups decorated with the monogram of Nicholas II. The chief concern of this Russia was collective security—by which it meant, not peace preserved through an international police force, but regionalism of the Austen Chamberlain type.

The second Russia crept disregarded beneath the lighted windows of the first. Its ragged unskilled workers, moving silently along rutted by-roads, belonged to the ancient Muscovite world which traced its descent from the Tartars. Their inarticulate ranks provided "the faithful" who thronged the still open churches.

Beside these historic groups had grown up the third, modern, Russia, whose industrial shock-troops crowded the cinemas and workers' clubs. Hunger and misery were unknown to these finely-developed men and women, skilled in gymnastics and amateur theatricals.

No common characteristic united these different Russias, yet they composed one polity and were all dominated by the Kremlin. G. described this symbolic building, as he had first seen it, at night.

"In front is the blood-red marble tomb of Lenin, before whose doors the immense guards keep watch with bayonets. Behind are the white-washed walls, more white under the glare of the floodlights, which arise as though behind them lay some town of central China. At either end, toupee-like, are the corner-towers, vaguely red in the diffused light, utterly non-European despite their Italian builder."

Subsequent letters contained fewer details than his letters from Germany; information could still be conveyed more safely from Hitler's Reich than from Stalin's Russia. On the way to Rostov-on-Don he was reduced to describing the countryside and reporting the defects of the trains—"hot water as soap—you bump and a squirt comes; no plugs to basins; no toilet paper; otherwise just splendid."

From Yalta came a postcard of the Livadia Palace, a large white building flanked with cypresses. Vignettes followed of the Crimea— "a land of sharp limestone edges, like broken-off-biscuit"—and of Tartar villages with minarets which emphasised their eastward distance from Constantinople. Apart from my letters and occasional encounters with A. J. Cummings of the *News Chronicle*, he felt completely cut off from the western world and had seen no foreign newspapers on sale since his arrival.

(3)

Back in Moscow at the end of April, he dreamed that he heard church bells in Berlin, calling the people to last-minute prayers for averting war. He awoke with a certainty that war was coming, and wrote me that he did not know whether to be glad or sorry that this experience of Russia had not changed but merely strengthened his former opinions.

"I believe in a political system of democratic control and personal liberty, and believe so much more emphatically. Every belief of mine has been sharpened up."

A long break now occurred, and I received no more letters from Russia itself. On May 2nd the French Government signed a Franco-Soviet pact, and Pierre Laval, the Foreign Minister, arrived shortly afterwards in Moscow. During this period the strict security regulations temporarily relaxed through Ambassador Maisky's intervention had evidently been reinforced.

From Moscow G. took the decisive step of resigning his Cornell professorship. The attraction luring him back to England was not merely that of a wife and family; "semi-detachment", with all its problems, had been made to work and had become part of a settled routine. Active politics, that will o' the wisp which began to dance in the 1931 Election, now drew him from his University when I could without professional disadvantage have settled in America with the children.

"I came here to study politics and I will leave to do the same thing," he had written me from Ithaca four years earlier. If, he now added, one was going to take politics seriously, one must spend one's time on the spot. Cornell had been a grand experience, but though it had given him such early promotion and so many distinguished and agreeable colleagues, he believed that his utility there was over. So, for some years, he left the academic world for writing and practical politics.

In mid-May I received a new intimation of his existence, now freed from police-state supervision.

"At sea, off the Dardanelles and Troy," he had written on May 12th. "Yesterday Constantinople, city glorious—the most wonderful, the richest city I have ever in my life been in. Not a museum with a village attached, like old Rome, but a metropolis with infinite varieties of life. On Galata Bridge, watching the crowds pass, all nationalities, orthodox priests, Catholic priests, prostitutes, labourers, merchants . . . And at last quit of the sullen Muscovite tyranny with its everlasting brag of shoddy achievement. It has done something, but it believes it has done everything and watches with spy eyes to see who will contradict it. Police. Police. Police. Tanks. Tanks. Tanks. . . . Old barbarism in a new May Day finery."

Three days later—"running up by Corcyra, lovely sea, lovely land, lovely weather"—he followed this uncharacteristic outburst by another letter enclosing a poppy gathered beside the Parthenon.

"Came down by air to Athens the day before yesterday past

Olympus and Ossa. On the plane I saw in the paper of the fellow ahead of me, 'Le Maréchal Pilzudski est mort hier.' "

Had the purple poppy been red when he picked it? I wondered, envying his journey to Constantinople and Athens more than his knowledge of a dozen Russian cities. But perhaps I too would see those legendary lands when I had written my next book, and completed my next American tour, and the children had grown a little older. My reason knew that the clouds rising from Berlin and Rome could blot out the sky, but my intuition still did not warn me how far impending cataclysm would limit freedom of travel.

Late in May I met G. at Dover, where he came ashore wearing a black Russian beret which transformed him into the dignified semblance of a "comrade". We travelled to London together, and dined at the Ivy.

(4)

On May 6th, while G. was still in Russia, England had celebrated the Silver Jubilee of George V. In preparation for this festival, London became a panorama of jubilant decorations. Even the King's Road, Chelsea, which commemorates the amorous journeys of a less exemplary monarch, broke into a carnival of red, white and blue.

As the day approached, the newspapers forgot Nazi militarism and the nefarious designs of Mussolini upon Abyssinia. Instead they produced long essays, summarising twenty-five years of British progress, which featured wireless telegraphy, the suffragettes, Kipling's stories, the Veto Bill, and the Great War which had changed everybody's lives.

"A throne is never an easy inheritance," began an article by Horace Thoroughgood entitled *The King Has Seen Us Through a Quarter Century of Crises.* "When, just before midnight on May 5th, 1910, Edward VII died, he left to his son one of the ugliest political situations in English history."

Had the writer been a prophet, he might have added that within a year George V would have bequeathed an even uglier political situation, not merely to one son, but to two.

The day before the Jubilee, the Labour Party held their annual May Day rally in Hyde Park. As I looked at the comfortable domestic scene, I thought how deep was its probable contrast with the demonstration which G. was watching in Moscow. The police, minus their helmets, sat on the ground in their own compound, munching buns while one or two supervised the horses. They showed no readiness to go if called, and no expectation of being needed.

The Park contained the usual British crowd whose psychology is the despair of continental countries; tolerant, humorous, long-suffering; nobody out at elbows, yet nobody really well-dressed. Nothing could have been further from revolution than its air of patient respectability and its unrivalled faculty for turning everything into a picnic.

Perhaps, I thought, this crowd really does explain why we have had twenty-five years of the same king and queen when half the world's rulers have been flying for their lives. We are too agreeable and accommodating to do anything so drastic as overthrow a throne.

Like the rest of England, I had still to learn that the occupant of that throne was not necessarily so secure as I supposed.

Late that evening, listening with my mother to the broadcast service of preparation for the Jubilee, I hardly heard the Archbishop's eulogy of the Royal Family but thought with inevitable nostalgia of the years that I remembered . . .

When George V came to the throne Edward and I were children at school, not dreaming of what lay before us in France, in Malta, on the Asiago Plateau. Father was then a handsome man in his forties; now he's an invalid, lost and unhappy. And Mother, with whom I'm sitting here looking at the spring blossom in London's loveliest square, was a beautiful woman with chestnut hair and large dark eyes. She's still beautiful, and doesn't seem old though her hair is white . . .

In 1910 I took no interest in a future family; I did not picture John and Shirley, nor G. who was their father, nor Roland who might have been. Perhaps this Silver Jubilee will be their first vivid memory. Will they be alive twenty-five years hence—or will another Armageddon have swept us all away? If they're alive, what will *their* memories be? Shall I be with them still, and shall we have watched mankind draw nearer to civilisation or depart yet farther from it?

At home John and Shirley were not thinking about the future, but excitedly picturing the procession which they were to see from a window in Queen Victoria Street. Next day I described to G. the long morning which we had spent in the City.

"In a big ground floor window we were almost on the top of the Royal Family. The children have been acting Jubilee, soldiers, kings and queens ever since."

He would be amused, I wrote, to learn that after the King and Queen, the Prince of Wales and the York children, the persons who received the biggest cheers from our street were the Duke of Connaught and Ramsay MacDonald.

"He was in a carriage in Court dress," I added of Ramsay, "and looked rather sad and solitary, I thought, though a decorative figure which evidently pleased the crowd."

Shortly afterwards, I fulfilled John's long-standing ambition to visit Lot's Power Station, the great electrical plant at the unfashionable end of Chelsea. Coming back through the shabby streets which housed its workers, we saw chalked on a wall the prophetic words:

"FLAGS TODAY—GAS MASKS TOMORROW."

(5)

Throughout that spring I had worked steadily on my novel, *Honourable Estate*.

This book originated in some notes made before my marriage for a story entitled *Kindred and Affinity*, which had been inspired by my father's semi-apocryphal tales of his Staffordshire family. By 1925 the characters were already coming to life; the fictitious Alleyndenes bore a likeness to my forebears which they were eventually to retain.

Even earlier, another theme had attracted me still more. From G.'s conversation I had formed a clear picture of his mother, Edith Kate Orton, a turbulent, thwarted, politically-conscious woman who had died prematurely in 1917. When I met his father I understood why the explosive little clergyman, with his conventional judgments, had been unable to hold the gifted, rebellious girl sixteen years his junior who had joined the suffrage movement in spite of his disapproval. Inevitably, their marriage had foundered, and G. had endured the unhappy youth of an only child perpetually the target of conflicting parental claims.

Within a few months of our first meeting, I had made his mother the heroine of a projected novel called *The Springing Thorn*. This title owed its inspiration to the words of Jesus quoted by St. Matthew: "Do men gather grapes of thorns, or figs of thistles?"

During the first two years of our marriage, my interest in Edith Kate deepened as our own problems increased. In some ways, I thought, I was fulfilling in another generation my dead mother-in-law's aspirations for women. Later, when Shirley was two months old, the idea that the life of G.'s mother might justify itself in a third generation came to me through a short symbolic dream.

For G., who was then in Scandinavia, I put it down while I remembered it.

"I dreamt about your mother last night. She came to see John and Shirley. She had curious light blue eyes, but had a very old and extremely lined face (actually, I suppose, she would as yet be barely sixty). She said nothing, but just sat with Shirley on her lap."

From that time the idea of Shirley as her grandmother's future standard-bearer laid an increasing hold on me. By the age of three, she resembled Edith Kate's early portraits as closely as a human being can resemble a photograph. Might she not also grow up to resemble her in intellect and aspirations, and hence bring her as near resurrection as a frustrated person can be brought by one who is fulfilled?

At this stage I was wholly occupied by *Testament of Youth*, and put *The Springing Thorn* away, with my mother-in-law, into a mental pigeon-hole. But after my autobiography was accepted I began, as I have always done, to defend myself against the psychological consequences of publication by planning a new book.

Suddenly I captured the idea that I wanted. Why not marry *Kindred and Affinity* to *The Springing Thorn*, make the book a story of two contrasting provincial families calamitously thrown together by chance, and then, in the next generation, join the son of one household with the daughter of the other?

Thus the scheme for *Honourable Estate* was born. The period covered would be 1894 to 1930, and its revolutionary changes could be shown incidentally through their effect upon three marriages in two generations.

Before *Testament of Youth* appeared, this novel was in shape. To the notes made at Hardelot, my lecture tour added the idea of a young American soldier as a major character. Some valuable help came from my publisher, who as a former officer had been through the Argonne campaign. Before I left New York, I had collected some useful war stories and several military maps.

For weeks after my return I submerged myself in the personality of Edith Kate, whom I was to transform into Janet Harding. G. lent me her early letters and her diary, and I told him that I found these documents both absorbing and pathetic.

"What a tragedy of reason and intelligence versus the conventional interpretation of duty! She ought to have been born twenty years later and been a political organiser or M.P. It's so sad to read in her rather stiff, formal little letters her expression of the certainty that her marriage with your father would lead to her happiness."

Year by year I followed the conflict between G.'s parents with a growing sadness that so much fighting should have brought only failure and a premature end.

The later diaries were full of passion and introspection. They ended a fortnight before her death with the topical entry "Jerusalem captured." What a strange symbolism, I thought—one which I must certainly use in my book.

By May I reported to G. that I was now "well away with the story. It is going to be very large in scope, starting with obscure people leading an obscure life, and slowly opening out till it embraces half the world."

(6)

When G. returned from Russia we paid a short visit to North Staffordshire, so that I could refresh my memory with local details. For some time I had promised to show him the ancestral dwellings of my own family, of which the most fantastic was known as Ash Hall. This ornate mansion appeared in my book as Dene Hall, the home of the Alleyndenes.

In the year of Queen Victoria's accession my great-grandfather, a prosperous and eccentric cobalt manufacturer, had built this Hatter's Castle on steep rising ground near the main road from Hanley to Leek. By 1927 it had achieved reincarnation as a golf hotel. To G. I had then written:"Father's mother's people have just sold Ash Hall, and are joining Chesterton's 'last sad squires' who 'ride slowly towards the sea'. And the sooner they ride in, the better for all of us, say I."

Now we spent a few days at the "golf hotel", and thence walked to Bucknall churchyard to find the much-embellished but dilapidated vault of my ancestors inside iron railings. Nobody appeared to mourn them any longer, for the pompous sarcophagus was green with moss.

Nor, it seemed, had the modern world much use for their homes or their tradition. On a hill-top between Keele and Newcastle-under-Lyme we looked for another mansion, smaller than Ash Hall but still substantial, known as The Cloughs. In this dwelling my father, as the eldest of eleven, had spent his boyhood. He had proved a difficult child, unmanageable by his prematurely widowed mother, and his grandparents had brought him up.

One of my earliest memories centred round a Victorian daguerreotype of The Cloughs which hung on my father's dressing-room wall; it showed a three-storied house of sulphur-coloured brick flanked by a Spanish fir. At last we discovered the gate and went in, expecting to find an old-fashioned but still attractive home. Instead we saw a ruin awaiting demolition.

The window panes were smashed and the floors covered with broken glass; the ceilings had fallen in, and bats haunted the upper rooms open to the sky. Piled-up bricks surrounded the remnants of the stables; brambles and thistles choked the roots of stately old trees rising from rough grass which had once been a lawn. G. put a stone in his pocket as a souvenir and we walked down the weed-covered drive in silence, realising that we ourselves were part of the new forces which had written "Finis" to the domination of such families as mine.

We returned home by way of Buxton, which I had quit in revolt against the provincial young-ladyhood that the First War abolished for ever. I wanted to put it into my book as "Sterndale Spa", the Derbyshire health resort which provided the Reverend Thomas Rutherston with his first modest living.

My parents told me that it had altered little since the eighteen-nineties, in which the beginning of my story placed it. With its Pavilion Gardens and Pump Room, and the large cricket field against a background of austere hills, it seemed, unlike Staffordshire, to be the most unchanged place that I had ever revisited.

Only in one detail did I find it different. On the garden slopes above the Pump Room stood a cenotaph, adorned with bronze plaques and a Carinthian angel holding a laurel wreath. So far no cynic had added a swastika to the laurels.

On the bronze plaques I found the names of several boys with whom, in my 'teens, I had danced and played tennis. Amongst them was Edward's, though the local councillors had forgotten to record his Military Cross. Beneath the long list of vanished names and unfulfilled aspirations ran the orthodox inscription:

"Pro Patria. 1914-1919."

We returned in time to keep Shirley's fifth birthday. During her tea-party my father telephoned to ask for news of our journey, and I tentatively suggested that he should come over to see her and hear our impressions. To our surprise he agreed; although he had not felt well enough to visit Chelsea for months, he and my mother arrived within half-an-hour.

No one would ever write "Pro Patria" under my father's name, though the debonair parent of my youth had died with Edward. But to-day he seemed better, and delighted by the children; and when G. offered him the stone retrieved from The Cloughs, he accepted it and took it away.

When we made our usual Sunday expedition to Kensington the

following afternoon, he produced the familiar picture of his old home and we studied its now disappearing landmarks. Its demolition did not appear to distress him, though he insisted that he was too ill to accompany my mother and the children into the Square garden.

I stayed with him indoors, peacefully mending stockings and talking about France, where three days later I was taking John and Shirley for their first continental holiday. When we left that evening, he seemed more like his former self than he had been for years.

(7)

Feeling less than the usual anxiety for my parents, I crossed the Channel with the children, their German governess, and Winifred's adopted sister Edith de Coundouroff. G. was to follow us two days hence, and Winifred still later.

Two years previously I had explored from Hardelot the hay-scented country round Wimereux, and found a pleasant hotel with a large paved garden divided by a shallow ornamental pool. In the sunlit space between flowering trees, its fringe of nasturtiums looked at their scarlet faces mirrored in the water. Here, I decided, I could write *Honourable Estate* in the tranquil beauty which doubles the progress of any book.

For two days I wrote happily, though freedom from minor disturbances was not complete. On our second night a large white moth entered my bedroom window, and flapping round with tedious stubbornness eluded capture. At last I drove it away but lay shivering all night, unable to sleep for restlessness and a persistent feeling of cold. I assumed I had caught a chill, but after a morning's work in the sunshine felt as well as usual.

The next evening I had arranged to meet G. at Boulogne. He was spending ten days with us—all he could spare, for he now had the political opportunity he had so long desired.

Five weeks earlier he had been selected by the local Labour Party to fight the next election at Sunderland, a "marginal" but promising two-Member constituency represented by two Conservatives since 1931. He therefore planned to spend most of August in getting to know his constituents. In the event he did not come to France even for the promised ten days; instead it was I who travelled back to England.

At noon on the day he was due to arrive we were sitting at luncheon when, roused by an exclamation from John, I looked through the glass doors of the restaurant and saw Winifred in the entrance hall. This sudden arrival could only mean disaster, since she was not due for another week. I pushed back my chair and ran to her, hardly able to put into coherent language the fear for G. which suddenly darkened the sunlit garden. But her first words dispelled that major anxiety.

"No—it isn't G. It's your father. He disappeared two nights ago and still hasn't been found."

She explained that my mother, going into his room to call him, had found his bed empty, and remembered hearing a noise in the night which she thought came from the Square. Now she recognised it as the sound of the iron bolt which fastened the front door dropping against the wooden panel.

"He might have lost his memory," I said. "He's had so many delusions."

"I know. At first we all hoped he'd be found wandering about. That's why I didn't come yesterday; we didn't want to fetch you back unnecessarily. But the police have been looking for him now for a day and a half, and if it was only loss of memory they think they'd have found him."

She hadn't wanted to telegraph the stark news, she said. So she had come over to bring me home, while G. looked after my mother and dealt with the police.

From that moment I felt certain that my father was not only dead but drowned; the extraordinary feeling of cold which had kept me awake on the night of his disappearance could mean nothing else. Even the large flapping moth which would not be banished now appeared as an inarticulate messenger of death.

(8)

We crossed the Channel by the evening boat, and reached London at midnight, delayed by Bank Holiday crowds. I soon realised that Winifred should never have come; all afternoon, while I repacked my bags and put together my dishevelled manuscript, she lay on my bed wrestling with sickness, and recovered only just in time for the journey. Perturbed for her, and anxious about the children left behind in a country to which they were not yet acclimatised, I almost forgot my father until G. met us at Victoria and took me to Kensington.

Then indeed, alone and sleepless while G. and my mother retired exhausted to bed, I found myself submerged in a grief which surprised me by its depth, though it was less the grief of a daughter for a father than the sorrow of a mother for an attractive but spoiled and unstable child who has at last done something irreparably disastrous. This picture of my father, little changed by subsequent memories, remained uppermost in my mind during the next twelve months, in which I drew his portrait—a loving though realistic memorial—as Stephen Alleyndene in *Honourable Estate*.

For two more days we waited, pursuing inquiries and learning nothing. Then, on Bank Holiday, the telephone rang and I answered it. The message came from the police; a body answering my father's description had been found in the Thames at Twickenham.

Days followed of a nightmare quality so grotesque that it was difficult to grasp as part of our lives. Police officers, undertakers and lawyers came and went. A short funeral service at Richmond, where for some reason known only to himself my father had wished to be buried, followed the brief inconclusive inquest at which a doctor's letter made inevitable the verdict then passed on victims of melancholia: "Suicide whilst temporarily of unsound mind."

That inquest had been incongruously held in the billiard-room of a white-painted inn overlooking a lovely reach of the river at Isleworth. Oars for the boats moored to the bank littered the floor; beneath the windows the dark-green water reflected the willows growing at its edge. Above woods enclosing lush meadows fragrant with summer flowers, the spire of Richmond Church pierced the placid sky.

Only G. gave evidence, but I asked if anyone knew how my father —old, invalid, mentally disturbed and long dependent on others— had reached the river so far from home in the early hours. No one could tell me, though we knew that he had left the house in his nightclothes without overcoat or hat, taking only thirty shillings. The driver who picked him up could hardly have mistaken his intention, but evidently found it more convenient to pocket his money than try to save him.

Still less could anyone explain what incident had made the cruelty of living seem finally unendurable, for he left no message. It is one of the unanswered questions which have haunted my life.

Perhaps, in Eternity's unseen pattern, some illumination might lie which I should never know. In the hope of divine understanding, we inscribed on the sundial which later marked his grave the psalmist's prayer: "Comfort us again now after the time that thou hast plagued us, and for the years wherein we have suffered adversity." And round the face of the sun-clock, not for him but for ourselves, we added the sterner behest: "So teach us to number our days, that we may apply our hearts unto wisdom."

Soon afterwards, as the beginning of wisdom, I joined the Voluntary Euthanasia Legalisation Society. Surely, I thought, when an individual's life has run its course, or owing to mortal illness he knows that he can make no further contribution, a civilised community should provide, with sufficient safeguards, the means of exit? He should not be compelled to face the terror of self-destruction, or to inflict tragedy and humiliation upon those whom he loves.

(9)

Back in Kensington, a new anxiety confronted me.

Throughout the inquest and funeral, G. had kept to himself the painful symptoms of an oncoming malady; now they could no longer be concealed. Shortly after the invading lawyers had departed, he retired to bed with a high temperature. A doctor diagnosed an obscure form of glandular poisoning, with the risk of total septicaemia.

I telegraphed for the young married couple who now looked after us to return from their holiday and open our house, for my mother could not be asked to accept the strain of another invalid. I persuaded an aunt to offer her temporary refuge, helped her to close her house, and took G. back to Chelsea.

Already Amy and Charles Burnett were waiting for us with beds made, hot-water-bottles filled, meals prepared. The quiet of our own home brought a sense of freedom beyond belief. For three weeks, unaided by trained nurses for whose alien presence none of us felt disposed, we fought the threatening septicaemia. Winifred, meanwhile, characteristically returned to France to supervise the children and take what she described as a much-needed holiday.

More exacting even than G.'s treatment, and more inconvenient than the importunate literary agent who at this moment demanded an article for the *Daily Mirror* entitled "My Mother and What She Has Taught Me", were the constant visits to Kensington which I had to undertake. Almost daily my mother telephoned, asking me to make sure that a light was put out, a tap turned off, the windows properly fastened. The first time I entered the dark, shuttered house, I heard my father's voice summoning me from his dressing-room.

"Is that you, Jack?"

That this illusion should disturb me seemed irrational; at such a time my father would never have wished to alarm or distress me. But I knew that my life had always been a pitched battle between ancestral tendencies and personal values, and now I had learned the final consequence of domination by nervous fears. Beyond them, if they once established control, lay death—a self-imposed death because life to the seeker was even more terrible.

From Winifred I sought reassurance—the conviction that fear could be overcome; that I had not contributed to my father's death by negligence; that I need feel no horror of the beautiful river which I had always loved. And, as usual, she sent that reassurance.

She herself, she wrote, had thought that she heard her father speaking in his bedroom when she knew that he was dead. And she felt certain that I had been right to walk beside the Thames after returning to Chelsea, "for to get a horror of any place or action is to curtail freedom and utility". A day later she added: "Don't blame yourself for your father's death. Love never yet cured melancholia any more than it cured any other disease. Nothing more than you did could have helped him."

In the third week of August, I was able at last to report a change for the better in G. But she replied offering to keep John and Shirley in Wimereux for another week, where they would disturb him less. She herself, she said, had completely recovered her own health, and felt "quite different from the worm who went to France".

And she did indeed look bronzed and fit when I met her and the children at Victoria, one month and one day before her death in a London nursing-home on September 29th.

(10)

On a mild morning of mid-October, I sat alone beside a shallow creek at Fowey in Cornwall, and tried to grasp intelligently the events of the two previous months. Though mentally numb I was not conscious of physical fatigue except when I tried to write my book, only to find that five hundred words used up a whole day.

When G., after three weeks of serious illness, began drafting memoranda for Sunderland, the doctor said firmly that he must take a complete holiday before starting work again. But this, owing to the sudden onset of Winifred's final illness, had been reduced to one distraught weekend at Brighton. A month later, after her funeral in Yorkshire, he was still pale and easily tired. As autumn had now come, the doctor advised a short Mediterranean cruise.

I was anxious myself to get away from London with its too raw memories, and my mother, her days now empty, was glad to take the children. G. and I therefore arranged a fortnight's expedition to Egypt and Palestine in a ship called *Excalibur*, but six hours before we were due to leave, we had to cancel the trip. We were having breakfast when a telephone call came through from the Labour

Party Office. A familiar voice summoned G.; it was Ellen Wilkinson. "You mustn't leave the country on any account," she told him. "There's going to be a General Election in November."

A few minutes later our friend F. W. Pethick-Lawrence confirmed the news. Why, I reflected, must there always be a General Election when one or the other of us wanted to write, or rest, or even recover quietly from sorrow?

Next day we travelled glumly to Fowey, chosen because Devon and Cornwall were G.'s favourite counties. It would also, we believed, be distant enough to guarantee privacy while still accessible to the news of political developments. These occurred so fast that we were able to stay only for a week, but by the end of it we no longer minded.

The soft misty atmosphere ought to have been restful, and our bedroom window, looking over the small harbour, framed an evening picture of dark smooth water spangled with lights. But the lovelier appeared the autumn-scented gardens and grey village churches with their soaring towers, the more overwhelming became the sense of loss—less ours than Winifred's, for she had loved life so keenly and found the world so beautiful.

For the time being the swift sequence of calamities had destroyed our capacity for appreciation, and our frustrated attempts to arrange suitable convalescence for G., a minor tragedy compared with the others, had yet been exasperating enough to seem the last straw. G.'s illness had left him with a touchiness quite unlike his normal conciliatory temper, and we squabbled wearily as people will who have reached the end of their endurance.

When he suggested that he should leave Fowey a day before me in order to compare the hunger-stricken area of the South Wales coalfields with the homes of the Durham miners, I welcomed our temporary separation with mingled relief and shame that the mutual help and comfort which we usually gave each other should have broken down so completely.

After he had gone I walked to a quiet creek half a mile from the hotel, and there, released from argument and reproach, remorsefully sought peace in the healing silence. I had now begun to read the uncorrected typescript of *South Riding*, which Winifred had received just before going to the nursing home, and at last was able to devote my thoughts to her.

How sadly conscious I felt that I had always accepted from her so much more than I gave, and now could give no more! None of her books published in her lifetime had sold remarkably, so she helped mine to sell magnificently. The only man whom she really loved had failed her, so she identified herself with my married happiness. Her burdens were great and intolerable, so she shouldered mine which were often trivial. When she learned that she must never have children, she shared in the care of ours.

Sitting beside the calm water, I recalled the sculptured benevolence of her face in the mortuary chapel. In February 1926 she had written from South Africa to my mother of "Uncle Bill": "I am so glad that you saw his beauty after death. I do not know what the meaning of that change may be, but it often seems as though the real soul shone through the body . . . and one looked, not 'through a glass darkly', but 'face to face'."

I could not pretend that this was how Winifred in death had appeared to me. Her innate nobility had given her face a sweetness which persisted, though it had now the colour and fixity of a beautiful waxwork; she looked serene with the serenity of a statue, but the life and the light of her had gone clean away. That eagerness, that lovely kindness, had departed, and its place knew it no more.

At the time of her death I had read only part of *South Riding*, which was to bring her back to me, and I found no reason to change the words which I had written in my notebook as she lay dying.

"There is no God and no hereafter; no angels guide our steps nor protect our paths. The only benevolent force in the Universe is man himself, a tiny indefatigable unit persistently fighting against the hostility of Nature and the malevolence of fate. And yet how much, throughout the centuries, he has accomplished. . . . So long as individual men and women continue the struggle, battered yet undefeated, hope remains and life, in a world of disaster, is still worth-while."

To a sympathetic friend who wrote that once the election was over she hoped I should be able to "escape" into my book, I replied that writing seldom represented an escape to me. It was a method of coming to terms with life, of reconciliation with the all-but-irreconcilable. But the attainment of this catharsis was always a slow process, working itself out through time and perspective. Some day I should write of Winifred, and perhaps even of my father; of neither could I write at once.

Yet that seemed to be exactly what several publishers hoped to persuade me to do. I had hardly reached Fowey when two or three for whom I had never written invited me to produce a short biography of her for publication as quickly as possible. But I had no mind for a topical study, even if I had then felt equal to writing it.

A superficial biography would put out of court the large future book which already I dimly perceived; a book which would show Winifred and her writings in relation to the contemporary scene.

Harder to resist than publishers were earnest appeals from one or two of Winifred's influential friends, who felt sure that if I did not write about her immediately she would be forgotten.

I regarded this judgment as a total underestimate of her real quality and its effect on those whom she met. As recently as 1953 Mr. Andrew Dakers, our former literary agent and later a publisher, confirmed this opinion, and told me of the extraordinary impact which she had made on him the first time he saw her.

"She was like a flame," he said. "Some kind of light inside her seemed to be burning her up." And, referring to his own psychic powers, he added that she appeared to him to be a "visitant" to this earth rather than part of it.

He sought for a word to describe the vivid ethereal personalities who belong only briefly to mortal life, and I reminded him of Maeterlinck's phrase, "*Les Prédestinés*".

The delay in writing *Testament of Friendship* was abundantly justified. A quick topical study would necessarily have omitted *South Riding*—from which, with the typescript in my possession, I perceived possibilities that others could not guess. Winifred's last novel eventually created admirers for her work not only in Britain but throughout the world. In 1940 a far bigger public awaited her biography than the small, specialised group which would have read it immediately after her death.

(11)

When deep sorrow smites human life and personal faith is insufficient for religious consolation, I know of only three ways to sublimate grief.

The first and best, for any creative person whose vitality has not been extinguished, is a new piece of work—a book, a painting, a concerto, the organisation of a business. Such compensation may also come through a new child who atones for the loss of its predecessor.

A second-best expedient lies in travel to scenes unconnected with the tragedy, bringing new contacts, new vistas, the transformation of a sorrowful design into fresh patterns of experience.

Yet another road to recovery may be found in a political or social campaign, if its demands are absorbing and it carries, in spiritual or material terms, the possibility of sufficient reward. Though such a crusade may be impermanent, by the time it is over its incidents have displaced catastrophe from the centre of recollection.

During the autumn of 1935 I had tried in vain to continue my novel, and our sorry attempts to travel had been doomed. But ahead of us lay a political campaign which appeared at least relevant to the darkening international background.

For the past three months, intimations of the Italian-Abyssinian conflict had kept breaking in upon our personal troubles. Back in June, when the Peace Ballot showed an unexpected national confidence in collective security, Mussolini had openly threatened the military domination of Abyssinia, and League of Nations supporters faced an ominous test.

Two days after Winifred's funeral, Mussolini attacked Abyssinia. At the Labour Party Conference, which opened on September 30th in Brighton, little else but the threat of war had been discussed. There, where the delegates endorsed the Government's foreign policy, G. had witnessed a Socialist convulsion. Lord Ponsonby, a convinced pacifist, gave up the Party leadership in the House of Lords, and George Lansbury, savagely accused by Ernest Bevin of "carting his conscience from conference to conference", similarly resigned the leadership of the Commons.

On October 24th, after the Dissolution of Parliament, I saw G. off at King's Cross by the night train for Sunderland. I now felt ashamed of the indifference to the election which I had expressed at Fowey; for this cause and all its implications, G. had sacrificed academic security. He was still physically unfit for a hard political campaign; the least I could do was to throw off the crippling paralysis of grief, and help him.

For a week I remained in London, finding speakers, organising Press publicity, and trying to place articles for G. in the much-bombarded Socialist Press. Early in November I travelled north myself. As soon as I reached Sunderland my mood, like G.'s, changed abruptly. Here was all the clatter and clamour of a developing political campaign; no one, least of all ourselves, had time for recriminations or nostalgic sorrow.

Unhappily the prospects of a local Labour victory were less hopeful than we had imagined. Sunderland was one of the few towns recently captured by Labour in municipal elections, and its Borough Council included six Socialists who had been returned unopposed. At the time of G.'s selection the previous June, there seemed a reasonable probability that he and his Socialist colleague, Leah Manning, would defeat the two Conservative sitting members.

Ten days before the campaign opened, one of those marginal manœuvres had occurred which cast dubious shadows over the rutted field of party politics. The Co-ordinating Committee of the National Government put strong pressure on the older of the two Tory candidates to stand down, and he reluctantly made way for a young "Simonite" Liberal who could be guaranteed to attract the Liberal votes given to Labour in 1929.

There was now no chance for Labour to win the seat unless some fortuitous event created a marked swing in public opinion. Had G. known in June that he would have to face two candidates from different pro-Government parties, he would not have accepted Sunderland's invitation to the Selection Conference. Now he was obliged to carry on the campaign against overwhelming odds.

(12)

This political jugglery was not the only handicap of which, on an unfamiliar scene, we had been ignorant. When G. reached his constituency, he found that one of his opponents owned the *Sunderland Echo*, which now began to publish articles amounting to a daily Election Address.

Other members of the Government parties sowed ingenious suspicions of ourselves among the Sunderland voters; implications that we were foreigners and anti-patriots circulated round the crude suggestion that G.'s English name (which I was subsequently to find in three centuries of Bedfordshire records) had a Polish-Jewish origin. Even our recent misfortunes were skilfully and ruthlessly exploited. One local newspaper castigated G. for spending so little time in the constituency while avoiding any mention of his recent illness, and implied that our intended cruise showed indifference to Sunderland's welfare.

We tried to ignore these malicious pin-pricks, for the constituency, a seaport hard hit by the depression, deserved a dignified and serious campaign.

The previous July, Arthur Greenwood had proposed a vote of censure on the Government, based upon the Report recently issued by the Commissioner for the Special Areas of England and Wales. Mr. Greenwood's speech emphasised the number of persons receiving poor relief, which had increased from under a million in 1931 to over a million and a half in 1934. The debate had been "talked out", but the Government had received a bad Press for its inadequate policy.

"The total of these ameliorative and restorative measures is very considerable . . .", ran a *Times* editorial, "but they are not in themselves fundamental remedies; they are palliatives."

At Newcastle-upon-Tyne, the nearest big town to Sunderland, catastrophic unemployment had been registered the previous March. In Sunderland itself, demoralised young men who had never worked loitered at street corners or clustered round public houses. During a teachers' meeting held by the Young Men's Christian Association, a gymnastic instructor told G. that most of their members were too under-nourished to profit by physical training.

The local Labour Councillors included no women, but the wife of one took me canvassing round filthy basement dwellings with holes in the floor and no heat or light. Another escorted me up the worn stairs of dilapidated tenements where we fell over tin buckets on the pitch-black landings and the unseen walls felt damp and slimy.

At successive meetings we struggled to interpret these facts, more real to Sunderland than the troubles of Abyssinia. Several well-known candidates were contesting adjacent constituencies; we exchanged platforms with Ellen Wilkinson at Jarrow, Chuter Ede at South Shields, and Emanuel Shinwell, who successfully opposed Ramsay MacDonald at Seaham Harbour. Hoping to spare G. some of the perpetual talking, I made thirty-three speeches in ten days and earned from our opponents the sarcastic designation of "the third Labour Candidate".

But it was all quite useless. A final canvass showed that the more depressed the district, the more certain were its inhabitants to vote for the lethargic administration which had failed to cure their mortal sickness. As we listened after the poll closed to the broadcast results declared that night, we knew that our own constituency would follow the lead of the great northern towns which still supported the National Government.

A letter to New York described the end of our campaign:

"G. was defeated after one of the most exhausting fights that I ever remember, and we have lost a large sum of money in return for nothing but some rather bitter political experience.

"The result is our third major catastrophe this year, and it is difficult not to feel discouraged. No doubt you yourself endorse the verdict of this country in returning the National Government, yet I cannot believe that you or any other thinking American really admires the lethargy and vacillation of their foreign policy during the past four years. Now that they are returned, I personally see war in Europe within five years unless some unforeseen change occurs.

"I am thankful to have my novel to turn back to. I only hope that this at least will bring us a change of fortune."

(13)

We returned to a London confidently expecting Government support for the dynamic application of sanctions against Mussolini by the League of Nations. The election had been a resounding triumph for Mr. Baldwin's so-called policy of "Safety First", and the public had characteristically failed to ask itself how safety and sanctions could live together.

Within a month the soothing picture had changed, and the honest bulldog leader ("You know you can trust me!" ran the caption under David Low's vitriolic cartoon) had sacrificed his Foreign Secretary to the rage of disgruntled voters scandalised by the cynical Hoare-Laval Pact for the partition of Abyssinia. Meditating on those fortuitous occurrences which the poet Henley called "the bludgeonings of chance", I have often reflected that if this crisis had happened six weeks earlier, G. would probably have been a Member of Parliament for the rest of his life.

Our finances and the need for mental reinvigoration alike compelled a return to my novel. But national events remained obtrusive; on January 20th, 1936, the most preoccupied worker could not escape the mournful reiteration of the radio: "The King's life is moving peacefully towards its close." Two days earlier Rudyard Kipling had died, but the readers who bought his writings now ignored him in another period of preoccupation with the Royal Family.

Late that evening, G. was due at a theatrical party. To escape the increasingly lugubrious tone of the broadcast bulletins, I drove part of the way with him and walked back to Chelsea past Buckingham Palace. Though the King was dying at Sandringham and a snow-laden wind howled through the streets, large crowds stood patiently outside the Palace waiting for news. Silently they pressed against the railings while photographers with flashlights irreverently climbed Queen Victoria's statue to get a better view. Above the Palace, with its drawn blinds, the clouds occasionally parted to reveal a solitary star.

Fragments of conversation drifted towards me from the edge of the crowd.

"It's very sudden."

"Yes—it is sudden, isn't it?"

"They say he really died this afternoon."

"Oh, but the 9.30 bulletin didn't say so."

"They never does. Look at Queen Victoria! She was dead a fortnight before the people was ever told."

"Oh! . . . but what about buryin' her?"

It was now past midnight, and halfway home I picked up a taxi. The driver told me that a 12.15 a.m. radio message had announced the King's death. He had actually died at 11.55 p.m., as I stood outside the Palace, and thus missed dying on the same day as Queen Victoria by twenty-four hours and five minutes.

A Canon of Westminster had given me a ticket for Kipling's funeral in the Abbey. Three days after the King's death I sat in the North Transept, watched the clergy and choir move with uplifted crosses to the Poets' Corner before the marble urn containing Kipling's ashes, and heard the Dean utter the Committal Prayer standing beneath the outstretched hand of Addison's statue.

After the quiet singing of the "Recessional" I moved with the congregation to the South Transept, and saw the purple-covered tomb, surrounded by wreaths of spring flowers, situated in odd companionship between the graves of Charles Dickens and Thomas Hardy.

By now we nearly all wore official mourning for George V. Shortly after the service for Kipling I overheard a conversation between the children initiated by Shirley, who disapproved of my sombre garments.

"I wish Mummy wouldn't wear black."

"Why not?"

"I don't like black. It isn't a colour."

"Don't be silly!" John responded, with a logic which seemed the more infallible the closer I analysed it. "If it wasn't a colour Mummy wouldn't have a dress on."

How well worth-while that long struggle for his life had been! He had recently been promoted to a preparatory day-school in Sloane Street, while Shirley, who had outgrown the Glebe Place Nursery School, followed him at the South Kensington Kindergarten which we called "Mrs. Spencer's". She was the only member of her class who could read, she told me proudly.

One day the previous summer G. and I had found her sprawled beneath the dining-room window, talking to herself as she turned over a succession of brightly-coloured pages. But the gaudy illustrations did not come, as we had imagined, from one of her picture books; they belonged to a seed-catalogue, retrieved from the wastepaper basket, with which she was giving herself reading lessons. Syllable by syllable, as we listened, she repeated the long Latin names of the flowers.

On the afternoon of the King's funeral, my diary briefly records that we "gave a tea for P. Nehru, President of the Indian Congress". Lord Lothian, recently Under-Secretary of State for India, had asked us to arrange a gathering where this distinguished rebel, not long out of prison, could meet some of the younger Socialist leaders.

We selected a group which represented most variants of the Left-wing parties. One ebullient guest, who normally wore black, appeared with scarlet collar and cuffs pinned to her dress to show her Republican independence. At the other end of the political scale were one or two future Ministers, such as Arthur Creech-Jones and Hugh Gaitskell.

Probably no one present pictured Jawaharlal Nehru as a future Premier of India who would often speak for all Asia. But I found myself impressed by the composed intelligence with which the olive-skinned young-looking man with sombre eyes answered our guests' questions for over an hour, and stayed without impatience till everybody had gone.

"Your *Testament of Youth* was one of the last books sent to me in prison," he told me. He did not mention that as a prisoner he himself had written an autobiography, of which H. N. Brailsford was to comment in the *New Statesman* the following May: "This book . . . is the most vital contribution that any Indian has yet made to political literature."

Before he left, at G.'s request, Jawaharlal Nehru inscribed his name on the back of a picture of Thomas Jefferson. Eighteen years afterwards his sister, Mrs. Vijayalakshmi Pandit, then President of the United Nations Assembly, was to put her signature beside his.

(14)

In Winifred's short will, drawn up on a threepenny printed form two years before her death, she had appointed me her literary executor. Before doing so she consulted me, and I readily accepted the responsibility.

The work involved brought a perpetual dull heartache, strangely combined with the exhilarating sense that she who had died was speaking to me again. But it also meant, owing to the brevity of her will, a series of legal and psychological complications which she certainly would not have imposed on me had she foreseen them.

The clause which most concerned me gave me "full authority" to publish any manuscript unpublished at her death, and after a legacy from the royalties to compensate me for my trouble, bequeathed the remainder to Somerville College "for scholarships".

If "by any chance" the sum exceeded £3,000, it was to endow a "Dorothy McCalman Scholarship" to be offered to students who had earned their living for three or more years before going to college.

Other short clauses appointed her mother as executor and bequeathed small legacies to friends and relatives. With my copy of the will she had enclosed an affectionate covering note:

"I want you to have as little trouble as possible. . . . I think there should be no confusion."

That typical and kindly wish proved incapable of fulfilment, for a will is not necessarily simple because it is brief. Legal lucidity, unlike literary simplicity, is often attainable only through a mass of verbiage. Authors making wills, if they cannot afford good lawyers, should forget all that they have ever learned about style. In order to make themselves clear they should use as many words as possible, if necessary saying the same thing over and over again.

It was natural that Winifred should make me responsible for her manuscripts; we were mentally and spiritually so close that each could correct the other's proofs without consultation. She knew I had the technical qualifications to complete any work that she was obliged to lay down; she also, I believe, calculated that I alone amongst her friends was prepared to stand up to her formidable mother.

Winifred loved her mother with loyal affection, but she fully recognised her literary limitations. Once, when G. tried to help me by arguing the claims of *South Riding* to its place in English literature, Alice Holtby responded: "Literature be damned!"

This attitude was comprehensible in an elderly farmer's wife of feudal outlook and marked practical ability, who thought of writers, when she thought of them at all, as neurotic and temperamental. Winifred knew her mother too well to ask her direct for the material that she needed for *South Riding*. Instead she extracted the Agenda of East Riding County Council meetings from the dining-room waste-paper basket after Alice had gone to bed.

Knowing Winifred's tolerant but clear-sighted realism, I am sure that in giving me "full authority" she intended to make me independent of her family. But her legal knowledge did not equal her literary skill. She was unaware that a "literary executor" is a creature unknown to the law, which recognises only "executors", plain and unvarnished.

A literary executor whose duties are not explicitly defined possesses legal obligations but remains largely at the mercy of any other executor whom the will may appoint. When executors agree on policy this confusion is unimportant, but Winifred's executors—her mother and myself—viewed the management of her literary work from opposite poles.

Her will confronted me with a conflict of loyalties and values in which not only my training but her own expressed wishes inexorably committed me to one side. The more earnestly I tried to avoid creating antagonism, the more catastrophically I seemed to sink with both feet into the mud of misunderstanding.

Directly I received the typescript of *South Riding*, I plunged into a series of dilemmas which I should never have surmounted but for the brilliant, sympathetic support of Harold Rubinstein, the solicitor-playwright of Gray's Inn, whose benevolent skill has brought help and comfort to many writers of my generation.

Mr. Rubinstein's interpretation of his duties went far beyond ordinary legal obligations, and involved much delicate arbitration with Winifred's family. Her mother's solicitor and relative, Thomas Holtby of Driffield, was an old and amiable man who candidly admitted his ignorance of literary technicalities and humbly allowed himself to be guided. Alice Holtby's literary inexperience equalled his, but she knew what she wanted and belonged to a human type which is less ready to be guided than to guide.

At an early stage Mrs. Holtby—generously, from her own standpoint—conceded to me with evident hesitation and pain the powers which Winifred had intended to give. As conscientiously as I could in a life burdened by work and correspondence, I reported every major action that I took. But it was physically impossible to discuss each minor step, and whenever a Press paragraph contained vague rumours about Winifred's publications a reproachful letter would descend on my breakfast table.

But these pin-pricks were negligible compared with the problem which arose over *South Riding* itself.

(15)

Just before she died, Winifred asked me to give her mother the beautiful "Prefatory Letter to Alderman Mrs. Holtby". I did as she requested, but found, as I had feared, that Alice Holtby was less moved by its pathetic loyalty than concerned with the effect of a book about a County Council on her own position in the East Riding. With difficulty she was persuaded to refrain from criticism while I told Winifred untruthfully that her mother had loved the Prefatory Letter, and (with complete veracity) that I thought the last pages were the most moving work that she had ever done.

Even before Winifred's death, Mrs. Holtby had made up her mind that *South Riding* must not be published.

"It makes a mock of my work," she said with blunt bitterness.

So firmly did she believe this, until she found herself the applauded guest of honour at the first night of the film and other functions connected with the book, that she resigned from the East Riding County Council when *South Riding* appeared.

Since the chief duty which Winifred had laid on me was to publish this book, and the interests of Somerville College and her publishers alike demanded that it should come out quickly, my dilemma at times became excruciating.

When Alice Holtby sent letters imploring me to publish a collection of Winifred's articles instead of *South Riding*, I was compelled miserably to disregard them. I have never found it easy to be ruthless, and ruthlessness to an ageing mother who had just lost the last member of her family seemed intolerably cruel. But I could only satisfy Mrs. Holtby by sacrificing Winifred and repudiating her last behest.

In desperation I resorted to the same type of subterfuge which had driven Winifred to her mother's waste-paper basket. Obtaining legal permission to "negotiate" *South Riding* before the probate of the will went through, I sent the typescripts corrected at Fowey to Collins and Macmillan, Winifred's English and American publishers, without further delay. When Mrs. Holtby subsequently inquired about them, I laid the responsibility, to my secret shame, upon the Collins firm, which she knew and liked. They had already sent the book to the printer, I said; to recall it now would be costly and difficult.

How far Alice Holtby suspected the truth I never learned, but after this painful conflict I was not surprised that she endeavoured to arrange for the publication of Winifred's *Letters to a Friend* without reference to me. My permission proved to be legally necessary and I gave it, though the editorial policy was not precisely of a kind that I should have chosen. To the version intelligently produced by the owner of the letters, Miss Jean McWilliam, Mrs. Holtby added another of her own, and the publisher, uncertain which to choose, asked if I would collate the two.

This I agreed privately to attempt, though the many incompatibilities between the two versions made it the most difficult literary task that I have ever undertaken.

In carrying out the section of the will relating to Somerville College I had a simpler duty, for here I was dealing with mentalities which I understood. Dorothy McCalman, after whom the scholarship left by Winifred was named, had been a conscientious teacher who went late to Somerville after earning her living, obtained Second Class Honours in History, and died after only a year as a tutor at the Oxford Training College.

Not many students seeking to enter college belong to this restricted category, and Somerville was not altogether happy about Winifred's provision. With time academic knowledge tends to deteriorate, and I sympathised with the College; it did appear that Winifred's share of her family's impulse to help "lame ducks" had perhaps triumphed over her respect for scholarship. But Somerville perceived my obligations as clearly as I did, and the two Principals with whom I negotiated—first Miss Helen Darbishire and later Dr. Janet Vaughan—made my task as easy as any executor could wish.

Eventually Winifred's conditions found abundant justification. One of Somerville's most distinguished students, Margaret Hubbard—who obtained a Double First and a series of academic awards never previously won by a woman—was a Dorothy McCalman Scholar who had earned her living in Australia. She received much additional help from Winifred's royalties, for after the profits of *South Riding* had far exceeded the £3,000 visualised by the will, the College authorities and I agreed that these funds should be allocated on a wider basis as additional grants.

Today a memorial tablet to Winifred adorns the walls of Somerville College chapel. Its inscription records both her literary status and the gift that it brought.

WINIFRED HOLTBY
Student of the College
1917-1921
Author of *South Riding*
and Benefactor of the
College Born 1898 died 1935
Sursum Corda

(16)

In the New Year I went to Sidmouth for a short period of work on *Honourable Estate* and the proofs of *South Riding*. Numerous papers connected with Winifred's will followed me there for signature; it seemed strange to be reading about "Winifred Holtby Deceased" within sight of the red cliffs and tossing waves which we had watched together from the same house with its seaward-looking balconies.

"How lovely Winifred's book is!" I wrote to G. "Such a strange and sad communion, correcting these proofs."

But they also had their humours, of a kind that Winifred would have appreciated. In her race with death she had wisely ignored all trivialities, including spelling, and gave several minor characters one name in the first half of the book and another in the second. Collins's conscientious printer increased my confusion by faithfully reproducing all her mistakes.

As I re-read the tragi-comic love story of the headmistress, Sarah Burton, and the farmer-Councillor, Robert Carne, some phrase recalling conversations between us would make me start and look round, as though she were standing behind my chair. Towards the end I found so quiet an acceptance of death and so clear a solitary conquest of pain and terror, that I knew she had "paid" for this book a sum-total of spiritual effort far exceeding the cost of mine. Everything that she believed, all the lost experience of the years in which she would have done so much, had to go into one novel because there was no more time.

Soon after I returned to London with the corrected proofs, Mr. W. A. R. Collins telephoned me that *South Riding* had been chosen by the Book Society as "Book of the Month" for March. I reported this news to Alice Holtby and rang up Violet Scott-James, who like myself was more conscious of life's bitter irony than of posthumous reward.

When the book was published in England it had an immediate success; five days after publication 16,000 copies had been sold. Even the national shock administered by Hitler's reoccupation of the Rhineland on March 7th did not interrupt these sales, which had reached 25,000 by March 25th. On that day I telephoned Harold Rubinstein that I had just sold the film rights for £3,000 to Mr. Victor Saville, representing Alexander Korda.

The sale occurred on an afternoon beset with typical household problems and dominated by prospective drama.

(17)

In February 1936 Ellen Wilkinson had flown to Germany, and published in the *Sunday Referee* an article which described Hitler's plans for marching to the Rhine.

Six days later, the long luminous pencil of a searchlight stabbed the clouds above South London, and a small frightened voice summoned me upstairs.

"Mummy! Mummy! I can't go to sleep with that thing in the sky!"

"Don't be ridiculous, Shirley," I said briskly, "it won't hurt you." Not yet, added an inner voice.

In spite of the many warnings which we had received, the actual reoccupation created an international uproar. Protests poured from the Press; public meetings were hastily organised; in America an article in the June number of *Harper's Magazine* entitled "Too Late for World Peace" opened on an ominous note.

"With Germany's rearming of the Rhineland there has been swept away the last shred of an illusion eighteen years old. The so-called peace structure has finally toppled."

In Britain there was still little support for sanctions against Germany; too many people felt that the Versailles Treaty which Hitler had infringed should long ago have been scrapped or revised. Early in March the Italian bombing of Red Cross units in Abyssinia caused greater indignation.

On March 16th a secret meeting of the League Council took place in St. James's Palace. There G. and I found many international journalists known to us from visits to Geneva; they included John Gunther, Konni Zilliacus, W. N. Ewer of the *Daily Herald*, Gordon-Lennox of the *Daily Telegraph*, and von Kriess, the London correspondent of the *Berliner Tageblatt*. Eventually the Council went into public session and declared that Germany had violated the Treaty of Locarno. My diary for that day recorded some immediate reactions.

"All the people I met seemed to be divided into: (1) Those who hate murder in Germany but don't mind it in Russia. (2) Those who hate murder in Russia but don't mind it in Germany. (3) A few minoritarians like myself who hate it anyway. . . . As Winifred wrote in *South Riding*, I feel 'the deep fatigue of those whose impersonal ideals do not march with history'."

Next day a prophetic instalment of American opinion came to me from my publisher in New York.

"I feel that the Allies should have immediately occupied the bridgeheads when Hitler tore the Treaty in half by announcing to the world that he was going to rearm. But I am afraid that, now he has torn it in little pieces, the diplomats will not call his bluff and will let him go on with his preparations which will result in time in a conflict far worse than that of 1914-1919."

This view appeared to be shared by John Gunther, who dined with us that night at the Gargoyle Club. A tense argument which developed between him and von Kriess sent me home with a ferocious headache, but gave to G. and myself the idea that this was the moment to go to Germany and try to get behind the news. We could return by way of the Argonne battlefields, which I meant to describe in my novel.

An assignment offered me by Allied Newspapers confirmed our decision; they wanted three articles for the *Sunday Chronicle* on German reactions to the occupation, and a personal impression of a speech by Hitler. Three days before we departed Sir Oswald Mosley held a giant Fascist demonstration in the Albert Hall, and the police broke up an anti-Fascist meeting in nearby Thurloe Square.

On March 25th, leaving the children with my mother, G. and I travelled to Germany—but not without the usual eruption of family complications. That morning our housekeeper's young husband had to be rushed into hospital with appendicitis; immediately afterwards a literary agent telephoned to ask if I would see Victor Saville, who wanted to discuss the film rights of *South Riding* at once.

A few minutes after he arrived, these rights were sold. Our immediate departure compelled a decision on the spot; there was no time to wonder how Mrs. Holtby would respond to a large commitment made without consultation. But I wrote at once, and in France eventually received her reply. So flabbergasted was she by the sum offered, which in the modest context of our lives seemed enormous, that she quite forgot to criticise.

(18)

The following day, as we breakfasted in a restaurant car of chromium and green leather, I observed with interest the flat tranquillity of Holland. The clean agreeable cities—Rotterdam, Utrecht, Deventer—emphasised with their calm prosperity the disease of poster-politics now afflicting Germany. At the frontier a giant placard informed us that the Führer had increased the number of railway waggons, and outside Hanover another announced in black and red the forthcoming General Election:

"Der Führer hat Wort gehalten: Deutschland dankt ihm 29. März."

A red ball lying on a black swastika carried above it in huge scarlet letters the single word *"So!"*

In Berlin we called on the American United Press, which had arranged to relay my articles to the *Sunday Chronicle*. These articles were to appear under my name, but as a routine precaution Allied Newspapers had agreed that I should send them out of Germany unsigned. The helpful Americans told us that Goering was booked for a major election speech in Berlin next day. On Saturday Hitler would make an eve-of-the-poll speech in Cologne, where we decided to follow him.

Already Berlin had become a city of flying flags and election posters in variations of black, white and red. This vast, insistent propaganda terrified us by its incongruous emphasis upon peace and honour; hardly a slogan that we read failed to mention the one or the other.

"*Arbeit—Ehre—Frieden.*"

"*Wir schützen die Welt vor dem Bolschevismus.*"

"*Der Geist des neuen Deutschlands ist der Geist des Friedens.*"

"*Ein Volk—ein Reich—ein Führer.*"

That night we walked down the Hermann Goering Strasse, once named after Friedrich Ebert, to the West End *Taverna* where Berlin journalists met. As we passed an ornate building defaced by a large "To let" notice, G. suddenly exclaimed: "That's where I lunched with Treviranus in November 1933!"

It was the Herrenklub, Berlin counterpart of London's Carlton Club. Once the meeting place of the Right, this Club was now closed, and G. told me that Treviranus, one of Bruening's Ministers, had fled to exile in Scotland. Protests from the Right had been silenced by this formidable tyranny as completely as clamour from the Left.

At the *Taverna*, amongst journalists from many nations, we found a woman representative of the *Chicago Tribune* carrying on a discussion with an elderly Nazi. The talk, frank and realistic, turned on the crisis and the elections; these hard-bitten newspaper colleagues suggested a gathering of conspirators who had all tacitly agreed to spy on one another. When I remarked on the politeness of the Germans I had met, the American woman responded drily: "Ah, yes! They're expecting your country to do something for them next week!"

"There will be a new Locarno," commented the Nazi. "Then Hitler will get his twenty-five-years' Peace Pact and all will be well."

But the American continued to drop hints to me on the unreliability of peace promises.

"Go to Aachen," she said. "I've heard they're fortifying there, and have armies of workmen."

A large fair young writer from an American Press agency yawned and stretched when we inquired about the election campaign.

"Hitler's getting damned dramatic. He always does, but his voice is holding out. He hasn't got this cancer of the throat people try to give him, and if he doesn't stop talking soon he'll have us all in strait waistcoats!"

The next evening, after drafting my first article in a café, I went with G. to Goering's Charlottenburg meeting. We reached the Deutschlands Halle, a gigantic modern building in grey concrete which recalled Olympia, amid swarming detachments of Brownshirts and uniformed Stormtroopers wearing black steel helmets.

From our Press seats near the red-draped platform we watched the gathering audience of 20,000, which across the vast distance suggested a restless swarm of ants. On an enormous black flag behind the platform spread a silver German eagle above a black swastika on a silver ground. Round the galleries hung white sheets with slogans in huge black letters:

"*Die Garnisonen Deutschlands sind Garnisonen des Friedens.*"

The audience sprang noisily to its feet as Goering entered, in Brownshirt uniform with red swastika armlet. A few minutes earlier we had observed his wife, a tall woman smartly dressed in grey with a large hat. After him, a kaleidoscopic display of ruthless power, came an interminable procession of Fascist flags and pennons.

"Surely," I remarked to G., "this must be the most highly organised pageantry in the world! It makes Mosley's Wagnerian displays look like children's charades."

Through opera glasses we examined Goering as he began to speak. He appeared even bulkier than his photographs indicated, a heavy masculine type with no particle of Hitler's neurotic femininity. One deep furrow creased his shallow forehead with its dark, brushed-back hair, and his small slit-like eyes were oddly placed high above the level of his ears. Beneath his hard flat mouth a prominent chin disappeared into rolls of fat.

The deep raucous voice began with a shout; soon it became a sledge-hammer, rasping, exhausting, overwhelming. Automatic and inhuman, it conveyed the impression of a highly geared mechanical instrument in spite of the demagogic gestures which accompanied the words. Behind him the Fascist legions, black and brown, stood motionless with their pennons, like robots controlled by clockwork.

I found this speech one of the most terrifying experiences that I had known. It suggested the release of some enormous impersonal force, amoral, undirected, overpowering. But at least no simulated love of peace and righteousness inspired the harsh staccato phrases which reached us through the loudspeaker.

"Germany, once powerless, can now say No. . . . No peace with weakness, no peace without honour. . . . A weaponless people is everyone's victim. . . . Pacifism is a phrase—what matters is honour and freedom."

Listening to the applause which punctuated these comments with the thunder of a gigantic waterfall, I thought of all the books I had read on herd-instinct and mob-psychology. That meeting was surely no mere example of pageantry raised to the nth degree of decorative hysteria; it was a sub-human phenomenon, invincible as a flood or an earthquake. But G., who had met the Nazis before, was less disconcertingly impressed.

"This," he remarked to me under cover of the colossal roar which greeted the end of the oration, "is a political meeting reduced to the level of a football crowd."

(19)

In Cologne, Hitler's meeting was no football demonstration; the emotions which he aroused were more subtly demonic. His gods might be pagan, but their challenge had a perverted spiritual appeal which must, I thought, be irresistible to vulnerable and aspiring youth.

On the morning train from Berlin, I noticed the unadorned faces of the women travellers. They had all "gone pure"—if that was the correct description for severely dressed unwaved hair and greasy unpowdered skin. It was odd, I reflected, that when a woman lost every asset except her sexual qualities, the accepted methods of emphasising these qualities also disappeared.

As the train crossed the Lüneburger Heide in pale sunshine, woods and scattered orchards displayed the tremulous tokens of spring. Delicate shades of green emerged from clumps of spruce; blackthorn like snowflakes on bare branches softened the austerity of the untamed heath. Beyond it, against hillsides and trim farm-houses, gleamed the tender mauve of pear-blossom in full flower.

We reached Cologne about three o'clock but found that the road between the station and the Dom Hotel, where we were staying, was already impassable. In half-an-hour Hitler was due at the hotel for a meal, and we were obliged to wait with the excited crowds surging through the main thoroughfares leading to the Domplatz. Seven hours elapsed before we were able to occupy our room.

This was not my first visit to Cologne. Eleven years earlier Winifred and I, newly-fledged free-lance journalists, had stayed here during a tour of Central Europe in which we had sought, as G. and I were now seeking, to penetrate through the news and obtain authentic material for our writings. In the *Weekly Westminster* I had then described British-occupied Cologne as "A City of Sorrow and Hate".

Wherever we went, we had found the German people sullen and depressed from shame, poverty and malnutrition. The only visible displays of food were in the Army canteens, where cheerful Tommies ate beef-steaks before the envious infantile eyes of the future Nazi youth.

One Sunday evening I had looked from our hotel window on to Cologne's main thoroughfare, the Hohed Strasse. There, in the half-lighted road beneath the sinister black shadow of the cathedral, the morose population walked up and down in couples, hardly speaking and never laughing. Without money, entertainment or hope, they resembled a troupe of shades condemned to patrol some lampless Teutonic inferno.

The whole story of German Fascism lay in the contrast between the two Colognes. In a note dated March 15th, 1936, I recalled a history-book comment that the Bourbons, restored to the throne of France after the downfall of Napoleon, had "learnt nothing and forgotten nothing". "But we," I added, "have surpassed even them in idiocy; we have learned nothing and forgotten everything."

Amongst the facts we had forgotten was the unconquerable spirit of a proud and vigorous people too long humiliated. Denied the chance to rebuild through peaceful cooperation, it was now recovering its soul by the short cut of force. Throughout Cologne, in the exhilarating spring sunshine, an air of cheerful animation prevailed. Everywhere red swastika flags flew and music sounded; yellow forsythia gleamed vividly against the grey Cathedral walls. Wild cheering broke out as Hitler passed; the dense crowds concealed from us even his car.

We had now to acquire our Press tickets promised by the Propaganda Ministry for Hitler's meeting at the Messehalle across the Rhine. After a vain expedition to the Press Office in the Gürzenich Halle, where Hitler was receiving a Rhenish delegation, we found the tickets at the Ministry itself and drove to the Messehalle.

By now we felt tired and hungry, but could obtain only two ham sandwiches for which G. queued with a crowd of Brownshirts at a beer-house. In this provincial metropolis the "Press Gallery" proved to be somewhat primitive; it consisted of two wooden benches and a few hard chairs ranged beside the platform. Ten yards away we observed Anne O'Hare McCormick of the *New York Times* vainly endeavouring, like ourselves, to wriggle into comfort.

The great modern building, though less vast than the Deutschlands Halle, held perhaps ten thousand people. Its walls had been hastily draped in red, and a red satin curtain with a huge silver-painted swastika decorated the rear of the platform. Just before Hitler arrived, a Nazi officer beat behind it with a stick; other officials scrutinised the Press from the wings. We learned later that Hitler dreaded attack in this Catholic city; he feared not only the devout population, but the wives, still living here, of several leading Communists who had been liquidated.

(20)

If I had not expected a fanatic, I should not at first have put Hitler into this category. Below the platform he stopped, smiled, and saluted the crowd; his brown-uniformed figure suggested an amiable sergeant-major in the prime of life. Here was no sledge-hammer bully thumping on the nerves of the audience. Even the Nazi ballet which surrounded him—Ley, Frick, von Blomberg in blue uniform, and limping dark-haired Goebbels—left a theatrical rather than a military impression.

He began to speak in a low sonorous voice, restrained and clear, building up the familiar case against the Versailles Treaty. Then, as the atmosphere in the hall grew tense, his demeanour suddenly changed; it was as though he had pulled out a new psychological stop or deliberately turned on a tap inside his brain.

"I am the best democrat in the world!" he screamed. His voice cracked and shrilled, and the sentences which we struggled to take down became more incoherent. "A new community to build. . . . I must go this way, I could go no other. . . . This senseless war must be ended . . . we have waited sixteen years. . . ."

As he reached the final words, he clenched his fists, waved his arms, and beat his breast like a penitent in the last agonies of religious fervour.

"A people of sixty million stretches out its hand. . . . No man has worked more for peace than I have. A war is not a useful event. Peace, by God's help!"

When the speech ended the audience broke into fervent singing. Throughout Germany the radio stations relayed *Das Niederländische Dankgebet* which they sang, and the bells of every German church started to peal for fifteen minutes as they reached the last verse:

> *"Wir loben Dich oben, Du Lenker der Schlachten,*
> *Und flehen, mögst stehen uns fernerhin bei,*
> *Dass Deine Gemeinde nicht Opfer der Feinde,*
> *Dein Name sei gelobt, O Herr mach uns frei!"*

The bells were still ringing when we struggled through the crowd outside the hall, and crossed the Hohenzollern Bridge on foot with a throng of listeners mostly in uniform. Beside us thundered flag-draped Nazi lorries; from the high centre of the curving bridge we saw a panorama of flood-lit buildings stretching along the left bank of the Rhine. Against the dark sky the twin pinnacles of the Cathedral, no longer a sinister black shadow, scintillated in tune with the delirium of the night.

Next morning—March 29th, the day of the Rhineland election—we woke to see flying flags and hear the sound of jubilant bands. Beneath a clear blue vault flew the *Graf Zeppelin* and the *Hindenburg*, aerial prodigies dropping pamphlets over the city. In the Cathedral that Sunday morning the congregation surged round the doorways and crowded the aisles below the vivid orange and pellucid green of the tall East window. Again, as in 1924, their singing echoed back from the vaulted roof, but their spirit had experienced a complete transformation.

To recover from our exhaustion, we drank coffee and cognac that afternoon at an outdoor café overlooking the Rhine. On our way G. had visited the Bahnhof polling station, and obtained a voting paper and the gold button given to electors who had been to the poll. It was very quiet, he said; he had found no crowd and no excitement.

Over our coffee we observed that a number of insanitary buildings facing the river were being demolished. Above our heads a poster designed for women showed a cheerful-looking boy and girl beside their mother, who kissed her latest offspring with a sentimental smile.

"*Unsern Kindern die Zukunft durch Adolf Hitler*", ran the caption beneath.

A Reuter's correspondent to whom the American United Press had telegraphed from Berlin gave us potent cocktails at six o'clock and entertained us with stories of the crisis. Cologne, he said, had been taken by surprise when the coming of the troops was announced about 5 a.m. on the day of the occupation. At the Rhineland frontier the soldiers had alighted from the trains; many were compelled to march long distances, and had reached the city in the afternoon half dead with fatigue.

Before Hitler's meeting at the Messehalle, the Gauleiter Grohe who acted as Chairman had visited the Cardinal-Archbishop of Cologne and implored him to come. The Archbishop had refused; his appearance there, he said, would create a false impression that he countenanced the wrongs done to Catholicism by the régime.

After a late dinner at our hotel, we listened to the election results which from ten o'clock onwards began to come over the radio. Claps and cheers endorsed the expected 99 per cent vote for Hitler; the whole of Cologne appeared to be applauding this triumph, though the streets outside seemed strangely empty.

"I expect they're all at the Neumarkt," said G., referring to the central square where the results were being relayed to the population. "You stay here, and I'll go and see."

Half-an-hour later he returned. In the Neumarkt he had found six loud-speakers blaring announcements and cheers into an empty square. Whether the enthusiasm for the Rhineland's "liberation" came from the Propaganda Ministry or a studio in Berlin we never knew. It certainly did not originate in Cologne.

(21)

Before leaving Germany for the French frontier, we visited three other German cities.

At Aachen (Aix) we followed up the suggestion of the *Chicago Tribune* representative and spent a day in the shadow of Charlemagne's Basilica, but found neither the workmen nor the fortifications of which she had spoken, though we walked three miles to the Belgian frontier through wooded meadows white with anemones. Only a global conjuror, we concluded as we looked across the striped wooden road-barrier towards Belgium's church spires and tranquil fields, could have concealed in that open country the ten thousand blue-overalled workmen supposed at intervals to throng Aachen's streets.

In this former capital of the Holy Roman Empire, Nazi propaganda seemed even less appropriate than it had appeared in Cologne. From the tower of the green-roofed Rathaus hung two gigantic sheets showing the painted futurist figures of soldiers. Beneath the typical slogan which divided them—*"Unsere Garnisonen sind Garnisonen des Friedens"*—we noticed a tiny seated statue of Christ, with one hand holding a sceptre and the other uplifted in blessing.

On the road to the frontier we had similarly observed the sculptured figure of the crucified Redeemer above a stone fountain; before it a large glass frame displayed anti-Jewish propaganda which included pages from Julius Streicher's obscene journal *Der*

Stürmer. The local authorities, unless deliberately blasphemous, had evidently failed to develop a perception of incongruity.

The election results published in *Mittag* had shown only two cities which registered a substantial anti-Nazi poll—Hamburg with 37,000 votes and Frankfurt-am-Main with 10,000. We felt sure that the 5,000 anti-Hitler votes recorded in Cologne represented only a token figure, but could never discover the total numbers entitled to vote in the larger cities. This vain search for abstentions took us to Frankfort past the hillsides of Bad Godesburg, now white and mauve with blossom.

A German representative of Reuter's to whom we carried an introduction volubly escorted us round Frankfort. He accompanied us to the office of the *Frankfurter Zeitung*, to Goethe's house, and to the residence of Mr. Smallbones, the British Vice-Consul. Finally he used his status as a newspaperman to take us to the Café Rothschild reserved for the Jews.

A mingling of rich and poor customers, driven together by common misfortune, crowded the upper and lower floors of this restaurant. Their collective sense of humiliation oppressed me like those obstinate nightmares which refuse to be shaken off in sleep, and I felt as though I were in a gathering of Girondins under the Terror.

In Heidelberg, still a serene University city with its old bridge over the Neckar, and the ancient *Schloss* of the Electors Palatine crowning a hillside where cherry trees gleamed pure as a recent snowfall, we believed for a few hours that we were back in pre-Nazi Germany. But a slip pasted over a name on a list of local attractions aroused our curiosity, and we walked to the Pfaffengasse to identify the offending memorial.

We found a small workman's cottage with plants in the window. Judicious inquiries revealed that the obliterated plaque above the doorway had proclaimed the birthplace of Friedrich Ebert, Germany's President under the Weimar Republic. An adjacent cake-shop displayed a conspicuous notice: "*Juden sind hier unerwünscht*".

Even Heidelberg had not escaped the octopus grip of the Nazi régime.

(22)

In April we crossed the Rhine to Strasbourg, and with almost tangible relief found ourselves in France. Throughout Germany we had been conscious of letters opened, telephone calls tapped, conversations overheard. I still did not know whether my three articles had reached the *Sunday Chronicle*, though I found later that the American United Press had efficiently done its job.

From spacious Strasbourg, with its red sandstone cathedral and pink-and-white azaleas, we travelled to Metz in a Zürich-Amsterdam Pullman. Subsequently I described this day in a published article entitled "It Rained in Metz". The deluge began as we stood disconsolately regarding the shabby yellowish-brown cathedral, which was closed. Soon reaching waterfall dimensions, the rain eventually drove us into a local cinema.

Here an extremely long and drearily informative film of the French Soudan, entitled *Le Pays de Soif*, showed endless pictures of laden camels tramping over acres of sand where the superfluous water in the streets of Metz would have been a welcome gift. Finally came a news-film of the German elections, preceded by a notice imploring the audience to *"prenez le grand calme"*.

That evening, as rain blotted out the wooded hills which formed the natural frontier between France and Germany, we reached Verdun, the fortress-town of the First World War, standing high above the olive-green waters of the Meuse. Next day was Passion Sunday, and a "Pilgrimage of Peace", initiated by *La Ligue des Anciens Combattants Pacifists*, filled the restored cathedral. The pilgrims had come to tour the battlefields, and their local organiser explained that the *Anciens Combattants* brought together the various left-wing organisations—Socialists, Radicals, and Communists—which composed *le front populaire*.

"Tell the English people about our pilgrimage," he implored us, "for the French Press will be silent."

We promised that we would. Eventually G. wrote to the *News Chronicle* and I to the *Manchester Guardian*, reporting that this gesture by 1,600 French pacifists had been made in spite of the Nazi elections.

Beyond Verdun lay the French-American battlefields, where yellow butterflies flitted over the ancient trenches and hawks soared above them. How real, yet so far how indefinable, was the contrast between this old war and the threatening new one which I had left round the corner at Cologne!

In the deep tree-filled ravines of the Argonne Forest, brambles concealed the former dugouts, and the experimental notes of the first cuckoo echoed uncertainly over half-opened anemones and budding broom. But in the sector where the American Army had fought in 1918, broken trees and dead brown bushes still lay in heaps amid clumps of silver birch. Near Haragée, in the centre of the forest, a French monument saluted the American divisions which had tackled this formidable barrier when everyone else was tired:

"Aux Morts de l' Argonne."

How soon would tramping feet sound through these ravines again? I asked myself as I filled a notebook with descriptions of the baneful forest and the American cemetery at Romagne, which had assembled beneath neat white crosses those half-forgotten dead. But, in the event, the Argonne was spared; it was to the Ardennes, Luxembourg's similar wooded frontier, that destruction came through von Rundstedt's armies. This too I should one day see.

That night, in the small Coq Hardi Hotel at Verdun, a notice pasted on the lounge wall seemed already to answer my question. In spite of the *Anciens Combattants* and their pilgrimage, it advertised *"Précautions individuelles en cas de chute des bombes"*.

(23)

After ten days in England I was back on the Continent to lecture for the Anglo-Netherlands Association. Though the Italian armies had now captured Addis Ababa, no premonition of war seemed to disturb the robust serenity of the Netherlands cities where I gave my addresses.

The Dutch, one of Europe's adult nations, seemed confident that their neutrality would again defend them, and more than wishful-thinking lay behind this opinion. I met several families whose members had intermarried with Germans. Their relatives, they said, often visited them and talked freely, leaving an impression of deep discontent with the Nazi régime growing inside Germany. Meanwhile the little nation cheerfully cultivated its bulb-fields, superb patchwork-quilts of colour laid at intervals between The Hague and Enschede on the German border.

In the modest homes of young civil servants and teachers, I was entertained very simply by New World standards. But my hosts were as benevolent as the Americans and quite as persistent, since they all keenly desired to learn my language. One distinguished earlier lecturer had lugubriously warned me that I should receive "working-class hospitality", but this, though I should have welcomed it, was never forthcoming. I stayed at only one hotel, the unpretentious Ruimzicht at Apeldoorn, where the Queen's summer palace stood half hidden by low hills and fir-fringed sand-dunes rare in Holland. The little hostelry was bare, cold, and innocent of hot water, but as clean as an operating theatre.

At Amsterdam just before seeing Rembrandt's pictures *The Night Watch* and *The Jewish Bride* in the Rijks-museum, I received a letter from G. He wrote that he was "ecstatically happy" working on a book called *England Must Choose* (subsequently *The Anglo-Saxon Tradition*).

His next letter reached me in Groningen, Holland's northern University city, where I stayed at the house of the Dutch-Jewish Professor of Philosophy, Leo Polak. The Professor and his family—a tall, dark, keenly feminist wife, three young daughters, and an eighty-year-old mother who spoke only German—welcomed me like an intimate friend to their home.

He showed me his remarkable library, which contained first editions of Luther, Hobbes, Locke and Rousseau, and I promised to send him one of G.'s books for the Political Science section. This was my happiest visit in Holland, and I left the family with a regret untinged by any foreboding of their tragic fate.

Apart from the Polaks—a highly-cultured household where conversational judgments were intellectual rather than moral—my various hosts gave me such candid impressions of previous lecturers that I wondered what they would say about me after I had gone. Travelling home I reflected—as so often in the United States—that there ought to be a Public Relations Officer at the Foreign Office specially appointed to "brief" British lecturers going abroad on their responsibility as unofficial ambassadors; the risk of leaving them to do their worst seemed to be too great.

The little tour, like all tours, had been exacting, but, though physically tired, I felt happier than I had been for months. Three crowded weeks of colourful adventure on the Continent had restored my vitality, and I was now ready to finish *Honourable Estate*.

(24)

My novel was completed on August 2nd, but this much-harassed story—it ran to 200,000 words and had occupied two-and-a-half years—did not reach its end without further tribulation. In May my stalwart aunt and godmother, who had supported my decision to go to America in 1934 against parental opposition, had died from the delayed effects of an earlier operation.

Soon after Winifred's death, Shirley had startled me by a strange remark during her evening bath.

"Two nice people gone—Grandad and Auntie Winifred. I expect Auntie B."—the children's name for my godmother—"will be the next."

"But, Shirley," I protested, "you surely don't want Auntie B. to die, do you?"

"No," she said. "No, I don't. But," she added reflectively, "I do like you a bit better."

Evidently "Auntie B.'s" fate and mine were inexorable alternatives in her mental logic. Now "Auntie B." was gone, and her pleasant home would see the children no more.

At the end of October G.'s father followed her, the fourth member of our family to leave us in fifteen months. For two years he had lain in an Oxford nursing home, his memory only occasionally reawakened by G. Though sorrow seemed inappropriate for the end of a life so deeply shadowed, G. was much distressed, as we all are by the loss of a load which we have carried so long that its weight becomes part of ourselves.

In the Isle of Wight, where I took the children for their summer holiday I revised the typescript of my book, and with more than the usual feeling of relief sent copies to its respective publishers, who had both planned to bring it out for the Christmas market. So long had I now existed without a break in the cycle of work and sorrow that G. decided upon a genuine holiday in another, more glamorous island.

Early in September we departed for Capri, hoping to repeat the enchantment of Portofino. But the Italy of 1936 was not the Italy of 1934. The Abyssinian campaign had divided that lovely spring from this mellow but menacing autumn; the forked lightning which accompanied our steamer from Naples seemed all too symbolic of the political climate.

At the exuberantly-named but peaceful Eden-Paradiso Hotel in the village of Anacapri, high above mosquitoes and tourists amid fir-shadowed olive groves, the proprietor and staff were courteous enough. Nor could politics detract from the spectacular beauty of steep untrodden cliffs above sapphire seas, or chill the warmth of the sunny water on the Piccola Marina. But Italy was already supporting the rebels in the Spanish Civil War; the Rome-Berlin Axis had been born; and embarrassed British debates on non-intervention only offered the customary weak provocation to the Fascist powers.

Scrawled on the white walls of Anacapri and the island's harbour, we read inscriptions as ominous as the slogans in Germany:

"*Il grido d'Italia è un grido di giustizia ed un grido di vittoria.*"

"*L'Italia non farà più una politica di rinuncia e di viltà.*"

"*Molti nemici, molto onore.*"

Soon after our return, we attended the P.E.N. dinner at the Savoy

Hotel for the seventieth birthday of H. G. Wells. In spite—or perhaps because—of a long, elaborate, and indiscreet joke retailed at Wells's expense by Bernard Shaw, the occasion seemed less of a gay celebration than a sad memorial. To coincide with his birthday Wells had published *The Anatomy of Frustration*, and his own speech reflected frustration rather than triumph as he recalled the long-ago injunction of a nurse in his childhood:

" 'Now, Master Bertie, put away your toys.' . . . So little done, so much to do!"

Honourable Estate was published early in November both in England and in America. On a train to Birmingham during a series of autumn lectures, I opened my *News Chronicle* to find that it headed the fortnightly list of best-sellers. It also "crashed", in Macmillan's phrase, the New York *Herald-Tribune* best-seller list.

Nevertheless it remained, as it had been all along, a "fated" book. In America it was eclipsed by *Gone With the Wind*; and in England it joined the many minor victims of the Abdication.

(25)

The younger generation which reads the still widely disseminated story of Edward VIII must sometimes wonder how it affected his near contemporaries, and why, two decades afterwards, the world should take so unflagging an interest in his mature love-affair. One curious feature of the Abdication was the effect of its human emotions upon individuals like ourselves who normally paid little attention to the Royal Family, monarchs, and thrones.

Apart from this human quality, the drama became a contest between relatively youthful, rebellious informality, and the staid Victorian conventions personified by Stanley Baldwin and his colleagues. It also cast an uncomfortable light upon the deep gulf between Christian charity and the top-level ecclesiastical policy denounced by H. G. Wells in an article headlined "The Church Militant and Rampant". The sinister bias of *The Times* under the editorship of Geoffrey Dawson was not fully recognised for several years.

Those of us who were authors of recent novels soon realised that national tension had killed the Christmas market in the fortnight when book sales normally reach their peak. One of the biggest British booksellers, whose average sale was 1,000 copies a day, found these reduced to 50 during the Abdication period.

Travelling to Scotland on December 9th, I emerged from fog into bright winter weather. Between Carlisle and Edinburgh the sun shone from a clear pale-blue sky upon olive-green fields and brown woods covered with a thin layer of snow.

That night I spoke in Dunfermline, where the news had virtually obliterated the audience. The Nonconformist Minister with whom I stayed immediately stimulated my sympathy for Edward VIII by his adamant disapproval of the pilloried lovers and his undisguised commiseration with Queen Mary.

"I'm sorry for her," he said righteously. "She must feel she has utterly failed as a mother."

On my journey south to Yorkshire, I changed trains at Edinburgh. Newsvendors selling special editions ran up and down the cold bright length of Prince's Street; from large placards the words confronted me: "ABDICATION FEARS GROWING." Outside the railway station, I glanced up at the towers and spires of Scotland's capital and the silhouette of the Castle, focus of the bloody records of Scottish kings, outlined against a grey and vermilion December sky. How strange in our annals was today's event upon which those monuments of history looked down! Even reigning monarchs, it seemed, could not always escape from the truth of Burke's disillusioned words, recalled to me by a barrister cousin after my father's death: "What shadows we are, and what shadows we pursue!"

At Middlesbrough, where I was due to lecture for the Literary and Philosophical Society, I heard the King's decision announced in the crowded restaurant of a department store. After a silence broken only by the opening and shutting of lift gates, the expected words came over the radio:

"After long and anxious consideration I have determined to renounce the throne to which I succeeded on the death of my father, and I am now communicating this, my final and irrevocable decision. . . . I have accordingly this morning executed an Instrument of Abdication. . . ."

That evening my lecture, selected months earlier by the organisers from a list of titles, dealt by peculiar coincidence with "Changes in Manners and Morals during the Past Thirty Years"; it was the "background" theme of *Honourable Estate*. Quoting the familiar dictum: "Happy is the country which has no history", I remarked that I belonged, like Edward VIII, to a generation which was still on the early side of middle age but had already seen almost more history than any generation could bear.

How much more of it we had yet to see, my contemporaries and I were soon to learn.

In London a jaded sense of anti-climax prevailed, but on December 15th a Foyle's Literary Luncheon featuring the descendants of classical writers was crowded to hear John Drinkwater and Rose Macaulay. Replying to the toast of "The Classics", John Drinkwater nonchalantly observed: "My ancestors came from Canterbury, but thank God they were only publicans!" This comment went down well with an audience which that morning had read in *The Times* a summary of the Archbishop's bitter broadcast on the departed King.

Shortly afterwards Dr. Cosmo Gordon Lang of Canterbury became the subject of a ribald epigram by Gerald Bullett, of which various versions were subsequently quoted on both sides of the Atlantic:

> "My Lord Archbishop, what a scold you are!
> And when your man is down how bold you are!
> Of charity how oddly scant you are!
> How Lang, O Lord, how full of Cantuar!"

The essence of the whole drama, as I saw it in common with many other British citizens sickened by sanctimonious hypocrisy, lay less in the King's attitude to his ministers, which was strictly correct, than in the attitude of the ministers to the problem. Mrs. Simpson, we believed, had merely been made a convenient excuse for removing a monarch whose informality, dislike of ancient tradition, and determination to see things for himself had affronted the "old gang" from the beginning.

After so much obnoxious moralising in the English Press, it was refreshing to find the Paris *Herald-Tribune* leader of December 11th frankly stating:

"Political chroniclers will probably say that the King was constitutionally bound to conform to the clearly-expressed wishes of the Ministers of the British Commonwealth. But historians seeking the truth will read in the abdication the defeat of a sovereign who belonged to his generation before the forces representing generations long dead or dying."

CHAPTER FIVE

THE LIGHT ABOVE THE STORM-CLOUDS

"When the war clouds gather
 And the day grows dim,
The seekers after God shall trust in Him.

"Though ruin threatens
 The bounds of space,
The lovers of the Lord shall see His Face.

"Hell and its legions
 Go thundering by,
But the peace-makers carry His standard high.

"Beyond death's night
 Lies the hour of birth,
When they, the meek, shall inherit the earth."

V.B., 1950.

(1)

IN THE SUMMER of 1936 an episode had occurred which appears in retrospect as a turning point of my life.

Its challenge, once accepted, was to carry me far from the bright pinnacles of worldly success which I had just begun so hopefully to climb.

At first there seemed to be no special significance in an invitation to address a large open-air peace meeting. This demonstration appeared to differ from others owing mainly to its size—it was to be held in a natural amphitheatre near Dorchester which could seat 15,000 people—and to the unusual distinction of the platform.

My fellow speakers, I learned, were to be George Lansbury, the veteran Labour politician; the Reverend Donald Soper, already the best-known young orator in the Methodist Church; and Canon H. R. L. Sheppard, formerly Vicar of St. Martin-in-the-Fields. Our chairman was Laurence Housman, novelist and dramatist, who had just obtained permission from Edward VIII for his long-banned series of plays, *Victoria Regina*, to be shown on the London stage.

As I travelled to Dorchester through a sudden shimmering heat-wave, I felt intimidated by the status of the other speakers and especially by the overwhelming reputation of Canon Sheppard. This man of genius—preacher, broadcaster, peace crusader, and one of the most popular human beings ever to tread London's crowded pavements—was known throughout the world as Dick Sheppard. A young Army chaplain broken in health by direct contact with war at its worse, he had been appointed to St. Martin's in November 1914.

Within months he transformed a moribund city church into England's most vital Christian centre. Being a faithful and uncompromising follower of Christ, he also believed that war, however "righteous" its alleged cause, was contrary to the will of God and the spiritual welfare of man.

When the demonstration at Dorchester began, a huge audience from all over Wessex crowded the great Ring in beating sunlight. On the raised platform, scintillating with heat, the speakers addressed their listeners from beneath a striped sun umbrella.

George Lansbury followed the chairman; shrewd and benign, sturdily erect in his black alpaca coat, he appeared in spite of his seventy-six years to be the only person unaffected by the temperature. At the end of the row sat Dick Sheppard in his customary informal attire. As he listened to George Lansbury he inhaled oxygen from a rubber apparatus which he carried to relieve his chronic asthma.

With half London I had seen and heard Dick Sheppard preach at St. Martin's. He had entered more directly into my consciousness when, simply and tenderly, he conducted Winifred's funeral service. Now, as he rose to speak in his light, friendly voice with its underlying note of infectious laughter, I realised that he could play on the emotions of a crowd with a master's skill.

By the time that my own turn came I was panic-stricken. This Christian pacifist platform was like no other on which I had stood; here my customary little speech in support of collective security would strike a discordant note. Its basis was political, but the message of my fellow-speakers sprang from the love of God.

Yet I had prepared nothing else. Struggling to my feet I quoted Bunyan, improvised a feeble little story about the pilgrimage of the *Anciens Combattants* at Verdun, and sat down—the biggest disappointment to thousands on that spectacular afternoon.

The hilarious gaiety of the journey back to London all but obliterated this humiliation.

A cavalcade of organisers and audience accompanied us to the station, and insisted upon photographing us before we boarded the train. Being the only woman speaker, I had been presented with a bouquet of luxuriant roses. As Donald Soper was then a young man and I still appeared deceptively immature, the finished picture suggested a bride and bridegroom being seen off for the honeymoon by their respective fathers.

In the train the four of us shared a restaurant table, and talked all the way home. George Lansbury described his recent American tour, and Dick Sheppard told me about the Fellowship of Reconciliation formed during the war to preserve the Christian ideal of peace. He also spoke of his own Peace Pledge Union, initiated by a letter sent two years previously to the Press. It had invited men who shared his outlook to send him a postcard simply stating: "I renounce war, and never again directly or indirectly will I support or sanction another."

The response to this appeal, and to a second similarly addressed to women, had been so enormous that the signatories of the Peace Pledge had now grown into a great movement supported both by ordinary citizens and by leaders of opinion. Their revolutionary conception of peace had nothing in common with the cowardly policies by which the politicians of the nineteen-thirties created animosity in neighbouring countries, and then purchased immunity from the consequences at other people's expense.

"I hear Ellen Wilkinson, after a prolonged struggle with herself, has come over to it, together with Aldous Huxley, Gerald Heard, and Siegfried Sassoon," I reported to G., who had returned to Heidelberg for a period of writing.

In the railway carriage, though our conversation was glorious, the heat became excessive, and one after another we took off all the outer garments that we could decently remove. Dick Sheppard's popularity sprang from his deep humanity and magnetic charm; he was not a handsome man, and even in his canonicals did not look impressive. Now, with his coat thrown on the table and shirt-sleeves rolled up, he resembled a tipsy cricketer going home at the end of a too enjoyable afternoon.

The railway officials had immediately recognised both him and George Lansbury, but not all the passengers were equally enlightened. One sour-faced elderly woman at the next table appeared particularly scandalised by Dick's informality.

"Pick up your coat!" she reprimanded him severely. "Fancy putting it down where people have to eat!"

With a sidelong wink at me, Dick meekly obeyed her. When we reached Waterloo the porters ushered us off the train as though we were Royalty, and we shook hands and parted.

Soon afterwards my mother, who occasionally helped at St. Martin's tea-parties, heard from one of the parish workers a story which I have always treasured. On the way to Dorchester it appeared that Dick had drawn George Lansbury's attention to my name in the list of speakers, and remarked with characteristic frankness: "You know, George, I have a feeling I shan't like that young woman."

"So have I, Dick! So have I," Lansbury responded gruffly.

At the end of the day, when I had left them at Waterloo, Dick turned to George Lansbury again.

"George, I take back everything I said about that young woman."

"So do I, Dick! So do I."

This generous recantation was as typical of Dick as it was undeserved. Characteristically he gave me the credit for a joyous journey which owed its sparkle chiefly to him, his racy stories, and his unqualified enjoyment of the disapproving lady. Certainly his reconsidered judgment could not have been due to my speech, which was easily the worse that I have ever made.

(3)

Shortly after the Dorchester demonstration, Dick invited me to become a sponsor of his Peace Pledge Union. Looking back on his letter, which for me was to have such momentous consequences, I have always believed that, if I had spoken at Dorchester in the usual competent fashion, he would not have written.

Dick Sheppard never "judged" people as the intolerant majority of us are accustomed to judge, but he was eminently capable of shrewd intuitional assessments. From reports by others, he had evidently diagnosed my character as controversial and belligerent. But the confused embarrassment of the little speech which the local Press and I alike deplored had also shown him that I was able to perceive the significance of his message. In that moment I saw that my study of peace had been too superficial; to delegate responsibility to a set of fallible politicians at Geneva was to over-simplify the problem of human violence and repudiate personal guilt.

167

Since Dick was soon using me to address some of his largest meetings, his long experience of the peace movement must have shown him that it contained many disciples of a type similar to mine. They suffered from the deficient confidence which is the root of all aggression, and in order to discipline their unruly selves required the inexorable standards of a spiritual creed. They also knew that, although a man does not automatically become a better citizen because he has seen a vision of the truth, he must inevitably become a worse citizen if he fails to follow that vision where it leads.

In the summer of 1936, I had not fully confronted this challenge. Disingenuously I sought to postpone the issue which Dick had raised, and I told him that I could not decide whether to join his group until I had finished *Honourable Estate*.

During the war my hospital service had often meant pain, and sometimes terror, for which an easy provincial upbringing had not prepared me. But that sorrowful ordeal had always lain safely within the confines of social approbation; it had been an accepted expression of patriotism, a form of humanitarian co-operation with the war machine. Though the conclusions to which my experience led had been unequivocally stated in *Testament of Youth*, such work for peace as I could combine with writing had been offered to organisations which were politically "respectable" because they were ultimately prepared to compromise with war.

"Collective security," Dick Sheppard used to say, "means that if war comes everyone will be in it"—a dictum justified long after his death by the war in Korea.

For fifteen years after the First War, this wide moral division between the supporters of collective security and the exponents of revolutionary pacifism had always existed but had not been emphasised. But with the threat of a second World War, the gulf became clear. Individuals who believed that war was wrong in all circumstances could no longer join with those who were prepared to fight in the last resort.

Many intelligent persons who made a different choice from mine, or never finally accepted either the one position or the other, were coming at this time to perceive the basic conflict of principle involved. One of the best analyses came from Kingsley Martin in the *New Statesman* during 1938.

"The difference of philosophy is fundamental. The pacifist regards the refusal to fight as obedience to a universal obligation, while the advocate of collective security is a politician whose attitude is determined by circumstances. . . .

168

"If you would command attention in world politics today you must show an ultimate readiness to fight. Obviously a threat may keep the peace at a particular moment, but equally obviously it brings no hope for the world in the future. . . .

"It is ideas and systems of thought that we have to combat, and war has become a monstrously inefficient instrument for that purpose. If the last war was fought against Prussianism and produced Nazism, what incredible horror are we likely to get out of a war against Hitler? . . .

"The job—the only one worth attempting in the world and becoming daily more difficult to accomplish—is to defeat Fascism without war; if it comes to war the battle is lost. The division lies between those who think that it is still worth while making this attempt to defeat the Fascist peril by . . . that nice adjustment of threat and concession which is called diplomacy, and those who are so sure that any display of force will only breed war that they retire from the immediate struggle, hoping that . . . they may at least direct men's attention to the choice of better methods in the long run. Ultimately it is a clash between two religions. In a crisis people find out what they are."

This able exposition did not help me with my own dilemma, for it appeared two years afterwards. Another seven were to pass before the "incredible horror" of totalitarian domination merely transferred from one part of Europe to another by six years of disastrous warfare was to justify the writer's prophecy.

My war service had never brought me into contact with the minority groups which accepted the obligation to obey, as Lord Hugh Cecil recognised between 1914 and 1918, "a Higher Authority than the State." But my recollection of newspaper paragraphs jubilantly describing the fate of pacifists reviled, imprisoned, or hounded from public meetings were clear enough to show what happened to those rash individuals who turned from well-trodden roads into unorthodox paths.

For three years now I had enjoyed outstanding success in different parts of the world, and had savoured that rare experience the more fully owing to the long period of frustration before it. Everything in me recoiled from the prospect of exchanging this welcome stimulus for public disapproval. I was still far from realising how obstructive such disapproval could be, but I suspected that, once I stepped outside the borders of officially endorsed peace-making, there could be no turning back.

Whatever might be possible for others, integrity as I understood

169

it would never permit me the periodic compromises of those who shouted for peace in peace-time and for war in war-time; such moral gymnastics would involve a self-contempt even harder to live with than social ostracism. For what Dick Sheppard and his friends offered to their followers was not, in the last resort, a policy but a principle—the revolutionary principle put forward, and still rejected by the majority of mankind, in the Sermon on the Mount.

It was a simple idea which derived its validity not from political calculation, but from the prophetic challenge of an inner compulsion; it was the belief, for which Christ died, in the ultimate transcendence of love over power.

(4)

Dick's letter had been a summons which gave a new insistence to the rumble of approaching war. Once my novel was finished, I could not honestly postpone the obligation to think out anew my own position.

Passionately and repeatedly I wished that I had never gone to Dorchester to be thus diverted from the accepted policies, endorsed by millions who desired peace but did not want to pay for it, which stopped short at the final sacrifice. As I had perceived all too clearly on that pacifist platform, to follow Dick meant treading the Way of the Cross in modern guise. He pointed to a path which might end, not in crucifixion or a den of lions, but at internment, the concentration camp, and the shooting squad.

It was not surprising that the rulers and most of the people in Britain—for three centuries an aggressive country which had lived by conquest and domination—could not receive Dick Sheppard's message. They could no more accept it than they or any other powerful nation had ever accepted the teaching of his Master and Friend—for "to take him seriously", as H. G. Wells wrote of "this Galilean" in *The Outline of History*, "was to enter upon a strange and alarming life, to abandon habits, to control instincts and impulses, to essay an incredible happiness. . . ."

But it seemed that a beginning could indeed be made, as it had been made in Galilee; not by saints, but by ordinary men and women, the twentieth-century equivalents of fishermen and taxgatherers, publicans and sinners. Just as the followers of Jesus, beneath the shadow of a great imperialist tyranny, had formed and maintained their "little flock" to bear witness to a revolutionary creed, so a handful of modern pioneers could form theirs, and bear

170

witness to the same dynamic faith even in a community which had gone to war.

By chance there happened at this period to be an interim test to which I could submit my painful hesitations. On my desk lay several requests to address League of Nations Union meetings; I had postponed replying until *Honourable Estate* was finished. Now I accepted five of these invitations in order to discover whether I could still conscientiously uphold the collective security position which I had hitherto expounded.

That brief tour was the most disconcerting that I have ever undertaken. Wherever I went, members of local Peace Pledge Union groups turned up to heckle me. The more resolutely I sought to fend off their questions, the more deeply I grew convinced that they were right in their view of the League. It had become a mere French-dominated instrument for continuing the unjust *status quo*, set up at Versailles, of which Hitler was the appalling consequence. Clearly the road to goodwill on earth no longer lay in this direction, if it ever had.

Only one thing now stood between my former work on peace platforms and the reply to Dick's invitation; it was a letter written by G. from Heidelberg in answer to mine describing the Dorchester rally:

"As to the radical issues you raise, the ultimate object of political organisation is peace. The abolition of war and poverty are the two imperative tasks of our generation; the major political aim is how best at this time to further these ends. I will not stop to inquire whether pacifism as an *absolute* principle is sound. In measurable time you will not convert to it the majority of this great nation and therefore (whatever one's private view) it will not, as a public fact, avert war."

If a long-term policy conflicts with a short-term policy, I asked myself, which does one choose? Obviously one cannot work—as the League of Nations Union now seemed to be trying to work—in two directions at once. It was characteristic of G. and myself—and in no way destructive of our relationship, which had so long absorbed without friction many religious and political differences—that he saw the short-term policy as essential, while I was coming to believe too deeply in the long-term policy to accept the short-term policy for myself.

G.'s letter had embodied the argument of pacifism's best opponents; mankind would not be converted to it "in measurable time". But the same argument applied to all forms of revolutionary teaching, costly and often dangerous to its interpreters, which visualised life in terms of a society still to come. The fallible Apostles could never have hoped to convert the great Roman Empire to Christ's doctrines "in measurable time". But surely few would now say that the early Christian Church should have abandoned its task as too difficult, even though neither the lands once ruled by Rome nor the rest of humanity were converted even yet?

I could find no argument more fundamental than this. I was very far from sainthood and not even sure that I believed in God; but the effect of Jesus upon human history was a fact of experience. As a man He had died on the Cross believing that, whatever the immediate results of a course determined by conviction and ending in apparent total defeat, His Father would reveal in time's long perspective that an action performed in accordance with the Divine Will would produce the results that He desired for His world.

Soon after Christmas I wrote to Dick and told him that I would become a sponsor of his movement.

(5)

It now seems unbelievable that I attended for barely a year the sponsors' meetings at the Regent Street office where Dick was chairman, walked in poster-parades, and joined a late night deputation to the Archbishop of Canterbury. Still less is it credible that this man, who could dissolve with a jest the grievances of his distinguished but temperamental sponsors, was not only sick but sad, lonely, tempest-tossed, and faced with the break-up of a home crushed by his own overwhelming popularity.

It has remained for his biographer, the late R. Ellis Roberts, to tell the millions who admired and envied Dick Sheppard of the sensitive little boy terrified by a relentless grandparent, and afflicted through the sarcasm of a brutal schoolmaster with a permanent sense of inferiority which the final tragedy revived and reinforced.

During the spring of 1937 I shared platforms with Dick in many cities. At Bristol, by a characteristic stroke of genius, he invited Siegfried Sassoon to read his poems in the gentle, diffident voice which seemed to symbolise the lonely pathos of the war generation.

To Manchester Dick travelled from London in order to appear for fifteen minutes and tell his entranced hearers: "Last night I had a dream. In it George Lansbury and I were playing tennis against Hitler and Musso. George had a game leg and I was asthmatic, but we won six-love, six-love."

On the midnight train to Euston I could not rest in the sleeping compartment next to his because, throughout the night, I could hear him coughing, groaning, and fighting for breath.

At these meetings which he addressed with such painful consequences for himself, he was grave as well as gay. "Not peace at any price," he would insist, "but love at all costs." How many members of his audiences reflected what that favourite slogan really meant, or understood that he was inviting them to become the spearhead of the Christian conscience?

At *all* costs. . . . Though my enemy slay me, I will die rather than hate him. Though my country go down before an invader, it will find in non-violent resistance to evil the final answer to occupation and war. By accepting crucifixion my nation and I will return through suffering to a new security rooted in spiritual power—"safe where all safety's lost".

The dilemma of 1937 was not that we had forgotten our dead who died in "the war to end war", but that it had become so difficult to be true to them; the accumulating catastrophes of Europe rebuked each endeavour to remember them constructively. The unquiet world which mocked their sacrifice had again come close to me, for shortly after the Bristol meeting G. departed for the scene of another revolution even more bloodthirsty than those which he had already explored in Germany, Italy and Russia.

(6)

When the Spanish Civil War broke out in July 1936, several left-wing British groups vehemently adopted the Republican cause. Their policy, in the accepted fashion of that time, was dominated by fellow-travellers.

Today we recognise the Spanish War as a dress-rehearsal for the life-and-death struggle between the Fascist and Communist varieties of totalitarianism which was to rend Europe for the next nine years, and leave Stalinist Russia one of the only two Great Powers to benefit by the Second World War. But in 1936, with these crowded pages of history still to be written, the true character of the Civil War had not clearly emerged. Many good democrats, like G. himself, accepted Republican Spain as a genuine symbol of persecuted democracy.

Soon after the war began, G. attended an international gathering summoned to Brussels to discuss the "Spanish question". The following month he joined the delegates at the Edinburgh Labour Party Conference who declaimed against the Government policy of non-intervention, and in December served on a Spanish Aid Committee which met in Paris.

After these activities the National Joint Committee for Spanish Relief invited him to visit Spain as their representative, and investigate the needs of the population in the war areas. They hoped ultimately to raise funds in the United States, where G.'s contacts would be valuable, and he agreed to go to Spain for three weeks.

From Paris he sent a ribald story to cheer me after this sudden departure.

"Madame de M. had two most pleasing tales of Mr. Baldwin offering to sacrifice Mrs. Baldwin if Edward would sacrifice Mrs. Simpson."

He had now seen Señor Araquistain, the Spanish Ambassador in Paris, with whom he subsequently travelled to Valencia.

"I have got a direct introduction from the Ambassador to Señor del Vayo," he wrote, "and I am informed that I shall without question see him and Caballero and President Azaña."

Six days after leaving London, he telegraphed me that he had reached Valencia. It had surprised him, he told me later, to hear "Wake Up and Sing" suddenly echoing from the total darkness outside his bedroom, and to see Shirley Temple films being shown in the refugee villages.

On January 30th the American Press Association telephoned me that G. was broadcasting to the United States that evening from Madrid, where the front line, stabilised after the November fighting, now ran through the University City. He described to me later the nightly bombardment of the substantial Telefonica Building in the "West End" of Madrid, its million inhabitants increased by three hundred thousand half-starved refugees.

The front line was now only twenty minutes' walk from the Gran Via; G. travelled by tram to see trenches and barricades, derelict buildings, and shell-torn walls on which machine guns were periodically trained to catch the unwary. The fighting had relapsed into trench warfare, and only a piled embankment in a park indicated the enemy stronghold.

"I have seen the Ministers of Justice, Foreign Affairs and Health (a woman), and hope to see the President," G. wrote me on February 2nd. "As touching my own mission I am exceedingly happy. Things are moving in terms of an international Commission of the Hoover magnitude."

In Barcelona he found another city overcrowded with refugees, sad harbingers of the homeless millions whom Europe was to know in the next decade. After two days there he flew to Marseilles, and was back in London on February 8th.

(7)

To his Committee G. reported the need of bread and meat in the industrial areas, milk for children everywhere, and a large consignment of medical supplies.

Neither rebel nor Republican forces, he had found, could escape responsibility for the nightly slaughter of "suspects" or the new practice of holding hostages, soon to be developed into a diabolic art all over Europe. But whatever disillusionments he might have suffered regarding the innate nobility of Spanish democrats, he agreed to fulfil the second half of his mission, and in mid-February sailed for America to discuss the establishment of an international Commission modelled on the relief work of Hoover and Nansen.

In Washington he talked with Edgar Rickard, the Director-General of Hoover's Commission for Russian relief, and had a short interview with President Roosevelt. Francis Sayre, the Assistant Secretary of State, assured him that American collaboration could be counted on if a Commission was set up.

A month after his return to England the Nazi "volunteers" in Spain tested their bombing powers on the defenceless city of Guernica, ancient capital of the Basque territory. They razed the small town to the earth, obliterated its defenders, and blew to pieces or roasted alive scores of helpless non-combatants.

British opinion, unable to conceive how rapidly its own sensitivity would be hardened by daily examples of "frightfulness" from all the leading belligerents in another war, boiled up into an orgy of pious indignation. More realistically, a *New Statesman* editorial warned its readers that this raid was a portent of carnage to come.

"No good is done by pretending that such horrors will not be perpetrated, if once war breaks out, by every country, including our own. . . . Nor is it any good to shirk the fact that Guernica is a rehearsal not only for Bilbao and Madrid, but also for Oxford and London. We are all awaiting the fate of the people of Bilbao; our only notion of evading it is to equip ourselves, in Mr. Baldwin's own phrase, to bomb the women and children of other countries more thoroughly and quickly than they can bomb ours."

Though thousands of Basque children took refuge in England and Bilbao was brutally raided in June, G.'s projected International Commission for Spanish Relief had not yet been created to shelter the homeless and feed the starving. Actually, it never took shape at all.

In Spain he had discovered that the Spanish Government's chief deficiency was not so much money as organising power. For weeks he worked to draw up a scheme which would be acceptable to both the Spanish Government and the National Joint Committee, but, in current terminology, "the answer was a lemon".

The Spanish Government, it appeared, had welcomed the creation of relief committees as a form of propaganda. It owned, or professed to own, ample resources for its refugees, and objected to being controlled—"like Abyssinians", as the Ambassador put it—by an international commission.

The beneficent scheme which had cost so much time and money eventually foundered on the rock of Spanish obstructionism. How necessary it had been, I was able to judge three years later when I, passed through Spain on a roundabout journey to the United States.

(8)

Towards the end of 1937, a group organised under the title of *Left Review* sent out to over 150 "Writers and Poets of England, Scotland, Ireland and Wales" a "Question" on the Spanish War. This inquiry was made in the names of twelve authors, who included Nancy Cunard, Heinrich Mann, Ivor Montagu and Stephen Spender.

Presumably these writers had never read the French critic Julien Benda, who nine years earlier had prophesied in a famous book, *La Trahison des Clercs*, that mankind was heading for the greatest war which the world had ever experienced. It would come, he wrote, because Europe's intellectual leaders had departed from their supreme function of disseminating impartial wisdom; they had begun to "take sides" and, by adopting materialistic values, to represent evil as good.

The "Question" posed by the *Left Review* followed precisely the direction that M. Benda had deplored.

"It is clear to many of us throughout the whole world that now, as certainly never before, we are determined, or compelled, to take sides. The equivocal attitude, the Ivory Tower, the paradoxical, the ironic detachment, will no longer do. This is the question we are asking you: *Are you for, or against, the legal Government and the People of Republican Spain? Are you for, or against, Franco and Fascism?* . . . . Writers and Poets, we wish to print your answers."

The subsequent replies, not surprisingly, were mainly of the kind which the editors desired to publish. They appeared, with small additional sections headed "Neutral?" and "Against", in a mustard-coloured booklet, *Authors Take Sides on the Spanish War*, which opened with twenty-three pages from Spanish Government supporters.

In December a brief review of this pamphlet appeared in the Quaker magazine, *The Friend*.

"Probably most of our readers," wrote their critic, "will share the opinion of Vera Brittain, classified as 'Neutral?'—but why? In the course of this she says: 'I hold war to be a crime against humanity, whoever fights it and against whomever it is fought. I believe in liberty, democracy, free thought and free speech. I detest Fascism and all that it stands for, but I do not believe we shall destroy it by fighting it. And I do not feel that we serve either the Spanish people or the cause of civilisation by continuing to make Spain the battle-ground for a new series of Wars of Religion.'"

But the most forthright neutral, though described as "Unclassified" and given a place to himself inside the yellow cover, was George Bernard Shaw.

"In Spain," he wrote, "both the Right and the Left so thoroughly disgraced themselves . . . in trying to govern their country before the Right revolted, that it is impossible to say which of them is the more incompetent. . . . I as a Communist am generally on the Left; but that does not commit me to support the British Party Parliament system and its Continental imitations, of which I have the lowest opinion.

"At present the capitalist powers seem to have secured a victory for the General by what they call their non-interference, meaning their very active interference on his side; but it is unlikely that the last word will be with him. Meanwhile I shall not shout about it."

(9)

In January 1937 I had begun to work systematically on the biography of Winifred. So far I had only produced a scaffolding of chapters and a large quantity of unorganised notes.

Night after night I sat in my study with her work spread over my desk—typescripts, proofs, volumes of novels and stories, letters embodying her concern for South Africa's black population which showed her to have been a young, inquiring forerunner of Michael Scott and Trevor Huddleston. Often I experienced the sensation, familiar after the war, of being left stranded by the tide when the full sea flood had carried so much that mattered away.

All publishable material had now been extracted from her papers

177

and made available to her public. Not only had *South Riding* taken the critics by storm and earned the James Tait Black Memorial Prize for the best novel of 1936; in April *Letters to a Friend* would appear and, like a speaking voice suddenly stilled, leave a silence so deep that the reader seemed to fall into it headlong. A volume of short stories, *Pavements at Anderby*, which I had edited with the help of our Somerville contemporary, Hilda Reid, would follow in the autumn. Now I had only to persuade Winifred's publishers to issue her work in a collected edition—a purpose which, owing to the publishing problems created by the Second World War, I have yet to achieve.

As executor and biographer, I had still to go through her large correspondence, and soon discovered that even the best-intentioned deputy has difficult problems of tact to solve.

"I know one or two of her correspondents," I wrote to a friend, "who would just writhe at the thought of my even seeing their letters. Nearly all the great seem to have written to her—even Shaw and Wells—and though some of these letters deal with private matters, I think they should be kept for the importance of their writers. Time, in the end, reduces all private things to history, and it seems to me pure vandalism to destroy what posterity will treasure."

Mrs. Holtby, like other efficient persons guided by common sense, was a wholesale destroyer of letters. Generously she lent me the few from Winifred which she had kept, but when I came to describe the early Yorkshire background, I found the lack of family material a serious handicap.

Years afterwards I felt much sympathy for the historian G. M. Young, who wrote the life of Stanley Baldwin. After Baldwin's death it was alleged in the Press that a member of the family had made a bonfire of personal correspondence, covering the events of fifty-three years.

As my search into Winifred's life progressed, I found that there were four main problems to be faced. The first concerned her status as a writer, which I must neither over-estimate nor underrate. Because she had been not only an author but a saint with a passion for justice, she was peculiarly liable to disparagement by the "official" type of literary mind.

Official bodies, whether cultural or political, do not like crusaders. Their warmth and ardour, their deep convictions and keen concern for the victims of power, are inconvenient to the slow-moving caution always characteristic of orthodox authority. Even when their causes have succeeded—as in time all worthwhile causes do—the distributors of conventional rewards prefer to regard them as

178

persons without discrimination in the arts or professions which they have made their own.

In the end history sometimes achieves a kind of rough justice. John Bunyan, that doughty crusader for righteousness whom his learned contemporaries despised, was finally admitted to the ranks of "English Men of Letters" three hundred years after his death; Tolstoi and Dickens received from the twentieth century a warmth of appreciation denied by their less revolutionary contemporaries in the nineteenth. But how many significant figures in art or science vanish during the winnowing process because their own epoch has rejected them?

Apart from estimating Winifred's status as a writer, I had also to register an impartial judgment on a person very close to me whom I had loved and admired. Only the passage of time could make such a judgment possible, though G.'s occasional comments, with their greater detachment, helped me to perceive and assess.

"She was one of the sanest people, most completely expressive of 'sweetness and light', that I would ever expect to come across," he wrote me when I was already engrossed in research. But a periodic lack of confidence puzzled him, and he added: "I suspect great sexual diffidence passed off as a joke on 'outsizes'."

After my book had been published, a letter from Virginia Woolf confirmed his observation.

"I feel that, thanks to you, I know her much better than I did before. I was puzzled by something about her when we met. . . . I felt that she was oddly uncertain about something important—perhaps you'll understand. I think I see now what it was. And having never read her books because I felt this, I'm now going to.

"I am very grateful to you for giving me this fresh insight. It's so seldom that a biography does that, but yours does. More than ever it makes me feel, just as I did when I read a book of her letters, that she was only at the beginning of a life that held all sorts of possibilities not only for her but for the rest of us."

I had thirdly to consider how far I was entitled to cause pain or annoyance to Winifred's friends, whose private contacts with her must be exposed to public appraisal in order that she might be better understood. Her contemporary "Bill", whose unpropitious relationship with her I had analysed in the book, especially raised this problem, and though I concealed his name, my estimate of his influence on Winifred subsequently produced some protests.

No biographer, I concluded, could satisfy every reader; the interests of truth must be the only criterion. If the truth about the dead could not be established without sacrificing the living, then the living, however regretfully, must be sacrificed.

Finally I asked myself how far I ought to bring my own relationship with Winifred into a book designed as the story of her life and work. At first, foreseeing criticism from her friends if I appeared at all, I decided to leave myself out entirely, but here again G. helped me by introducing a perspective which was not theirs. He realised that the biography, if it was to be more than the slick "memorial volume" for which so many people had clamoured, must be a study not only of Winifred and her epoch, but of friendship itself. To the extent that this theme required my presence, and no further, I must bring myself in.

It was he who suggested the title under which the book appeared in 1940—*Testament of Friendship*, inspired by his recollection of Cicero's *De Amicitia*.

(10)

In May 1937 we moved from 19 Glebe Place to an even more attractive part of Chelsea.

After Winifred's death we decided to reconstruct our lives in another house which would not hold persistent memories, and I looked hopefully for an unpretentious alternative. But our new home was chosen the moment that G. saw a "Lease For Sale" notice outside 2 Cheyne Walk.

This house—now scheduled as an "ancient monument"—stood at the east end of the long terrace facing the river where some of Britain's best known writers and artists had lived. They included George Eliot, Sir Arthur Sullivan, D. G. Rossetti, A. C. Swinburne, Elizabeth Gaskell, J. M. Whistler and John Turner.

Number 2, a typical eighteenth-century dwelling with one or two rooms on each floor, was tall rather than large; it acquired a vicarious opulence from the impressive neighbours which divided it from Chelsea Manor Street. Like several of the others it was put up about 1720 by Sir Hans Sloane, the famous scientist and speculative builder of his day, whose ornate tombstone, dominating the highway, survived the destruction of Chelsea Old Church in 1941.

The "speculative" quality of the house appeared in the banisters, adorned on the first floor with finely carved fruit and flowers which became rough-and-ready on the second floor, and disappeared altogether on the third and fourth. In the tiny front garden two pink prunus trees flanked an ancient damson; at the back a strong luxuriant vine climbed an old red-brick wall.

To any housewife this "period" residence, with its relentless staircases and large basement kitchen, threatened nightmares of inconvenience, but its beauty reduced these practical objections to birdseed. Its perfectly-proportioned rooms, looking south across the Thames to Battersea Park, brought a sense of serenity combined with a consciousness of sunlight that I have known nowhere else. Once G. had seen it, he refused to look at any other house.

We moved in just before the Coronation of George VI. Instead of attending this revised function, we went to Laurence Housman's play *Victoria Regina*. Its beautiful *décor* and costumes, and the gay but sagacious dialogue, caught London's imagination and fitly celebrated the doomed cultural richness of the vanishing thirties.

At 2 Cheyne Walk, John and Shirley acquired the first conscious memories of their adventurous childhood. From their earliest years they had met and mingled with all our guests, ranging from Cabinet Ministers and international writers to members of local Labour Parties and visitors of all ranks from India, Africa and China. They never developed a superstitious belief in the superiority of a white skin, and they sharpened their wits on every type of literary and political argument.

After the long war-time separation in which they reached adolescence, our family discussions were sometimes less amicable but remained always vital. They supplied the basic experience which turned both children into articulate human beings.

(11)

That summer G. and I set out together for a twelve days' walking-tour in Cornwall which proved to be one of the happiest holidays that we ever shared.

Already the international portents were darkening through successive weeks of radiant skies. In July a new conflict between Japan and China had brought fighting in Shanghai and official protests to both belligerents on the bombing of open towns. After the Coronation Stanley Baldwin had retired in favour of Neville Chamberlain, that successful Minister of Health with a sincere passion for social reform who saw Europe as a more troublesome version of his native Birmingham, and orientals as "lesser breeds" which impinged on his consciousness as indirectly as the inhabitants of Mars.

But the evils which might arise from the limitations of human vision were not yet immediate. Our tranquil mood and the serene consciousness of being completely at one matched the summer weather; our pleasant undisturbing conversations subsequently appeared in nostalgic contrast to the anxious discussions which the near approach of war was to precipitate a year later in south-west France.

In Cornwall we chose four centres—Launceston, Bodmin, Boscastle and Bude—and a fifth, Bideford, in Devon. From these we walked over the surrounding country, travelling from one town to another by train or bus in order to avoid long stretches of highroad. In brilliant weather the richly-coloured flowers and leaves of early autumn jewelled the lanes and cliffs; everywhere we breathed the hot intoxicating scent of newly-reaped corn. Even the bleak expanse of Bodmin Moor—the *Jamaica Inn* country—seemed kindly in the sun. Beside a stream which ran through a wood on the hither side of the small county town, we sat talking for a long afternoon while the sunshine cast dappled leafy shadows across the pleasant glade.

Three weeks later I carried these English memories to the United States for my second lecture tour, which took me away till Christmas from our newly-established home.

(12)

On September 18th, 1937, I sailed from Southampton in the *Georgic*. Four days earlier President Masaryk had died in Czechoslovakia, fortunate in missing the future eclipse of the State which he had built.

Familiarity with my manager's routine had removed the apprehensions which preceded the first tour, but I travelled reluctantly to my forty lectures without the comforting reassurance of G.'s presence. He accepted my departure with greater equanimity, for he had just begun one of his major works, *The History of the Political Philosophers*. Five days after I sailed, the New York firm of McGraw Hill accepted his scheme, and when I reached America I found them enthusiastic about the book.

Within a few hours of my landing, publicity encompassed me like a warm shower-bath, for I was the only Macmillan author on tour that autumn. I found my audiences really interested in only one subject. Whether I was officially talking on books and authors, war and peace, or social revolution, the discussion always returned like a boomerang to the Abdication. A supposed likeness to "Wally", based solely on slight proportions and dark hair with a centre parting, largely accounted for the good attendances at all my lectures.

Behind this universal preoccupation with the troubles of Royalty, a serious-minded America anxiously debated the drift of Europe towards war. Its concern, and the not-yet vanished possibility of preventing war at the highest levels, was probably responsible for the ten minutes' private talk with President Roosevelt which represented the climax of my second tour. This short interview, unforgettable in both human and political terms, followed a mid-December luncheon at the White House which I attended as Mrs. Roosevelt's guest.

In my book *Thrice a Stranger* I have described these events, and recorded how Eleanor Roosevelt's duchess-like dignity at first inspired me with an alarm which disappeared as I came to know her better and to understand the deep sincerity of her approach to human problems. But when I wrote my book immediately after returning to England, I was unaware of a fragment of history then undisclosed which in retrospect gives my brief contact with the President a special significance.

It is now known that, throughout this period, President Roosevelt was considering how far the United States could use its influence to reconcile the gathering conflicts of Europe. For him the chief obstacle to such an endeavour apparently lay in the isolationist Middle West and the still widespread American suspicion of European entanglements. Early in October he had made in Chicago his famous "quarantine" speech which contained the following significant passage:

"When an epidemic of physical disease starts to spread, the community approves and joins in a quarantine of the patients in order to protect the health of the community. . . . We are determined to keep out of war, yet we cannot insure ourselves against the disastrous effects of war and the dangers of involvement."

Travelling through Indiana and Ohio immediately after his speech, I had compared the anti-Roosevelt sentiments of these States with the warm endorsement of the Eastern seaboard. On the President's face, when I saw him, this struggle appeared to be written; the pale, drawn countenance behind the mercurial smile impressed me even more than the large immobile figure supported by a huge arm-chair behind an outsize desk.

"A great man, with one of the most charming expressions I have seen on the face of any human person, and exquisite manners," I wrote to G. after the President had interrupted a dispatch to Japan on the sinking of the American gun-boat *Panay* in order to question a visiting lecturer on her experience of Middle Western isolationism.

Today the President's inquiry suggests that he was seeking information from every available source about the possible effect of his interventionist policy on American opinion. But in the end it was not his own country which frustrated an initiative that might have changed the course of history.

Contemporary historians such as Sir Winston Churchill and Lord Templewood have recorded that, in January 1938, President Roosevelt made a proposal for a general peace conference which Neville Chamberlain rejected without even consulting the Foreign Affairs Committee of his Cabinet.

(13)

This second tour differed from the first only because it took me, for two weeks, through the South-west and Deep South, with its luscious flowers, intoxicating scents, and spectacular sunsets.

Train schedules were hard; even today the backward railway services south of the Mason-Dixon Line reflect the economic consequences of the Civil War. But the lovely cities never yet revisited—Tulsa in Oklahoma, on the shallow Arkansas River; fabulous New Orleans with its green palms and white oleander in paved court-yards; Tuscaloosa set amid the virgin woodlands of Alabama; the spreading city-garden of Atlanta beneath copper-hued oaks and golden maples—made temporary fatigue a small price to pay for so much remembered beauty.

From the Louisiana swamps I sent my mother a handful of the grey feathery moss which festoons the forest trees; fifteen years afterwards I was to find its surprising toughness, like leathery string, unaffected by time. At Atlanta I failed to see Margaret Mitchell, who vanished from the city before my visit. Had I known that her phenomenal career was to be ended by a street accident in 1949, I should have tracked down the elusive author of *Gone With The Wind* with greater persistence.

Before I returned home these colourful travels had been shadowed yet again by sudden death, for in October Dick Sheppard, the friend of a year whose example had changed my spiritual perspective, finally succumbed to his chronic illness.

The first half of my travels had been cheered by pleasant thoughts of our ripening friendship. At exactly the right psychological moment, when G.'s waving figure had disappeared and I descended to my cabin in the *Georgic* feeling deeply dejected because I should not see him again for three months, I received a farewell cable from Dick, though I had never told him the name of my ship.

Soon afterwards he accepted an invitation to stand for the Rectorship of Glasgow University, where his fellow candidates included Winston Churchill and Professor J. B. S. Haldane. At the

184

outset of the campaign, he explained his convictions in a letter to the *New Statesman*:

"It is my belief that the Spirit of Life now requires of every man that he should call his soul his own and witness quite simply to the truth as he knows it. . . . All I want to appeal for is this response from those who have hitherto had hopes that a way of avoiding war might be discovered through social and political means which did not entail their complete personal devotion and severance from the existing so-called 'order'. Pacifists must live within that 'order' not as baffled idealists but debonair and courageous—as rebels against the world as it is. . . . If they will, truly I believe the miracle of peace may even now be achieved."

Travelling to St. Louis on October 24th, I opened the *Chicago Sunday Tribune* to find two remarkable pictures of Sir Oswald Mosley. The first showed him addressing a crowd at Liverpool from the roof of a radio van; in the second, struck by a hostile stone, he was lying sprawled among the loud-speakers with his hand to his head.

Savage doctrines, it seemed, were already breeding savagery in retaliation. I turned to the letterpress and there found a totally different item. Under the caption "Pacifist Beats Churchill in Glasgow U. Election", it told me that on the previous day Dick Sheppard had been chosen as Lord Rector, polling 538 votes to Churchill's 281.

Throughout the journey to St. Louis, where I cabled him, the heavy train seemed a celestial chariot wafted on air. Characteristically, his warm acknowledgment of my cable ended with the words: "As my constituents hadn't seen or heard me, I romped home."

Before this letter reached me, his light had been extinguished. But the Alabama newspapers, absorbed in speculations about the Windsors' proposed visit to the United States, failed to report that on the morning of All Saints' Eve a Canon of St. Paul's had been found dead in his study chair with a half-finished letter before him. Only when a long journey involved a night in New York did I open a waiting packet of family letters and confront this heavy news.

"I have just learned of Dick Sheppard's death and am over-whelmed by it," wrote G. "A dear, great man—one of the greatest that has come my way this five years. . . . Five years—and how much richer we should all have been. The Devil seems out reaping this year and especially among our friends."

Like the rest of England ten days earlier, I too felt overwhelmed; for a few hours the foundations of my work, so lately reinvigorated by his single-minded faith, seemed to crumble and disappear. To all who cared for spiritual values, the shock of Dick Sheppard's death to his own country was comparable to the blow dealt to India a decade later by Gandhi's.

"God certainly seems to have retired from the scene at the moment and left the Devil to do his worst with the big battalions," I replied to G. from the depths of dismay. Dick's life had represented England's only powerful challenge to the impulse of death in society. Who would take his place?

At first, struggling to assimilate this fresh disaster, I found the facts of his death almost unbearable. To die all alone, with no friend beside him, when so many people had loved him! Certainly there was One who had said: "When thou passest through the waters, I will be with thee", but being so much further from Him than Dick, I forgot that for the true believer the river of death may also be the waters of comfort.

(14)

From G.'s letters and my mother's, I sought those fragments of consolation which alone sustain us after some unexpected blow. For two and a half days, G. told me, the people of London had passed by Dick's coffin in St. Martin's. He had attended the farewell service in the church—"all those clerics non-committal, using generalisations like blankets, but the service effective".

From Trafalgar Square he had followed the funeral procession along the Thames Embankment to St. Paul's Cathedral—"with police holding the traffic . . . people standing hatless, the police on point duty saluting; most touching of all, Thames barges and tugs, and the men coming up on board and taking off their hats. Up Ludgate Hill to the thousands, four deep, standing round the churchyard—into the Cathedral crowded to the doors, all that immense area; never since the King's funeral, and this without pomp or commerce, have I seen anything like it."

After describing the service and the crowd flowing out afterwards "into the London that he had made his own", G. asked of himself and our troubled epoch some implicit questions which went to the root of Christian experience.

"Nothing I think is more extraordinary than the way in which this man had power. Those who utterly disagreed with him were swayed by him. Those who most thought him wrong, dangerous, almost treasonable, conspired to honour him. . . . And one is left thinking about it—very seriously.

"I suggest that we have now to find *both* a discipline for the few *and* a way for the world. I suggest further that the analogy is extraordinarily close with early Christian history—there again the fights of democrats and aristocrats and followers of this and that dictator, all looking for salvation in force and all men of blood. And the issue of their actions increasing chaos. The cradling of the new civilisation not their work, but that of the pacifist church."

Some years afterwards, when I attempted in a novel to show what might have happened to a character comparable with Dick's if he had lived through the Second World War, Canon C. E. Raven sent me a letter containing the phrase *"felix opportunitate mortis"*— "happy in the chance of his death". Another year, with its burden of the Austrian invasion and the Munich crisis, might have found Dick's prestige as England's leading Christian assailed by the hysterical accusations of fear, and though his spirit would never have failed he would have suffered acutely in body and mind.

His passing in 1937 appears today as a tempering of the wind to the "shorn lamb" whose domestic life already lacked those private consolations which help us to endure public criticism. He departed at the height of his incomparable popularity, leaving us who lacked his spiritual gifts to confront the problems intensified by both his leadership and its loss.

When a leader dies his followers must become leaders themselves, trained by his example just as those imperfect men, the twelve Apostles, were trained by the example of Christ. Only thus does a leader differ from a dictator, and a great crusade distinguish itself from an ephemeral campaign.

The task of writing Dick's biography fell to Ellis Roberts, whose comprehensive study, based on painstaking research, appeared in 1942. In spite of its conscientious attention to detail it was not a well-balanced book, for it emphasised Dick's tragedy at the expense of his charm. But one memorable passage underlined G.'s first impression of the effect of his death upon contemporary London.

"My wife was motoring along Upper Regent Street, her mind full of Dick, when she realised that she had passed a group of out-of-work singers . . . and, on an impulse, gave the man who was collecting a ten-shilling note. The man looked surprised and she found herself saying, 'Take it in memory of Dick Sheppard'. To her astonishment the man burst into tears."

In the United States Dick was less well-known, but I who had personally mattered to him so little struggled on with my lectures in that autumn of 1937 feeling that the sun had gone down. How implacable a foe death had been for the past two decades! It was the universal enemy, of course, challenging one's work and perpetually threatening to write *Finis* against achievement. But from those near to me it had taken not merely the old whose term was ending but, in Carlyle's phrase, "the eloquent, the young, the beautiful and brave".

Into my mind as I travelled through New England came some lines by an author whose name escaped me, which I had read soon after the war:

"Behold, my God, I am a little thing.
 My life is little, compassed round with death;
 I am too weak to fight Thee, or to fling
 Back in Thy face Thy mocking gift of breath. . . ."

But no, I thought, as night eclipsed the deeply indented Connecticut coast. That impotent defiance is true neither of me nor of my dead. No life is little in terms of its potential accomplishment, however limited the sphere; and if God exists—a dubious proposition, but one that I dare not rule out—He does not mock us with His gift of experience even though it be short like Edward's and Winifred's, or shadowed with bereavements like mine. If the baffling scheme of things is ordained by Him, He must still have work for His servants Winifred Holtby and Dick Sheppard, and in His many mansions even my poor father may find a place.

(15)

I sailed home in time to attend the first night of the *South Riding* film at the London Pavilion, where Winifred's name appeared among the brilliant sky-signs dominating Piccadilly Circus.

According to the standards then expected by film-goers, Victor Saville had made a memorable picture, renewing Winifred's spirit through the candid Yorkshire scenes rather than by an over-romantic treatment of her moving but astringent story. A more realistic film could be made today, showing Sarah Burton and Robert Carne as the star-crossed middle-aged semi-lovers whom Winifred created, and depicting Alderman Mrs. Beddows as a patriarchal seventy-four instead of the glamorous sixty-six presented by young-looking Marie Löhr.

I brought back to England another lecture invitation for 1940 from the Leigh Bureau, and with the Macmillan Company's contract for *Testament of Friendship* carried another for a short immediate book on the American scene as I had known it since 1925.

During my journeys through the South I had suddenly perceived that a fascinating travelogue could be written which not only contrasted the forty-five States that I had now visited, but compared the epochs of prosperity, depression and normality that I had known. Ever since I first lived in the United States I had realised how little we in England understood the American people; this story would provide an opportunity for interpretation. It would also help to finance the research still needed for my biography.

I found the Macmillan Company attracted by the suggested travelbook, which we agreed to call *Thrice a Stranger*. It finally turned out not to be "short" at all, but a volume of 120,000 words. The £1,000 it eventually earned "carried" the writing of *Testament of Friendship* for a long period, though like its predecessor it encountered misfortune by appearing in the middle of the Munich crisis. Ironically these royalties came chiefly from England, where international tension did not stop the sale of two editions before publication. By September the American public had given up reading, and had its collective ears glued to the radio at meals, on car rides, and even in bed.

From the beginning of 1938, political events made a too-convulsive background for literary composition. In February Anthony Eden's resignation as Foreign Secretary, which Churchill has since described as a consequence of Chamberlain's rebuff to President Roosevelt, was then attributed to the vexed course of contemporary negotiations with Italy. But the events of the following month soon eclipsed the sensation created by this manœuvre.

On Saturday March 12th, with the unadorned brevity appropriate to sudden disaster, my diary recorded: "Germany marched into Austria", and next day continued: "Germany annexed Austria. Hitler appeared in Linz and Vienna". By Monday I was noting, more subjectively, "the oppression of the bright beautiful days of this amazing March when the international situation is so precarious".

It had been precarious since early February, when Hitler summoned the Austrian Chancellor, Dr. Schuschnigg, to Berchtesgaden in order to demand that the leading Austrian Nazi, Seyss-Inquart, be made a member of the Cabinet. The Chancellor's submission had not prevented Austria's conversion into a virtual Nazi province, which now increased the epidemic of fear spreading throughout Europe.

On March 16th the new American Ambassador, Joseph P. Kennedy, spoke grave words during a Pilgrims' Dinner held at this inauspicious moment to welcome him.

"Good neighbourhood is not a one-way street," he concluded.

"The decline in international morality has alarmed our people in recent years. . . . My country has decided that it must stand on its own feet, at least until regard for treaty obligations has again become fashionable."

Immediately after the rape of Austria, the continuous trickle of refugees who had been coming from Central Europe since the rise of Hitler turned into the flood which Britain was to sustain for the next decade. A clipping by chance preserved since June 1938 from *The Times* advertisement columns contains five successive notices from would-be exiles with addresses in Vienna.

"Three Children's Doctors (Non-Aryan), with large practice, seek position."

"Two Building Constructors (Non-Aryan) . . . seek jobs."

"Viennese Brother and Sister of good Jewish family, seek work."

"Viennese Cutter-out (Male) . . . seeks post any country."

"Viennese Doctor of Philosophy, 24, Jew . . . seeks position as Tutor."

(16)

In June the International P.E.N. held its annual Congress of writers in the most vulnerable of Europe's threatened citadels. This summer G. had again gone to Central Europe on another fact-finding journey that might well, he thought, be the last of its kind which an itinerant philosopher could undertake for years. He joined the P.E.N. Congress at Prague, and sent me some vignettes of the beautiful doomed city just before long night blotted it out from the West.

"The Czechs are optimists—on a superficial judgment much less alarmed than London. Last night I went to the *Romeo and Juliet* play (a few war-planes overhead!) amid the so-green and gold illuminated trees of the Waldstein Palace—that Waldstein, in the days of Richelieu, who aiming at the throne of Bohemia was murdered by his General Piccolomini. What a background! . . . And beyond, illuminated Prague."

At this play the Czech writer, Karel Čapek, appeared for one last happy interval before his death the following December.

The Secretary of the Czech Social Democrats, G. reported, had told him that they would benefit from the concessions proposed for the Sudeten—"which perhaps throws some doubt upon their worth". Senator Dundr had shown a pleasant confidence in the future; there would be no war, no revolution, though British support was of course essential. The Chairman of the Czech Agrarians,

Beran, in an interview of nearly an hour had been equally optimistic.

Only Jaksch of the German Social Democrats, and Otto Strasser, the brother of Gregor Strasser, had prophesied war—"perhaps in August over the Minorities question. They also were sure that within six months of war Germany would break up from within. They were nice fellows but I doubt their political judgment."

Czech optimism, like Czech miscalculation, was doubtless an important counter in Hitler's game of skill. Today it seems incredible that so many "nice fellows" could have been wrong about so much.

From Prague G. went on to Vienna, where he now found the Monarchists being persecuted with the Jews, and *Der Stürmer* on show. Except for two great flags in front of the Rathaus, he saw not a banner from the Austrian border to the capital so recently occupied by Hitler.

On the way to the Hungarian frontier he asked for whom the flags were flying at half-mast, and was told "the Treaty of the Petit Trianon". The editors of the *Hungarian Quarterly* cheerfully expected war, and rescue from the Germans by the British. On this series of journeys one of the few realistic comments came from a Viennese Jewess in Rome to whom he offered sympathy.

"We went through the Red Sea, and I suppose we shall go through the Brown Mud."

Before G.'s return I went to a much-discussed play, Norman Macowan's *Glorious Morning*, attended the Canterbury Festival to see *Christ's Comet* by Christopher Hassall, and afterwards visited Dick Sheppard's grave. To G. in Rome I described the square of emerald lawn within the cloisters, a framework of grey stone beneath the cathedral tower. Two vases of delphiniums and sweet peas rested upon the spot which covered Dick's mortal remains.

How quiet that grey pile—to bear only five years later the scars from Nazi bombs—appeared beside the troubled countries of which G. had written; how fitting it seemed that Dick's spectacular pilgrimage should end in this peaceful acre! Above the storm-clouds gathering over Europe his faith in God's love shone like a beacon star, often dimmed but never eclipsed, which symbolised the one hope of threatened mankind in a foundering world.

(17)

Later that year G. and I had arranged to spend three weeks in the Basque country at St. Jean de Luz. A holiday never seemed to us complete unless it took us abroad, but this time we made a more political choice than usual.

In August 1938 the Spanish War was still in progress, and all the country south of the Bidassoa River had fallen into Franco's hands. Though the Labour Party, like Bernard Shaw, constantly protested that "non-intervention" really meant support for Franco, the Non-Intervention Committee had relapsed into coma. In the spring a series of successful attacks by the rebels had culminated in the bombing of Barcelona. Franco's early victory now seemed certain, though Dr. Negrin, the Republican Prime Minister, had stated in a policy declaration on May 2nd: "We will fight to the bitter end."

At St. Jean de Luz the shadow of the Civil War seemed to lengthen from across the frontier. We found the little town almost empty of foreign visitors, but filled with Basques and Spaniards who had settled there after war began.

"It seems queer," I wrote to my mother, "to sit on a balcony looking across a valley of green trees and white houses to the cloudy ramparts of the Pyrenees which mark the Spanish frontier, and think of all the tragedy still being enacted on the other side."

G. found St. Jean too melancholy for his taste, and after a week he suggested that we should move a few miles north and sample Biarritz as a brief respite from politics. I was not enthusiastic, but since St. Jean had proved depressing I agreed to migrate. We soon discovered, in that critical year, that even Biarritz had no diversion to offer.

The American newspapers described Europe's situation as "more difficult than at any time during the last twenty years", and the weather in France matched the news; thunder, heavy gloom, downpours of rain and a driving gale followed one another in quick succession. Great rollers came in from the Bay of Biscay carrying bitter winds; the waves broke on the rocks and crashed against the hotel. One evening a copper-coloured sunset between purple clouds over the desolate sea suggested that the flames of war were already consuming Europe.

As we watched the rolling breakers, G. put to me repeatedly one agitating question.

"What are you going to do? If war comes, what are you going to do?"

Till then it had not occurred to me that one did anything about danger except confront and endure it. I now learned that to him, in the darkening international night, this stoical acceptance seemed highly unintelligent. When he put his question, I knew that he was not concerned about ourselves. He meant: "What are you going to do for John and Shirley? Shall we leave them to share our fate in Europe, or take them to America, our second country?"

At ten-and-a-half and eight, the children were too young to go to the United States unless I took them. To this, even though I might be able to put them in the care of others and quickly return to England, I felt most reluctant to agree. I knew that by temperament I was a physical coward; and the only way for a coward to conquer his cowardice is to stand his ground and look perils in the face.

G.'s moral problem was totally different, for he was immune from personal fear. He had been unperturbed by bombardment in Madrid, then considered very alarming, and was to remain equally unmoved in worse future ordeals. His political perspicacity told him (correctly, as we realised when the Gestapo List was published in 1945) that neither he nor I was likely to survive for long if the Nazis won the war or, at any stage of it, landed in England.

He had been the international Treasurer of the Burned Books Committee and an active supporter of the Spanish Republic; I had formulated, in my writings, a philosophy which was anathema to Nazi ideology, and I was now identified with Dick Sheppard's movement. Although I never knew until I toured Germany in 1947 that the burned books had included my autobiography, it was clear that if the war went badly for Britain we should both be "for it". We also realised that the children of political victims were likely to suffer—as they subsequently did suffer in their thousands on the occupied Continent—a fate from which no sacrifice of scruples could be too great to save them.

To G. my moral doubts seemed trivial compared with the children's danger, which in his opinion wholly justified their education in the United States. Of this he was in favour for its own sake, since he loved America as a man loves a beautiful woman who is no less attractive for sometimes being a little spoiled. And as a rational opponent of impulsive choices, he believed that only distance and detachment would enable us, if war came, to see where and how we could most effectively bear witness to our own convictions.

Thus we approached a deeply emotional problem from conflicting standpoints, involving a difference of opinion such as we have never since experienced. Because G. was sure of the right course while I remained uncertain he had his way, though I still recall as a physical pain the violation of the instinctive judgment—described by a contemporary as "sheer romanticism"—which ceaselessly cried, No!

When the autumn crisis deepened towards Munich and silent Londoners knelt before the Cenotaph in Whitehall to pray that Chamberlain would save them from war, we took the bewildered but philosophic children for a brief visit to the United States. If war broke out we intended to leave them in American schools, arrange with friends to care for them in the holidays, and return home as soon as possible.

While the issue remained uncertain, we stayed at the small hotel opposite Columbia University where G. and I had lived in 1926. Then, when the risk of immediate war was over, we brought the children back.

Owing to the dangers inflicted upon them by their return, it might well seem that this was a foolish decision. So, throughout the war, it appeared to me. But now, in time's perspective, I realise that we were right. In the event we did lose John and Shirley for three years, but after that period, though nothing could atone for the loss of continuity, our family life was restored. A total absence of five years would have meant an irreparable break.

(18)

Throughout the winter following Munich I remained, like many others, so stunned by the sudden crescendo of international tension that hardly a memory of that dismal Christmas remains. By the spring, G. was already on his way back to the United States. An invitation to deliver a course of lectures at the American University in Washington had followed our autumn journey, and his *History of the Political Philosophers* was awaiting proof correction in New York.

"We go to U.S.A. in much the same way as other people go to Brighton," I commented in my diary, for this was G.'s thirty-third Atlantic crossing.

But though he sailed on a bright February morning, I felt even more than the usual depression when his ship, the *Queen Mary*, slid smoothly out of sight. The apprehensions of that spring were too acute for any wife to welcome the consciousness of a wide ocean between her husband and herself.

Passionate controversies aroused by the Munich settlement continued to create strained relations within families and political parties. One newspaper coined the phrase "crisis-teria" to describe the universal mood in which nobody dared to look ahead for more than a few weeks at a time.

A main source of apprehension in the New Year had been Hitler's speech to the Reichstag, scheduled for January 30th. Ten days before, an Underground advertisement of Madame Tussaud's Waxworks Exhibition showed pictures of Stalin, Hitler and Mussolini above the caption: "The only place in the world where they all live together at peace." On the evening of the speech G. and I had listened to the broadcast from the Reichstag until we could no longer endure the raucous, provocative voice, but subsequent analysis showed its general tone to have been more pacific than anyone expected.

The respite was only temporary: within a fortnight rumours and their consequences had begun again. Just after G.'s departure a Sunday newspaper reported Roosevelt's return from a fishing holiday owing to "ominous reports". So far no clear indication had appeared of what these might be, but throughout Britain air-raid precautions were now going ahead in every large city, and a January campaign launched by the Prime Minister to enrol volunteers for National Service had turned by April into an announcement of early conscription.

In March I realised a long-standing ambition to meet Compton Mackenzie, whose early books had helped me, a young V.A.D. nurse in revolt against the limited vision of Army matrons, to endure "the war to end war". At a P.E.N. dinner I sat beside him, and questioned him about the "lighted door" in his novel *Guy and Pauline*.

"During the war," I told him, "when I gave up Somerville for nursing, that 'lighted door' always symbolised Oxford for me. Was it really in Oxford?"

"It isn't in Oxford in the book," he said, "but it *was* an Oxford door."

The original, I learned, had been in Worcester College, and the Provost's daughter was the model for "Pauline".

After its long preparation my own book, *Testament of Friendship*, was now close to the final version.

I began the last of several drafts on March 20th, and was destined to write it from start to finish against a background of mounting tension.

Often I sat up until the small hours, periodically dropping the manuscript to wonder how I could make the future tolerable for John and Shirley. Sometimes I blamed myself for their existence; I had known one war, and the Treaty of Versailles, which I had often criticised for its vindictiveness, had warned me that unless it were revised there would probably be another.

Early in 1938 the newspapers had reported the death of Will Dyson, whose famous 1919 cartoon—"I think I hear a child crying"—had shown Clemenceau and Lloyd George leaving the Hall of Mirrors at Versailles while a naked baby labelled "Class 1940" shivered sobbing behind a pillar. Dyson had not lived to see his prophecy fulfilled, but that fulfilment was coming none the less.

Because Roland died of wounds at Louvencourt, John and Shirley had escaped belonging to "Class 1940", but the air-raids in the Spanish War had suggested that even "Class 1950" could not count on survival. I had meant to make such a promising life for them, buttressed by the security which all children need, but my work for peace, like my books, seemed now to be threatened with ruin.

These periods of defeatism were only occasional, for many people needed help more urgently than the children. Much of my correspondence with G. that spring concerned a Czech-Jewish woman dentist whom he had met the previous summer on the train from Prague to Vienna. When he left for America I took over the prolonged negotiations with the Home Office and Foreign Office which he had begun in the hope of bringing her to Britain.

From rumours and rescuers I escaped for John's half-term at the Downs School in the Malvern hills, where we had now sent him. During the past half year he had grown into so responsive a companion, with such a keen enjoyment of life, that I missed him hourly after the school train left Paddington, while Shirley, as always, roamed the house like a lost soul without him.

We spent Sunday morning exploring the hillsides, where the strong champagne-like air was brightened but hardly warmed by the cold brilliance of the February sun. On the highest hill, near an historic site known as the British Camp, John saw a finch with a green head, and in the village we passed a farm orchard where the coral-tipped ears of baby pigs gleamed like gems amid the trees.

He shared the absurd happiness which these trifles brought me, and I returned to London convinced that we had been right to send him away from distraught headlines and screaming posters into the peaceful normality of the countryside.

I returned to find Shirley with a high temperature, and the doctor advised a tonsils operation. I had just arranged for this to be done immediately after G.'s return, when Hitler marched into Prague.

(19)

His act of aggression on March 15, 1939, followed days of uneasiness, which had begun on the 10th with Slovakian demands for separation and autonomy. The consequent crisis ruined, amid so much else, a Queen's Hall mass meeting arranged for March 18th to celebrate the collection of over a million signatures to a National

Petition for a new Peace Conference. Within hours of occupying Prague Hitler had declared Bohemia a German Protectorate, and Czechoslovakia had been wiped off the map.

On this calamitous day G. wrote me from Washington: "The really serious news is Stalin's gestures to Hitler. . . . Perhaps because of lack of inoculating exhaustion, America seems to have more sense of humanity going to perdition than England."

He added that he did not think there would yet be war—not even about Roumania, which the Press was now spot-lighting as the next potential victim. But in London the news suggested the possibility of an outbreak at any moment. The final fortnight of G.'s absence seemed to last for two months instead of two weeks.

As soon as the crisis broke I had redoubled my efforts to save the Czech dentist, Dr. Schreiber. She had been unable to get an aeroplane passage out of Prague and dared not risk rail travel through Germany; innumerable telephone calls to the Home and Foreign Offices elicited the news that all Czech airports were now in Nazi hands. About 6,000 would-be refugees, it seemed, were similarly stranded in Prague, and I heard through the P.E.N. that fifty Czech writers had passed beyond reach of communication though their papers had been in order for weeks.

"Have thought, talked, and worked Dr. Schreiber exclusively for the past three days—what a world!" I reported to G.

Eventually, after continued persistence, the young dentist actually reached England ten days later. Since professional regulations forbade her to practise dentistry in Britain, she trained as a maternity nurse under the National Midwives Scheme initiated by Ruth Fry.

The day after the annihilation of Czechoslovakia, I took part with Lord Ponsonby—Under-Secretary at the Foreign Office during Ramsay MacDonald's first Government—in a peace demonstration at Brighton. All day I felt scared, expecting a rough house, but the audience which crowded the great Pavilion listened keenly and seriously when Arthur Ponsonby gave the best intellectual exposition of pacifism that I had ever heard.

Even at that hour our enthusiastic reception was not surprising, for the educational work done in its early idealistic days by the League of Nations Union had produced its maximum effect by the late nineteen-thirties. A real will to peace existed throughout Britain, and few people now took the pre-1914 view of war as a glorious activity redounding to national credit. During the Second World War this pacific sentiment was to be driven underground but not extinguished.

In one area of Europe hatred had now exhausted itself; Franco occupied three-quarters of the Spanish Peninsula, and on February 28th the British Government had recognised the Burgos administration as the *de facto* government of Spain. The official ending of the Civil War, once the source of so much bitter controversy, passed almost unnoticed in the shadow of the greater conflict which now seemed inevitable. Engaged in his final Washington lectures, G. commented, resigned rather than reproachful, on my determination to stay and face the cheerless future rather than organise a new family expedition to America.

"It may be you're quite right, that your job is to do your work in contact with the stresses of the country in which you chanced to have been born. Personally I don't care a rap about nationalism; I am *weltbürgerlich*. But I do care a lot about certain values."

To this rational argument, which did not affect my own intuitive judgment, there was still time to reply.

"I am as *weltbürgerlich* as you, but such influence as I have is based upon the fact that I have lived close to events, experienced them and suffered them. Even though the Roman Empire is ending life itself will not end, and something else must be born. And I want to be in at the new birth and have some part in shaping the world that follows it."

(20)

On April 3rd, G. returned to England in the German liner *Bremen*. It was a strange choice at that hour, made stranger still by Chamberlain's guarantee to Poland on March 31st, 1939.

"No one who understood the situation," Churchill afterwards wrote of this guarantee, "could doubt that it meant in all human probability a major war, in which we should be involved."

But Shirley was due to have her operation, and the incongruous ship had been the only one after G.'s lectures ended which would bring him home in time for it. So acute had the tension again become that I wondered whether by taking a German boat he ran the risk of internment in Germany should war suddenly start.

When he arrived I took John, just home for the Easter holidays, to Southampton to meet him. A blustering wind slapped the sea against the docks as the tender from the *Bremen* crept up Southampton Water, unwelcomed by the red and green flag usually run up on the jetty. It brought to England only thirty-four passengers, mostly an odd assortment of Germans and Japanese. But at least G. was with them, and war had not come with the Atlantic between us.

The huge ship, he said, had been practically empty, but never had he been more courteously treated. All the Germans on board were hoping desperately that war might still be averted. A number of Czech passengers had at first resented having to travel by the *Bremen* and carry German passports, but by the end of the voyage Germans and Czechs were dancing amicably together each evening after dinner.

The special coach run by the German Line to Waterloo carried the usual external placard: "*Norddeutscher Lloyd*", and as we passed through the stations along the line, passengers waiting for trains stared at us as though we were a collection of German spies. At Waterloo the porter who took G.'s luggage inquired how he had fared on the voyage. When he replied that all the Germans with whom he talked had been hoping for peace, the porter's response showed that the British man or woman-in-the-street still shared these hopes.

"I'm glad to hear it, sir," he said. "Who wants war? This last crisis has hit us like anything. There's nobody travelling and we haven't enough jobs to keep us busy."

The next afternoon we took Shirley to the Children's Hospital in Tite Street. Two days after her operation, on a Good Friday which had seemed so peaceful with its freedom from letters, newspapers and rumours, the six o'clock broadcast news reported that Italy had invaded Albania.

An American journalist whom we knew passed on successive bulletins; the Albanian invasion, he said, was probably a "blind" to distract attention from Hitler's manoeuvres. Germany might well march into Denmark or Poland before the week-end, and within a few days we should be in the pre-ultimatum period.

Throughout that incongruously beautiful Easter, the loveliest for a dozen years, similar alarmist reports filled the Press. We never mentioned them to Shirley, but we could not prevent her, alert and intelligent, from seeing the headlines on newspapers brought into the hospital. London with its apprehensions had clearly become no place for a convalescent child. On the day after Easter Monday, the first that she was well enough to travel, I took her and John to Bournemouth until the summer term started at Oldfeld, a P.N.E.U. school at Swanage in Dorset where she had cheerfully agreed to go after seeing it with me in March.

When we reached Bournemouth she was tired, and wept a little because, she protested, I "treated her soft". But two nights later she appeared in my room from her bed across the passage in the early hours, frightened and, shivering after a nightmare. She had dreamed, she said, that a sudden air-raid had come to Chelsea, and a "headless body" had fallen on her cot.

The following night the dream recurred, but a few days by the sea soon banished these after-effects of war scares and posters, and she played contentedly in the garden of the hotel, once an old manor house, which stretched along the East Cliff.

"I don't like this hotel!" John had remarked airily after observing the usual seaside nucleus of elderly ladies in the lounge when we arrived. "It's too full of the outgoing generation."

But he forgot his pre-adolescent cynicism in games with Shirley amid the spring flowers. One radiant day spent with them on the sands below the cliff remains a cherished memory of their childhood. I took some work down to the shore, and the children, busy with buckets and spades, left me as free to write as I should have been in my study at home. Beyond their sand-castles the placid sea stretched smooth as blue silk, and tiny rivulets on the water's edge reflected the pale yellow brilliance of the sun.

(21)

During this brief holiday I realised a long-standing ambition which I had never pursued effectively, until the near approach of war made urgent the need to find some place outside London where I could take John and Shirley between their school terms.

I had often dreamed of buying a country cottage in order to escape from London's demands, and achieve real concentration; now I sought one which would be, I calculated, far enough from town to deter those car-driving visitors who "drop in" unannounced to torpedo a working day.

A house-agent showed us several small properties with miniature gardens, but they were all too conventional for my mental picture. Eventually I agreed to look at a game-keeper's cottage, once part of a large estate which no longer needed it, two miles from Lyndhurst in the New Forest.

It was further from railways stations and urban "amenities" than I had intended, not being a car-driver, to go. The garden was unkempt and the kitchen dilapidated, and the proximity of Southampton made it less than secure for the children. But the moment I saw it, and walked straight out of the front door into the unspoilt forest with its virgin miles of beech, oak and heath, I knew that this was the place for me.

John and Shirley, picking anemones beside a woodland trail and romping round the quarter-acre garden where daffodils and periwinkles gallantly emerged from the over-grown grass, eagerly confirmed my judgment, and begged me to buy it.

Since the little house badly needed reconstruction it was going cheap, and the vendor promptly knocked off a further sum because she had so much disliked the other would-be buyers. The hamlet where it stood was known as Allum Green; afterwards I remembered that R. C. Sherriff had mentioned it in his play, *Journey's End*. I returned to London the owner of the cottage, later named "Allum Green Corner" and purchased with the final savings from my autobiography. At last I had something of my own from *Testament of Youth*.

For the moment the threat of disaster seemed to have receded. On April 15th President Roosevelt—whose message to Congress on January 4th had been a vigorous fighting speech—now changed his tone, called an international conference, and invited the dictators to pledge themselves to abstain from further aggression for ten years in return for economic benefits.

"If only Roosevelt's invitation to a conference had come earlier!" I commented in my diary, not knowing then that it had. George Lansbury, I noted with satisfaction, had cabled the President asking him to add such an invitation to his message. "In this state of tension," I continued, "one can hardly expect the dictators to accept Roosevelt's definition of them as the two naughty boys who are causing all the trouble."

At the end of April I saw John off to Malvern and Shirley, with especial thankfulness, to Swanage. She would now, I calculated, be secure against poster-panic and dreams of air-raids, for I learned that the last experience of war known to the small seaside town had been a landing of the Danes in the time of King Alfred.

(22)

Now that the children were safely at school, a weight like a Sisyphus stone seemed to roll off my back. So completely did their new security relieve my mind that I hardly troubled to read the papers.

Remembering August 1914, which had broken like a thunderclap into my preparations for college, I felt instinctively that if war came it would come in the summer holidays. I resolved to subordinate everything to *Testament of Friendship* before John and Shirley returned, and for this the cottage at Allum Green seemed to have been designed by Providence.

Much of May was spent in wrestling with leisurely solicitors and builders. When I had pushed through the legal negotiations, reconstructed the old-fashioned kitchen, replaced the hand pump by a motor, and equipped the little place with the necessary minimum of cheap furniture, I took Amy and Charles Burnett to the New Forest and left one of their relatives to look after G.

While they decorated the house, tidied up the garden, and provided for our routine domestic needs, I wrote hour after hour, day after day, week after week, in an open south-facing summer-house which I had installed beyond the miniature lawn. At first the small garden was a jungle, for the grass had grown apace, and Forest ponies had broken through the wooden gates and eaten the bushes. Many of them had foaled since I first saw the hamlet; little grey and brown creatures the size of a large dog staggered on spindly legs over the smooth green beyond my windows.

The intrusive ponies had not impaired the ravishing beauty of the white and yellow broom, purple lilac, and crimson rhododendron, now all blossoming together. Nor had they disturbed the graceful poise of the turquoise and black dragonflies already darting in the late spring sunshine over the buttercups which had invaded the lawn. Twenty yards from the hawthorn hedge surrounding the garden, giant beeches like the flying buttresses of a great cathedral cast their shadows over me each evening as the red sun descended behind them.

Why, I wondered, had I unenterprisingly spent each summer in London because G. preferred urban surroundings, when every instinct inherited from my countrybred Staffordshire ancestors cried out for trees and fields and sunshine? Even the gathering war clouds could not spoil the rapture of this new possession.

Not only the hawthorn hedge, but the attitude to strangers shared by the conservative Hampshire inhabitants with the natives of Cornwall, preserved my privacy. Even when I had owned the cottage for several years and was on friendly terms with tradespeople and neighbours, I had perforce to accept the continued status of an alien. Towards the end of the war Amy Burnett lost her ration-book and asked me, as a "responsible person", to witness her application for another, but the girl at the local Food Office remained unimpressed.

"We don't know that name in Lyndhurst," she said to Amy. "Can't you ask the Vicar?"

In spite of being regarded as an interloper from London, I came to love so deeply this unpretentious cottage, and the surrounding woodlands where my few neighbours so seldom walked, that it became the only place I have inhabited in which I consciously grieved over the certainty of death.

It was not that I resented or feared that inevitable ending which might now be so near, or failed to remember the many centuries which had passed over this lovely oasis of trees and moorland before I had known it. But on the long summer evenings, when the sanguine after-glow of the sun lingered above the quiet glades fragrant with the smell of warm earth, I thought with regret of the countless future sunsets over the tranquil forest which I should not be there to see.

(23)

Now freed for an interval from conflicting claims, I wrote 100 pages of *Testament of Friendship* in the first ten days at the cottage, and had done nearly 500 at the end of another month.

From time to time the "bush telegraph" repeated rumours which suggested that the impending conflict had already begun. Unable to concentrate on my work until I knew, I would lay down my pen and hurry through the Forest into Lyndhurst, only to find after walking two miles each way and losing an hour that the afternoon papers contained no word of the threatened alarm.

As I raced to finish my book with a sense of the oncoming crisis at my heels, I began to understand the quality of Winifred's race with death to complete *South Riding*. Who knew, indeed, what form of death might not be coming with the outbreak of war?

In July news of death came indeed, from a quarter quite unexpected. On the 11th a letter from Yorkshire told me that Alice Holtby, now over eighty, had just undergone an emergency operation for appendicitis. At first her magnificent constitution caused the doctors to believe that she was pulling through, but she gradually weakened and on July 31st I received a telegram to say that she was dead.

I had finished the actual writing of my manuscript on July 14th, and with intense relief had then written to G.

"Now, at least, if I die, the world will know what I know of Winifred. It isn't more, perhaps, than the sum-total of what a great many other people know, but no other *individual* has anything like the same knowledge. Hence my fear of being drowned, bombed or blown up before I finished it. I've had to fight my own fear to refrain from 'getting it done' instead of doing it well."

When the last chapter had been written, two concentrated weeks had to be spent on revision, and this I finished, by a strange coincidence, on the day I learnt that Winifred's mother had followed the family which she had survived. Since none of her relatives felt able to undertake the minor but expert task of composing an obituary, I wrote two short paragraphs and hoped that they were just.

Two days later G. and I attended her funeral at the Priory Church in Bridlington, and afterwards I described the service for a friend who had known both Winifred and her mother.

"I went for Winifred's sake—just as for Winifred's sake I wrote about her in *The Times* and the *Yorkshire Post*. What I said, I meant. That generation of Yorkshire women was narrow, intolerant, unimaginative—and magnificent. She wanted so badly to control my control of Winifred's work, and in the end was defeated, not by any skill or superiority of mine, but just by time. Sitting in the Priory Church I could feel no satisfaction in the departure of a permanent critic, or even reflect that the one person who might really have ruined the biography was gone.

"I kept thinking of that poignant passage in the 'Miss Sigglesthwaite Sees the Lambs of God' chapter of *South Riding* which begins 'O time betrays us', and reflecting that I, too, shall one day be defeated by John and Shirley and their friends."

(24)

On August 4th, the twenty-fifth anniversary of the First War was forgotten in the approach of the Second.

Long afterwards I remembered that in 1932 I had gone to the Embassy Theatre at Swiss Cottage to see Hans Schlumberg's drama, *Miracle at Verdun*. The author never knew of its overwhelming success when it was produced at Leipzig in 1930, for he died after a stage accident—a fall into a deep orchestral pit—just before the performance.

The play visualised the world celebrating the twenty-fifth anniversary of the war, showed some of the much-belauded dead coming back to a life where nobody wanted them, and pictured them as ultimately returning whence they came. Schlumberg's savage pessimism was abundantly justified that August, for far from welcoming back the dead mankind was preparing to double their number, and throw in several million civilians as a make-weight.

Already a selection of "Public Information Leaflets" had been delivered at the cottage by the local Civil Defence organisation—"Evacuation, Why and How?"; "Your Gas Mask—How to keep it and how to use it"; "Masking your Windows". A London friend who had also received them commented that this preliminary barrage of instructions was getting people accustomed to the idea of war.

Early in August, I arranged to deliver to Macmillan, its English publishers, the book which I had begun nearly four years earlier. Harold Macmillan himself received the typescript on August 9th; they hoped to publish in the New Year. He advised me not to send the script before publication to persons interested in the story, or allow them to influence my judgment.

"A book designed to offend nobody loses all its life," he concluded wisely.

I walked down St. Martin's Street into Trafalgar Square with the mingled feeling of thankfulness and anti-climax which follows the completion of every large book. Whatever happened now, Winifred's story would be told; I had won my race with the on-coming war. But who knew whether I, or any of us, would survive to write any more books?

(25)

Both the children were now at Allum Green, and G. periodically came down from London. On August 13th the European representative of *Collier's Magazine* spent the day with us in the country. The crisis, he told us, would develop between Hitler's Tannenburg and Nuremberg speeches on August 27th and September 2nd, and would be "very hot".

"But there's still a chance some way out will be found," he added, trying to reassure us. "Mussolini's getting more and more anxious —he's said to be quite frantic for peace."

The chance didn't seem particularly good, I thought, looking at the moist purple buds of the Michaelmas daisies which the July rain had brought prematurely to flower. But I may as well enjoy this loveliness while I can—like a soldier on leave.

A week later, with the "war of nerves" on Danzig providing "noises off", Hitler and Stalin signed the German-Soviet Pact. It fell like a thunderbolt from a sky which had seemed no darker than before, since the secret intrigues between Germany and Russia had not leaked out. Instead, the Press had spotlighted the Anglo-Russian negotiations which had dragged on since April. In spite of Litvinoff's dismissal as Foreign Commissar in May, British hopes had centred round William Strang's mission to Moscow.

Throughout the country a brief panic followed the news of the Pact. One young friend from London, fearing she knew not what, arrived at the cottage with her nurse and baby. Alarming telephone messages periodically came through for various members of our growing household. G. was now back in town, and I implored him to ring me late each night when these "jittery" calls were over, so that he could convey his well-balanced judgment on the course of events.

The "jitters" were not without cause, for after the Pact the Government itself speeded up its precautions and issued repeated orders to intimidated civilians through the cultured voices of B.B.C. announcers. In a letter written when the terms of the Pact were published, I set down some conclusions which appear, in the light of subsequent experience, to have been relatively close to existing realities.

"The people who really sold us are the militant Liberals, who persuaded everyone to put their faith in Soviet Russia, and yelled for a 'Peace Front' which has actually proved to be a weak war front. While the Leftists were accusing the Peace Pledge Union of being 'used' by the Fascists, they themselves were being used by the Communists, and never even suspected themselves of being pawns in the Russian game! It is clear now that the Russian game has been to set Middle and Western Europe by the ears, and, since neither side can win without the help of Russia, to step in when both are exhausted and create revolutions in all the countries concerned.

"That doesn't mean I hold any brief for Chamberlain—a Tory imperialist who is, as you say, no pacifist, and never pretended to be anything but what he is. But I believe he saw the Russian game more clearly than the 'peace-loving' Left. The whole business is just one more instance of the incredible cynicism with which power-politics are conducted."

The response of rural Hampshire to this cynicism proved to be typically and equably British. In late August I took John to the Lyndhurst cinema to see *Pygmalion*. Before the film came some ancient news, such as small picture-houses in remote places had then to accept, which began with a "shot" of the British Mission leaving for Moscow.

Owing to the inappropriate optimism of the old news-reel the operator wound up this section to top speed, but it was not fast enough to conceal the self-satisfied smiles of the British delegates or extinguish the complacent accents of the narrator: "And we wish them every success in their friendly talks with the Soviet Government".

John and I waited with interest for the reaction of the crowded audience. Would it be boos, hisses? It came—a spontaneous and unanimous outburst of derisive laughter.

At Allum Green the local air-raid warden told me that, if war came, children from Portsmouth would be packed into every corner of the village. We were a "neutral", not a "safe" area, I learned, for the whole south coast lay within range of German bombers, but any village was better than a busy port. Later, after the fall of France, the New Forest became a "defence" area, and only residents were allowed inside.

John and Shirley, hardly affected by the crescendo of events now that they were out of London, played contentedly in the Forest. From the hollow trunk of a fallen tree they constructed a "submarine" which occupied them for hours, and organised a "Bracken Club" with blackberries for coins. It was now my mother whose welfare most concerned me, for I feared that she might be involved in a panic rush out of London if raids began.

Eventually G. persuaded her to leave town and spend the rest of the summer with her youngest sister in Kent. A year later this south-eastern section of the coast was to become a maximum danger area, but in 1939 it appeared a less probable target than London or Southampton. From Kingsdown she wrote appreciatively of G.'s kindness; he was always so calm in a crisis, she said, and had been "such a strength and stay."

(26)

In the last week of August, the crisis effervesced after a swift series of ominous events. On the 25th an Anglo-Polish Treaty and the hostile movement of German troops towards the Polish frontier followed Chamberlain's message to Hitler two days earlier. This message had renewed the Government's plea for a peaceful settlement of the Danzig dispute, but clearly defined Britain's attitude towards Poland.

Twenty-four hours before the Treaty, Parliament had passed an Emergency Powers Bill, and shortly afterwards over a million mothers, children, expectant mothers and blind invalids were warned to prepare for evacuation on September 1st. Rumour, persistent and irrepressible, reported that the German liner *Europa* had been seen racing at full speed past Southampton without stopping to disembark her passengers, while the *Bremen*, ordered to turn round in mid-Atlantic on her way to New York, had been compelled to go on by a thousand rampageous American travellers.

On August 28th, the main Southampton-Bournemouth road became a study in crisis traffic. Standing at the end of the rough track which led from our cottage to the highway, the children and I watched buses filled with troops, huge removal vans, small cars almost submerged under cots, perambulators and suitcases, motor dispatch riders with steel helmets, and cyclists bent beneath the weight of overloaded packs. All through the night, heavily-laden lorries crashed towards unknown destinations. Everyone on holiday seemed to be going home, and everyone at home to be migrating somewhere else. How thankful I felt, this time, to be able to "stay put"!

Three days later the crowded road was deserted; a strange waiting silence followed the racket. A lovely late summer had succeeded the rain, and an incredible beauty, which seemed to transcend life itself, illuminated the rich countryside. Peacock butterflies and Red Admirals, like animated jewels, danced above the sunflowers; from village gardens drifted the faint astringent smell of early autumn bonfires. Standing on the small Roman Bridge near our cottage over the Forest stream oddly known as the Highland Water, G. and I spontaneously kissed as though saying farewell.

The newspapers now reported that the King of Belgium and the Queen of Holland had offered themselves as mediators; the lives of millions seemed to hang on the thread-like chance of a "face-saving" formula being found which would satisfy Hitler's Danzig claims without involving another Munich. The International P.E.N. cancelled its Stockholm Conference, though its President, H. G. Wells, was already on his way. During that week of suspense a Swedish citizen, Berger Dahlerus, flew almost without food or sleep between Germany, Sweden and Britain in a final effort to save the peace which he has described in his book, *The Last Attempt*.

On September 1st, as G. and I stood outside Lyndhurst Post Office, a rumour that Germany had invaded Poland flew through the village. We went into the Crown Hotel, listened to the one o'clock news, and learned that this time the rumour was true. Polish towns had already been bombed, and Hitler had nominated Goering as his successor if he became a casualty.

Next morning G. was summoned north to keep an appointment in Lancashire. At Southampton we observed the complete balloon barrage which now encircled the docks. An immovable traffic-jam blocked the entrance to the station, where tearful parents, buffeted by young men joining their regiments, took leave of their resigned evacuee children carrying school satchels and gas-masks. Platform

208

tickets and cross-country trains had alike been suspended; I was obliged to remain outside the ticket-barrier when G. pushed his way on to the platform for the train to Waterloo.

"Never before," he remarked as we parted, "have I seen an English town that reminded me of Madrid."

That afternoon thunder and lightning broke over Lyndhurst, and at Westminster Arthur Greenwood, urged by Leopold Amery to "speak for England", passionately commented on the period of inaction which had followed the invasion of Poland. A week later, the English cities which resembled Madrid had multiplied with astonishing speed.

At ten o'clock on the morning of September 3rd, the B.B.C. announced that Britain's ultimatum asking Germany to leave Poland would expire at 11 a.m. If no reply had come by then, the Prime Minister would speak at 11.15.

After two years of scares, rumours, crises, prophecies, and head-lines, this final tragic certainty came almost as a relief. Incongruously the Sunday church bells, so soon to be silenced, echoed through the Forest from Lyndhurst, and Shirley, by now acclimatised to incomprehensible disturbances from unknown countries, raced to the window to watch a red-brown foal scamper downhill across the empty green.

Whatever happened I knew that Dick Sheppard's followers, with the Quakers and other Christian believers in the power of the spirit, would bear their witness, and I hoped that I should find enough courage to bear it with them. At eleven o'clock the children and I joined the others already in my upstairs study. Grouped round the loud-speaker as the hour approached, we waited in silence for the coming of war.

PART II

O Divine Master, grant
That I may not so much seek
To be consoled, as to console;
To be understood, as to understand;
To be loved as to love.

For it is in giving that we receive;
It is in pardoning that we are pardoned;
It is in dying that we are born to eternal life.

ST. FRANCIS OF ASSISI (traditional prayer).

CHAPTER SIX

THE CLOUDS DESCEND

The purple asters lift their heads
Beneath the azure autumn skies;
Above the sunflower's golden cup
Hover the scarlet butterflies.

Not in the sandbagged city street
Where London's silver guardians soar,
But through the cottage garden throbs
The aching grief of England's war.

v.b., September, 1939.

(1)

WHEN THE ECHO of Neville Chamberlain's trembling voice had died away, the paralysis which held us motionless in the study suddenly broke. John and Shirley—bored as children always are by the anxieties of their elders—vanished into the Forest and the rest of us dispersed.

Escaping from the crowded cottage, which now held eight people, I too set out on a Forest trail. Everything had changed, yet nothing was different. No counterpart of the first siren—a false alarm which startled London within twenty minutes of war's declaration—disturbed the quiet glades round Southampton. When at last I sat down to write an article—"Lift up your Hearts and keep your Heads!"—which had been asked of me in the event of war, its urgency seemed as unreal as the news.

Only when the radio next morning announced the sinking of the liner *Athenia* did we realise that war had indeed begun.

My diary for September 4 gives the news as originally reported: "She remained afloat for some hours and everyone was saved except those killed by the explosion." Actually 112 passengers were lost, including twenty-eight Americans. In the Twilight War, as Churchill afterwards called it, the first quality to move into the shadows was truth.

On Sunday night I had sent a letter to catch G. in London.

213

"As I write this date, I think to myself incredulously that before long it will be as familiar as August 4th, 1914, and stand for as great significance—but what significance? More misery? A longer or shorter period of terror? Victory or defeat or revolution?"

We were to wait six years for the answers to those questions. Meanwhile we could only live for the moment and its emotions, which permeated the first broadcast speeches.

"Chamberlain's actually making the declaration of war I found moving because he was obviously so greatly upset," I wrote. "But everyone else might have been back in 1914. The same 'devil' who is to blame for everything; the same invocation of 'God and the right'—as though either had anything whatever to do with this business. I had the impression that nobody really meant quite what they were saying and were repeating parts like parrots for the benefit of history. It is so quiet here to-night—unbelievable that we are on the edge of chaos."

In the persistent sunshine of the next few days the wireless announcements seemed grotesque, but they made a bitter mockery of the belated summer. To G. I commented sadly on "the utter failure of all the sincere efforts made for peace through twenty years," and could not yet imagine how time would reveal that this ostensible failure had not been "utter".

Failure is only complete if the hearts and minds of men remain totally untouched. But in September 1939 the Nazis racing towards Warsaw in perfect campaigning weather appeared to have defeated much more than Poland.

(2)

Submerged in the sunny quiet of gorse and heather, I tried vainly to take in the size of the catastrophe. War came closer when searchlights from the coast flashed meteor-wise across the midnight sky, brilliant streamers which briefly outlined the black beeches outside my bedroom window. Along the pitch-dark country roads, newly-painted white lines sprang suddenly to life as bemused drivers ran into the open beneath the stars, but became part of the all-enveloping black-out under the trees, where cars had to crawl for fear of colliding with Forest ponies placidly incapable of adaptation to war.

"I think this war will last either ten weeks or ten years," a friend wrote to me from the outskirts of London. The radio endorsed her more melancholy forecast; we must prepare for a long war, the announcements insisted.

My correspondent had recalled August 1914, of which we both

214

dimly remembered the incredulous excitement. In September 1939 the expected had happened, and was accepted with philosophic pessimism.

One Sunday that autumn I lunched at Eton with a schoolmaster and his wife who had been my Oxford contemporaries. During the afternoon, a few of the previous summer's Sixth Form who had just been called up came in to say good-bye. Their attitude of casual resignation, and the master's deliberate optimism which concealed his disappointment over their frustrated promise, seemed one with the melancholy of dying chrysanthemums in river gardens and fading virginia creeper on grey college walls.

Civilians everywhere displayed little alarm, though air warfare had put them all in greater danger than any non-combatant had thought possible in 1914. Even the new regulations, over a hundred in number, which limited freedom of speech and opinion passed without opposition through a stunned House of Commons. By the time that Parliament awoke to this curtailment of our liberties, a few small amendments to the Emergency Powers Act were the most that Members could achieve.

But if the Second War brought less excitement than the First, it created far more confusion. While an unreal peace enveloped our isolated hamlet, the large-scale evacuation of children and invalids had been followed by the movement of government offices, commercial firms and schools from "danger" areas.

The conflict soon revealed itself as less a struggle of men with men than a contest in methods of mass production which were to debase the intrinsic value of martial daring. It was also from the start a bewildering duet, and later a whole orchestra, of propaganda carried out by all the new instruments of communication developed between the wars.

As radio reports became shriller, the Royal Air Force dropped millions of pamphlets over Germany. Ten days after the outbreak of war, the British and French governments made a virtuous declaration "solemnly and publicly affirming their intention to conduct hostilities with a firm desire to spare the civilian population and to preserve those monuments of human achievement which are treasured in all countries".

Governments were not alone in the scruples which they discarded so rapidly when the war began to move. One contrast between the First Armageddon and the Second lay in the moral dilemmas again imposed on all citizens. These problems no longer centred on the obligation of "volunteering"; no "key" person in civilian clothes had to suffer the humiliation and self-reproach endured between 1914 and 1918 by my "Uncle Bill" at his City bank. Conscription had lifted this painful choice from the shoulders of all but the few who became conscientious objectors.

Gone was the ferocious hatred which atrocity stories had aroused in our elders who sat out the First War in armchairs; gone too the self-righteousness of non-combatant public opinion with its sorry stock-in-trade of sneers and white feathers. The risk of qualifying for a white feather had now become all too general.

Instead, tormenting doubts assailed civilians of all ages and both sexes. Most members of the middle generation carried responsibility not only for the young but for the old, who were far more difficult to organise than children. As early as September 5th, my mother announced that she was returning to London from Kent. For the next six years she moved perpetually in and out of danger areas, a source of anxiety when in them and of restless agitation when out.

But John and Shirley, my cherished but perturbing obligations, inevitably concerned me more. Should one stay out of danger with one's children, or remain in it and keep them there too? Should one put their interests before everything else, or accept risks which involved the possibility of leaving them motherless?

"Lord, how difficult it is to draw the line between courage and responsibility!" I wrote to my correspondent who remembered 1914.

In similar mood, she replied. "What a world, in which every mother has the same frightful anxiety. The simple lives of simple people are destroyed, everywhere."

When John and Shirley went back to school and released me from the relative immobility which their care had demanded, the moral problem remained. From the cottage, now so silent without their footsteps and voices, I defined it to G.

"So long as one has dear human beings to live for one is a potential coward, and courage is the more costly."

(3)

Even before the children's departure left me free to consider what "war work" to do, an approach to writers by the newly-formed Ministry of Information had faced me with a challenge.

Literary agents were mobilised early. On September 7th a letter signed A. D. Peters requested me, as an author "valuable" to the Ministry, to refrain from any other form of national service until I received their instructions.

This approach did not surprise me, for a scramble to conform had already shown itself among many conspicuous persons hitherto dedicated to the work of peace. Before long it was even to affect some of Dick Sheppard's distinguished sponsors, and one of his more cynical disciples was to produce a private aphorism: "There is more rejoicing in the Ministry of Information over one repentant pacifist, than over ninety and nine good militarists which need no repentance."

I meditated on the Ministry's invitation as I sat in the summer-house correcting the proofs of *Testament of Friendship*. How would Winifred, I wondered, have responded to such a summons? She, like myself, had been deeply concerned with problems of peace and war. But when she died the word "pacifist" was seldom used; it had not become, as it was now becoming, a term of abuse.

Winifred had simply been pro-peace and anti-war, regarding with disdainful pity the bankruptcy of statesmanship which declarations of war revealed. Would she, deeply distrustful of passion with its loud, angry voice, have been willing to join the Ministry of Information and stir up hatred even against a hateful Germany?

I did not think that she would and I felt sure that I could not, for every instinct resisted this appeal. I did not intend to lease my mental integrity to the Government for the duration; this was not, I thought, the function of writers, who should surely try to provide an oasis of sanity in the spiritual desert created by warring ideologies.

Years afterwards, I was to discover the *Declaration of the Independence of the Mind* issued to his fellow brain-workers by the French writer, Romain Rolland, from Villeneuve in 1919.

"The war has disordered our ranks. Most of the intellectuals placed their science, their art, their reason, at the service of the governments. We do not wish to formulate any accusations, to launch any reproaches. We know the weakness of the individual mind and the elemental strength of great collective currents. . . .

"Let us point out the disasters that have resulted from the almost complete abdication of intelligence throughout the world, and from its voluntary enslavement to the unchained forces. Thinkers, artists, have added an incalculable quantity of envenomed hate to the plague which devours the flesh and spirit of Europe . . . They have worked to destroy mutual understanding and mutual love among men. So doing, they have disfigured, defiled, debased, degraded thought, of which they were the representatives. . . .

"Mind is no one's servitor. It is we who are the servitors of mind. We have no other master . . . Our role, our duty, is to be a centre of stability, to point out the pole star, amid the whirlwind of passions in the night. . . . Truth only do we honour; truth that is free, frontierless, limitless; truth that knows nought of the prejudices of race or caste."

This statement embodied the concept of my function towards which I was struggling in 1939. I wrote to the Ministry of Information that I could not do war propaganda, but would gladly join any group studying peace aims in cooperation with the neutral United States. With this purpose in mind, I attended one or two of the dinners held that autumn by the English-Speaking Union to discuss Anglo-American relations.

I was now tormented by indecision about my prospective lecture tour, which the Leigh Bureau had fixed for the spring of 1940 at the time of our unhappy trip to New York during the Munich crisis. In August a cable had asked me to come before January, the month tentatively arranged, and lecture till the end of April. Mr. Leigh added the significant words: "Think important for Anglo-American friendship".

Although this friendship, from the standpoint of peace aims, was now more vital than ever, the conviction that I should not leave the children at all had become equally compelling. Eventually I cabled that I could not come before January. If no great campaign had then begun, it seemed unlikely to start before the Easter holidays. So far, apart from rapidly collapsing Poland, a strange immobility appeared to paralyse the opposing forces.

"What a queer war this is!" I wrote to a friend on September 19th. "I feel all the time in a kind of fog, with a sense that immense things are happening (though hardly any of them the things we expected) of which we learn only the fringe."

(4)

A lecture tour, in any case, was an isolated event. I had still to consider what special work, if any, the war demanded from me.

I had already put down my name for a volunteer "Service Corps" which the Society of Friends was organising, but I knew that a decision "to go and be a V.A.D. again", as one acquaintance put it, would mean a waste of training and skill. An article by Bernard Shaw that autumn reinforced this conclusion. Why, he inquired, when a war broke out did most people abandon the work for which they were equipped, and rush to volunteer for other jobs in which they were quite inexperienced?

Practical work of this kind would merely provide a means of shirking the issue which now confronted me. In the First War I had faced dangers, then considered more perilous than they now appeared, with the support of public approval; but before that war ended I had come to see the enemy, not in terms of the dying Germans whom I had nursed at Étaples, but as war itself.

Ever since Armistice Day 1918 had found me alone, with my young and dear contemporaries gone, I had been trying to understand why they died. Was not the unthinking acceptance of an aggressive or short-sighted national policy, followed by mass-participation in sociable war-time activities, one of the ingredients which created a militant psychology and made shooting wars possible? I had studied their consequences too, and knew how rapid a deterioration of civilised values followed the initial nobility and generosity, until the Christian virtues themselves came to be regarded with derision.

Surely the path which I had trodden for two decades now summoned me to struggle against that catastrophic process? Though I still underrated the cost of such a stand, I knew that the routine performance of dangerous duties would be stimulating and congenial compared with the exhausting demands of independent thought and the task of maintaining, against the deceptive surge of popular currents, a conscious realisation of what was actually happening.

And where, apart from the usual writings and speeches, could I newly begin? An idea suddenly came from my endeavours to answer the daily quota of letters from unknown correspondents which had increased so rapidly since the outbreak of war. Some wanted to help, others to be helped; all were eager to stop hostilities. One correspondent hopefully suggested that the women of the world should immediately unite, and call a truce.

By means of a regular published letter I could not only reply to these anxious, bewildered people, but seek out and rally such independent-minded commentators as the author who wrote to deplore the lack of vision among Britain's rulers.

"Even if they can't treat with Hitler they could, they ought, to proclaim what sort of peace they are willing to make . . . I think people are feeling desperate listening to Chamberlain maundering on about stating our specific aims *some time*, and other Ministers making war speeches, and the Labour leaders joining in the chorus."

A periodic word to similar correspondents, if based on determined research behind the news, could elucidate vital issues for the doubting, galvanise the discouraged, and assure the isolated that they were not alone. Its title, I thought, might be "Letter to Peace-Lovers", for the group that I hoped to reach was much wider than the small bodies of organised war-resisters.

I found considerable support for this project, and by September 12th had shown to G. the draft of an introductory circular with which I planned to approach possible subscribers. This circular explained that my purpose was not to give information, which could already be obtained from many sources both good and bad, nor yet to criticise the Government and its military machine.

> "What I do want is to consider and discuss with you the ideas, principles and problems which have concerned genuine peace-lovers for the past twenty years. In helping to sustain the spirits of my readers (and through writing to them to invigorate my own) I hope to play a small part in keeping the peace movement together during the dark hours before us. By constantly calling on reason to mitigate passion, and truth to put falsehood to shame, I shall try, so far as one person can, to stem the tide of hatred which in war-time rises so quickly that many of us are engulfed before we realise it. . . .
>
> "In a word, I want to help in the important task . . . of keeping alive decent values at a time when these are undergoing the maximum strain. . . .
>
> "My only object is to keep in close personal touch with all who are deeply concerned that war shall end and peace return . . . and who understand what Johan Bojer meant when he wrote: 'I went and sowed corn in mine enemy's field that God might exist'."

Two small advertisements produced a shoal of enquiries, and when, with the help of friendly volunteers, I sent out the introductory circular, I had a hundred subscribers—at 2s. 6d. each for six months—by the next day's post. Until I could acquire an office of my own I borrowed a desk at Dick Sheppard House in Endsleigh Street, where Dick's followers were now established.

The Letters seldom ventured on prophecy, but the third issue, sent out on October 25th, contained a forecast which now seems worth recalling.

> "Even supposing that we do destroy Hitler, we shall not again

be confronted by a Europe agreeably free from competitors for power. The disappearance of Herr Hitler will probably lead instead to a revolutionary situation in Germany, controlled by puppets who own allegiance to another Power. We, the democracies, will still be faced by totalitarianism, in a form less clumsy but no less aggressive, and even more sinister in its ruthless unexhausted might."

Whether or not such predictions helped to secure subscribers, I had a thousand by the end of October; the better-known included the future Colonial Secretary, Arthur Creech-Jones; Dr. Maude Royden; and Vernon Bartlett. The Letter, I reckoned, would pay for itself by the time I had collected two thousand regular readers. Their actual number never quite reached this figure, but was always near enough, together with intermittent donations from supporters, to bridge the narrow gulf between subscriptions and costs. My circulation was not confined to England; soon after the Letter began, I obtained a permit to send it to neutral countries. One or two American libraries subsequently filed it as an historic "document".

This small publication owed its success to two devoted secretaries, first Winifred Eden-Green, and later Irene Mills. We began with a weekly issue, but owing to the steep rise of costs had finally to raise the subscription to 3s. 6d. and come out every fortnight.

In spite of my periodic travels we never missed an issue, though technical difficulties due to air raids sometimes delayed publication. I carried on the Letter until the second year after the war, when the need for it seemed to be over.

(5)

Soon after the Michaelmas term began I went back to London, and stayed with my mother before re-opening our closed house. On a previous visit to discuss the Letter with possible supporters, I had dismantled our pictures and laid them face downwards on the floor.

In brilliant heat my train had reached Waterloo beneath a shining galaxy of barrage balloons. Piled sandbags already protected the doorways of hotels and offices, and A.R.P. shelters were under construction in all the main streets. G. and I discovered our old acquaintance, Oswald Garrison Villard of the American *Nation*, staying at the Ambassadors' Hotel. We learned that he was on his way to Germany.

"I came over for a peace mission," he told us, "and arrived to find war."

By late September, the London evenings were closing in. Night brought the pervading depression of the black-out, which caused innumerable minor casualties and disguised even the familiar outlines of our own homes. Though air-raid warnings had been few and abortive, a timid Government refused to allow jaded minds the distraction of theatres and cinemas, which it had closed on the outbreak of war. In the *Sunday Times* for September 12th, a letter of protest from Dame Marie Tempest had coincided with another from G., who described the contrasting practice of the Spaniards in the Civil War.

"I hope," he concluded, "that we shall act on this experience available, and abandon the policy of sitting at home in the dark telling each other rumours."

When I opened 2 Cheyne Walk in October I was alone with Amy and Charles Burnett in the tall empty house, for G. had again gone to America.

Soon after war began, when I was contemplating my Letter, an idea had simultaneously occurred to him of a regular publication which would explain, each to the other, the psychological response to war of Britain and the United States. The official censorship which limited freedom of expression in newspapers caused several similar projects to be born at that time.

G. embodied his proposal in a memorandum to Arthur Greenwood, and received considerable encouragement. "A.G.," my diary recorded on September 4th, "would like him to go to America in a week." G.'s idea was a larger proposition than my modest Letter to Peace-Lovers; it needed substantial American support which could only be collected across the Atlantic. Following Arthur Greenwood's suggestion he arranged an early visit, though he reported to me in dismay that "ocean fares are extravagantly up —£100 single for a 4-berth cabin."

On October 24th he sailed from Southampton in the S.S. *President Roosevelt*. Before he left we lunched at the South-Western Hotel beside the docks, and drank a toast to his scheme in a bottle of Chambertin. From the ship he wrote me of his hopes and plans.

"What is the position? To have a clear view of what one wishes to issue from this war. To press that view in America. To report to England what America thinks, not excluding what it thinks that will conduce to righteousness. . . . America will shape the peace of Europe. Only those with a foot in both worlds will help in that process."

He could have carried out his project; not his own failure, but the nervous fears of distrustful officials were to thwart his adventure. But neither of us foresaw that future frustration when I received, with enormous relief, a cable announcing his safe arrival.

(6)

I had not much time for missing G., owing to an autumn so strenuous that it soon submerged me in a permanent morass of work.

In addition to the weekly Letter and the large correspondence which it brought, I was obliged to fulfil a series of speaking engagements booked long before the war. Several had been arranged by peace societies which now wanted to consider how war could be ended and peace aims defined. They sought to maintain the vision of a united humanity which Wendell Willkie, the American would-be President who died too soon, was to incorporate in his book, *One World*.

So far, owing to a difference of opinion between the British and French Governments about the future of Germany if they conquered her, the people of both countries had been provided with no peace aims and only one war aim—the destruction of Hitlerism. Not even the bargain basements of an earthly city could be founded upon so negative a purpose.

Summoned to "give a lead", as best I could, to more constructive thinking, I set off on long journeys to the North and Midlands in slow overcrowded trains now deprived of restaurants. Policemen in plain clothes attended some of these meetings, for "peace" had become—as it was to be for so much more of our lives—a disreputable word.

I shared one trip to Manchester with Maurice Browne, the producer of *Journey's End*. After the warmth of September, a chilly late autumn foreshadowed one of the coldest winters for years. Long before we reached our destination, darkness enveloped the blacked-out train; the tiny blue light in the railway carriage barely enabled me to see my companion's tired, kindly face above the decorative fur collar of his overcoat.

Being unable to read, we talked all the way. In the beautiful voice which was later to move our audience to tears, he told me that he had spent the previous war in the United States. From the outbreak until America came in, he had travelled from coast to coast with a cast which included Sybil Thorndike. They played *The Trojan Women*, in Professor Gilbert Murray's translation, before large audiences in every important city. This poignant protest against war's destructive tragedy had been made by the Greek dramatist Euripides four hundred years before Christ.

"Pity is a rebel passion," Gilbert Murray had written in a famed Introduction. "Its hand is against the strong, against the organised forces of society, against conventional sanctions and accepted gods. It is the Kingdom of Heaven within us fighting against the brute powers of the world."

How much of that rebel passion would be left when the war ended? A few days earlier six women, of whom I was one, had sent the Prime Minister a letter asking that, whatever the Nazis might do to us, we should not sink to the level of bombing German women and their children in open towns. Mr. Chamberlain had replied that he "fully sympathised" with the object which we had in view. With his answer he enclosed a copy of his own cautious statement on bombing made in the House of Commons on September 14th.

Only the *News Chronicle* and the *Manchester Guardian* published our communication. Though I had not initiated it, I received an abusive letter from an unknown woman contemporary.

"We are at war with the German nation. If we suffer setback and calamity and individual misery at the hands of German bombers, then let us, without hesitation, BOMB THEM in return. . . . There is no reason whatsoever why German women should be spared anything that our own people have previously experienced."

This vengeful spirit was conspicuously absent from our Manchester meeting, though one local paper had appeared that morning with a monster headline splashed over its front page:

"PACIFISTS AND NAZIS MAKE UNHOLY ALLIANCE."

Two thousand listeners crammed the hall from floor to ceiling, and the queue waiting outside became so long that a large overflow meeting was held nearby. At neither gathering did one voice expostulate against the plea for humanity made by Maurice Browne and his fellow speakers.

(7)

Shortly afterwards I returned to the New Forest for a final week-end before closing the cottage for the winter.

In a last brief burst of Indian summer, the orange and gamboge of the changing beeches rivalled the challenging beauty of America's golden maples and scarlet oaks. The Forest had never been more lovely, but the evacuated mothers and children were not there to see it: they had all returned to Portsmouth.

Not even the inspired optimism of official journalists could persuade reception areas that evacuation had been a success, yet every item of news which emerged from the fog shrouding the Western Front suggested that within a few months the evacuees would again be seeking refuge. Even the peace move by the Queen of Holland and the King of Belgium had spluttered as ineffectively as a torch in the rain.

Now that only seven weeks divided me from January and the strange war still refused to develop, the dilemma of a lecture-tour which meant leaving John and Shirley weighed ever more heavily on my mind.

"Last week-end," ran my next letter to G., "I almost prayed (for purely selfish reasons) that Hitler would walk into Holland, so that I would have a really good reason to cable Leigh and say: 'Cancel tour'. I am beginning to feel that I am crazy, crazy, to put myself out of reach of the children in wartime."

The very next day, a responsible presentation of the case for going increased the difficulty of decision. A week earlier, I had attended the third of the Anglo-American dinner-discussions at Dartmouth House. Usually I had listened rather than talked, but this time I contributed quite vehemently to the discussion because, I told G., "I was so infuriated by S., who took the view that all war aims beyond the destruction of Hitler were quite idiotic."

This lampless outlook seemed to emphasise the importance of visitors to America who expressed a different opinion. To Roger Eckersley, then Assistant Controller of the B.B.C., whom I had met at a previous dinner, I confided my problem. Had my tour any significance, apart from the modest financial return which it was likely to bring? He suggested immediately that we should put this question to his American friend Ed Murrow, the young, dynamic representative of the Columbia Broadcasting Corporation.

On November 15th, after we had seen Edward Murrow, I described the visit to G.

"Mr. Murrow had a handsome, man-of-the-worldish, slightly cynical exterior, but he turned out to be an idealistic near-pacifist who deplored the outburst of hatred to which the U.S.A. is giving way. Roger Eckersley sat quiet and let us talk. And after we had talked for half an hour, the American assured me it was my job to go over. He *urged* me to go, and said that no one of any standing would attack me if I took the line in U.S.A. that I had taken with him.

"So now—having all but reached the point of cancelling my tour—I don't know what to do. . . . I hate refusing adventures; but I hate even more leaving the children in a dangerous country while I go to a safe one."

(8)

Back from Germany, in late November, came Oswald Garrison Villard to add to my perplexity. In a lecture at Friends' House he spoke of a new Blitzkrieg timed to start on May 1st, and designed to overthrow England in Polish fashion by the end of the summer. His series of *Daily Telegraph* articles, subsequently republished as a small book called *Inside Germany*, caused a sensation by supplying chapter and verse for this prophecy. If he was right, ought I to leave home at such a critical moment? My dilemma remained unresolved, but I had in any case already cabled Colston Leigh that I would take no lecture engagements after April 5th.

Soon afterwards came news of the death of our old friend Mrs. H. M. Swanwick, who as editor of *Foreign Affairs* had given me some of my first commissions. A lifelong peace-worker, and British substitute-delegate to the League Assembly under the first Labour Government, she had been greatly distressed by the return of war, which seemed in her old age to extinguish all her hopes. Leaving a note to say that she thought "the best thing to do was to remove myself from the world", she achieved her object by an overdose of medinal.

Grieving that her brave and valuable life should have ended in this conviction of defeat, I wrote to G. in America that I thought "one must carry out arrangements unless there is some reason other than personal peril for cancelling them." A recent murder trial, which I had attended as a potential witness and was later to use for the theme of a novel, *Account Rendered*, hastened the process of decision, for the tragedy had its origin in neuroses caused by the First World War.

"The X trial," my letter continued, "has convinced me that the kind of phobia which comes from the rejection of things is more ruinous to one's whole make-up than rational fears over the risks from which such fears arise."

On November 30th the Russian invasion of Finland, like the preceding liquidation of the Baltic States, created a grim climate for this resolve. Nor was it made easier by G. himself. I had been counting on his return to our household before my departure, but now he wrote that to come back so soon would be "completely catastrophic" to his remaining chances of launching his publication.

Soon after his arrival he had spent three hours discussing the project with our friend Lord Lothian, the British Ambassador to the United States. Other talks produced enthusiastic but purely moral support from such "key" Americans as Thomas Lamont, Raymond Gram Swing, and Stacey May of the Rockefeller Foundation. By December he was still ruefully reporting "limitless encouragement but no finance. If blessings justified a scheme it would blossom like the rose."

In spite of the blessings he thought that American opinion was hardening against participation in Europe's affairs, though the effect of the Finnish news had been "electric". He was finally obliged to abandon his idea of an Anglo-American letter as financially too ambitious, but was saved from total disappointment by an invitation to lecture in Canada. His recent books were also prospering. In the United States his *History of the Political Philosophers*, published in December, had already gone into a second printing, and, like *The Anglo-Saxon Tradition* in England, had received a Book Society Recommendation.

Abandoning all hope of shared responsibility for the children, I arranged with their respective schools to keep them, in any emergency, until I came back from America. Their return for the Christmas holidays brought very close the tour which I had now mentally accepted.

It was indeed so near that I had to risk keeping them in London. From Allum Green I could not have contended in time with the travel formalities, which seemed daily to grow stricter, though war operations were virtually at a standstill and Franco-British casualties on all fronts barely exceeded 2,000. It now took three weeks to get an exit permit, while money, food, baggage, trains and cross-Atlantic passages all required multiple forms. I lost count when I had filled in nineteen.

(9)

The tour was due to begin in Boston on January 14th, and Colston Leigh had arranged for me to travel by Clipper. This first transatlantic passenger air service now left Lisbon twice weekly, and took twenty-eight hours to reach New York. My manager hoped that air travel would ensure a punctual start in spite of war-time delays. He was even more anxious to make sure of the lecturer, for Germany was now using a new "secret weapon". Between November 18th and 25th, magnetic mines had sunk 60,000 tons of Allied shipping.

Like most of my contemporaries I had not yet pictured myself taking long air journeys, let alone flying the Atlantic in winter, but the sudden precariousness of all life meant that a guaranteed arrival at any destination had become an unattainable ideal. In a choice between air travel and magnetic mines the Clipper seemed preferable, not least because it would enable me to be in England for the New Year publication of *Testament of Friendship*.

On New Year's Day, 1940, Mr. Harold Macmillan gave a small luncheon for me, to which he invited Desmond MacCarthy and other literary figures of equivalent standing. Main page reviews in the *Observer*, *Reynolds News* and the *Sunday Chronicle*, and a warm tribute in the *Yorkshire Post* to both Winifred and the book on publication day, counteracted a colder douche from the *Times Literary Supplement*. But one advantage of my impending departure was that it lessened, by putting it into perspective, the painful alarm which usually preceded the appearance of any major book.

New obstacles now made the journey before me even more intimidating than I had expected. For the first time bad weather held up the Clipper, and the accumulation of passengers already waiting in Lisbon made it impossible to say when my turn would come. Since I already had French, Spanish and Portuguese visas, and there was no time to make new arrangements, my travel agents advised me to go to Lisbon, and take the first ship sailing for New York. An American-bound Italian liner, the *Vulcania*, was putting in there on January 10th; if I flew to Paris as planned, I should be able to catch it and begin my tour with the loss of only three engagements.

At times I felt sorely tempted to follow my mother's repeated exhortations and "give up the whole thing", but always before me hovered the image of my father. Because he had tended to "give up" whenever an obstacle appeared, life itself had ultimately seemed too difficult and had been abandoned.

I had already persuaded my mother to keep John and Shirley for the few days before their schools reopened. She agreed reluctantly, obviously convinced that my departure would be the signal for a full-scale Blitz on London. On January 5th, before going to the air terminal for the Paris plane, I put both children on the bus for Kensington, and said good-bye as casually as I could.

What a world in which to be twelve and nine, I thought, recalling my own uneventful childhood in Macclesfield and Buxton. But whatever might happen to England before I returned, the immediate risks, as I well knew, were mine rather than theirs.

(10)

At the air terminal I learned that the Paris plane had been cancelled owing to "low visibility". By now heartily cursing the inauspicious conjunction of war and weather, I took the cross-Channel night steamer which offered the last chance of reaching Lisbon with time to spare.

From the air officials I also discovered that no writing or photographs could be carried through France, which meant a last-moment rush to the Censorship Department at the General Post Office, where my lecture notes were censored and sealed. Had the Paris plane flown as usual, all the material prepared for my tour would have been confiscated immediately I landed.

In the company of Mr. and Mrs. Frank Sheed, of the publishing firm of Sheed and Ward, who had also been Clipper passengers, I crossed a calm, misty Channel. Neither mines nor submarines disturbed us; only the weather obliged us to anchor for an hour outside Calais until the dawn fog lifted. Steel grey against the pale blue morning sky, our escort of six planes swooped low over the ship. When we finally landed we found Calais very cold and its streets covered with hard-frozen slush.

Our midday train stopped at every station on the way to Paris; by the time we reached the crowded Gare du Nord in darkness, the journey from London had taken twenty-one hours.

"It was queer," I wrote afterwards to my mother, "to see once more the cemetery at Étaples, with its dead of two decades ago, looking exactly as it looked in the winter of 1917-18 when I was there, with the bare brown pine trunks and snow on the ground."

Over late dinner at a small restaurant in the Boulevard des Hôpitales, the Sheeds and I decided that Paris looked much more cheerful than London because "black-out" material was actually royal blue. The city seemed completely different from the tense, tragic Paris that I had known in the previous war; its inhabitants displayed an equilibrium, even a gaiety, which had been totally lacking in 1917.

On the walls of restaurants and stations hung large maps of the world, with British and French possessions coloured red. Below ran a sanguine caption:

WE SHALL WIN BECAUSE WE ARE THE STRONGEST.

Confident in their Maginot line, the French were waiting for history to repeat itself. But history is seldom so obliging. Four years later, the walls of Paris under the Nazi occupation were still to show the tattered remnants of this hopeful prophecy.

At the Gare d'Austerlitz we learned that extensive Portuguese floods round the Tagus had held up the Sud-Expresse for two days. In spite of this discouraging information, I slept so soundly in the Wagon-Lit to the Spanish frontier that when the conductor brought me coffee and rolls at Bordeaux, I thought we had only just started.

As the train passed through Bayonne, the soft air and warm sunshine seemed miraculous after the raw cold of war-time London. A French paper which I read beside the open carriage window conveyed the unexplained news of Leslie Hore-Belisha's resignation as Minister for War.

Another disconcerting adventure awaited me in Spain, a country which still seemed, under the universal supervision of Franco's portrait, to be more truly at war than England or France. The cruelty and desperation of battle remained alive in the ruthlessness of officialdom at wayside stations, and in the lorries hurtling down muddy tracks regardless of human life.

At the frontier village of Irun, much damaged by the Civil War, the Spanish police—Anglophobe like the rest of the Peninsula—detained me in the station guard room. Innocently I was carrying pesetas at an illegal rate supplied in good faith by my travel agency, and for two hours wearily endeavoured to convince Spanish officials who knew no French that this crime had not been intentional. Eventually my travelling companions rescued me by vouching for my *bona fides*.

After a belated lunch, only one hour remained for exploring Irun before the Lisbon train. But it was enough. The little town provided a comfortless foretaste of sights and smells still to come in my own country, and later to be re-encountered on the devastated Continent. Gutted buildings stood amid heaps of rubble, their twisted iron balconies pointing like skeleton fingers into the air.

One large deserted mansion, facing the main street, must once have been an elegant home; now its impressive exterior was blackened with fire, its windows gaping, its roof blown away. As the evening mists rose from the Bidassoa River they carried a stench once familiar to me—the stench of French villages where the unburied dead rotted anonymously beneath heaps of fallen stone.

Next morning the sight of half-starved ragged children at village stations, and the milkless *ersatz* coffee served beside the line, recalled

G.'s abortive efforts in 1937, and the bitter need of the Spanish people for the internationally-controlled relief which had been so arrogantly refused.

Such was war. The comfort of moving from this ferocious, poverty-stricken country into Portugal defied adequate words. Why had no one described to me those lovely landscapes of pines and rushing streams, with their vistas of rocky valleys climbing to rugged ranges of cloud-capped violet hills?

Further south, tangerines glowed like miniature lanterns against their dark leaves, and for the first time I saw European mimosa in bloom. The exuberant galaxy of magnolias, marigolds, roses and geraniums all flowering together brought back the memory of Portofino in a far-off peace-time spring.

At twilight the train sped past the flooded Tagus, running for miles through a vast shallow lake. As we suddenly crawled over a mended section of the line which appeared as fragile as matchboard, the short crooked reflections of olive trees looked back at me from the waterlogged land in the red afterglow of sunset.

Late that night I sat beside my open hotel window in the mild Lisbon air, drafting the next issue of my Letter. Gazing up the broad slope of the Avernida da Liberdade with its line of brilliant lights, I though incredulously: "This is peace. How long before London knows its solace again?"

(11)

Throughout my visit the crowded spy-ridden city, just beginning its long era of prosperous neutrality, remained as warm as an English June.

I found that the story of my Spanish adventure had preceded me. That night three calls from newspaper offices were put through to my bedroom; next morning the front page of *Il Secolo* carried an account of my arrival. I also read a description of my fellow train-traveller, Eve Curie, a handsome woman in her thirties whose biography of her mother had been a recent best-seller. She too was lecturing for Colston Leigh, and later appeared on the *Vulcania*.

A telephone call from Susan Lowndes-Marques, the daughter of Mrs. Belloc Lowndes, followed the newspaper story. From tea at her flat she and her husband, a handsome Portuguese editor, took me to an outsize cocktail party given by *The Times* correspondent. There I met most of the English colony, including the British Ambassador.

On January 10th the *Vulcania* came in, and duly went out again

231

with the Sheeds and myself on board. Up to ten o'clock that morning nobody knew whether the ship was coming, or when she was leaving if she did arrive. In addition to her small contingent of first-class passengers, she carried 900 Polish, Czech and Jewish refugees. At the vaccination inspection before we sailed we all undressed together while a Portuguese doctor, sternly supervised by an American immigration officer, examined our previous scars.

Towards evening we sailed, looking back from the wide Tagus estuary at Lisbon glowing in the flame-pink sunset. White-walled with roofs of vermilion tiles, its cypress-crowned hills disappeared as we slid into the Gulf Stream.

For three days we passed no other passenger ship; no fishing vessel; no sign of human or animal life.

"I have the feeling of being hundreds of miles from any other set of living souls, at sea or elsewhere," I wrote to my mother, sitting on the small verandah outside my cabin beneath a pale blue cloud-flecked sky. What unknown terror did that incongruously placid sea conceal, I wondered, recalling my wartime journey to Malta in the doomed hospital ship *Britannic* on the voyage before she was sunk. Who would come to our rescue if we struck a magnetic mine?

Courage was a quality I could never claim; to a writer, except when he or she is writing, imagination is more often a curse than a blessing. But the danger, though trivial, did exist; war-histories have since recorded that two-thirds of the shipping losses caused by magnetic mines fell on neutral countries.

When we stopped for two hours at Porta Delgarda on the island of St. Michael in the Azores, I collected a new item of geography. I had pictured a series of fishing villages on barren semi-tropical beaches; instead I learned that these Portuguese islands formed a unit of Atlantic civilisation two hundred miles long, with a population of seven hundred thousand.

Not even Eve Curie was allowed to go ashore in the clean white town, though the French Consul came on board to greet her. Standing on the top deck, I contemplated the yellow roofs of square-towered churches, half concealed by small closely-packed houses colour-washed in jade or terra-cotta. Beyond the roofs, little walled fields climbed towards sugar-loaf hills of a vivid unbelievable green. With their strange irregular shapes, which recalled the Mountains of Mourne, they suggested the haphazard lines of a child's painting-book.

We sailed on through the tail of a hurricane which had passed two days earlier, leaving cold rough weather behind it. Huge waves continually struck the ship with the sound of subterranean explosions.

"Once," I reported to my mother, "it was so loud that everybody thought we had been torpedoed; she stopped and quivered for about three minutes."

A year afterwards G. was similarly to mistake, until almost too late, the sound of a torpedo for the impact of a wave.

When the cyclone drove me from the dining-room I talked in the cabin with my stewardess, a pleasant, buxom young woman whom I had taken for thirty. Instead I learnt that she was a widow from Trieste, with a twenty-year-old son at college in Venice. Her husband had lost his life in the Trieste and Fiume "troubles" which so closely resembled our own "troubles" in Ireland.

I told her in return how my brother had been killed on the Italian front, and lay buried in the pine forests of the Asiago Plateau. For his sake especially I was glad that Italy had so far kept out of the war.

"How thankful you must be," I added, "that your son doesn't have to fight."

"Indeed, but I am!" she cried, spreading out her plump, comely hands. "It is no good, ze warre! In all countries it is ze same—ze governors only want ze warre. For ze common people—no use!"

The mothers of London's East End, I suspected, would strongly agree.

(12)

We reached New York in a snow-storm, but this did not prevent reporters and photographers starved of European visitors from hurrying some of us out on deck. Equally unflattering pictures of Eve Curie and myself appeared next day on the front page of the *New York Times*.

At the docks G. met me with representatives of the Macmillan Company and the Leigh Bureau, all looking frozen. He had finished the Eastern half of his long tour for the Canadian Institute of International Relations; my ship conveniently arrived just before he began the Western section.

We arranged to meet in California, for I had now no time to talk either with him or with my publishers. Already the failure of the Clipper had cost me five lectures; next morning I was obliged to leave for Louisville, Kentucky. Interviews arranged to advertise *Testament of Friendship* had to be crowded into a few moments, but I learned that the advance sales had reached 5,000 and took with me an encouraging collection of early reviews. Ten days later a mass of notices reached me from London, where Macmillan reported that their first edition of 10,000 copies had sold out during publication week.

From a bundle of newspapers carried to the train, I learned more about the war in a few hours than I had gathered from the semi-fog of the last five months. America tacitly expressed her opinion of tendentious information by a small inset caption on the main page of every paper:

REMEMBER THAT ALL NEWS FROM EUROPE IS SUBJECT TO
CENSORSHIP AND PROPAGANDA

Outside Washington another snow-storm, overwhelming even for that phenomenal winter, delayed my train for two hours. In the lounge car I asked a conversational business man what interest that section of the near-South felt in the war.

"It's the main topic of every intelligent discussion," he told me. "We all listen eagerly to radio programmes from Europe—though not perhaps with quite the excitement of the first few weeks."

That night, for the first time in my experience, the heating system failed in my Pullman car. Too cold to sleep, I struggled into some clothes soon after dawn and sought warmth in the empty dining-car. When I reached Louisville the mercury had fallen to 13° below zero, a temperature unknown in Kentucky for forty years.

At luncheon the Women's Club demanded a talk on my journey instead of the scheduled topic. Later I sent my mother a clipping from the Louisville *Courier-Journal*, whose woman reporter had been present.

"British Vera Brittain," she began dramatically, "kept an engagement to speak in Louisville even though . . . she went through hail, rain, fire, sleet, wind and the rest of it to do so. . . . She was looking forward with true British fortitude to anything else that might come her way."

Actually, I had long lost all confidence in my "fortitude", and still felt uncertain whether I had any right to take even such minor risks as my travels involved. John and Shirley weighed heavily on my conscience, a secret burden of cold, racking fear. The news of the fresh Nazi threat to frozen Holland had reached me on the *Vulcania* through brief radio reports so badly translated that I could not estimate their importance. I was disturbed especially by the threat from the air, for every attempted raid on England was reported in detail in the American papers, and sounded much more alarming than it had appeared at home.

Weren't the children an unfair responsibility to lay on two head-masters and an ageing grandmother? Back and forth raced my unquiet speculations until the tour, with the leviathan-like inevitability of all tours, finally overwhelmed them.

Two days later, passing through Chicago to a lecture in Lake Forest, Illinois, I met G. by accident during a short walk under bright sun in an icy wind which froze Lake Michigan a quarter of a mile from the shore. We lunched together at the Union station, fascinated by the strange chance of encountering each other in a city of three million people. He was putting in a few hours on the way to Winnipeg, he told me.

Travelling in the Middle West, I soon realised that all America was by no means watching the European conflict with deep sympathy for the Allied cause. In the current Letter, I recorded what one well-informed citizen of Wisconsin had described as the typical reactions of his own community.

"The lessons of the last war, the futility of it, have sunk deep out here," he said. "What people remember are the secret treaties, the vindictiveness of Versailles, the defaulted war debts and the post-war blindness of France and England. There is also a deep-seated suspicion of British and French motives: people here feel they are up against something they don't understand—the European system."

The next card to my mother went from El Paso on the Mexican frontier, where I changed trains for Los Angeles after a lecture in Dallas. Even the Texas temperature had fallen to 12° above zero; from the train the huge State slid by in an interminable vista of chocolate-coloured earth and cinnamon-brown woods lightly powdered with snow.

Years later I was to find that every detail of these travels, like the journeys of the First World War, had been burned into my memory by anxiety and tension. Much of this anxiety was caused by the newspapers, which exaggerated American events for my mother and British events for me. The heightened consciousness of war-time still leaves a clear-cut picture of the lovely desert cities in the South-west, and especially of Tucson, Arizona. There, during a long halt, I watched the sun set in a vermilion glow over vast horizontal miles of hard-baked earth, prickly cactus, and dry brown scrub.

Even the names of the desert flowers, supplied by a fellow passenger, remained in my mind. Ocotillo opened like a scarlet butterfly from slender leafless stems taller than a man; yucca stood straight and challenging, like a white flambeau; beavertail trailed its tiny red blossoms along the ground. Still stranger were the shapes of the all-green cacti; the Joshua tree with waving arms; the sinister spears of the sahuard pointing upwards; the cholla like a mass of pine-cones sprouting from one branch.

Next morning the train left the desert to plunge through long ranges of low mountains, the southernmost spurs of the Rockies. Some were round, some sharp, some jagged; in the clear brilliant atmosphere their vivid colours shaded from sapphire to violet. At sunset they turned indigo and purple, with a deep rose glow on their distant summits.

"We were among them all day," concluded the letter to my mother, "giving a new meaning to the phrase 'the everlasting hills'."

(13)

From Chicago onwards I had become conscious of a growing discomfort, due, I thought, to the violent changes of climate which I had experienced since leaving home.

When I reached Los Angeles on January 27th the thermometer registered 85°. My own rising temperature gave me a less than just appreciation of that sprawling metropolis reaching out like an octopus to its famous suburbs—Hollywood, Pasadena, Santa Monica, Beverly Hills—where the palms grew as large as oak-trees, and scarlet poinsettias flowered richly in front of the humblest shack. In spite of the mountains and the sea, it seemed to me less beautiful than New Orleans, and even Minneapolis.

This experience of Californian sunshine, when harsh winter at home made war even more cruel, recalled the phrase by which Winifred had justified her departure from Somerville College in 1917 to join the Women's Army—"the horror of immunity". Amid the warmth and beauty of the Far West, war seemed only the more evil, and man's folly in denying himself the glories of his lovely world the more crassly stupid.

The next day brought thunder, lightning and heavy rain, followed by cold, damp weather. Simultaneously I went down with an attack of grippe so severe that for two days I thought I had pneumonia. Alone in the noisy, fashionable hotel where the Leigh Bureau had sent me, I fought the virulent germ with aspirin and brandy. I dared not send for the hotel doctor owing to the probable size of his bill, and eventually I telephoned the Bureau's Los Angeles representative. She hurried to my room with a local physician, whose emergency treatment put me shakily on my feet in time for the opening lecture at Hollywood.

By contrast with the heat of my blood as I lay tossing behind half-drawn blinds in a bedroom as restful as a main line terminus, G.'s letters described winter-bound Canada, lying beneath endless miles of snow, "an eternity of it under the moon". On February 6th he joined me from Vancouver, a journey of two and a half days to be with me for less than a week. By that time I had moved to a quieter hotel overlooking the green slope outside the palatial Public Library, and had given three lectures with a fluctuating temperature on a diet of orange juice, soup and tea.

Already I had found that the Californian papers gave far more space to the war than the journals of the Middle West. But it was an educative experience for a British traveller to read publications which presented England's naval misfortunes with the same laconic detachment as Germany's aerial defeats, and treated Winston Churchill's dramatic speeches with hardly more respect than the picturesque pronouncements of Dr. Goebbels. In the imposing Los Angeles window of the Hamburg-Amerika Line, a large placard invited Americans to help in breaking the British blockade.

"YOU CAN NOW SEND FOOD PARCELS TO GERMANY."

As soon as I could promote myself to normal meals, Macmillan's local representative gave a dinner for G. and me at Hollywood. The guests included Victor Saville, as friendly as he had been when I sold him the film rights of *South Riding*; Paul Jordan Smith of the *Los Angeles Times*; the novelist, James Hilton; and Rachel Field, author of *All This and Heaven Too*. A vague discomfort surrounds the memory of the late James Hilton, the fleeting impression of too long a sojourn among the flesh-pots of California.

Other recollections of Los Angeles have been dimmed by two encounters which still cast their vivid images across the years.

(14)

At our hotel a letter awaited us from Bertrand Russell, now on the Faculty at the University of Southern California. With his O.M. still nine years ahead, he was becoming, at sixty-seven, increasingly conscious of his isolation from an England at war. When a press paragraph reported our presence he invited us to dine with him and his wife Patricia, whom I had last seen as an undergraduate.

The famous sea-food restaurant where we met remains the only eating place that I recall in Los Angeles. Almost immediately, his dark brows bent under an impressive halo of white hair, Lord

Russell plunged into a dissertation upon the contrast, as he saw it, between the motives of the Allies in the two World Wars. His pacifism during the First had caused him to be expelled from Trinity College, Cambridge, but Hitler, he felt, had made pacifism impossible for a thoughtful agnostic.

This was clearly no expedient conversion, no lining-up for admission to orthodoxy and public approval. The intellectual wrestlings to which we listened were all but visible and tangible; doubt was excruciating and pain authentic. Those soul-searchings still incongruously recall to me the appetising smell of cooked lobster and the sight of live trout plunging casually through sea-green tanks.

Shortly afterwards we were the guests, at another dinner in Pasadena, of Upton Sinclair and Charlie Chaplin. The two men, long close friends, were already known to G.; in 1935 Sinclair had arranged for him to meet Chaplin and see his latest film.

"What chiefly struck me," G. had written of that occasion, "was the vital energy displayed, like the blue flashes sizzling in an electric wire, in every gesture, in the rapid shooting-out of ideas. A really remarkable extroverted creature."

Not realising the time needed to keep engagements within the 450 square miles of Los Angeles, we arrived extremely late from a cocktail party in Santa Monica. Had our hosts been lesser men they would probably have gone home, but the owners of these world-renowned names, familiar with British miscalculations, awaited us patiently for over an hour. When we entered the now empty hotel dining-room they were still there, Upton Sinclair tall and spare, with the responsible seriousness of the social historian; Charlie Chaplin small, puckish, and effervescent.

The four of us sat talking all evening; G. and I eventually returned to Los Angeles at 3 a.m. in Chaplin's car. On the way back he described to us, with characteristic eloquence, a recent journey through Indo-China. Soon its native inhabitants, in the world of ironic fantasy which he created for us, became larger and stranger than life.

"Big, silent, *vicious* men!" he hissed with sibilant enthusiasm. "Padding behind you in the dark!"

Between these lively engagements I had sandwiched lectures at Pomona and Santa Barbara, a seaside Eden of orange groves, hibiscus and mimosa, with which G. fell so deeply in love that when his own tour was over he spent three weeks at its Margaret Baylor Inn making the first draft of his new book, *One Anglo-American Nation*. There I read of Sumner Welles's peace mission to

Europe, but a few days later at Fresno, the home of Sun Maid Raisins in the long San Joachim Valley, I heard of the new Soviet onslaught against Finland's Mannerheim Line.

In San Francisco I appeared at the Town Hall Forum of the West, and during the luncheon which followed the lecture sat beside Gertrude Atherton, the ageing yet ageless author of *Black Oxen*. My visit coincided with that of Alfred Duff Cooper, of whom G. had newly invented a *mot*: "No Englishman should visit America for the first time."

With its steep hills, sunlit air, and the splendid bay which reminded G. of Constantinople, I found San Francisco the most enchanting of America's beautiful cities. How sad distant England seemed in this heaven of California, with its tiny, gay humming-birds and vivid butterflies! Yet it was the gloom and glumness which summoned me back; the beauty which would keep me conscience-stricken until I had renounced it.

On our last evening before G. returned to Canada and I went north to Seattle, we dined together in the Chinese quarter where the pagodas and dragon-decorated houses suggested Shanghai rather than America. Leaving next day at sunset, I looked from the train across the Pacific to see the Golden Gate exactly as it should be seen between the twin columns of the mighty bridge, with flaming bars of cloud above them and the deep blue skyline of the city fading into night.

This lovely land turned towards the West, pacific in its outlook as in its mild radiant climate, seemed to symbolise the level of civilisation which might be universally achieved if men could settle their differences by the deliberate exercise of good-will—that powerful political weapon so often belauded in fair words, but so seldom tried.

(15)

During the next four weeks my letters reflected a series of kaleidoscopic experiences. The temperature and trees of Seattle might have belonged to a glorified Hampshire in spring, I wrote to G., now back in New York where he had seen the secret arrival of the *Queen Elizabeth*. An eminent local professor, I added, had described a recent visit by Harold Laski.

"He nearly caused a revolution here," my acquaintance commented glumly. I gathered that Laski, preaching Marxism, had involved the University in trouble with the Legislature, which appointed an abortive commission of enquiry after he had gone.

At Washington State College in Pullman I suffered another ignominious collapse, attributed by a local doctor to food-poisoning and the neglected after-effects of influenza. Owing to his intravenous injections and the kindness of a college "house-mother", I was able, again without missing a lecture, to struggle on weak legs to an engagement at Spokane.

Even more than the medical treatment, some letters from England restored my confidence that I could carry on. One from my publishers reported 15,000 copies sold of *Testament of Friendship* and a third large printing in hand. Among 200 reviews and notices, another clipping from the *Yorkshire Post* remarked on the astonishing persistence with which Winifred remained "news" when so many writers, once dead, were forgotten.

On the long journey from Spokane to Laramie, the capital of Wyoming, I passed through Boise, the chief city of Idaho. In this small community of 20,000 inhabitants beneath the snow-capped foothills of the Salmon River Mountains, Senator Borah, the great isolationist, had been buried after a fatal seizure the previous month. The State Offices and the white rounded dome of the Capitol gave the little town a top-heavy dignity.

My train passed within sight of the cemetery, a humble acre difficult to distinguish from the drab-coloured earth and grey-white frame houses of this scrubby land. Yet 11,000 people, a fellow passenger told me, had passed in silence before Borah's coffin when it was brought home from Washington. At the end of January a long series of newspaper columns had contained the most moving obituaries of an American statesman that I had ever read. His sudden collapse in his apartment was soon to be recalled by the similar end of another great man who died shortly afterwards—Lord Tweedsmuir, the Governor-General of Canada, whom most of us knew better as John Buchan.

That evening, three business men joined my table in the dining car. I kept silence lest my "English accent" should reveal my nationality, for sooner or later most American travellers were liable to talk about Britain and the war.

I was not disappointed. The inevitable discussion of the Finnish campaign led by rapid stages to the expected criticism of England.

"They say they're for the small countries," observed one company director. "Why, they've sold every small country down the line up to date!"

"H'm," growled another, "those people never won a war yet without gettin' somebody else to help 'em out. You mark my words, if Roosevelt gets a third term, we'll be in it same as we were in '17!"

And I was moved, like any militant patriot, to raise my English voice and defend my country, as I always did in the question periods that followed my lectures, with a series of excuses which would never have seemed valid had I uttered them at home.

Later, as the train passed over the highest point of the Union Pacific Railroad near Cheyenne in the Rockies, I looked from my sleeping car at the field of brilliant stars amid the snow-covered peaks; from 10,000 feet the familiar planets seemed tremendous and very near. Was William Borah, the just man with the vehement prejudices, now able to view the warring earth with the same magnificent detachment as the midnight stars?

After the engagement at Laramie, where the 7,000 feet altitude increased a convalescent's problems by temporarily destroying the power of concentration, I stayed in St. Paul, Minnesota, with Ruth and Woodard Colby. Now firm friends with whom I corresponded regularly, they were deeply concerned by newspaper prophecies of the coming Blitzkrieg and almost as anxious as myself about John and Shirley.

In their care the poet Paul Engle, whose *America Remembers* I had quoted in *Thrice a Stranger*, had left a folder of his recent poems for me. One seemed to recall the friend, now in Broadmoor, whose murder trial I had attended in November:

> "I leave the house. Big winds from northward blow
> Darkly against the open door, to find
> And scare me from my walk. They do not know
> That there are wilder weathers of the mind . . .
>
> "Let the rain ravel through the beaten leaves,
> I turn it back with heavy coat and leather.
> It is a little thing to him who grieves
> Harried by a more savage human weather."

Passing through Chicago for a brief visit to Canada, I found the windy city damp and grey. Bleak gusts from the still frozen lake blew melting icicles off slowly thawing trees with the strange effect of a violent hailstorm.

That day's *Chicago Tribune* published a cartoon as savage as the wind. Inflamed with contempt for the countries which Thomas Jefferson denounced as "nations of eternal war", the artist had drawn a demented monster labelled "Europe" kneeling on a stool. Round his neck, a thick noose called "British Opposition to Peace" hung from the ceiling. To his ear he held a pistol ticketed "German

Opposition to Peace", while his other hand clutched the label "French Opposition to Peace" on a bottle of poison.

The laconic caption ran: "Determined to do a thoro job of it this time."

Toronto seemed friendly after Chicago, though American neutrality had presented Canada with a problem of divided loyalties. Her civilisation, dominated by the United States, recalled Europe only in the Province of Quebec, yet her traditions tied her emotionally to Britain. Three members of the Toronto Press who interviewed me stated frankly that Canada had joined in the war mainly for "sentiment". Yet Union Jacks decorated my lecture platform, and the evening opened with "God Save the King".

In Boston, where I now went to make up the lectures missed at the beginning of my journey, I found my hosts discussing the Hitler-Mussolini meeting on the Brenner Pass and the new series of raids on Scapa Flow. Did these portents signify the opening of the spring Blitzkrieg?

I should soon know, I reflected with relief, as I walked to my hotel through a radiant spring morning from Scollay Square, where a passport photograph had been taken for the now imminent journey. On my way I passed Trinity Church, a celebrated circular building of red-brown stone which is old as America reckons age. I pushed open the heavy swing door, and stepped into a mellow twilight beneath golden stained-glass windows.

So much had I travelled that I had lost count of dates and seasons, and was abruptly recalled to Holy Week by the Lenten service proceeding within. The clergyman conducting it had begun to read the passage from St. Luke's Gospel which describes the Last Supper, the betrayal of Judas, and the denial of Peter. As I sat down at the back of the Church, he reached a familiar verse now so charged with meaning that I felt I had never heard it before.

"While I was daily with you in the temple, ye stretched forth no hands against me; but this is your hour, and the power of darkness."

No words could more poignantly have emphasised the contrast between the doctrine which the worshippers professed and the actions of their fellow men in the world outside. Into my mind flashed the *New York Times* headlines which I had read over breakfast that morning.

"WHITE HOUSE FINDS PEACE TALK EMPTY." "CHAMBERLAIN IN A FIGHTING SPEECH THREATENS DIRE REPRISALS ON REICH." "WELLES RETURNING, NO PEACE IN SIGHT."

This, it seemed, was indeed their hour—the dictatorships which betrayed Christ; the democracies which lacked the courage to confess and follow Him. Had mankind ever drifted so far from the civilised conduct demanded of His disciples by the Teacher in the temple?

"This is your hour, and the power of darkness."

(16)

The final third of my tour involved a series of lectures to college students, who nearly all chose the subject "Youth and War" from my list of topics.

These boys and girls had followed the war news with keen intelligence, but like their elders they felt deeply suspicious of propaganda, and did not want their generation to be "let in for it" as their still young fathers had been. Yet their immunity gave them an unhappy sense of guilt towards their European contemporaries. Short of fighting, there seemed to be nothing that they would not do to help the British cause.

At one college after another, they asked me almost identical questions.

. "How long will the war last? Will Mr. Chamberlain continue as Premier? What does English youth think of German youth? How is conscription affecting your students?" And finally, with memories of the Abdication, "What do the young feel about the Archbishop of Canterbury?"

Suspense still immobilised the Western Front, but from all available portents it seemed clear that this strange paralysis would not last much longer. Dominated by anxiety to get home before the respite ended, and struggling with energies still impaired by two breakdowns to finish a closely-packed schedule, I had paid insufficient attention to several disquieting episodes emphasised by a newspaper cutting which my mother had sent me.

This was a Press attack—one of several, as I eventually found—on Dick Sheppard's Peace Pledge Union and, incidentally, upon myself. On February 21st I had even figured in question-time at the House of Commons.

"What duties," inquired Sir Henry Page Croft, "are performed at the Ministry of Information by Miss Vera Brittain, and is she being sent to America by the Department?"

"Miss Brittain is not employed by the Ministry of Information and has no connection with it," Sir John Reith had answered blandly. He did not add that America's interest in my lectures had long ante-dated the Ministry, or that I was fulfilling an invitation issued months before the war.

The following day, by a peculiar coincidence, Sir John Anderson, the Home Secretary, had announced in Parliament that the Peace Pledge Union was being "carefully watched", and the question "whether special measures are called for will be kept in view."

Under splash headlines, "2 WOMEN HELP TO CONTROL THE PEACE PLEDGE UNION", the paragraph sent by my mother published the names of its Council, which then included George Lansbury, Lord Ponsonby and Canon C. E. Raven. Beneath a conspicuous photograph of myself appeared a caption: "The novelist wife of Professor G. C., who was economic adviser to Sir Oswald Mosley in the days of the New Party."

This endeavour to identify us both with Mosley's Fascist policy was of course mendacious. G. had ended his brief connection with Mosley immediately Sir Oswald left the Labour Party, though other conspicuous Socialists had joined him for a time. But only the post-war publication of the Gestapo List was finally to dispose of these tendentious suggestions.

In my thirteenth Letter, published on January 18th, I had written prophetically: "One of militarism's subtlest and most damaging weapons is misrepresentation; that is, the presentation of an honest opinion or activity in such a fashion as to arouse the suspicions of others."

I now wrote to G.: "I think you should deal with this Mosley lie in some conspicuous place," and added that their early association had been used against us before. But I was too busy to analyse this attempt to discredit me. More perturbing, because at the moment closer, was a strange communication from the Secretary-Treasurer of an organisation which I was shortly to address in New York. Whether his letter arose directly from the British Press attacks, I never discovered.

"I have been requested by the Chairman and Board of Directors," it ran, "to ask you . . . whether you have been correctly quoted in the papers in stating that you would not stay in England to help her in any way to win the war. The officers had not known of this newspaper remark, and in view of the proposed tea for you on March 29th felt that they should be accurately informed."

On March 18th I replied as follows:

"Since I arrived in this country on January 17th and have given literally dozens of interviews in all parts of America . . . I should be fortunate indeed if no journalist had produced a garbled version of my remarks. As you do not give the date, the name of the newspaper, or the exact quotation of my alleged statement, it is a little

244

difficult for me to identify it. But I cannot imagine how anyone could quote me as saying that I would not stay in England, since I only left on January 5th and am sailing back there on April 6th."

With this communication I enclosed a copy of my twelfth Letter to Peace-Lovers, which answered the common accusation that advocates of non-violent resistance did not love their country.

"This Letter," I added, "makes quite clear both my philosophy of life and my attitude towards England. I have given no interviews here which contradict this view. As for my lectures, they were submitted to the chief British Censorship Office before I sailed . . . and were passed without criticism."

The organisation professed itself satisfied and did not accept my offer to cancel the talk, but neither then nor later was I supplied with evidence for my supposed statement. Friends suggested that I should refuse to appear, but the maintenance of my dignity seemed less important than the restoration of good relations.

When the day came, derogatory rumours had clearly preceded me. One guest thrust her angry red face close to mine and exclaimed censoriously: "I hope you're not going to talk about *peace*!" Her hope was realised; my innocuous discourse on the British Government's scheme for evacuating children and invalids would hardly have been recognised under that now inauspicious word.

During this tense period of mounting suspicion, Bertrand Russell, whom we had seen such a short time ago, also found himself in trouble. His recent appointment at New York City College had been vehemently challenged by some powerful religious bigots, though whether the cause lay in his atheism or his views on morals did not clearly emerge from the spate of indignation.

"Bishops also belong to the mob," G. wrote me of this controversy. "I doubt whether Russell will get his post even at City College. Bishop Manning is on his track. So powerful is convention, and so ruthless, that Manning will probably win."

As an object of criticism I was certainly in good company. At a lecture on "Changes in Manners and Morals" for New York's Town Hall Club, I gave my frank opinion of the anti-Russell faction.

Lord Russell's troubles proved to be short-lived and to end happily with a return to Cambridge contrived by his friends; my own were still to come. Even now I did not clearly interpret the accumulating signals which afterwards made a letter written to G. on a final journey to North Carolina read like an epitaph on the past decade.

"What a lovely State this is! It was 85° in Charlotte yesterday.

The gardens of a charming road here where I walked this afternoon were so beautiful that, as I thought of returning to Europe from their colourful serenity, Walter de la Mare's words came into my head: 'Look thy last on all things lovely . . .' "

Neither G. nor I anticipated the frustration which awaited us in our own country because we chose to go back to it. But he, now freed from the exacting travels which still deprived me of time to think, had begun to recognise how quickly a State fighting totalitarianism becomes affected by the enemy's values.

"I think the physical risk too small almost to be worth the counting," he had written me from Santa Barbara of our impending return. "The real risk lies in suppression of what one has an obligation to say. That really frightens me. Where there is war there can be no freedom of speech—and like Shaw I prize it. I do more than prize it —it is what I exist for. A political philosopher who distorts his utterance is worse than a liar; he is a criminal against humanity."

In spite of his apprehensions, I reached the end of my tour with deep relief. Apart from the physical fatigue created by anxiety and illness, it had been much harder than its two predecessors. Every British lecturer in America, whether belligerent or otherwise, was now liable to a cross-fire of criticism from the Isolationists who assumed that he would talk war propaganda, and the Interventionists who attacked him if he did not.

On April 5th, our last evening in New York, G. and I dined together in a Fifth Avenue restaurant and there saw a British author whom we knew. He came over to speak to us, and we told him we were sailing next day.

"I do envy you, going home so soon!" he said.

"Why not come with us?" we suggested. "There seems to be plenty of room in our ship."

But this, he explained, though desirable, was really quite impossible. He had a film script for Hollywood which he must deliver in person, and then there were people whom he'd promised to look up. . . . However, he'd be seeing us in London very soon.

Four years later the author was still in America, but I had no impulse to join in the uncharitable comments on his prolonged absence. I had learned a bitter lesson during the reluctant flight from Europe with the children in 1938, and knew I should never have been brave enough to live with the knowledge that I was afraid to return.

Next day we sailed; the American friends who came to the docks to say good-bye treated us with respectful melancholy, as though we were going back to the front.

Our ship chanced to be again the Italian *Vulcania*; she was the first liner to sail for Europe after my tour ended. Almost empty, she carried a staff with manners totally transformed from the amiable courtesy shown me three months earlier. The officers, foreseeing Italy's impending entry into the war, had become cold and silent; the stewards, alive to every unexpected sound, showed a palpable fear of Allied torpedoes. They did not even attempt to disguise their apprehension after we read, in the ship's newspaper dated April 10th, the reports which told us that our return had come only just in time.

"Great Britain intensified her raid precautions Tuesday night in anticipation of early Nazi air attacks after the Allied Supreme War Council ordered full aid rush to Norway to resist Adolf Hitler's lightning invasion of Scandinavia."

Beside me on deck lay Storm Jameson's new novel, *Europe To Let*. When he realised that I had read the news, the Italian purser pointed sardonically to the book.

"There'll be more of Europe to let before long!" he said.

Half-way between the Azores and Lisbon, we passed the *Vulcania's* sister ship, the *Saturnia*, sailing westwards; laden from bows to stern with European refugees, she appeared to be racing from the wrath to come. But why, we wondered, had the attack developed in Scandinavia? From January onwards we had dreaded the invasion of Holland and Belgium, and even, despite the Maginot Line, of France. What threat to Hitler's grandiose ambitions for the Third Reich could have come from pacific Norway and Denmark?

Captain Liddell Hart, the military historian, has since supplied the answer to that question.

"Clumsy efforts to forestall a fear aggression have too often provoked it . . ." he wrote in 1951. "We now know that Hitler was very reluctant to embark on an invasion of Norway until Churchill's speeches and preparatory steps so alarmed him as to convince him that we were about to occupy the neutral country on his flank."

Perhaps on account of the new disturbance, our journey northwards from Lisbon took only half the time needed in January; formalities had been shortened, trains speeded up. But in Paris the French, still Maginot-minded, continued to drink their coloured *sirop* with unabated optimism in their roadside cafés.

When G. and I boarded a plane for England I made, at last, my first flight, and triumphantly recognised the contours of Brighton as we crossed the South Coast. Behind me I had now left for over half a decade the American continent with its scenes of friendship and triumph, and was soon to descend from the precarious pinnacle of popularity on which I had balanced for nearly seven years.

CHAPTER SEVEN

MIDNIGHT HOUR

"As soon as you find yourself on a path which can lead to no worldly advantage, you are freed at last from the competitive scheming of seekers after office or place. . . . Your road to salvation lies through pain and dishonour, for which there is no competition."

V.B., Humiliation with Honour, 1942.

(1)

How GLAD I was to come back to the kindliness and tranquillity of England; to find the cottage, where my mother had taken the children for their Easter holidays, as peacefully unimpaired against its background of spring blossom as it had been the previous year.

It seemed to be the nation three thousand miles from danger which had shown agitation; the one so close to the war displayed a calm which gave the strange illusion of perfect safety. No wonder men, and women too, were ready to die in the service of this peaceful, patient country without inquiring too closely into the motives and methods of her government; to lay down their lives

> "for some idea, but dimly understood,
> Of an English city never built with hands,
> Which love of England prompted and made good."

With those lines I had ended the *Letter to Peace-Lovers* which I had sent to the New York organisation where my patriotism had been questioned.

That Easter even my mother seemed less anxious than I had feared; to her the Scandinavian invasion was a bagatelle compared with the early closing of the children's schools owing to an epidemic of German measles. To this illness, the one minor infection which they had hitherto avoided, John had mildly succumbed and thus put Shirley restlessly in quarantine.

"They *would* get an infectious disease just when the invasion period began," wrote a friend who had helped my mother to take care of them. Pessimistically she added: "You will find England changed and changing. The Norwegian tragedy has begun to embitter people."

But so far nothing appeared to be changed for the worse; some weeks had still to pass before I observed that increase of intolerance which is a pathological symptom of war. An influx of distinguished Norwegians appeared to be the chief consequence of the Scandinavian attack; they were the advance guard of the Dutch, Belgians, French, Poles, Czechs, and other foreign nationals who in ten years were to transform England from a compact homogeneous island into a cosmopolitan State.

Late in April, Harold Macmillan, destined for the highest national honour, invited me to have lunch at Claridge's and give him a précis of my tour. I told him that I thought an important work of conciliation had still to be done in America by English friends of the United States. It was needed there because American contempt for Europe's failure to avoid wars sprang from an underestimate of European problems. The similar criticism of America in England owed more to complete ignorance of her domestic conflicts.

In exchange Mr. Macmillan gave me his own impression of Britain's contemporary shortcomings, which I subsequently recorded.

"He does not feel that we, the public, are being told or facing what we should. It seems to me from what he said that we may have to stiffen ourselves to confront things that our victorious (and vainglorious) history makes peculiarly difficult for us."

From the luxurious sofa which seemed so unsuited to the bleak realities of the military situation, I put the question then universally asked of anyone likely to possess inside knowledge.

"How long do you think the war will last?"

With grave deliberation the future Prime Minister replied: "Twelve months if they win; five years if we do."

Precisely five years and twelve days after that conversation, the war in Europe ended.

(2)

A fortnight after the children's return to school the Nazis marched into Holland and Belgium, thus initiating the period of acute danger which was to change history for John and Shirley and their generation.

Within weeks, owing to the strange confusion in official minds between religious conviction and political treachery, I was to find myself a "suspect", haunted by police supervision, thwarted by prohibitions in an England no longer tranquil or friendly. Often, in the years which followed, I asked myself a fundamental question. If I had believed that, by staying in America, I could have saved my reputation for integrity, my freedom to travel, my power as a writer to earn money abroad, should I have remained and had the children sent out to me?

I still think that the answer is No.

The new Nazi invasion, foreshadowed the previous January in plans captured from a German major whose aeroplane made a forced landing in Holland, coincided with a change of government and the death of George Lansbury.

On May 7th came the historic debate which released the emotions of a House of Commons disillusioned and exasperated by the catastrophic Norwegian campaign. Two days after Leopold Amery had ended his critical speech with Cromwell's impatient words to the Long Parliament—"For the love of God, go!"—and David Lloyd George had made his last decisive contribution to his epoch by insisting that Mr. Chamberlain should sacrifice the seals of office, I lunched at the House with Arthur Creech-Jones.

Though the division had given the Government a majority of 81, he thought it certain that Chamberlain would go. Over thirty Conservatives had voted with the Opposition and sixty had abstained; their vanished confidence could hardly have been more clearly displayed.

On the evening of the debate George Lansbury, with whom I had shared so many platforms since the Dorchester rally, died in the Manor House Hospital, aged eighty-one. In the words of his old friend H. Runham Brown, he had laid down his task "unfinished—in the midst of war—rejected of men but not despised. Loved by all men, respected by most, he had no enemies."

While the Nazis obliterated the centre of Rotterdam and flood waters spread from the opened dykes to add to Holland's nightmare, G. and I travelled to Bow Road to bid our friend farewell. The door of his pleasant East End cottage, later to be destroyed by a flying bomb, stood open to welcome callers.

Behind the purple-lidded coffin standing in his living-room against a bank of spring flowers, the raised window showed a green radiance of garden where birds were singing. As we wished him good-bye I realised, with a dismay which the future would soon increase, that he was the last great figure of his generation to bear the witness which we, their unworthy successors, must try to maintain without them in a period unrivalled for disasters even by the 1914 war.

On the day of his funeral the flag over the Bow Conservative Club flew at half-mast, and his local fellow-Socialists lined three miles of road to the garden where his ashes were taken before being scattered at sea.

"I am a convinced internationalist," he had written in his will, "and like to feel I am just a tiny part of universal life which will one day break down all divisions . . . and make mankind one great eternal unit both in life and death."

His dignified Parliamentary colleagues, excluded by the crowds from the parish church, paid their tribute at a Westminster Abbey Memorial Service where even the new Prime Minister, whose values "G.L." had so often challenged, sent his Secretary, Brendan Bracken, to represent him.

In the book, *England's Hour*, which I wrote later that year, I called the chapter describing this ceremony "Memorial Service for Civilisation". By that date, May 23rd, the Dutch resistance had long collapsed, the Belgians were about to capitulate, and mechanised Nazi armies had raced through Abbeville and Étaples to Boulogne. On May 14th the news was already so bad that, as Lloyd George's secretary later told G., Duff Cooper and his colleagues at the Ministry of Information did not know how to present it.

Four days earlier, when Mr. Chamberlain resigned after Clement Attlee and Arthur Greenwood politely declined to serve under him in a National Government, the Labour Party had already been Cabinet-making. A hint from Hugh Dalton sent G. that afternoon to Bournemouth, where the Party Conference was scheduled to open on Whit-Monday. I followed him next day to find the delegates assembling in a mood of suppressed jubilation, since the prospect of power is an excellent substitute for personal safety.

The Party stood, said Barbara Ayrton-Gould in her Presidential address, for "the right to fight for the things we believe in without being victimised because we believe in them". Long before the opening of another Conference, many honest citizens had reason to doubt whether the support of some leading Socialists for that admirable sentiment was still unshaken. In Bournemouth successive delegates emphasised the terrible responsibility of taking office at such a time; it was, of course, purely in the public interest that the Party had consented to serve. . . . One future statesman proclaimed that we had a moral duty to wring Hitler's neck; this was, I assumed, the modern version of hanging the Kaiser.

On the hotel terrace G. and I talked to Ellen Wilkinson beneath a gaily striped sun-umbrella as incompatible with the news as the calm sea, serenely blue beyond the shimmering hedge of gorse adorning the cliffs. Half-consciously we listened for the distant thunder of battle so soon to come within earshot of the threatened South Coast.

(3)

From the Conference G. and I went to the cottage and awaited, with the rest of England, the impact of the news. That night a raider appeared over Southampton; about 2 a.m. the anti-aircraft guns opened up all through the Forest. I awoke to hear their thumping from my bed under the window, and to see a network of search-lights round the fire-flashes in the sky.

"I shall have to get used to this," I thought, feeling slightly sick; our faculty for choosing abodes in unsafe areas seemed certainly to be outstanding. At present London appeared less frightening than the country, for the possible descent of parachutists had become a topic of conversation, and rumour, overworked as usual, reported them as likely to use the Forest. Many bewildered motorists now lost themselves in Hampshire lanes suddenly deprived of signposts.

On May 27th, a Sunday set aside as a day of National Prayer, I went with G. to the small Catholic Church in Lyndhurst where the local priest preached a simple sermon much less militaristic than Cardinal Hinsley's radio address. Though the weather remained radiant the graceful village, usually crowded at week-ends, appeared almost empty; the few passers-by were silent, and their faces looked white and strained.

To my publisher in New York I wrote that afternoon: "In all my experience there has been no tension like the tension of this wait-ing." Next morning, from an English friend, came a telepathic communication.

"I expect you feel like a piece of elastic which has been stretched until it has perished. I do. The stretching process has gone on too long."

In the cottage garden the vivid butterflies, flitting in hot sunshine from white broom to crimson rhododendron, made the likelihood of soon dying in cold blood as fantastic as it had doubtless seemed to the Dutch, Belgians and French a month ago. No one had then realised that the Maginot Line was only half a line, and a poor half at that.

Across the Channel a British garrison in Calais fought unrelieved for three days to protect the bridge-head at Dunkirk, and a strange armada of large and small ships passed over the sea which had looked so serene at Bournemouth. Even from Emery Down, the highest point of the New Forest, we could not see any part of that improvised flotilla, which varied from armoured destroyers and unarmed lifeboats to the "Saucy Sallies" of the summer season.

By June 4th, history's most dramatic rescue expedition had brought home an army of over 300,000 men. The "hard and heavy tidings" of which Churchill warned the British public had not taken its dreaded shape, but other terrors remained. Their personal aspect began to occupy our minds now that a temporary break had come in the story of national disaster. Ever present in my mind was one question: how soon would the tide of war rolling from France begin to threaten John and Shirley?

(4)

On June 5th the Press reported a new German offensive along the congested French roads, where the Nazi bombers, almost unopposed, impartially attacked both the disorganised troops and the terror-stricken civilian refugees. This formidable thrust had been made on a seventy-mile front from Abbeville towards Paris, which appeared to be the next objective before our own turn came.

Two days later we travelled to Dorset for Shirley's half-term at Oldfeld School.

"What a relief," I said to G., thinking of the uneventful centuries which had passed over Swanage since the Danish landing under King Alfred, "to be sure of three days without a raid!"

That night a loud explosion, followed by a spectacular but futile display of searchlights, woke me rudely from sleep. At breakfast our fellow visitors conjectured uneasily where the bomb could have fallen. "Snug and sunny Swanage", as our hotel brochure described it, appeared to have entered a new historic period of which snugness would not be the outstanding feature.

Shirley, racing along the sands with her class-mates, looked brown and fit, and seemed quite unperturbed by potential raids. Catching sight of us she waved gaily, but at the school play that evening she appeared to have as little use for us as any other nine-year-old confronted by visiting parents.

The following day I carried back to London the mental picture of a fair-haired child with limpid blue eyes, hugging our parting gift, a toy brown horse, against her red check frock, and swinging her

253

gas-mask in the other hand as she ran uphill to school. Beyond her flaxen head the sunlit cliffs conveyed the same illusion of tranquillity as the Cornish coast that framed the dream-like camouflaged ships in the tragic summer of 1918 which I was now painfully to remember.

Our return to the cottage coincided with Italy's entry into the war. How far, asked the newspapers, would Mussolini's long-conditioned soldiers differ from the Italians defeated at Caporetto in 1917? It was that defeat which had cost Edward his life.

"Twenty-two years ago on Saturday," I wrote in my diary that evening, "Edward was killed fighting for Italy. What a damned silly ironic folly war is, making the greatest fools of those who fight it! I hope they'll take care of his grave among the pines on the Asiago Plateau."

The handsome little boy from Bassano who had picked a bunch of scabious and white clover for me when I first visited that grave in 1921 was now, no doubt, a member of Italy's Fascist youth, and had become my "enemy". Two years afterwards, when I was writing a fortnightly Letter on the communion of saints, the idea suddenly came to me that the small British graveyard at Granezza—tended, as those mountain cemeteries would have to be, by local villagers— was actually a symbol of common suffering; a link perhaps lasting through war to peace to reconcile the Italians and ourselves.

Shortly after the Italian declaration of war, President Roosevelt broadcast an account of his abortive negotiations with Mussolini to the accompaniment of Nazis "cutting in" with their Horst Wessel song. At Lyndhurst the Civil Defence announced that church bells throughout England were now to be rung only to warn the population of airborne enemy troops. It seemed a strange use for instruments designed to summon the faithful to worship their Lord.

John's half-term, a week later than Shirley's, began on the same day as the fall of Paris; at Colwall the French-born wife of our hotel-proprietor greeted us, weeping, with the news. But John was naturally more interested in the antics of the Marx Brothers at the Malvern cinema. Before going in the three of us climbed to the top of the Priory tower, whence the rich Worcestershire countryside, stretching to the Welsh Border, gave the same unbearable impression of serenity as the Dorsetshire headland beyond Shirley's school.

In London we learned that the Pétain Government had asked for an Armistice, and read Churchill's speech which told the House of Commons that this was our finest hour. If only, he urged, we stood up to Hitler, "the life of the world may move forward into broad, sunlit uplands". Ten years afterwards that eloquent prophecy was to read strangely against the threat of a Third World War fought by other global antagonists with atomic weapons. But in 1940 those new levels of military attainment were still unforeseen; the tension already described, I wrote to New York, had now reached an all-time high. It seemed more like two years than two months since I had left America.

"We still wait, with the sense of being the last ninepin in the row, but everyone here faces the prospect with extraordinary calm. Whether the explanation is courage, fatalism, or a phlegmatic inability to picture things which have never happened here before, it is difficult to tell."

I added that I too could face everything with equanimity "if it weren't for the children. They are my Achilles heel."

(5)

During the Dunkirk evacuation, the Press had reported a discussion between Lord Lothian and Mr. Cordell Hull, the Secretary of State, on the possibility of American ships evacuating thousands of British children before the maximum danger period now at hand.

From that time onwards, newspapers and radio described the progress of a "seavacuation" scheme in which the United States and the Dominions would share. Troubled parents and anxious teachers began to contemplate the rescue of at least the young on the largest possible scale. During our half-term visits to John and Shirley, their headmasters at Colwall and Swanage were wondering whether it might not be right to move the schools overseas.

Inevitably these speculations revived the dilemma which had divided G. and myself during the Munich crisis, but now the danger, then merely potential, was on our doorstep. With looming invasion, the shadow of the concentration camp already menaced G. and me. If this did not mean death for the children too, it could bring terror and insecurity ending in moral and spiritual corruption.

Ought they to go to America again, and this time stay there? The Press did not lack its happy-go-lucky critics of "jitterbugs", but the United States, which recognised the portentous odds against us more clearly than ourselves, failed to share the comfortable belief of the British public in England's guiding star.

Into this new period of uncertainty came a discreet cablegram from Ruth and Woodard Colby in Minnesota. Their message struck a note of quiet insistence.

"Dearest Vera, please send us John and Shirley for the summer."

One practical reason for taking advantage of the evacuation

scheme seemed determinant. So much of my work had lain in America during recent years; at any moment a summons to return there for a time might come. Never again, as in the "phoney" war, could I risk being across the Atlantic with the children in England. My Letter for July 4th reflected these weeks of psychological struggle.

"War brings perpetual conflict. . . . Not one of the agonising choices which it compels us to make is ever simple and straight-forward. To volunteer or not to volunteer; to move or 'stay put'; to part from children or keep them at home; to wind up a business or carry it on at a loss . . . these are problems which practically everybody has now to solve."

To the moral quandary of our choice for the children was added another, even more acute. In 1938 they had been too young to leave England without me, but now they were just old enough to travel alone under supervision. Should I go with them, or stay behind? There seemed no right decision to be made; whichever course I took would involve bitter regrets.

At last I decided that I could not live safely across the Atlantic while the friends with whom I had worked might have to face ostracism, prison, and, if Hitler landed, the gas chamber. But this decision was easily the worst that I have ever taken, and I gave up all attempts to justify it. How could I explain to casual acquaint-ances, without provoking derision, that I had a sense of being under orders which I could not disobey?

Years afterwards the matron of the Chelsea Babies' Club, whose wisdom had sustained me through John's exacting babyhood, retrospectively supplied unforeseen reassurance. As we discussed the after-effects of evacuation on the children who went, I men-tioned my own painful doubts in June 1940.

"I was so glad you stayed," she said immediately. "I *should* have felt let down if you'd gone with John and Shirley."

Eventually G. and I arranged for them to travel alone, and stood for two hours in a long queue of distressed parents to obtain their passages in an unnamed liner sailing for Canada on June 26th. We now took up a recent generous offer from my New York publisher, and asked him to act as one of the American guarantors required by the organisers of the scheme.

John and Shirley, returning separately from their schools to London, realised that this time they were going alone and might not come back for years, if ever; the "summer" of Ruth's cable had been a judicious fiction. Amy Burnett, meeting Shirley at Brocken-hurst to say good-bye three weeks before the birth of her own daughter, cried all the way back to Allum Green in the car. The driver, she said, had been very kind to her; he drove her to a neighbour's house so that she need not return to the cottage alone.

At first Shirley too looked pale and miserable; she did not want to go to America, but recovered as soon as she saw John. The philosophical acceptance of disaster common to their buffeted young generation did not desert them on the journey to Liverpool.

In the train G. and I met Jan Struther, the author of *Mrs. Miniver*, who was joining the ship with her two younger children.

"Are you going too?" she inquired, and looked crestfallen when I answered: "No. I'm only seeing them off."

"I feel as if I were running away," she said brokenly. "But I thought if I didn't go I might never see them again."

I looked at John and Shirley, and felt sick at heart. In that inexorably speeding compartment, familiar words seemed to hang in the air between Jan Struther and myself.

"Lord, let this cup pass from me!"

How many times, all over the world, had our women contemporaries uttered that prayer during their numerous Gethsemanes?

Who was right, she or I? We had made different decisions, but so great was our mutual anguish of irresolution that neither could blame the other for her choice. She was an idealistic, intelligent woman, a writer of sensitive hymns; I cannot believe that the profitable unreality of the Miniver film ever appeared to her as a great patriotic service.

In two books, *England's Hour* and a novel, *Born 1925*, I have described our parting with the children, and I do not propose to repeat it here. In those chapters I never succeeded, as I have so often succeeded elsewhere, in "writing out" a bitter experience from my recollection. The carnation pressed in my diary from the parting bouquet which John and Shirley gave me remains a poignant relic, for the lost years of their childhood are lost to me still.

The small gallant figures which disappeared behind the flapping tarpaulin of the grey-painted *Duchess of Atholl* have never grown up in my mind, for the children who returned and eventually took their places were not the same; the break in continuity made them rather appear as an elder brother and sister of the vanished pair. Nobody was to blame for this; it lay in the logic of a world situation with by-products which neither the magnanimous Colbys nor ourselves could prevent. But I have often wondered whether other parents of sons and daughters sent abroad have shared my experience.

Five days after they sailed with several hundred other children, the *Arandora Star* was torpedoed while taking interned civilians to Canada, and a number of London's most famous *restaurateurs* perished in the Atlantic. I noted this incongruous sacrifice of amiable Italians to the Moloch of revenge and, like an emotionless automaton, fulfilled that week's engagements. As the days slowly passed, I became aware that I could not go on living if John and Shirley were drowned.

(6)

But this time destiny was merciful. On July 5th a cable reported the children's arrival at Montreal, where some medical friends of the Colbys met and entertained them before putting them in the care of railway officials for the two days' journey to St. Paul.

Shirley's first letter exuberantly described the kindly interest taken in two young British evacuees by their fellow-passengers.

"In the train all the people were awfully friendly and gave us meals and iced drinks and sweets at their own expense. Indeed they kept coming one after another and didn't stop until the train did."

Subsequent letters from the St. Paul household, though increasingly delayed by the slow wartime mails, assured us that both children, acclimatised from babyhood to family adventures, had settled down without apparent homesickness and were going in the autumn to local schools.

I had now firmly to ignore heartache, for much work awaited me. In gratitude for the safety of John and Shirley I had volunteered to help the Children's Overseas Reception Board, a Government body set up at the headquarters of Thomas Cook & Son to arrange the large-scale emigration of British children. My cousin Geoffrey Shakespeare, then Under-Secretary for the Dominions, had become the official head of this organisation, which was popularly known as "Corb".

Only a small percentage of the expected 50,000 "seavacuees" actually went, for the Government abandoned the scheme after the *City of Benares* was sunk in September 1940 with eighty-five children on board.

. I was already spending several hours daily in choosing escorts from hundreds of applicants to accompany the children, when my English publishers suggested a successor to *Testament of Friendship*. The mounting sales of that biography had been singularly unaffected by the Blitzkrieg, and the firm now invited me to write a short book giving a picture of contemporary civilian England under the impact of war. The idea appealed to me and also to the Macmillan Company of New York, who cabled offering a contract.

I had barely started work, when G. announced that he must revisit America.

During July a Harvard colleague, Dr. Raymond Buell, had cabled him reporting his own appointment as adviser to Mr. Wendell Willkie, the Republican Presidential candidate, and requesting information on "Britain's needs and powers to resist". G. immediately consulted several members of the Government, and from them collected a dossier emphasising the importance, at that critical hour, of an American loan to Britain of fifty outdated destroyers. Winston Churchill had already made this suggestion in two recent memoranda to President Roosevelt.

An earlier cable, which G. received while Hitler was still behind the Maginot line, had asked him to lecture that autumn at Kansas City University. This invitation now made it possible for him to cross the Atlantic and give Raymond Buell his collection of private documents.

With a growing desolation which obstinately refused to be banished by G.'s new opportunity, I accompanied him to the office of Thomas Cook and Son to investigate the secret and scanty Atlantic sailings. Some of their posters, I observed, were as much outdated as the optimistic placards on the walls of Paris.

"VICHY—ALL THAT A SPA SHOULD BE", announced the most conspicuous, while another exhorted us to "VISIT BEAUTIFUL POLAND".

Our next engagement, at the Ministry of Information, which now sponsored applications for exit permits, proved more disconcerting. A recent letter from Colston Leigh had offered to arrange further lectures whenever I could return to the United States, and though I did not intend to quit England with invasion looming and my book —tentatively entitled *England's Hour*—still to be written, I thought I might usefully revisit America and see the children if the danger had lessened by the time the book was finished. So, to G.'s request for an immediate permit, I added a provisional application for another at a distant date.

G.'s mission, with its Ministerial support, created no problem, but my own reception was unexpected. An embarrassed official whom I had known for years told me that I was unlikely to be again allowed to visit the United States for the duration.

"But why?" I exclaimed aghast, for my probable future journeys had been a strong argument in favour of the children's departure. "It's almost as much my country as this!"

259

After much evasive bush-beating, the official explained that I belonged to the Peace Pledge Union, and had been the subject of a Parliamentary question by Sir Henry Page Croft which had embarrassed the Ministry. But, though disconcerted, I did not take this explanation seriously. A group founded by Dick Sheppard could hardly be a "suspect" organisation, while everybody regarded Sir Henry as the "Colonel Blimp" of the House. I concluded that I was a temporary victim of official pomposity, increased by the exceptional powers given to Government departments in war-time.

I had still to learn how far a frightened democracy will go in using such powers to impose conformity upon its intellectual or moral dissenters, and thus repudiate the very ends for which it professes to be fighting.

(7)

By now the aerial battle round the British coasts had reached a crescendo which diverted my mind from autocratic threats. Two weeks after the children left, heavy attacks had begun on ports and convoys, changing on August 8th to daylight raids between the coast and London. Rumour had selected August 15th as the date on which Hitler proposed to make peace from Westminster, but as this ceremony depended upon the defeat of the British Air Force the day was marked instead by a series of engagements fought all over the country from Tyneside to Southampton.

"Yesterday," I reported to New York, "when the air battles were raging all round our south and east coasts and the barrage balloons above this city were so numerous that you couldn't count them, a newsvendor stood in Sloane Square displaying the following notice: 'BIGGEST RAID EVER. SCORE 78 TO 26. ENGLAND STILL BATTING.'"

At this inauspicious period, when Croydon, Malden and Wimbledon had already received visitations which then seemed appalling, Winifred's posthumous play, *Take Back Your Freedom*, was given its first performance at the small Neighbourhood Theatre in South Kensington. Frank Allenby and Beatrice Wilson played the parts of the dictator and his mother, and several leading critics, including James Agate and Desmond MacCarthy, were present. But the raid-obsessed audience seemed unenthusiastic, and the subsequent notices were tepid.

"Complete flop," I noted in my diary for August 20th. "Glad W. is not here to see this."

But the play, inspired by the political antics of Sir Oswald

260

Mosley, proved strangely indestructible; performances by amateur dramatic societies, continuing to this day, were subsequently to justify the time and skill given to its revision by Norman Ginsbury.

By the end of August, London sirens had become continuous. On the 24th G. and I watched from the Embankment a sinister glow, like a flaming sunset at midnight, spread over the raided City; four days later two delayed-action bombs whistled over Cheyne Walk into nearby Burton Court. Again the anguish of indecision racked us both. How, said G., could he go to America, and leave me alone to this? But how, I asked, could I give up my book and the obligation to record these days which was my real war-work? My passion for experience, perpetually at odds with my natural cowardice, had again come out on top.

Finally he decided to go and do his job, and I resolved to stay and do mine, but the eve of his going found us in as deep a mutual melancholy as we had ever shared. Almost silent, we sat dejectedly over our tankards on the balcony of an old riverside inn near Bermondsey Settlement where G. occasionally worked and had a room, and watched twilight eclipse the slate-grey curve of Tower Bridge. As a parting mascot I had bought him a miniature Chinese lion carved from lapis-lazuli, and he promised always to carry it in his pocket.

Nostalgically revisiting the place a few weeks later, I found the little inn a heap of ruins, with wrecked cranes and burned-out warehouses surrounding it like baleful ghosts.

Next day, just before G.'s departure, the siren sounded at Euston; as the train slid out of the station he gazed back at me, standing alone on the platform, with an expression of despair, half-protesting and half-resigned. Struggling northward through the now perpetual raids, his train took eighteen hours to reach Glasgow, and he caught the *Cameronia* with only minutes to spare.

Gripped by the same emotional tempest which seized me in London when I tried to picture the incalculable experiences dividing us from our next meeting, if it ever came, he wrote to me that morning: "I do send this to say that I love you very much. . . . One's mind so often is tired, one's emotions dulled, and what one feels does not come across clearly. I admire your determination to hang on till the book is written."

(8)

When I emerged from the Underground at South Kensington, the Alert was still in progress. Uncertain, as we then all were, how much it meant, I spent the next half-hour in a shelter under Onslow Square, contemplating the threatened ban upon my movements which had cast its incredible shadow over the parting with G.

"It is INSANE," a fellow P.E.N. member to whom I reported this warning had written. "The country is full of pro-Nazi people, allowed to live freely and do any mischief possible, even, in some cases, apparently protected by the authorities, and the internment camps are filled with passionate anti-Nazis, and you, whose integrity could not for one split second have been in doubt, are refused a permit to lecture in America. I think that most of us have treated much too lightly the grim prophecies of such people as Kingsley Martin about fascism-in-our-time."

Some weeks earlier, Roger Eckersley had remarked to me that the current misrepresentation of the peace movements was probably inspired by the real Fifth Column as a screen for their own activities; the newspapers, he thought, by focussing attention on the wrong people, had fallen into the trap. Meanwhile the status and rights of the individual were challenged by the Emergency Powers (Defence) Acts; these permitted any "suspect" to be detained indefinitely without appeal, and provided no machinery by which the prisoner could discover the grounds for his detention.

Accompanying these regulations, several ludicrous varieties of hortative propaganda gave unusual scope to both knaves and fools. The "Silent Column" advertisement campaign, announcing that "chatterbugs" talked about the war but only "defeatists" discussed the peace, conferred its unBritish blessing on the eavesdroppers who were invited to denounce these offenders. The "Mr. Sensibles", publicly urged to pass on authentic news by word of mouth, seemed likely to emulate the platoon once ordered to circulate verbally the message: "We are ordered to abandon the attack on the hill." When it reached the last member, the instruction ran: "The band can go home if it feels ill."

Within a few days the long-suffering public decided that even victory was not worth a revival of the seventeenth century "informers". Very properly they ended the brief authority of the eavesdroppers by a derisive soubriquet—"Cooper's Snoopers".

But behind these foolish expedients existed the real danger of overwhelming powers unsuitably employed. Shortly before G. left, the semi-official threat which I had encountered appeared from another quarter. In quest of material for my new book I had recently applied for the necessary permit to visit defence areas, but though Mr. Daniel Macmillan endorsed this request it had been abruptly refused. Was it really possible that an intellectual position adopted four years ago after a sudden religious illumination could now cause me to be credited with a treacherous willingness to give away official secrets discovered by chance?

In my book I had hoped to describe the battles developing round the coast; now the story had perforce to concentrate on the war as seen from London. But reasons other than departmental obstruction already made it difficult to write.

The night following G.'s departure soon became the noisiest up to date. While the Burnetts, who had brought their infant daughter from Lyndhurst in the belief that London was safer, occupied the basement, I sought uncomfortable refuge in the coal cellar. As I listened to the periodic "crumps", I reflected how strange it was that within a few weeks children, husband, and official support had all vanished, leaving me alone amid bombs and threatened invasion. Many other women experienced a similar fate, but an overdose of adversity is seldom made more tolerable by widespread repetition.

The persistent bombs—as I was to discover after G. returned—were a trivial affliction compared with the loss of my family at a time when mistrust added bewilderment to increasing peril. Of all those closest to me, only my mother remained in England. She had been, I knew, very anxious about us owing to the number of "incidents" already recorded in Chelsea, and though I could not lay my burdens upon her, I could at least relieve her mind and save us both from loneliness by joining her for a time.

She welcomed me thankfully when I arrived with my manuscript, but within a week chaos had come. On September 7th, 1940, the Battle of Britain changed to the Battle of London; that night the first concentrated air attack killed four hundred Londoners and set the docks on fire. My mother and I were observing the red glow through the black-out when a loud roar and a crash shook the old house to its foundations. As we hurried down to the fragile basement, hopefully shored-up by timber, a second and louder crash brought the sound, so soon to be familiar, of falling glass. Through the open windows the fierce blast, pressing behind us like a scorching hurricane, gave us the uncomfortable sensation of being blown downstairs.

After a sleepless and terrifying night, we found that the bomb had demolished the roof of the house which adjoined our small garden. My mother was badly shaken, and after listening for three more nights to the crash of bombs and the heavy hiccuping drone of the Nazis overhead, I persuaded her to take refuge with her sister in

Woking. In the same area I found a temporary home for the Burnetts and their baby.

Now truly alone, I closed both our unsubstantial eighteenth-century houses, and took a service flat which a friend had found for me in a modern block near Portland Place. Amid these intensified domestic problems, I almost forgot the risks of G.'s journey until his cable arrived from New York.

"Safely in. Benedictions. Anxious you safe."

So perturbed indeed had he been by the dramatic American head-lines, which suggested the imminent demolition of London, that he exhorted me urgently in a second cable: "Go instantly to Lakes."

But this—though frightened almost out of my wits—I replied that I could not do. Safe areas were no part of my scheme for living; normal life, comfortable and unthreatened, now seemed as abnormal as bombs had once appeared, and contributed nothing to a book about the war. Nor, from the security of a relative's home amid lakes and mountains, could I write fortnightly Letters for readers under bombardment, or cut myself off from the risks taken by my young secretary and the courageous printers.

In Kansas City, G. found Wendell Willkie's campaign for the Presidential election already in progress, and the election caravan just arrived from Chicago. As Willkie's voice was exhausted by speeches in Indiana and Raymond Buell had suddenly fallen ill, the organisers invited G. to act temporarily as a foreign affairs adviser. In a *Yorkshire Post* article he subsequently described his three days on Willkie's campaign train, with its eleven cars and freight of one hundred politicians, journalists, and stenographers.

"By his deliberate policy," wrote G. of Willkie, "he renders politically possible the transfer to Britain of the fifty U.S. destroyers."

To me he reported a breakfast with Lord Lothian, and a cheerful telephone conversation with the children in St. Paul. Shirley's fondness for riding had full scope there, it seemed, while John had entered a new phase of passionate painting.

In my flat close to the B.B.C. I learnt, during the next few days and nights, what it meant to be in the same area as a major target. Bombs fell so incessantly that the between-raid periods when it was possible to get some fresh air or take a bath became perpetually fewer.

On Sunday, September 15th—later to be recorded as the decisive day of air victories which finally caused Hitler to abandon the invasion of Britain—an outburst of noise exceptional even for that period brought me up at noon from the basement restaurant where

I was struggling to write my book. I found an air battle in progress immediately over the block of flats; curiosity overcame panic and, looking through the doorway, I saw a large brown bomber driven almost to the ground by British planes. Almost immediately came a sickening explosion; two minutes later the hall porter jubilantly announced that the bomber had crashed near Oxford Circus.

To G., still obstinately propagating the claims of safe areas, I wrote with rueful apology.

"I do have moments when I feel that, if only I see you and the darling children again, I shall be glad to have been through all this at first hand."

(9)

Some days afterwards an old friend, who before the war had wisely left the centre of London for a home county, called at my flat.

With unanswerable good sense she pointed out that I was not in fact getting on with the book which I had stayed in England to write, and had now surely experienced as many air-raids as it needed. This was true enough; continuous wakefulness, added to the sheer terror of the noisy nights, had virtually destroyed such creative powers as I possessed. Even at the cost of self-contempt for cowardice, I knew that I must somehow command a period of quiet if my book was to be ready within sight of the contract date.

My friend invited me to go home with her, and eventually suggested that I should stay until the book was finished or G. had returned. Stupefied by a sleepless week, I accepted the proffered hospitality with gratitude.

Her busy household provided intermittent companionship, a sunny attic where I could work undisturbed, and a large overgrown garden, filled with apple-trees, which seemed further from the clamorous autumn battles than it actually was. Munition dumps in the surrounding woods brought evening raiders, whose onslaughts tilted the bath-water with the same effect as a rough sea during an ocean crossing. On the near horizon rose nightly the shooting star-shells of London's barrage.

The house lay on the Nazi air-route to the Midlands, now known as "Hell's Corridor"; when the raids spread north and west of London, the hours of darkness became more clamorous. On November 14th, the night of the great attack on Coventry, the sky hummed for four hours like a hive of gigantic bees; from dark to dawn the barrage flashed all round the horizon. Pulling aside my

265

black-out curtains, I watched for an hour the anti-aircraft shells bursting ineffectively beneath the unseen raiders.

A week after the death of Neville Chamberlain, whose spirit left his ravaged city just in time, 800 people in Birmingham were killed and 2,000 injured on three successive nights. By the end of the month the towns attacked included Southampton; following a visit to the cottage at Allum Green, I read that another heavy raid had started only an hour after I left.

For ten weeks I divided an uneasy existence between London and my temporary refuge. The first civilised institution to suffer from the air-blitz had been communications; after September 7th stations were periodically closed, bridges barricaded, mails delayed; in the London area telegrams and long-distance telephone calls were invariably refused. Unable to picture these drastic changes, G. protestingly attributed to negligence his non-receipt of my regular letters.

Many of my London visits took me through shattered streets ankle-deep in glass to Government offices, for I still could not believe that my work abroad, which in pre-war years had achieved such useful results, was arbitrarily and curtly to be ended. Where was now the kindliness of England? Eclipsed, it seemed, with some other vulnerable qualities, such as compassion and truth.

"This is a problem of a kind I have never been up against—a black mark against me as a writer and a citizen," I confessed to G. He responded drily that it seemed odd to have helped so many refugees to go abroad through one's influence, and then be forbidden to travel one's self.

In October, after a bomb on the Square made her house uninhabitable, my mother had joined an old acquaintance from Buxton in a Dawlish hotel. There in mid-November I paid her a week-end visit, travelling to Devon through a cloud-burst which caused huge waves to break right over the small seaside station.

She too, now old with all her nearest gone but me, knew what homelessness meant; after the lonely weeks marked by a sense of deprivation too deep for full expression, I found her presence more comforting than I had ever known it. Though we had few values in common we shared many transcendent memories, and in her repressed fashion she loved me with a unique affection. The years of grieved comparison between myself and her lost Edward had long gone by; I had become her mainspring, and in so far as such self-restraint was possible for her she had ceased to criticise me.

"If by any unexpected chance I do find I can get to America," I wrote to her on my return, "don't forget that *you are to survive* the war, so that whatever happens to me you can make certain of seeing the children again."

I had not yet told her that another invitation, more adventurous than the standing offer of lectures from Colston Leigh, had recently come to make the dogged quest for an exit permit worth-while. Out of the blue, a letter from the All-India Women's Conference invited me to attend, as a British delegate, their annual meeting under the chairmanship of Begum Hamid Ali at Mysore in late December 1940.

"Believe me," wrote their secretary, Mrs. Lakshmi N. Menon, "to whatever schools of thought my countrymen belong we are all united in our great sympathy with England in its hour of trial. May God be with you."

Over luncheon at my flat I discussed this proposal with Agatha Harrison, long recognised as unofficial Quaker ambassador to the India which had been involved in war against her will, and was now pressing for self-government. She promised her help, but the organisers of the Conference, unfamiliar with wartime travel problems, had left me insufficient time to make plans for the journey.

By using the primitive air lines of that period it might just have been possible, with full official co-operation, to reach Mysore by the scheduled date, but government obstruction soon used up what little margin there was. Shortly after I finished my book I learned from Arthur Creech-Jones, who with Colonel Josiah Wedgwood was my stoutest ally in fighting the official attitude which was making it impossible for me to travel and difficult to carry out my work, that this new opportunity of usefulness was also to be denied me.

Through other friends trying to help came a rumour that the Home Office had compiled a "dossier" about me. No doubt it registered the usual information that I belonged to the Peace Pledge Union, now blindly accused of Nazi associations, for which not the slightest evidence has ever been produced. But the "dossier", if it was supposed to be a truthful record, must have contained some strange omissions, including the anti-fascist Foreword to *Honourable Estate*; the *Sunday Chronicle* articles which not only described but derided the Nazi circus; and the contribution which I had written for Victor Gollancz's symposium, *Fascists at Olympia*.

A letter to G. reported the latest set-back, and added: "This business of being treated as a suspicious character is very exhausting and depressing—especially as no one will supply an explanation."

But just when resilience was almost extinguished by repeated disappointment, new encouragement came from G. himself. He was returning, he cabled, in a Cunard ship sailing early in December.

(10)

On December 15th I read in the Sunday newspapers that a liner called the *Western Prince* had been torpedoed between Ireland and Iceland.

With relief I noted that the lost vessel was not a Cunarder, but I did wish that G. had waited for a Clipper passage instead of coming by sea at such a dangerous time. With the Nazis commanding the French Atlantic ports, shipping losses were known to compare with those of the worst period in the First World War.

By now I was becoming anxious for news, and a friend inquired at the Cunard office whether G.'s ship and arrival time could yet be disclosed. There he learned that the Cunard Company had taken over all civilian Atlantic sailings, and that G. had been a passenger on the torpedoed liner. Whether he had been saved would not be known till the rescue ship arrived, for one lifeboat filled with survivors was lost. For two days which seemed a hundred years, I kept in touch with the shipping line, and waited.

Just after their final telephone call, a telegram signed by G. himself reached me from Gourock.

"Splendid health despite slight mishap shipwreck open boat eight hours entirely safe but in pyjamas. Cable America, lunch with me Dorchester Hotel London to-morrow."

An hour later he telephoned me from Glasgow, and I arranged to meet him next day. Reaching London early, I made a provisional booking at the Dorchester, which I knew would provide comfort and a deep air-raid shelter where G. could sleep. Then I went to Euston and waited for his train, which was already four hours late, amid a crowd of reporters and photographers.

When at last the train came in, I did not recognise him until he spoke to me; five days of shipwreck had transformed my elegant husband into a battered tramp. His face was grey with fatigue; he had a black eye, acquired as he was climbing out of the life-boat; and, having lost all his suitcases, he still wore his sea-stained greatcoat over his pyjamas.

Both now inarticulate, we took a taxi to the Dorchester, where I inquired about my reservation. After one look at G., the room-clerk said hastily that the hotel was full up—a statement untrue of all London hotels during that period of maximum raids. When I explained G.'s plight, the booking was immediately confirmed and all possible co-operation given; "the staff there couldn't do enough for him," I wrote later to my mother.

That evening G.'s name appeared in several newspapers, and the *Star* recorded his rescue in its front-page headlines. This publicity brought us a large mail which continued till long after Christmas. Amongst other American friends, my publisher wrote from New York.

"We, of course, knew that he was on that boat and were worried stiff. We hadn't an idea what to do. We just sat by and waited, watching for the survivor list. Ruth Colby apparently went through the same stitches as I went through, for she too reads her newspaper. She had had a letter from G. and knew of the boat he was on. . . . It was a four-or-five day period, I can tell you!"

Directly the newspaper headlines appeared the B.B.C. tracked G. down, and asked him to broadcast to America. On December 22nd, over the National Broadcasting Company's wave-length, he told his story.

The *Western Prince* had been torpedoed just before dawn, beneath a moon so bright that the submarine could hardly have missed its target. The vivid beams outlined the ship like a stage spotlight, and threw the shadow of its rigging on the white foam of the waves.

G. was awakened by the heavy thud of the torpedo, but the alarm-bells, perhaps damaged, failed to function. Deciding to investigate, he and his cabin companion put on their coats, found the corridors deserted, and went up the companion way to their lifeboat station. There, looking over the rail, they saw the lifeboats already down and filled with passengers. Hurrying to the other side of the ship, they found the one remaining boat still not lowered. G. was almost the last passenger to get into it.

A strong sea was running in bitter December cold. Every few moments the lifeboats ran into squalls of rain, and huge waves swamped the sailors trying to head them into the wind. G. spent the first part of his eight hours on the sea in baling out water.

Half-an-hour after the first torpedo had struck, he saw the flash of the submarine's conning-tower among the boats. The sailors saw it too; "a terrible tension like a white shadow passed over their faces," James Bone, a fellow-passenger, wrote afterwards in the *Manchester Guardian*. But the submarine commander waited for the boats to get clear before putting another torpedo into the *Western Prince*. A violent explosion followed, and in half a minute, amid a roar of flame, the liner was gone.

Her captain, a heavy man injured in the first attack, went down with his ship, blowing three farewell blasts on her siren as she sank. In his broadcast G. questioned the wisdom, especially during war, of the tradition which involved this loss of experienced captains; pilots, he said, had been taught to bale out because they were considered more valuable than their planes. With the captain perished a honeymoon couple who had gone back to their cabin for some wedding presents, and his personal steward who returned to get the crew's £100 Spitfire Fund.

Towards evening, when the one motor-vessel among the life-boats had continuously sent out the S.O.S. and doubts were growing whether they could survive the night in a rising sea, the ship-wrecked passengers saw a 3,000-ton collier appear on the horizon. Her crew had observed the explosion and flares, but as ships were then officially instructed to avoid danger areas the captain consulted his men. Without exception they volunteered to face the risk, and reached the life-boats shortly before dusk.

At first the only method of embarkation was to jump, as G. did, for a rope-ladder from the crest of a wave, but the few babies and one or two women were eventually hauled up in a huge fish-basket. No one would have been lost had not the motor-boat drifted under the freighter's waste-pipe. A sudden jet of water overturned it and drowned its seventeen occupants.

The freighter's crew provided hot tea and bully beef for their shivering guests, but a boat designed for thirty occupants could not easily accommodate one hundred and thirty-two. The half clad men and women lay where they could, on chairs and tables; their chances of rescue would have been non-existent if the collier also had encountered a submarine. During four days on board G. had only one night's sleep, on a bunk in the powder-magazine.

To the end of the voyage, danger pursued the ship-wrecked travellers. Struggling through thunderous seas outside Gourock the little ship cut the corner of a mine-field, and the crew felt her side scrape the edge of a mine.

G. landed without possessions except for his passport and re-entry permit, and my lapis-lazuli lion in his overcoat pocket. With his suitcases had gone down the gold fob and ikon which had been his father's wedding gift, and the Christmas presents for their family enthusiastically purchased by John and Shirley from pocket-money saved up for weeks. Since Ruth withheld from them the news of the sinking until G.'s rescue was known, these lost Christmas gifts represented their real tragedy. Some weeks later, a pathetic list of purchases reached me from John.

"We sent to Mummy," he concluded, "two plates with Currier and Ives prints on them, these were about 80 years old. To Daddy we sent a lapis-lazula [sic] owl. It was meant to be a companion piece to the lion you gave him and was just as beautiful, but never mind because we don't much mind any more."

G.'s broadcast had been uncensored except for one passage; he was not permitted to pay a tribute to the submarine commander whose delayed action had spared their lives. This officer, it was plausibly alleged, might be penalised if his humane conduct became known to his Nazi masters. G. told me afterwards that, though several passengers spoke bitterly of the attack which nearly cost them their lives and destroyed their possessions, the sailors themselves showed no resentment. In their opinion the German had simply done his job, and it was all part of the fortune of war.

(11)

On Christmas Eve we went down to Cornwall, where my mother now shared a cottage in Carbis Bay with her youngest sister who had moved from Kent. As soon as she learned that G. was a passenger on the *Western Prince*, my mother had fatalistically assumed him to be drowned until I firmly reported his rescue.

It seemed strange to move straight from his sombre Atlantic drama to an overcrowded "reception area" where bored and querulous evacuees pushed each other off the St. Ives pavements. Not for anything, I thought, would I exchange London for this. At night, acclimatised to the habits of danger areas, I still listened half-consciously for the heavy hesitant bump of the Nazi bombers, like a car climbing a steep mountain road.

G., to my relief, slept well and seemed unimpaired by his adventure. But two months later the delayed effect of shock and cold brought on severe influenza followed by jaundice. Before Easter we came back to Cornwall for his brief convalescence.

Early in January 1941, we had returned to a London newly scarred on December 29th by the great incendiary raid which broke the City water-mains and started fifteen hundred fires. Round the blackened surviving Colossus of St. Paul's, pigeons with burnished necks and pink-rimmed eyes toddled as placidly as though the devastated scene were a normal picture of civilised living. In the half-erased streets which divided the gutted buildings between Ludgate Circus and St Paul's Churchyard, a forest of twisted lamp-posts and signboards rivalled the desolate French towns on the Western Front in the First World War.

I learned later that among the minor casualties of that lurid night had been the new cheap edition of my novel *Honourable Estate*, destroyed in Simpkin Marshall's warehouse amongst the three million books lost by publishers and book-sellers in the catastrophe.

After the City raid London flats, already a drug on the market, became even easier to find. The sum then asked for a modern West End apartment is to-day demanded for ramshackle top-floor "conversions" in the ancient dwelling-houses of North Kensington. In Piccadilly we now made a temporary home. G. expected to return to America—though not, if he could help it, without me—but transport at present was almost non-existent. The submarines discouraged civilian sailings, and the Clipper was booked fourteen months ahead.

Soon after we had settled into our new flat overlooking Green Park, *The Times* announced the death from a heart-attack of my old acquaintance, Archie Macdonell. The previous autumn he had moved from London to Oxford because, after fighting without a break from 1914 to 1918, he could not endure the air-raids. Irresponsibly he had brought much trouble to others during his forty-five years, but I owed him only gratitude for constant and generous literary support.

A week later, another death came still nearer home. Early in February one of the two elderly writers who attended Robert Leighton's funeral telephoned me to say that Marie Connor Leighton had died in hospital at Aylesbury. Alone because Clare had emigrated to America and Evelyn, her younger son, was stationed overseas, she had sought companionship only from her old and savage Alsatian. At last she had become too eccentric to live without supervision.

"But I didn't even know she was ill!" I cried, distressed and remorseful. "If I'd known, I would have gone to her."

"She wouldn't have recognised you," he said gravely. "She lived solely in her memories, and her mind at the end was in total eclipse. Nobody seems to have known her age. I gave it as seventy-five, but I am sure she was older."

Two days afterwards I wrote to Clare during an air raid, enclosing a paragraph about her parents from the "*Star* Man's Diary" and a short appreciation which I had vainly sent to *The Times*. In our ruthless era, Roland's mother no longer interested readers too busy trying to stay alive to be attracted by the cloying sweetness of Edwardian romance.

My letter too was a war-time casualty, for Clare never received it.

At the end of January Mr. Wendell Willkie, defeated the previous November by the undefeatable Roosevelt, arrived in England to see British resistance for himself. In response to a cable from his campaign manager, Russell Davenport, G. went to Bristol to meet the plane from Lisbon.

Summoned to the Dorchester next day he found Mr. Willkie in bed, and talked with him while he read his letters. To me G. reported that we were both on his list of breakfast guests for the following morning; but, checking up on the invitation later that day, we found that our names had been crossed off the list by an unknown hand. It was the first of many similar "incidents" which were to haunt our lives till the end of the war. After this visit, though he corresponded with him, G. never saw Mr. Willkie again.

By now I had acquired a new variety of "war-work" in which to find compensation for official setbacks. Released from the prolonged concentration demanded by *England's Hour*, I offered my services to several organisations which cared for the much-bombed inhabitants of London's East End. Many January and February evenings were spent in these derelict areas, where only the fires from incendiary raids lighted the dense wintry black-out.

One night found me in the secure warmth of a model shelter run by the Friend's Ambulance Unit beneath Lloyd's building in Leadenhall Street; another took me on a soup-serving expedition in a mobile canteen through the roofless and windowless streets of Bermondsey. The eight shelters served included the Spa Road Arches which formed part of the five hundred railway arches carrying trains over the once marshy ground between London Bridge and New Cross. Here a thousand people nightly sought refuge, indifferent to the traffic roaring above their heads.

More frequent were periodic visits to Kingsley Hall, a Settlement founded in memory of their brother by Muriel and Doris Lester at Bromley-by-Bow. Impatience and disappointment could not long survive in the serenity of its daffodil-decked Meeting Room—"'safe where all safety's lost' in the heart of Poplar," I wrote in the fiftieth issue of my Letter. Many houses in this dangerous area had been demolished; the remaining inhabitants led a cheerless existence by day, and spent the long cold nights in primitive shelters.

"I wish," my Letter continued, "Mr. Wendell Willkie could have seen one series of trench shelters, flooded to a depth of two or three inches, that I visited under Bromley-by-Bow Recreation Ground. Though the duckboards squelched in the liquid mud and large drops of water fell down the back of my neck from the roof . . . many young mothers and small children sleep nightly in this miasmic atmosphere."

One February evening we had just served these shelters when the siren signalled the first raid for several nights. As I set out with the Warden and his colleague through the black debris-strewn streets for other trench shelters ten minutes' walk away, the Blitz appeared to develop all round us. While the Nazi bombers whined overhead the "noises off" increased, and the moonless vault above us flickered with each flash of the guns. Further east, a fire started by incendiary bombs illumined the sky like a truncated dawn.

As we passed under a railway bridge a badly-screened train ran over it, and with terror I heard the drone of a bomber swooping low. A momentary tension seized even my experienced companions, who never jumped as I did each time the guns went off, but the crash, when it came, sounded far away. For me this journey through the Blitz and the black-out was an occasional experience, but for the Settlement workers it had become a nightly occurrence carried out with a tranquil courage which made light of its perils.

(13)

On February 11th the English edition of *England's Hour* appeared. In spite of the war-time regulations which were fast transforming books into utilitarian products, it carried a striking jacket in black, white and scarlet showing the night pattern of London's searchlights.

Preliminary omens had been favourable; an enthusiastic letter had come from my American publishers, while in England a second edition was put in hand before publication. But the book was far from popular with its British critics, for it did not conceal the chaos and distress caused by the air-raids. Even more injudiciously, it pleaded for the humane values now threatened by war propaganda. As I wrote it I had analysed the growing influence of that propaganda, and my conclusions might have been summarised by the passionate protest of Edna St. Vincent Millay: "I know, I know, but I do not approve, and I am not resigned."

Civilisation, I thought, might well be defined as the widening area of man's sensitivity and the development of his capacity to view human problems with imaginative compassion. "Taking it", now universally extolled as a major virtue, seemed to be the exact reverse of this process. It meant submitting our standards, our consciences, and our capacity for thought to progressive brutalisation.

This outlook was naturally anathema to those practitioners of psychological warfare whose job compelled them to lash the amiable British people into rage against their enemies. Especially selected for attack was a passage in the concluding chapter, "Forever London", in which I commented on a recent angry editorial in a Sunday newspaper. Under the title "Can we Forgive?" the writer had repudiated forgiveness as a contemptible form of sentimentality.

"Leaning at sunset over the wide arches of Westminster Bridge," I wrote, "we can still look lovingly upon the city which appears as an old engraving delicately etched against a tranquil sky. The cranes, though some are now charred ghosts, still lift their pinnacles above the Pool of London . . . and the sea-birds flap their wide grey wings over the ancient barges in the Bay at Chelsea. But London's immortality lies not only in these eternal things; the spirit of men and women from generation to generation matters even more than they. It is my faith in my countrymen which makes me repeat the question: 'Can we forgive?' and try to supply a different answer.

"I believe that we must indeed learn to forgive; that if we do not, we shall sacrifice an essential part of our national quality. 'A nation,' affirms our leader-writer, 'cannot watch its holiest monuments being battered . . . and then meet the enemy afterwards in a forgiving, tolerant spirit.'

"Can it not? If not, then it has already lost the peace; and if it loses yet another peace, the war of 1965 will annihilate our children and our London too . . . If we fail in forgiveness, something that is forever England, and forever London, will have departed from our land."

For the first few days after publication the reviewers industriously did their worst; "emotional", "egotistical", "sentimental" and "hysterical" were only a few of the adjectives hurled at me like a prepared collection of verbal rotten eggs. I had anticipated this response and accepted it philosophically, if wryly; the person really upset was my mother, who occupied her over-abundant time by pasting in my press-cuttings.

Fortunately she was soon able to add an encouraging collection of reviews from the neutral United States, which produced one hundred laudatory criticisms in the week of publication. Typical of them were the *New York Times*, which commended "a poignant and moving book in which hatred and revenge have no place", and the *Philadelphia Bulletin*, whose critic declared: "She strikes a chord that finds a harmony overseas; such an England must be saved."

Even more comforting, because unexpected, was an animated observation sent by Shirley, aged ten.

"From your book," she wrote, "you seem to be rather in the midst of things. . . . I think it was *lovely*. I wish I was there in some of the experiences you were in."

(14)

Apart from the evening shelter-work, I felt myself summoned at this time to another form of inconspicuous service. Through my Letter I had hoped to bring fellowship to isolated groups and individuals who could not accept the official attitude towards the war. In February and March I decided to visit some of these groups in places which had suffered continuously from heavy raids.

They received me gladly and arranged a number of small gatherings, usually in the local Friends' Meeting House, to which I spoke. The cities that I visited included Coventry, Birmingham, Manchester, Hull, Sheffield and Plymouth. I must not describe what I had seen, I wrote afterwards to my American publisher, "but it was enough to endorse my conviction that the human race is going through the worst period of insanity that it has ever perpetrated."

In each bombed city the now familiar pattern of destruction appeared, presenting an identical appearance of squalid desolation whatever the original value of the property. Everywhere I found the same acrid smell of wet charred wood; the same acres of twisted girders; the same littered streets ankle-deep in bricks and glass.

"Sometimes," I wrote to a friend after leaving the ninth blitzed area, "I feel as if the debris from the whole lot were lying on top of me."

At Coventry, where a Shakespeare First Folio and the manuscript of *The Mill on the Floss* had been destroyed with the Central Library, G. and I stayed at the home of a young silk-worker from Courtauld's factory, which had suffered three million pounds' worth of damage. When the raid began, he and his wife were at a private house where a small group of friends had met to read aloud Norman MacGowan's play, *Glorious Morning*. After the All Clear the whole of Coventry appeared, from this house two miles from the centre, to be burning down.

After four more years of British air-raid damage and the sight of far worse devastation on the post-war Continent, it is now difficult to recall the cold horror brought by the first view of Coventry three months after the great raid. This was, of course, the normal human reaction; later, the repeated experience of ruin brought a grim familiarity, and we all became unnaturally immunised against pity and terror.

The middle of the city seemed to be laid flat, apart from the remnants of the Market Tower and the three distinctive spires which soared serenely above the havoc. In the bombed cathedral pious hands had replaced the wrecked High Altar with a rough heap of stones, and had lashed two charred beams together to form a Cross. Amid the debris of the shopping area less reverent citizens had stuck a corpse-like dressmaker's dummy at the end of a pole, and on a hoarding between two blasted buildings had pasted a placard showing a smiling film-star countenance above the caption: "Bette Davis uses Lux Toilet Soap."

At my meeting in the upper room of a local chapel, the able Baptist Minister who took the chair summed up in a sentence the psychological effect of the raid.

"It made everybody feel more vehemently exactly what they had felt before," he said. But he added that many members of his congregation had been distressed by the assumption of a B.B.C. announcer that the retaliatory bombing of Hamburg had been "good news for the people of Coventry". This city which had endured so severe a visitation seemed already to have formed, like London's East Enders, a fellowship of the bombed whose attitude was far less bitter than the vengeful spirit of the safe areas.

After similar expeditions to Birmingham, with its widespread damage, and Manchester, which had suffered acutely at Christmas, I found the centre of Sheffield comparable with Coventry. Before the raid, a false "Sheffield" with faked lights ten miles away on the moors had given the city's inhabitants an illusion of safety. On the bombed wall of the demolished Friends' Meeting House, charity and self-discipline had been responsible for a poster which quoted a text from St. Paul's Epistle to the Ephesians: "Be ye kind one to another, tender-hearted, forgiving one another even as God for Christ's sake hath forgiven you."

(15)

When I visited Hull and Plymouth their major onslaughts were still to come, though both had been constantly attacked. In Hull my lecture for the Literary and Philosophical Society coincided with the worst raid yet experienced there. Uneasily conscious at the Station Hotel of being almost on top of a legitimate military objective, I listened to several bombs noisily exploding nearby. One fell on a coal dump, scattering sooty fragments all over the city.

Plymouth looked handsome and prosperous, for the war had given good jobs to many skilled workers. After my visit there I went on to St. Ives, where G. was convalescing from his attack of influenza and jaundice. In January, my mother told me, two bombs had fallen on the astonished little town, shaking evacuee morale owing to the absence of shelters. But when the prolonged ordeal of Plymouth began in March 1941 before I left the St. Ives hotel, I felt oppressed by the defensive atmosphere of complacent indifference which I now thought of as "the safe area mentality".

In the First War, returning to London from service in France, I had noticed a deep spiritual gulf between the soldiers and nurses in the fighting areas, and the civilians who remained at home. That same gulf seemed now to be growing between different sections of the population.

"Isn't it awful about Plymouth!" lamented one woman in the hotel lounge. "They say the centre's all gone, and there are no policemen left!"

But after that isolated protest, concern seemed to end; out once more came the novels and the knitting. The rattle of windows when a stick of bombs fell on Redruth ten miles away caused more agitation than the heavy casualties in Plymouth.

As I worked on the current Letter next morning in the clear spring sunshine, I found the Riviera-like beauty of North Cornwall unbearable amid the rumours of catastrophe. Though the guns sounded all day from the sea, St. Ives stretched like a perfect pastel painting beneath the pale cobalt sky adorned with pink-tinged clouds. I resolved to go to Plymouth, where normal communications appeared to have ceased, and find out what had happened to the hospitable policeman's family who had entertained me.

Next day I hired a car and drove through the primrose-filled woods between Bodmin and Liskeard; in the hedgerows the pussy-willows were bursting like miniature spools of grey silk from the bare black branches. Devonport seemed almost untouched, but signs of severe damage began as soon as we approached Plymouth Hoe.

My friends were safe, but their home, like hundreds of others, had become a charred ruin. Nothing remained of the hotel where I had slept but fragments of wall round a crater. The commercial buildings, formerly so handsome, loomed like derelict castles from the inaccessible city centre. On the Hoe, blitzed motor cars lay along once elegant terraces like the discarded bully beef tins of trench warfare.

In a damaged house I found an energetic business woman who had attended my meeting; the large modern store where she worked had burned down after the "All Clear". Brisk and unembittered, she sat with a note-book open on a dusty table making plans to start all over again.

As I drove away, I passed the funeral of an air-raid victim going towards the naval cemetery. Behind the long line of mourners, a bank of daffodils in full bloom scintillated unspoiled in the sun.

When I returned home and reflected on these visits to England's worst-bombed cities, I found I had brought away an impression of something quite other than tragedy. I recalled some words once uttered in a public speech by Sybil Thorndike: "There is always an altar on my stage." On the platforms of the small chapels and Meeting Houses where I had stood, there had seemed always to be an altar too.

Though acres of houses might be demolished and famous public buildings reduced to ashes, the men and women of these bombed areas impressed me as bravely cheerful and spiritually undefeated. An attitude of affirmative courage dominated the minority which had been brought up to oppose war no less than the majority which accepted and supported it.

Six years earlier Winifred had written me from Hornsea: "I know that moving and incomparable sensation of feeling one's self to be part of a small group gathered together in the face of disaster". In different cities on different evenings, I had discussed with just such groups over the glowing coal fires which even the Blitz had not banished from the Midlands our mutual reasons for feeling unvanquished.

We agreed that we did not look for absolute triumph in the long struggle of love against power; we recognised that the battle for civilisation had to be fought anew in each epoch so that future men and women could draw fresh courage for their contemporary conflicts. In some such affirmation lay the best answer to the hatred and fear of a divided world. We rejected war because we affirmed the unity of mankind and the value of the struggle, against all temporary obstacles, for its final achievement.

(16)

Between the journeys to Birmingham and Manchester in February 1941, I recorded in my diary a cable from Phyllis Bentley, who was now in America lecturing for the Ministry of Information.

Phyllis strongly disagreed with my attitude towards the war, but

279

unlike other authors attached to the Ministry she did not publicly criticise me, or get hold of *England's Hour* for an onslaught called a review. On the contrary, she went out of her way to show me continuing friendship. Her cable announced that she had taken the opportunity of an engagement in St. Paul to visit the children.

"I saw John and Shirley on Tuesday," it ran. "Their lovely characters and talents are thriving in favourable air."

On her return to England some weeks later, she called to tell me more about them. John, she thought, had not wholly accepted the new surroundings, though he loved his painting lessons and liked his school. But Shirley had completely settled down and seemed to be jubilantly happy.

With well-justified confidence Phyllis concluded: "Shirley will always bounce!"

Soon afterwards, yet another attempt was made to clear up the persistent refusal of the Government to give me an exit permit. This time my benefactor was Mrs. Vyvyan Adams, later to be a key figure in the development of television. In May she left the Ministry of Information owing to a disagreement on policy, and telephoned me volunteering to provide some light on the Home Office attitude towards myself.

When she came, she repeated explanations previously given; the real difficulty lay in my membership of the Peace Pledge Union, which had led to the question in the House.

"But of course," she added, "no person of integrity could give up their convictions and affiliations for the sake of material advantage."

We discussed possible methods of overcoming prejudice, and she promised to see the Under-Secretary at the Home Office on my behalf. But before she could carry out her generous intention, a new invitation from India again raised the exit permit problem from another angle. Refusing to take my compulsory "No" for a final answer, the President of the All-India Women's Conference—this year Mrs. Vijayalakshmi Pandit—cabled a second cordial request for my attendance as British delegate at their 1941 meeting in December.

The long struggle for self-determination in India, where Jawaharlal Nehru was again serving a harsh prison sentence, had become a deep concern to all men and women who cared for freedom. In their eyes, Indian independence represented a basic test of Britain's alleged reasons for fighting Hitler. Hence this second invitation brought me not only the renewed support of Agatha Harrison, the Quaker friend of India who had previously tried to help me, but a fervent backing from several much-respected citizens who accepted the war.

In June an influential group known as the Women's Liaison Committee summoned me to discuss my projected visit; it included such well-known political women as Mrs. Corbett Ashby of the International Alliance and Miss Daisy Solomon of the British Commonwealth League. To my own surprise I convinced them that in India I should seek only roads to reconciliation, and would create no difficulties for the British Government. Shortly afterwards Mrs. Corbett Ashby approached the late Mr. L. S. Amery, then Secretary of State for India, and persuaded him to see me.

When I called at the India Office Mr. Amery—the only Minister who ever went so far—allowed me to state my case, but it was clear from the start that he meant to refuse my request for an exit permit.

"I do not doubt your sincerity," he said, "but the Congress Party would make propaganda hostile to the Government from your views on the war."

Surely I was not so influential as that, I thought! But obviously nothing would change Mr. Amery's mind, and ignominiously near to tears I hurriedly left his office.

Even before this interview, G. told me that one night I had wept in my sleep, and cried aloud: "What's the good of living when one's so ineffective!" But I assured him that whatever self-pity my subconscious might indulge in during the night, my waking thoughts were free from defeatism. However long we had to wait for the end of the war, I felt certain that eventually I should be able to vindicate myself and carry words of friendship to the peoples of other countries.

But to Mrs. Pandit, it was not I but the British Government which required vindication. With a cold anger quite uncharacteristic of the warm personality which in saner years was to make her the most attractive of Indian High Commissioners, she commented at the Conference on the Government's refusal to let me come.

"The decision was unfortunate. At this critical period in the relationship between the people of India and those of England, human contacts are important. Miss Vera Brittain would have forged another link in that chain of friendship between our peoples which this organisation has been trying to create."

(17)

On April 15th I had almost forgotten the now intermittent raids owing to an absorbing fortnightly Letter on Virginia Woolf. Her sudden death at the end of March had shocked the literary world, for she was presumed to have committed suicide when her body was found in the River Ouse near her Sussex home.

Before starting to write, I had received a broken-hearted and almost undecipherable communication from Virginia's closest friend, Dame Ethel Smyth, now in her eighties. Remembering the three benevolent letters which Virginia herself had written me, I struggled to compose a better-considered memorial than some of the hasty and embarrassed notices which had appeared in the newspapers.

"The minds of those who deliberately seek death are seldom open to analysis . . ." I wrote. "Her end was perhaps a kind of protest, the most terrible and effective she could make, against the real hell which international conflict creates for the artist. . . .

"The only method of adaptation for the artist under present conditions is to acquire what the Quakers call a 'concern' for the problems that war creates for mankind—an essentially political pursuit. . . . She could no more compromise with the brutalised values which are now being accepted . . . than James Joyce, the protesting invalid exile who made long lists of proof corrections for *Finnigans Wake* with the Germans at the gates of Paris, could compromise with the circumstances that sent him out of tottering France. She preferred to say—in words written ten years ago at the end of *The Waves* which might stand for her epitaph—'Against you I will fling myself, unvanquished and unyielding, O Death!' "

That night a heavy outburst of gunfire followed an early siren; on the next, April 16th, came one of the violent assaults which had caused Virginia Woolf to escape from the disorderly barbarism of contemporary life. It appeared to be a retaliation for the recent R.A.F. bombing of Berlin's Unter den Linden.

By 10.30 on the evening of London's heaviest raid, the crackle of incendiaries and thunderous roar of guns seemed so close that, for only the second time, G. and I decided to take refuge in the basement shelter. At midnight the high explosives began to come down, and rained round us, thud after heavy thud, for five successive hours. One or two bombs fell so close that the tall block of flats rocked like a ship at sea.

Gone now was the cold terror inspired by the early raids; a mixture of familiarity and resignation had taken its place. Throughout that night of April 16th-17th, in which the occupants of the crowded shelter recognised that they might not live till morning, I felt as detached as though I were watching some wholly impersonal drama.

Even when one bomb seemed to lift the entire building from its foundations and glass from the hotel next door cascaded around us, not a man or woman in the typical war-time assembly of British, French, Dutch, and other exiles uttered a sound.

When at last the All Clear came and we went upstairs, I heard what I took to be heavy rain, and thought: "This is what stopped the raid." Then, pulling aside the curtain, I saw the still vivid moon in a clear sky; the sound of water came from a broken main pouring down Piccadilly. On the east side of Green Park, a succession of burning buildings made a scarlet glare of the sky. Further away, half Jermyn Street and St. James's appeared to be in flames.

One of G.'s former Cornell colleagues, Professor Allan Nevins, was then staying at the Athenaeum Club, which seemed to be enveloped in smoke. As the telephone was out of order we decided to go on foot to find how he had fared, and bring him if necessary to our still undamaged flat. Imbued with the strange exultation which the aftermath of a heavy raid always brought to those who survived it, we dressed quickly in old clothes and strong shoes, and went out to a scene such as I had not yet witnessed even in a winter of continuous bombing.

By this time the half-moon was waning and the sun beginning to rise; in a moment the flamingo-hued mists of dawn mingled with the red-tinged clouds from countless fires. Six of the numerous "crumps" which shook us had made craters within a hundred yards of our windows; in Piccadilly a trail of desolation spread from Hyde Park Corner to the Circus. On the pavement outside a once elegant men's shop lay a glove stretched over a wooden hand, fortuitously symbolising the human debris which rescue workers were discreetly removing. Still in the shop, a half smashed bowler hat balanced precariously on a drunken stand.

As we plunged towards St. James's Street through surging water thick with glass and splinters, an acrid smell of burning wood and escaping gas half choked us.

"Poor Nevins!" exclaimed G., looking at the smoke clouds pouring from the south.

But Professor Nevins had spent a better night than ourselves in the basement of the B.B.C.; from a tired and grimy porter at the Athenaeum, we learned that he had left for a broadcasting engagement before the raid began. Eventually he joined us for breakfast, which our restaurant, though deprived of gas and electricity, somehow produced. As rumours of heavy damage in Chelsea had reached us, we took a circuitous taxi-ride to see if 2 Cheyne Walk still stood.

Again our house had been fortunate, though a bomb on the corner of an adjacent roof had blown the nursery windows with their frames into the room. But further west one of the loveliest landmarks of our lives had become a grotesque heap of rubble; Chelsea Old Church, demolished by a parachute mine, lay across the Embankment like the ruins of history itself. Only the embellished tombstone of Sir Hans Sloane complacently surveyed undamaged the shattered past to which he had belonged.

That morning the B.B.C. for once broadcast the news of London's "long and heavy raid" with savage frankness, and I sent a reassuring telegram to my mother at St. Ives.

(18)

Two nights later a second ferocious raid smote London, but most of the damage occurred further East. This time, though we left our beds and lay on the floor with the writing-table over us ("This is civilisation!" I commented later in a letter), we felt too tired to stir when the scream of a bomb sounded outside the window.

"How funny—I never heard it go off!" G. murmured drowsily a few minutes later.

"It must have," I said. "You mixed it up with all the other noises."

In the morning we saw soldiers digging for a time-bomb just inside the railings across the road. We had slept peacefully for half the night only twenty yards away from it.

The next day a surviving creator of civilisation's vanishing beauties joined us for lunch. Some time previously G. had boldly written to Sir William Rothenstein, the painter, now attached as official artist to the Royal Air Force, asking if he would paint my portrait. I feared he might think the request impertinent, but to my surprise he accepted the commission and now came to arrange for sittings.

"Sir William is like an intelligent-looking small monkey," I wrote to my mother of the seventy-two-year-old painter in his Air Force uniform.

Throughout that summer, which saw the institution of clothes-rationing and the disappearance of sweets and cigarettes from shop-windows deceptively adorned by empty boxes, I travelled to Chalford in the Cotswolds and sat for Sir William. The completed

284

picture now hangs in our living-room; it shows me in a black dress against a semi-ecclesiastical screen of coloured embroidery. I thought the rendering too demure and pensive, the typical work of an ageing artist who died three years later, but most of our acquaintances praised it as a good likeness. These differing opinions represent, I believe, a typical conflict between candid friends and the subject of a family portrait.

Sir William's grey stone house, Far Oakridge, overlooked a wooded valley now vivid with the fresh emerald of birch and larch. When G. and I arrived we met the Irish poet James Stevens, with whom I had crossed the Atlantic in 1934. He and his wife had been driven by raids from Wembley to make their home in a disused Cotswolds chapel.

As the portrait developed, Far Oakridge became the background for several historic events. Our first visit, on May 10th, coincided with the third great spring raid on London. Almost immediately came the aerial descent, like some semi-mythical apparition from the Twilight of the Gods, of Rudolf Hess.

While successive editions of the newspapers clamorously discussed his arrival, G. and I returned to London to find the debating Chamber of the House of Commons demolished, the roof of Westminster Hall destroyed, and an ugly gash across the stonework which framed the blackened face of Big Ben.

I was staying at Far Oakridge on the Sunday, hottest of recorded June days, when Hitler made war on Russia. From the garden where roses, lupins and passion-flowers had sprung into blossom overnight, I looked across lush buttercup meadows towards the brilliant beeches in the wooded valley. As the portable radio announced that the Nazi armies had attacked the Soviet Union at dawn on a front of 1000 miles, I seemed to be back in the resplendent May which had accompanied the conquest of France with shining seas and sparkling skies.

That evening, through the same wireless set in the peaceful garden, I heard the Prime Minister address the nation on the Russian invasion and describe Herr Hitler as "a bloodthirsty guttersnipe". Unhappily many British people regarded his new victims as guttersnipes too. Long before the political Left began its clamour for a Second Front, the embarrassed B.B.C., faced with the problem of playing the Internationale in its nightly selection of National Anthems, decided to substitute a judicious programme of patriotic Allied music.

After Hitler's attack on Russia, the air-raids virtually ceased and the shelter work ended. Throughout that summer I found new scope for practical service at an old Essex manor house known as Langham Oaks, where some personal friends had founded a community centre. Its warden was Max Plowman, the author of *A Subaltern on the Somme*, whose death that summer added another member to the communion of saints.

Langham village lies near the sea, in the Constable country between the rivers Colne and Stour. As this part of the coast was still officially expecting invasion, its children had been evacuated and the countryside seemed very quiet. The community managed a co-operative farm where conscientious objectors could obtain the agricultural work now legally permitted as alternative service, and the large house sheltered a number of aged evacuees bombed out of the East End.

Here I stayed for long periods, caring for the evacuees and tending the garden, and found a healing contentment in the open country, reminiscent of Holland, where pageants of cloud marched over the wide horizons and wild flowers filled the lanes with their blue and yellow. The nights were less happy; lying awake in semi-darkness I listened to heavy British bombers flying out to sea, and wondered how many German children would die before the morning.

To suffer damage might be grievous, but to inflict it was detestable. When the great tits with black bullet heads twittered sociably at dawn from the leafy boughs in the garden, I would reflect—as so often in the First World War—on the heightened consciousness created by everyday life lived under the shadow of death.

I was at Langham when G. experienced a second naval adventure. Owing to the Presidential loan of the fifty outdated destroyers which had been the subject of G.'s "dossier" on his last cross-Atlantic journey, the American newspapers followed the progress of all destroyers with keen interest. Hoping for a chance of lecturing on their actual work, he arranged through the Admiralty to make an observation trip, and late in July departed for a "destination unknown".

For ten days I had no news of him; then I received a telegram from Belfast when I expected one from Liverpool. His convoy, I learned later, had headed for the Azores when the crew discovered that the *Scharnhorst* and a number of submarines had been seen in the area. On the last of several vigilant nights, G. lay down to rest at

4 a.m. in the Captain's cabin. Within an hour a monstrous explosion wakened him, rocking the ship and pitching the Captain's possessions on the floor.

"Torpedoed again!" he thought philosophically.

He hurried upstairs to find the ship on fire and listing so badly that one deck was within six feet of the water. But this time the "missile" was not a torpedo; in the dawn haze another destroyer accompanying the convoy had rammed them. The prow had penetrated the engineer's cabin which adjoined the Captain's, and torn a large hole in the oil-chamber. The hot oil flooded the cabins to knee depth; it resembled thick molasses, and caused everything that it covered—including one of G.'s newly-purchased suitcases—to disintegrate completely.

The crew released the lifeboats, but managed to put out the fire before it reached the store of high explosives. Eventually the destroyer limped into Belfast under her own steam, but was "laid up" for weeks. For the second time in six months, G. faced the problem of partial re-equipment in a coupon-dominated era.

No Pressman dared to report this incident, but a fellow "observer" on board subsequently described for me G.'s response to the emergency. With his remaining white suitcase in his hand, said my informant, he stood on deck as calmly as though he were waiting for a bus in Piccadilly.

The crew of the destroyer liked him as much as he liked them, and gave him the ship's old ensign as a keepsake. For years, a counterblast to the Gestapo List, it adorned our dining-room wall at 2 Cheyne Walk.

(20)

That summer, in which the publication of the Atlantic Charter incongruously coincided with memorial meetings for Rabindranath Tagore, two famous Americans came to London.

The first, Raymond Gram Swing, a long-standing acquaintance, crossed the Atlantic in a bomber. He talked with us one July evening in his room at the Savoy Hotel, where we described the raid of April 16th–17th which Americans had heard on the radio.

"What does it feel like to listen to a raid when there's no chance of your being involved?" I inquired.

With a vehemence which astonished me, he replied: "It's just hell . . . Believe it or not, London's a far happier city to-day than New York."

I had not previously known Thornton Wilder, though I had been

287

among the thousands who read *The Bridge of San Luis Rey*. When he arrived with John Dos Passos to attend the International P.E.N. Congress held in London that autumn, he brought with him the same contrite mood as Raymond Swing. Describing the impression made upon an American by the first sight of bomb-damaged London, he suddenly gripped the desk and exclaimed: "Forgive us our immunity!" with a note of real anguish in his pleasant voice.

When I recalled this cry of remorse in the fortnightly Letter that described the Congress, I quoted some relevant words which Winifred, in her short story, *The Comforter*, had made Judas Iscariot utter in hell.

"Heaven is only tolerable to those who have learned how to forgive themselves. So I came here, where, if we are in torment, we may at least share the pain we have inflicted. We are not called upon to suffer the horror of immunity."

But now the danger period, for Londoners, was temporarily over. With no immediate services needed by an unbombed population, G. and I contemplated another move. In spite of his destroyer trip and the book, *One Anglo-American Nation*, which he had published that summer, his prospects of an early return to the United States had become unpromising, and he began to meditate on a new book as a constructive alternative.

In my own mind the idea for an unconventional small work had also been germinating. In it I wanted to express my hope of seeing something better than "the destruction of Hitlerism" come out of the war, and like G. I needed more quiet than Piccadilly could offer.

G. had spent part of his boyhood in Kew and Richmond, where his father had been Vicar of St. Luke's, Kew Gardens. As his book was to be autobiographical and he hoped to recapture the atmosphere of this lovely outer suburb, we moved in September to a flat on Richmond Hill which overlooked the silver scythe of the Thames from its front windows and the eastward sweep of London from the back. Though half Richmond Park housed some of London's largest defence guns and the local damage rivalled Kensington's, the beauty of the riverside borough remained unimpaired.

We went to Richmond for three months, and stayed for twenty. Shortly after we had settled there, the Japanese attack on Pearl Harbour brought America's "immunity" to an end. The night after the onslaught, we listened over the radio to President Roosevelt's challenge to Congress in the name of "our righteous might". This inflammatory speech now reads somewhat strangely in the light thrown by subsequent revelations on preceding events.

Once again the children were part of a country at war; a main justification for sending them away had gone. But at least they were living in the middle of the American Continent and not near the threatened coasts. Peaceful Minnesota, with its well-balanced Scandinavian population, was a safe distance from the new centres of war hysteria.

CHAPTER EIGHT

VALLEY OF HUMILIATION

The sands run out; no dawn light stirs the sky;
From North to South flicker the fires of hell;
Within the walls of Europe's citadel
A million mothers watch their children die.
Themselves half-famished, haunted by the cry
Of stricken youth for bread, they lift their prayer
To friends who from starvation and despair
Have saved themselves, but now all aid deny.

For ruthless in their pride the statesmen go;
Indifferent that their noon is Europe's night,
They disavow compassion for the plight
Of babes abandoned both by friend and foe.
O women of the West, rise now and speak,
Lest pity die, and strength betray the weak!

V.B., *Europe's Children.**

(1)

"It is an hard matter," wrote John Bunyan in the *Pilgrim's Progress*, "to go down into the Valley of Humiliation."

By 1942 I had almost grown accustomed to the climate of the Valley, in which it seemed clear that I should have to remain until the end of the war. Distrust did not only come from official quarters; friends who had known G. and me for years coldly avoided me at public gatherings, and a growing spate of abusive letters increased the pain of such rejections.

To the pathological hate-mongers I never replied, but when a famous writer of "thrillers", now dead, asked in brutal language why I did not "keep my mouth shut", my answer inquired whether it was to shut people's mouths that we were fighting Hitler. In

* *The Friend.* October 22nd, 1943.

February a police visit to my Letter office at Blackheath suggested that perhaps, after all, it was. But in spite of this occasional supervision, no attempt was ever made to suppress or even to censor the Letter, though it had now quite an extensive circulation abroad.

It was comforting to reflect that I was again in good company. About this time I learned that, during the First War, Bertrand Russell had been refused an exit permit to lecture at Harvard, and forbidden to visit towns in "prohibited" areas.

And there were other compensations. More numerous than the "poison-pen" products were letters from readers who found encouragement in my writings for their own midnight hours, or judged them from the relative detachment of distant countries. Among the latter was Nora Waln, the American Quaker who wrote *Reaching for the Stars*, and gave my fortnightly Letter some timely financial help. At Christmas that year one anonymous correspondent sent me a card with a printed message which had probably been designed for a different type of recipient.

"We think of you daily with gratitude. What you do and endure is never forgotten by all who love truth and peace."

Among these compensations was the continued loyalty of a few unintimidated friends. In the New Year "Jos" Wedgwood—recently promoted to be Baron Wedgwood of Barleston—lunched with us in town and gave me a ticket to watch him take the Oath in the House of Lords. Arthur Creech-Jones, now Parliamentary Private Secretary to Ernest Bevin at the Ministry of Labour, assured me after the police investigation that there was no real "drive" against my Letter.

"Jon thinks it is performing a really useful function in trying to put people in a decent mood for peace-making," I wrote of him at this time to G., "and will take up the matter with vigour if any attempt to suppress it is made."

From a speaking tour in South Wales, G. sought to bring me encouragement. The miners, he wrote, were disillusioned by Party doctrines, and waiting for a new vision.

"They don't like Mr. Stalin's atheism—and they are not taken in by our Ministry of Propaganda. There are the seeds of a great and hopeful movement here. . . . Audiences overflowing, people standing . . . If you had heard, as I have, of the respect in which your books are held in Wales, I think you would be tempted to do more."

Another book seemed indeed to be due. For some time a belief had been growing that I might perhaps find the writer's characteristic "compensation" in an attempt to comfort other inhabitants of the Valley of Humiliation who faced with me the danger of self-pity.

The idea of "redemptive suffering" voluntarily shared, so often put forward during the war in the writings and speeches of Canon Raven, was then a conception quite new to me. But some such instinctive conviction had produced the sense of being "under orders" which compelled me to stay when John and Shirley went to America.

During the autumn of 1940, a keen sense of injustice had brought me much bitterness. I had been "deceived", as it seemed, into parting with the children before learning that I should no longer be allowed to do the work abroad which the previous winter had been represented as my duty.

One October week-end I had walked through a country lane considering, with the ready indignation of a combative temperament, how I could "get my own back" on the obstructive bureaucrats who had made such havoc of my personal life.

Suddenly, in an empty valley covered with fallen leaves, something seemed to check the direction of my thoughts. Within my mind, an inconvenient second self addressed me firmly.

"Don't you realise that this is a spiritual experience? For the past few years you have had far more honour and appreciation than you deserve. Now you know what it is to be humiliated; and this gives you a new kinship with those to whom you have hitherto felt superior—prisoners, refugees, the unemployed, the down-and-outs, and all the despised and rejected of men."

And I remembered that, when I wrote *Honourable Estate*, I had made one of my characters express a similar idea.

"I suppose, if we took a long enough view, we should feel that any sorrow bears its own compensation which enlarges the scope of human mercy. Some of us, perhaps, can never reach our honourable estate—the state of maturity, of true understanding—until we have wrested strength and dignity out of humiliation and dishonour."

Now, after meditating for a year on that resurrected philosophy, I felt impelled to embody it in a book more closely related to the war-time needs of 1942.

(2)

I called this little volume *Humiliation with Honour*, and dedicated it "To the Victims of Power" in the words of Rabindranath Tagore:

"Be not ashamed, my brothers, to stand before the proud and the
    powerful
With your white robe of simpleness.
Let your crown be of humility, your freedom the freedom of the
    soul;

Build God's throne daily upon the ample bareness of your
  poverty,
And know that which is huge is not great and pride is not everlasting."

Each of the short chapters was designed for a different type of
victim—the "mass-man"; the transgressors of two wars against the
dominant State; prisoners; internees; refugees; the bereaved who
mourned; the young paying with life and limb for the sins of their
elders. The brief Epilogue concluded:

"War begins first in the human soul. When a man has learned
how to wrest honour from humiliation, his mastery of his own soul
has begun and by just that much he has brought the war against
war nearer to victory. He no longer looks to the men on the heights
to supply him with evidence that God exists. Instead he himself,
from the depths, becomes part of that evidence. He has proved that
power itself is powerless against the authority of love."

I began this work, as a series of short essays, in March 1942. At
the end of May I decided that the essays were lifeless, scrapped the
manuscript, and started the book again in the form of letters to
John. It came alive immediately, although John, then absorbed in
painting and other forms of mental development more appropriate
to fourteen, never attempted to read it.

Humiliation with Honour, finished in August 1942, had an unexpected publishing history. My current British and American publishers, committed in their different ways to the war effort, asked me
to excuse them from doing it. I had, indeed, no desire to challenge
their normal cooperativeness with such an embarrassing proposition. Eventually the work was issued in England by Andrew Dakers
Ltd. and in the United States by the Fellowship of Reconciliation,
which added an Introduction from Dr. Harry Emerson Fosdick,
the distinguished unorthodox Minister of New York's Riverside
Church.

Mr. Dakers betrayed no misgivings when the manuscript first
reached him.

"It is a shining thing in a dark world," he wrote me, "better and
lovelier than I had dared to expect. Your restraint gives it power,
and it will shake the complacency of many who have not bothered to
think out a conclusion for themselves. . . . There is nothing in the
book to offend any Christian citizen."

He published it in October; the striking black and white jacket by
Arthur Wragg showed a gyved figure with its head uplifted to the

light. We expected a total sale of perhaps 3,000 copies from a highly selected group of readers, but by publication date the first edition of 6,000 copies had gone, and a second and third edition brought the sales up to 10,000 by February 1943. Some striking reviews by such well-known writers as Laurence Housman and Arthur Ponsonby added prestige to circulation.

In occupied Norway *Humiliation with Honour* was also read. After the war, I learned that it had been smuggled over from England and circulated in typescript throughout the Resistance movement.

(3)

From the beginning of 1942, I wrote my book against a back-ground of national humiliation seldom relieved by compensatory honour.

"What a New Year's Day!" ran my diary for January 1st. "More countries at war than ever before in the world's history. Hong Kong gone; Sarawak going. Penang gone; war surging into Malaya; Rangoon and Singapore bombed. Manila burning, and the Americans fighting a hopelessly outnumbered battle in the Philippines. . . . A year ago this country faced the Axis alone; now we have the United States, Russia and China as allies. By next year—what?"

As the victorious Japanese advanced on Singapore, Australian agitation increased British dismay. No cheers now greeted Churchill's face on the cinema screens, and everywhere voices asked: "Will Australia go? Will New Zealand? Will Burma? Will India?"

In beleaguered Singapore, one million people experienced an in-tensified version of Britain's mood after the fall of France. Day after day, the consciousness of their apprehensions cast a shadow, like a palpable presence, upon our work. By March an empire built through two centuries had vanished in two and a half months, and we felt as though we were living through the closing chapters of Gibbon's *Decline and Fall*.

Four days before Singapore surrendered, three German battleships sailed unimpeded from Brest through the Straits of Dover. The exasperated Press, compelled to record Britain's declining prestige in the Far East, loudly lamented our worst humiliation at sea since the Dutch sailed up the Medway in 1667.

In the United States, the first passionate enthusiasm for the war had yielded to consternation. Vehement anti-British recriminations followed the expulsion from Malaya of an American commentator who refused to broadcast false statements about imperial air strength.

My New York publisher gloomily reported "dislocations"; the

paper industry had given to munitions 60 per cent. of the chlorine needed for books. In the *Evening Standard*, Major-General Fuller commented acidly that the gigantic forces being raised in America suggested preparation for the next war rather than this. A Canadian reader of my Letter wrote unhappily from Vancouver.

"Our immediate problem is with the evacuation of 22,800 Japanese from the coastal areas. It is being done with little regard for the feelings of the Japanese, even the Canadian-born. At present they are in a sort of concentration camp in the Exhibition grounds and buildings. It all seems so like Fascist methods."

From India, where British defeats in Burma threatened national security, Mahatma Gandhi addressed an incisive pamphlet "To Every Japanese".

"You have been gravely misinformed, as I know you are, that we have chosen this particular moment to embarrass the Allies when your attack against India is imminent. If we wanted to turn Britain's difficulty into our opportunity we should have done it as soon as the war broke out. . . . You will be sadly disillusioned if you believe that you will receive a willing welcome from India. The end and aim of the movement for British withdrawal is to prepare India by making her free for resisting all militarist and imperialist ambition, whether it is called British Imperialism, German Nazism, or your pattern."

In March Sir Stafford Cripps took his Mission to India in the hope of relieving the deadlock; his journey followed the fall of Rangoon. He returned unsuccessful, to find many British people recalling the appeal made the previous year by Mrs. Pandit: "Has freedom a double meaning—does it mean one thing for you and yours, and something different for us?" That summer she was again arrested, and detained at Allahabad.

The spring weather matched the news; between January 6th and February 21st came the twentieth century's longest spell of cold, and the coldest day (January 15th, when 46 degrees of frost were recorded) since 1881. Richmond Hill with its frosted trees resembled an old-fashioned Christmas card; frozen snow covered the Park, and the Thames locks turned to solid ice beneath the bitter wind. On the slippery roads the distribution of our scanty coal broke down; in my tiny north-facing study I struggled to write wearing a thick woollen shelter-suit with long trousers and a Pixie hood.

Austerities and shortages accompanied the cold; soap rationing was announced just before Singapore fell. The Japanese conquest of Malaya cost the Allies their main supply of rubber and tin, but the buzz of conversation among the women at the small hotel where G.

and I took our meals showed that Singapore left them indifferent though soap roused them to fury. They realised the meaning of the capitulation only when they were obliged to ransack the local shops for fast-disappearing hot water bottles and rubber-soled shoes.

With March came more cuts in our fruitless diet and rationed clothes; April brought fuel rationing and five-inch baths. Over the whole melancholy scene a mental fog due to scarce and unreliable news lay like a blanket.

"The censorship here is so close that I depend for most of my information upon *Time* and *Life*," I wrote to New York that summer. "Even in this tiny country one part doesn't know what is happening in another. You can get information about a place only by going there. . . . There is endless talk about a Second Front and constant pressure for it from Russia."

Throughout that year the ruthless struggle between Nazis and Communists gave a distant dark background to events nearer home.

"Whether the kind of Europe that will emerge if the Russians do successfully stand up to the Germans will be of a type to please the present powers that be, is another question," I had written in an earlier letter. "I do not imagine that the Russians are fighting their war to restore Franco-British domination of the Continent!"

Even when Stalingrad was seriously threatened, Stalin's own animation seemed unimpaired. On April 1st, G. brought back a lively story from a luncheon with Sir Richard Acland and Victor Gollancz.

"When Eden was in Moscow, Stalin was telling him and Cripps his plans for post-war Europe. Eden interposed nervously: 'But, M. Stalin, what about the Atlantic Charter?' Whereupon Stalin turned to Molotov and chuckled: 'Ha! Ha! the Atlantic Charter!' He went on making this interjection throughout the conversation."

By now the healing spring had come at last. The sudden singing of birds, and the smell of moist earth beneath snowdrops and crocuses in the Terrace Gardens, accompanied the heavy-type announcement of Japanese atrocities and a newsvendor's poster outside the cinema on Richmond Hill.

"WAKE UP ENGLAND. GIVE THE B JAPS A BLOOD BATH."

In April daffodils covered the lawns; vividly in blossom against the blue backcloth of the sky above the Thames, magnolia, forsythia, prunus and almond-blossom sang their chorus of colour to the strengthening sun.

Yet this loveliness seemed only to emphasize the unbroken tale of reverses, which in June's "Black Week" culminated in the surrender of Tobruk and the loss to Rommel's forces of all Cyrenaica. For many British families these national defeats had their personal cost; to us they meant an indefinite postponement of the long-hoped-for date when the children could return.

The weary Press caustically reported a current quip: "Good news at last! Two of our generals were captured at Tobruk!" and the *Sunday Express* philosopher, Nathaniel Gubbins, produced a characteristic comment: "The worse the news is, the more we talk about what we are going to do with Germany after the war."

(4)

Now that the supply of practical workers exceeded the demand, I used my pen increasingly for a special form of "psychological warfare." It endeavoured to mitigate the ferocious propaganda which had now developed its own brutal vocabulary, and to plead, in George Eliot's phrase, for "one draught of simple human pity that will not forsake us".

The critics of efforts such as these dismissed them as spiritual arrogance, but the workers in this discredited field were so few that each learned to ignore the disparaging labels which he attracted. Their ranks included many good citizens of varied outlooks who believed that acceptance of war need not involve the total debasement of Christian values.

Amongst them were R. R. Stokes, M.P., whose outspoken protests in the House of Commons undoubtedly deprived him of ministerial status in the first post-war Labour Government, and H. N. Brailsford, whose beautiful essay on Brahms' *Requiem*, "All Souls' Day", appeared in the *New Statesman* for November 14th, 1942. This article recalled for its readers a German nation quite different from the "butcher birds" which inspired Lord Vansittart's hectic propaganda.

Much of this diverse witness was directed against the "saturation" bombing of great towns and the British blockade of Occupied Europe. It rejected the popular demand for "retaliation" in the belief that to inflict suffering corrupts, while the best Christian precedent exists for enduring it. The current journalistic method of recording British air raids in jubilant sporting terms which ignored the human anguish involved also seemed to be due for revision.

Two small organisations, the Bombing Restriction Committee and the Food Relief Campaign, were formed to resist the cruelties imposed by bombing and blockade. The second worked, in so far as it was allowed, with a larger and more orthodox body known as the Famine Relief Committee.

The Bombing Restriction Committee began as a protest against the night bombing of civilians. In May 1941 its founder, the indomitable Quaker, T. Corder Catchpool, had written asking me for help.

"Have you thought of taking any action in connection with the Bishop of Chichester's letter in *The Times* on the bombing of civilian populations, which has recently received strong support by a joint letter from Bernard Shaw and Gilbert Murray? It seems to me almost like a last despairing cry of humanity before all such considerations are completely lost in the increasing welter of horrors."

The Bishop had suggested an offer by the British Government to abandon night bombing if the German Government would do the same. It seemed even then not too late to return to the position adopted by Churchill in the House of Commons on June 7th, 1935: "It is only in the twentieth century that this hateful condition of inducing nations to surrender by massacring the women and children has gained acceptance . . . among men."

In 1942, when I had worked with Corder for about six months, his Committee enlarged its purpose to meet the change in British tactics which followed the appointment of Sir Arthur Harris to control Bomber Command.

On June 2nd, 1942, Winston Churchill made a pronouncement totally different from the civilised utterance of 1935.

"As the year advances, German cities, harbours and centres of war production will be subjected to an ordeal the like of which has never been experienced by any country in continuity, severity or magnitude."

"Bomber Harris" was appointed to carry out this Cabinet policy. His own broadcast on July 28th left no doubt of its purpose.

"We are bombing Germany, city by city, and ever more terribly, in order to make it impossible for you to go on with the war. . . . Obviously, we prefer to hit factories, shipyards and railways. It damages Hitler's war machine most. But the people who work in these plants live close to them. Therefore we hit your houses and you."

(5)

As soon as "obliteration" bombing became part of Allied war strategy, atom and hydrogen bombs "lay in the logic of history". It was the first step towards the policy of genocide which in the nineteen-fifties would threaten mankind with extinction. Such a course utterly repudiated the value attached by Christian teaching to the human soul. If one national group was entitled to destroy another, what became of God's concern for the individual and his struggle for righteousness?

The moral consequences of the new strategy were instantaneous. Press and B.B.C. alike hailed the devastation of working-class suburbs as Allied triumphs. The cultural treasures of the ages— Cologne's museums, Münster's cathedral, the Römer at Frankfort, Monte Cassino—became less important in the eyes of war-leaders than a temporary national advantage. Protests were ignored or condemned as the voices of traitors. Nevertheless, they continued.

Two old Hanseatic cities were the first to suffer from "saturation"; in March, according to the communiqués, the R.A.F. "devastated" Lübeck. In April, for "four nights of horror", they "plastered" Rostock, a supply base for the Russian front where the supplies were not kept in the workers' homes. According to R. C. K. Ensor's *Miniature History of the War*, "the annihilating raid on Lübeck . . . and the raid of 1,130 bombers on Cologne . . . each marked an epoch" in Allied achievement.

During 1947, when I visited Lübeck, I found that this particular "epoch" had been marked chiefly by the demolition of churches, all old and historic.

"We were unlucky with it," a member of the Control Commission, for which I was lecturing, said plaintively. The port, I learned, was thirteen miles from the centre of the city. In the first great Cologne raid, the news bulletins boasted, 70,000 people were killed or injured, and I commented in my Letter: "Beside such a massacre, St. Bartholomew's Day looks like a picnic."

The unconcealed gloatings in the communiqués were now causing widespread, if suppressed, disquiet. One provincial clergyman wrote me that he had recently been stopped by a stranger who turned out to be a local tram-driver.

"T'ain't right, them raids," this man had muttered uneasily. "They ought to be stopped."

These mutterings increased when the raids brought inevitable retaliation on some of England's loveliest cities, of which Exeter, Bath, Norwich and York were the first to suffer. A Nazi announcement indicated that these reprisals were aimed at "works of art, monuments and residential districts . . . everything with three stars in Baedeker."

I saw the results for myself in Bath, where the Lantern Window was shattered in the abbey and gargoyles lay in heaps on the ground. Casualties, I was told, amounted to 400 killed and 1,000 injured. When I came out of the warehouse where I had been to discover the fate of our London furniture, which was stored there, a bus passed me advertising "Worth's Mourning Wear".

As 1942 passed into 1943, the R.A.F. "saturation" raids included Nuremberg and Munich as well as the industrial cities of Turin, Bremen and Essen. When our "biggest ever" attacks on Berlin began in March 1943, the Nazis retaliated with "sneak raids" on the coast and a new series of onslaughts on London. In one occurred the strange and terrible accident where nearly two hundred persons were suffocated during a panic rush to an East End shelter.

Night after night, with G. away lecturing to troops, I watched the fireworks from our window on Richmond Hill, while the little Bombing Restriction Committee bravely produced one of its unpopular pamphlets, *Stop Bombing Civilians!*

"The Nazi planes came right over this flat twice, flying very low," I wrote to G. after one of these raids. "Much nervousness among the occupants—lavatory chains pulling all over the place! I was glad when the 'All Clear' went; I have been alone in too many raids to enjoy the experience or find any excitement in it any more."

(6)

From the beginning of 1942 until the Allied invasion of the Continent in 1944, I acted as chairman of the small Food Relief Campaign, with Roy Walker, the young author of a book called *Famine Over Europe*, as its energetic secretary. None of its members supported the war, which caused occasional clashes with the larger Famine Relief Committee. This more orthodox organisation included bishops, headmasters and impeccable social workers, with the Bishop of Chichester as their chairman.

Though the two groups differed in outlook and methods, their purpose was the same—to persuade the Government to allow small quantities of special foods to pass through the British blockade to the children, mothers and invalids of the German-occupied Continent. They confronted an adamant ministerial conviction that all such food must benefit the Nazis, though the large Hoover Mission to Belgium in the First War had avoided any such leakage. To the official mentality which had now developed, the widespread starvation of children appeared to be preferable to some dubious and infinitesimal advantage to the enemy.

Whenever I recall that constantly thwarted struggle to help the suffering youth of Europe, two small episodes come back. In March 1942, returning from an Easter visit to my mother, I saw a little girl on the station platform gaze with longing eyes at the automatic sweet machines. Her mother pulled out the drawers to show her that they were empty, and the child's face crumpled with disappointment. In my bag I carried a small basket with two or three marzipan fruits, the remains of a gift from Shirley to my mother. When I gave it to the child her smile came back and she ran gleefully to the train, holding the basket before her like a trophy.

Three months afterwards, on Hammersmith Underground Station, a husky young man, thinking himself unobserved, crept up to an automatic machine which sweet-hunters had missed, emptied the entire contents into his haversack, and hurried away. Watching from the opposite platform, I remembered the little girl and seethed with impotent rage. In my recollection the greedy youth became a combined symbol of the Nazi invaders and the British Government, which were both denying its normal privileges to helpless childhood.

Greece and Belgium now suffered most acutely from undernourishment, while France, Holland and Norway also struggled miserably to live on ever-diminishing rations. In December 1942, when Dr. Raymond Gautier, the Swiss member of the League of Nations Health Section, addressed a private meeting at Friends House, he stated bluntly that two hundred million Europeans were waiting only for the day when they could have a square meal again.

Twelve months earlier, the expected average of deaths from starvation in Greece had been 200 a day; nine months afterwards, the deaths of Greek children alone totalled 110,000. Just before Christmas 1941, *Life* published a report by a former American Ambassador to Belgium which warned the world that two million young Belgians were threatened with stunted physique and mental degeneration. By Christmas 1942, the Swedish Committee for the relief of Belgians declared that the whole nation was "heading for catastrophe".

Through my work for Food Relief I came to know Professor Emile Cammaerts, the Belgian poet and scholar who had lived in England since 1908. In the long *Times* obituary which appeared on November 3rd, 1953, his wartime endeavours to assist his half-starved fellow countrymen went unmentioned, though they lasted for over two years and must have drawn from him, in pamphlets, articles, and letters to the Press, many thousands of vehement words.

Professor Cammaerts officially worked for the Famine Relief Committee, but I shared many platforms with him and a former Governor of Equatorial Africa, Mr. Martin Parr. One speech, which I made in the Aeolian Hall, was transcribed by an American listener and appeared in the New York magazine *Fellowship* under the title "Has Pity Forsaken Us?"

"Nowadays," I had said, "some people seem to regard compassion as a form of Fifth Columnism." Later I quoted some words spoken by Dr. Fridtjof Nansen, the saviour of Europe's prisoners and refugees after the First World War, when he received the Nobel Prize in 1923.

"They called us fanatics, soft-heads, sentimental idealists because we have, it may be, a grain of faith that there is some good even in our enemies. . . . I don't think we are really very dangerous. But the people who are ossifying behind their political platforms and who hold aloof from suffering humanity, from starving, dying millions—it is they who are helping to lay Europe waste."

(7)

Early in 1943 the Director of Relief in Europe for the American Friends Service Committee, Dr. Howard Kershner, came to London from France, and strongly supported the Famine Relief Committee's modest proposals for sending two thousand tons of dried milk and vitamins to Greece and Belgium each month.

Over an austere war-time meal, we discussed his own limited relief project for the ten million most needy children, mothers, and unemployed in France, Belgium, Holland and Norway. He returned to America to write his booklet, *One Humanity*, and to conduct a national campaign for food relief which culminated in a mass meeting in New York addressed by ex-President Hoover.

Soon after Dr. Kershner left England, I learned that the new Archbishop of Canterbury, Dr. William Temple, had joined the Cardinal Archbishop of Westminster in a plea to the Foreign Secretary for Greece and Belgium. They made little progress, and the Archbishop arranged to address both Houses of Parliament on February 17th.

The previous autumn I had acted as judge in a competition held by a parents' magazine for "Britain's Bonniest Babies", and the contrast between the lovely children whose photographs I saw, and the European children of whose sufferings I read, haunted my mind for weeks. Surely these self-congratulatory parents and editors could not have been so pleased with themselves had they realised that millions of young Europeans were slowly dying of hunger?

Now, with the famine reports before me, I felt suddenly impelled

301

to drop everything I was doing and urgently appeal to other parents to help in saving Europe's children. Firmly an inner voice commanded "Write!" So I put aside my half-finished novel and began a long pamphlet, designed for the uninformed public, which I called *One of These Little Ones*.

In order to get it published before the Archbishop made his appeal in February, I collected the necessary material and wrote 10,000 words in three days. Andrew Dakers, humane and co-operative as always, agreed to put 50,000 copies on the market before the Archbishop's address, and I arranged to divide the profits between the Famine Relief Committee and the Food Relief Campaign. Later the Fellowship of Reconciliation published the booklet in America.

When February 17th came, the politicians at Westminster paid more attention to the debate on the Beveridge Report than to the Archbishop's plea, but the widely-distributed pamphlet helped to rally support for a statement issued by the Archbishop to the Press after his abortive meeting. The Friends' House bookshop displayed it in their Euston Road windows; Professor Cammaerts welcomed it in a friendly letter; and the North Welsh Women's Peace Council produced a Welsh edition translated by their Nationalist author, Kate Roberts.

All over the country, local relief campaigns sprang up, and as the night grew darker for Europe's children behind the iron curtain of Government indifference, Richard Stokes revived the subject of famine relief in Parliament during the November debate on the adjournment. This time relief measures were urged from the Government side of the House by Harold Nicolson, the civilised author-politician who remained a discreet opponent of blockade and saturation bombing throughout the war. He had just returned, he said, from Sweden, where searching questions had been put to him on the harshness of Britain's official attitude towards feeding Europe.

Shortly afterwards, with two other members of the Food Relief Campaign, I called on Harold Nicolson in his room amid the impressive ruins of the Temple. He spoke of the Minister of Economic Warfare and his Parliamentary Secretary as personally humane and we accepted his judgment, though we felt that if humane men could support the Government's policy they must have split personalities.

We had hoped to persuade Mr. Nicolson—later Sir Harold—to ask a question in the House, but this, he told us, as a former Civil Servant he had resolved never to do.

"Arrange for one yourselves, and go on pressing," he urged us in conclusion. "However obstinate the Government seems, something may come of it."

On New Year's Day 1944, we received the news that Greek relief, permitted on a minute scale since January 1942, was to be extended by 1,000 tons of food each month. It was not much—in the light of Europe's needs it was almost nothing—but the small concession enabled a number of young Greeks to survive the war.

(8)

Of the two chief personalities associated with these humanitarian efforts, one has survived to an active and saintly old age. The other died on a mountain top in 1952.

As chairman of the cautious Famine Relief Committee, the Bishop of Chichester had some misgivings about our dynamic little Food Relief Campaign, but his Committee used my booklet and gratefully accepted half the royalties that it earned.

On June 6th, 1954, under the heading "George Cicestr", a paragraph in *The Observer* contained the following comments:

"Next Friday the Bishop of Chichester will celebrate his twenty-five years as 'George Cicestr' . . . George Kennedy Allen Bell may seem, for a moment or two, to have walked out of Trollope, but he has come hard and boldly up against the problems of his time. He has spoken out often on vexed public issues.

" 'Only lately,' said a Sussex church councillor recently, 'have I forgiven our Bishop for the way he criticised the bombing of German cities,' adding, 'Mind you, I think he was right.' His friends believe that if he had not been so forthright at that time, he would now be Archbishop of Canterbury."

The Bishop who thus sacrificed preferment in the cause of humanity remained for me a respected chairman, but Corder Catchpool became a personal friend for whose memory I can thank God with a gratitude that few human beings inspire.

Corder belonged to an old family of Leicester Quakers, and had trained as an engineer when the First War challenged him to bear witness to the Quaker peace testimony. At first he served in France with the Friends Ambulance Unit, but this socially approved occupation soon appeared to be too easy a choice. In 1916 he proclaimed himself a conscientious objector, and for three years endured courts-martial followed by imprisonment with hard labour. His books, *On Two Fronts* and *Letters of a Prisoner*, described those early experiences.

Between the wars, Corder and his wife Gwen dedicated themselves to relief service in Germany. After Hitler came to power they remained in Berlin; although they were suspected and spied upon, they continued their work till 1936. When the Second War broke out they were living with their four children in Hampstead, where Corder characteristically became a stretcher-bearer attached to the local Hospital. He also served in East End shelters, cycling imperturbably through the raids from Hampstead to Bow and back. During 1940 and 1941, I occasionally met him at Kingsley Hall before I joined his Bombing Restriction Committee.

Corder was then about sixty, a quiet man of middle height with almost white hair and an unexpected passion for mountaineering. Though he presided at many public meetings he was not an impressive speaker; his shy smile and gentle humility seldom suggested the firmness with which he could act within the field of his convictions. Only gradually did his colleagues in any project come to realise the strength of his inner dedication.

He never knew when he was beaten; this sublime lack of realism cost him his life but was also his glory. It made him a man fitted only for the heights of human experience, and the standards he exacted from himself he took for granted in others. He assumed their readiness to give up personal advantages for principles, including such apparent assets as popularity and prestige. "Good publicity" meant nothing to him at all; the bad publicity given to Christ by His contemporaries was good enough for him.

It was inevitable that, with such a man, I should discuss the possibility of joining the Society of Friends. Amid the pressures of wartime, the Church of England seemed to me to compromise precisely where a truly Christian body would take a firm stand.

"I am terribly tempted to desert the Anglicans and apply for membership of the Society," I wrote him in February 1942, "but Nora Waln tells me that no one at all 'prominent' is accepted now for fear they go back on their undertakings, as so many well-known people did at the outbreak of war."

Two months later Corder invited me to discuss the problem at his home, and I spent a week-end in Hampstead with his family. When the others had gone to bed we talked long after midnight, but eventually I decided—though reluctantly—to remain an Anglican.

One difficulty was professional. Literary achievements, whether major or minor, seldom emerged from the group-thinking which seemed to be an essential part of the Quaker philosophy.

"No creative work can be done without a routine that appears selfish because it is self-centred—or rather, work-centred," I wrote to G. during this period of indecision. The same view, reiterated in a letter to *The Friend* during 1954, produced a long correspondence which eventually bore fruit in the Friends' Fellowship of the Arts.

Apart from the egotistical obligations of writing, I thought myself personally unsuited to the Quaker community. Frivolous clothes and the use of cosmetics were not consistent with their sober habits, yet I recognised these forms of vanity as too habitual to be eradicated.

Equally inconsistent with the Quaker way of life was my combative disposition. This, within limitations, I could learn to discipline by accepting the standards of conduct which Dick Sheppard had shared with the Quakers, but I could not provide myself with a placid temperament or become uncontroversial by wishing that I were. (And anyway, did I really wish it?)

When Corder received these explanations he was disappointed, but his friendship remained unchanged. After our Committee had ended with the war I saw him less frequently, but we met from time to time and the consciousness of his existence lighted a beacon in every dark hour.

One September morning in 1952, a newspaper paragraph headed "Climber Aged 69 Dies of Exhaustion" immediately caught my eye.

"Zürich, Wednesday. A 69-year-old Englishman, Mr. Thomas Corder Catchpool, of Parliament Hill, N.W., set out with his wife and an Italian guide three days ago to climb the 14,500 ft. Monte Rosa. To-night he was brought down dead to Zermatt.

"Mr. Catchpool slipped in the dark into a 15 ft. crevice during the descent and injured his eyes. He died of exhaustion as his wife and the guide tried to lead him to an overnight shelter.

"Mr. Catchpool was planning to travel to Berlin in November as the official British representative of the Society of Friends."

For an incalculable period I sat stunned at the desk, my work totally forgotten. Returning at last to painful consciousness, I wrote the short tribute which appeared in both *The Times* and *The Friend*.

The following April, on the way to a short holiday in Italy, G. and I spent the night at Zermatt. There we found Corder's grave among tombstones commemorating mountaineers and guides in the village cemetery beside a mountain stream swollen with melting snow. During the warm afternoon we climbed the foothills of the Matterhorn until we saw, through a gap between the mountains on the Swiss-Italian frontier, the snowy peak of Monte Rosa, like a full-blown flower. Appropriately cradled by those celestial snows, Corder had died.

That night I sent to England a Sonnet, "Suggested by the grave of Corder Catchpool at Zermatt", which *The Friend* published a week later.

> "Death is no enemy to those who seek
> And scale the mountain-tops of life and time,
> To meet their end upon some mighty peak
> Of man's experience, ruthless and sublime.
> Yet not their end; for who that sees this place
> Can doubt the Maker's pattern, shade and sun,
> Defeat redeemed by victory, triumphs won
> Which light the blazing glory of His Face?

> "And how should we forget thee, undismayed
> By years or peril, whose untarnished soul
> Soared free to find its own allotted goal;
> Leaving the mortal man, his ransom paid,
> To sleep serene amid the snows untrod
> Where dwells the awful Majesty of God?"

(9)

Though the struggle for the victims of bombing and blockade lasted nearly three years, I was usually also at work on a book which provided a sure refuge from disappointment. While *Humiliation with Honour* was still unfinished, I started to plan a novel which had been in my mind since the outbreak of war.

In the autumn of 1939, I was summoned to a murder trial as a potential witness for the defence. The prisoner, a sensitive and intelligent professional man, had caused his wife's death and then attempted suicide, but afterwards claimed that he could remember nothing of the tragedy. A team of psychological specialists traced back this amnesia to a bomb explosion in 1918, and my acquaintance was found "Guilty but Insane". Though I was never actually called, I remained for three days in the Midlands town where the trial was held, and heard all the evidence.

Moved by gratitude for his escape and my subsequent visits to Broadmoor, the prisoner agreed that his strange and tragic story which linked the First War with the Second would make a significant novel. I promised to postpone it until the events of the war, which had virtually relegated his misfortunes to the local newspapers, had dimmed the public memory of the trial, but I discussed the book with both my publishers. Three years later, they suggested that the time to begin it had come.

This new commission coincided with my mother's return to London in June 1942. Deciding for the second time that she could no longer endure being evacuated, she wrote to me with the pathos of an elderly exile swamped by incomprehensible events.

"How difficult it is for me to be so far from anyone to advise me to do what is right. . . . I feel old, frail, and feeble."

Now she travelled to town, and found a hotel that she liked. Her choice subsequently became notorious for its association with the Kensington murderer, John Haigh, but her residence there pre-dated his arrival. Since Haigh selected well-to-do elderly widows as his victims, this was fortunate for my mother. I helped her to settle in, and two months later went away with G. for a brief golden holiday.

This time we chose Llandudno, where his father in an early mini-stry had won an outstanding reputation as a preacher. G. took me to see his former church; a small picture of him preaching still stood on the vestry mantelpiece.

I found I had forgotten the spectacular beauty of this normally crowded but now empty Welsh seaside town. Over the great green hills the shadows of clouds, driven by the vigorous wind, sped briefly to extinguish the scintillating gold of gorse against a sapphire sky, and the setting sun gleamed blood-red from countless small rivulets in the Conway Estuary beneath Penmaenmawr.

As the big hotels were all occupied by evacuated Civil Servants, we stayed at a glorified "pub". The Grand Hotel had appropriately become the headquarters of the super-tax authorities, but it wore a desolate air for the home of officials who were presumably dealing in millions. Undaunted by the absence of visitors, Krishna Menon, later the first High Commissioner for India in Britain, held a propaganda meeting while we were there, and a cinema showed the film of "Mrs. Miniver", which we went to see.

Although I knew that the script-writers, Jan Struther and James Hilton, had described our Blitz from the safety of America with a sentimentality which it had not possessed, I found myself moved with envy for the men and women whose simple patriotism, like mine in the First War, inspired them with the belief that by reci-procal violence they could conquer the powers of evil.

(10)

I felt that I could now leave G. for a time and begin my book, for he had recently started his autobiography, which deeply absorbed him. From Cheddar in Somerset I wrote to him gratefully:

"I have loved more than one man besides yourself, but I have never known one whom I could have married with such experience of toleration and full understanding."

I now made a practice of going to country hotels or the Allum Green cottage when starting or trying to finish a book. London, I had learned, was no place for a writer, but G.'s preference for urban living obliged me to use it as a base.

As the cottage was now let I went to a small hotel near Cheddar Gorge, which I had discovered the previous year after a meeting in Weston-super-Mare. It stood over an artificially-widened mountain stream, which suggested a lake and ended in a waterfall at the bottom of the garden.

My room, looking up the stream towards the gorge, lacked morning sun owing to the great overhanging rock, and as central heating had been abolished for the duration it was often cold. But the small back garden above the waterfall provided a sun-trap where green dragon-flies flitted actively over Michaelmas daisies and golden rod. Here I read the three-year-old newspapers which described the unusual murder trial, and studied a "background" book, *The Neuroses in War*, published by the Tavistock Clinic, for the psychology of my chief character.

During the month that I spent in Cheddar, many Somerset scenes and skies found their way into my novel, then called *Day of Judgment*. Sometimes, as I walked through the gorge and the huge rock chimneys seemed to close above my head, I felt with the Biblical Jacob: "How dreadful is this place!" It was more reassuring to climb the stone stairway, and watch the vast herring-bone pattern of sunset clouds spread cerise and purple above Axbridge reservoir from the top of the cliffs.

To G. I described the derelict "tourism" of the village. Tearooms, souvenir shops, and the caves in the cliffs were closed, for the cheese which once attracted week-end trippers had been commandeered by the Ministry of Food. But their absence at least guaranteed my privacy. As *The Neuroses in War* reminded me how much of my own life had been a battle against fear, I entered ever more deeply into the soul of my convicted "hero" and understood how easily his position might have been mine.

I returned to London just in time for the Anglo-American landings in North Africa which followed the defeat of Rommel's tanks at El Alamein, and the final loss of German initiative to the Russians before Stalingrad. On Thanksgiving Day in late November, the Stars and Stripes flew from Westminster Abbey for the first time in its nine hundred years of history; within, three thousand khaki-clad

Americans heard their Ambassador, John G. Winant, make the Thanksgiving proclamation. Among the few British invited, G. and I stood beside them, singing "America the Beautiful" and thinking with nostalgia how significant was this ceremony for the descendants of the men who shook England's dust from their feet three centuries ago.

In a totally different fashion, Christmas Day was memorable too. When I arrived at St. Martin-in-the-Fields, where I had arranged to meet my mother, she already occupied her usual seat in the crowded church. At once she asked me: "Have you heard any more about Darlan?"

"No," I said. "What about him?"

"He's been assassinated," she whispered. "I heard it on the wireless."

The unhappy Admiral had indeed been shot in his Algiers office, and never received from the Allies the credit due to him for bringing the French overseas forces to their side.

"It seemed a strange piece of information to be given me in church on Christmas morning," I recorded that night.

By determined concentration, I managed to finish my novel on a radiant April day of 1943. So far an unusual quality of inspiration had carried the book to the final scene in which the rehabilitated victim of catastrophe set out for an unknown future, but it soon ran into dire misfortune.

When the revision was finished and the American copy of the manuscript had been dispatched, I sent my acquaintance, now released from Broadmoor, a typescript at his own request. In reply he told me for the first time that he had been freed on conditions which rendered impossible the publication of the book in its existing form.

As soon as I had recovered from this extinguishing blow I notified my publishers that the manuscript must be withdrawn, though it could perhaps be rewritten. With the expected regrets from America came a brilliant report.

"Our reader is lyric in his praises, and incidentally thinks the book might be expected to have a wide sale. It will be too bad if you have to do it all over again, because the book seems tops just as it is."

From the abyss of disappointment, I tried in my reply to be philosophical.

"It is just one of those literary catastrophes which actually do seem to occur quite frequently, but I hadn't run into myself before. The story was based on about four years' psychological reading. I regard the theme as so important that I am going to try to write it again and make it publishable. I should be glad however if you would keep the original manuscript, as I do not feel that a rewritten version is likely to be as good as the original, which was written under very strong inspiration. I should, therefore, hope that some day, even if it is after we are all dead and gone, this book might be published by your firm in its original form."

Some months afterwards, I tackled the painful task of rewriting the story under a new title, *Account Rendered*. A musical friend, Dennis Gray Stoll, the son of Sir Oswald, generously helped me to transform the central character into a musician. I completed this second manuscript to the sound of British bombers going out to raid Germany beneath the clear stars of January 1944, and my friend and solicitor, Harold Rubinstein, passed it as fit for publication within the limits imposed.

Though a strange and spectacular success awaited this novel after initial failure, the quality of the first version was irretrievably lost.

(11)

The unfamiliar sound of church bells which followed the Allied victories of November 1942 in North Africa at first meant for us only a new postponement of the time when we should see the children again.

All the Mediterranean was now ablaze, and every possible ship and plane had been diverted from the Atlantic routes. But gradually it became clear that the Allied change of fortune would eventually make the seas safer by turning the Nazis' attention from submarine warfare to the crises looming on land.

From the time that the prospect of invasion ended, G. and I, in co-operation with the children's American guardians, had been considering how to bring them home. Though a "token" contribution of £3 per month per child had been permitted since January 1942, their cost to their foster parents alone made it desirable that they should return. It now seemed likely that British financial regulations would postpone for years the cross-Atlantic transfer of compensating funds.

For months innumerable letters crossed the Atlantic discussing alternative expedients. Should we venture to bring the children by sea, or try to get them on the Clipper, with its waiting list of would-be passengers nearly two years long? Risks and delays were endlessly weighed against our consciousness of their expense to their guardians. Our desire for their presence became a mere "also ran" amongst the arguments for their return.

"Sometimes," I admitted to G. in August 1942, "I can't believe that this endless period without them is not a dreadful nightmare from which I must soon wake up."

But the approach of Shirley's twelfth birthday—her third since she left England—had already galvanised us into action that summer. In June we registered the children with Thos. Cook & Son as intending travellers and applied for a Treasury permit.

Though life without John and Shirley resembled a double amputation, the continuing tragedies of Europe and Asia compelled long periods of impersonal detachment. In September 1942, G. wrote to Mrs. Eleanor Roosevelt to suggest American intervention in India. Mr. Amery reprimanded him with a severe note, but he received a cordial reply promising to consult the President. Four months later, against a background of reports from the Casablanca Conference, I took the chair at the Trades Union Club for a significant address by Edward Thompson on "Bankrupt Statesmanship in India".

It was bankrupt indeed. Within the next few weeks, stories of Mahatma Gandhi's spectacular fast in his Poona prison filled the newspapers, and a reader wrote me ironically quoting a current British slogan: "Freedom is in peril; defend it with all your might!" Gandhi's English friends prayed for him at an Intercession Service at St. Martin-in-the-Fields, which I described in a fortnightly Letter.

"When the history of our time comes to be assessed from the standpoint of the centuries," I added, "the part played by the Viceroy may appear not dissimilar from that of the Procurator of Judea."

These periodic reminders of the values for which the British Government claimed to be fighting gave G. the idea of a short anthology which we could compile together. It would include whatever contemporary stories we could collect, from newspapers and journals and books, of compassionate action between war-time enemies, and poems which reflected the survival of charity. The title, I thought, might be *Above All Nations*, recalled from a carved quotation from Goethe on a Cornell building: "Above all nations is humanity". When we put the suggestion to Victor Gollancz, he warmly welcomed it.

My subsequent extensive reading of wartime poetry for the purpose of collecting material led me to some significant comparisons between the writers of two wars. A wide gulf stretched between the poets of 1914 and their successors from War No. 2. The men and women serving in its military forces would clearly regard with pitying amazement the romantic idealism of a Rupert Brooke or a

Julian Grenfell. The only older poet who came near their mood was Siegfried Sassoon.

Realism and disillusionment marked the work of these young contemporary writers. Some were tough and others sensitive, but even the sensitive never allowed aspiring remorse to become romantic. Their idealism did not concern itself with the glamour of war, for to them it had none. Instead, as in the work of Emanuel Litvinoff, they resolutely counted the cost and determined that from present suffering must come a re-dedication to the lost ideals of humanity if man was to survive.

After reading *Poems from the Forces* I understood far better my own son and daughter, who with unruffled self-possession accepted perils and perturbations which I, in spite of my early war service, would have found hair-raising at twice their age.

(12)

A providentially mild winter changed almost imperceptibly into the astonishing spring of 1943. By St. Valentine's Day the Terrace Gardens had become a hallelujah chorus of blossom, and on March 16th I watched a Tortoiseshell butterfly alight on a crocus.

Encouraged by the weather we increased our efforts to recover the children, and learned from Cook's office that Portuguese ships regularly crossed the Atlantic to Lisbon. Several hundred children had already returned in these boats, and Britain even provided a connecting aeroplane. Finding that single passages were the easiest to obtain, we booked a cabin for John on a June sailing and another for Shirley in July.

While our American friends endured the ordeal of form-filling which this decision involved, acquaintances at home offered advice that ranged from irresponsible optimism to the darkest forebodings. For weeks they sent me up and down the entire gamut of maternal emotions, and after one outburst of gloomy prophecy, I wrote to New York in deep discouragement.

"The whole business gives me a pain in the neck. Taking risks for one's self is nothing; to ask a young and probably rather nervous creature to take them is terribly hard. We have all made mistakes in trying to solve the enormous problems of the war, and in trying to save the young from harm have laid heavy burdens of loneliness and readjustment upon them. My fear is that if they are away any longer they will never succeed in readjusting themselves, and the unity of our family will be broken for ever."

Now that the prospect of their early return really seemed hopeful, we decided to reopen 2 Cheyne Walk. Charles Burnett had gone with the R.A.F. to North Africa, but Amy agreed to join us with their three-year-old daughter.

Though the house had been closed since 1940 and successive raids had shaken dust and plaster all over the rooms, it felt, as always, warm and serene, and our historic railings had been spared from seizure for scrap-iron, since the building was later to be scheduled as an "ancient monument". When the Borough Council surveyor told us that the coal-cellar where I had taken refuge in 1940 was extremely dangerous and would probably have buried me alive had the tall house been hit, we installed a double Anderson shelter in the small rear garden.

My mother now announced that she was tired of the hotel, and asked me to find her a flat near our house. London flats were still easily obtainable, and I soon discovered a six-room apartment in Rossetti Gardens Mansions round the corner. Three rooms looked north, but the other three faced south over green back gardens, and when I first saw them were filled with a spring ecstasy of sunlight. In spite of their pleasant aspect, she decided to use the north rooms which were larger, though she found them cold.

We returned to our own house on April 27th, 1943. A walk to the Food Office showed Chelsea as half empty, and more damaged than I remembered; I felt like a *revenant* going back to the ruins of Pompeii. That evening G. and I crossed the Albert Bridge into Battersea Park and the English Garden. It was strange to see the great gap where the Old Church had been, and to watch the sun which it used to hide sinking above the wreckage like a huge red globe. Later in the year these shattered foundations would be adorned by purple rosebay—London's "fire-weed", which came like a benison on some country wind to soften the starkness of flame-scarred debris.

When we re-entered our still half-empty house, the moon was almost full. The bombers were going out in resounding squadrons, and I asked G. to put Beethoven's Violin Concerto, which Edward had played years ago, on the gramophone to drown the noise.

Soon after our return a reader wrote me a letter of which I realised the full significance two years later, when the results of the general election seemed to bear some relation to the books that the troops had read.

My correspondent described an incident related by her fiancé, a young political officer in the Sudan who had been given the task of clearing a battlefield "somewhere in Abyssinia". Within the shadow of a wall he had found a British soldier lying dead; in his hand a copy of *Testament of Youth* was open at the Villanelle, "Violets from Plug Street Wood", sent me by Roland from Flanders in 1915.

> Violets from Plug Street Wood,
> Sweet, I send you oversea.
> (It is strange they should be blue,
> Blue, when his soaked blood was red.
> For they grew around his head;
> It is strange they should be blue.)
>
> Violets from Plug Street Wood—
> Think what they have meant to me—
> Life and Hope and Love and You.
> (And you did not see them grow
> Where his mangled body lay,
> Hiding horror from the day;
> Sweetest, it was better so.)
>
> Violets from oversea,
> To your dear, far, forgetting land
> These I send in memory,
> Knowing you will understand.

A few weeks earlier Victor Gollancz had reissued this book in a war-time format, and the new edition had sold out before publication. This news surprised my New York publishers when I suggested a similar reprint in America; they would have "to get a long way further in this war", they wrote, before that book could be republished in the United States.

On how many battlefields was it now being read? And was not this story of a dead British soldier the final answer to bureaucratic suspicion?

As we waited for John, the year ticked on with its burden of events. On April 30th our impressive acquaintance Beatrice Webb had died; four years afterwards she was to become the first woman, apart from Royalty, to have her ashes buried in Westminster Abbey. In May the war in Africa ended; almost simultaneously a specially trained force of Lancaster Bombers destroyed the Eder and Mohne dams in an "incident" which was to make, in the nineteen-fifties, an oddly popular film. That evening a series of Alerts, combined with the sound of heavy gunfire, kept us all night in the shelter.

The next morning, reading of the Ruhr floods and looking at the heavy clouds which seemed to press down upon Chelsea, I felt for the first time a stir of misgiving about the possible retaliation for Britain's increasingly ruthless policies which might await the children's return.

(13)

On June 5th two hundred readers of my Letter gathered at 2 Cheyne Walk to celebrate its hundredth issue, which had actually appeared on January 14th.

In a short conference before tea, we discussed how to make the Letter more widely known in the absence of funds to spend on publicity. But throughout the crowded and sunny afternoon, my heart was heavy and my mind preoccupied owing to the possible private implications of a recent national tragedy.

Four days before the "Centenary Party", the hitherto unmolested passenger plane between Lisbon and England—safely used by many children—had been shot down with its thirteen travellers. Amongst them had perished the sensitive film-actor, Leslie Howard, who had been lecturing in Spain for the British Council. At once a tormenting uncertainty arose. Could we now risk this route for John, whose arrangements for leaving Philadelphia in July were almost complete?

Much perturbed, I sought advice from Lord Ponsonby, the courteous and cultured ex-diplomat with whom I had shared Dick Sheppard's platforms. Now nearing the end of his long life, he had become my faithful friend. When I once asked him if he intended to compile a sequel to his book *Falsehood in Wartime* from the propagandist inventions of World War II, he told me that his famous "debunking" First War classic had taken ten years to write, owing to the difficulty of finding the origins of several atrocity stories.

"I shall be dust long before that," he said to me with prophetic realism. In January 1944 a strange little letter told me that he was in a nursing home, the victim of a stroke, and two years later he died.

Now, to help us in our dilemma, Lord Ponsonby asked Lord Cranbourne (the present Lord Salisbury) whether he regarded the loss of Leslie Howard's plane as an isolated episode or the consequence of a new Nazi policy. Lord Cranbourne replied that he believed the tragedy to be a unique mischance, and if his own son were coming he would take the risk. No doubt he had private information, for in Volume IV of his War History Winston Churchill described this incident, which followed his own presence in North Africa.

"The regular commercial aircraft was about to start from the Lisbon airfield when a thickset man smoking a cigar walked up and was thought to be a passenger on it. The German agents therefore signalled that I was on board. . . . A German war plane was instantly ordered out, and the defenceless aircaft was ruthlessly shot down. . . . The brutality of the Germans was only matched by the stupidity of their agents. It is difficult to understand how anyone could imagine that with all the resources of Great Britain at my disposal I should have booked a passage in an unarmed and unescorted plane from Lisbon and flown home in broad daylight."

In spite of inevitable misgivings we took Lord Cranbourne's advice, and on July 3rd received a cable saying that John was on his way. During the interval of waiting, my mind dwelt on the evidences of his mental development during recent months; the many drawings and poems which he had sent us; his enthusiasm for Blake's *Book of Urizen*, my latest Christmas gift; and finally a letter written at Easter telling me how much he wanted to come home.

Early on Sunday, July 18th, a telephone call from Cook's office told us that the Lisbon plane, with John on board, had safely reached Bristol, and that afternoon we met him at Paddington.

At first, when I saw him standing imperturbably in his black rubber coat beside a pile of luggage, I did not recognise him. Dark, sunburnt and handsome, he was now five inches taller than myself; his absence had coincided with three vital years of adolescence which had changed him from a boy of twelve into almost a young man.

When he spoke his American intonations, though we had expected them, made him seem even more of a stranger. With the slight shock of dismay which hundreds of other mothers must have experienced in similar family crises, I realised that it would take some time to get to know him again.

He had travelled from Philadelphia without incident and in fifteen days, the bare minimum of time. At Lisbon, he told us, the interval between ship and plane had been so short that he had seen nothing of the city.

One period of suspense was happily over. The other remained.

(14)

Eight days after John's return came the downfall of Mussolini and the death of my intrepid friend, Lord Wedgwood of Barleston.

Like Beatrice Webb, "Jos" had grown old; our generation was

316

now taking the places-filled by him and his contemporaries. At his commemoration service in St. Margaret's, Westminster, I remembered that he had once cheerfully said to me: "I unveiled Arnold Bennett's memorial at Hanley, and I took forward to the day when you'll unveil mine at Stoke-on-Trent."

Early in September came Italy's surrender to the Allies. As we read of the Salerno landings, G. and I recalled a steamer journey to Amalfi from Capri in 1936. We had spent two nights at the *Albergo della Luna*, where Ibsen wrote *A Doll's House*, walked up the hill to Longfellow's favourite hostelry, the *Albergo dei Cappucini*, and from Ravello had taken a car along the steep mountain road to Sorrento overlooking the Bay of Naples. Which of these beautiful cities and villages would future generations have cause to mourn?

By this time John had joined us in planning his future education, and we had visited Eton where G. had registered him soon after his birth. He now reacted vigorously against his housemaster's expectation that he would fit into "the system" and specialise in classics, which he had dropped in America. To take up Latin again would oblige him, at nearly sixteen, to join a class of thirteen-year-olds.

He was also depressed by the small ground-floor study, looking into a back-yard, which he was told would be his, and inevitably compared it with his fine room at the American boarding-school where the Colbys had sent him. It became the final argument against Eton which made him decline to go there.

To any Old Etonian, his criticisms would certainly appear unreasonable. What else could an evacuated boy, returning much older than the normal age of admission, expect of the School authorities who from their own standpoint were treating him so tolerantly? Yet it is perhaps desirable for the time-honoured customs of British traditional education to be viewed occasionally from the larger perspectives of the enterprising New World.

Since I had always preferred day-schools to boarding-schools where family life had anything to contribute, I hoped that we should now consider the claims of Westminster and St. Paul's, G.'s own old school. But G., as a gifted teacher, had always disliked the vast educational area, with its nebulous gradations, which lies between the few most famous public schools and State education. One or the other, he said, but not a compromise. Since Eton had fallen through, he decided to try Harrow.

The Headmaster of Harrow was then Dr. Ralph Westwood Moore, appointed the previous year at the age of thirty-six. When the post fell vacant the Governors had received only three applications, for Harrow, on the edge of London, was considered so vulnerable to bombs that the more eligible schoolmasters preferred safer billets. Eventually the Governors approached Dr. Moore, then Head of Bristol Grammar School, and he agreed to come. He himself had been educated at Wolverhampton Grammar School, and was the first headmaster of a great public school who had not attended one.

As soon as I saw Dr. Moore, my prejudice against Harrow disappeared. To the end of his short life, this young man with the pallid face and jet-black hair made a similar impression on most people who met him. Pomposity had been omitted from his disposition; he wrote neat manuscript notes to the parents of prospective pupils, and his clothes and manner were equally informal.

After talking to John for half-an-hour, Dr. Moore offered him the last remaining vacancy in his own House. He imposed no rigid conditions about classics; he would arrange a reasonable continuity with the excellent if unorthodox education given to John in Minnesota. The opportunity was too good to miss, and with John's agreement we accepted it.

When we returned to Chelsea, he announced with characteristic American energy: "I'm not going to stand around here till school starts! I want to take a job." The next day G. saw Christina Foyle, who co-operatively engaged John as a temporary assistant at the large book-store in Charing Cross Road. For the rest of the summer he worked contentedly in the second-hand book department, dusting ancient volumes and waiting on customers.

He still seemed happy when I visited him on the Hill during his first term, and found a demi-American modern youth transformed by Harrow's peculiar variety of fancy dress into a mid-Victorian schoolboy. At least his study did not look on a back-yard; from an upper floor it commanded a wide panorama of suburban London.

The following term, by one of Dr. Moore's inspirations, John shared a larger study with Marian Mikolajczyk, the son of the Polish Premier. This sturdy, amiable boy had recently escaped from a concentration camp after much grim experience, and knew no English. The two exiles, past and present, now shared the process of mutual adaptation to a conventional English school with an unconventional Head.

(15)

Notwithstanding Dr. Moore's dynamic youth, he remained Headmaster of Harrow for less than a decade.

In October 1951, a mass radiography unit visited the Hill. Dr.

Moore explained the importance of routine X-ray examinations to the boys, and, to set them an example, took the test himself. When the plates were examined, only one issued a warning—his own. Further tests showed that he suffered from lung cancer, the disease which had recently attacked King George VI.

Like the King, Dr. Moore submitted to an operation, and recovered sufficiently to present the prizes on his last Speech Day the following summer term. That afternoon, in a vehement address which the newspapers reported, he told his distinguished audience to "hate and detest" the most cynical slogan produced by the post-war period—"I couldn't care less".

"If only we care enough," he said, "then, by the grace of God, no limit is set to what we might achieve."

In the late autumn of 1952, the Oxford University Press published a volume of poems, *Trophy for an Unknown Soldier*, which Dr. Moore had written over fifteen years. John gave me a copy, and the contents moved me so much that I sent Dr. Moore a letter. Although he was dying, his wife afterwards assured me that he understood and appreciated what I had tried to say.

These simple and poignant lyrics should be better known to poetry readers. To his threnodies for the young men who died in the Second War, Dr. Moore added some valedictory verses in which, as a deeply convinced Christian, he faced and tried to accept his own cruel fate. I have often re-read the last lines of one poem, "O that this bitter cup might pass", since his death in January 1953.

"The other garden waits for me,
     The Sabbath trumpets call,
 But winter's in Gethsemane,
     And winter is my all.

"Yet not for me the Friday's pain,
     The Cross, the crown of thorn;
 All that is His, to take again
     And shed on Easter morn.

"My bitter hour is not complete
     Till willingly I run
 And lay my sorrow at His feet
     And say Thy will be done.

"Lord, take this bitter heart away,
     Lord, bring again the sun,
 Lord, give me courage yet to pray
     Thy will, Thy will be done."

While John and Shirley were in Minnesota they had once heard my voice, for at Christmas 1941 I took part in a cross-Atlantic broadcast between parents and evacuated children. Afterwards Shirley wrote me affectionately that, though my time was "so precious", the effort had been well worth-while.

Throughout 1942 and 1943, her letters referred to 2 Cheyne Walk and the New Forest cottage; our "crimson dining-room" in Chelsea was her favourite room, she said. Another letter turned into a thesis on England, which she described as "the home of a great nation". These spontaneous communications left us with no uncertainty about her readiness to return to Britain's hardships. The problem now was to get her.

Early in September an air letter from George Brett told me that, after many delays, a member of his own domestic staff had seen her off at Philadelphia on the so-called "August sailing", and had put her in the charge of a British wife sailing alone. Her Portuguese ship, the *Serpo Pinto*, was the same as John's, but her journey, in every detail, was to be far more difficult and adventurous than his.

The family relics of that period include a British Information Service pamphlet, headed "Since You Are Going To England", which was evidently given to Shirley as she left the United States.

"You will find yourself," it began, "in a country that has been at war for more than three years. The war effort has changed the whole pattern of life to an extent that is hard to picture from the other side of the Atlantic."

After some depressing comparisons between American and British food, clothing, tobacco, and toilet articles, the booklet continued bravely:

"In the material sense you will be giving up much. . . . But you will also find, we believe, that the country is a happy place in which to live, for the sense of a common effort, and the consciousness that every deprivation contributes a concrete part to the war effort, exhilarates the people as it will exhilarate you. . . .

"But you may also find that many people are easily tired and sometimes, therefore, abrupt in their manner . . . because the cumulative pressure on nerves and physical and mental endurance during the last two years has been considerable. We know you will understand this and meet this fatigue . . . with sympathy and patience."

Whatever Shirley at thirteen may have thought about the dangers and discomforts, thus graphically presented, to which she was returning, she soon had plenty to contend with on the *Serpo Pinto*. At the end of October, a paragraph by the *Daily Mail* Correspondent in Lisbon "revealed" the peril which she and her fellow evacuees were fortunate to survive.

> "Lady Howard de Walden, who is travelling home from the United States with her four grandchildren, told me to-day how a party of British children escaped death by a narrow margin during an Atlantic cyclone.
>
> "Most of the children were travelling unaccompanied to Lisbon in the Portuguese ship *Serpo Pinto*. Half-way across the Atlantic the cyclone struck. The captain said afterwards it was the worst he had known in 26 years.
>
> "All the lifeboats were swung out from the davits ready for launching—but the voyage had ended before the master of the ship told anyone of his fears that none of the boats would have survived in the raging sea."

In London we knew nothing of the cyclone, which roared on for five fearful days and drove the ship as far south as Madeira, but long after we thought that Shirley should have reached Lisbon, disconcerting messages from Thomas Cook and Son reported inexplicable delays. At last, on September 22nd, they notified us that the *Serpo Pinto* had landed its passengers, but cautiously warned us not to expect Shirley at present, "as all the big air transports have gone to the Mediterranean".

The Allied offensive in Italy which John escaped had developed in time to hold up the travellers on Shirley's delayed ship. In Lisbon 370 children had now accumulated, and though Shirley, as an unaccompanied child, might expect priority, 200 of these passengers remained from the previous voyage. Just at this moment, some prolonged negotiations between the Allies and Portugal concerning the use of the Azores by British and American naval and air forces reached fruition. The agreement undermined the neutrality of Lisbon, where "jitters" took the form of trial black-outs and A.R.P. exercises.

We realised this threat, and the period of waiting which had seemed long during John's voyage now became interminable. Reassuring letters came periodically from Susan Lowndes-Marques, whom I had met in January 1940, though she must have wondered whether the child in whom she was taking so kindly an interest would remain in Lisbon for the rest of her life.

Impatiently I walked round Battersea Park; the leaves were falling fast, and only one or two melancholy birds remained in the aviary which had been a popular family rendezvous on long-ago happier Sundays. While Cook's apologetically described the bottle-neck in Lisbon and assured us that the children were well cared for, I wondered how Shirley was actually spending her time.

With an intrepid contemporary, Rosemary Roughton, the daughter of a Cambridge doctor, she had been sent to the Palacio Hotel at Estoril, fifteen miles outside Lisbon. Nominally the children received official supervision; in practice they were left entirely on their own.

Day after day, the two tough little girls rioted round Estoril. Occasionally they varied this lively routine with expeditions into Lisbon, where by an unlikely miracle they escaped misadventure. When geographical explorations palled, they added spice to their lives by taking the lift to the top floor of the tall hotel, and climbing over the unprotected parapets on to the roof. Each evening at dinner they finished a bottle of Madeira between them, and wondered why they always slept so soundly.

During the period in which we expected Shirley I had refused engagements outside London, but with mid-October came a series of lectures booked long before we knew the date of her voyage. On Sunday, October 17th, a day of wild rain, I addressed the Birming-ham Co-operative Society and returned home late, discouraged, and soaking wet.

I had hardly turned my key in the front door when G. called to me from our first-floor living room.

"Come up here! I've got something to show you!"

"In a minute," I said. "Just let me get my wet coat off," but he called again more insistently.

"Don't wait. Come up at once!"

I opened the upstairs door to see him standing alone, smiling, in the large empty room. Suddenly the drawn window-curtain was thrown aside, and a small figure in a plaid frock danced into the firelight. How pretty she seemed, with her softly rounded features and blonde hair! A fairy-like little girl, full of gay animation, had replaced the round-faced, good-natured child of 1940. Clasping her tightly in a surge of emotion which I never allowed myself to show again, I felt as though, after years of unbearable climbing, I had reached the summit of my Everest.

She had flown from Lisbon on a very rough night, but neither this uncomfortable passage nor the long series of adventures since she left Philadelphia appeared to have disturbed her poise.

More than ten years afterwards, when we were discussing whether Ruth Colby would be able to leave her work for the United Nations to attend Shirley's wedding, I chanced to ask her whether she had remembered me when she came back from America.

"No," Shirley said, "you weren't real to me at all. You seemed more like a person in a book."

I knew then that in spite of inevitable pain for the generous Colbys and grave risks for the children themselves, we had been right to bring them home. In another year or two, those disappearing images of a father and mother would have vanished for ever.

(17)

Although that December marked our fifth wartime Christmas, it seemed a happy season to us. For the first time since 1938—a melancholy winter shadowed by well-justified apprehensions—the whole family kept Christmas together.

But on New Year's Day, when Arthur Greenwood and his wife came to dinner, his prophecies for 1944 set our personal reunion against a larger perspective. It would be a fearful year of Allied casualties, he said. Within a few weeks the Second Front would start, and revive the heavy bombing of London.

This gloomy forecast took our thoughts back to the catastrophic famine in Bengal, which modified current rejoicing over the mounting victories on the Russian front. Angry political protests against Herbert Morrison accompanied these major events; as Home Secretary he had permitted, on medical grounds, the "conditional release" from detention of Sir Oswald Mosley. Upon these shrill bickerings I had commented in a recent issue of my Letter.

"The crowds which gathered in Whitehall to protest against Mosley's removal from Holloway might more usefully have raised their voices against the employment of young British airmen to commit abominations of ruthlessness characteristic of that very Fascism of which Sir Oswald is the symbol."

Arthur Greenwood's prediction followed a series of "nuisance raids" on London; one of the worst had actually occurred on the night of Shirley's return. Throughout that autumn and winter we were constantly obliged to hurry her, with Amy and little Marian, into the cold garden shelter. Often we did not reach it until the bombers were overhead and the shell splinters, a lethal hail, tumbling into our back garden.

From America Shirley had imported convictions about her education as clear-cut as John's reactions to Eton; raids or no raids, she wanted to live at home and go to a day-school. Since these strong opinions matched our own, we sent her at half-term to St. Paul's Girls' School in Hammersmith, but the decision left us wholly responsible for her safety and was to have some awkward consequences when the next series of heavy raids began. In term-time the Harrow masters shared the liability for John, though after his sixteenth birthday on December 21st he could no longer be regarded as a child.

Throughout the Christmas holidays he sat at the piano, passionately improvising, or putting long classical records on my father's old gramophone. Whenever he played the Beethoven Violin Concerto he brought back the ghost of Edward, whom in a dark emphatic fashion he strongly resembled. The rough Norfolk jacket, brown eyes, black eyebrows, and slight stoop of the shoulders over keys or gramophone, carried me to the distant past in which Edward for me was never a soldier, but a tweed-coated musician permanently aged sixteen.

(18)

At this stage of the war, two recurrent problems dominated the newspapers. One was the obstinate official emphasis on Germany's "unconditional surrender"; the other the ever-increasing violence of Allied bombing.

The phrase "unconditional surrender" had first been used at a Press Conference held by President Roosevelt in Casablanca. The *New Statesman* described the exponents of this policy as "Bitter-Enders"; their high priest was Lord Vansittart, whose propaganda seemed guaranteed to defeat the struggling German Resistance movement. As a challenge to his vociferous disciples, the still small voice of Quakerism proclaimed an unpopular alternative.

"That way of peace is not to be found in any policy of 'unconditional surrender', by whomsoever demanded," stated the Friends' London Yearly Meeting in April 1943. "It requires that men and nations should recognise their common brotherhood, using the weapons of integrity, reason, patience and love, never acquiescing in the ways of the oppressor, always ready to suffer with the oppressed."

Many "Bitter-Enders" believed that Allied bombing would

enforce total surrender, though the stiffened resistance of Britain during 1940 and 1941 suggested that the unity of Germany behind Hitler was a more likely result. The totemistic official faith in "obliteration" now sent government expenditure on bombs up to prodigal levels; the 2,000-lb. bombs of 1942 had reached 12,000 lb. by 1944. In August 1943 Mr. Brendan Bracken, now Minister of Information, told the Press at the Quebec Conference: "Our plans are to bomb, burn and ruthlessly destroy . . . the people responsible for creating this war."

His statement followed a series of massive raids on Hamburg which left the working-class suburbs in ruins, though, as G. and I had discovered in 1936, the great port had a largely Jewish population and was hence the most anti-Nazi city in the Reich. In a post-war record entitled *Bomber Offensive*, Sir Arthur Harris himself described the ordeal of Hamburg, which caused civilian casualties variously estimated at between ten and sixty thousand.

"The alternative dropping of blockbusters, high explosives and incendiaries made fire-fighting impossible, small fires united into conflagrations in the shortest time . . . developing into a fire-typhoon such as was never before witnessed, against which every human resistance was quite useless."

Several observers reported to neutral countries the cost of this policy in human agony.

"Charred adult corpses had shrunk to the size of children. Women were wandering about half-crazy," stated an account in the Swiss newspaper, *National-Zeitung*, and a stoker who deserted from a German ship told the Stockholm correspondent of the *Daily Telegraph*: "People went mad in the shelters. They screamed and threw themselves, biting and clawing, at the doors which were locked against them by the wardens."

Lest British "squeamishness" should be disturbed by such details, the Sunday Press took a hand in supporting the bombers.

"NO PITY! NO MERCY!" shrilled one outsize headline shortly before the Hamburg raids. The writer continued: .

"If we are to succeed we must not harbour cant and humbug. Voices are already heard, crying that mercy must temper justice, that vengeance belongs alone to God. . . . All these sentimental appeals are bunkum and hypocrisy . . . whether they come from a familiar prelate or some unsuspected quisling."

In another Sunday paper Hilary St. George Saunders, author of a

Government publication, *The Battle of Britain*, reinforced this exhortation with the assumption that the Hamburg massacre encouraged his readers.

> "The figure of 50,000 dead may well be a conservative estimate. . . . Is it too much to believe that a similar success will be repeated not only in the case of Berlin, but also in those of the 22 other cities of Germany with over 300,000 inhabitants?"

"Are we to infer from this article," I asked in the next Letter, "that there is secret rejoicing in official circles when thousands of German children are burned or drowned?"

In spite of the Press, a few "quisling" voices more powerful than mine continued to make similar comments.

"Women and little children are women and little children to me, wherever they live, and it fills me with absolute nausea to think of the filthy task that many of our young men are being invited to carry out," R. R. Stokes courageously insisted in the House of Commons.

By 1944 Lord Lang, the former Archbishop of Canterbury, was supporting the persistent protests of the Bishop of Chichester in the House of Lords, and the ageing Dean Inge predicted in an *Evening Standard* article that "when the war is over we shall be very sorry for what we have done".

These voices went unheeded. "Saturation" bombing continued, occasionally varied by a precision raid—such as the August 1943 attack on Peenemunde, where experiments were in progress on "doodlebugs" and rockets—which made sense from a military standpoint. In November 1943 began the "Hamburging" of Berlin, reduced to rubble by February after fifteen heavy raids. In January 1944 a raid lasting only three minutes "obliterated" the smaller city of Brunswick, about the same size as Coventry.

After reading a description of this raid in the *Sunday Express*, I listened on that calm frosty evening to the roar of our heavy bombers going east and recalled an episode of the previous September. I had just posted a letter to the similar sound of day bombers overhead in the sunshine, when a small elderly woman whom I had never previously met came from the block of flats across the road and spoke to me.

"Sounds as if they meant business," she said, pointing to the unquiet sky. "It isn't right! There's room in the world for everybody."

326

That autumn a friend sent me a booklet entitled *The Bases of Civilisation*, by Dr. G. S. Spinks, one-time editor of the *Hibbert Journal*. Reading it I found some sentences which, in the Quaker phrase, "spoke to my condition".

"The spirit of humanity is disappearing. The belief that human life is valuable, and sacred, that belief is dying. . . . Whole sections of the human race have become merely so much raw material to be nationalised, transported, deported, liquidated and 'mopped up'. . . . At times it looks as if the stage of history were being prepared for a new Dark Age. And in a Dark Age there is only one thing that individual men and women can do and that is to keep the little glimmers of reason and humanity alight."

Although I had still to complete the revised version of *Account Rendered* and was helping G. to collect material for *Above All Nations*, I felt compelled to make a final appeal, through a companion booklet to *One of These Little Ones*, against the policy of "area bombing". As Dr. Spinks had perceived, this policy denied the sacredness of man exactly as the Nazis had denied it to the Jews, and thus rejected the God in whose image man was made. From the Christian standpoint, no military or political advantage could justify that fundamental blasphemy.

I began this pamphlet in November 1943, and called it *Seed of Chaos* after Pope's couplet in Book IV of *The Dunciad*:

"Then rose the seed of Chaos, and of Night,
To blot out order and extinguish light."

The plentiful material supplied by the Bombing Restriction Committee eventually turned the pamphlet into a small book. So appalling were the details of mortal anguish which I was compelled to read, that to the Pope quotation I added a verse from the Book of Jeremiah:

"Were they ashamed when they had committed abomination?"

(19)

The bombing of Berlin naturally brought reciprocity, though the Nazis could no longer produce it "in kind". During January I spent many nights in the shelter with the two little girls, who listened with the stoicism of contemporary childhood to roaring guns and crashing bombs. The London barrage, reported the Press, was now as heavy as the barrage before the Battle of the Somme. On

January 29th, shell-splinters fell over us with the effect of a violent hail-storm; next morning Shirley and I found several in the garden and on the roof.

Wondering how much longer we should be justified in keeping the children in town, I sat over a tiny gas-fire in the unheated house and struggled with frozen fingers to get one or the other of my three books a stage further before the evening raid. Especially I wanted to complete *Seed of Chaos*, since it sought to achieve, in Professor Grensted's words, that "self-contradictory humanisation of war" which eventually creates a more favourable atmosphere for war's abolition.

This booklet related the history of the Allied bombing offensive, described the development of "obliteration" tactics, and explained precisely what this meant in innocent suffering even more deadly, in spiritual consequences, to those who inflicted it than to its helpless victims. It pleaded for a return, even while war continued, to the standards set up by Hugo Grotius as a protest against the cruelties of the Thirty Years' War. The precepts of international law which he initiated still maintained that it was ultimately better for a nation to accept disadvantage in war than to descend to those depths of barbarism in which the most savage expedients are condoned if they lead to victory.

The human damage was not the whole terrible story. On February 15th the Allied demolition of the Monte Cassino monastery, which had symbolised religious aspiration for forty generations of men, typified a growing mania for the wholesale destruction of irreplaceable treasures as a short route to some hypothetical military gain. Even the *Annual Register*, a semi-official publication, was moved in its 1944 issue to record "the intense regret of all in England who were aware of its historical associations." The commentator did not add that the commander in charge of operations disapproved on military grounds of his subordinate's policy, but his account concluded:

> "The military results hardly justified this action. The Germans continued to make no less effective use of the building . . . and the Allied progress was not accelerated in the least."

With February the raids on London reached a crescendo of violence subsequently described as "the little Blitz". From the top of 2 Cheyne Walk, when the attacks ended, we saw large fires ringing our own district. Again we watched the sad little processions of bombed-out families to the Rest Centre, and the crowds reading the casualty lists outside Chelsea Town Hall.

One evening, immediately after the All-Clear, Shirley disappeared with Amy Burnett's young sister Sheila into the lurid night. After an hour in which I waited unhappily for the next of the now frequent sirens, she returned to tell us excitedly that she had watched a tobacco factory burn down on the other side of the river. Next morning, as her school was temporarily out of action, she vanished on her bicycle and spent the day with two school-friends exploring perilous ruins in devastated Fulham.

As she had clearly no concern for her own safety and was too young to be allowed to throw her life away, we felt she would have to leave London when Amy announced that she must take Marian to the country. Again we decided to close our unwieldy house, and find a flat whence G. could continue his Chelsea fire-watching. I persuaded my mother, shaken by wakeful nights, to visit some old friends in Staffordshire; I hoped she would stay till the raids diminished, but like a recurring decimal she was back in a few days.

(20)

While we looked for somewhere to live and considered what to do with Shirley, some hospitable friends who owned a spacious West End apartment invited us to stay until we had solved our problems. Though they were near-millionaires, they claimed several acquaintances among Labour Party leaders. When I appeared before dinner on our second night and saw Herbert Morrison, the Home Secretary, amongst their guests, I was tempted to excuse myself and depart, owing to a recent interchange in the House of Commons.

A Conservative M.P., Mr. Purbrick, had asked the Home Secretary to intern the members of the Bombing Restriction Committee, since their activities were "clearly evidence of their pro-German sympathies". Herbert Morrison replied: "If people think obliteration bombing is wrong, I cannot see that it is terrible to say so." He continued: "There is no danger that the bombing will leave off, anyway."

After dinner, when our host put on some gramophone records, Herbert Morrison crossed the room and asked me to dance. As we took the floor he said, amiably reproving: "It's no good, you know!" But his eye almost twinkled, for he was well aware that I should not change my outlook because of anything he said. As a First War conscientious objector, he understood that penalties do not abolish convictions.

That night, as though they had located the Home Secretary, the Nazis selected the West End for their regular visitation. When pandemonium began we all moved down from the penthouse flat to a safer apartment on the third floor, and there, unperturbed by the raid, Shirley entertained Herbert Morrison with a spate of animated conversation until the "All Clear" sounded.

His kindly affection for her, as schoolgirl and adult, dated from that evening; he called her "a remarkable child", and a few weeks later invited her to lunch at the House of Commons. After the West End raid she went to Cambridge to stay with her *Serpo Pinto* friend, Rosemary Roughton, leading a black-and-white mongrel collie puppy which I had rashly given her.

Soon after closing our house, G. and I found a tiny furnished flat on the top floor of Sloane Avenue Mansions, a modern block off the King's Road, Chelsea. Its south-facing window gave us an impressive view of Thames-side London, but its height meant constant nocturnal migrations to a lower corridor. We expected to leave the flat in a few weeks, but actually kept it for eighteen months.

On the day we moved in, a shock awaited us. There had been an exceptionally heavy raid the night before, and a "block-buster" had fallen in the road thirty yards from our new flat, wrecking a row of small houses and breaking three hundred windows in Sloane Avenue Mansions. When we had struggled through the blasted outer door and climbed nine flights of stairs because the bomb had damaged the electric lift, we found our little apartment filled with smashed china and glass from the owners' crockery and the kitchen window. There was nothing to do but put on an apron and tackle the debris.

As I swept it up, I quoted to G. a sentence that I had written of the First War in *Testament of Youth*.

"Its permanent symbol, for me, is a candle stuck in the neck of a bottle, the tiny flame flickering in an ice-cold draught, yet creating a miniature illusion of light against an opaque infinity of blackness."

"Surely," I added, "the symbol of *this* war is a broken window!"

(21)

As soon as the children returned from America I had planned to recover our New Forest cottage, let since 1940, as a refuge for them outside London. Late in March 1944, I reopened it as a war-time home for five children—Amy's Marian; her fifteen-year-old sister Sheila; the small son of another widowed sister; John in the holidays; and Shirley at week-ends. For the remainder of the war

330

she went as a temporary day-girl to a school in Bournemouth, where friends put her up during the week.

The cottage, as we immediately discovered, was now in a "defence area" of a special kind; a fortnight after we reoccupied it, only householders were allowed to enter the district. We were soon to realise that the only homes which we could offer the children still represented a choice between the frying pan and the fire.

A Second Front, I remembered, had been discussed as early as 1942. It was already obvious that the "Little Blitz" had been a defensive manœuvre on the part of those about to be attacked.

The afternoon before our return to Allum Green a new oratorio—Michael Tippett's *A Child of our Time*—had been performed at the Royal Adelphi Theatre. On page 12 of the published libretto, the Narrator uttered two lines which seemed to me at that time of swiftly deteriorating values to have a special significance.

> "Men were ashamed of what was done.
> There was bitterness and horror."

These words symbolised one answer to the question from the prophet Jeremiah which I had quoted in *Seed of Chaos*—"Were they ashamed when they had committed abomination?" Another type of answer now arrived in a fashion which made me, with twenty-eight unorthodox Americans, an astonished scapegoat of collective misgiving.

The first hint of strange happenings reached me on March 10th, 1944, through a bundle of press-clippings. These included excerpts from the *News Chronicle* and *Manchester Guardian*, which reported that a so-called "article" of mine on saturation bombing, supported by a signed statement from twenty-eight Protestant "leaders of opinion", had created a "furore" in the United States, and had even inspired three and a half columns of adverse criticism in the *New York Times*.

I then recalled an episode of the previous winter which I had almost forgotten. Before Christmas, when the first draft of *Seed of Chaos* had been typed ready for revision, a discreet supporter of the Bombing Restriction Committee offered to take a copy with him to the United States. If the Censor passed the material, he promised to give it to the Fellowship of Reconciliation in New York for possible notice in their monthly magazine.

The Censor retained the typescript, but agreed to send it after our friend if he felt that he could release it. Its ultimate arrival in New York testified to the respect shown by the Censorship Department for the democratic right to voice unpopular opinions which Herbert Morrison had so recently endorsed in Parliament.

Six weeks before its English publication, extracts from *Seed of Chaos*, under the more challenging title of *Massacre by Bombing*, appeared as a supplement to the magazine *Fellowship*. This Supplement also contained an "American Postscript" by Dr. John Nevin Sayre and a "call to repentance" by the group of Protestant leaders. They included Dr. Harry Emerson Fosdick of Riverside Church, Dr. Paul Scherer of Holy Trinity, Professor Georgia Harkness of the Garrett Biblical Institute, Dr. Rufus Jones of Haverford College, the Bishops of Western Massachusetts and Arizona, and my staunch friend Oswald Garrison Villard.

In a letter which I received early in May, Mr. Villard described the Supplement as causing "a terrific sensation".

"As the matter," he wrote, "was only mailed into the New York Press offices in a most casual way the outcome was most astonishing. In my whole journalistic career I have never seen a more remarkable phenomenon, which in itself is the clearest proof that people's consciences are troubling them, and that we struck home."

My first real understanding of the "terrific sensation" came from an article published in the *Sunday Chronicle* on March 12th by the American columnist, Dorothy Thompson. It was the protest of the twenty-eight, at least as much as the accompanying plea by an alien, which in Miss Thompson's words "roused U.S. fury". Her article continued:

> "There have been two types of reactions—those of professional editorial writers, columnists and radio commentators—and that of the public itself. We can say generally of both types of reaction that the repercussion was enormous; everybody talked about it and 98 per cent. rejected it. . . . Actually, the letters from the public are much harsher and more furious than the comments of professional publicists. . . . The public did not cut any fine lines."

(22)

For the next three weeks I was swamped by Press clippings from American correspondents. After reading them I felt as though I had turned on a tap expecting the usual thin trickle, and found that I had released Niagara instead. As the controversy raged on, President Roosevelt himself took part by issuing, through his secretary, Mr. Stephen Early, a "stinging rebuke" to the intrepid twenty-eight.

Presumably international etiquette forbade him to reprimand me, but a syndicated attack on my work as "Nazi inspired" by William

L. Shirer, the author of *Berlin Diary*, became so abusive that I was compelled to reply in another long article, "Not Made in Germany", which *Fellowship* also published. A main reason, then unknown to me and the Bombing Restriction Committee, for this frenzied indignation among the knowledgeable probably lay in their belief that massacre bombing was "conditioning" popular opinion to accept the atom bombs so soon to be dropped on two helpless Japanese cities.

When the dust and clamour of the dispute at last diminished, I became aware of a few quiet voices which had expressed a different view from that of the shrill majority. In May an American monthly, *The Catholic World*, published a carefully reasoned editorial article on the logical fallacy, *Petitio Principii* ("begging the question"), of which, it said, my booklet had been the victim.

> "It was a sober presentation of a crucial moral problem. It employed little rhetoric and displayed no hysteria. . . . It deserved either endorsement or patient refutation. Yet it was almost universally rejected out of hand; its author and its sponsors derided and vituperated. . . . I must have read a couple of hundred attacks on Miss Brittain and her theme. They ranged all the way from expostulation to diatribe, but I'm blessed if I found one which correctly reported the precise position she had taken."

About the same time a correspondent sent me a copy of *Human Events*, issued weekly from Washington by Dr. Felix Morley, a former editor of the *Washington Post*. Amid the hurly-burly of abuse, his publication had maintained a quiet detachment.

> "The violence of the response is disproportionate to the humility of the protest. This vehemence of itself indicates public uneasiness. . . . The tragedy of our time, highlighted by two fratricidal wars, is that the concept of Nationalism has first submerged and is now destroying the inheritance of a common Western civilisation. . . .
>
> "In this suicidal process is found the 'Seed of Chaos' to which Vera Brittain refers, now drawn to public attention as a 'call to repentance' by twenty-eight prominent and responsible Americans. These voices, crying in the wilderness, may be shouted down. . . . That would not stay the spread of general anxiety, ever more pointedly demanding intelligent and intelligible civilian leadership to the end that the basis of Western civilisation may be saved."

The "furore" had its consequences. For several weeks, letters from American friends became embarrassed and perfunctory. Ruth Colby, almost alone, remained unchanged, but when she reported that an angry acquaintance in St. Paul had said to her: "Well, what do you think of Vera Brittain *now*?", I could guess how much courage had been needed for her reply, "More than ever!"

In England a small idealistic firm known as the New Vision Press published *Seed of Chaos* for the Bombing Restriction Committee on April 19th. Except by a few specialist publications it remained unreviewed, and created not a ripple on the deceptively quiet surface of British public opinion. The collective sense of guilt existed, but it was less passionate than the American sense because the burden of the war had been borne longer, and those who carried it were now too tired to protest.

But the time was coming when they would throw off their fatigue, and react in a totally different fashion from the United States against the terrible deeds which had been done in their name. For them also Michael Tippett spoke, in the words of his Alto Soloist in *A Child of our Time*:

"The dark forces rise like a flood.
Men's hearts are heavy; they cry for peace."

(23)

After the war the policy of "obliteration" bombing, which had caused the death of so many young British and American pilots and reached its moral nadir in the destruction of Hiroshima and Nagasaki, was discredited by both Church and State.

The aftermath showed it to have been not merely wicked but stupid. "Bomber Harris", omitted from post-war Honours Lists when other military figures of comparable status were rewarded, appeared to be the scapegoat for collective remorse.

This remorse did not prevent the illogical development of hydrogen and cobalt bombs by nations terrified to desperation of the very mass genocide which they were helping to prepare. Many post-war pronouncements and conclusions nevertheless endorsed the spiritual foresight of Corder Catchpool and his American counterparts.

In 1948 the Report entitled *The Church and the Atom*, issued by a Commission which the Archbishops of Canterbury and York had appointed, condemned "massacre" bombing in uncompromising words.

"The Commission is agreed that the 'obliteration' bombing of whole cities with high capacity and incendiary bombs, the success of which is measured by the number of acres devastated, must be condemned. It is inconsistent with the limited end of a just war; it violates the principles of discrimination which we have established; and it is not necessary for the security of the attacking aircraft. In fact it constitutes an act of wholesale destruction that cannot be justified."

The isolated protests of the little Bombing Restriction Committee would have been enormously strengthened if this weighty ecclesiastical pronouncement had been made while "obliteration" was actually a policy. But of the sixteen eminent Churchmen who drew up the Report, only the Archdeacon of Stoke had supported the stand made by the Bishop of Chichester during the war.

For other than moral reasons, the Allies had cause to regret the delirium of destruction which they had inspired in the name of "retaliation". In the end the war was won—if in the larger perspective of another decade it could justly be described as "won" at all—in traditional fashion by land forces. Their progress had been assisted by the relatively intelligent precision bombing of aircraft factories and railway junctions, but the mountains of urban rubble left by "saturation" merely impeded their advance. Even the most patriotic of historians, Sir Robert Ensor, described the razing of German cities, though he clearly approved of it, as "incidental".

In 1943, soon after Britain adopted "obliteration" as a policy, an article in *Time* reported that "the German home front morale had grown stronger"; bombing "united" and "stiffened" the German people just as the Nazi Blitzkrieg in 1940 had united and stiffened the British. During 1944 German armaments production was higher than in any previous war year, but every bomb dropped on North-West Germany—as I was to see for myself in 1947—ultimately created a severe headache for some harassed British official.

Britain, the chief bomb-dropping ally, acquired responsibility for the devastated Ruhr among other decimated areas, and the British Control Commission had then to face the social problems created by the lost houses, schools, churches and hospitals which British bombs had destroyed.

The Americans developed a different but equally excruciating headache. When Allied bombs overwhelmed Western Germany, the Nazis pushed their armament industries constantly further east, and built great factories in Upper Silesia and other provinces bordering the Soviet Union. At the end of the war these territories fell into Russian hands, and the great eastern industries became a valuable Communist asset at the very time when American fear of Russia was reaching its zenith.

The development of atom and hydrogen bombs—lethal especially to the industrial West—finally warned everybody with any prophetic capacity that, without a determined rejection by mankind of the genocide policy which massacre bombing had initiated, the human race would disappear in an orgy of universal suicide.

Long after the bombing controversy had vanished from American minds and newspapers, it continued to have a decisive effect on my position there as a writer. No one remembered exactly what I had done—I was a Communist or something—but such writings as I could still publish never emerged from the shadow which had darkened my name.

Should I have allowed the draft manuscript of *Seed of Chaos* to cross the Atlantic if I had foreseen what the cost was to be? Often, in these post-war years, I have asked myself that question.

I think I should; but I am still thankful that chance took the choice out of my hands.

CHAPTER NINE

DAWN OVER CHAOS

"You have no more pity or scorn for human folly.
Your lips and hands are still.
War cannot wake you, nor the vain trumpets of victory
Echoing from the city to your grave under the hill."

V.B., *Lines to W.H. on V. J. Day.*

(1)

IN THE SPRING of 1944, our cottage was certainly the worse for war and neglect. The garden, ignored by our elderly tenants, had turned into a field; next door the once attractive country house whose owner had sold us our small property was now a bomb-scarred ruin.

No chance hit, but a feat of precision bombing, had caused this damage. In 1940, Allum Green House had been commandeered for troops; their indifferent discipline, said the local grape-vine, had cost them several lives. By day they sat on the green carelessly dismembering their Bren guns; by night their lighted cigarettes defeated the black-out. One evening a German plane came over and planted a bomb neatly on the house, killing seventeen soldiers.

The cottage itself had no shelter, but it was at least an insignificant target, and by day the countryside preserved an illusion of peace which would, I thought, reassure the children.

John and Shirley, however, appeared to need no reassurance.

"The children," I wrote to New York, "mind the raids far less than I do, and seem to feel far more the contrast between the shortages and restrictions here, and the relative comfort of life in U.S.A. Shirley, for instance, just can't get used to making 12 oz. of candy last for a month, or washing in little kettlefuls of hot water because the coal ration won't run to more than an occasional bath."

She nevertheless asked me, at the end of April, whether she could not spend the summer in "this heavenly Paradise"—a phrase which made me feel oddly flattered.

Paradise, if sometimes apparent, was only relative. At every turn of every glade, we found waggons and ammunition dumps, vainly sought by the Nazi observers, which the late-budding trees concealed. Our nights echoed to the ceaseless clatter of heavy tanks lumbering down the Bournemouth-Southampton road. If ever I had doubted where the "Second Front" would start I could speculate no longer, and at times became ironically conscious of the chance by which the frustrated suspect of 1940, forbidden to enter "defence areas" in quest of literary information, possessed this vital knowledge.

Clearly our area was a top "security risk", yet because I owned a modest property I was not only permitted to come in unquestioned, but to go out. Shuttling between G. and my mother in London and the family of children at the cottage, I could have disclosed a dozen military secrets on every townward journey. Doubtful whether to award the palm for idiocy to the crazy suspicions of the invasion period or the irresponsible complacency of the present, I found the danger of inadvertent "careless talk" a constant threat to my peace of mind. Never had I been obliged to be silent about so much for so long.

"*Taisez-vous! méfiez-vous!*" I would exhort myself in the words of the placards in First War France. "*Les oreilles ennemies vous écoutent!*"

We learned later from the Press that the invasion forces began to travel by special trains to the South coast opposite the Cherbourg Peninsula on March 26th, six days after we recovered the cottage. Now, assembled off Southampton, lay a large part of the four thousand ships and innumerable smaller vessels to be used on D-Day.

Southampton itself was a half-razed city in which weeds smothered the trail of the Blitz. Throughout that summer I found it difficult to negotiate the grass-grown ruins of Above Bar, where the wreckage of the largest local store carried a gallant notice: "Plummer's Fashion Centre". The unhappy town, though so often the first to be seen by visiting Americans, was to become a Cinderella among bombed cities; even by 1956 many wartime scars would remain unhealed.

The contrast between the awakening spring and the massive slaughter of youth which Allied policy would involve brought an atmosphere of deepening suspense to the Hampshire countryside. How many of the uniformed young men who looked casually upon the bare branches of oak and beech against the cloudless blue would be dead before those boughs were heavy with summer foliage? Into my mind came a letter, long forgotten, which I had written during my first spring as a college student to Roland who died at the end of that year.

"I think it is harder now the spring days are beginning to come to keep the thought of war before one's mind. . . . At this time of year it seems that everything should be creative, not destructive, and that we should encourage things to live and not die."

From the United States Mr. Oswald Garrison Villard, inspired by the same thought, sent me an article called "Last Plea for Europe" which he had published in *The Christian Century*. There he implored Britain and America to abandon the policy of "Unconditional Surrender"—a plea which Edward Murrow was to reinforce in July—and to substitute the publication of "Peace Points", comparable to President Wilson's, for the coming holocaust of young men.

"Once more I appeal for dying Europe—and for America too. I dare not suppose that my plea will carry far but I must make it. . . . Just because the voices of my fellow-countrymen are still, I must cry out in behalf of millions who are now condemned to die. . . .

"I plead not only for Europe. I plead for England. For England cannot survive the destruction of Europe upon which it depended for so large a proportion of its trade, for its intellectual stimulus and for its inspiration in art and music. . . . So I plead for the British boys who are destined for immolation. Their country suffers deeply to-day because of the generation lost in the First World War. I plead for the England that I love more than any other country save my own—that it may yet be saved."

In 1944 such voices went unheeded. On May 15th, four days after the death of Dame Ethel Smyth, whom I had recently visited for the last time, the Government announced that many passenger trains would be curtailed owing to the heavy transport going South. Persistent Allied bombing attacks now began on the French coast between Dunkirk and Cherbourg, eighty miles from our cottage. As the Nazi reconnaissance flights also intensified, I had a front-line view of spectacular battles, illuminated by searchlights, from my seaward-looking study window. Sometimes, when the planes were driven inland by coastal guns, it seemed the better part of valour to take refuge with the children under the stairs.

The news of a fresh offensive in Italy brought further apprehensions, for Charles Burnett was now there with the Royal Air Force. The Anglo-American troops on the Anzio beaches, we learned, had broken out against the opposing Germans and joined the Americans marching along the Appian Way.

Three days before the Fifth Army entered Rome, the cottage doors and windows rattled for ten minutes though we could hear no sound to explain the vibration. During the next few nights, I lay in bed and listened to the incessant booming of guns. They did not sound like our usual coastal defences, and I realised later that the noises must have come from intensified bombing or shelling on the coast of France.

(2)

On June 5th, when invasion tension had reached its peak, I joined G. in London for a series of engagements. John and Shirley had long departed from Allum Green for the summer term, but I was obliged to leave the rest of our household at the cottage to face increasing nocturnal pandemonium.

We had no radio at Sloane Avenue Mansions, but next morning G., who was out keeping an appointment, telephoned me that the invasion had begun. Anxiously I rang up Allum Green, to learn that nothing untoward had occurred and the noise had palpably diminished.

When I left the flat for a luncheon engagement with Christina Foyle, the streets were quieter than usual; an odd hush which was almost silence seemed to have descended on London. In the bus the invasion was not discussed; I heard no one mention it until Christina Foyle and G. and I listened to the one o'clock news at the restaurant. Londoners had known many crises in the past five years: this was just one more. Only the rush for the early editions of the evening papers betrayed their suppressed emotions.

That afternoon I had to travel from King's Cross for two lectures in Grimsby and a meeting at Lincoln. The station was almost deserted; the ruins of offices and waiting-rooms left by the direct hits of earlier years looked even bleaker than usual. Few trains were running, though these fortunately included mine. By the time I reached Grimsby, I was the only passenger left in a long coach of several compartments.

At Grimsby I learned from the Vicar, who had arranged an informal gathering, that the whole East coast had expected raids immediately the invasion started. One late Alert did finish our meeting, but nothing further happened. After a quiet night I gave the two morning addresses; then, as my train had been cancelled, the local Medical Officer drove me to Lincoln.

How superlatively English was that East Anglian country, with its flat ploughed fields and windmills stretching their long arms against a huge expanse of opalescent sky! Many of the thousands of men now landing on the Normandy coast must have thought of home in terms of the fen-lands which I now saw, recalling the umbrella-like elms, the quietly feeding sheep, the clusters of red-roofed houses round isolated impressive churches. The high central spire of the church at Louth, rising straight from the ground to meet a cluster of smaller spires, suggested a tall gladiolus.

An audience which seemed indifferent to raids crowded my Famine Relief meeting in a Lincoln picture gallery, but later it rushed to buy newspapers which reported that the invasion was going "according to plan". That night I lay awake from midnight till dawn in my room at the Saracen's Head, listening to successive waves of heavy bombers going over the city towards the coast.

Back in London, I found the daily papers of June 8th commenting on the failure of the Luftwaffe to attack the large invasion fleets now spread between the Isle of Wight and the Cherbourg Peninsula, but four nights later three quickly repeated Alerts in the early hours proclaimed the unrecognised beginning of flying bombs. During the next two days I addressed two meetings, took Shirley and her Cambridge friends to see the Ballet Jooss at the Haymarket Theatre, and finally returned to Allum Green still unaware of the new peril threatening "Southern England".

A now keenly-developed instinct for danger nevertheless made me deeply uneasy. Throughout that night I heard the sound of distant guns; as I stood at my window looking over the silent Forest, the horizon seemed to be periodically illuminated as though by sheet lightning. Next day the B.B.C. broadcast a statement by Herbert Morrison officially reporting the arrival of "pilotless planes"—a new secret weapon which created terror by its uncanny behaviour until the long-suffering British public, growing familiar with its obnoxious boom and meteor-like trail, characteristically invented the ironic name of "doodlebug".

Only on July 6th came Winston Churchill's official explanation; this weapon, he said, had been developed since 1943, and would have been used earlier had not the experimental stations been located and bombed at Peenemunde. Though my mother wrote incoherently of "constant raids", G. as usual made light of them; the uneasy and expensive progress of the struggling armies on the opposite coast seemed more worthy of attention.

After the first ten days of the invasion, the weather had turned pro-Nazi; though Bayeux, ten miles inland, had been taken in the first advance, low cloud and strong winds accompanied the costly battle for Caen. Even the secret pre-fabricated ports could not compensate for this resistent stronghold; with sorrow I read that four thousand American soldiers and five thousand French civilians had already been lost in the struggle to take it.

Nor was death the only price of invasion. During the second week of the battle, a Letter reader sent me from that day's *Evening News* a clipping which contained only two headlines:

CHILDREN SEE GERMANS DIE.
"C'est bon," they say. *"C'est bon."*

"It is obvious," I wrote in the next issue, "that the most difficult function which will fall to the relief workers now preparing in their thousands to enter Europe will be, not to feed the hungry or to comfort the suffering, but to transform into civilised beings the young people brutalised by years of privation and peril."

To coincide with the Second Front which they had so long demanded, the Russians now launched a new offensive at their end of Europe. Within the next few weeks, long-forgotten names came back into the news—Mogilev, Minsk, Vilna, Przemyśl, Brest-Litovsk. By August I was to awaken to their significance and venture upon another published prophecy:

"The chief consequence of this war will be the domination of Europe by Russia, strengthened and enlarged to a degree which already leaves her with nothing to fear from Britain and America. What conduct can we expect in Germany from Soviet soldiers whose hatred has been aroused by acts of cruelty committed within their own territory, and nourished on a propaganda more brilliant and ruthless than that of any other nation? Possession is nine points of the law—and the citizen armies of Stalin may take that law into their own hands, whatever the theoretical decisions previously reached far from the battlefront by leaders of the United Nations."

Before the Russian victories captured my consciousness, the battle developing round Cherbourg continued to provide an uneasy challenge. Sometimes the noise of the guns in France seemed to be carried to my ears by the wind, reminding me of the strange shudder, half sound and half sensation, which penetrated to the Base Hospitals at Étaples from the front line during the First World War.

Not until the port was taken on June 26th did the ghostly echoes diminish and finally cease.

(3)

From the middle of the month, air-raid sirens became constant both in London and in the New Forest. On June 19th the Paris radio announced that one series of attacks by the new robots was directed especially against Portsmouth, Southampton and Bristol. Warned by the Press that danger arose chiefly from flying daggers of shattered glass, I laid the cottage pictures face downwards on the floor with the feeling that I had taken this precaution in a continuous nightmare which had lasted all my life.

The nights now became restless with strange noises and the days with rumours of "P.-planes" crashing all over Hampshire, though nobody I met had actually seen one. But the reported destruction with many casualties during the morning service of a London "church" (later identified as the Guards' Chapel) showed that this "secret weapon" possessed serious lethal qualities, even if they were not so effective as the Nazis claimed.

According to their radio, the customary crowds going to the Derby represented a "mass evacuation of London", while the entire South Coast was said to lie under a "pall of smoke". With G., who came down for the week-end, I climbed to the highest point of the Forest at Emery Down, to see the Isle of Wight basking in afternoon sunshine and looking even more peaceful than usual.

As time moved on, the claims acquired rather more substance. On June 23rd, G. and I reached Waterloo two hours after a crashing robot had damaged the station and the nearby County Hall. Concealed by heavy clouds, several flying bombs boomed over our heads as we walked to the Underground.

"They sound like a mixture of an angry bee and a broken-down tug on the Thames which keeps you in suspense as it gradually nears," I recorded that night in my diary. "The engine stops—a light flashes, and someone is 'for it'; the explosion follows immediately, causing its own cloud of smoke, but there is no smoke pall over London."

Unlike my Hampshire neighbours, I had an immediate opportunity of seeing a fallen robot next day in Russell Square; it bore a curious resemblance to a huge dead bat with a broken back. Only the use of their eyes and ears and a careful scrutiny of Press obituary notices told Londoners where the bombs had struck. A reported death "by enemy action" at Kenyon, near Harrow, made me anxious for John, whose school had already been damaged by incendiary bombs followed by continuous raids; and a letter from him disclosed that the boys were again spending their nights in the shelter and diving under their desks during classes. After one flying bomb had landed on the cricket field the Headmaster gave parents the option of removing their sons; but John elected to stay till the end of the term and take his School Certificate examination.

Public engagements again became difficult to fulfil. An attempt to board a morning express for three lectures at Doncaster showed me that evacuation, if not on the scale reported, was at least in progress. London's unhappy children were again on the move; giving way to them I cancelled my evening lecture, and travelled to Yorkshire by a late night train. On my return I found London tense beneath its sixth Alert since dawn.

It was our nineteenth wedding anniversary. Before celebrating it with G. at a quiet hotel dinner, I had promised to take the chair for a meeting "Towards a Christian Peace" at Whitefield's Tabernacle in Tottenham Court Road. Periodic boomings and distant crashes punctuated an uncomfortable two hours, but neither the audience nor the German refugee speakers—a Pastor and a Quaker relief worker—betrayed any sign of fear.

Halfway through the meeting Corder Catchpool came in and sat quietly beneath the platform; from time to time he smiled encouragingly, as though to reassure me that I did not appear as scared as

I felt. Some months later, the Tabernacle was demolished by a V.2 rocket.

(4)

Throughout that summer, G. and I experienced many raids at Sloane Avenue Mansions. We usually slept in our beds with coats and flashlights beside us, and a fireman's whistle lest we should suddenly find ourselves buried beneath the ruins of the huge block. But the flaming comet-like objects which scorched past our ninth-floor window sometimes made sleep unattainable, and we descended to a reinforced room on a lower corridor.

These so-called "diabolical" weapons, I explained to my Letter readers in quieter areas, were really just a new kind of shell.

"Up to date it is at least a shell which can be intercepted, and there is no essential difference between its objectionable buzz and the whine of a whizz-bang."

At the end of the term I thankfully saw John off for a quiet fortnight with a relative in the Lake District. On one of his London visits we had found Piccadilly ankle-deep in glass, and at tea-time in my mother's flat had flung ourselves face downwards while a "doodlebug" cut out overhead and fell with an earth-shaking crash on the opposite bank of the river. At the time our house appeared undamaged, but some weeks later I found a great crack in the outer wall and my study ceiling in dusty fragments all over my books and papers.

"You really must get out of London for a bit," I told my mother before returning to the cottage for Shirley's holidays. Like many elderly people she tended to wait until precautions had become difficult, and she now made the laborious journey to Allum Green with marked reluctance.

That week, which coincided with the unsuccessful attack on Hitler's life by the German Resistance, saw George Lansbury's house in Bow destroyed by a flying bomb, and our Letter office put finally out of action by a fourth severe blasting. Philosophically my secretary removed the essential files, and carried on from her own basement in Lewisham.

My mother remained in Hampshire only a few days, for the Nazis inconsiderately selected that week to deliver a doodlebug half a mile from the cottage. She might as well have stayed at home, she declared indignantly, and would not even wait for Shirley's return for the holidays. Eventually I persuaded her to go to Wales, where a favourite former maid had offered her refuge.

Together Shirley and I searched for the spot where the robot had fallen, though I had an irrational dread of finding it. We soon discovered that the bomb had devastated the uninhabited loveliness of a woodland glade. The place appeared as though a mathematical circle of blight had descended from heaven. Everything within it was burnt and brown, the leaves stripped from their boughs and the grass consumed by a sweeping flame. The explosion had blown off the tops of the nearer trees, leaving only the shattered trunks and split branches to raise protesting arms to the sky.

We seemed to have walked from the sunlit forest into some strange island of desolation. This time there were no human casualties; the beautiful oaks and beeches, some hundreds of years old, had been the only victims.

"Thirtieth anniversary of August 4th, 1914 (the Second Thirty Years' War)," I noted a week later in my diary. Two days afterwards the newspapers announced that British, American and Canadian casualties since June 6th amounted to 116,139 killed, wounded and missing.

Soon we learned that the fighting in France had now turned definitely in the Allies' favour. Following a new Allied landing near St. Raphael and the "extermination" of the Seventh German Army inside the Falaise gap, the French Resistance had ordered a nation-wide insurrection, and an armoured force under General Leclerc had entered Paris. The evacuation of France by the Nazis now seemed to be imminent, and I began at last to contemplate an early return to the wider experience of pre-war years which I had visualised in a letter to New York on August 15th.

"I have the feeling of being back in October 1918. . . . I confess that I dread what we shall find in Germany and the occupied countries when the war is over; the roots of our so-called civilisation are very shallow. I hope to be able to get over to Europe as soon as I am allowed when the fighting ends, and to play some early part in the work of restoration."

(5)

At the end of August John and Shirley left Allum Green for a fortnight's farm-work at Compton Scorpion Manor in Warwickshire. The farmer, Adrian Beecham, was a son of Sir Thomas, and had married the daughter of our acquaintance Emma Tollemache.

Shirley departed on this mission with great enthusiasm, and John, who had no liking for agricultural labour, with unfeigned reluctance. But seven years afterwards, by an odd coincidence, he was to marry

345

his hostess's cousin, Jennifer Manasseh, a beautiful first-year Oxford student from Lady Margaret Hall, whom he met in his last year at New College.

On August 26th G. arrived from London to report a three days' lull in the flying bombs and the surrender of Roumania to the Russians. By September 1st the British and American armies were racing towards Germany; Amiens had been occupied and Dieppe taken without a fight. Slowly the Allies were encircling the "fly-bomb" coast; the Sunday papers which marked the fifth anniversary of the war's outbreak quoted American prophecies of its end in a month, and on September 6th wild rumours of a German capitulation flew round London.

Next day the Press cheerfully announced that black-out restrictions would soon be partially lifted and the Home Guard disbanded. From Washington a letter from Dr. Howard Kershner, forecasting an early change from his present famine relief campaigning to post-war plans for feeding stricken Europe, reached me in less than a week. Nothing could more forcibly have persuaded me that the war was really ending than this relaxation of a censorship which had often delayed American correspondence from three to six months.

But, as we were soon to learn, this mood of optimism was premature.

Coming up to London on the morning of September 8th, I read with the same happiness as my neighbours a *Daily Express* article by Duncan Sandys, M.P., the chairman of the War Cabinet committee on operational counter-measures against the flying bomb. He described how the "doodlebug" had been beaten, and proclaimed: "Except possibly for a few last shots, the Battle of London is over."

Late that afternoon I returned to Sloane Avenue Mansions at the end of a long Food Relief committee to await Corder Catchpool, who was coming to supper.

"Got home under lowering rainy clouds which looked like thunder," my diary recorded that evening, "and was just up in the flat when two terrific explosions occurred, shaking the whole building. Sounded like a large gun or time-bomb going off but I never got an explanation." After the entry a postscript dated 11/x/44 added: "This was actually the first V.2 rocket."

I looked at the sullen yellow sky and imagined that I saw puffs of smoke; in fact I could not have seen anything as our window looked south, and this rocket fell on Chiswick, four miles due west of Chelsea. When Corder arrived on his bicycle half an hour later, I questioned him without perturbation.

"Did you hear a strange explosion, about a quarter to seven?"

"Yes," he replied. "We heard it quite distinctly in Hampstead. I was just starting to come here, but I've no idea what it was."

Nor, for some days, had anybody else. The following week-end, as Letter No. 144 recorded, a gay relief on the faces of London's much-tried population was so conspicuous as almost to be tangible. In Piccadilly and Leicester Square, the holiday atmosphere suggested a normal peace-time Sunday.

Yet the strange noises continued and slowly multiplied, leading to uneasy speculations about broken gas-mains and unexploded time-bombs.

"It was hard to believe," a *News Chronicle* contributor wrote ten years afterwards, "that at this late hour Germany's battered, material-starved industries could produce yet another mechanical killer. . . . After the war it was learned that the bulk of the V.2 development staff had moved [from Peenemunde] to Poland. . . .

"It was an explosion that began a new era in warfare. The first supersonic rocket had struck."

(6)

Two months later, when "V.2" had been officially acknowledged, the disillusioned Londoners who bolstered their morale by inventing the term "doodlebug" had already named the invisible monsters "flying gas-mains". They had now grown accustomed to the ominous green flash, and the prolonged roar which smote their ears after the huge missile, faster than sound, had demolished the target which no device yet contrived could defend. But fortitude was harder to restore than ironic labels to invent. Most honest city-dwellers would probably have endorsed a confession made in November to G., then in St. Helens hopefully investigating his possible selection as Labour candidate for a safe Lancashire seat.

"The noise turns me cold and at the same time fills me with an intense exasperation. . . . For me it typifies all the horror and misery of this war."

In a letter to America I admitted that, of all the weapons with which we had been attacked, I detested most this unpredictable assassin which killed without warning. It seemed strange, I added, that so many Americans seemed to think that I opposed obliteration bombing because I had never suffered from German bombs.

"The opposite is the truth. I don't want to see inflicted on *any* mothers and children the constant anxiety for others which accompanied the sirens and the crashes, the dread of nightfall, the interminable waiting for dawn during the endless nights of the Blitz."

To depress jaded spirits still further, the autumn weather from early September turned cold and stormy, hampering the Allied armies and immobilising their pilots. A series of misfortunes, international and personal, accompanied the perpetual rain. They began when the costly disaster at Arnhem preceded the ruinous use of floods as a military weapon in Holland, but one month before the re-election of Franklin D. Roosevelt for his fourth term as President, tragedy struck nearer home.

On October 8th, the one o'clock news announced the death in New York of Wendell Willkie, aged fifty-two.

In April Mr. Willkie had failed dismally in the Republican Presidential primary elections in Wisconsin. "He will certainly continue the campaign, which he apparently regards as a crusade to reform the Republican Party," a current "American Diary" reported. But the heart had gone out of his crusade and him, and in June he was not even invited to the Chicago Republican Convention.

"In a sense," G. wrote sorrowfully from St. Helens, "it shears me of a kingdom. He was a great man and a world figure, the only one to emerge since the war. It will take many years before we are able to estimate our loss. Above all to me he was the man who had the right ideas. . . . We may yet find that his death counts in the same class with the premature deaths of Briand and Stresemann."

He added in a prophetic passage: "It is so oddly out of character. Gandhi dead would be Gandhi still more immortal. But Willkie so obviously was in love with life. It is like the death of Samson unbound."

The next day, by a chance irony, the newspapers published the first blue-prints for a United Nations Charter put forward at Dumbarton Oaks. Neither Wendell Willkie nor Archbishop Temple—whose equally unexpected and dismaying death followed Willkie's on October 26th—would share in this new attempt to create the "One World" for which each had laboured in his different fashion.

Late in November, the collapse of G.'s hopes at St. Helens inflicted another blow.

"As yet," he had warned me on November 12th, "we have only begun with the mud. St. Helens is 'real politics', not playing."

A fortnight later the mud had overwhelmed him, and he had lost all chance of being selected.

For me the post-publication fortunes of *Account Rendered*, issued in New York on November 8th, matched G.'s political disappointment. This novel, which a year later had brought in less than £400 in dollars, failed to provide even the modest reward on which I had counted. For the next three months, a galling series of tendentious reviews, inspired by the recent bombing controversy, were to send my battered morale down to zero.

(7)

Before I returned to the cottage for the children's Christmas holidays, it was clear that the war news would provide no fresh encouragement.

In mid-December von Rundstedt's surprise onslaught, under cover of perpetual fog, against the American Third Army in the semi-mountainous Ardennes where nobody had expected an attack, drove towards breaking point the rising tension between the tired and baffled Western allies.

At the end of the year, in his last regular Sunday night broadcast, Raymond Gram Swing spoke regretfully of "the unprecedentedly low state of Anglo-American friendship". The American people, he said, were now "at the lowest spiritual level of the war"; the massive German assault in Luxembourg had undermined American self-esteem almost as severely as the attack on Pearl Harbour.

From Eastern Europe different news brought other apprehensions. After September 1944 the Russians had steadily overrun the Balkans, laying impregnable foundations for the future Iron Curtain. When heroic Poles had died vainly in Warsaw during the premature insurrection staged by the Resistance, the Red Armies prepared for a new offensive. Soon they would dominate all Poland and capture Upper Silesia, abandoned by the Germans with its coal, oil and newly-transferred industries in the hope of saving Berlin.

During December we read of the Russian attacks on Budapest, that once splendid capital where historic buildings were successively sacrificed in the last desperate Nazi defence. Centuries ago, in a smiling war-free summer, G. and I had dined on the Margareten Island with Mr. Jacobi, the gay Jewish-Hungarian financier. Where was he now?

As the bleak New Year came in, isolating the cottage with heavy snowfalls, I realised that though this sixth wartime winter might be the least anxious, it was unquestionably the most miserable John and Shirley, at different stages of adolescence, found its normal problems exaggerated by the long-drawn discomforts of war. While

349

he developed a capacity for ruthless criticism, her natural good temper turned to a defensive obstinacy which expressed itself in monosyllables.

"Where are you going, Shirley?" I would inquire when she set forth on her bicycle, hoping to have some stamps bought or a letter posted.

"Out!" she would reply, asserting her claim to independence in a manner characteristic of adolescents from time immemorial.

The two now started a series of vehement arguments, and being extremely articulate drove each other to fury. Shirley, her logical mind oddly contrasting with her bouts of domestic anarchy, frequently triumphed in spite of her younger years; unconsciously she was practising, at her brother's expense, for the political speeches in which she was to prove so effective a few years later. When either child was absent the other tried to involve me in similar controversial discussions, until at moments of extreme fatigue I wished them both back in America. And the more persistently they baited each other, the more sedulously, wise in his own behalf, G. kept out of the way. He preferred the rockets to their arguments, he said.

When they had gone back to school, I struggled against incipient influenza and the remorseless cold to complete my part in editing *Above All Nations*. The rest of the household, snow-bound, depressed by food and fuel shortages, and apprehensive for Charles in Italy, provided a steady Greek chorus of discontent.

Our ragged nerves were typical of the exasperation now spreading throughout the Western world. Continuous cross-Atlantic batches of humiliating Press clippings both increased my discouragement and reminded me that Anglo-American strains could be personal as well as political. No self-evident connection seemed to exist between a fictitious murder due to a trench-mortar explosion in 1918 and a controversy about massacre bombing in 1944, but several critics ingeniously found it.

During the spring, another incident showed that in England too a writer could be repudiated in one decade for values acclaimed in another. The previous winter a well-known Quaker, Elizabeth Fox-Howard, had appealed on behalf of English-speaking German prisoners for books describing English life and institutions. I offered fifty copies, which were gladly accepted, of a forthcoming new edition of *Testament of Youth*, but the War Office refused to allow the book to enter the camps.

In the House of Commons, prompted by the Quakers, the Rev. Reginald Sorensen, M.P., eventually asked for an explanation, and the War Minister, Sir James Grigg, himself supplied it. *Testament of Youth*, he said, must not be read by German prisoners owing to its arguments against the Treaty of Versailles. I could not recall writing anything about the Treaty, but on going through 660 pages found two or three short references which viewed "fatal Versailles" in the same light as General Smuts and half the political world in 1933.

It was too much. If, after this, an English edition of *Account Rendered* brought another avalanche of critical onslaughts, I now feared that some quality of self-imposed restraint might crack. Accordingly, I asked my London publishers to postpone publication indefinitely, if not for ever.

Their cheerful response astounded me. Completely unintimidated by the American reception of *Account Rendered*, they wrote that they proposed to save the cost of several reprints by preparing one large edition of fifty thousand copies. They would be glad, they added, to delay publication till the autumn, as this would allow more time to collect the necessary paper. When I protested that such an optimistic venture would mean thousands of unsold copies, they assured me that the demand for books was now far greater than the supply.

My temporary panic, combined with their unruffled policy, brought some unexpected consequences, for when the book came out the war was over. Just as the New World, by its lyrical acceptance of *England's Hour*, had redressed the balance of the Old, so for *Account Rendered* the Old was to redress the balance of the New.

(8)

In February the Big Three met at Yalta and, led by President Roosevelt, dug still deeper the Iron Curtain's foundations. Shortly before the Conference opened, a letter reached me from Oswald Garrison Villard doubting whether the President ought to attend it at all.

"From one point of view he should not go; he looks shockingly in the movies, a completely altered personality, with the deepest of dark lines. If anything should happen to him he will be succeeded by an unfit and untried man."

At Yalta, according to the contemporary Press, the delegates consumed rich food and champagne cocktails, though fifteen members of Mr. Churchill's mission had died in an air-crash on the way to the Conference and millions of the peoples whose fate they were deciding lacked the barest necessities of life. Through implacable cold from the battle areas of Eastern Germany, forty-mile columns of hungry refugees, bereft of homes and possessions, struggled desperately westward. Setting out village by village, they varied from small groups with a few hand-carts to giant queues straggling behind long lines of vehicles. Women, children, and their aged relatives walked for hundreds of miles with scarcely a rest, leaving the weakest humans and animals to die on the way.

On February 13th thousands of these refugees crowded the railway station at Dresden, hoping for trains to help them on their westward journey. That night one of the heaviest "obliteration" raids of the war smote the city, hitherto considered safe owing to its cultural treasures. On May 5th the U.S. Forces' newspaper, *The Stars and Stripes*, quoted a description by British war prisoners of this fourteen-hour attack.

> "The British sergeant said: 'Reports from Dresden police that 300,000 died as a result of the bombing didn't include deaths among 1,000,000 evacuees from the Breslau area trying to escape from the Russians. There were no records on them. After seeing the results of the bombings, I believe their figures are correct. They had to pitchfork shrivelled bodies on to trucks and wagons and cart them to shallow graves on the outskirts of the city. But after two weeks of work the job became too much to cope with and they found other means to gather up the dead. They burned bodies in a great heap in the centre of the city, but the most effective way . . . was to take flame-throwers and burn the dead as they lay in the ruins.' "

The Bombing Restriction Committee issued its protest in a pamphlet entitled *The End of Dresden*, but we all knew now that our efforts were useless though we still determined to make them. As I had written to G. shortly after the American controversy, " 'pro-Nazi, pro-German, pro-Boer', are the typical labels applied to the critics of cruelty in war."

Early in March the American armies reached the Rhine, and the newspapers reported their arrival at the mountainous ruins which had once been Cologne. But in England the rockets continued; on a journey through Essex to lecture in Saffron Walden, I gathered a new picture of the effects of bombing upon the eastern outskirts of London. The attacks of different years could be identified from the water-filled bomb-holes covered with green scum, which recalled 1940, to the recent raw debris from flying bombs.

My numerous spring lectures were not important in themselves, but a series of new scenes and contacts restored me from a harassed author and badgered parent to a normal person interested in life. A visit to Bangor, where I spoke in a big chapel, drew the largest audience of the war, and recalled G's encouragement. Two days after my return to London, the Carnarvon valleys awakening to new life from harsh winter mourned the death of David Lloyd George.

That afternoon, as I left Waterloo to spend Easter at Allum Green, a heavy explosion shook the station. G. assured me that the noise came from an engine, but I knew better. It was nevertheless the last rocket that I had to hear; only two more were still to fall on Southern England.

Suddenly, with April, came the climax of the Allied advance, and renewed hope brightened in the sunshine of spring.

(9)

One of the main agreements reached at Yalta had provided for an international Conference to open at San Francisco on April 25th, in order to discuss the Dumbarton Oaks plan for a new World Organisation.

"We are told," I wrote in my Letter for March 8th, "that the difficulty of voting procedure on the World Security Council has been overcome, and that the sponsors . . . will be the U.S.A., Great Britain, Russia, France and China, though the difficult problem of who is to be invited remains unsettled."

Eventually the chief British delegates were announced as Anthony Eden, Clement Attlee, Viscount Cranbourne and Lord Halifax. This meeting, G. believed, would be the only Peace Conference that the world was likely to see; what more significant way of spending four weeks could he find?

Soon afterwards a group of Indian papers and the British news-magazine, *Cavalcade*, invited him to be their correspondent, and the technical facilities for going were his. On April 2nd he telephoned me that he was leaving for San Francisco three days hence.

Now that the hope of selection at St. Helens had foundered, the decision to go, so attractive in itself, involved a political risk. We already knew that, when the war finished, a Dissolution followed by a General Election would end the longest Parliament in history. But the war was not yet over and all the available signs—editorial articles, "opinions" endorsed by famous names, and even personal advice from the Secretary of the Labour Party itself—pointed to an autumn election. When G. returned, it appeared that he would still have time to find a rewarding constituency.

As submarines continued to haunt the Atlantic, security regulations were still essential. The party of correspondents bound for San Francisco therefore left from Addison Road, a small suburban station in West Kensington. Here Shirley and I watched G. board a very dirty train with no provision for food. Sharing a compartment with Claud Cockburn of the *Daily Worker* and Philip Jordan of the *Daily Mail*, he travelled in this third-rate vehicle to Glasgow. It seemed a squalid prelude to a great adventure.

"I miss you very much and feel lonely," I wrote him three days later to the Palace Hotel Press office in San Francisco. "But it's no use expecting sympathy from the children, who regard such feelings as 'soppy' and don't see it as their function to be comforting (though they sometimes are by accident!). At least everyone else seems to envy you and would give anything to be in your place—as I would, instead of feeling solitary, and egregiously overworked at dull jobs."

One immediate job was not dull, though intimidating. The Prime Minister of New Zealand, Mr. Peter Fraser, was then visiting London, and the Central Board for Conscientious Objectors asked me to see him and plead for more official tolerance towards New Zealand war-resisters. To my surprise, Mr. Fraser agreed to the interview.

I found a large, benevolent man whose courtesy, like that of President Roosevelt seven years earlier, put me instantly at ease. Our discussion was nevertheless difficult, for Mr. Fraser proved to be an interested reader of my books. He was much more anxious to discuss them than the conscientious objectors—for whom, he said, he couldn't do much anyway, owing to public sentiment—and it was hard to keep him to the point.

After the interview I suggested to A. J. Brayshaw, the secretary to the Central Board, that it might be wise to tackle New Zealand public opinion before making further approaches to politicians, and a letter with several responsible signatures went off to the New Zealand Press. Eventually their Government slightly modified its harsh regulations, but how far my talk with Mr. Fraser was responsible I do not know to this day.

G.'s voyage proved to be almost as uncomfortable as his train journey, if more adventurous. The correspondents and diplomats on board, he reported, included King of the Rothermere Press, Balfour of the Foreign Office, and Macdonald of *The Times*.

"A miserable ship . . . Greek," ran a letter, much mutilated by censorship scissors, dated April 6th. "Cabin for four. Thousands, it seems, of babies with their mothers . . . I have a profound conviction that the boat will be sunk, maybe for no more solid reason than that again I see I shall be at sea on Friday 13th . . . Depth charges being dropped last night and ordered to sleep in our clothes tonight."

But though the ship passed over the spot where a boat had been torpedoed the previous day, the catastrophe actually brought by Friday the 13th was not a sinking, but the news of President Roosevelt's death. While I, stunned, heard it at the cottage amid the incongruous beauty of spring blossom, G. listened to the ship's radio during a birthday celebration for Claud Cockburn. In less than three months, Mr. Villard's apprehensions had been realised; like Abraham Lincoln, Franklin Roosevelt had died when his country was on the eve of victory after a long campaign.

"What a setback for America, compared with which the advances of the victorious troops fall into their true proportions as minor factors," G. wrote me the next day. "And how dangerous the doctrine against which Willkie fought that any one man should regard himself as indispensable."

At home I heard the new President's broadcast address to Congress.

"The speech was simple, direct, sincere, without false modesty or inferiority complex and delivered in a pleasant friendly voice," I reported to G., adding in a similar mood to his own: "It may be that both Churchill and Stalin will accept a salutary reminder that the plans of great men to dominate their neighbours are subject to their own mortality."

G. landed in Montreal on April 17th, and travelled south-west through a forest of half-mast flags while the world's Press speculated whether the forty-five nations meeting at San Francisco would indeed lay the foundations of a new international order. One cynical headline—"San Fiasco"—seemed to typify the real expectations of a now disillusioned public.

On April 26th I bought a copy of *Cavalcade* containing G.'s first article, but more personal illumination eventually reached me in a letter dated the following day. To save time, he now lapsed into the "cable-ese" of his dispatches.

"Conference stupendous opera painful contrast European bloody muddle. Despite clouds incense plenty poker behind scenes and Molotov mighty tough. . . . Eden left admirable impression opera audience but this not reality. . . . Fever grips Conference but still not sure I am not playboying here. However, unexpected accolade, Ellen [Wilkinson] dines with me visit Chinatown together she and Mrs. Pandit my guests. . . ."

Further enlightenment followed on May 1st.

"Conditions still indescribable constant agitation pressmen milling round from 8 a.m. to past midnight press conferences called by rumour without notice experts complaining have no meals Molotov probably leaving next week . . . Had hoped to give some general reflections on conference but swirling rushing information roaring inflowing no possible chance reflect yet. . . . Broadcasting to-night after breakfast and lunch appointments Stassen press conference STOP whatalife."

When he returned on May 20th he found an England totally changed, and a Europe already beginning its long and painful convalescence.

(10)

Two days before the San Francisco Conference, Victor Gollancz' published our short anthology, *Above All Nations*. The sub-title described its contents: "Acts of kindness done to enemies, in the war, by men of many nations".

From early February, when the end of hostilities again came in sight, Victor had been anxious to go to press. A pre-publication sale of 45,000 copies now justified his foresight and, by contrast with recent literary experience, brought a lifting of my spirit though I could claim, at most, only a quarter share in this experiment.

The idea had been G.'s and the title mine, but Victor and one of his younger directors, Sheila Hodges, had done half the work, and many of the best stories from the Press were his discoveries. He had also contributed an Introduction which referred, in its conclusion, not only to the national differences that divided the "enemies", but to the varying political opinions of the four anthologists.

"Deeper than this division, a faith unites us: the faith which answers with a calm and sure affirmative the ancient question 'Are we not all'—Germans and Englishmen, Gentiles and Jews—'Are we not all children of one Father? Has not one God created us?' "

A letter in the *Jewish Chronicle* subsequently assailed Victor for publishing and commending *Above All Nations*. ("Here in a subtle way an attempt is made to soften the righteous indignation felt by every decent-minded person at the beastly atrocities committed by the Germans . . . What excuse has Victor Gollancz?")

Victor disregarded this attack; his impassioned sincerity provided all the "excuse" that he needed. He was, as usual, impervious to criticism when he believed an action to be right.

By the end of April, the sales of this half-crown book had reached

50,000 copies; after one journey from Lyndhurst, a large pile on Waterloo Station bookstall caught my still incredulous eye. These sales, had we realised it, were a clue to public thinking, already deeply influenced by other Gollancz "yellow books", of which the first had been *Guilty Men*. They formed part of the writing on the wall which those to whom it most mattered were still unable to read.

In May Muriel Lester, founder of Kingsley Hall and travelling lecturer for the *Fellowship of Reconciliation*, offered £50 for the anthology to be circulated in German prison camps and British military hospitals if someone else would give the same amount. Through my Letter I collected the second £50, and the Friends' Aliens Council subsequently assured me that this time the War Office had raised no objections.

On Sunday evening, August 26th, the B.B.C. broadcast a half-hour programme, based on *Above All Nations*, in which twenty extracts were quoted without alteration. By that date we all understood better the reasons for the little volume's success.

(11)

During the Easter holidays I took the children to a Southampton cinema, hoping to see the current news-reel of Franklin Roosevelt's life. Instead we were shown a film of his Memorial Service at St. Paul's Cathedral, followed by scenes of devastation in Hanover and the Ruhr.

If these pictures were intended to fill British film-goers with feelings of jubilant triumph over their expiring enemy, they totally failed. Southampton audiences were accustomed to damage, but when the frightening ruins of Hanover appeared on the screen, a gasp like the sound of a sudden wind through reeds filled the large cinema.

Ten days later, the same picture-house showed the visit of a British Parliamentary delegation to Buchenwald Concentration Camp. Mrs. Mavis Tate, M.P., handkerchief to nose, gazed at closer quarters than ourselves upon a gruesome assemblage of living skeletons and disintegrating bodies; her death a year or two afterwards was said to have originated in an infection acquired at that time. A "close-up" of Mrs. Clare Luce, America's future Ambassador to Italy, followed immediately. Incongruously beautiful and elegant, she declaimed with passion on the magnitude of the Nazi crimes.

Within the next few days I read a new Gollancz pamphlet, *What Buchenwald Really Means*. In the *Left News* for July, 1944, Victor had also published a document from Underground France on the future of Germany.

"We have not forgotten," it ran, "that the German resistance movement was the first to rise up against the Nazis. . . . We shall not forget you, our murdered friends. We shall try and help your children to create a new fatherland."

I recalled that Victor himself, by publishing *The Brown Book of the Hitler Terror*, had been in 1933 one of the first to emphasise the "beastly atrocities" which were then as wholly disregarded by right-wing British politicians as by German civilians. These civilians, for whom protest meant death or prison, were now being condemned for "tolerating Buchenwald" by many of the safe British who had done exactly the same.

How far, I asked myself, were the discoveries in the camps being "played up" by news-reel and radio to prevent the development of a growing sense of guilt for Germany's razed cities? What essential moral difference divided the murder of prisoners in concentration camps from the incineration of refugees in Dresden or the drowning of mothers and children in the Ruhr valleys below the shattered dams?

Beside me, on my desk at the cottage, lay a collection of dispatches, which I had used for recent Letters, from perturbed war correspondents attached to the advancing armies. They could all, I thought, have been summed up by the glum description of barbarism in the book called *Leviathan* by the seventeenth-century philosopher, Thomas Hobbes.

"No arts, no letters, no society, and which is worst of all, continuall fear and danger of violent death, and the life of man solitary, poore, nasty, brutish and short."

On March 14th the *News Chronicle*'s correspondent, S. L. Solon, had called Cologne "End-of-the-World City". His dispatch had continued: "When the sun grows cold and the last cities on a crumbling earth are dying ruins, I suppose that the surviving remnants of human life will live as they live to-day in the bowels of Cologne."

To the *Evening Standard* Anne Matheson had contributed a later and similar description of Nuremberg. "It is as though some giant had crashed his fist down. . . . Nuremberg has been wiped from the face of the earth."

Even George Orwell, who had dismissed *Seed of Chaos* with contempt the previous year, now expressed deep misgivings in *The Observer* for April 8th.

"The people of Britain have never felt easy about the bombing of civilians . . . but what they still have not grasped—thanks to their own comparative immunity—is the frightful destructiveness of modern war and the long period of impoverishment that now lies ahead of the world as a whole. To walk through the ruined cities of Germany is to feel an actual doubt about the continuity of civilisation."

Other correspondents described the near-famine in Belgium and France, with their dying invalids and children; the helpless agony of half-drowned Holland, robbed of food, heat and light; the marauding "displaced persons" crowding the roads of Europe. An army thirteen million strong of Poles, Russians, Czechs, and other miscellaneous Europeans, they had spent years as slaves of the Nazi machine and now, penniless and starving, lived by terrorising the helpless civilian population into parting with their last scraps of bread. Just so the pillaging soldiers had massacred, raped and looted after the Thirty Years' War.

Who, I inquired of the silent Forest, would help these people? Who would feed them when the end came? Mrs. Luce, I remembered, had courageously supported with her voice and pen the Famine Relief movement in the United States. My handful of politically-conscious Letter readers had been so anxious to help that, when I reported the willingness of *Entr' Aide Française* to receive a limited quantity of food for undernourished French children, they had almost overwhelmed the little relief organisation with gifts from their rations.

But they were not typical. The previous autumn I had noticed, in correspondence published by a Sunday newspaper on the preparations being made to help post-war Europe, a letter from two "Bournemouth mothers":

"WHAT ABOUT US? While no one is averse to feeding the starving peoples of Europe (in reason), it is surely too much to expect us to undergo a prolonged period of food rationing after the war. Let some of the 'fruits of victory' be tangible and edible—quickly!"

When I published a short reply the following week, maintaining that we and our families should be ready to face rationing for another decade—as in the end we had to—if this would help Europe's children, a spate of abusive letters swelled my post-bag. Expressions of gratitude came, it was true, from a Norwegian, a Belgian, and a German refugee, who stated briefly: "I am one of Germany's starved children of the last war. Many of us have never recovered." But my fellow-countrymen tended to suggest that if I did not object to further rationing I must be a food-hoarder, and ought to live in Germany where I should be welcome. An anonymous postcard inquired: "Are you simple, or just plain 'nuts'?"

From that time onwards, my question had repeated itself. Would U.N.R.R.A., the new international relief organisation, be able to fulfil all Europe's post-war needs? If not, who else would feed the starving? Who else would care?

(12)

In the midst of hell, heaven surrounded me. A letter to G. in San Francisco described "a week of mid-June in mid-April".

"The loveliness of the blossom and the young leaves is impossible to take in properly. All the budding trees seem to be shouting 'Alleluia!', as though the war were quite over and the world recovering, instead of still bleeding so profusely from its wounds. Our purple lilac is covered with blooms and filling tne little garden with scent, and the oak is out before the ash, meaning according to the wiseacres a long hot summer. But somehow all this loveliness makes me miss you more."

The serenity of the Forest lent an incredible quality to the news now racing in from Europe: the meeting of Russian and American troops at Torgau, where the last sanguinary battles of the Seven Years' War had been fought; the surrender of Dittmar, Berlin's famous radio commentator, to the Americans; Goering's flight with his family, and valuables worth five million pounds, to an "unknown destination".

Mussolini too had tried to flee, and been captured by Partisans on the Swiss frontier. Next day they shot him on the spot where fifteen of their colleagues had been executed by Fascists, and strung him up, like a slaughtered turkey, beside the body of his young mistress in the streets of Milan.

"During the past few weeks I . . . have had the sense of being continually banged on the head with a very large bludgeon," I wrote to my Letter readers a week later. Listening on Sunday April 29th to the grim details of Mussolini's end being reported in suave tones by the B.B.C. announcer of the midnight news, I felt disturbed because I reacted so little. Having spent nearly six years in attempting to help keep alive the sensibilities of others, had I ended by losing my own capacity for horror and pity?

When rumour, outrunning the papers, reported that Hitler too had died, raving mad, in Berlin, the pace of events overtook the power to follow them. That night a mournful broadcast, relayed from Schleswig-Holstein, confirmed the astonishing news: "Our Führer, Adolf Hitler, has fallen this afternoon at his command post in the Reich Chancellery, fighting to the last breath against Bolshevism for Germany."

Bolshevism, personified by the victorious Russians, now held Berlin; behind them the huge German armament factories fed the Soviet machine.

Innumerable attempts to forecast the end of these world-dominating personalities had been made during the past decade, but not one prophet had ventured to predict that, within three critical weeks, Roosevelt, Hitler and Mussolini would all vanish from the international stage. Yet even the sensational coincidence of their exit—so grandly dignified for the one, so grimly brutal for the others—was soon submerged in the cumulative story of German chaos, defeat and surrender.

It seemed strange to be alone, separated from my family, with the war ending in sombre drama. Inevitably I compared these final days with the last hours of the First War, but then I had been alone indeed. At the forthcoming victory celebrations I should only be physically alone; though Edward and Winifred, who might have shared these cataclysmic weeks with me, were gone, G. was in San Francisco, and John and Shirley no further away than their schools.

Long ago, before I married G., I had feared that if we had children a new series of catastrophes such as I had known between 1914 and 1918 might involve them in their turn. Those catastrophes had come, but the children, however uncomfortable their armour-growing processes might be for others, had accepted them as their destiny and faced the future unafraid.

(13)

One of the reporters who described the final capitulations in Montgomery's tent on the Lüneburger Heide and Eisenhower's headquarters in a school-house near Rheims wrote quite simply: "It was all over now." When the B.B.C. announced that V.E. Day was imminent, I hurried through sudden rain to the Southampton bus and went up to London.

"According to A.P. flash war ends 2.41 a.m. this Monday," G. wrote me next day. "After the penny-dreadful dramas and horrors of Mussolini and the Wagnerian end of Adolf, the end of the war, in a San Francisco concerned with the Pacific and depressed about the Conference, finds no excitement and the 'extras' scarcely being bought up."

He told me later that the *New York Post* announced the conclusion of the war in Europe under the headline: "Now We Must Crush the Japs!" But to the much-enduring citizens of London, it was the Japanese war that seemed unreal. Long before it started, they had suffered and died from the bombs which, after six interminable years, had ceased to fall on their heads.

On the afternoon of V.E. Day, I went to Whitehall alone. I had promised, after hearing the announcement, to go to my mother for tea; again, as in 1918, I should leave Westminster for the parental home. My father was dead and my mother lived in Chelsea, not Kensington; these seemed to be the only personal differences between the two Victory days. For a moment, as I made my way to Whitehall through the multiplying throng, the years which divided those days vanished like a puff of smoke blown away by the winds of time.

No doubt, through friends in the Government, I could have watched the crowds from the comfort of a ministerial window, but I preferred to join them on the pavement. I had been with them there—the "poor plain people" who suffered most from war—in 1918, and there, standing on almost the same spot, I would be with them again in 1945.

But in 1918 it had been chill, dreary November, with the street lamps, after four years of darkness, shining like a fairy-tale through the London gloom. Now it was May, a sultry afternoon with beams of warm sunshine struggling through thunder-clouds which pressed down like a low ceiling upon the unforgettable scene.

In spite of the flags, bells and streamers, the now harmless bombers circling Westminster Abbey, and the sense of danger departed which London at the close of the First War hardly knew, the waiting multitudes never surged into that outburst of relief known to history as Armistice Day.

When Winston Churchill, complete with bowler hat and cigar, left Downing Street for the House of Commons, they surrounded his car and cheered him with an enthusiasm which convinced him that he was destined to remain their Prime Minister in the years immediately ahead. But they listened to his voice announcing the end of the war in a silence which, for a long moment, remained unbroken.

It is only civilians far from the line who burst into noisy rejoicing. The people of London had seen their fellow-citizens killed and their homes destroyed; they had known danger, terror, apprehension and relief. Because of these things, their attitude to war's end resembled the attitude of soldiers at the front.

They had acquiesced in evil deeds and at their worst were capable of cruelty and greed, but they had also endured with patience much wrong done to them by others. Suddenly I had an overwhelming impression of their essential goodness; a goodness which could transform the world if they worked with their Creator instead of blindly joining His enemies.

And then came a strange experience, the confirmation of a long-growing certainty which even now was not instantaneous. Not for days could I begin to put it into words, and many months were needed for its full realisation. Just how the change had occurred I still cannot explain; I knew only that through humiliation had come an assurance which I had learned neither from deep grief nor from resounding success, and had sceptically repudiated after Winifred's death. Now, out of all the errors and confusions, had emerged a certainty so immense that the sad record of human fallibility dropped back into its appropriate though significant place.

Walking dumbly and blindly up Whitehall at the end of the First War, I had felt no conviction of any divine principle, any Easter morning, any meeting again. Now, walking up Whitehall at the end of the Second, I became deeply aware that, in the past five years, my attitude had changed.

I could not yet believe in the Easter morning and the meeting again; I did not expect to see Edward or Roland or Winifred in any future conceivable by human consciousness. But of the existence of a benign Rule, a spiritual imperative behind the anarchy and chaos of man's wilful folly, I was now wholly assured; the superficial faith which the First War destroyed had been replaced by an adult conviction. Like the girl student in *Glorious Morning*, I knew that God lived, and that the sorrow and suffering in the world around me had come because men refused to obey His laws. The self-interested, provocative policies which had driven mankind to the edge of the abyss seemed to supply incontrovertible testimony that an opposite policy—the way of God, the road of the Cross—would produce an opposite result.

He was not, I thought, omnipotent in any magic or automatic sense, but only with the co-operation of the creature whom He had made in His image and endowed with free will. So far, throughout the centuries of human history, that co-operation had been rejected by all but a few, but it was none the less attainable; it lay in the divine potentialities with which we, sinners as we were, had been invested by the mere fact of our humanity. And once it was attained, but only then, God's Kingdom would come and we should build Jerusalem on earth as it was in Heaven.

(14)

Before the war ended, the National Peace Council had arranged a mass meeting for May 30th, 1945, at the Central Hall, Westminster. Professor Norman Bentwich had promised to be chairman, and the speakers, who included Victor Gollancz, the Rev. Leslie Weatherhead, C. E. M. Joad, and myself, were asked to support a demand for "Real Peace This Time!"

To the astonishment of the organisers, this meeting turned into one of the largest demonstrations ever known in the history of the peace movement. Over five thousand people tried to get into a hall which held less than three thousand; the unsuccessful crowded two overflow meetings, and the residue attempted to hold a rally in the street. The police eventually moved them on to Hyde Park, where at about 11 p.m. I made my fourth speech.

Even outside a popular cinema, I had never seen such a crowd. As I struggled to penetrate through the milling hundreds blocking every entrance to the Central Hall, an elderly woman stood firmly in my way.

"May I get by?" I pleaded. "I'm one of the speakers."

She glared at my insignificant person with the utter scorn due to an unscrupulous imposter, and hissed at me angrily.

"Oh, yes! You're *Vera Brittain*, I suppose!"

I gave it up and appealed to a policeman, who piloted me round the large building to a back entrance.

Inside the hall, even standing room was at a premium; scores of young listeners crowded the platform steps and hung precariously over the balcony rails. When Victor Gollancz, in a vehement and uncompromising speech, demanded the return of the Left parties in the forthcoming election, the response was a waterfall roar such as I had heard only at a stadium. Hardly less impressive was the answer to my own appeal for the end of the "non-fraternisation" order now imposed on the British troops occupying Germany.

One or two weekly publications subsequently referred to that expression of mass emotion, but the meeting, spectacularly successful though it had been, was virtually boycotted by the ordinary Press. This policy was not only unimaginative, but completely stupid from the standpoint of the Press itself. A perspicacious reporter at that meeting could have forecast the result of the General Election.

The imminent dissolution of Parliament was already filling the newspapers when G. returned from San Francisco, and we travelled together to the Labour Party Conference at Blackpool. Already, on October 6th, 1944, the Party had issued a statement repudiating the 1918 expedient of a "coupon" election. Labour, it declared, would go before the country "with a practical policy based on the Socialist principles in which it believes".

In April this policy had been expounded in a new manifesto, *Let Us Face the Future*. Four days after publication, Parliamentary recriminations between Ernest Bevin and Brendan Bracken heralded the break-up of the Coalition.

At Blackpool the atmosphere was tense with expectation. In an impressive speech which staked his claim to the Foreign Secretaryship if Labour were returned, Ernest Bevin, still Minister of Labour, told his audience that if the war had lasted a few months longer, rockets at the rate of five a minute would have devastated London.

On May 23rd Churchill resigned, and a brief "Caretaker Government" assumed control. Three weeks later the longest Long Parliament passed into history, and the election campaign began.

Though G. found this early election disconcerting because its date cut out all hope of a new constituency, both he and I, still dominated by memories of the 1918 "khaki election", expected a Churchill victory. At a mass meeting to support Herbert Morrison in Lewisham he plunged into the campaign, while Shirley, with even greater zeal, devoted all her out-of-school hours to her local contest.

By the time G. left London to support Labour in Staffordshire, blue election posters appeared on hoardings throughout the country.

HELP HIM FINISH THE JOB!

From the standpoint of a people hoping to share in the constructive shaping of the post-war world, this slogan was as uninspired an example of backward-looking propaganda as the cry of "SAFETY FIRST" which lost the Tories the election of 1929.

On the eve of the poll, G. returned to take the chair at a mass demonstration in Chelsea Town Hall. Then, on July 5th, the shrill crescendo of propaganda throughout the country gave way to sudden silence.

They were all voting now—the young soldiers who had read

Guilty Men and *Testament of Youth* on distant battlefields and, unlike my reader in Abyssinia, had survived the war; the young airmen compelled to do deeds demanding superhuman heroism which some at least had abominated; the elderly women who believed that there was room in the world for everyone; the working men who had murmured: "T'ain't right, them raids!" when they met a friend whose discretion they could trust.

And their verdict was to be decisive.

(16)

In order that the votes from the Forces might be collected, an interval of three weeks divided the election from its announced result. Between the poll and the declaration I paid a visit to Gloucestershire, and came back with the outline of a new book.

For the first time since 1924, I had taken no part in an election campaign; I could not, I wrote to G., throw off "a curious complete numbness" about politics. Although, this time, the war had deprived me of no beloved relative or friend, I found myself overwhelmed by an abysmal fatigue which recalled the sorrow-stricken automatism of 1918.

In June I learned that my former benefactor, Sir John Marriott, to whose encouragement I owed the original escape from Buxton to Oxford, had died at a great age, but I could not rouse myself to attend his funeral or even write to his family. The news that his younger Oxford contemporary, the Principal of Hertford who as Dean coached Winifred and myself in International Relations, had died tragically in a mental hospital left me even more indifferent. I reawakened only later to the debt which I owed Mr. C. R. M. F. Cruttwell, and realised how pitiful was the breakdown from which his brilliant brain never recovered.

My remorseless spate of daily letters now became a crushing burden. Nothing seemed to stop the flood, which had started after *Testament of Youth* and twelve years later was almost undiminished. To G. I confessed myself defeated by the avalanche of mail which had followed the Central Hall meeting.

"Just how to deal with people with genuine needs but no sense of proportion, whose attentions if they are encouraged even the tiniest bit become like the consequences of pulling a large lavatory chain, is a problem I have never solved."

Struggling ineffectively to satisfy my correspondents, I did not believe I was suffering only from the war-weariness which I shared with everyone else. This abnormal lethargy was not to be explained

366

by bombing, or shortages, or prolonged periods of suspense, or even by G.'s political setback at St. Helens, which I felt the more keenly for not wishing to appear disappointed.

Three months afterwards I was to find a similar lethargy in Norway, whose unarmed civilians resisted the Nazi invaders to the end and then fell into untypical inertia. Gradually I began to suspect that for myself also the long struggle against hostility and suspicion was exacting its cost. While opposition continued I could sustain my part, but now it was ending I felt as though I had just emerged from a serious illness. Finally recognising the reason, I remembered too that the help I needed was there on request.

The previous year my Quaker friend Stephen Hobhouse, periodically incapacitated by physical weakness arising from prolonged imprisonment during the First World War, had written me of the benefit that he had derived from a nature-cure home at Coleford, in the Forest of Dean. I had visited the place myself for a few experimental days, and now asked if I could be received for more thorough treatment.

Thomas and Dorothy Elliot were well-known naturopaths, who had worked in Bristol until their hydro was commandeered by the Government. Like the Chelsea Babies' Club, they concerned themselves with the prevention of illness rather than its cure. Though they were not Quakers, they had a similar conception of mental and physical health, and they did not find my ideas about human behaviour revolutionary or strange. Years afterwards I wrote Dorothy Elliot, a handsome woman with an incomparable serenity of manner, to acknowledge my real debt for that visit to Coleford.

"I shall never forget what it meant to come into a community where I was regarded neither as a fool nor a traitor, and how well you understood that what I needed then was just rest and that complete unquestioning acceptance of all I was and tried to be."

She replied in her usual kind and comforting fashion.

"How well I appreciate what you say about your work during the war. If some of those who were hostile could see the young people as I saw them eagerly look forward to your peace Letter, they would realise what a work you were doing apart from anything else."

(17)

At Coleford, wrapped in a quiet happiness which I had not known for years, I walked or rode over the fertile Gloucestershire country, visiting Chepstow Castle and Tintern Abbey against its background of wooded hills.

"The Abbey," I noted in my diary, "tall, grey, slender, the stone tracery of its East and rose windows still perfect, with a carpet of green grass, and green plants springing from its high stones, is like a perfect anthem, an aspiring oratorio."

As I walked and dreamed, I thought out the plot of my new novel. The idea had first come to me, during the grey months of the preceding winter, by way of "compensating" for the bitter reviews of *Account Rendered* and the impatient onslaughts of the war-weary children.

Shutting out those painful distractions, I began to collect notes for the story subsequently called *Born 1925*. By making its older central figure a clergyman with a position and ideas similar to Dick Sheppard's, I could "write away" the humiliations arising from war-time unpopularity. By giving him a son and daughter of comparable age to John and Shirley (actually I made them two years older because I wanted the book to end with the boy a full-fledged adult), I could rid myself of the soreness caused by the critical attacks of ruthless adolescence.

In this novel the Elliots' house became Evansford Manor, where Robert Carbury, V.C., spent his convalescence after the all but fatal wounds received at the Battle of Loos. On Symonds Yat, the giant rock which overlooks five counties above the circular curve of the Wye, Robert experienced the "conversion" which sent him into the Church and ultimately exposed him to war-time execration.

Had Dick survived to see the Second War he would have been treated, I thought, as a quisling, for I did not believe that he would have made his Christian witness with the discretion which kept the brave Bishop of Chichester within the confines of respectability.

One late evening as the sun was setting, I climbed a stile leading to a meadow opposite the Elliots' home. On the path through long lush grass now luxuriant with meadow-sweet, I met a young man with his arm round a girl.

The girl was crying, and the man said "Good-night"—to distract my attention, I thought, from her to himself. I answered "Good-night", and walked away.

At the end of the field I leaned against another stile, and watched the sunset turn rose and flame above the Welsh hills beyond Monmouth. Somewhere, invisible in the wooded valley, lay the twisting Wye. The boy and girl had taken my thoughts far back into the past, and I remembered how Roland had put his arm round me on a cliff at Lowestoft in the last summer of his life.

Returning to the present of which he had been deprived, I meditated on the Elliots' work, and the well-founded conviction of their

368

staff that life, healthy and energetic, could be defended by sane living against the onset of disease. I remembered G.'s lost friends, Lord Lothian and Wendell Willkie, dying in their fifties from illnesses which could have been prevented soon enough to give them many more years of valuable service. I thought too of our celebration, the previous Sunday, of the eightieth birthday of the ever-young, ever-vigorous, playwright Laurence Housman.

Then I recalled the state of the world, and gazing at the deep afterglow above the Monmouth hills, found myself passionately praying for a further share of time.

(18)

From literary and religious contemplation, I returned to London for the declaration of the poll with its tremendous practical consequences for Britain.

Throughout July 26th, we sat beside the radio and listened to the astonishing results coming in. That night the evening newspapers appeared with bumper headlines.

SOCIALISTS IN. BRITAIN SWINGS TO THE LEFT AND THE
TORY GOVERNMENT GOES OUT IN A LANDSLIDE.

The Left Parties boasted a majority of 199 over all their opponents; more than 200 seats had been won.

When the result was certain we took Shirley to Transport House, where she congratulated a jubilant Herbert Morrison. Then, at the Central Hall, we heard the newly-elected London Labour M.P.s make two-minute speeches. Not only they but all the other Labour Members were overwhelmed by the support they had received. Former M.P.s came back with majorities of twenty and thirty thousand; the winners of "marginal" seats were safely elected by five or six thousand votes.

"Whole Churchill clique defeated except the old man himself," my diary noted that night, but went on to record the cold douche administered to our own calculations. "Amid surging feelings of excitement we both felt personally stricken because G. hadn't stood."

The Staffordshire constituency of Bilston, where a couple of years earlier he had lost the nomination by two votes, had been won with a majority of 16,000.

Apart from the safe Bilston, we had discussed other less-than-marginal seats of which most—though only until the next election—had gone Labour. San Francisco, a natural attraction after years of isolation, had triumphed over these slender chances owing to the

369

counsel offered by official advisers, genuinely deceived as we nearly all were. In June 1942 I had been wiser, and in Letter 84 had committed myself to a prophecy which had now come true.

"Once the war is over, official British disclaimers of all present interest in discussing the post-war world will certainly be remembered against this country by a forward-looking people. . . . Most governments behave as though they were immortal; they even endeavour to intimidate the ordinary citizen and crush his initiative by this wishful presumption. Actually, in any democracy, it can almost be guaranteed that a government which has been over long in office will be thrown out of power immediately the people are able to re-assert their will, and supplanted by another with a totally different outlook for perhaps a decade."

Why had I subsequently been blind to the illuminating portents—two by-elections won by Independent candidates in the spring of 1944; the astonishing sales of *Above All Nations*; the crowds struggling to attend the peace meeting at the Central Hall? Now G.'s chance of getting into the House was gone for several years; again he would have to look elsewhere than to Party politics for the opportunity to implement his constructive thinking.

For several days the excitement, no longer suppressed, of ordinary Londoners overflowed into their acts and conversations. Typical of many others was the response of my Chelsea hairdresser, a small middle-aged Socialist who had secretly hated the war. He had palpably found my visits a relief amongst those of other local residents who did not share his sentiments in that Conservative borough.

Keeping an appointment shortly after the Labour victory, I found him almost in tears with joy. When I noticed in the window a few packets of scarce "invisible" hairpins and asked if he could spare me one, he seized the precious bundles with both hands and held them out to me.

"Take two!" he exclaimed. "Take three! Take four!"

And in spite of my protests that I was getting more than my share, the four packets of hairpins were thrust exuberantly into my purse.

(19)

For months after the election, post-mortems continued. The United States especially found the result inexplicable.

"It seemed incredible to millions in this country," announced a typical syndicated article on July 30th, "when news came that the

British people, not long since in deadly peril from a ruthless foe, had rejected at the polls the man without whom there would have been no free election. . . . Not even his political opponents question that the British people, and the world as well, owe him a mighty debt. And yet, at the first opportunity following the German collapse, the British electorate overwhelmingly vote him out of power."

Why did they? Innumerable explanations of that silent revolution were offered in scores of newspapers. The election, they said, had been forced too early; the common citizen wanted a change; the campaign, unskilfully conducted, had used "bogeys" and "stunts" insulting to the intelligence of an electorate which looked for a positive programme of reconstruction, and could not be stampeded into distrusting the honest men and women who had shared Churchill's responsibilities for five perilous years.

All these arguments were relevant, especially the last. But the real clue had been given by Howard Spring in an unpretentious article which appeared in *St. Martin's Review*, the monthly magazine of St. Martin-in-the-Fields, for September 1942.

"I think there was a breach, for some time before the war, between what the people wanted and what the politicians were doing. It was the sense of the widening of this breach that produced the dreadful feeling of frustration in so many minds. If ever again comes the chance of thinking about these things, we shall have to ask ourselves how this may be avoided."

Throughout the war, like the seed growing secretly, the thinking had been done and the private questions asked. As one of the inquirers, I had recalled in Letter 127 the reaction against cruelty and hatred which created the League of Nations in 1920, and suggested that we should see such a reaction again—"probably the more intense and prolonged just because the war has been longer drawn out and its leaders have sunk to even deeper levels of callousness and brutality."

The election of 1945 embodied this reaction; it gave the British people the first opportunity to voice their mute revolt against the evils committed in their name. Most of them had regarded these evils as "necessary", but that did not mean that they approved, or wanted any longer to be led by the men responsible for political vengeance.

This mute revolt was a manifestation which Churchill, so grieved by his rejection, never understood. In his War Histories—like Sir Samuel Hoare in *Nine Troubled Years*—he denounces as criminally irresponsible the drive towards peace and disarmament in which, during the nineteen-thirties, the Labour Party, the orthodox peace groups led by the League of Nations Union, and their revolutionary pacifist wing then combined. But that widespread impulse was far from irresponsible; it represented a desire to apply new standards to politics which was none the less sincere and significant because the times were out of joint. This desire and the reasons behind it, difficult to understand by old-style politicians who saw national power as their country's greatest good, explained Churchill's defeat at the polls.

In the first volume of *The Second World War*, Churchill subsequently stated that a responsible Minister cannot be guided by that "last word in Christian ethics", the Sermon on the Mount. This admission that the leader of a sovereign State could not also be a good Christian possessed at least the merit of frankness.

But between the wars the British people had been educated by innumerable peace meetings to desire a new kind of State with a different type of leader. When civilisation again broke down and war followed, they chose an old-style politician to deal with an old-type situation. But once the war was over, they no longer wished to uphold the reactionary standards which had been imposed but never wholly accepted. They wanted to renew the endeavour to bring, as Mahatma Gandhi had brought, religious values into political life; they desired a new Britain which at least attempted to take the Sermon on the Mount as its guide.

Churchill could not interpret his dismissal because he never percieved the fundamental difference between the pacifism which he scorned, and the pre-war appeasement pursued by lethargic politicians anxious to avoid uncomfortable contact with reality. Throughout his history of the Second War, he confuses a creed with a timid political expedient.

The nation was grateful to him for rescuing it from a predicament in which it need never have been placed, but the individual who had won its love, its allegiance and its tears had been Dick Sheppard, the uncompromising follower of Christ who in 1937 had defeated Churchill at the Glasgow Rectorial Election. It knew— dimly or clearly according to the measure of each person's political consciousness—that the Second War did not begin with the miscalculations of Neville Chamberlain or even with the paranoiac dreams of Adolf Hitler. Its origins lay in the errors and humiliations which followed the First, and for these the old-style politicians had been responsible.

The Labour Party was not of course equal to the overwhelming demands now made upon it; the war-weary, fallible men and women who composed it could not suddenly develop into the archangels for whom the electorate looked. In their eagerness to get back to the pursuit of moral objectives, the British people credited the Party with ideals which it had pursued earlier in the century, but was now gradually to relinquish under the corrupting influence of power.

The processes by which "power corrupts" are perhaps inevitable, since the idealistic blue-prints offered by unelected leaders too often prove incompatible with the actual exercise of authority. But the purposes of those leaders, though impaired and truncated, were never wholly lost. For the next five years the astonished statesmen expected to play the part of Titans continued, amid the incredible chaos of a disintegrated world, to visualise as in a glass darkly their intractable ends.

(20)

The new Parliament was sworn-in on August 1st, the day before the Potsdam Report announced that an Allied Control Council would exercise supreme authority over the Germans. Already the Iron Curtain concealed prodigious tragedy in the Eastern half of Europe.

After the election results had been announced, the children and I went to the cottage for their summer holidays. They were happy now because warm weather had replaced the winter's cruel cold, and there was no more tension either at home or at school.

By his own wish John had left Harrow, though Dr. Moore had wanted him to sit for a Cambridge Scholarship; next term he would make an experimental beginning at the London School of Architecture. While we were still counting the years, the European War had ended seven months before his eighteenth birthday.

With peace would eventually return many once familiar accessories of daily living which Shirley, at least, could not remember; unrationed petrol, butterscotch and bananas, and a plentiful supply of the books and magazines which she now read perpetually in trains, buses, her bedroom and her bath.

At Allum Green, between the devastation of Hiroshima by the atom bomb and the two "V.J." days which celebrated victory over Japan, I learned what was happening to the English edition of *Account Rendered*, which amid the pressure of events I had almost forgotten.

To my publisher in New York I now described the totally new atmosphere in Britain since I had last heard from him early in June.

"In two months everything has changed beyond recognition. . . .

The strangest thing here has been the complete change of political climate for some of us, and the breath of fresh air that blew through the country when everyone realised what everyone else had been thinking and it was at last possible to say it aloud. One of the odd minor results (though not quite minor for me) has been the effect on *Account Rendered*."

The 50,000 copies which comprised the first edition had, in fact, all been sold before publication. The results were breath-taking, for Macmillan announced a prospective royalties cheque of over £5,000.

After receiving their letter I ran through the Forest to the bridge over the Highland Water, where a series of excited dreams temporarily eclipsed the collapsing war. Enough money could now be set aside to cover both children's college expenses, and I could send my friends in the Peace Pledge Union a more substantial gift than the £50 saved for their treasurer, Corder Catchpool, as a thank-offering for the war's end. We could reconstruct the bomb-shaken, dilapidated cottage, and repair immediately the raid damage at 2 Cheyne Walk, where we were returning in September. G. and I would travel far and wide, which at last was possible even for me . . .

Then I remembered. This large, unexpected sum, not provided for in my contract by advance royalty payments, had all been technically earned in one income-tax year.

By the oddest of ironies, the chief beneficiary from a story which had grown in my mind for half a decade, occupied two full years because it had to be done twice over, been condemned in America for reasons which did not exist when it was written, and finally achieved a spectacular sale in England, was the British Treasury.

(21)

On August 12th G. wrote me briefly: "We used to 'liquidate' classes; we now 'vaporise' humanity."

Six days earlier the first atom bomb had fallen on Hiroshima, to be followed by a second on Nagasaki. This, the logical development of obliteration bombing, was genocide, naked and without compunction. The unpopular protests against "saturation" now appeared, not merely as an attempt to limit the cruelty of war, but as a plea for the continued existence of mankind.

The evening papers of August 7th breathlessly announced in gigantic headlines: "THE WORLD WAITS". It was to wait for ten years before the full consequences of that superlative atrocity became apparent. Even from a military standpoint it had no justification; Japan's offer of surrender through Stalin before the bomb fell subsequently emerged from the fog of contemporary uncertainties. Four days after the massacre at Hiroshima she surrendered officially, and the Far Eastern War ended at another turning point in history.

Shortly afterwards a letter with 31 signatures appeared in the British Press; they included the names of Benjamin Britten, Sir Osbert Sitwell and Lady Pethick-Lawrence. Among the rest were G.'s and mine.

"The perpetration of this crime," it ran, "reduces to hypocrisy the self-constituted right of the Allied Nations to put 'war criminals' on trial. What moral difference is there between Nazi 'extermination camps', and the mass extermination of helpless civilians in Hiroshima and Nagasaki? The Allied leaders and those whom they represent should rather be entreating God's forgiveness for their misuse of the cosmic forces which He alone can be trusted to control."

Nine years afterwards, when the "H Bomb" succeeded the "A Bomb", H. M. Tomlinson wrote with bitter truth in the British Press that "the laboratory has had priority over the altar". On the same day an Oxford correspondent sent in an even more relevant comment; it consisted only of a short quotation from *The Tempest*.

> "The cloud capp'd towers, the gorgeous palaces,
> The solemn temples, the great globe itself,
> Yea, all which it inherits, shall dissolve;
> And, like this insubstantial pageant faded,
> Leave not a rack behind."

Sitting in the cottage garden on August 10th, 1945, I tried to compass with my finite mind the infinite event, and, failing completely, fell back in a letter to G. on personal issues.

"Just heard that the war with Japan is over—but at what a cost. Well—thank God! . . . John should live his span of life out now, if only we can achieve moral control of the atom bomb, which automatically makes armies, navies, and frontiers things of the past."

In spite of the world cataclysm beyond comprehension, I became increasingly aware of a deep thankfulness which submerged even the guilty sense that too many others were sad and suffering for joy to be appropriate. How different was the end of this war from the end of the last! Then, everybody who really counted for me was gone; now, our small family circle had survived intact the raids, shipwrecks, and perils of war-time travel by land, sea and air.

The Second War had taken only a privilege far less important

375

than those whom I loved—prestige. I had lost, especially in America, the asset which publishers and lecture agents called "good publicity".

It did not matter. Though the confidence in continuous achievement created by the success of *Testament of Youth* had vanished, a new confidence in man's relation to God had taken its place. Sooner or later the small band of war-time witnesses would find their niche in history's temple, even though the same anonymity which shrouded the cathedral-builders of Europe might eclipse their names.

I went on with my letter to G.

"I don't want to come up to town and rejoice over the Japs, who have been defeated even more brutally than the Germans. But I do feel almost as if, so far as I personally am concerned, the 'Poor Catherine' fairy-tale quoted at the beginning of *Testament of Youth* really was prophetic. However, there's still time to go before that can be proved. The atom bomb, and the fact that this horribly demoralised generation actually has the responsibility for deciding whether the human race is to continue or not, are not exactly sources of encouragement. Everything depends on how deep the revulsion against war really is, and how quickly it comes to the surface."

Outside the open summer-house where I was writing, the little garden drowsed in August sunshine. Red Admiral butterflies, their scarlet wings like jewels against the deep yellow of sunflowers and golden-rod, flitted from clump to clump exactly as they had flitted in September 1939. But only a few miles across the English Channel beyond the Forest, incredible devastation which I now knew that I was soon to see gave the lie to the illusion of serenity created by summer beauty. Could any of us hope for the "happy old age" which "poor Catherine", sacrificing joy in youth, had demanded of her Destiny in Andrew Lang's story?

If within the next few years mankind did not conquer the evil in itself which brought war and destruction, human civilisation would perish from its own wickedness, and the scene of the experiment vanish into the darkness whence consciousness had arisen. The vital conflict of the future would lie between the living philosophy of a spiritual faith, and the materialist philosophy of economic and military power.

The war was over; a new age was beginning; but man had learned how to destroy his life on earth, and sooner or later, unless he found and followed his God, he would use that knowledge.

PART III

"Experience is not what happens to a man; it is what a man does with that which happens to him."

MARGARET M. HARVEY, Swarthmore Lecture, 1942.

CHAPTER TEN

THE TRACK OF THE STORM

"You stood so proudly on the flowing Rhine,
Your history mankind's, your climbing spires
Crowned with the living light that man desires
To gild his path from bestial to divine.
To-day, consumed by war's unpitying fires,
You lie in ruins, weeping for your dead,
Your shattered monuments the funeral pyres
Of humble men whose days and dreams are fled.

Perhaps, when passions die and slaughters cease,
The mothers on whose homes destruction fell,
Who wailing sought their children through the hell
Of London, Warsaw, Rotterdam, Belgrade,
Will seek Cologne's sad women, unafraid,
And cry: 'God's cause is ours. Let there be peace!' "

V.B., Lament for Cologne*

(1)

IN AUGUST 1945 I said good-bye to frustration, though not, for months, to the war. During the two following years I was to see far more of its results than I had experienced in England, and even within the next few weeks was to learn how near the fabric of civilisation had come to damage beyond repair.

The war had lasted six years minus one month. It had been one year and eight months longer than the First War, which continued for four years, three months and seven days. For my "Class 1914" generation, war had claimed an entire decade of our active lives.

Throughout the world, huge casualty lists had wiped out many survivors from that generation, and in several countries had decimated, even to the youngest, its successor. These casualties, it was true, had not removed almost exclusively young men between

* *The Friend*, June 4th, 1942.

twenty and thirty; they had been more biologically distributed between soldiers and civilians, men and women, the old and the young. But their numbers were staggering.

Five years afterwards, statistics from official reports showed that the United Kingdom and the United States had each lost nearly a million men and women. But in Germany and Italy the figures, for dead, wounded and captured, amounted to eight and a half million; in Japan the loss of one and a half million included the 306,545 dead, injured and missing at Hiroshima. The war had reduced the seven million Jews who in 1939 lived in Europe outside Russia to one million and a half; in Poland the Jewish community of three and a half million could count only 100,000 survivors from gas chambers, concentration camps and mass starvation.

In the wake of universal death stalked widespread disillusion, revealing itself in a negative or ruthless attitude among adults, and amidst the young in the "toughness" which was their defensive response to successive disasters. England, though impaired by bombs and austerities, remained essentially herself, but beyond our island lay gigantic areas of devastation in which human suffering and intolerable memories had produced a psychology of despair.

In such a world nobody—least of all myself—imagined that 1945 would bring the "divine normality" which, a quarter of a century earlier, we had expected from 1919. But with the ending of suspicion and restrictions came the return of personal opportunity and the power to further opportunities created by others. How, I now asked myself, could I use my one gift of interpretation through writing and speaking to assist so many in such painful need?

One of the first post-war opportunities came, through the initiative of Victor Gollancz, from the organisation known as Save Europe Now. As early as September 1945, he and a group of colleagues who included the Bishop of Chichester, Professor Gilbert Murray, and Eleanor Rathbone, M.P., issued an "Appeal" to the British people which described the "8,000,000 homeless nomads milling about the areas of the provinces around Berlin", and concluded with a plea for their rescue from mass starvation:

"It is not in accordance with the traditions of this country to allow children—even the children of ex-enemies—to starve. . . . We ask, therefore, all who read this letter, and who share our concern, immediately to send a postcard . . . to 'Save Europe Now' . . . giving their name and address and saying that they will gladly have their rations cut, if thereby alone men, women and children of whatever nationality may be saved from intolerable suffering."

By the end of the month, 10,000 postcards had reached the organisation. Partly in order to help their work by telling my readers about the actual state of the post-war world, I began a new series of fortnightly Letters. I continued these to the end of 1946, and thus added 32 more issues to the 169 written during the war.

Even before we reopened 2 Cheyne Walk, several new invitations to go abroad had reached me. In October 1944 the American Friends Service Committee had asked me to undertake a lecture tour for them "at an early date", but even assuming the belated grant of an exit permit, I had felt that I should not leave while continuing war threatened the children with indefinite dangers. No such misgivings impaired the delight with which, soon after V.E. Day, I received a similar request from the Swedish branch of the Women's International League for Peace and Freedom, supported by my Stockholm publishers, Tidens Förlag. Their letters reached me at Coleford and contributed to the healing process which began there.

Invitations from Denmark and Norway quickly followed the approach from Sweden, and the outlines of a Scandinavian tour appeared. A helpful intermediary between these correspondents and myself was a young English Quaker, Myrtle Wright, now Myrtle Radley, who had been caught by the Nazi invasion while staying at Oslo and remained in Norway till the end of the war.

Re-reading those letters with their Scandinavian signatures— Naima Sahlbom, Signe Höjer, Karl Olson, Else Zeuthen, Marie Lous Mohr—still renews the sense of impending fulfilment which they brought after five years of curtailed movement. With the suddenness of a window flung open, the countries beyond the seas which I was once free to visit had come back within the ambit of my experience.

Not least astonishing was the unexpected co-operativeness of the British Foreign Office.

"Will you kindly let me know, as soon as all your arrangements are definitely made, on what dates you will be in each Scandinavian capital, so that I may inform H.M. Missions concerned?" wrote a representative of the Cultural Department. With this official support, my passage through the Scandinavian Legations was guaranteed.

These arrangements were continuing at an orthodox pace when a still more dramatic proposal came out of the blue. In view of my interest in Holland, wrote John Marsh, the Press Officer attached to the Help Holland Council, would I care to join a party of "half-a-dozen distinguished writers" who were going to the Netherlands in order to describe to the British public "the dire straits" of the Dutch people?

"The visit, which would last three or four days, would be in the second week in September," he added. "It would be made at the direct invitation of the Netherlands Government."

Would I care! As I realised with growing satisfaction that I could fit in the short tour before leaving for Sweden in late September, I wondered to what recent word or action I owed this suggestion. It was true that, by means of the Food Relief Campaign, I had struggled to get food to Holland through the blockade, publicised the agony of the starved and flooded Dutch in my Letter, and urged its readers to support the Help Holland Council.

Without thought of response I had cast my bread on the waters, and now found it after many days.

My travelling companions, I learned, were to be Marjorie Bowen, Godfrey Winn, Olaf Stapledon, and the popular novelist Henrietta Leslie, with her husband, Dr. Peter Schutze. When we had seen the flooded land, the bombed cities, the starving people—to whom an R.A.F. plane had first dropped food on April 29th—we were asked, by articles and lectures, to make them real to England. With undisguised eagerness, I accepted this chance to verify and interpret the facts which I had sought to convey.

(2)

The little Dakota plane skimmed over the North Sea through the fresh early morning of September 13th. Its periphery of hard bucket seats and wartime lack of "amenities" suggested a ramshackle bus loosely wired to a pair of irrelevant wings. In the London which we had left, the Conference of Foreign Ministers assembled to discuss the peace treaties had already reached deadlock.

Opposite me Marjorie Bowen, tall, gaunt, amiably shy, looked increasingly uncomfortable as the plane bumped on its way, but she would have endured much more for Holland, which she had made the scene of several historical novels. Looking down towards the sea through the narrow window, I saw what appeared to be a submerged sandbank a short distance ahead.

"What's that?" I asked a Dutch soldier who sat beside me.

"It is the coast of the Netherlands," he replied.

I realised that we were flying over the Island of Walcheren, still largely under water, though the floods had slowly receded as the gaps made in the dykes by the R.A.F. were closed. Perceiving the red roofs of houses and barns beneath the water, and seeing at intervals the once fertile fields left barren by the hostile sea, I had the strange impression of returning to the Creation and watching the primeval land struggle towards the light from the depths of the ocean.

As we flew over Holland with its bomb-damaged woods and wrecked planes scattered over the ground, I recalled the prosperous little country which had welcomed me in 1936. What had happened to its friendly citizens?—to the cultured Jewish household at Groningen; the cheerful bourgeois family who had entertained me in Amsterdam; the editors, doctors and school-teachers who could then discuss, with a detachment now unbelievable, the Nazi reoccupation of the Rhineland? To-day, thanks to the terrible paradox by which a people's homes and happiness were the cost of "liberation", that past fortune had become a wistful memory of "happier things".

Our plane, by an error, took us on to Eindhoven, which meant a long drive back to our headquarters at The Hague. We piled on two official cars the suit-cases filled with cigarettes, cocoa, toothbrushes, needles, cotton and tape which we had brought for the Dutch people instead of a change of clothing for ourselves.

Everywhere we discovered that bridges were down over the roads and railways which linked the shattered villages along the Waal River; their broken backs trailed in grey water beneath a steel-grey sky. Long stretches of electric railway lay grass-grown and silent, for the Nazis had looted the miles of copper wire which connected the cables. Near Eindhoven the only "trains" we saw had been improvised from painted horse-boxes and were jammed to the doors with standing passengers.

Our programme for the next four days was continuous and exacting; it began at 8.15 a.m. and ended after dark. Since our official guides were naturally concerned to emphasise the sufferings of their country, I received an immediate impression of material devastation in varied forms which suggested a nightmare of destructive ingenuity. Sometimes the devastation was human; at two cemeteries being constructed in a rough field outside Breda for British, Canadian and German dead, blanketfuls of human remains collected from temporary graves lay with their identity disks piled beside them awaiting burial.

We drove on to Walcheren, where heavy rain fell dismally on floating trees and half-submerged houses. A dank smell of sea-saturated earth pervaded the flood-ravaged streets and bombed buildings of once lovely Middelburg. When the rain ceased, Olaf Stapledon hired a small boat and rowed to a half-submerged island; Henrietta Leslie, motherly, lame, over sixty, but indefatigably enterprising, insisted on joining him with her husband.

Meanwhile Marjorie Bowen, Godfrey Winn and I called on the Mayor at Veere. Being a member of the local commission to assess damage, he soon became eloquent over its cost.

"Who is going to pay for all this?" he demanded, including in one dramatic gesture the dreary miles of saturated soil. "The Germans stole our sons, our bicycles, our horses. England must put her foot down and demand that the Germans pay!"

That night, in a small hotel at Breda, I wakefully meditated. After twenty-four hours of bewildering impressions I was beginning to observe what I had come to see—the Dutch people.

Already the lavish meals provided for us by the Government at clubs and hotels had produced a collective bad conscience in our party. But food was not the main problem, for Canadian rations now helped to sustain the people who, whatever their social class, had been driven the previous winter to devour tulip bulbs. The chief shortage appeared to be clothes; so far the Help Holland Council had been able to supply only a fraction of Dutch needs in this comfortless land whence fuel had vanished. Before we left Holland Marjorie Bowen had given away the coat from her back, and the rest of us returned half-clad, with empty suitcases.

At Vucht next day I met, with Godfrey Winn, an even sadder problem. The head of the local Underground, Mrs. Timmenga—the highly respectable image of a ducal housekeeper known to the whole population as "Aunt E."—sent us to inspect the notorious local concentration camp where Dutch collaborators had been collected from all over Holland. There, indefinitely interned, we found a number of small boys who at ten or eleven had been taken from orphanages by the Nazis to work on balloon sites.

On our first night at The Hague, Dr. Hugenholtz of the Dutch Fellowship of Reconciliation had told me that in Rotterdam a thousand delinquent children, orphaned by the air raids, had lived for years on sabotage and looting. Now, under the protection of a Children's Court Judge, they faced a future hardly less uncertain than that of the young collaborators.

The plight of all these helpless children seemed so pitiful that after returning home I wrote to the Press supporting a recent plea by J. B. Priestley for an International Children's Charter. This, I suggested, might fix an age-limit beneath which the responsibility for political error would not fall on children but be borne by the whole community.

From Vucht we drove to Nijmegen and stood on the high green bridge—saved from destruction by nineteen-year-old Jan van Hoof, whom the Nazis shot after he had cut their fuses—and looked into Germany. Although I had visited the crowded cemeteries of Northern France after the First War I had never seen that country as I now saw Holland, with its uncollected dead lying in improvised graves and its fields still perilous from unexploded mines. Whenever we left our cars local guides warned us to stay on the road; the Allies and Nazis, they said, had between them laid five million mines in the Arnhem area alone.

Farmers, anxious to see their land again productive, worked in the fields at the risk of their lives, and parents, seeking food for their children, disregarded danger. In my notebook I recorded the story of a factory owner's family who watched their mother search for mushrooms in Arnhem's mine-infested woods.

"Daddy," inquired the eight-year-old, "will you marry again if Mummy steps on a mine?"

Not even Coventry and Plymouth had prepared me for Arnhem itself. Once reminiscent of Bath, it was now the grim caricature of a city, where the spires and towers of gutted churches rose like ghosts from the obscene rubble which marked the trail of modern war. On the shattered bridge, burned-out tanks lay disintegrating amid the remnants of barbed-wire entanglements half hidden by weeds.

Here the mines had been cleared. Scrambling to the top of the sloping wreck, I stared across the water towards the empty road which reinforcements never quite reached. Over the whole area lay an uncanny silence; no larks rose from the fields, no cattle munched the once blood-stained grass. Only the water bubbled eerily round rusting girders, fallen from the bridge like the jaw-bones of some prehistoric monster.

Long ago, in *La Belle Dame Sans Merci*, Keats had described this desolation:

> "The sedge has wither'd from the lake,
>   And no birds sing."

(3)

I drove back to The Hague with Kapitein Kalff, the Government envoy attached to our party. The memories of Arnhem were too overwhelming for much conversation.

My fifth-floor bedroom at the Central Hotel commanded a wide view of the city. I could almost see the devastated residential area, about the size of Chelsea, which the R.A.F. had accidentally "obliterated" in its search for V.2 sites. Not far away were the numerous empty houses, mostly evacuated by Jews, which a fuel-frantic population had stripped the previous winter of all the wood that desperate hands could tear away. I had seen a terrace where floors, ceilings and bannisters were all gone; from one house a half-staircase hung, as though protesting, unsupported in mid-air.

The bedroom was too high to show me the adjacent provision shops which displayed only cardboard imitations of milk bottles and Dutch cheese; but I knew that, hopefully pressed against these windows, were the faces of perpetually disappointed children with ragged handmade shoes tied to their feet, and their thin bare legs showing the sores left by scabies. This scourge was prevalent throughout Holland owing to the lack of soap and hot water.

Next day we drove to Amsterdam, and joined the Sunday crowds waiting at the Rijks-museum to see the Rembrandts and Vermeers rescued from their wartime hideouts in the sand-dunes. By now it seemed strange to find an undamaged city, but opposite the mansion in which we attended an afternoon reception ran a quiet green canal where many "accidents" had happened to Germans during the war. Its very presence had protected our host against billeting and looting.

From scholars and journalists amongst his guests, I inquired about friends formerly met in Holland. Where was Professor Leo Polak of Groningen? What had become of his wife and daughters?

"He's dead," said a Leiden Professor grimly. "I don't know about his family. Probably dead too."

At Scheveningen next morning we found the Atlantic Wall, a reinforced coastal dyke containing dug-outs, guarded by young boys from the wartime Underground. Near by stood the present residence of Queen Wilhelmina, a modest dwelling called "Sibilla". Affronted guards all but arrested Dr. Schutze when he tried to photograph it, and suddenly our whole party, discreetly but urgently, was tidied out of the way.

Slowly along the road came a broad figure in a voluminous white coat and skirt, informally riding home on a bicycle. At a respectful distance one solitary male retainer followed the Queen on another machine.

Later in the day I was surprised to find that Rotterdam, the very symbol of Nazi barbarism, appeared less damaged than Liverpool, but the ruins of the city centre—destroyed, we learned, in twenty minutes after capitulation—had all been cleared away. As we toured the warehouses where gifts from the Help Holland Council joined food and clothing contributed by many countries, we gathered that inconvenient European economics rather than bombs were the source of Rotterdam's immediate problems.

As the former main outlet for the commercial traffic of Western Germany, Rotterdam could not recover her pre-war prosperity without the revival of German industry—the last development which the Dutch, with their still raw memories, wanted to see.

On our final evening, over glasses of synthetic lemonade which cost 1s. 8d. each and tasted like hairwash, Marjorie Bowen and Olaf Stapledon and I discussed Holland's post-war mood, which we were now beginning to understand. Wherever we went, the better-educated and politically-conscious citizens had begged us to help them fulfil their need of new food for the mind.

The preoccupations of the Dutch people, deprived of international contacts for half a decade, still automatically revolved round the savage humiliations which we as a nation had miraculously been spared. Throughout our visit I heard only one individual—a young married woman whose brother, a military attaché, travelled regularly to London—mention the atom bomb and its implications for mankind. By receiving news of the outside world, she had escaped the deep mental introversion characteristic of peoples whose countries the Nazis had occupied.

Some of the intelligent Dutch with whom I spoke had uttered sentiments more reactionary than Lord Vansittart's, and then half apologised for the bitterness which they recognised as anti-social but were powerless to cure. For five years in which the fear of arrest and deportation had been added to the physical perils of battle and bombardment, they had lived on their nerves with memory and hope as their sole consolations, and now suffered from a spiritual sickness which time and understanding alone could heal.

Throughout the war years, mental stimulus had been virtually non-existent. Even in areas not smitten by war, such as Breda and Utrecht, education had been reduced to one and a half hours a day owing to the lack of teachers and buildings. Schools, universities and libraries had no text-books; cinemas, run by the Germans, were boycotted during the occupation. Nothing relieved the mental concentration on tyranny, torture and terror but the Underground publications and the private radio sets to which their owners had listened in mortal peril.

At an exhibition of Underground literature, we had seen the

poems of Emily Brontë and W. B. Yeats published in English, and "The Ballad of Reading Gaol" in French. During the war the sale of this literature had brought large sums for the Resistance movement. Now the Dutch longed once more to become the cultured members of a European community.

Shortly before our tour a Dutch teacher, G. M. van Rossum of Dordrecht, to whom a friend living in England had sent copies of my Letter, had written to me describing Holland's mental outlook.

"We never knew what the word 'barbarism' meant. But now we understand . . . Therefore we ask you other free peoples: Be patient with us for some time, for we have to *grow* again into liberty."

We finished our synthetic lemonade and returned to the hotel to be interviewed by two journalists from the Press Association. As soon as we entered the lounge, one of them rushed excitedly up to me.

"Do you know you're on the Gestapo list?"

"The Gestapo list?" I said. "What's that?"

He explained that several British newspapers had just published a memorandum, discovered in Berlin by the Americans, which contained the names of some 2,000 persons whose arrest was to be "automatic" after the Wehrmacht's victory over Britain. They ranged from Churchill to obscure Jewish refugees. My husband's name, he added, was there with mine.

"Are we all on it?" I inquired, indicating my companions.

"Oh, no! From the British authors here you are the only one."

This was not correct; I learned later that several organisations proscribed by the Gestapo included the P.E.N., to which all our party belonged. But I alone, it seemed, had been mentioned by name. I was then too deeply preoccupied by the Dutch scene to grasp the importance of this news for myself.

Before we left for the airport early next morning, a lightning flash rent the dark sky outside my lofty window and thunder rolled ominously over The Hague. Soon after leaving the Dutch coast, our plane ran into a thunderstorm; blackness enveloped us and lightning flickered alarmingly below.

Across the aisle, Godfrey Winn sat with closed eyes and a resigned expression. Of that party of six, he and John Marsh, our escort, alone remain to share with me the memory of those journeys through the uncleared havoc of war. Heavy gloves hid the scars left on Godfrey's hands by frost-bite during his war service with naval convoys to Russia. Once, in an unguarded moment, he had exposed them, and I knew him now for a man who concealed indomitable courage behind a convenient façade of affectation.

Suddenly the plane emerged into startling sunshine and sped safely home.

(4)

Partly owing to my continuous travels, the five authors who had visited Holland postponed until January their joint reports at the Caxton Hall. During the autumn, we added an urgent plea for books as well as clothing to many Press contributions describing the devastated Netherlands.

"You would be astonished if you saw how many bridges have been repaired already," Mr. van Rossum wrote me the day before the Caxton Hall meeting. A month later the first of a gift of bulbs which he had sent me in gratitude for our visit, a golden crocus, flowered in our small front garden.

Meanwhile, on September 27th, I had flown to Sweden. Though the Swedes had not suffered in comparison with the Dutch, Danes and Norwegians, they too, my correspondents assured me, had been deprived of international contacts and looked forward eagerly to a visitor from England.

The silver-grey Swedish plane flew over Western Denmark at dusk, but except from Aalborg no lights showed in the fuel-starved country. Intermittent circles of illumination immediately advertised the change to Sweden, and we finally plunged down into a pattern of lights so vivid that Stockholm seemed to be celebrating Europe's return to official peace by a firework display.

Two members of the Women's International League met me in a deluge of rain. The younger, Mrs. Inga Beskow, proved to be their Stockholm Secretary; the older, Elin Wägner, was one of Sweden's most distinguished writers and the only woman among the Swedish Academy's eighteen members. Recently she had published the official two-volume biography of Selma Lagerlöf, her sole feminine predecessor at the Academy.

Since Elin, with her perfect command of English, could read my books while I did not understand Swedish, she then knew more of me than I of her. But I soon learned that the young Elin had been a crusader of the same quality as Fredrika Bremer and Ellen Key; and that the mature Elin, before she published the Lagerlöf biography, had already been famous as the author of *Asa-Hanna* and subsequent epic novels which put the peasants of Småland on the literary map. All her life she was a vehement feminist and Quaker pacifist, and in an article I described her afterwards as "the Olive Schreiner of Sweden".

Now she had travelled from her home in Bergslund to greet me. At first, in the rainy darkness, I perceived only a small homely woman, older than myself, dressed plainly in tweeds beneath a battered felt hat. But I soon saw her better, for she and her companion straightway took me into a restaurant and ordered an omelette made with real eggs, and a bottle of red wine.

These almost forgotten luxuries and the warm room, furnished in crimson plush, immediately conquered my initial shyness. In fact I never really felt shy with Elin, for we took to each other instantaneously, and to the end of her life—which came all too soon—could never find enough time even in letters to cover all the topics we wanted to discuss.

After the meal, my companions took me to my room at the Hotel Plaza. Next day a Press Conference, where Elin introduced me, opened an exacting but fascinating series of functions. At a luncheon arranged by Tidens Förlag, which had published *Account Rendered* in August, the courses served suggested that the war had been a nightmare from which I had just incredulously awakened.

Other parties took place in the elegantly-furnished offices of the Women's International League, which provoked rueful comparisons with blitzed Britain's shabbiness. Everywhere the women I met put eager questions about Ellen Wilkinson, now Minister of Education, and British women writers. I gathered that though Swedish women had obtained the vote so early, they did not feel that they had made as much progress as they should.

Between engagements, my hostesses escorted me round Stockholm. As I had expected from G.'s pre-war description, I found myself enraptured by the loveliness of this sea-girt northern city, with its long lagoon-like inlets from the Baltic dominated by the dark spires of many churches, and the spectacular modern Town Hall designed by Ragnar Östberg to stand opposite the Old City on the cape jutting into the water between Riddarfjärden and Klaraviken. Some of the frescoes on its walls and ceilings had been painted by Prince Eugen, the eighty-year-old artist brother of King Gustav.

But, like any visitor from a war-scarred country, I felt less impressed by this beauty than by the reminders, in large and small shop-windows, of the material civilisation which so much of Europe had once achieved and wantonly thrown away. The unfailing courtesy of servants and officials, from the taxi-drivers who obligingly helped me to find my destination to the railway porters who carried my suitcases for long distances and then refused a tip, also constantly recalled the small kindnesses which war and fatigue had caused so many of my countrymen to abandon. Their graciousness reminded me that it is by behaviour, rather than by material possessions, that the quality of a civilisation can best be judged. The high standard of Swedish honesty aroused another regretful memory.

(5)

On October 2nd I set out from Stockholm to deliver eleven lectures on eleven successive evenings in the towns and cities of South Sweden. For the first two Inga Beskow accompanied me to interpret my lecture, "The Shape of the Future"; but later the task of translation proved unnecessary, as most educated Swedes understood English though it had become unfamiliar during six years of war.

For a quarter of a century Swedish politics had followed a Social-Democratic pattern, and the Prime Minister, Dr. P. A. Hansson, had held office almost continuously for fourteen years. After every lecture, questions on Attlee and Bevin rivalled the eager inquiries about the effects of the air-raids, the United Nations Charter, and the atom bomb.

At the hotels of these smaller towns, I learned from personal discomfort that Sweden, in spite of her neutrality, had paid with much inconvenience for the belligerency of others. Throughout that chilly autumn, only cold water flowed from the brightly-polished taps into the neat clean basins, for the whole country was short of the coal formerly purchased from England and Poland. Public buildings now depended for their heating on the piles of logs, which no one stole, openly stacked at the roadside. Private householders shivered in their coats over tiny log fires, for even in a land of endless forests wood was expensive; from a population of six and a half million no labour could be spared to cut down the thousands of available trees.

But the comfortable trains were warm, and the views superb; the spectacular landscapes of lake and forest showed me why most Swedes emigrating to America chose to settle in Minnesota and Wisconsin. The jagged tops of firs and pines continuously defined the horizon; amid these grand sombre trees, autumn-tinted silver birches stood out vivid and slender. If I half-closed my eyes, the forests appeared as a perpetually unfolding dark green tapestry threaded with gold.

When I tired of looking out of the window, I tried in vain to understand the long Press reports of my speeches. Amid the Oxford-like spires and towers of Uppsala, Sweden's great University city, I learned from the newspaper headlines, which alone I could follow, of the dismal ending of the London Conference. More stimulating was the reading of Somerset Maugham's short novel, *A Christmas Holiday*.

"Embodies Maugham's usual contempt for the safe and comfortable," I noted in my diary. "Made me think of contrast between lecturing in Sweden and the occupied countries. Lecturing in Sweden gives one the same feeling as lecturing in a comfortable provincial English town in a 'safe area' during the Blitz."

I had already observed the psychology produced by this contrast between the immune and the damaged; there had been a sense of uneasy guilt behind the well-justified pride with which my Swedish acquaintances had displayed their beautiful shops and well-stocked restaurants.

"Swedes, like British, have not much imagination," my notes continued. "Find it difficult to understand the savage hatreds caused by suffering in the occupied countries. Britain, which was not occupied but did suffer, stands halfway between the immune countries (in which one must include U.S.A.) and those which endured the Nazi invasion.

"Hence I have the feeling that I understand both. My conclusion is that suffering brings immediate knowledge but not immediate wisdom . . . George Saintsbury said: 'It is difficult to preserve the critical attitude when you love. That attitude is gone, beyond all hope of recovery, as soon as you hate.' Therefore, though the Dutch, Danes and Norwegians know what certain experiences mean which Sweden and Britain alike have been spared, I do not think they can assess the truth about Germany and the German people as clearly as the Swedes."

(6)

When my lectures took me near Elin Wägner's home, I spent a night there. In her dark-red frame house with verandahs overlooking a fir-bordered lake, no preparations had been omitted which the most honoured guest could desire. Fuel had been found for the stove which warmed my room against the October cold; over the fine bed-linen lay an exquisite pale-blue satin eiderdown.

Late into the night and all the next morning we talked; of books and writers, especially Olive Schreiner; of Henry Nevinson and other English personalities whom Elin had met in the London of the nineteen-twenties; of the possibility of getting her novels translated and introduced to British readers.

In middle life few experiences are more rewarding than a new friendship that seems likely to be permanent, and begins without the growing-up-together process on which lasting friendships are usually based. Elin was Swedish and I British; her background, her memories, her native language, were different from mine, and more than a decade divided us. But the same influences had shaped us; we had experienced the same type of spiritual growth. I was finally to leave Scandinavia eagerly wondering how soon I could go to Sweden again or persuade Elin to come to England.

In the small provincial town of Halmstad I found direct evidence of the concern for the war victims of many nations by which the Swedes sought to atone for their neutrality. Throughout the country I had come across refugees from the Baltic States, and learnt that among Sweden's guests were numerous Polish, Finnish and Dutch children, in addition to many former occupants of Belsen. After a fortnight in Sweden, I was no longer surprised at the large cases of food for Holland, stamped by the Swedish Red Cross, which I had seen three weeks earlier in Rotterdam.

At Halmstad I met two Polish women who were recovering from several years in Ravensbrück concentration camp. One, a small elderly woman with thin bony arms, was the wife of the former Polish Minister at The Hague, and had just learned that her husband was still alive. She had been arrested in Warsaw for helping the Resistance movement, and thought that this life, with its risks and apprehensions, had really been more exhausting than the prolonged endurance demanded by the camp. Towards her German captors she displayed a remarkable charity.

"We should not try to repay them in kind," she said. "I do not mean out of pity, but because killing is so terribly corrupting for the killer, especially if he is young."

"What did you think of the Nazi prison officials?" I asked.

"I could feel no special hatred. They had their orders from above, and were given no choice about obeying commands which damaged their characters."

At the end of my Scandinavian tour I had to return to Stockholm for my plane to England, since transport from Norway and Denmark was still under military control. An overwhelming final day included lunch with my publisher to meet the translator of *Account Rendered*, and a P.E.N. dinner at which I sat beside its President, Prince William, a very tall thin man who was the younger son of the King. From the frescoes by Prince Eugen in Stockholm City Hall I had learned that Sweden's unique Royal Family not only appreciated but practised art; now I found that to their intelligence they added a disarming freedom from "stuffiness".

393

The Swedish P.E.N., I discovered, had received no recent news of its counterparts in Denmark and Norway, for the Nazi invasion had divided the three countries from one another as effectually as three thousand miles of ocean. I was able to tell the Swedes that the Danish Centre had temporarily closed owing to collaborationist trouble, but the Norwegians were starting reconstruction from zero after the seizure of their records by the Gestapo. This capture of documents, said the Norwegian Chairman, Dr. William Keilhau, explained why the P.E.N. was among the proscribed organisations on the Gestapo List for the invasion of England.

(7)

Though my five days in Denmark involved three lectures and a speech at a literary club, its chief purpose was to attend the first post-war Inter-Scandinavian Conference of the Women's, International League. A strong Norwegian contingent and two representatives from Finland reinforced the Danish and Swedish delegates; and the Conference, which met in the Assembly Chamber used by the Upper and Lower Houses of the Danish Parliament, completely filled the long ornate *salon* with its gilded ceiling and frescoed walls. Mrs. Else Zeuthen, the future Member of Parliament who had arranged my visit, acted as chairman.

In Sweden I had been told that, since the Nazi occupation, the cheerful Danes had lost their gaiety. But much of their pleasant approachableness remained; it had not, like the once equable temperament of the Dutch, been impaired by a surfeit of cruel experience. Throughout the war, religious bodies and small pacifist groups, such as the War Resisters International, had continued their meetings undisturbed by the Nazis and unopposed by their fellow citizens, who regarded them, with their special concern for Danish Jews, as part of the Resistance movement.

The years of endurance seemed to have passed over this little nation as a bitter wind may ruffle the surface of a cornfield without disturbing its roots.

All the Danes whom I met had a comprehensible passion for large parties; I went to two, both in private houses, with forty or fifty guests. Such entertainment was possible because many foods, such as meat, eggs, milk and cheese, were plentiful and unrationed. But the accumulating stocks in this agricultural oasis did not contribute to the national advantage, since meat, a leading Danish export, could not now be sent abroad to earn money for clothing, books and cigarettes. Only that autumn 30,000 aead of cattle had been returned to the farmers as unsaleable. "What a monstrous world," I wrote to G., "in which the conquering nations won't purchase this food and send it across the border (no question of shipping) to the starving conquered!"

Like Holland and much of Sweden, Denmark was also a land without hot water owing to the fuel shortage which had accounted for the opaque darkness beneath my plane. As all the hotels were still occupied by British and American troops, I stayed with the family of Dr. Knud Jessen, the Director of the Botanical Gardens, who told me that they had washed in cold water for the past two years. I now felt guilty when fatigue produced an irritation which I should have assuaged at home by a hot bath or a cup of tea.

Coffee and chocolate, like tea, were all synthetic, apart from gifts constantly brought by Swedish friends across the Öre Sund. Denmark had also to feed and indefinitely maintain a quarter of a million German refugees who had fled before the advancing Russians in the final months of the war. My Danish friends begged me to publicise their plight in England, and when I returned I wrote to Eleanor Rathbone and the exiled German educationist, Minna Specht.

On October 20 I crossed the Sound from Helsingor to Hälsingborg, and travelled by night to Oslo through Sweden. As the ferry passed beneath Kronborg castle in the light of a nearly full moon, I seemed to see the ghost of Hamlet's father solemnly pacing the dark sea-girt battlements.

(8)

Norway brought a series of surprises. I had imagined the tolerant Norwegian delegates at the Copenhagen Conference to be internationally-minded exceptions from a nation living in a post-war atmosphere comparable to that of Holland. But though the Nazis, in the far northern province of Finnmark where Norway and Russia shared a frontier, had systematically laid waste an area the size of Denmark and made twenty thousand farmers homeless, I found a hopeful spirit alive in a mystical and courageous people.

I had to allow for some personal contrasts. In Holland our official guides had represented the Dutch government; in Norway I stayed with Sigrid and Diderich Lund, who had led the pacifist wing of the Resistance movement. Diderich, whom I was to meet four years later in India, had now joined the reconstruction teams in Finnmark, but Sigrid, a tall, affirmative woman with humorous eyes, made me instantly at home. With me from Copenhagen had come Myrtle Wright, who had spent the war with the Lunds.

Round their modern house in Vinderen, a pleasant suburb of Oslo, the autumn leaves were turning gold above the wide tree-bordered roads. After Sweden and Denmark their warm home was comforting; though Norway's shortage of food, clothing and books far exceeded our own, hot water was plentiful owing to the abundant cheap electricity produced by swift rivers flowing from high mountains. Adjacent hills gave a clear view of the long fiord, with its many islands, running due south to the Skaggerak.

I soon perceived even the Lunds to be less exceptional than I had supposed. Norwegian Resistance appeared to have taken, in general, a non-violent form, which had stimulated and united the people while saving them from the introvertedness of the Dutch in the areas blighted by fire, flood and starvation. I recalled Ruskin's words in the Preface to *Sesame and Lilies*: "Let heart-sickness pass beyond a certain bitter point and the heart loses its life for ever." Much of Holland reached that point; most of Norway did not.

Several Norwegians spoke critically to me of John Steinbeck's recent novel, *The Moon is Down*. Norwegian Resistance, which included many women, was never so ferocious, they said, as the book suggested, and seldom involved murder. At a party in the Lunds' house I met a Government Minister, Fru Kirsten Hansteen, and Fru Martha Larsen Jahn, who had presided over the largest women's organisation in Norway. Some of its members told me first-hand stories of Resistance methods.

I knew already of the part played by Norwegian judges and clergy, who resigned their official positions under the Occupation. Now I heard of the girl couriers who secretly carried messages all over Norway, and of the inspired obstruction of the teachers, backed by their pupils, who quietly disobeyed Nazi decrees until the Germans were obliged to accept the teachers' terms. One effective strike against an attempt to impose a Nazi version of European History upon the schools owed its success to the secret work of Fru Dalen, later a Norwegian delegate to U.N.O.

Even the public transport system had given opportunities for minor forms of non-violent resistance. Some passengers, one woman told me, had been arrested because they ignored the vacant seats next to Nazis in trams.

"We even had posters in the tram-cars saying that any person who did not sit down beside a German would have to leave the tram. This did happen occasionally. Then usually all Norwegians left as well and took the next tram. After some time the notices were taken down, but people still never noticed the vacant seats."

Though the women resisters refused to kill, they often died. The day after I arrived in Oslo, my hostess took me to the crematorium for a memorial service in honour of Birgit Nissen, the part-time editor of an Underground newspaper who had been arrested, put in Grini Prison for women, and then went to Ravensbrück. After her release she had died suddenly of typhus contracted in the camp.

The dome-shaped building was crowded with men and women, many of whom wept during the prayers and hymns. Beyond the lectern with its dark wooden Cross stood the small urn covered by the Norwegian flag; the only light came from the double row of candles which surrounded it. On a carved wooden chair sat the Lutheran priest in black gown and pleated ruff, and high above the urn hung a huge red banner, the standard of the Labour Party to which the dead woman had belonged.

(9)

During a talk at Oslo University, I encountered the now familiar continental passion for English books and newspapers. The students, I found, ran an English magazine, since they could not purchase British literature with money valueless outside Norway. When I spoke at the Nobel Institute under the chairmanship of Marie Lous Mohr, a handsome and elegant teacher who had spent part of the war in Grini Prison, the large crowd which came seemed to understand my address without an effort. Many of its members stood in the hall throughout the evening; others patiently thronged the vestibule in the hope of catching an occasional word. The implicit tribute was not to me but to England and the English language, but I found it very moving to speak on peace and the future in such a place.

The most stirring moment came when, taking a risk, I described our Save Europe Now movement, which included Germany, and mentioned the ten thousand supporting postcards which had already come in. There was a brief, tense silence; then the audience, only five months after the long occupation of their country had ended, burst into applause.

I understood the quality of that silence, for its emotions were directed towards problems other than German starvation. Throughout my visit Oslo was awaiting, with a sense of guilt heightened by the brutal dispatch of Laval in France a few days earlier, the unannounced but imminent execution of Vidkun Quisling.

Pre-war Norway had abolished capital punishment, and its

revival for the destruction of collaborationists gave all Norwegians a bad conscience. Even though Quisling had added a new word to the language of treachery, his early idealism and co-operation with Nansen on relief service in Russia were clearly remembered, and his plea at his trial that he had sincerely believed himself to be acting in Norway's best interests had been made with courage and dignity.

When I left Oslo on October 23rd he was still alive, but the mounting tension in the city pervaded every conversation. Late that night, eight hours after my departure, the execution took place. Reading of it in Stockholm next morning, I reflected with sympathy on the anguish of my kindly Norwegian friends. I was not surprised to learn that, shortly afterwards, the Women's International League had organised a mass meeting in Oslo which sent a resolution to the Government asking that the death penalty be rescinded as early as possible.

On my homeward flight I meditated on the contrast between the three peoples whom I had come to know. The reserved, socially-conscious Swedes, the lively, approachable Danes, and the vital, imaginative Norwegians, seemed each in their own fashion to be striving towards a new interpretation of freedom.

The frequent bumps from the rising wind put an end to these absorbing speculations, for immediately after crossing the British coast we ran into a full gale which tossed the small plane up and down like a cork. Never had our island appeared so long. At last, after my worst flight up to date, the plane circled Croydon for half an hour trying to avoid the air pockets.

"Weren't you sick?" exclaimed G., greeting me with relief when I finally emerged into drenching rain and raging wind.

"Certainly not," I said truthfully. "I was much too frightened!"

(10)

Now that six weeks of eventful travel were over, I had time to reflect on the Gestapo list which had roused so much interest on the Continent. I had been questioned about it in radio interviews at both Copenhagen and Oslo, for G.'s name and mine had appeared, alphabetically, on the same page as the names of Churchill and Chamberlain. This page, reproduced all over the world, had answered the war-time heresy-hunters more effectively than any argument.

Our inclusion brought a sudden spiritual catharsis, justifying G.'s political perspicacity and our decision to send the children to

America in 1940. Himmler's addition of conspicuous pacifists to the list of Nazism's arch-enemies showed also how clearly the Gestapo realised that the advocates of non-violent resistance were at least as dangerous to their authority as the belligerent politicians who fought Fascism by its own methods.

Norway had taught the Nazis that psychological opposition could be a more deadly weapon than guns. British pacifists, I perceived, had remained "suspect" in their own country precisely because England was not invaded. Had the Nazis landed, the little company of war-resisters would have become, like their counterparts in Norway, Denmark and Holland, a respected branch of the national Resistance movement.

The Gestapo List, it appeared, was now regarded almost as a Roll of Honour, and I could understand why some impeccable patriots who had not been on it wished that they were. We procured from the *News Chronicle* a copy of the page containing our names, and for some time that abortive death-sentence hung on the dining-room wall. Eventually we banished it to the lavatory, which seemed more appropriate.

After a day or two at home, the normal domestic routine of 2 Cheyne Walk closed about me as completely as though the epic eighteen months just past had never occurred. Shirley was back at St. Paul's Girls' School, and John, now within a few weeks of his eighteenth birthday, was awaiting his call-up.

For months, during that summer and autumn, he and I had discussed his attitude to military service, which was never a foregone conclusion either *pro* or *con*. At Harrow he had refused to join the Junior Training Corps, and spent their exercise-periods sawing logs in the congenial company of the School Chaplain, Edward Bryant, brother of Arthur Bryant the historian. This behaviour, oddly enough, did not make him unpopular with the boys, but merely gave him a reputation for eccentricity.

During 1945 an approach to the Friends' Ambulance Unit brought keen disappointment when he learned that he was too young to serve with them in China. Eventually he decided that if he registered as a conscientious objector it would be for the wrong reasons, and he must allow the undiscriminating military machine to take its course.

I respected him for the honesty of his decision, though I could not endorse it. But when eventually I watched him depart—philosophically resigned as the youth of our turbulent epoch had learned to be—to catch an early train from Euston in the grey light of a

January dawn, I felt only the more conscious how young eighteen was to make any political decision whatsoever.

This problem was not irrelevant to *Born 1925*, perforce laid aside for the past two months, and I now sought to banish anxiety for him by continuing it. Though I could not believe that prestige or popularity would ever come back, I went on with my book because I had no alternative. Writing had always been the road to fulfilment; only with a pen in my hand was I fully alive. The fortunes of *Above All Nations* and *Account Rendered* suggested that, at least in England, I could count on a limited public which would read what I wrote.

But the continental deprivations which I had so recently seen also gave urgency to the claims of Save Europe Now, and throughout that winter I appeared on its platforms. The day after I left Scandinavia, the Nobel Prize for Medicine had been awarded to Sir Alexander Fleming and his colleagues for the discovery of penicillin, but how many of the half-fed, half-clad Europeans to whom winter would bring pneumonia could hope for its benefits?

On November 9th, 1945, the Prime Minister, speaking at the Lord Mayor's luncheon, uttered a prophecy which time was grimly to endorse.

"Science applied to warfare," he said, "might discover other weapons even more terrible than the atom bomb."

This forecast lent a sinister light to the opening, ten days later, of the Nuremberg trials, which seemed unlikely to remove the risk of future war, and precipitated a series of uneasy questions.

Who were the war criminals? The difficulty of truthfully answering that question had led nineteenth-century statesmen to include, in most of their great treaties, clauses giving free pardon to the political offenders of the preceding war.

"It has been left for the twentieth century," I wrote in a subsequent Letter, "to enthrone and crown moral indignation as though it were an admirable virtue."

Had not the Nazis and their country suffered enough, without belated vengeance on selected scapegoats being authorised by judges who would themselves have been the criminals had the Axis defeated the Allies? With millions of homeless nomads invading Germany and a large mass of its population living in unrelieved squalor, the Third Reich which was to last a thousand years had become four occupied Zones administered by the victorious armies of its foes.

Whatever might be going on at Nuremberg, in London no postwar frenzy of jingoistic excitement, similar to that of 1919, impaired the hopes raised by the first meeting of U.N.O. within the sober walls of Central Hall, Westminster, in January 1946.

Even its soberness had been transformed for the occasion; this austere resort of Nonconformity now resembled a social worker who had temporarily borrowed the glad rags of the local beauty chorus. In a wintry wind, the flags of the United Nations quivered above the blue and gold awning which hopefully endeavoured to give a touch of San Francisco's splendour to the sombre entrance. The President, M. Spaak of Belgium, and the delegates, who included urbane Jan Masaryk of Czechoslovakia, mounted a platform with gold-embossed cream steps which suggested a marriage between the Earl's Court Exhibition and the Mappin Terraces at the Zoo.

By the time that Mr. Churchill's Fulton speech and Marshal Stalin's reply had confronted this gilded idealism with the spectre of a Third World War, John had been called up. In the late spring of 1946, his unit left Sudbury for the South of France. As a humble "A/C2" he finally reached Port Said, and with two or three boys of equivalent age constituted the "Port Authority" for the R.A.F.

I could not see him off, for by the time I received his six-page letter, begun at Toulon and finished on the *Duncannon Castle*, I had been for nearly a month in the United States.

(11)

When the first invitation from the American Friends Service Committee reached me in 1944, I had agreed to come as soon as the war ended and I could obtain an exit permit. After the General Election of 1945 had transformed the political atmosphere, I arranged a speaking tour under their auspices for May and June 1946. Letters that spring to the now friendly Foreign Office brought the news that exit permits had been abolished; not sponsorship, but shipping, was the current problem.

The American Friends, deeply concerned for European relief, asked me to speak on my recent visits to ex-occupied countries; at my lectures they proposed to appeal for funds to send food across the Atlantic. Early in the year Washington experts had announced a world wheat shortage, and in May the President invited Herbert Morrison to come to America with representatives of the U.N.R.R.A. countries and discuss the threatened famine.

In April my shipping problem finally reduced itself to a choice between the *Ile de France*, sailing with thirty "G.I. brides" to a cabin, and the *Cavina*, a little Canada-bound liner of 6,500 tons formerly used on the Elder-Fyffe line to Jamaica. This glorified banana boat took twelve days to reach Montreal, but experience justified her choice; she was clean and peaceful, and offered a good selection of travelling companions. In order to save storage space, deck chairs were not provided; during the first quiet and sunny days I prepared my speeches propped against a coat on the bare boards.

In the crowded bar of the small ship, unlimited wines and spirits were available without tax at 1s. a glass. I soon tired of the free drinks offered me by travellers exuberantly released from austerity; our relative abstemiousness was responsible for the automatic choice of one of my two constant companions, a paper manufacturer from Aylesbury. The other, George Woodhead, had no inhibitions about using the bar, and was calling me "Vera darling" within forty-eight hours.

As a former editor of the *Oriental News*, this sixty-three-year-old journalist had been imprisoned and tortured by the Japanese until he was paralysed. Now, broken in health and looking ten years older than his age but full of courage and vitality, he was going to Hong Kong as *The Times* Correspondent.

Throughout the voyage, small adventures abounded. Five days from the Irish coast, my two friends and I watched a midnight storm of green streamers springing fountain-wise from the North; like a neon light the aurora borealis illuminated the sea and sky. Next day we ran into the ice-fields which the captain expected, for this was his first voyage to the St. Lawrence since November.

Uneasy memories of the *Titanic* came back when thick fog closed over the ship and the drifting bergs. At midday an iceberg the size of a cathedral loomed from the mist just ahead of us, causing a sudden reversal of engines and change of course. When sunshine temporarily dispersed the fog, another great berg two miles away assumed the sinister beauty of a spectral white galleon in full sail.

That night the captain stopped the engines; submerged in fog we drifted south with the ice. For four days, until we entered the Gulf of St. Lawrence, he remained on the bridge while the fog-horn blew without cessation.

To G. I wrote that five years of intermittent bombs had at least dispelled my former fear of the sea.

"All things are relative, and compared with the German pilots who were seeking one's death deliberately, the icebergs seemed just clumsy if spectacular natural phenomena."

After a heavy thunderstorm which blacked out the river, we reached Montreal in clear sunshine on May 1st. My thirteenth

Atlantic crossing had brought me back to the American continent which I had left precisely six years ago. On the docks a cable from G. told me that soon after I sailed he had taken a flying boat and gone for a month to India in response to a cabled message from Maulana Azad, then President of Congress.

This possibility had laid in his mind since he had drafted, two years earlier, an "International Declaration in Support of Indian Independence" which two Ministers and several M.P.s had signed. Judging with his usual political intuition that evidence of co-operation would be most useful to the Indians before Independence was granted, he now followed discreetly in the wake of the Cripps mission. His airmail letters described talks with Gandhi and Nehru; meals with the Sardar Panikkar of Bikaner and the Maharajah of Dholpur; an interview with Lord Wavell the Viceroy; and a half-hour meeting with Azad in Simla.

(12)

Glamorous New York seemed oppressive and disturbing after the war-ravaged countries which I had seen. How, I wondered, could a people accustomed to buy unlimited candies in glittering tinsel boxes ever understand what hunger meant? The crowded city made me feel like a poor relation, tired, shabby and unwanted.

But New York, as usual, was not the United States. In New England I soon rediscovered the second America always lying behind the façade of ruthless prosperity set up by the first. The Friends in Boston, and later at their Philadelphia headquarters, received me so kindly that my sense of being a poor relation disappeared. And so wide was the concern of thoughtful Americans for what was happening in Europe that my travels took me from New England to North Carolina, and thence through the Middle West to the Pacific coast and back to Washington, D.C.

At the University of New Hampshire, and Concord, its capital, I found that two addresses had been arranged to support Food Conservation programmes for starving Europe.

Like all British visitors, I had already noticed the waste of food against which these "drives" were directed. Breakfasting on the train from New England, I saw with horror a Negro waiter throw away with the debris left from the meal a half-carton of cereal which I could not finish. I had touched only the cardboard package, but American sanitary regulations forbade the collection of these substantial remnants from tables all over the country to feed the famished.

But articles in American magazines had begun to challenge the deficient imagination which made such regulations possible. *Fortune* devoted its entire May issue to an illustrated essay on "The Food Scandal", with a sub-title which proclaimed that "Political Cowardice and Public Waste Make the U.S. Welsh on its Promises to a Hungry World"; *The Christian Century* publicised articles with such titles as "If Thine Enemy Hunger" and "Feed Germany Also". Instead of appearing at clubs and hotels I spoke in college halls and churches, and on radio interviews answered questions designed to elicit information about Europe's plight.

By May 23rd I had acquired enough experience to justify a letter, published by the *Manchester Guardian*, which sought to answer English criticisms of well-fed America's indifference to famine in Europe.

"I hope," I wrote, "you can find space for some account of the deep and growing concern for European suffering in U.S.A. . . . for once the generous American people becomes alive to a need, their native speed of living and thinking makes their response immediate."

After giving details of "Food Conservation Days" and relief campaigns, I concluded by quoting some words spoken by ex-President Herbert Hoover at Chicago on May 17th: "The saving of these human lives is far more than an economic necessity to the recovery of the world . . . Such action marks the return of the lamp of compassion to the earth."

(13)

One of the first engagements in the so-called "Middle Atlantic" area took me to Wilkes-Barre in New York State. To satisfy my sudden desire to see Ithaca again, the young ex-teacher who drove me to the next lecture in Syracuse obligingly made a ninety-mile detour from the direct road along the Susquehanna River.

An unbelievable nostalgia seized me when I saw the familiar silhouette of Cornell University, with its library tower, looking down on steel-blue Lake Cayuga from the heights above the town. The Campus, with its mammoth grey and terra-cotta buildings, seemed even larger than I remembered; round the old frame house in Oak Avenue which had been our first home, the young grass, spangled with dandelions, gleamed beneath the tall oaks and maples. As I gazed from the high suspension bridge on to the budding tree-tops in the ravine below, I suddenly returned to my first months as a bride.

There had been no airfield then beside the long lake where we now drove, passing the spectacular waterfalls, Buttermilk and Tuchannock. Both, I noticed, had been converted into "parks"; I preferred their natural wildness. With G. I had climbed the gentle slope of Buttermilk Falls, moving from stone to stone over the thin trickle of water till we reached the woods at the top.

Why had I so signally failed to appreciate this grandeur twenty years ago? A letter written to G. from Switzerland in 1947 subsequently gave the answer in a phrase: "Ithaca—that beautiful scenic railway leading away from life."

When we are young, ambitious and frustrated, the beauties of nature do not compensate for the unattained prizes of experience. We appreciate them only when we have achieved a measure of fulfilment, combined with a philosophy of humble acceptance.

Another kind of nostalgia came later at St. Paul, Minnesota, where I stayed with the Colbys. This great food-producing area, known to Americans as their "bread-basket", had arranged a lecture at the University and two talks for the local Famine Relief campaign. It was already difficult to believe that John and Shirley had spent three years in the prosperous Twin Cities, though I talked with the heads of both their schools.

From St. Paul my train moved steadily through the great prairies of North Dakota, where for hundreds of miles the young wheat which would be the lifeblood of Europe was pushing its green shoots. Contending against an on-coming railway strike, typical of many in the disturbed United States that spring, the train successfully reached Montana, a new State for me, and ran for hours beside a swift green river between forest-clad peaks where I felt I should be happy to stay for ever. Eventually we made our way through the State of Washington and arrived in Seattle, one of the last trains running in the whole country, to face a barrage of Press photographers.

Here, for the first time since I had left New York, I found opposition to the idea of food relief for Europe; it came from two women whose sisters, housewives in England, had assured them that the British were grievously under-nourished. I ought to be appealing for my own country, they said indignantly, instead of talking about other people's! They would, I felt later, have been delighted to see the comment of one journalist who, reporting a meeting in Toronto during my brief visit to Canada, acidly described me as "a thin dark woman who looked as if she could do with some of the rations which she was so anxious to give away".

On May 27th I started on the long journey to Los Angeles between hedgerows covered with wild roses. Next morning, in the

Californian desert, saffron-coloured cactus flowers the size of lupins stood like small sentinels against the rocky foothills of the High Sierras.

In Pasadena I stayed at the Green Hotel, where G. and I had dined six years ago with Charlie Chaplin and Upton Sinclair. From the garden, now brilliant with roses and bougainvillea, I sent him the petal of a Californian poppy. Then once more I travelled north, to Mills College across San Francisco Bay, where I received the honorary degree of Doctor of Letters, and gave the Commencement address in an open-air amphitheatre surrounded by capped and gowned members of the Faculty and students. Before me an audience of fifteen hundred occupied tiers of seats rising to a low hill; the scent of the eucalyptus trees on the Campus filled the dry, sunny air, and chrome-coloured Swallowtail butterflies added their informal decoration.

In a large church at Berkeley next day my audience raised $800 for European relief, and directly afterwards I caught a midnight T.W.A. plane for a Friends' Summer School at Wichita, Kansas. The ferocious headache produced by the oven-like temperature of the crowded cabin in tropical sunshine seemed in retrospect a small price to pay for the memory of flying over the High Sierras at dawn.

Plane travel now added a new urgency to American tours, and the growing popularity of radio interviews made them more exacting. Already I had flown over the Blue Mountains of North Carolina in a tiny machine carrying only three passengers and the pilot. Now, above a more formidable mountain barrier, we seemed to steer by a distant orange glow which gradually spread until the sun blazed across the horizon.

Below us the great rocky mountains lay like a colossal relief map, their heights measurable only by the length of their shadows. Gradually they changed to foothills and then to the red brown immensity of the Arizona desert. After Albuquerque, the prairies of Texas and Kansas stretched endlessly to the horizon like huge chequer-boards of green and brown felt.

"This journey," I wrote to G., "brought a quite terrifying realisation of how little of America is inhabited compared with the size of its mountains, deserts and prairies."

From Wichita I worked my way back to the East, and after the short expedition to Canada where six programmes had been arranged in twelve hours, recovered from this exacting time-table in the languorous heat of Washington. There I met Dr. Felix Morley, my supporter in the bombing controversy. I found that, as a former

Rhodes Scholar, this vigorous, broad-shouldered man with reddish hair had been my Oxford contemporary.

(14)

I had now a fortnight to wait in New York for the *Queen Mary*. After twenty-eight lectures, eleven talks and nineteen radio programmes, I relaxed through July's humid heat in a spacious top-floor room which my publisher had skilfully obtained for me in a hotel near Washington Square.

G. and I exchanged wedding anniversary cables on June 27th, which, I told him, I had spent at the sweltering Federal Building obtaining a sailing permit.

"When I explained why I gave the Philadelphia address of the American Friends Service Committee, the hard-boiled official said of them spontaneously: 'Those people are the only ones that haven't got an axe to grind. Everybody else tries to make something on the side, but they don't grind no axe.' And I was handed my permit almost with a bow."

The previous January, during the United Nations meeting in London, G. and I had given a small dinner for Mrs. Roosevelt. Now, seeing my presence reported by the Press, she asked me to have lunch with her at Hyde Park and bring a friend.

I travelled to Poughkeepsie with Marian Putnam, an established sculptress married to a Macmillan editor. Mrs. Roosevelt, now informal and unintimidating, received us at her own cottage, Val-Kill, and after lunch drove us round Hyde Park. She showed us the large family house, closed for cleaning after the week-end sightseeing crowds; the small church where Franklin Roosevelt's parents were married; and his private retreat in the woods at the top of a steep incline with a view of the Catskills. Finally she took us to his grave between the tall hedges which surrounded the rose-garden, where roses shading from flame to crimson were now radiantly in bloom. By his own instructions, she told us, the President was buried beneath the green sward in front of his unadorned white monument.

"He couldn't bear the idea of lying under a heap of marble," she said.

It seemed strange to me to see her own name—"Anna Eleanor Roosevelt, Born 1884"—also on the tomb beneath her husband's, with a blank space for the date of her death. But this, Mannie Putnam explained as we returned to New York, was an American custom.

Late in June, Mr. Oswald Garrison Villard invited me to spend my only July week-end at Rockledge Farm, his property at Thomaston, Connecticut. Now seventy-four, he was growing deaf and his shoulders were bowed, but his mental energy appeared undiminished.

"The possibility of never seeing the old man again seems so great that I feel I must go," I wrote to G.

As the temperature shot up to 90° that week-end, it was pleasant to sit talking with this valiant champion in his garden which overlooked a placid green pool. His house, typical of New England in its modern comfort, was unique in its period furnishings and the many historic relics of his grandfather, William Lloyd Garrison, the slavery Abolitionist.

We talked of the Baruch Plan for the control of nuclear energy, and the fourth atom bomb dropped over Bikini Atoll on June 30th, which was typically a Sunday. Beneath the glare of that explosion, Americans had begun to see in perspective this ominous phenomenon of an age in which poverty amid abundance created a new drift towards war. Responsible journalists issued warnings which appeared as yet to have little effect upon the military experimentalists.

On the day of the Bikini test, the bulky Sunday edition of the *New York Times* carried an authoritative article by Hanson W. Baldwin which described without camouflage the blast effect of atom bombs and the physical consequences of exposure to gamma rays. Three months earlier, Lewis Mumford had contributed to the *New York Herald-Tribune* a desperate warning entitled: "Gentlemen: You Are Mad!" Almost simultaneously, the Commission appointed by the Federal Council of the Churches to study the relation between atomic warfare and the Christian faith produced its Report.

"The atom bomb," it began, "gives new and fearful meaning to the age-old plight of man. His proudest powers have always been his most dangerous sources of peril, and his earthly life has been lived always under the threat of eventual extinction . . . Our latest epochal triumph of science and technology may prove to be our last."

(15)

Thirty-six hours after leaving Mr. Villard, I was due to sail from New York. As I packed in the suffocating heat, I meditated on the cumulative experiences of the past ten weeks. Though post-war America had little in common with hungry, battered Europe, I perceived some likenesses between her psychology and that of Sweden which had produced their effect upon Anglo-American relations.

Even by the reassuring Quakers I had been warned of widespread anti-British sentiments, though these appeared to be vaguely directed against the nation rather than specifically visited on individuals. The relatively few Britons now in the United States were hospitably welcomed as I had been, and commended to fellow guests as representatives of a country which had endured and sacrificed.

Politically, this much-publicised hostility could be traced to two contemporary "facts of life", the British Labour Government and the American Loan. To one large group of Americans, our General Election provided disastrous evidence that Britain had gone Bolshevik; to another, the new régime was a sham which barely concealed the old-style imperialism.

"I am consistently acting on public platforms here as the Labour Government's friendly interpreter," I had written to G. on June 6th. "Endlessly I give verbal vignettes of Attlee, Bevin and Morrison, patient and complimentary, explaining their difficulties, their sincerity, their statesmanship."

The American Loan Agreement—a hard bargain signed at Washington on December 7th, 1945—had tied Britain's economic future to America's fiscal policy, but was still endlessly discussed. Listening to these arguments, I concluded that the Loan was not so much a grievance in itself, as an opportunity for keeping other and deeper grievances aired. Of two psychological reasons for British unpopularity, the first seemed to be a subconscious sense of inferiority towards a closely-related people which had suffered more deeply than America from the war.

In 1940 distant Britain, struggling for her life against overwhelming odds, had been an object of deep emotional admiration. But post-war Britain, bomb-damaged, shabbily clothed and drearily fed, gave most Americans, like most Swedes, a feeling of undeserved exemption. For though, since 1941, the United States had itself been at war, this historic fact had not meant trouble on its own doorstep.

America's youth, it was true, had paid for their country's policy much as British youth had paid from 1914 to 1919. On my journeys I had met some of these young veterans, usually silent and preoccupied. One or two seemed barely able to tolerate the presence of their elders, and I recalled the deep spiritual gulf which had developed in the First War between my contemporaries and myself on active service, and the safe, though deprived, civilians at home. No such gulf existed in Britain after 1939; death and injury had come alike to soldiers and civilians, men and women, the young and the old.

American civilians had paid heavy taxes, bought War Bonds, endured suspense, and yet had not earned the compassionate respect given to those who face and accept death together at home or abroad. Many whom I met seemed to feel an inarticulate envy of their British contemporaries who had trembled in shelters and shivered in food queues. Since it is natural to dislike those who make us feel mean and uncomfortable, this shamefaced exasperation had reached articulateness in the shape of an anti-British prejudice.

But if the first cause of strain lay deep in American psychology, the second was wholly a British importation. It arose from the wartime presence of English exiles who varied from deliberate danger-dodgers to the adult relatives of dependent children turned into cadgers against their will.

"The generous and hospitable people of this country," I wrote to G. just before sailing, "have been at the mercy of countless British scroungers, whose log-rolling for themselves has been helped by the short-sighted (psychologically) Defence Finance policy of successive British Governments. Nobody tells you this direct. They tell you that they had as their house-guest a perfectly lovely British person whom they just adored—and only by degrees do you learn that said lovely guest used to get up late, put upon the servants, expect to be waited on, and was always cadging for this, that and the other.

"Do you recall Phyllis Bentley's letter about this in *The Times* soon after the policy of sending mothers and children over began? It could have been far more forthright than it was. The debt of gratitude owed by us as a nation to the Americans in war-time is so enormous that anyone who knows any American must try to repay him or her in personal terms."

On July 9th, 1946, cheered by a cable from G. and warm-hearted letters from American friends, I sailed in an austere *Queen Mary* with frescoes defaced by countless troops and plumbing almost defunct from exhaustion. I arrived home just in time for an incongruous conglomeration of events—the institution of bread-rationing, the ninetieth birthday of George Bernard Shaw, and the death of our beloved revolutionary friend, James Maxton.

(16)

Immediately I returned, the Women's International League invited me to be a delegate at their Annual Conference in Luxembourg.

I accepted in the hope that Elin Wägner would be there representing Sweden, but she was already committed to engagements in

Italy. Eventually Ruth Colby's presence with the American delegation atoned for this disappointment, and we spent some agreeable evenings together at an open-air café in the capital which provided meals that only Sweden and Switzerland could have rivalled. At each dinner we shared a bottle of Moselle, which in this wine-growing country beside the Moselle River cost the equivalent of 5s.

The city of Luxembourg appeared to be a near-relation to Strasbourg, but I thought it more beautiful with its ancient fortress towers built on either side of a wide and deep ravine. Here the narrow River Petrusse, a tributary of the Alzette, flowed between rocks fringed with vivid flowers and shrubs under the spectacular Pont Adolphe. The Duchy itself—one of the few European states that managed to balance its budget—impressed me as a surprising little Ruritanian oasis in the midst of continental misery. There was plenty of food, though most of it was rationed; the shops contained sweet creamy cakes and apparently unlimited wine.

But if the Duchy was prosperous, most of the delegates were not. At this Conference of two hundred women from twenty-two nations whose members had not met since 1939, it was easy to tell by the clothes of their representatives which countries had suffered damage and occupation, and which had escaped. Within forty-eight hours the expensively-dressed Americans, sitting beside the poorly-clad French or Dutch or Jugo-Slavs, found it tactful to appear more modestly attired.

The discussions at the various sessions brought equally sharp contrasts arising from experience.

"As you might expect," I wrote to G., "the Conference roughly divides between the Scandinavians, British and Americans, who want to be reconciled with their former enemies and go forward, and the French, Czechs, Poles and Jugo-Slavs who want to go on living in the past, emphasising their grievances and fighting 'Fascism'."

The Luxembourg Reception Committee, I told him, had refused to admit any Germans into the city, though the German would-be delegates invited to the Conference had been anti-Nazis for many years.

In another letter to John I developed this outline of post-war European tensions, and described how the French delegation had walked out of the Conference for twenty-four hours because a Norwegian delegate had protested against tyranny in the Baltic States.

"You got to know," I added, "how each delegation would react to every Resolution—e.g. if the British or Americans proposed that conquered peoples should be so treated that the seeds of future wars should not be sown, the French delegate popped up and said this didn't apply if they were Fascist beasts; and if the Americans proposed that all prisoners of war should now be sent home, up jumped the Czechs and said, Oh no, they ought to stay and repair the lands that they had ravaged.

"So it went on, with one half of the Conference continually pleading for reconciliation, and the other half insisting on revenge."

Between discussions, I learned some problems of individual delegates. One Jugo-Slav seldom spoke because she believed that a younger delegate had come to spy on her. A Finnish representative admitted that if her group had supported the Norwegian protest on the Baltic States, they would all have disappeared after returning home. But a Pole, Anna Szołagowska, the once wealthy owner of three hundred acres who now worked at a bank in Wrocław, believed that the agrarian reforms which compulsorily divided the estates under Soviet rule had actually benefited Poland.

With Ruth Colby I joined the official visit to the military cemetery, a huge meadow where eight thousand white crosses covered the young Americans who fell in the von Rundstedt offensive. Among them, with a raised platform before his grave, lay the remains of General Patton, incongruously killed after the war in a motor accident near Mannheim. One delegate told me that the Duchy had suffered severely from damage by troops, but the Luxembourgers who put flowers on the American graves had decided to forget it in gratitude for their rescue from invasion.

Afterwards we drove north-east through thick beech woods to the Ardennes, where most of the dead in the cemetery had met their end. Leaving the car we walked to the top of a high hill with strange rock formations; here the heaviest fighting had occurred. These dense forests and dramatic ravines brought back memories of the Argonne; there, too, rank weeds and tussocky grass had grown over the roots of shattered trees and their broken trunks piled at the roadside.

"Just think what it must have meant to collect the dead from a place like this," I said to Ruth.

She looked down through the top branches of beeches and pines to the half-concealed gorge.

"Yes. A great many of our boys have been missing since those battles. Probably their bodies are hidden there still."

Our guide told us that more than half Luxembourg's built-up area had been destroyed in von Rundstedt's advance.

After the Conference, I flew home in an evening hour of calm following successive thunderstorms; at sunset we looked down on the Dunkirk beaches between rose-tinged clouds while a full moon rose serenely above the red glow reflected from the west. We reached Northolt at dusk, with the lights coming out all over London.

Amid those farewell beacons, his eighty-year-old mind "at the end of its tether" and his "open conspiracy" a diminishing hope, H. G. Wells lay dying.

(17)

Throughout my travels John had written me long regular letters, recording in detail everything that he saw and did. He also sent me numerous essays and poems to criticise. This creative phase evoked by solitude seemed to bring him even nearer than he had been at home, and impelled me to include in the correspondence some fragments of the writing philosophy by which I lived.

"The achievement of a first-rate thing is so rare that it is worth doing second-rate work for a lifetime in order to produce one or two perfect things. Even if the perfect thing is never actually produced, the life of second-rate achievement is justified by the quest for first-rateness which inspired it."

Articulate as always, John vividly conveyed the bleak realities of his life in the Canal Zone between the two chief storm-centres of the Middle East. Anti-British riots in Cairo the previous February had been followed by the Labour Government's undertaking to withdraw all British troops from Egypt, where a delegation led by Lord Stansgate, the Air Minister, was now discussing the revision of the Anglo-Egyptian Treaty. In Palestine continuous outbreaks of terrorism and sabotage culminated during July in an explosion at Jerusalem's King David Hotel, killing a hundred officers and men.

The uniformed children in Port Said, scapegoats for the bitter tangle of political events between the wars which were to produce a major international crisis in 1956, had been warned not to walk alone through "native quarters", where the hostile Egyptians bombarded them with missiles of every kind. At eighteen John could not refrain from contrasting his normal life with this perilous loneliness; not many people of his age, he wrote, had been reduced "from a background of cloth-of-gold to a stone wall".

At Wichita, Kansas, I had met a young Quaker poet, Kenneth Boulding, who had recently published a book of Sonnets, *There is a Spirit*. Each Sonnet was inspired by a sentence from the dying message of James Naylor, the saintly fanatic who in 1655 rode into Bristol imagining himself to be the Messiah entering Jerusalem, and was ruthlessly flogged and imprisoned. I now sent John the Sonnet entitled "I found it alone, being forsaken":

> "There is no death but this, to be alone,
> Outside the friendly room of time and space,
> Forsaken by the comfortable face
> Of things familiar, human, measured, known.
> Not in raw fires, nor in the imagined groan
> Of tortured body-spirits, do we trace
> The shape of Hell, but in that dreadful place
> Where in the vision naught but self is shown.
>   And yet—he found it there, as on the Cross
>   When even God had fled, Love did not die;
>   So from the last despair, the extremest cry,
>   Flows the great gain that swallows all our loss.
>   And from the towers of Heaven calls the bell
>   That summons us across the gulf of hell."

Seeking further to reassure him, I added: "If the dreary monotony and loneliness of Port Said make you see your normal assets as 'cloth of gold', you cannot wholly regard them as loss. Happiness comes from within and from nowhere else—though there are certain external things which can increase it, and, perhaps most of all, the consciousness that one has behaved magnanimously and somehow managed to overcome the Satan within one's self."

Soon he was writing more cheerfully, for in July he had a great privilege to record; our benevolent acquaintance Lord Stansgate had invited him to lunch at the Antoniades Palace in Alexandria. Sending me afterwards a pressed rose from the garden, he contrasted with understandable cynicism the friendly gardener who gave him roses because he was the Air Minister's guest, and the other Egyptians who threw bricks at him as an ordinary aircraftsman.

In October I went away for three weeks' writing at a newly-discovered hotel which overlooked Maer Bay, half a mile from Exmouth in Devon. Hutchinson's, the publishers, had recently commissioned a short manual of advice for the young would-be writers, now so much handicapped by the shortages which made publishers "play safe". As this 60,000-word book could be written in three months, I put *Born 1925* temporarily away. Beside a lily-covered pool in a garden divided from the sea by Riviera-like firs, I sought to combine with practical instructions enough inspiration to stimulate easily-discouraged youth to surmount its problems.

In Exmouth I learned that my loyal friend, Arthur Creech-Jones, was now Colonial Secretary; his enlightened and disinterested policies were to have too brief an opportunity owing to his Parliamentary defeat at Shipley in 1950. I also read John Hersey's *Hiroshima*, recently published by the *New Yorker*, which had created a resounding sensation in American journalism. Beside this human document, the official Report of the British mission to Japan on "The Effects of the Atomic Bombs at Hiroshima and Nagasaki" seemed anaemic indeed.

These accounts of man's ingenuity in torturing his fellows threw a lurid light on the concluding stages of the Nuremberg trials, where for months a group of individuals held responsible for collective national crime had provided a barbarous public spectacle for their conquerors. During July G. had flown to Nuremberg to write an article, commissioned by a Sunday newspaper, which compared these legal antics with the Reichstag trial. Now, in October, the prosecutors of the first melodrama had become the condemned criminals of the second, and with one exception were executed by slow strangulation described in gruesome detail by the Press.

On October 17th I wrote G. that these ferocities haunted my dreams, and I couldn't help feeling a grim satisfaction in Goering's suicide, "which showed up the whole business for the bogus law and actual vengeance that it was. The Greeks were more civilised; they let Socrates drink the hemlock."

In the *New Statesman* for October 5th, "Sagittarius" had already penned the Nazis' epitaph.

> "They with their empire pass into the dark,
>   But now their conquerors, at least in thought,
>   Upon preventive massacre embark;
>   Their victors have embraced the creed they taught."

I had hardly returned to London, my short manuscript almost complete, when a letter from John announced that he was in hospital at Fayid. Soon after visiting Alexandria he had begun to suffer from a chronic ailment which he called "enteritis"; now a Mediterranean germ was to involve some months of illness.

Later he wrote to us from a hospital on the Mount of Olives where he had been transferred; laconically he recorded that the railway station at Jerusalem had been blown up on the afternoon of his arrival, and his ambulance had taken him round two road-craters where mines had exploded that morning. A pine forest hid his hospital from the turbulent city, but from the window of his ward he could see in the distance the lifeless blue of the Dead Sea.

By the late autumn we had received no official word of his illness from the R.A.F., but in December the Air Ministry at last telephoned us that he was being evacuated to England. Soon after Christmas he reached Southampton and was sent to an R.A.F. hospital camp in South Wales. There I periodically visited him in a remote village amid the piled-up snow-drifts of an arctic spring.

Six weeks before his return, I wound up my fortnightly Letter after publishing it without a break for over seven years. In spite of national troubles soon to come, the long reign of war psychology seemed at last to be over in Britain. On parts of the Continent, as I was to discover the following summer, its atmosphere still prevailed.

(18)

John's return coincided with the severest winter for sixty-six years and an acute fuel crisis. The "Cripps Plan", designed to solve the nation's economic problems but torpedoed by zero temperatures and successive blizzards, had to be abandoned till April. At a party G. met Aneurin Bevan, soon to be involved in acute controversy over his new National Health Service.

"God is obviously a Tory," he remarked, explaining that the Government had gambled on a mild winter, and lost. The New York *Herald-Tribune's* London representative, Don Cook, described our crisis for the benefit of Americans living in comfortably heated homes.

"Economically, psychologically and meteorologically, the fortunes of Britain were just about at an all-time low last week.

"But as the temperature fell, the coal-stocks went down, the heat and light went off and the queues formed outside Labour exchanges, there was at the same time that stiffening of morale which saw this country through Dunkerque, the Battle of Britain, and the blitz.

"The economic crisis through which Britain is now passing has struck a country ill-prepared for the blow."

At the end of January, my series of spring lectures began in Dublin. I found a city of snow-capped roofs and slippery streets which enjoyed even less gas and electricity than London. Recent blizzards had made the peat-bogs inaccessible, and thousands of families shivered in their houses before fireless grates. I addressed

416

the Royal Dublin Society in a huge cold library where the weather had put even the microphone out of commission.

A week later, when I visited the Midlands and North, they were enveloped in a snowy blanket several feet deep. At Grantham the station roof, overweighted with snow, had collapsed on the York-shire Pullman by which I was supposed to travel. When I finally reached Ripon by a slower train, the open countryside hidden under drifts suggested Wisconsin in January.

From Manchester I travelled in cold trains to Paisley and Greenock, and learned from the Glasgow evening papers that Ellen Wilkinson was dead. Huddling over the half-stoked grate, I recalled the five-foot red-haired dynamo who led the hunger marchers from Jarrow to Hyde Park during the Depression; the incongruously respectable administrator of Home Security who drove her own car through the raids, but was embarrassed by accidentally meeting me in a West End restaurant; the post-war Minister of Education who co-operatively supplied me with details of her work for a lecture in Sweden.

In the final months of deteriorating health, her concern had been for the school-children whose welfare lay in her hands. After her death another Cabinet Minister, remarking that private Cabinet discussions seldom inspired eloquence, described the last meeting to which Ellen came. She pleaded, he said, with such passion for the school-leaving age to be raised to fifteen that several waverers were converted and the Cabinet agreed to support the proposal. In America *Time*, correctly diagnosing her claim to remembrance, published her photograph over the caption: "Death of a Champion"

In March, after weeks of frost, came intermittent thaw and floods. Below Chertsey the Thames was three miles wide; the Trent burst its banks and inundated the Midlands. When I paid a visit to John in South Wales, I found the country road a torrent which sprayed like a fountain round the bus, and on returning to London discovered that the Severn Tunnel was blocked by a landslide. My train, diverted to branch lines barely visible above deep water, eventually reached Swindon after a long detour through the Cotswolds, which resembled the Alps.

A week later, passing the town which the newspapers described as "Bedford-under-Ouse", I saw blocks of ice floating through the streets. This Midland expedition involved a visit to Buxton, where the forgiving Public Library had invited me to lecture at the Winter Gardens Pavilion. I felt indeed a *revenant*, and was surprised by a warm ovation from the crowded hall.

T.E.–O

At Brighouse in Yorkshire, a fellow-guest in the house where I stayed was a Lincolnshire farmer's wife who told me that, towards the end of the frost, wild pigeons hopelessly seeking food would flop dead outside their windows. When they picked them up, they found only skeletons huddled in feathers. According to a Farmer's Union report, over a million sheep and thirty thousand cattle had died throughout the country in snowdrifts and floods.

As I passed through York on my way home the swollen York-shire Ouse surrounded the Minster, which seemed to emerge from the centre of a lake. Much delayed, I reached Chelsea to find my guest, Dr. Felix Morley, whom I had invited to break his journey to Geneva, being entertained by Shirley with a discourse on current politics.

"Felix Morley's flying visit has left me with a quite extraordinary feeling of warmth and happiness," I reported later to G. Adding that my New York publisher had also been in town and had taken me to dinner and a play, I concluded: "Thank God for Americans who turn the long night of winter into spring!"

(19)

From Luxembourg in August the International Conference had sent a message to three Indian women, Mrs. Pandit, Shrimati Kamaladevi Chattopadhyaya, and Begum Hamid Ali, which expressed the hope that "for you the hour of victory approaches, a victory doubly glorious since it will have been won through non-violence, and we rejoice in it as though it were our own."

The following March, when G. made his second visit to India, that hour was approaching with unexpected speed. The year 1947 was to see the greatest voluntary surrender of political power ever made in history; by its end British troops had left Egypt, British administration had been wound up in Burma, and three new Dominions, India, Pakistan and Ceylon, had come into being. When Churchill complained of the "hurried scuttle" which added "the taint and smear of shame" to the break-up of the British Empire, Attlee told him bluntly that he was fifty years out of date.

Before G. left England, the Government had stated its intention of withdrawing from India not later than June 1948. A fortnight after he arrived, Lord Mountbatten became the new Viceroy, and the transfer of power was hastened by almost a year. The price of "agreement" was the division of India, which Gandhi, for whom Hindu-Moslem unity represented a cardinal principle of non-violence, reluctantly accepted.

In December 1946, Calcutta University had invited G. to deliver a course of lectures. Three months later, when an English publishing firm commissioned a book subsequently entitled *In the Path of Mahatma Gandhi*, he was able to accept since the advance royalties covered his travelling expenses.

For him this type of political experience provided the "significant living" of which he had written me from Italy the previous summer, affirming that it meant "to express effectively the ideas within one's self, to promote the rule of peace, the restoration of Christendom, the Union of the West." These objectives guaranteed a sympathetic reception from the Mahatma, whom he saw three times. On the last occasion Gandhi summoned him to Delhi from Allahabad, and gave him ten minutes while taking his bath. This was his only free time in a very busy day.

"It shows what confidence I have in you," he added as G. departed.

From an England still covered by six inches of snow, G. had flown to tropical Calcutta to stay with Sarat Chandra Bose, "the Hindu political boss of Bengal". Bose's six servants, he wrote me, talked English "rather as in the Middle Ages the clerics talked Latin."

"Everybody, including S. C. Bose, seems to be quite convinced that we are on the verge of another war," he continued. "Everybody here knew from the British army that Churchill would lose the election."

At the Inter-Asian Relations Conference, he met his old friend George Yeh with the Chinese delegation, and in ten minutes had arranged an immediate journey to Shanghai, Nanking and Peking before spending a final week with the Mountbattens at Viceregal Lodge. As I did not know of this plan, the sudden break in his correspondence gave me three weeks of anxiety. He had not allowed for the chronic delays which held up his letters, but eventually I located him through Reuter's Far Eastern correspondent and a cable to Sarat Bose. Two letters describing Shanghai and Peking—"not a city but a caravanserai, with wide open spaces of rubble"—brought compensation for uncomfortable suspense.

"They speak of dust blowing in from the Gobi desert", he wrote of Peking. "I say it is the grey dust from their own five miles square of unmade-up streets. You go over the uneven pavements which recall Moscow, to see little shops mostly selling spare bicycle parts, rice, lemonade, tobacco brands. There is a vague smell of garlic and sewage. You can turn a corner and find it by no means vague. . . .

"But you know that you are in one of the earliest planned cities. Along the roads, displacing the dromedaries, run a succession of fast, smart cars. Then you see above the cypress trees the sixty-foot-high tiled gable, yellow the tiles and red-painted the building, of one of the four gates of the Forbidden City. On beyond is the Palace of the Manchus. At one corner is the palace, rebuilt by the Ming Emperors, where Kubla Khan entertained. You are in the world of Marco Polo."

In his letter he enclosed some violets, gathered for me in the Forbidden City.

(20)

By the time G. returned in May, a sudden heat wave had replaced the ruthless cold; during one of the hottest week-ends ever known in England, the Labour Party Conference opened at Margate.

The Government had now become unpopular owing to its long enforcement of austerities and bans, which included private electrical heating, greyhound racing, and the B.B.C. Third Programme. All over England, unwelcome posters insisted that "We're up against it. WE WORK OR WANT." Casualties amongst the Party's leaders had also added to its troubles. When Ellen died, Herbert Morrison was in hospital with thrombosis; for months Arthur Greenwood acted as Leader of the House.

After the Conference I went again to Exmouth, this time for three weeks' work on *Born 1925* which had occupied my thoughts for over two years. By the end of June I had completed the story except for the Epilogue. This I intended to lay in Germany, where G. and I had been invited by the Foreign Office to do a short joint lecture tour for the Education Department of the Control Commission.

I had long wanted to see for myself that tragedy of defeat which I was so often asked to describe at public meetings on "the German Question" organised by Save Europe Now. Amid the growing depression which crept like a miasma over Western Europe, British concern for Germany centred upon the still inadequate rations, the sordidness of life in the worst-bombed cities, and the general breakdown of communications. At the end of April, when Lord Pakenham took over J. B. Hynd's responsibility for twenty-two million Germans, the British Zone was still struggling against hunger marches and token strikes.

In July, when we were due to leave, G. was unexpectedly offered the chance of selection as Labour candidate for a London constituency. Communist influence there, he thought, would work against him as a Catholic, but he felt that he should not ignore the opportunity.

I agreed, and on July 19th left for Germany alone.

From 1943 onwards there had been much talk about the "re-education" of Germany. Discussions on this theme were often carried out in an atmosphere of complete psychological idiocy, as though no one but the Germans needed re-education.

No doubt the Education Department of the Control Commission —on the whole a devoted and sympathetic body of men and women —had been founded with this process in mind. But apart from merely conveying information, I did not see myself as "educating" the Germans; it was they who were going to educate me. I went to learn what they had suffered and how they had endured; to discover their attitude towards the past and the future. It might even be possible to mitigate in small ways some effects of Britain's political and social mistakes, which I had seen described in newspaper articles and such first-hand reports as Victor Gollancz's *In Darkest Germany*.

After discussion with the Foreign Office I took over the typescripts of three lectures—"Rebuilding Culture in Post-War Europe"; a revised version of "Shaping the Future"; and "The Progress of Women in Britain". This last topic was requested in order to meet the contemporary needs of German women, who owing to their sheer numerical preponderance of seven to one had now to assume the very responsibilities of which Hitler had deprived them. The Teutonic tradition of female inferiority also gave point to the story of our successful feminist revolution, which had written women's emphasis on human values into Britain's welfare politics.

As my German, though adequate for rough-and-ready conversation, was not sufficiently expert for lecturing, the Control Commission provided an interpreter from their "pool" at Bad Pyrmont. This interpreter—an attractive dark girl called Margaret Brown— subsequently joined me at my Kiel hotel. As a species of glorified secretary she accompanied me everywhere, coped with the excruciating problems of transport and telephone, and turned an experience which without her might have been a nightmare into a valuable adventure. Together we tackled the local youth groups, women's organisations, and university students, which the Control Commission particularly wanted me to address.

When G. saw me off at Liverpool Street, we found a noisy pandemonium of returning troops and officials which accompanied me all the way to the Hook of Holland. That night I shared a large cabin minus a washroom with eight other women.

"If Norfolk House tells you again that you will be looked after all the way to your destination, don't you believe it," ran a subsequent letter to G. "On arrival at the Hook we were called at 5.30 a.m. for a train that went at 8.56. I still didn't know how to get to Kiel; the Railway Transport Officer on the dock didn't know either, so told me to go to Hamburg and report to the R.T.O. there."

As we passed through Holland I noticed a remarkable change after two years; cattle browsed in the fields; roads and bridges had been repaired; little grey steel trains ran along the railway lines beneath restored copper cables. In contrast to the Dutch, now well-dressed and well-fed, I saw hungry Germany for the first time on Osnabrück station in the shape of porters with yellow skins and lined, shrivelled faces.

At Hamburg the Railway Transport Officer, an irresponsible Scottish youth about John's age, disclaimed all interest in me; I was part of the civilian set-up, he said, and he was concerned only with the military. As it was now nearly midnight I decided, tired and exasperated, to assert my status.

"Look here," I said, "I'm a V.I.P. and you're the same age as my son. I'm going to talk to you as if you were my son. You can't leave me on the station all night. You must get in touch with the appropriate authorities and find me a room in a Transit Hotel."

This vehemence actually appeared to impress him, and eventually a car took me to the nearby Reichhof, dark, crowded, and businesslike. I fell instantly asleep, too weary to be troubled by the strange room or the desolate heap of rubble outside my window. In the morning the local Education Officer, contacted after a long struggle with the telephone, said I wasn't supposed to be in Hamburg at all, and must drive instantly to Kiel where I had to lecture at midday.

The journey from Hamburg to Kiel normally takes two hours, but my German driver, disregarding both my safety and his own, made it in one and a quarter. In spite of this helter-skelter, I noticed as we drove into Kiel past fantastic ruins the rusting hulk of a German-American liner on its side in the harbour. Later I was told that the R.A.F. had bombed the ship when it was packed with internees being sent to Norway. Presumably the corpses of these anti-Hitler victims were still inside.

The large barracks, Schleswig-Holstein headquarters of the former

Luftwaffe, appeared by contrast to be quite untouched. Here I reported to the local "Mil. Gov.", where the Education Officer informed me that I had not been expected till midnight, and had no lecture that day. Half disconcerted and half relieved, I telephoned the local Friends' Relief Unit and spent the unexpected free afternoon at their headquarters in Schleswig, a lovely undamaged old town on the Baltic. Here they took me round one of the two hundred camps of expellees, tragic flotsam of war, which they supervised in co-operation with the International Voluntary Service for Peace.

At Kiel University next day I met Dr. Gerhard Mackenroth, the Professor of Economics and one of the most enlightened Germans I have ever known. A tall man in his early forties, with a handsome appearance and sensitive face marked by much suffering, he had already been in touch with G. about a German edition of *Above All Nations*. This he now agreed to translate and edit, as a response to the wartime tragedy which had wrecked his personal life.

I learned that he had lost his wife and three young children in the Dresden raid; he had sent them east to escape the bombing, and in February 1945 they were on their way back to Kiel before the advancing Russians. Caught by the raid, they perished with thousands of anonymous refugees; though he sought them for three days amid the ruins of the city, visiting hospitals, rest-centres and cemeteries, he learned only that they had been seen at the railway station on that fearful night. Now he had no relative left but a seventy-three-year-old mother living half-starved in the Russian Zone.

Above All Nations brought him a brief compensation. To help in the translating, he engaged a young war-widow with three children to support. They fell in love and married, and had two children to take the place of his lost family before his own premature death in 1955.

(22)

From Kiel I returned to a Hamburg programme made the more strenuous by G.'s absence. The Education Branch, following a self-imposed rule which forbade them to cause the Germans any avoidable disappointment, had added his engagements to mine, and as the summer temperature rose my lectures, each followed by a long discussion, increased to three a day.

"The discussions help to ventilate German grievances and hence mitigate the tense atmosphere," I wrote to John, "but they are extremely exhausting as one is a target for every kind of bitterness and one *has* to answer, explicitly, honestly and discreetly. Each discussion takes at least two hours, so on Friday I was on my feet literally for six."

Outside the Reichhof, a steep street led downhill to a small lake known as the Binnen Alster through a heap of debris where a black cross marked the remains of a doorway.

An Education Officer had told me that all corpses were systematically cleared, but local rumour insisted that these crosses indicated the presence of unburied dead. From the rubble a hot effluvium gave substance to the report, bringing back the memory of French villages on the Western Front and the wrecked main street of Irun beside the Bidassoa River.

Round the Binnen Alster some relatively intact buildings maintained the appearance of a city, though a distant colossal skeleton indicated where the Blohm and Voss ship-building yard had stood. But it was the Wandsbek and Hamm suburbs which showed me the real consequences of "fire typhoons". For twenty minutes I drove through the Hamm area without seeing anything but acres of rubble, seldom varied by even the framework of a building. Estimates of Hamburg's casualties, said the Chief Education Officer, varied from 150,000 to 200,000. After each big raid the S.S. Guards went round the city, shooting the worst-injured victims and throwing their bodies into the Elbe.

Innumerable animals had also suffered; these included nearly two hundred lions, tigers, leopards and buffaloes in Hagenbeck's famous Zoo. Many had been poisoned by licking phosphorus from firebombs; twenty-five others were burned in a railway train while being evacuated. Birds of prey, including eagles, escaped, and were shot after eating the pheasants and ducks which formerly roamed the park. The seals all died in the early raids; terrified by the noise, they swam wildly round until their hearts gave out.

I drove to Hanover through the Lüneburger Heide, where the Germans had surrendered; pines dotted the wild heath, and the boughs of the mountain ash were already heavy with scarlet berries. Beside the sunny road, its blue-grey surface broken by shadows of trees like dark delicate lace, grew clumps of the same magenta rosebay which adorned the ruins of Hamburg and of Chelsea Old Church.

At one of my meetings in Hanover where I deputised for G., my audience was a predominantly male student class at the Veterinary College. With engaging honesty, they treated me as an Aunt Sally for two strenuous hours, catechising me sceptically about reputed shortages in Britain and our failure to release our German prisoners.

Like other audiences in the same age-group, they also displayed a deep distrust of the Marshall Plan.

That evening, feeling exhausted and inadequate, I was glad to return to the quiet Transit Hotel in the encircling forest which concealed the wreckage that I had once seen pictured in a Southampton cinema. The next day a German driver took Margaret Brown and me in a Volkswagen over the 360 kilometres between Hanover and Cologne.

I had already learned that zealous competition existed throughout the British Zone for these regular driving jobs, made necessary by the widespread destruction of railways and bridges. Most British travellers, ignoring the official prohibition against feeding the Germans, added to the driver's meagre ration by ordering sandwiches for two at the Transit Hotel. As we handed over our own "extras" at a suitably secluded corner, I reflected that nothing becomes the British nation better than its habit of quietly disregarding regulations which offend its fundamental decency.

On the great Nazi-made Autobahn, which by-passed all the big cities and divided the country like a sweeping sword, secluded corners were not easy to find. Continuously along the road wound a broken ribbon of traffic—Army lorries, small military cars, steel-helmeted motor cyclists, German farm carts with the driver on a high seat between two horses. After fifty kilometres of flat fields we emerged into wide rolling country, darkened by thickets and sprinkled with little red-roofed houses.

Late in the afternoon the Volkswagen reached the Ruhr, running between slag-heaps and tall narrow chimneys. On the outskirts of Dortmund the drunken spires of derelict churches loomed above shattered houses.

At Bochum in the same area I was to meet Frau von Scharfenberg, the sad, shy daughter of Josefine von Reitzenstein, a refugee German friend with whom I had watched the searchlights at midnight on V.E. Day. Josefine's daughter was a young widow with a baby son whose husband, an anti-Nazi officer, had been shot for his part in the conspiracy to remove Hitler.

Soon after my return to England I approached the Home Secretary, Mr. Chuter Ede, with the request that she might be allowed to join her mother, but—good and humane though he was—he felt unable to give his permission owing to the number of similar requests reaching him from Europe. Later Josefine brought her daughter over, but it was then too late; she died in a Sussex hospital after giving, for too long, her scanty rations to feed her child. I was

425

to find it difficult to forgive either the Home Secretary or myself for this avoidable tragedy.

The little utilitarian car, travelling through the Ruhr, had soon to interrupt its steady fifty miles an hour for Bailey bridges and "diversions". One of these took us four kilometres out of our way through wrecked Duisberg, where the bridge which had spanned the Dortmund Canal trailed in the water like the broken skeleton of a prehistoric animal.

Here the meaning of "obliteration" had become visible and tangible. In my notebook I recorded a sardonic quip then current in Germany. "The Russians have the food, the Americans have the scenery, the French have the wine, and the British have the rubble." Writing in the *New Statesman* for January 18th, 1947, Ritchie Calder had commented caustically on the omission at that time of "Bomber Harris" from post-war Honours Lists:

"Perhaps the British taxpayer . . . will consider £80,000,000 a year (which is what the British Zone is costing us) a generous enough testimony to the thoroughness with which Harris did his job. And he cannot complain about his memorial. You can go to the Ruhr and look around you."

In the same weekly review H. N. Brailsford recorded two months later that fifty thousand "open" cases of tuberculosis existed in the British Zone, for which only twelve thousand hospital beds were available. Throughout this area wreaths were still laid on ruins and rough wooden crosses with black-lettered names stuck into anonymous heaps of rubble, though the sharp agony of mass-annihilation had been replaced by the slow agony of living death.

Shortly after we had by-passed Düsseldorf, the dark silhouette of Cologne Cathedral appeared against the sultry evening sky. Gradually the suburbs, skeleton buildings rising from sordid weeds, encroached like the ruins of a lost world upon the car. We crossed the Rhine at sunset by the only available bridge, and drove through Marienburg to the Linden Club on the outskirts of the city.

After the brilliant exhausting sunshine, this grey stone building with green-shuttered windows looked inviting and cool. But throughout my visit I could not forget that, according to local gossip, the dispossessed owner had committed suicide, or become unaware of the chaos concealed by the tall clumps of weeping willows which overlooked the neatly-trimmed lawn.

In the gathering twilight as we drove from the Rhine, those spectral fragments of chimneys had seemed to be part of a forgotten civilisation peopled by ghosts.

Cologne had become part of my experience. I had seen it with Winifred in the bitter atmosphere of 1924 during the first British occupation, and with G. at the time of Hitler's triumphal entry in 1936. On this third solitary visit, it made the most appalling impression of any German city. By contrast with the two thousand years of history which it had enshrined in stone and gold, it epitomised all the horror and loss of the Second World War. The damage suggested Arnhem multiplied by ten; the ultimate limit of destruction where civilisation finally broke down.

In the rainless heat of early August, my first impression had been one of dust and weeds. Then, looking up from the huge obscene growths choking the remnants of doors and windows, I noticed the fantastic shapes of the ruins themselves.

All over the derelict city, these caricatures of roofs and gables pointed like accusing fingers at the sky. They seemed to be calling down vengeance on the crazy humans who had wantonly obliterated their heritage from the past. Piles of debris concealed thousands of rotting corpses whose flesh had long been consumed by rats from the Rhine. The Messehalle where I had heard Hitler speak in 1936 was now a broken shell; below the cathedral the once magnificent Hohenzollern Bridge still trailed in the Rhine.

During the first thousand-bomber raid, I learnt, Cardinal Schultze, the great Archbishop of Cologne who boycotted Hitler's Rhineland election meeting, had died from a heart-attack.

Of the myriad museum-pieces which Cologne had possessed, the Cathedral alone remained, but as a much-publicised example of careful British bombing it did not quite live up to its reputation. The junior official who showed me over it admitted that, being close to the railway station, it had received fourteen direct hits, of which one had shattered the splendid West window and another the organ. Inside the building, thirty tons of steel scaffolding supported the roof. From a pinnacle far above my head, a startled falcon swung into the air through a large bomb hole and disappeared.

Many builders were now at work, clearing fragments of ornamental stonework and piles of melted lead which resembled solidified waterproof sheeting. They were endeavouring, said my guide, to repair the structure in time for the seventh centenary celebrations in 1948.

Climbing nearly five hundred steps to the top of the sound twin spire, I looked down on an unimaginable panorama of broken bridges and dusty ruins. Among them, like a modern variant of Childe Roland's Dark Tower, stood the bomb-proof bunkers with which Germany, unlike England, had saved thousands of her population. Now they were used to shelter the homeless.

My conductor took me to see the Bunker Vogelsang at the Pädagogische Akademie in the Bickendorf suburb. There for an hour I talked to Heinrich Seise, the leader of the eighty students—a tall, spare young man with flushed cheeks and spectacled eyes.

Heinrich, though an anti-Nazi Catholic studying for the priesthood, had been called up in 1939, sent to the front, and badly wounded. After he recovered, the Gestapo found him leading a semi-underground existence at Aachen, and again took him from his studies to be a stretcher-bearer.

During the fight for the bridge at Arnhem, several shell splinters entered his head and chest. Now, with his lungs damaged as though by galloping tuberculosis, he obtained oxygen from weekly visits to the hospital, and went on reading theology. In his cell, on the small shelf containing his scanty books, stood a vase filled with sunflowers—always a sign of unextinguished hope in the Germany of 1947. I had even seen flowers in the basement cellars where whole families lived beneath the rubble.

Subsequently I related the story of Heinrich Seise in three small magazines circulating in England, America, and New Zealand. It captured the imagination of their readers, who kept Heinrich alive with food parcels until the hunger period in Germany ended. After that, his faith in God and his indomitable powers of endurance enabled his impaired body to survive till 1955.

When I drove from Cologne to Aachen, that unconquerable spirit showed itself in a different fashion. On the way our car passed through Düren, a once prosperous city of 50,000 people now destroyed and vanishing into weeds. There I saw a small crowd, containing many children, hurrying along the cleared main road. Their destination, I discovered, was a travelling circus incongruously set down amid scattered stones and encroaching thistles.

Two days afterwards, driving to Münster, we stopped for a meal at Recklinghausen, an oddly undamaged industrial oasis on the edge of the Ruhr. After the usual expedition into a quiet street to hand our rations to the driver, Margaret Brown and I bought our lunch at the Salvation Army Canteen. Before leaving I sought the Ladies' Cloakroom, but the military authorities, characteristically

428

indifferent to female requirements, had provided only a "Gentlemen's." On its door a placard assured me, with doubtful accuracy, "Christ Will Provide For all Your Needs."

(24)

In gabled Münster, the once lovely Westphalian capital where three centuries ago had been signed the treaty which ended the Thirty Years' War, I stayed for the first time at a German hotel. Formerly it had been part of a crowded cathedral city; now it appeared to be set down in a large country field. Rosebay and sorrel waved round it in the breeze; during a sudden rainstorm the wind whistled through ill-fitting doors and broken windows.

At the East end of the Cathedral, a ruined shell now open to the sky, two *prie-dieu* stood beside a flat buff-coloured stone surrounded by begonias. This was the grave of the heroic Bishop of Münster, who had consistently defied the Nazis in his sermons. I bent down to read the inscription.

"CLEMENS AUGUSTINUS
DE GALEN
SRE PRESBYTER CARDINALIS
EPISCOPUS MONASTERIENSIS
1878-1946."

My assignment at Münster was an international vacation course on "The World and its Problems as seen from without Germany", where I found myself the only woman lecturer. In the ruined city sleeping quarters had somehow been found for two hundred and fifty of the four hundred students, who included British, French, Swiss, Scandinavian, Dutch, and Canadians. Lecturers and students alike fed on pooled British and German rations at a priests' refectory.

After Herr Karl Arnold, the Minister-President of Land North/Rhine Westphalia, had given the first address, the Vice-Chairman of the Students' Representative Council, Bernhard Rosenmöller, a student of theology, made a noteworthy speech.

"The interests of individuals seeking for the common values of life outweigh national differences," he began. "The victors must carry their victory with modesty and moderation, the defeated with dignity and tolerance. We do not look on you as strangers, but as companions on our way."

Rosenmöller belonged to the age-group from which Germany had most to expect; many of them, evacuated during the air raids,

429

had escaped the intolerable memories of their parents, whom a few sympathetic questions often reduced to tears. Being small children when Hitler came to power they had no hampering sense of guilt, and their protests at my discussion classes about their standard of living seemed puzzled rather than bitter.

The effect of the epoch in which Hitler had tried to put the clock back to the Middle Ages seemed to vary with the age of the citizen. I had met some fine men and women among those who reached political consciousness before the Nazis came to power, but the majority appeared to be exhausted by years of harsh experience; they were glad to join in progressive work, but too tired to take the lead. Those who were somewhat younger, in the twenty-five to forty group, found it hard to shake off the immediate past; during their most impressionable period the Nazis had ruled Germany.

Could the civilised outlook expressed by Rosenmöller prevail over the disruptive influences now at work amongst the German people? A great question-mark, to which no one yet knew the answer, dominated not only this vacation course, but all Germany.

On August 8th I bade a regretful farewell to Margaret Brown, and travelled by night in a locked railway coach through the Russian Zone to Berlin.

(25)

The Savoy Hotel in Berlin did not remotely resemble its illustrious namesake on London's Victoria Embankment; it was a workmanlike residence similar to the Reichhof in Hamburg. Here the organisers of Youth Groups called on me, together with British and American Friends waging their characteristic battle against the moral nihilism which is born of despair.

In May 1945 Clifford Webb, the *Daily Herald*'s correspondent, had written of Berlin: "This is no longer a city. It is a desert of dreadful destruction. I was sick with horror and frightened." It would, I was told repeatedly, take fifty years to rebuild, but this estimate underrated German vigour once hunger and tuberculosis, Berlin's worst enemies, had been overcome.

Yet even in the post-war wilderness created by British bombers, the city seemed to retain its peculiar formality. The tall façades of gutted houses which lined the main thoroughfares recalled the ageing, cadaverous, pre-Hitler teachers, steeped in the Prussian tradition, who had been resuscitated to assist the process of denazification in the schools of the British Zone.

Ellen Wilkinson, visiting these schools as Minister of Education, had returned to tell the typical story of a senior German inspector with whom she had discussed the importance of developing mental freedom in the young.

"I entirely agree with you, Miss Wilkinson," was the earnest response. "And now, perhaps, you will give us some directives for independent thought?"

In the Berlin of 1947 four nations, whether they appreciated their position or not, stood at the judgment bar of history. The Germans also were watching and judging them; questions put to me by Youth Groups in the British and American Sectors, and by the writers invited to meet me at the home of the Berlin publisher, Peter Suhrkamp, reflected this vigilance.

"Do you really think," inquired one young German at a discussion meeting arranged by the Quakers, "that constructive human fellowship is possible between the members of two nations who stand in the relationship of conquerors and conquered?"

A middle-aged Berlin Countess, to whom a music-loving reader from the Army of Occupation had introduced me, insisted that, in spite of everything, such fellowship was possible. She was a good-looking intelligent widow, who had lost her only son on the Russian front, and during an evening spent at her flat, she assured me that the British were still the best-respected of the Occupying Powers.

"You see," she said charitably, "you are both adult and just."

Of this conversation I wrote later in the *Manchester Guardian*:

"Admittedly the standard of comparison must be distressingly low if our prestige has survived our unhappy failures to maintain supplies, and the pervasive inefficiency which causes the whole machinery of the Control Commission to creak like the worn-out Volkswagen for which transport-starved officials compete so desperately. But if my informant's opinion is representative, the opportunities in Germany to-day appear to be especially ours."

My Transit Hotel, if unpretentious, was conveniently central; between the conversations and organised discussions which multiplied like snowballs I set out, usually on my feet, to try to identify the Berlin that I remembered.

A few months before marrying G. I had walked with Winifred in the Tiergarten, where the lime-trees in their shining autumn glory had scattered leaves like golden paper coins upon the sculptured monarchs in the Siegesallee. To-day this area, half-converted into allotments, with the stumps of its shattered trees providing no screen for the derelict houses which ringed the park, looked strangely small, and the royal statues, many of them headless, struck ridiculous attitudes among the cabbages. The gilded Goddess on the Victory Column of 1870, which had survived the bombing, seemed to belong to a past as distant as the Holy Roman Empire.

One afternoon I took a taxi through the Brandenburg Gate to the Wilhelmstrasse in the Russian Sector, for I wanted to see the Reichskanzlerei where Hitler and the surviving members of his entourage had spent their last days. No special permit was needed for this expedition, but the streets beyond the gate looked strangely empty, and my taxi-driver seemed nervous. When I alighted at the Chancellery, he drove without stopping round the adjacent squares until I was ready to return.

The wrecked edifice, with its gaping stone window-frames, offered gruesome evidence of the sombre destiny to which aspirants after power can descend. Like enormous dead insects with their legs in the air, fallen chandeliers covered the bare boards of the Diplomats' Room. In the great reception lounge between tiers of marble pillars, a continuous pool along the floor dismally reflected the bomb-holes which pockmarked the ceiling. The rusting machinery of the heating plant emerged from deep water that suggested a bottomless pit, and everywhere the Russian conquerors had systematically stripped marble or brocade from the walls. I retrieved a fragment of egg-shell blue tile from a heap of debris on the bathroom floor.

Outside, in the desolate ruins of the garden, an elderly woman was searching for edible weeds amid anonymous piles of overgrown stones. Across an unkempt stretch of grass, dirty water which looked and smelt stagnant in the August heat flooded the lower rooms of Hitler's concrete bunker. Round a dank hollow in the soil, where a pursuing guide assured me that the bodies of Hitler and Eva Braun had been burned, lay some rusty kitchen utensils. Adolf might have experienced, as G. had remarked, a Wagnerian end, but a singular squalor dominated its aftermath.

On August 13th, owing to a successful "wangle" by an amiable Air Force sergeant, I obtained a seat in the morning plane to London. Two days later, India and Pakistan would win their independence; to my German audiences I had commended this voluntary transfer of power as an example of current British policy at its best.

As we rose into the smooth upper air, I reflected how much the past two years had done to atone for the previous five. Though the nine countries that I had visited had brought me so close to the avoidable tragedy which war creates, I owed to them and their people a series of kaleidoscopic experiences, unique in their enrichment.

Flying homewards over demolished Bremen on the silver streak of the Weser and across resurrected Holland where the Zuider Zee appeared as an oddly-shaped geometrical lake, I followed once more the track of the storm.

CHAPTER ELEVEN

THE CITADEL OF TIME

"Not least interesting . . . is his treatment of the spiritually impaired. Not one fails to reach the Celestial City, though Mr. Ready-to-Halt gets to the River bank on his crutches, and Mr. Despondency and his daughter, Mrs. Much-afraid, have to be rescued by Mr. Great-heart from Giant Despair."
v.b., In the Steps of John Bunyan, 1950.

(1)

BEFORE HE WAS called up for National Service, John had decided that he did not want to be an architect; and during his months in hospital it had been agreed that he should go to Oxford while he made up his mind about a career. In September I took him to Switzerland for a holiday before he sat for the New College examination.

At Wilderswil, in the Bernese Oberland between Lakes Brienz and Thun, we stayed at a small hotel which Christina Foyle had recommended. Twelve miles to the south, the immaculate peak of the Jungfrau dominated the lovely valley sweeping up to Mürren.

After the dust and debris of Germany, the cheerful village two thousand feet above sea-level seemed a paradise of clear, sunny air. Trim fountains and small beer-gardens glowing with salvia and geranium adorned its spotless central square. Through rich meadows spangled with autumn crocus, a winding path led downhill beneath sun-scented firs to Interlaken two miles away—"a beautiful little town with much too beautiful shops," I wrote G. with a cautious eye on our limited currency allocation. But Wilderswil, I told him, was "not in the least 'gosmopolit', with cows attached to large bells

433

(so seems the proportion) wandering down from the mountains, and late at night villagers replying to the plaintive piping which comes across the valley from the next village, Gsteigwiler."

Neither Shirley nor G. could join us in Switzerland, since she was still at St. Paul's for the term which proved to be her last, and he was on his way to America to lecture for the Canadian Institute of International Relations in a new phase of the work for Anglo-American friendship on which he had spent so much of his life.

Against their picture-postcard background of blue skies and snow-clad mountains, the Swiss offered a way of living which for many nations had become the vanishing memory of a dream. Their currency provided the dollar with its only rival; their plentiful food was virtually unrationed. What explained this prosperity in a small country with large mountain areas impossible to cultivate and no natural advantages but beauty and water-power? How had neutrality been preserved through two Great Wars started by belligerent and excitable neighbours?

One answer seemed to lie in the hard work upon which national existence depended. Swiss Trade Unionism had never become its own Nemesis, perpetually counting the number of nails knocked into the wall. Our hotel proprietor, M. Zurchmiede, and his wife rose daily at 6 a.m., though their restaurant which served the village remained open till close on midnight.

Another explanation came from the solid bourgeois residue of un-ruffled morality in spite of the temperamental differences of three races and the problems created by four languages. In this land of calm nerves, tranquil courtesy, and model family life, I became ashamed of the irritable manners created among the warring nations by prolonged austerity in the wake of bombs.

A week after we arrived, the Marshall Plan had been signed at the Quai d'Orsay; simultaneously Andrei Vyshinsky at Lake Success had accused the British and Americans of hindering disarmament. From the stronghold of Swiss serenity, these events and their implications appeared even more distant psychologically than physically. It seemed odd that this adult nation still denied its women the vote.

While I climbed the foothills with John in the sunshine, a number of our friends at home, including Arthur Greenwood, suffered political eclipse. A new spate of austerities followed the Cabinet changes, and foreign travel was suspended outside the sterling area. All over Switzerland the big hotels were obliged to close; by mid-October Interlaken, with its shuttered shops, resembled the British seaside in January.

Having always believed that freedom of travel, so essential to the mutual understanding of nations, should be the last and not the first liberty to be sacrificed to compulsory thrift, I listened with sympathy to M. Zurchmiede's laments. Without some modification of the ban, he protested, Swiss economy would be ruined; the tourist industry was their chief source of income and more than half of it came from Britain.

"I can't help feeling that this economic blow at a friendly country is the height of folly," I wrote to G.

How much currency would the ban save anyway? It seemed to carry too far the drastic expedients which Ivor Thomas, M.P., who had now left the Labour Party, described as "Strength through misery".

(2)

As usual when I could escape to the peace of the country, my mind had become a ferment of ideas for novels, short stories and articles. I knew that I could do them if I could but achieve the prolonged concentration which is the first condition of excellence.

"I want only two things," I had written to G. in a new mood of revulsion against London's interruptions just before he left for the United States. "To do my work as it ought to be done, and to be with you whom I love more than anyone in the world. I have just picked you these Alpine flowers on the steep valley road going from Wilderswil towards the Jungfrau; the smooth blue one is a gentian. Take them to America and think of me there."

That autumn Hutchinson's published On Becoming a Writer; in N.w York, re-edited for American readers, it was to appear later with an altered title, On Being an Author. It was not however this practical book, but my novel Born 1925, which had inspired the sudden passionate yearning for a quiet seldom attainable by mothers responsible for households and families.

Ever since the story had come to me in the closing months of the war, no book except Testament of Youth had so persistently eluded the quest for time to get its substance into words. Repeatedly it had been taken up and put down, not only for the journeys abroad which brought their own compensation, but for a series of household dilemmas so trivial that, had they not impeded my work, the memory of them would have long disappeared.

Discussing this book with John in letters before he left hospital, I had sought to counter his conviction that the younger male "hero" was a portrait of himself.

"It is and it isn't," I told him truthfully. "I don't think I could have written the story of a boy who in the book grows from three to twenty-two without having had a son. In one or two cases when you annoyed me (chiefly about two years ago) I did deliberately use the incident because I wanted to get it off my mind. But having said that, I come to an end of any resemblance you might find. Like most fiction characters Adrian is a complete hybrid, and what matters about him is that he should be typical of his generation."

At Exmouth, taking this tale of family life to the point where only its epilogue in Germany remained to be written, I had held long conversations with my characters on seaside walks, and listened to them talking amongst themselves. They had become so real to me that the final dramatic incidents seemed to unfold spontaneously, and I had written to G. about the astonishing independence of these fictitious personalities.

"One thing that surprises me is that my Dick Sheppard character, whom I intended to be the element of tragedy in the book, has passed this character on to his actress wife; he ends his life praising God for its richness despite its many tribulations; but she, losing her first husband in the first war, loses with him the power to love, and the story's real tragedy is that when Robert Carbury (Dick Sheppard) dies, she cannot even grieve for him. It is queer how stories take these things on themselves."

Now at Wilderswil I began the epilogue, in which Robert's son Adrian goes to Germany with the Army of Occupation. Sitting beneath the trees in the outdoor restaurant, I sought to convey to English readers who were indifferent or still hostile the realities of life as lived to-day in Hamburg and Cologne.

Nowhere, I thought as I wrote, had war appeared more brutally undiscriminating than in the Germany of 1947; aimed at the guilty, it had exacted similar penalties from the good and the great, the young and the innocent. I remembered some who had suffered or died: the three young children of Gerhard Mackenroth; the Cardinal Archbishop of Cologne; Heinrich Seise; Bishop von Galen. Yet human ingenuity was devising weapons even more imprecise, as though mankind had still not paid enough for its descent from grace.

Eventually the English edition of this book was to sell 20,000 copies; even in the United States its fate would not be negligible. But I did not foresee this minor success when I finished my epilogue and sent a typescript from Wilderswil to New York. With it went a letter to Harold Latham, who had been my friend from the time that he transformed my life by accepting *Testament of Youth.*

"This book deals with one conflict which must, I feel, be universal in an absolute sense; the conflict which arises from the dichotomy which exists almost everywhere between family life, and public and professional achievement. Why public insignificance should be the price of family unity, and family discord so often the price of eminence, is surely a problem that must have exercised thousands of families all over the world. All the members of my Carbury family escape from each other into work—the father into his ministry, the mother and ultimately the daughter on to the stage, the son into astronomy. The tragedy of the story is that the father does not want to escape; he wants his family to be his emotional mainspring, and it refuses to become one.

"In this book I have sought to work out some of my own problems vicariously and it is to me the most important novel I have written (which does not mean that I regard any of my novels as important)."

(3)

I felt glad to be quit of *Born 1925* because I had immediately to tackle another contract, which though long overdue seemed likely to make an unusually light demand on nerves and emotions. Some time ago I had been invited to contribute a book on John Bunyan to Rich and Cowan's *In the Steps* Series. These volumes combined the biographies of famous historic characters with excursions into their topographical background.

I accepted largely because I was tempted by the serenity of an historic topic after the writing of *Born 1925*, which had revived so many public and private tensions. But when some initial reading at Wilderswil had brought back into focus a period untouched since my years at college, I discovered that the seventeenth century was neither so psychologically distant, nor so comfortably irrelevant to current predicaments, as I had supposed.

Writing in the deceptive afterglow of the Edwardian sunset, Mark Rutherford had commented that Bunyan's era, with its passionate revolutions, "was a time in every way inconceivable to us now, and it is farther off from us in reality than the age of Julius Caesar". A few years after his book appeared, the First World War and the subsequent political errors that created the Second had brought mankind abruptly back to those "realities" which the men and women of the Puritan Revolution had faced in their own epoch.

As soon as I re-discovered that the vigorous seventeenth century Independents and the passively resistant Catholics had defeated the totalitarianism of their day, with its roots in Church and Crown, and between them saved Britain's liberties, I was captured by the topical charm of my subject. Seeing John Bunyan as the great Conscientious Objector against orthodoxy and oppression, I worked with energy at a scheme which carried him from his birth in the year of the Petition of Right to the last chapter, suitably entitled "The Relevant Pilgrim".

Late in October, John and I returned to an England preparing for Princess Elizabeth's marriage, an event overshadowed by the unexpected suicide of John G. Winant, the wartime American Ambassador. Other portents of wider significance cast a deepening shadow over the wedding preparations.

Through the Swiss newspapers and belated copies of the *Daily Mail*, echoes of the Cold War had penetrated to Wilderswil. Soon after we arrived, the formation of the Cominform had re-emphasised the Communist campaign. Persistently, during the autumn, the Soviet Union had charged Britain and America with a German policy hostile to itself. In London the Foreign Ministers' Conference, summoned for late November, had adjourned in December, after a prolonged unconstructive duel between Bevin and Molotov, without agreeing on the basis of a peace treaty for Germany.

A series of treason trials in Poland had recently caused M. Mikolajczyk, the father of John's school-friend, to flee to Britain; he fared better than Petkov, the Bulgarian Opposition leader, who on September 23rd had been executed in Sofia. One review of the year subsequently compared these ominous incidents to "the dull thud of rubber truncheons heard from outside the prison walls".

Already this threat of a Third World War had brought some odd reactions. Demi-Communist organisations began plausibly to seek the co-operation of pacifist groups in the name of "peace", which thereby became a suspect word. In America the columnist Dorothy Thompson, changed by a post-war visit to Germany from war acceptance to war repudiation, appealed to mothers through the columns of the *Ladies' Home Journal* to join the war-resisters. Shortly afterwards she surprised me by a personal approach on behalf of her World Organisation of Mothers of All Nations.

"I find it hard, God forgive me, to take all this at its face value," runs a note made in my diary at the time. "I have known so many peace-time pacifists, and I cannot forget D.T.'s wartime belligerence; her opposition to the anti-bombing campaign when her support would have done so much to mobilise American opinion against 'the mass murder of mankind'. And yet I must give her the benefit of the doubt. I too saw Cologne and Hamburg and Berlin, and realise the terrible shock to the spirit that the ruin and desolation and corruption caused."

On December 14th, two days after the ashes of Beatrice and Sidney Webb had been buried in Westminster Abbey, the newspapers reported the death of eighty-year-old Earl Baldwin, who by the negative appeasement policy which Neville Chamberlain made positive had done so much to create the problems facing the world. At whatever level these were confronted, neither my generation nor the children's could hope to enter a Land of Beulah for years to come.

(4)

But the younger generation, though occasionally cynical about its chances of survival, remained unintimidated by current omens. In December Shirley sat cheerfully for the Somerville examination; like myself long ago, she had wisely decided to take the higher standard Scholarship papers as her Entrance.

For once circumstances had given a girl advantages which a boy did not share; no disruptive period of conscription handicapped Shirley's education. The moment was auspicious for women students; on December 6th the University of Cambridge, twenty-seven years behind Oxford, at last decided to give degrees to women on the same terms as men.

Shirley departed for Oxford with stockingless legs and flying hair, looking as usual like a tomboy of fourteen. She might do quite well in her papers, I thought, although her school considered that at seventeen and a quarter she was a year too young for the examination; but even if she did well enough to be summoned to the interview with the Principal which was given only to "possibles", that experience would undoubtedly finish her. As the days lengthened after her return, I concluded that she had produced one of those "marginal" results which have to be assessed after the majority of candidates are placed.

But I was doubly wrong. She returned from her belated interview to announce casually: "I think I've got a Schol." She had indeed; and this open History Scholarship had been awarded less on her papers than upon the interview. I learned afterwards that she and the Principal, Dr. Janet Vaughan, both sitting on the hearthrug before the fire, had discussed the state of the world from A to Z.

Faithful to her determination to follow her own path, she decided not to go back to school for her final year, but to work on a farm. I realised that she knew her own mind. She had already made a preliminary chart of her course through life; for a would-be Parliamentary candidate, the experience of everyday work among ordinary people would be more useful than three terms in the top form at St. Paul's.

The day after the green, white and saffron flag had flown half-mast from India House to mourn Gandhi's assassination, she departed on her bicycle for the village of Frating, near the Essex coast.

Throughout the benign weather of that eventful spring, in which railway transport and electricity were nationalised and controversy boiled on the National Health and Steel Bills, she worked on the community farm run by J. H. Watson, whom I had met at Langham. Soon afterwards Joe Watson became the part-time political agent for the Harwich Labour Party, and Shirley helped him to work for the Socialist candidate, Morris Janis.

When, four years later, Mr. Janis moved to Luton, the Harwich Party selected Shirley, at twenty-two, to be its candidate. Fifteen months afterwards this Tory constituency had to fight a by-election, which gave her a premature but useful political baptism.

During April G. atoned for his absence the previous summer by a short series of lectures in Germany; his tour for the Religious Affairs Branch of the Control Commission took him, with "all Germany in white blossom", to Hanover, Hamburg, Bunde, Düsseldorf and Berlin.

From Berlin he sent me a pessimistic judgment on post-war Germany.

"My first impression is that occupation of a conquered country corrupts and unconditional occupation corrupts unconditionally. The situation here is very alarming. All the Germans seem to expect war."

In May Shirley followed him, temporarily dropping her farm-work to attend a conference in Bavaria for the Labour League of Youth. She and a twenty-year-old fellow-delegate, Tom Deacon, travelled by air to Frankfurt, and then motored two hundred and fifty miles with a German driver of their own age.

When I was seventeen, my mother had regularly arranged for me to be "met" in London and shepherded into the Buxton train on my way home from school. Those nervous apprehensions which hampered my youth had been replaced by this gay, glorious independence; that was something to thank God for, though like most privileges it had occasional risks. Owing to the failure of the car lights in a Bavarian village, Shirley and Tom took nine hours to reach Hof. Eventually arriving after midnight, they were both dumped into a hostel for American G.I.s. On the return journey they smuggled with them to Frankfurt a young Czech refugee who had escaped from Prague.

"She certainly sees life," I wrote to G. "Do you realise that the Party spent £100 on sending those two kids to Hof, and that they were the first British delegates to go officially to any foreign Youth Conference since before the war?"

In July, Shirley decided that she ought to learn something of northern England, of which she knew nothing. For six weeks she worked as a housemaid at an hotel on the coast near Newcastle upon Tyne, sharing an unventilated semi-cupboard with another girl, and accepting sixpenny tips from facetious male customers. In September she returned to London, and spent a month at a Chiswick factory which produced container-tops for a well-known brand of boot-polish.

From this stimulating experience of tin-lid making, she went straight to Somerville.

(5)

Early in May, G. had returned to America to take a series of lectures at a Middle Western University. This time John went with him to fill a vacation post at the Macmillan Company's New York bookstore.

The two had barely reached New York after a stormy flight, when my mother's failing health began rapidly to deteriorate. One morning in April she had awakened with her speech indistinct and the use of her right hand impaired; to me she seemed much the same as usual, but Miss K., her companion, thought she had suffered a slight stroke.

This was the first of many successive small attacks of the cerebral thrombosis to which she eventually succumbed. The doctor reported an interference with the blood-supply to her brain; when this happened, he said, the patient sometimes lived only for a few more weeks.

One day the previous year she had suddenly wept at the prospect of "coming to an end", and I had tried to comfort her by recalling how firmly she had always rejected self-pity. Her unwillingness in her seventies to say farewell to life surprised me, for it had brought her much tragedy and continuous disappointment. Perhaps, I reflected, only those for whom life has been full and rich are ready to face death as part of experience. Perhaps the frustrated secretly dream of some golden moment, some bright compensation for past disillusionment, which will ultimately be theirs, and in that hope cling to life.

Now some half-conscious acceptance of physical decline seemed to have calmed this restless expectation. Once she inquired why John had not come to see her, but never in those final weeks did she mention my father or refer to Edward, though all her affection had centred upon him and his loss had been her greatest sorrow. She talked only of the trifles which surrounded her, and turned to me for every conscious need.

Death, it seemed, "which taketh all away", had removed perspective from memory even before he came. Thus, at the last, I was the only person in her life, and witnessed its end.

During one of Miss K.'s half days in the late spring, I sat beside my mother as she drowsed in a chair; her disturbing habit of escaping from us both and losing herself in the King's Road traffic had now ceased. Her white hair, the grey curls at the back so carefully dressed, framed a face which still wore the evidence of its former delicate beauty. She did not suggest to me a dying elderly woman but someone familiar and ageless, so much a part of the daily picture that I still could not imagine it without her.

Yet my mother had climbed the citadel of time, and I was now ascending its slopes; already my past years lay spread behind me like a landscape. When I die, I thought, no one else will ever see the rich and vivid pattern which is the panorama of my life.

My mother opened her eyes, and suddenly spoke.

"Whatever happens," she said slowly, "you've always been wonderful to me."

It was not, of course, true. Remorsefully I recalled the many times when, hardening my heart, I had left her and gone abroad; the Sundays on which, truthfully pleading work, I had allowed her to struggle by herself up the difficult steps outside St. Martin-in-the-Fields.

During my rebellious girlhood, having little in common, we had been constantly at loggerheads, but now the sorrows of our era and our mutual memories had drawn us together. I was glad that the approach of death had eliminated, with so much else, the consciousness of my failures, and after the years of criticism felt that I had received a superb and moving reward.

The mental picture of the steps at St. Martin's reminded me that I had heard—vaguely, for I was not then a member of the congregation—that a new Vicar had recently come to the parish. Remembering how much my mother had valued a visit which his predecessor, the late Eric Loveday, had paid her when she was ill on an earlier occasion, I wrote to ask if one of St. Martin's clergy could spare the time to see her before she died.

Next morning, when I was working at home, the telephone rang. It was Miss K., an Irish Catholic by birth and tradition, and she seemed unusually agitated.

"Can you come round at once? It's the Vicar!"

"What Vicar?" I said, temporarily confused.

"I don't know, but he's here—in the flat!"

She sounded as though the whole place were about to blow up, so I hurried round the corner of Flood Street to Rossetti Gardens Mansions. And there, making the modest dimensions of my mother's living-room look smaller still, stood the tall clergyman with the young face and white hair who eight years afterwards became Bishop of Worcester.

Beneath strongly-marked eyebrows his kindly, quizzical eyes brought unforeseen reassurance. Chelsea was not in St. Martin's parish, but on receiving my letter he had characteristically come at once, himself.

"Just fancy!" said my mother when I explained that her caller was the new Vicar. On his next visit she was totally unconscious, and at his invitation I remained during the short prayers for the dying. When I took him to the door, he remarked almost casually: "I recently lost my own mother," as though to emphasise that emotion was quite appropriate at such a time.

From the Church itself the social workers who ran the old people's tea-parties sent me a letter which showed that amongst them, unknown to her family, my mother had found a niche.

"We all loved her for her kind interest and sympathy with the members, who are mostly aged. . . . Many of us will lift her up to God in our prayers."

Early in June another stroke deprived her of the power of speech and the use of her limbs. As I dared not now go farther away than my own house, where I was constantly on call, I spent many of those strange summer days in correcting the proofs of *Born 1925* on her dining-room table. Though she could not utter my name,

443

a sudden joy came into her eyes whenever she found me sitting beside her. A quiet dignity, deeply moving in its utter defencelessness, had replaced the fatalistic pessimism always so ready to distrust the best and believe the worst.

The persistent echoes of the Cold War now gathering round the Russian blockade of Berlin and the Allied air-lift seemed to come into the hushed apartment from very far away. That spring I had found in a heap of papers a copy of *Cavalcade* containing one of G.'s San Francisco articles; on another page a news paragraph jubilantly reported the end of the war.

"So the Hitlerite reign of terror which at one time threatened to become universal draws to a close, and when accounts with Japan have been settled, the earth will be once more a place where free men can walk in peace."

It was difficult to know whether to laugh or cry. In the First War people had really believed that they were making the world safe for posterity; from the Second, though they had long ceased to credit "all that nonsense", they had hoped for a reasonable period of tranquillity. In this third variety which had not yet warmed up from cold controversy to heated shooting, all that apparently mattered was to come out on top in the current manoeuvres.

During the past six months, international tension had been accelerated by a series of untoward events. In February we had read of the Communist *coup* in Czechoslovakia and the death—was it murder or suicide?—of genial Jan Masaryk. During April an air collision over Berlin between a passenger aircraft and a Soviet fighter had cost fifteen lives without markedly disturbing the ironic apathy of a Europe exhausted by perpetual crises. On May 28th the Speaker of the House of Commons hopefully laid the foundation stone of the new Chamber.

At least my mother, who had suffered so much in two wars, would escape a third. To G., concerned because I had been left to face this crisis without his support, I wrote that I had reached a mood of "acceptance of inevitable human mortality", and he must not reproach himself because his work called him abroad.

"The death of the old is sad, but it is not like the death of the young, of which I have seen so much too much. But I do wish she could go and be released—only life in her is so strong, as it always has been, and even now that she cannot control it, it seems as if it won't release her."

Amy and Charles Burnett were helping me devotedly, I told him, and on the afternoon of June 23rd Shirley appeared at my mother's flat from Frating, though I had not sent for her. That night, in the small hours, the summons came.

To G. I wrote that she had gone very fast at the end, leaving us after three long slow breaths which ceased without resistance.

"The strange thing was that though her cheeks were sunken and her mouth twisted, she looked really beautiful—not cyanosed as she had been, and so peaceful that I felt for the first time that perhaps in her soul there was a fundamental peace (a peace to which the poor aged women at St. Martin's somehow reached down); and that all the restlessness and inability to take pleasure in the usual sources of enjoyment was due to superficial physical causes which she perhaps could not help.

"The years seemed to have fallen away, and she looked like a still lovely woman of no more than forty or fifty—just lying against the pillows and dying so quietly without any fuss. That is how I wish to remember her."

(7)

At dawn I unlocked the small leather suitcase which my mother had told me to open after her death. It contained her few private papers, with a careful description of its contents written on each; in spite of the confusion with which her failing mind had wrestled, she had made a most conscientious effort to spare me trouble.

After various minor legacies, she had left me the residue of her modest personal estate and made me her sole executor; clearly she trusted nobody else. A final letter contained precise instructions for a funeral followed by cremation.

". . . Then my ashes, do not have them put in an urn and buried . . . I want them scattered to the winds and be no more seen."

When I telephoned St. Martin's to ask if the funeral could be held there, the Vicar, owing to the early hour, answered himself. Immediately he volunteered to conduct both the small private ceremony in the Church and the Committal Service at Golders Green.

On June 28th, a cool day of heavy thunder-showers and occasional gleams of sunshine, the little cortège left Chelsea with my cross of Ophelia roses lying on the purple-lidded coffin. My mother would have been pleased, I thought, that on the way to St. Martin's her mortal remains passed through Piccadilly, where afternoons of window-shopping had been one of her few real enjoyments.

Beneath a sudden downpour the Vicar and I drove from the

445

church to Golders Green, with Shirley and my aunt from Kent in the car beside us. Getting leave from her farm, Shirley had insisted on staying with me at 2 Cheyne Walk for the past four days. But at seventeen a grandmother's death is seldom a tragedy; while my aunt and I sat silent, she entertained the Vicar all the way to the crematorium and back with lively conversation.

His sustaining presence quietly dominated the Duke of Bedford's private chapel, now used for family cremations and decorated with blue and pink hydrangeas. While he spoke the final words of the Committal prayer—"Through our Lord Jesus Christ; who shall change our vile body, that it may be like unto his glorious body, according to the mighty working, whereby he is able to subdue all things to himself"—the heavy shower ended. As the doors behind the altar opened and the coffin passed under a glass roof, the sun shone brilliantly on the purple pall and flame-coloured roses.

"One had the extraordinary illusion," I wrote afterwards to G., "of the gates of heaven opening to take her in."

The following afternoon I returned alone to Golders Green. Several friends offered to come with me, but I wanted no one there who was not close to me; nor did I wish to impose the final weight of human destiny upon my young Shirley who had been so good.

When the small heap of ashes was scattered between the rose-garden and the sundial, I seemed to see all my past life dissolving into dust. A strong breeze was blowing; in a moment my mother had her wish and was "no more seen". Suddenly I found myself weeping as I had never wept for Roland or Edward or Winifred.

Today a stone tablet close to the spot bears beneath my mother's name the words: "*Fiat Lux*."

(8)

The usual avalanche of immediate business followed the funeral.

"I am really thankful to have so much to do that I have had no time for the inevitable self-reproaches that death always brings," I wrote to G. I added in a letter to John, who with youthful detachment from the heritage of the past had assumed that I should be relieved by my new freedom, "You must realise that it is possible to miss even constant demands and handicaps. It will be more than a week or a month before I lose the feeling of utter strangeness when I pass Rossetti Gardens Mansions and realise that no one is waiting there perpetually longing for me to come. Like Christian in the *Pilgrim's Progress*, I shall have to learn to walk without my burden."

As I systematically cleared my mother's flat, giving away her elegant clothes according to her written instructions, and distributing the odd little collections of medicines and matches which she had continued to hoard long after the war, the tensions in Europe approached a new crescendo.

With Bevin and Vyshinsky maintaining a noisy duel at the United Nations Assembly against the overall clatter of the Allied air lift, the shadows deepened until September. The other Powers occupying Germany then referred their dispute with Russia to the Security Council. In the United States the Un-American Activities Committee captured the headlines with spy-ring allegations, and the long series of recriminations began between Whittaker Chambers and Alger Hiss.

Throughout the summer I went through family documents; this involuntary research into my parents' star-crossed lives seemed even stranger than the vigil at my mother's bedside. She had kept, I found, every item associated with Edward; old examination papers set by our governess; preparatory school photographs; and even the bullet-torn uniform, with its blood-stains still visible, in which he had been wounded on the Somme.

From a handful of old receipts I discovered that he had sent five guineas to the Uppingham War Memorial from the Asiago Plateau ten days before he was killed himself. One document, in its conjunction of age and date, epitomised the history of a generation: "Brittain, Edward H., aged 18, passed the Oxford and Cambridge Higher Certificate in the month of July, in the year 1914."

To G. I confessed that I had spilled some tears over the scanty mementoes of my father. He had sent a small Easter card enclosing a pressed rose to my mother just before their wedding; after that she had kept almost nothing until the last months of his life. One letter from a nursing home where he had struggled for health in the care of a well-known neurologist pathetically attempted to explain his melancholia.

"Dr. R. tells me that I have a highly skilled technical brain, and not having been able to use it for so long, it has turned upon me."

When all my mother's possessions had been distributed, I went to Rossetti Gardens Mansions for a final inspection before handing over the keys to the company's office. Now that the flat was empty it looked just as it had done when I took it for my mother five years earlier, with the sunlight streaming into the south rooms, overlooking the green and peaceful back gardens, which I had thought that she would use instead of the larger north-facing rooms where she always felt cold.

447

In the bare apartment which I should never visit again, I realised anew how much, especially on Sunday afternoons, I should miss her. In spite of our profound differences of tastes and values, the shared experiences of half a century had as deeply united us. There was no longer anyone near to me who remembered Edward and Roland, or Victor and Geoffrey; no one with whom to speak of the small things that made up a picture of my childhood—the pug-dog called Koko with which Edward and I had played; the bicycle rides over the Buxton moors; the journeys to Uppingham. Except in the solitary recesses of my mind these things were gone, scattered like my mother's ashes upon the wind.

I closed the door on the sunlit rooms, and went down into the street.

(9)

Early in September I settled temporarily in Bedford, where Bunyan lived for thirty-three years, and with determination began to read for my biography.

In July the Society for the Propagation of Christian Knowledge had celebrated its two hundred and fiftieth anniversary with a special performance of the *Pilgrim's Progress* by the Covent Garden Choir and Ballet. I had seen this beautiful programme, in which Robert Speaight played the part of Christian, and on August 31st, the 350th anniversary of Bunyan's death, had visited his grave in Bunhill Fields off the City Road. That experience had been less inspiring than the Covent Garden ballet, for I had found Bunhill Fields severely blitzed and Bunyan's effigy defaced by splinters.

A residential hotel in Bedford's De Parys Avenue offered friendliness and calm; its intelligent proprietress took so keen an interest in my book that she subsequently drove me in her own car to historic sites all over the county.

"Not the least part of the fun of this job is the kindness of the Bedford people," I wrote to G., whose own ancestors came from Bedfordshire. "The Deputy Librarian has constituted himself my Evangelist. After the grim summer I am enjoying it greatly. I have never known any town other than a university town which takes so much interest in its own history and has documented itself so well."

The Deputy Librarian, Cyril Hargreaves—a keen young Lancashire man with spectacled humorous eyes—took charge of the John Bunyan Library presented to the town by the Bunyan specialist, Dr. Frank Mott Harrison. Here, under Mr. Hargreaves's enthusiastic guidance, I spent my mornings. He proved to be a skilled amateur

448

photographer, who provided most of the illustrations which subsequently adorned the book.

During the afternoons I strolled beside the Ouse through the peaceful Midland town, placarded with Bunyan memorials, or explored the pleasant villages, often only a mile or two apart, which gave its fascination to a county thought commonplace by uninformed travellers.

At Elstow, where the splendid Abbey Church represents Bedfordshire's cathedral and a still rustic lane leads straight from the main road to the Middle Ages, I stood before the brick and timber Moot Hall on the village green where Bunyan heard the Voice which led to his conversion. In Stevington I found the ancient Gothic Cross that tradition identified as the place at which Christian lost his burden, and from the ruins of Houghton House ("House Beautiful") on Ampthill Heights overlooking the Chilterns saw a typically tranquil view of "the Delectable Mountains". I understood now why Bunyan had looked no further than his native county for the scenes of his Pilgrim's adventures.

One warm September day sent me in search of Bunyan's reputed birthplace amid the semi-cultivated fields round Harrowden hamlet. With the growing excitement of an amateur detective, I struggled through waist-high brussels sprouts to a weed-covered mound concealed by tangled bushes on the banks of a narrow stream. The Vicar of St. Martin's, a Bunyan devotee, subsequently told me that he had also made this journey with my book in his hand.

No sign-post then informed the traveller that he was treading historic ground. Today a placard perpetuates the legend that the heap of stones beneath the bushes was once a rough cottage with a thatched roof overhanging its narrow windows.

Soon these minor preoccupations, perhaps because I really needed their solace, became so absorbing that I almost forgot the Cold War. But when the newspapers reported the death of Mohammed Ali Jinnah, who had so soon followed Gandhi from the turbulent scene of political partition, and the assassination of Count Bernadotte, appointed Mediator in Palestine by the United Nations in May, I realised that Europe could claim no monopoly of the tragedies which cast their shadow over the sunny autumn days.

Only G.'s return from America made a break in this uneventful routine; during October he came to Bedford for the day and cheered me by his presence. Like John he had expected my mother's death to mean release rather than sorrow, and I found difficulty in explaining the degree to which it was both. But he understood why, tired out by the twentieth century and its problems, I had temporarily escaped into the now academic perturbations of the seventeenth.

While I worked on my book amid the quaint idiosyncrasies of the residents at my Bedford hotel, John and Shirley had gone up to Oxford for their first term at New College and Somerville.

John was eventually to become a member of the new Psychology School and to join the advertising profession as a research worker; now, assisted by a grant from the Ministry of Education, he represented one example of that "flow of ex-servicemen to the Universities" which had not yet reached its peak. Shirley wrote me from a new experience of delight that "Oxford is heaven and heaven is wonderful". Already she was an active member of the Oxford University Labour Club.

Reading Philosophy, Politics and Economics, she found Philosophy the weakest of her three subjects and, unconsciously selecting her future husband, sought the help of a Balliol Philosophy Scholar a year her senior. In her second year she became one of the Feature writers of *The Isis*, the famous University magazine, and during the Long Vacation toured the United States with the Oxford University Players as Cordelia in *King Lear*. At the beginning of her third year, she was elected the first woman chairman of the Labour Club.

These extra-curriculum activities were to rob her of her First as certainly as my literary preoccupations at college had deprived me of mine. But I was not entitled to lament this loss for either of us; the Labour Club, like my editorship of *Oxford Poetry*, pointed more appropriately to the future than a high academic degree. I rejoiced in her happiness, and the spiritual home which she found at Oxford represented for me a form of fulfilment that coincided with her own.

Although, in the circumscribed Buxton existence, Oxford had meant the realisation of an early dream which once seemed unattainable, its achievement was never complete until Shirley went to college. There she experienced the loves and friendships of which history had robbed me; the gorgeous normality that in a war-time and post-war university had never been mine. Her three years at Somerville proved that everything I had believed of Oxford could really come true.

Gone, for her, were the foolish and suggestive chaperone rules of my undergraduate days; gone too the ridiculous regulations which had prevented even Edward from visiting me in college. Men and women now found their natural level in a university which had become, at long last, a true microcosm of the adult society for which its youth was preparing.

Equally typical of modern Oxford were Shirley's married Principal and Economics tutor; wives and mothers who understood the humours and exasperations of normal family life were partially replacing the unmarried women who had once figured almost exclusively in female Senior Common Rooms. Even the Commission of Human Rights, now functioning under the chairmanship of Mrs. Roosevelt, and the Status of Woman Commission set up by the United Nations, seemed both to be part of Shirley's Somerville.

That spring, before either John or Shirley went to college, the Oxford University Labour Club had invited me to be one of its "distinguished visitors" during the Michaelmas Term. I had accepted largely because this engagement would give me an opportunity of seeing the children without the appearance of unwelcome curiosity. As the subject of my address I chose "Some Values of British Socialism", and for several weeks beforehand sought G.'s co-operation. I was well aware, I told him, that "I mustn't 'muff' this speech. Shinwell's reception by the O.U. Labour Club has made me rather apprehensive, though I don't flatter myself I shall attract the same amount of attention!"

On a sunny morning with a cool November breeze, three days after Harry S. Truman's unexpected victory for the Democrats in the American Presidential Election, I walked with Shirley through the familiar streets to my luncheon engagement. I was thankful to find a good attendance, but as she listened to my speech she tore a programme slowly to pieces for fear I should let her down before her friends. When the talk went well, and the discussion continued until the chairman stopped it at 3.15, her relief was manifest.

"She thought you were going to make a fool of her," said John later; the idea seemed to amuse him.

"I daresay I wasn't asked to speak because I was her mother," I said, sharing his mood. We recalled that the Labour Club had first approached me when she was ten months old.

Three weeks after the luncheon, when I was finishing my work at the John Bunyan Library, she telephoned me that she was coming to Bedford for the night. I booked a room for her at my hotel, and eventually she arrived on her bicycle. What was the reason for this visit, I wondered, since we should both be back in London within a few days? Had a financial difficulty arisen, or some sudden love affair in which she actually wanted to consult me?

But when she had eaten a large tea and curled up comfortably before my bed-sitting room fire, she mentioned no problem and appeared to be in her usual friendly mood. Finally I inquired as casually as I could: "What made you decide to come? Was there some special reason?"

"Oh, no," she said amiably. "I just thought how fond of you I was, so I came."

Long ago indeed seemed the days in which she was never going to the shops or the Post Office, but only "out". That night I went to bed feeling abundantly repaid for all the years since 1930.

(11)

In December I returned to Chelsea, with my book a huge scaffolding of references, organised in chapters, to a year's notes. The shape was there, but the task of transforming this framework into narrative seemed formidable indeed. Yet it would have to be done in four months if, as G. was now insisting, I was to go to the West Indies for a "real holiday" in May.

In spite of the paper restrictions and binding problems which handicapped English publishers, my novel *Born 1925* was at last due to appear, and for Christmas I sent an advance copy to Elin Wägner. This gift was acknowledged by a friend; Elin was very ill, she said, after a difficult operation four weeks ago, and there was no hope of her recovery.

Elin died on January 7th, 1949, the publication day of *Born 1925*. The Swedish Press distributed her unpretentious picture under banner headlines; the Swedish Academy mourned its one woman member, and replaced her by a man.

We had known each other for three years and three months.

From my publisher I soon learned that *Born 1925* was selling well, and one or two translations were already under discussion. The normal contingent of reviews followed publication, but my mother's death and the loss of Elin's stimulating friendship had left me without the courage to read them. So I put the clippings into a folder for some future date when I should feel better able to face the critics.

There, untouched, the elastic-banded bundles remain to this day.

That autumn, following the retirement of the Welsh writer George Llewelyn Davies, the Peace Pledge Union invited me to become its chairman. I accepted, and held the position for two years.

It seemed strange now to reflect on the cost to myself of this small group with its dedicated membership; to recall how dangerous it had been considered by excitable bureaucrats and other persons anxious to discover traitors where none existed. There were difficulties still, of course; though the slur of "Fascism" had evaporated, Communist organisations with subtle skill were confusing peace aims with Soviet propaganda. But this type of misrepresentation was now a familiar weapon. As Mrs. Vyvyan Adams had recognised during the war, the problems which it raised were not of a kind to change the course followed by any person of integrity.

Although the Peace Pledge Union was no longer the large and prosperous organisation of which Dick Sheppard had been chairman, it had still, with its supporting newspaper *Peace News*, a revolutionary function to perform in a society still dominated by traditional behaviour. In March 1949 the end of Save Europe Now, whose diminishing obligations had been taken over by the Society of Friends, meant one group less in which the underlying violence of normal political values did not obtain. And though the Berlin dispute had been referred to the Security Council, American-Soviet differences, with the atom bomb as their final argument, continued to darken the international horizon.

In December the arrest of Cardinal Mindszenty, Primate of Hungary, had renewed the apprehension, and in February the controversy which followed his sentence of life imprisonment had kept it alive. On April 9th, Great Britain and the United States, with nine other countries, signed the North Atlantic Treaty which represented an important Allied manoeuvre in the Cold War.

Yet the spring brought reassurance too; the counter-blockade of Berlin continued to be effective, and in May the Soviet Union lifted its ban. That same month saw the end of military government in Germany and a new Constitution signed at Bonn.

Against this background I had finished the story of John Bunyan's distant turmoils, putting myself on a strict routine of one large chapter every six days. It meant six daily hours of continuous writing, but, as I had written to G. from Bedford, "this West Indies trip is like a perpetual carrot in front of my nose, driving me on to work for fear of losing it."

I sent the manuscript to Rich and Cowan just as the newspapers announced the end of clothes rationing and the return of neon lighting, which made Piccadilly itself again. With relief I learned that the publishers thought well of this book which had demanded so little of the usual tension, and at last could leave for the Caribbean holiday on which G. had so long insisted.

A minor political campaign prevented G. from accompanying me at the outset of our journey, so he arranged to fly and meet me in New York. I travelled alone in the new *Mauretania* and among the passengers discovered Ruth Draper, a small observant middle-aged woman, in the company of Mrs. Charles Dana Gibson. Taller than her sister Nancy Astor, Mrs. Gibson appeared, at seventy-five, as upright and clothes-conscious as a girl of seventeen.

When we stopped on our first evening at flood-lit Havre, I saw that it had been worse damaged than Calais or Boulogne. Looking down from the harbour into the bustling streets, I noticed many new buildings rising from the ruins left by the last ferocious battles, and remembered that the playwright, William Douglas Home, had voluntarily accepted a prison sentence as an officer rather than obey an order which would have meant the large-scale death of Havre civilians.

At New York G. duly met me, and we stayed for a few days. We found that, as in 1946, the British were not conspicuously popular; the worst sterling crisis since 1947 was now in progress, and a section of the Press was conducting a vehement campaign against the economic policy of the Labour Government.

One friend remained unaffected by the periodic acerbity of Anglo-American squabbles; Mr. Oswald Garrison Villard invited us to his flat, but I was shocked and saddened by the change in my loyal supporter.

A stroke had followed the period of failing health which had coincided with my last visit to America; now, white and shrunken, he lived in a wheel chair under the care of a nurse. When he died that autumn I could not regret his passing as I had regretted Elin's, for his vigorous life, like my mother's, had run its course. But I wrote to G. in October that I should always miss his letters, "which, pessimistic though they tended to be in recent years, were always full of such illuminating comments on current happenings."

We travelled south to Miami in a new stream-lined train known as "The Silver Star", and flew for seven hours to Ciudad Trujillo, capital of the Dominican Republic. Once this city had been familiar to Caribbean travellers as Santo Domingo; its new name flattered the Republic's pocket dictator. Packed into the picturesque islands of which it was part were most of the world's races and nations, washed up on these sunny shores by the current of history as it rose and receded.

Like many recent adventures, this visit to the Dominican Republic resulted from a "fan-mail" letter. In Bedford the previous autumn I had opened an envelope with a beautiful postage stamp showing a map of the West Indies, and found that my correspondent, Carol McAfee Morgan, was the wife of an American Presbyterian minister in Ciudad Trujillo.

She and her husband, she wrote, ran an interdenominational mission which included twenty-one churches, a hundred-bed hospital, and "the best bookstore in the Caribbean". If ever I were near the West Indies, she hoped I would come and stay. When I replied that we were planning to visit Jamaica in the spring, an invitation to fly first to Trujillo followed by return mail.

The Morgans awaited us at the airport, and took us to their cream-coloured villa. It was set in the midst of a real tropical garden, moist and verdant because the rains had started; my book had kept me at work until the fashionable season for the Caribbean was over. Palms abounded, and cactus as tall as trees; the flowers recalled New Orleans; an arch of "heart of man", white in the morning but crimson in the evening, divided the lawn. Swallows wheeled over it, and lizards, green and brown with white shirt-fronts, leaped such long distances that at first I took them for swallows too.

Our correspondents proved to be easy and generous hosts; visits to their schools and churches occupied only a small part of the time spent in meeting local personalities. These included the Archbishop and an aged Latin-American poet, Amerigo Lugo, who told us that years ago he had been appointed to write the history of the Dominican Republic. When the present Government ordered him to include President Trujillo in his book he refused, saying that this was not the brand of history which he wrote. His notes were thereupon seized as "the property of the government".

The sweltering sunny days and the nights of heavy rain, like noisy tea-trays being banged on the villa roof, inevitably ended in the regretful hour when we left Trujillo for two days in Port-au-Prince, the capital of Haiti, on our way to Jamaica. But there was nothing to regret in a visit to this lively Negro republic, one of the few French-speaking territories on the American Continent.

Here, in the Citadelle Hotel run by an American-Haitian couple, high above the town and the bay, we really rested for the first and only time. Except for M. Dantes Bellegarde, the writer who had once represented Haiti at Geneva, nobody knew us or understood either our English or our French.

Lying on my bed in the heavy, humid air, I looked sleepily down on the huge semicircular basin of the city, surrounded with low hills backed by high-mountains. Amid the olive-hued palms stood white tropical buildings with red-tiled roofs; from our window the primitive mud-huts beside the half-made roads, which gave one, said G., an idea of the Far East, were hidden by the dense green counterpane of trees.

Black and yellow butterflies flitted over their summits beneath the Citadelle's white terrace, and lizards made sudden zigzags over the stones. Conspicuous in the middle distance the palace of the President, enormous coffee-black, kingly Paul Magloire, stood out like a wedding cake against the pale buff-grey of the twin-spired cathedral.

It might have been a town in French Equatorial Africa, and we were sorry to leave it.

(13)

In Jamaica our hotel overlooked the harbour. Beyond the wide lawn stretched a green-tiled swimming pool, fringed with outsize palms permanently inhabited by avaricious-looking kites. Whenever I bathed there I felt that the kites were patiently waiting for me to drown.

Every morning and evening Jamaica's habitual trade winds ruffled the palms, bringing a perpetual restlessness to the island. Close to the hotel, Kingston's red light district stretched indefinitely from a corner of the main road.

When the plane descended over the city, it appeared as a haphazard collection of unfinished shacks. This impression was not wholly unjust; walking that evening through the streets, we felt that British colonial civilisation compared sadly with the Spanish dignity of Trujillo and the French insouciance of Haiti. Over all Kingston an impression of squalor lay like the faint but indelible stamp of a postmark.

Beyond the main fruit market, a drive took us past Jamaica's "cardboard city", otherwise known as "wapem-bapem" or "the dungle". Here the police periodically burned down the cardboard shacks, erected on the remnants of grass amid indescribable debris, which housed a nondescript population. Since the municipality did not provide alternative shelter, the ejected occupants were compelled to return and live as best they could in the charred ruins.

This society with its decorative upper crust and sordid fringes

456

nevertheless appeared to be the one British territory which, at least officially, had abolished the colour-bar. On the fashionable hotel terrace, the white visitors entertained Jamaicans of all hues from coffee black to pale cocoa brown. Much of Jamaica's wealth appeared to be in Syrian or Jewish hands; our hotel proprietor, Mr. Elias Issa, was an energetic Syrian who had lived in the island for fifty years.

Among numerous invitations came one, promised before we left England, from the Governor to visit his residence, the King's House, on the beautiful slopes of palm-clad mountains. Sir John Huggins, tall, handsome and dignified, proved to be an expert on West Indian cricket. His wife Molly, one of the most glamorous of "First Ladies", was away in Washington arranging a lecture tour. At dinner he told me of a visit which the Roosevelts had made to the King's House in 1944, and immediately we returned to the hotel I recorded in my diary the incident that he had related.

"They" (the Roosevelts) "said then that Franklin D. must and would stand for a fourth term as he alone knew the whole set-up, but (quite calmly) they both realised that it would kill him and accepted the fact that it was a sacrifice he was called on to make."

Sir John continued by saying that he greatly admired Eleanor Roosevelt, and felt furious when the local Opposition newspapers deliberately published her worst photographs. From the Roosevelts he went on to discuss West Indian politicians. I carried away clear mental pictures of Alexander Bustamente, the shrewd First Minister who suggested a Jamaican version of Aneurin Bevan, and James Manley, the more restrained but able leader of the Opposition.

By chance these two made appointments with G. for the same afternoon, and he talked to the Irish-Jamaican Bustamente, full of uproarious life, with the disconcerting knowledge that his chief opponent was almost due. Considerable finesse was required; with some assistance from me, G. managed to usher the loquacious Mr. Bustamente into the hotel bar just as the handsome, gentlemanly Mr. Manley appeared at the garden door.

"What fun we do have!" said G. when both had departed.

One evening he chanced to meet a fellow victim of the *Western Prince*; recognising him, she invited us to visit Tate and Lyle's new sugar factory, where her husband was a manager. This journey through the old Spanish Town to the flat country surrounding an alligator-inhabited salt river forty miles away made real to me the isolated lives led by the managers of colonial industries and their wives. Level, insect-ridden fields surrounded the small settlement;

no roads fit for walking existed; available books and magazines were few and ancient. It seemed a strange little *enclave* of human desolation in a modern world.

On our return we attended a function at the local P.E.N. founded by a white resident, Mrs. Ormsby Marshall, and later addressed a Readers and Writers Circle for the Jamaican poetess, Una Marson, who had worked with the B.B.C. during the War. Her organisation, she said, encouraged the youth of Jamaica "to read and take literature seriously".

That evening two hundred brown-skinned boys and girls, packed into a small room and verandah, took us seriously enough to continue the discussion in extinguishing heat for over three hours. The dark young chairman, Victor Stafford Reid from the editorial staff of the *Daily Gleaner*, had recently published with Alfred Knopf a first novel, *New Day*, which told the story of Jamaica's struggle for independence.

Before we flew home, Mr. Elias Issa drove us across the island over hairpin roads, twisting and turning through deep green valleys lush with plantains and bananas, to his new Tower Island Hotel on the north shore. Here a coral reef protected the modern bathing beach from sharks, and pale orange sun-blinds adorned the green-tiled verandahs.

Only when I saw the sapphire waves breaking gently on the white sand, and felt the cool wind which stirred the bright curtains round the open windows, did I remember that the restful holiday of which I had dreamed was quite different from the functions, Press interviews and literary talks which had made Jamaica a miniature version of an American lecture tour.

(14)

We returned to a restless summer of dock strikes and financial crises, in which politically-conscious Londoners painfully discussed the international status of Communist China and the prospective devaluation of the pound.

At Allum Green, where Shirley joined me for part of the Long Vacation, I found as usual a quiet detachment from contemporary alarms and a swift recovery from the stress of travels which had brought more mental stimulus than physical rest.

In the summerhouse where so much of *Testament of Friendship* and *Born 1925* had been written, I corrected the proofs of *John Bunyan* and wrote an Introduction for the Classics Edition in which Collins had arranged eventually to publish *South Riding*. They reserved this series

458

for books likely to be permanent, an estimate justified by the continued success of Winifred's novel, which made the work for her literary estate almost as persistent as it had been ten years earlier.

That autumn I visited Hull and there saw the *South Riding* manuscript, handsomely bound in jade-green leather with her initials tooled in gold, which I had presented to the Central Library where so much of it was written. It was insured, the Librarian told me, for £500.

"How cruel that Winifred never knew of its success!" I thought once more as my train passed the sunlit estuary of the Humber which she had so often described. Yet her spirit which still seemed to haunt its flat marshy banks reminded me that she had always been concerned to create life rather than profit by her creation.

As I travelled about England, typical echoes of the Cold War continued to sound from Europe, where Heuss was now established as President of the West German Republic and Adenauer, once Mayor of Cologne, as its Chancellor. The news in late September that the Soviet Union had produced an atomic explosion appropriately coincided with the preparations for Stalin's seventieth birthday and the publication of George Orwell's *Nineteen-Eighty-Four*.

Questioned about these events on various platforms, I faced the usual critics who insisted that Gandhian methods could succeed only when used by spiritual giants like himself. The time available was too short, I believed, to wait for their chance appearance. We must use such imperfect moral equipment as the Lord in his wisdom had seen fit to give us.

"Someone," I wrote G. from Yorkshire, "must make a breach in the vicious circle of ever more destructive but still ineffective military weapons. Have not both the Government and the Opposition endorsed, in four short years, what we said during the war about both obliteration bombing and unconditional surrender?"

When I rejoined him in London, the problems which afflicted the Western world were already beginning to appear in a new perspective. At the end of November, invited by a group of Gandhi's disciples to study his revolutionary teaching, I was going at last to India.

CHAPTER TWELVE

TURN AGAIN HOME

"The whole world may be lost and if you remain to share the experience it is not lost. The whole world may remain and you go, and I am lost . . .

"Of our short play on the stage, so short before the actors are gone, the scenery decayed, the pretty dresses in rags, the actors dead and dust, this is the best, the climax of it. To whichever of us falls the lot to hold the other dead, their sorrow will be limited by the proud joy that the act was well played and they can recite their nunc dimittis *with an unfeignedly glad heart to the Creator who gave. This is marriage."*

G.C. TO V.B., 1927.

(1)

THE FORMAL INVITATION to visit India had reached me in 1948 when my mother was dying. For some time I had known that I was likely to receive it.

Soon after the war, a few of Gandhi's Quaker friends had suggested that perhaps fifty individuals from different countries who were interested in his technique should meet him to discuss the creation of peace through spiritual power. The Mahatma welcomed the idea, but insisted that the invitations should be confined to those whose witness had been, in his own words, "a hundred per cent reliable". He wanted to meet only those war-resisters who had stood firm against the basically fascist attempts of their communities to make them conform, and who saw the war against war as something even larger—a fight for the integrity of man's free mind.

In 1947, Gandhi decided to postpone the Conference until the "British bayonets" had been withdrawn from India. The chosen visitors would be asked to meet in two places in January 1949. At the first, Santiniketan in West Bengal, the poet Rabindranath Tagore had founded his long dreamed-of "university", Visva-Bharati, as a centre of world-culture; at the second, a village known as Sevagram in the Central Provinces, Gandhi had established his latest ashram.

Between the two sessions the guests were invited to travel round India, visiting especially places where reconstruction by Gandhian methods was in progress, and studying the needs and aspirations of the Indian people.

Had this programme maintained its original dates, my mother's death and the long-delayed fulfilment of my Bunyan contract would have prevented me from attending the Conference. The tragic chance of Gandhi's assassination enabled me to go, for though his friends decided that his scheme must not be abandoned, the necessary reconstruction of plans made postponement inevitable.

From the top of a bus on the morning of January 30th, 1948, I had seen with shocked incredulity the hastily-scribbled posters announcing Gandhi's murder, and later stood with the silent crowd which watched the green, white and orange flag flying half-mast from India House in that day's dismal rain. Shortly afterwards I went to the Memorial Meeting held for him at Friends House with the consciousness that this was one of those moments in the life of the world when some great event, terrible or glorious, summons men from their preoccupation with inessentials to confront the deeper realities of their day.

At that meeting were three of the friends who had helped me to play with greater understanding my small part in the campaign for Indian independence; Carl Heath took the Chair, Lord Pethick-Lawrence made one of the speeches, and Agatha Harrison sat silent on the platform. Inevitably I thought of others; H. N. Brailsford, whose articles I had read; Reginald Sorensen, M.P., of the India League; Edward Thompson, whose books I had reviewed up to his death in 1946. Before the meeting broke up we sang Gandhi's favourite hymn, "When I survey the wondrous Cross", which linked the aged Apostle of non-violence with the young Prince of Peace.

At the trial of Gandhi's assassin, which began in the Red Fort at Delhi the following June, Nathuram Vinayak Godse of the fanatical Hindu Mahasabha declared that he had been alone in his act.

"I thought it my duty," he said, "to put an end to the life of the so-called father of the nation, who had played a very prominent part in bringing about the vivisection of the country."

In spite of this uncompromising statement, it seemed unlikely that Gandhi would have endorsed the death sentence passed upon Godse on February 10th, 1949. The following November a few early delegates to the World Conference who knew the Mahatma's views on capital punishment pleaded with the Indian Government to spare Godse's life, but in spite of their intercession he was executed on November 15th. Two months later, Soviet Russia reinstated capital punishment.

By the time I left England for Calcutta, India and Pakistan alike had lost their patron saints, and Mrs. Sarojini Naidu, that rare combination of poet and politician who symbolised reborn India hardly less than they, had joined them both. In 1941 Rabindranath Tagore, Asia's Leonardo da Vinci, had preceded them all.

Of the great Indian figures well known to the West, only Jahawarlal Nehru remained.

For myself this flight to India had a twofold importance.

First, it would show me in a larger perspective those parts of the world that I already knew. Although I had not yet visited Africa, I had now travelled widely in Europe and America. I had seen war-shattered communities, their past torn up by its roots, seeking renewal through revolution though they might not always recognise the process by that name.

In Asia I knew that this pattern would not so much repeat itself as present a different facet of change. For two hundred years the West had dominated the subject peoples of the East; now, emerging into political consciousness and united less by a common philosophy than by universal awareness of oppression, those peoples were throwing off this traditional overlordship and choosing their own leaders. And in resisting domination they would teach the West that problems existed more fundamental than the quest for power which had unnecessarily produced two gigantic wars; remorseless problems of primary needs insufficiently satisfied by the semi-developed resources of a hostile soil or a primitive civilisation.

Secondly, I should learn more of Gandhi's philosophy and see it in action almost at first hand. Its underlying conceptions of love and non-violence were those which Dick Sheppard, for all his popularity, had preached in vain to militant England. It offered that "dynamism more important than communism" which a famous ex-editor, writing four years afterwards, was to define as the chief task of Western democracy.

Twice in my lifetime I had seen my country win a Great War and lose the peace. Why had this happened? One explanation, at least, could be perceived in the innate violence of leaders unable to find patience for the slow processes of reconciliation.

Gandhi had not made that mistake; his non-violent campaign against repression in India had been carried out by men and women who had first wrestled with the violence within themselves. His programme of *Nai Talim* ("New Education") not only provided an alternative to war more comprehensive and constructive than any previously used, but tackled the failure of individuals at its origins in home life and early upbringing. For him the attainment of world peace was one consequence, inevitable though distant, of the spiritual evolution of the human soul.

This teaching now seemed especially important for the British who had set India free, and not least because non-violence, taken for granted by millions of Indians, was untainted by the self-conscious minority spirit so often characteristic of peace movements in the West. England in Europe, India in Asia, had for the first time in history a similar function to perform; withdrawn for different reasons from the struggle for power, each had the opportunity of averting war between two nations greater than itself. And each, in this task of finding a middle way between the fears and ambitions of two restless Titans facing one another across Atlantic and Pacific, could perhaps contribute what the other lacked.

(3)

In the perspective of half a decade, India and Pakistan come back to me as a succession of sharp contrasts between regions and individuals. No more was it possible to say of any one section, "This is India", than to make the same generalisation about America in any part of the United States.

At Santiniketan, two hundred miles north of Calcutta, where the delegates assembled in November 1949, the Indian Press surprised me by its interest in our Conference; what English newspaper would have sent its correspondent to Ripon or Inverness to report a discussion on non-violence and the future organisation of peace?

A fabulous atmosphere surrounded this home of Tagore, where his family still lived amid the red rolling plains of West Bengal. Immemorial tracks traversed by bullock carts linked the ancient villages; palms and pampas-grass sprang from the dry rust-coloured soil. More privileged than many others, I stayed amid a forest of tents at the Tata House, a large hut with the luxury of a tub-and-bucket washhouse.

"Across the campus," I wrote to G., who had seen me off in a heavy fog from London Airport, "comes the sound of voices talking earnestly—in English with a foreign accent—about the state of the world. I learn that the room I am occupying was used by C. F. Andrews and that he wrote at the desk where I am now writing to you."

The same quality of legend enfolds the memory of Benares and Agra, where the white miracle of the Taj Mahal emerged from a

463

whirlwind of receptions and speeches. At Benares, the Hindu Holy City, I tossed gently with three companions in a launch on the Ganges. Opposite us, on the Burning Ghat a hundred yards away, Hindu corpses in bright silk shrouds lay on bamboo stretchers awaiting the primitive cremation carried out by their families amid the drifting acrid smoke. I noticed a large grey cow walk placidly down the steps which led to the city on the heights, and consume the garland of marigolds adorning the most expensively decked body.

"We then watched the ashes being sifted from baskets into the river—in which, I observed, the inhabitants also clean their teeth," I reported to G., and ended my letter with a description of the hospitable Indian household which at short notice had accommodated ten visiting delegates.

I added a fragment of local colour. "There is a European toilet here, but it doesn't work; the Indian toilet is in full view of the garden and the rest of the house; the doors don't shut. . . . One learns more about India and Indians from such incidents than by living in hotels for six months."

In Delhi the toilets worked, for I stayed magnificently at the home of Mr. Shiva Rao, who was away representing India at Lake Success. From this half-closed palace I accompanied Indian friends to functions across the vast open spaces of Lutyens's New Delhi; heard Mr. Nehru speak on the India Code Bill; and talked with him at a reception in his house for an Indian-American Conference.

Krishna Menon, then High Commissioner in London, had told me that I must not miss the South—the real India where no foreign invader ever penetrated, and even British civilisation had lain as lightly as morning mist. I was not disappointed; as I travelled towards the Indian Ocean until I reached Cape Comorin, India's Land's End, I fell in love with this country of violent colours and sudden gleaming vistas, the land of Pierre Loti's novel, Les Désenchantées.

South India had now become of personal concern to G. For some years Archbishop Mar Ivanios of Travancore had planned to establish a Dominican College in Trivandrum, the capital of the state, building it with the aid of the British Dominicans and making it a missionary centre from the East to the West. On G.'s second visit to India in 1948, the Archbishop had invited him to become its first Provost and help to organise it. He was then unable to remain, but promised to give what support he could. In 1951, when the College had been founded, he returned to Travancore for a period to fulfil his promise and became its Provost.

From the South I returned to Bombay, where I encountered for the first time since leaving Tagore's home the India of art and letters. Here I spoke to a meeting of the Indian P.E.N., and bought its books, edited by Sophia Wadia, on the Indian literatures. I also purchased for John's study the rosewood head of a Bali girl, and an ivory carving which showed the heads of Brahma, Vishnu and Shiva in a sandalwood frame.

At the craft centre founded by Annie Besant at Adyar, near Madras, I had already bought for Shirley a hand-spun white silk saree embroidered with gold thread. Five years afterwards she wore it, skilfully adapted by an Austrian refugee dressmaker, for her marriage to Bernard Williams of New College.

Leaving Bombay, I flew over the frontier between India and Pakistan, still closed to trains and cars, and landed in a dust-storm which effectually tested the skill of the Air India pilot. I found Pakistan's new capital, temporarily forgetting the Kashmir dispute, living in the aftermath of the Ceylon Commonwealth Conference. Receptions abounded, and at nearly all of them I met delegates from Colombo.

In October 1948 this Conference, then held in London, had been attended for the first time by three Prime Ministers of non-white Asian Dominions—Nehru of India, Liaquat Ali Khan of Pakistan, and Senanayake of Ceylon. Now it was the British who came to Asia; Ernest Bevin, shrewd, heavy, somnolent from ill-health, had been in Colombo with Philip Noel-Baker, the Commonwealth Minister. Unlike Bevin, Philip Noel-Baker came on to Karachi, kindly, conscientious, and wearing as usual the appearance of a still athletic but slightly distraught idealist.

(4)

"What of course first matters is people," G. wrote me of India in one of his letters, "and to sort out people is not easy in this swarming, deeply undemocratic land."

It was not easy. Who, at the end of the first few weeks, really stood out? The chief place had inevitably to be given to India's Prime Minister, Jawaharlal Nehru, who as a still young ex-prisoner had visited us at 19 Glebe Place in January 1936 and met some of Labour's future leaders.

How, nearly fourteen years afterwards, did India's leader appear? This Westernised, Harrow-educated Brahmin had lost none of the charm and poise conferred by his aristocratic origins, and his essential humility was still there, notwithstanding frequent bouts of feverish impatience. Highly organised and greatly intelligent, he had never suffered fools gladly, and now there were far more fools to contend with than ever before; they came not only from India herself but from other too-romantic Eastern countries which looked to him for leadership, and from the aggressive, sceptical, resistant West.

Nehru was not, like Gandhi, a saint with a revolutionary mission, but a national politician who possessed an unusual capacity for renunciation. He had already yielded ease and wealth in the cause of the half-starved masses, and had been ready to sacrifice freedom and life itself for his country's independence. Yet though politically normal he was spiritually exceptional; in spite of his rational agnosticism, he could not exclude from his vision for India the compulsion of Gandhi's religious aims.

In so far as their fulfilment was incompatible with his country's material progress he appeared to discard them deliberately, like the rich young ruler who turned away sorrowful; he abandoned Gandhi when confronting both Pakistan and South Africa. Yet whenever he could, he implemented the Gandhian teaching, taking no side in the conflict of East and West, but keeping India a resolute and affirmative neutral whose function was to mediate between rival ideologies when the opportunity occurred.

In December 1949 I still had not met Nehru's sister, Mrs. Vijaya-lakshmi Pandit, the first woman to be Ambassador both in Moscow and Washington. Four years later, when she became India's High Commissioner in Britain, I often visited her official home, and in 1954, during an address to the Overseas League, heard her make a quietly scathing comment on our over-eventful epoch which I subsequently recorded.

"We have behind us the experience of two World Wars, and I am afraid I have not been able to find out who actually won them."

At Santiniketan, and later in Delhi, I met two remarkable politicians whose names were then little known to the West. The first, Rajkumari Amrit Kaur, a Christian princess and social worker, had been Gandhi's secretary; now, as India's Minister of Health, she faced problems formidable for a Hindu Catholic. She maintained, I was told, the same discreet role of "hyphen" between Nehru and his stubborn deputy-Premier, Sardar Patel, as the saintly C. F. Andrews had fulfilled between Tagore, with his imaginative perceptions, and the shrewd, realistic Mahatma.

The second politician, Jivatram Kripalani, an ardent follower of

Gandhi, had already appointed himself as one of Nehru's gadflies. A representative from Sind who had been Congress President in 1946, he was soon to break away from the Prime Minister and found a new Party of workers and peasants. Although he was over sixty, Kripalani did not appear an elderly man; lithe, decorative and brilliant, he suggested an ageless figure from Renaissance Europe. At Santiniketan he had delighted us with his vivid human vignettes of Gandhi.

My fellow delegates from thirty countries were as difficult to estimate as the Indians. One of the most impressive and least communicative was Michael Scott, who came to India after presenting the case of the Hereros tribes to the Security Council at Lake Success, and already symbolised in his own dedicated person the cause of the oppressed races now staking their claims to equal membership of civilised communities. Legend attributed to Michael Scott some idiosyncrasies characteristic of the inspired C. F. Andrews; a trail of studs, buttons and uncollected laundry was said to mark the route of his travels.

Also from South Africa came Gandhi's third son Manilal, a small shy man in monk-like brown who sought with palpable humility to emulate by prayer, fasting and passive resistance his father's practical interpretation of the eternal values. At Phoenix, Natal, Manilal edited the magazine, *Indian Opinion*, which the Mahatma had founded early in the century. There, in April 1956, he was destined to die, his health broken by the struggle against the *apartheid* policy of the South African Government.

In contrast to these two reticent saints, the effulgent American Negro delegate, Dr. Mordecai Johnson, President of Washington's Howard University, relegated to obscurity his quieter colleagues. Never had I met a Negro whose share of his race's alleged inferiority complex appeared to be so small; his headship of the distinguished academic community which symbolised coloured America's approaching victory over segregation probably explained this fundamental confidence.

"Not only is he a very dominant and eloquent personality," I reported to G., "but to the Indians he is the Oppressed and his fellow delegates the Oppressors, even though they are good Quaker members of the American Friends Service Committee."

Dr. Johnson's endearing habit of boldly mixing metaphors in his dynamic speeches made them very popular with the other delegates.

"This tender plant," he declared exuberantly of Gandhi's Sevagram experiment, "should not be crushed by an international blunderbuss. We are trying to put too many babies to its tender breast."

Gandhi's own disciples were still able to convey the substance of their master's message, though since his death the non-violent movement had suffered from a national recession of which they appeared to be only half-conscious. Sometimes I felt that village industries and rural communities resembled the comfortable sand into which the ostrich thrusts its head.

The Mahatma's followers varied from the elderly, sage-like Kaka Kalelkar and the highly critical J. C. Kumarappa from Wardha who was always "agin the Government," to the young idealistic Sudhir Ghosh, who studied poetry and quoted James Naylor. It was perhaps unduly fanciful to think of these three as Peter, Thomas and John, but if an international assembly could have been held in Palestine under the auspices of the eleven surviving Apostles after Christ's death and burial, this meeting might have approximated in spirit to the gatherings at Santiniketan and Sevagram.

In death, as in life, Gandhi dominated his supporters; his memory gave a strange quality of resurrection even to the paving stone, honoured like a shrine by a long procession of modest devotees carrying African marigolds, that marked the spot where death confronted him in the Birla garden at Delhi. His ghost seemed to haunt the Raj Ghat in the Jumna meadows which commemorated the last resting-place of his bier, and to pervade the innumerable streets, colleges and schools all over India which, in spite of Nehru's protests, had changed their historic names to his.

Yet, by the time I left India, I was not sorry that I had never personally known Gandhi as G. had done; it was Rabindranath Tagore, the generous and original poetic genius whose family had welcomed me at Santiniketan, with whom I regretted having had no contact. I was content to have found throughout India living testimony, rather than dead memorials, to Gandhi's prophetic inspiration.

Though the creed by which he lived had illuminated my vision and transformed my life, I might have been oppressed if I had met him by the lack of poetry in his temperament. His writings, though creative and fundamental, expressed a Philistine matter-of-factness which sometimes seemed to be reflected in the lives of his friends. Not one of the essays in the Gandhi Memorial Number of Santiniketan's *Visva-Bharati Quarterly*, though they all presented him as a towering moral example, credited him with the imaginative insight which Tagore had possessed so abundantly.

Two years afterwards, I found in Manilal Gandhi's magazine one of Tagore's poems, called *Quiet Moment*, which conveyed to me the substance of the faith that survived his heavy burden of family tragedy.

"Deliver me from my own shadows, my Lord, from the wrecks
   and confusion of my days,
 For the night is dark and Thy pilgrim is blinded;
 Hold Thou my hand.
 Deliver me from despair.
 Touch with Thy flame the lightless lamp of my sorrow.
 Waken my tired strength from its sleep.
 Do not let me linger behind counting my losses.
 For the night is dark and Thy pilgrim is blinded;
 Hold Thou my hand."

(6)

Between visiting Delhi in December and travelling through the South in January 1950, I had spent Christmas and the New Year with the other delegates at Sevagram in the Central Provinces. In this last of Gandhi's ashrams, the bamboo and mud huts lighted only by oil lamps gave me, like the early rising in darkness, a sense of being back in the First World War.

"Luck and Agatha [Harrison]," I wrote to G. "here decided that I should have the great privilege of sharing with her the hut that was occupied by Gandhi's wife in her lifetime; it is also periodically inhabited by cockroaches, but one can't have everything. Luckily Agatha dislikes the cockroaches even more than I do, so we chase them out between us."

Apart from the cockroaches I was relieved to find few insects and no reptiles, though the air of the Central Provinces seemed mild and restful after the cold winds at Delhi. Vivid butterflies, hardly distinguishable from humming-birds, quivered over the dusty buff-grey paths leading to the prayer-ground from the headquarters of Gandhi's New Education experiment, the Hindustani Talimi Sangh; green parrots uttering shrill cries flew in and out of the stunted banyan trees. Solemnly parading along the modern dirt-road through the village occasionally marched a family of baboons.

G.'s Christmas was totally different from mine; it included cocktails with the Duke and Duchess of Windsor on board the *Queen*

Elizabeth, which was taking him to Washington for three weeks at a Political Science Convention.

"The conversation was chiefly political," he related. "And they were both as charming as they could be. For his age he looks extraordinarily young—and well. The pouchy eyes which the photos play up are largely merely the Guelph eyes. Today I gather he shocked them all in the cocktail bar by ordering tea."

Our New Year was to bring similar contrasts; it seemed typical of the varied world which we had so largely explored between us that he should have seen the new half-century in from America and I from India.

My own Christmas Day was one of the most memorable that I had ever spent, for early that morning I took part in an open-air service on the Sevagram prayer-ground which combined the Scriptures of four world religions. Our presence there, representatives from many nations with different creeds, was a tribute to Gandhi's belief in the need for toleration if human life was to realise its constructive possibilities. The ceremony began with "a call to worship" from the Book of Isaiah—"Prepare ye the way of the Lord, make straight in the desert a pathway for our God."

As the dawn sunshine climbed above the low hills of the Central Provinces, the prayer-ground was drenched in brilliant light. Beyond the head of the tall Quaker reading the summons, the thatched roofs of the mud-huts gleamed like metal.

The singing of Hindu hymns followed Vedic prayers and readings from the *Upanishads*; after them came the Buddhist "*Vision of Peace*". Like a pointer these verses led to the story of the Nativity, which found its place in the centre of the pattern. From the prayer-ground the young sacramental spinners listened with solemn dark eyes to an address by the Bantu Professor, Davidson Don Tengo Jabavu, whose father had been a friend of Olive Schreiner. The service ended with a hymn from the Koran and the Hindu *Invocation of Shanti*:

"Peace upon earth below; peace in the middle air; peace in the
    heaven above . . .
Upon the terrible, the cruel, and the evil of the earth.
Filled with that peace and grace be all the realms of Being."

In retrospect this service became one of the creative experiences which stand like signposts along the journey of my life.

The first, not fully understood until I knew Dick Sheppard, had come from the German war prisoners at Étaples in 1917; the sudden perception of a common humanity that they brought had sent me after leaving Oxford to work for peace and the League of Nations.

During 1936, when I met Dick, I had realised that peace meant nothing less than the total readjustment of previous values and a full acceptance of the revolutionary doctrines taught by the Sermon on the Mount; in that grander conception, the humility found in the German ward took its place. Dick Sheppard had indicated the road which eventually led me to India and Gandhi, though even he had left me uncertain whether a Power existed outside ourselves from whom strength might come to help us in our spiritual struggle.

In a Berkshire valley at the end of 1940 I had perceived humiliation to be a moral discipline, accepted by John Bunyan as a necessary part of his pilgrim's progress. Five years later had followed the illumination of V.E. Day, when the innate goodness of the men and women waiting patiently in Whitehall had shown me that God lived, but only with their co-operation could carry out His purpose.

To these experiences the Sevagram service made a fitting epilogue. I had long known that there were many roads to Jerusalem but now this truth came alive for me, and I saw that the Christian revelation was only a small part of the evidence accumulated, in different fashions and many languages, by the great religions of mankind that God exists.

(7)

Late in January I left Karachi for Liverpool on the seventh voyage of a new Anchor Line ship. On board went also a mildly depressing company of army officers and Government officials, with wives who after a dozen years in the East still looked as though they came from Streatham. G., on his way home from America, had pictured this residue of the British Raj.

"Occasionally," he had written of the Far Eastern officials, "you may find a truly significant man who can illuminate a whole landscape in history—but these be few. The great are so much simpler than the simple, who are shot with sordid jealousies. After all what *is* greatness, save getting on to a height from which at last one sees the proportions right?"

The conventional outlook of my shipmates troubled me not at all. After ten weeks spent amongst tense people discussing serious topics, I did not want to talk any more, but to rest and to think— particularly to think, for my travels in India had created a new orientation of outlook and increased the existing area of consciousness. As his biographers had written of C. F. Andrews, "once and for all the European perspective was left behind."

471

The warm sunshine and the smoothness of the Arabian Sea, its delicately ruffled surface the colour of steel, made the long-excluded occupation of thought easy to attain. At night, all the way from Karachi to Aden, I could see the Southern Cross through the open porthole of my small single cabin if I woke just before dawn. When we stopped at Bombay, adorned with flags for India's first Republic Day on January 26th, an affectionate cable from John and Shirley— "Happy voyage and much love"—brought a sudden lifting of the spirit.

After five days at sea, the air became moist and still. As we entered the Gulf of Aden magnificent sunsets, in which the orange disk of the sun plunged suddenly into the ocean as it had plunged at Cape Comorin, softened into a crimson afterglow. Alone among the life-boats on the ship's top deck, I reflected on the new field of knowledge which I had entered.

From the end of the First World War, I had seen my work ever more clearly as an attempt to enlarge "the consciousness of humanity". It had not brought me any special reputation, but I believed that it had played a small part in creating the mental revolution through which I had lived. The real cause of the two World Wars had been political unconsciousness; the too-slowly diminishing failure of the mass of people in all countries to perceive what was happening. If the peace-makers could extend, however little, this power of realisation, they had accomplished much of their task.

In those moments of depression which come to all would-be creators, my mind dwelt on the ends that I had set myself and my lack of success in reaching them. But in those happier times when a truer perspective sustained me, I remembered rather the distance that I had travelled from the "little girl" whose Staffordshire father had not thought her worth educating.

Humility, as I now saw it, did not lie in a constant regret for personal failure, but in realistic gratitude for the measure, against all probability, of substantial achievement, and the refusal—as Gandhi had refused—to count its cost. Once one began to say: "This will make me unpopular with the Party", or "That will put my name on a list", or "This will ruin the sales of my book", the battle was lost and the Devil took charge.

At least, I reflected, in the long struggle against heredity and temperament I had not wholly failed. Thanks to G.'s magnanimity, to the self-discipline demanded by my creed, and to the talent for writing with which, through the grace of God, I had been endowed, I had always been able to escape from ancestral impulses and become

472

myself. Constantly with me from the time I could hold a pen had been a second world of work and imagination, in which I could recover that sense of proportion which G. had described as the key to greatness.

(8)

A day later we stopped at Aden, first seen as a peninsula of rock half hiding the human settlement. Just visible over the water, a large white cross on the formidable hills with their saw-toothed edges commemorated for travellers the First World War. Except for a row of scrubby trees along the docks, no green appeared on this undesirable strategic colonial outpost at the foot of Arabia. The British inhabitants, we learned, carried boxes of soil from home and optimistically tried to cultivate little "English gardens".

Next morning I became aware that we had indeed turned the corner which divided Asia from Africa and Europe, and were going home. Although I had now learned to be at ease in so many countries, home was where G. was, and always would be; whether he survived me or died before me, it could never be anywhere else. At the moment it chanced to be London because he had just come back from America.

"I do long to see you," I wrote him in a final air-letter to be dispatched with the ship's mail from Port Said. "There is so much to talk about, and I have had to guard my words for so long."

Dear G.! I thought gratefully. How many adventures we had known and borne and enjoyed in each other's company; how perfect an integration, in nearly twenty-five years, we had achieved, and what enrichment beyond measure marriage with its shared experiences had brought us.

As Winifred had once prophesied, "friendships and opportunities beyond all dreams" had come, and were coming still. God had denied me peace, but He had indeed given me glory—in the loyalty of friends, the support of innumerable unknown readers, the love of husband and children, and the real value of all three to the society from which they sprang. Not the least of my privileges had been the power, surviving humiliation, to write and utter words which reached at least a few whose benevolence had power to change the state of the world. To-day those few included not only men but women, whose contributions were no longer crippled by the prejudices of the past.

The country to which I had just said farewell, so long thought of as backward and primitive, had appointed a woman as its leading

473

Ambassador; Mrs. Pandit symbolised the changes which had come for women in my lifetime. Through the conflict of marriage and career that revolution had been as costly, in achievements and opportunities, to G. as to myself. Yet however painful its personal consequences at the outset of our marriage, we had both, I thought, recognised their impersonal aspect.

The mistakes had been many but the treasures of mutual discovery had been many too, and the early years of conflict and occasional resistance were now far away. Our very problems had made us part of a concerned minority fighting against the dead-weight of convention for a woman's right to combine normal human relationships with mental and spiritual fulfilment.

That minority had done its work; the convention had been undermined, and the right, if sometimes grudgingly, admitted. Shirley, I believed, would no more find marriage an end in itself than I had done, but in the process of becoming a complete human being she would not meet with the criticisms, the obstacles, and the traditional assumptions which had handicapped my generation. Except for a period deliberately set aside for bearing and rearing children, the luxury of "checking out" at will from the world's work into private life would soon be as little expected from wives as it had always been from husbands.

Some day, I thought, I will make a book about the different kinds of progress which have come near fulfilment in my lifetime; it will be my last Testament. Of the great enemies of man which the crusaders of this century have fought, only war remains unconquered—and that has been spurned by the common people of all civilised countries in so far as they can make their will effective. Their best hope now is to multiply governments in which the Prime Minister carries out the resolute policy of a Nehru inspired by the enlightened teaching of a Gandhi.

(9)

Two days afterwards we reached Suez after sailing through a cool and breezy Red Sea which belied its tropical reputation. Some of the passengers, including myself, had been promised a trip to Cairo and the Pyramids if Egyptian unrest was no worse than usual; we were to travel by car from Suez, and return by train to Port Said while the ship was going through the Canal. Now I should learn, I thought, something of John's background as a conscript in 1946.

As I stepped into the launch which carried us over the glassy surface of the Gulf of Suez to the car waiting on the edge of the desert, the Purser gave me two letters from G. During the drive to Cairo, I opened and read them, and suddenly my whole body, warm with the expectation of a new adventure, turned numb and cold.

The first letter told me that he was "in bed with a mild attack of 'flu"; the second, written several days later, was more specific.

"Fifth day now in bed with this miserable painful influenza so that if you cough every muscle rasps like a nutmeg grater. Nor has one the energy or wit even to write letters, let alone anything more. I suppose it is the accident of infection plus the mixed effects of the foul London climate and of politics. . . . I am in a condition of general feverish misery."

From G. this was a most unusual letter, for he seldom complained of anything, and never about his health. There was no way of checking the information; he would not, I felt sure, have told the children about his illness. In any case, no one knew exactly where I was on the long journey home.

The pneumonia ward at Étaples was now more than thirty years away, but nobody who had once nursed twenty acute cases for two months could forget their symptoms. What G. had described was pneumonia, actual or potential. He would certainly not recognise it as such himself, for he had a rare immunity to painful symptoms and seldom felt ill. If he did, I knew that the trouble was genuine.

After Port Said the ship did not stop again till it reached Liverpool ten days later. Suddenly panic-stricken, I told myself that in ten days an over-tired person, smitten by pneumonia in the chill winter damp of England after stimulating, overwarmed America, could easily be dead. . . .

I dared not risk it. Then I remembered that Cairo was a leading airport; from here I could fly. Precipitately abandoning my companions as we were being shown Tutenkamen's jewels in Cairo's famous museum, I took a taxi to the B.O.A.C. office.

But here I encountered a major obstacle. Cairo was under martial law; Egyptian nationalism, directed towards the control of the Suez Canal, had recently broken out into spasmodic rioting. Not only was all communication with the outside world greatly delayed, so that I could not reach G. by telephone or cable in the short time before I had to rejoin the ship at Port Said; it also meant that Egyptian currency alone was acceptable as payment for all purchases from air passages to tooth-paste.

In my handbag—the only luggage I had brought—there was nothing useful except my passport, cheque-book, return steamship

475

ticket, and a small amount of English currency for the incidental expenses of the voyage. The B.O.A.C. clerk promised to keep for me until the late afternoon the last reservation on an Argonaut plane leaving next morning; and I took another taxi to the British Embassy.

It was now nearly one o'clock, and when I reached the building a tall red-faced man with prominent teeth, wearing a white suit, was about to lock the outer door before going to lunch. On the wide ornate steps of the Embassy I divulged my problem.

The official listened indifferently as I explained my urgent need for £73 of Egyptian currency in return for a cheque. Desperately I tried to establish my *bona fides*, but almost a sneer accompanied the words with which he dismissed me.

"Oh, I know your name and your books. But that does not mean that you are solvent. The British Government is not in the habit of lending money to stranded nationals."

Locking the door, he pushed me aside and departed.

By now I was not unfamiliar with obstructive patronage on the part of British officials, but this insolence, and this patronage, seemed altogether beyond what a realistic traveller might normally expect.

Fifteen months afterwards, when the world's newspapers published photographs of a British diplomat who had vanished with a companion behind the Iron Curtain, I recognised at once the red-faced man who had rebuffed me outside the Cairo Embassy.

It was Donald Maclean.

(10)

Nearly in despair, I took yet another taxi to my final hope, the office of Thomas Cook and Son. Here my luck changed at last; they agreed to accept my cheque and pay my plane fare. Thankfully I sent G. a cable; it explained my anxiety for him, reported my change of plans, and asked that Charles should bring a warm coat to the airport. Then, in order to fill an interminable afternoon, I rejoined the boat party for the trip to the Pyramids. Never had I felt less like an expedition, but the alternative was to stay dismally in Shepheards Hotel. I hardly saw the Nile as we crossed it, and without having consciously agreed, found myself suddenly hoisted on to the back of a camel.

As everybody who has ridden one knows, this animal has a gait similar to the motion of a ship on a rough sea. Clinging dizzily to its hump, I surveyed the swaying Pyramids and dusty brown desert with extreme discomfort. These immemorial monuments had been crudely commercialised; stalls selling miscellaneous merchandise at their base recalled the booths and public lavatories half-way up Milan Cathedral. Even the Sphinx disappointed me by its insignificance; it must, I thought, usually have been photographed from below the tawny slopes where it squatted to give it an impressiveness not conspicuous from a camel's back.

My good friend at Cook's had fixed me up for the night at Shepheards. G. had stopped there for a meal in 1946, and had written of this "Oriental Ritz" without enthusiasm. But though I had no luggage and was wearing only a thin silk frock under a light coat, the manager and clerks at this fashionable centre, so soon to be destroyed by violence, received me as courteously as though I had been a millionaire with forty trunks. They even sent a turbaned porter to accompany me to the airport before dawn next day, because I was a stranger and alone in the turbulent city.

The morning turned into one of those sunny, windless days which in early February appear a miracle, and I could only hope that the omen was good. We should even be able, I learned, to fly over the Alps.

The Argonaut Speedbird crossed the Mediterranean and soared above the snowy mountain-tops of Crete as though it had been made for the air from time immemorial. Then we crossed the tail of Italy, and flew over Capri, where G. and I had stayed in 1936; it was now a sombre island half eclipsed in mist.

The England to which I was returning had been absorbed for two months in preparations for the General Election on February 23rd, but though the Dissolution of Parliament occurred that very day, I did not for once give it a thought. Even G., it seemed, had become resigned to the idiosyncrasies of his fellow politicians.

"The Labour Party," he had written me from New York, "always reminds me of an immense saurian monster. If you kick it very hard it opens one lizard eyelid, regards you with lazy curiosity, and shuts it again."

More real than its unreliable rewards was the family life we had built up together—so happy, for all the sorrows which had shadowed it; so united in spite of the minor internal differences which were inevitable between four emphatic individuals. G. was a Catholic and I a Quaker-inclined Protestant; politically he stood to the right-centre of the Labour Party and I to the left, yet never had those fundamental issues been a source of controversy between us.

"Little love, who is about the only stable thing for me in my not so good world," he had written me from the Nazi-dominated Rhineland in 1933. That, I thought, re-reading this letter long afterwards, struck the authentic note of our relationship. In spite of their brief periods of glory, our years together had often been lived in a "not so good world", but at least we had not failed each other. "Here firm where all be drifting," each had offered to the other a loyalty, a certainty, an unshaken source of perpetual strength.

"All human love is a holy thing, the holiest in our experience," Dean Inge had written; it was the same thought which Father Bede Jarrett had put into words at our wedding a quarter of a century ago. Such a love, created by time and experience, was invincible against the disillusionments of the years. I had always found it difficult to understand the readiness with which some middle-aged couples divorced each other, and thereby cast away the accumulated treasures of their past.

(11)

For two hours we came down in Rome, comfortably enjoying a premature spring. Soon after we had started on the last lap towards home the Alps spread below us, but white clouds raked the giant peaks and hid them from view.

My thoughts were more troubled than the calm winter firmament, for I was haunted by an episode of which G. had written me from America less than a month ago. While he was in New York, he had promised to meet a valued elderly friend on his own return from Washington. He had arrived just in time to see his friend's coffin being wheeled away; in the interval the cheerful and generous old man had died from a stroke.

In spite of my attempts to forget it, this incident had suggested throughout my flight a vicarious foretaste of the experience which might be awaiting me. If indeed such a fate was ever to be mine, I should find no better epitaph on our married life than the concluding paragraph of a letter which G. had sent me as long ago as 1927.

"It is not joint success, it is not children to be proud of, it is not the dear relation of bodies, it is not the new job of co-working with its bright hope and energy; it is not memories of blue skies and bees buzzing in the thyme.

"As we look back it will be none of these, nor should it be as we look forward. It is that you are truly the sacrament of God to me and that I try so to be to you. For in our two selves there is communication, companionship, thought, intimacy, love, and when we part this flame dies down which we have lit to light us through life together."

While I meditated on the prophetic quality of this letter, the Argonaut swooped over France and across the Channel. Beneath the copper afterglow of the wintry sunset, the black outline of Beachy Head stretched like a long dragon with its tail curled round the sea. In a few minutes the lights of London Airport glimmered from the ground and we were fastening our safety belts and coming down.

Filling in the usual medical documents demanded an exceptional restraint. Then came the Customs shed, where the officials seemed surprised to see a hatless passenger without an overcoat, who truthfully asserted that she had nothing to declare because she had, in fact, brought nothing with her. Persuading themselves with difficulty that I really had no luggage, they let me through the barrier without delay. I walked into the lounge expecting to see the compact form of Charles with my fur wrap, and nerved myself to hear his news.

But beyond the barrier stood a tall familiar figure. In a letter which missed me at Port Said, G. had written that "after one of the most severe attacks of influenza I have ever had", his temperature had obligingly gone down and stayed there.

My cable had caught him when he was just beginning to feel like getting up. Cheered by my return ten days ahead of time, he decided to hire a car and come to meet me. And as I ran into his outstretched arms and he covered my thin summer clothes with the warm coat which he had brought from home, I knew that we should celebrate our Silver Wedding in June, and that our life together would go on.

THE END

"Long ago there lived a rich merchant who, besides possessing more treasures than any King in the world, had in his great hall three chairs, one of silver, one of gold, and one of diamonds. But his greatest treasure of all was his only daughter, who was called Catherine.

"One day Catherine was sitting in her own room when suddenly the door flew open, and in came a tall and beautiful woman, holding in her hands a little wheel.

" 'Catherine,' she said, going up to the girl, 'which would you rather have—a happy youth or a happy old age?'

"Catherine was so taken by surprise that she did not know what to answer, and the lady repeated again: 'Which would you rather have—a happy youth or a happy old age?'

"Then Catherine thought to herself: 'If I say a happy youth, then I shall have to suffer all the rest of my life. No, I will bear trouble now, and have something better to look forward to.' So she looked up and said: 'Give me a happy old age.'

" 'So be it,' said the lady, and turned her wheel as she spoke, vanishing the next moment as suddenly as she had come.

"Now this beautiful lady was the Destiny of poor Catherine."

Sicilianische Märchen, by Laura Gonzenbach.

(Included in *The Pink Fairy Book,* edited by Andrew Lang, and quoted at the beginning of *Testament of Youth.*)